Praise for the *The Art of Scalability*

"This book is much more than you may think ....out designing Web sites that don't crash when lots of users .... is about designing your company so that it doesn't crash when your business needs to grow. These guys have been there on the front lines of some of the most successful Internet companies of our time, and they share the good, the bad, and the ugly about how to not just survive, but thrive."

—Marty Cagan, Founder, Silicon Valley Product Group

"A must read for anyone building a Web service for the mass market."

—Dana Stalder, General Partner, Matrix Partners

"Abbott and Fisher have deep experiences with scale in both large and small enterprises. What's unique about their approach to scalability is they start by focusing on the true foundation: people and process, without which true scalability cannot be built. Abbott and Fisher leverage their years of experience in a very accessible and practical approach to scalability that has been proven over time with their significant success."

—Geoffrey Weber, VP of Internet Operations/IT, Shutterfly

"If I wanted the best diagnoses for my health I would go to the Mayo Clinic. If I wanted the best diagnoses for my portfolio companies' performance and scalability I would call Martin and Michael. They have recommended solutions to performance and scalability issues that have saved some of my companies from a total rewrite of the system."

—Warren M. Weiss, General Partner, Foundation Capital

"As a manager who worked under Michael Fisher and Marty Abbott during my time at PayPal/eBay, the opportunity to directly absorb the lessons and experiences presented in this book are invaluable to me now working at Facebook."

—Yishan Wong, Director of Engineering, Facebook

The Art of Scalability is by far the best book on scalability on the market today. The authors tackle the issues of scalability from processes, to people, to performance, to the highly technical. Whether your organization is just starting out and is defining processes as you go, or you are a mature organization, this is the ideal book to help you deal with scalability issues before, during, or after an incident. Having built several projects, programs, and companies from small to significant scale, I can honestly say I wish I had this book one, five, and ten years ago."

—Jeremy Wright, CEO, b5media, Inc.

"Only a handful of people in the world have experienced the kind of growth-related challenges that Fisher and Abbott have seen at eBay, PayPal, and the other companies they've helped to build. Fewer still have successfully overcome such challenges. *The Art of Scalability* provides a great summary of lessons learned while scaling two of the largest internet companies in the history of the space, and it's a must-read for any executive at a hyper-growth company. What's more, it's well-written and highly entertaining. I couldn't put it down."

—Kevin Fortuna, Partner, AKF Consulting

"Marty and Mike's book covers all the bases, from understanding how to build a scalable organization to the processes and technology necessary to run a highly scalable architecture. They have packed in a ton of great practical solutions from real world experiences. This book is a must-read for anyone having difficulty managing the scale of a hyper-growth company or a startup hoping to achieve hyper growth."

—Tom Keeven, Partner, AKF Consulting

"*The Art of Scalability* is remarkable in its wealth of information and clarity; the authors provide novel, practical, and demystifying approaches to identify, predict, and resolve scalability problems before they surface. Marty Abbott and Michael Fisher use their rich experience and vision, providing unique and groundbreaking tools to assist small and hyper-growth organizations as they maneuver in today's demanding technological environments."

—Joseph M. Potenza, Attorney, Banner & Witcoff, Ltd.

The Art of Scalability

The Art of Scalability

Scalable Web Architecture, Processes, and Organizations for the Modern Enterprise

Martin L. Abbott
Michael T. Fisher

♦♦ Addison-Wesley

Upper Saddle River, NJ • Boston • Indianapolis • San Francisco
New York • Toronto • Montreal • London • Munich • Paris • Madrid
Capetown • Sydney • Tokyo • Singapore • Mexico City

Many of the designations used by manufacturers and sellers to distinguish their products are claimed as trademarks. Where those designations appear in this book, and the publisher was aware of a trademark claim, the designations have been printed with initial capital letters or in all capitals.

The authors and publisher have taken care in the preparation of this book, but make no expressed or implied warranty of any kind and assume no responsibility for errors or omissions. No liability is assumed for incidental or consequential damages in connection with or arising out of the use of the information or programs contained herein.

The publisher offers excellent discounts on this book when ordered in quantity for bulk purchases or special sales, which may include electronic versions and/or custom covers and content particular to your business, training goals, marketing focus, and branding interests. For more information, please contact:

U.S. Corporate and Government Sales
(800) 382-3419
corpsales@pearsontechgroup.com

For sales outside the United States please contact:

International Sales
international@pearson.com

Visit us on the Web: informit.com/aw

Library of Congress Cataloging-in-Publication Data

Abbott, Martin L.
  The art of scalability : scalable web architecture, processes, and organizations for the modern enterprise / Martin L. Abbott, Michael T. Fisher.
        p.   cm.
  Includes index.
  ISBN-13: 978-0-13-703042-2 (pbk. : alk. paper)
  ISBN-10: 0-13-703042-8 (pbk. : alk. paper)
  1. Web site development. 2. Computer networks—Scalability. 3. Business enterprises—Computer networks. I. Fisher, Michael T. II. Title.
  TK5105.888.A2178 2010
  658.4'06—dc22

                                                2009040124

ISBN-13: 978-0-13-703042-2
ISBN-10:   0-13-703042-8
Text printed in the United States on recycled paper at RR Donnelley in Crawfordsville, Indiana.
Third printing, April 2013

Editor-in-Chief
Mark Taub

Acquisitions Editor
Trina MacDonald

Development Editor
Songlin Qiu

Managing Editor
John Fuller

Project Editor
Anna Popick

Copy Editor
Kelli Brooks

Indexer
Richard Evans

Proofreader
Debbie Liehs

Technical Reviewers
Jason Bloomberg
Robert Guild
Robert Hines
Jeremy Wright

Cover Designer
Chuti Prasertsith

Compositor
Rob Mauhar

To my father for teaching me how to succeed, and to Heather for teaching me how to have fun.
—Marty Abbott

To my parents for their guidance, and to my wife and son for their unflagging support.
—Michael Fisher

Contents

Part IV: Solving Other Issues and Challenges 409

Foreword

In 1996, as Lycos prepared for its initial public offering, a key concern among potential investors of that day was whether our systems would scale as the Internet grew; or perhaps more frightening, would the Internet itself scale as more people came online? And the fears of data center Armageddon were not at all unfounded. We had for the first time in human history the makings of a mass communications vehicle that connected not thousands, not millions, but billions of people and systems from around the world, all needing to operate seamlessly with one another. At any point in time, that tiny PC in San Diego needs to publish its Web pages to a super computer in Taipei, while Web servers in Delhi are finding a path over the information highway to a customer in New York. Now picture this happening across billions of computers in millions of locations all in the same instant. And then the smallest problem anywhere in the mix of PCs, servers, routers, clouds, storage, platforms, operating systems, networks, and so much more can bring everything to its knees. Just the thought of such computing complexity is overwhelming.

This is exactly why you need to read *The Art of Scalability*.

Two of the brightest minds of the information age have come together to share their knowledge and experience in delivering peak performance with the precision and detail that their West Point education mandates. Marty Abbott and Mike Fisher have fought some of the most challenging enterprise architecture demons ever and have always won. Their successes have allowed some of the greatest business stories of our age to develop. From mighty eBay to smaller Quigo to countless others, this pair has built around-the-clock reliability, which contributed to the creation of hundreds of millions of dollars in shareholder value. A company can't operate in the digital age without flawless technical operations. In fact, the lack of a not just good, but great, scalable Web architecture can be the difference between success and failure in a company. The problem though, in a world that counts in nanoseconds, is that the path to that greatness is rarely clear. In this book, the authors blow out the fog on scaling and help us to see what works and how to get there.

In it, we learn much about the endless aspects of technical operations. And this is invaluable because without strong fundamentals it's tough to get much built. But when I evaluate a business for an investment, I'm not only thinking about its products; more importantly, I need to dig into the people and processes that are its foundation. And this is where this book really stands out. It's the first of its kind to examine the impact that sound management and leadership skills have in achieving scale. When systems fail and business operations come crashing down, many are quick to look at hardware and software problems as the root, whereas a more honest appraisal will almost always point to the underlying decisions people make as the true culprit. The authors understand this and help us to learn from it. Their insights will help you design and develop organizations that stand tall in the face of challenges. Long-term success in most any field is the result of careful planning and great execution; this is certainly so with today's incredibly complex networks and databases. The book walks you through the steps necessary to think straight and succeed in the most challenging of circumstances.

Marty and Mike have danced in boardrooms and executed on the frontlines with many of the nation's top businesses. These two are the best of the best. With *The Art of Scalability*, they have created the ultimate step-by-step instruction book required to build a top-notch technical architecture that can withstand the test of time. It's written in a way that provides the granular detail needed by any technical team but that can also serve as a one-stop primer or desktop reference for the executive looking to stand out. This is a book that is sure to become must-reading in the winning organization.

Bob Davis
Managing Partner, Highland Capital Partners, and Founder/Former CEO, Lycos

Acknowledgments

The authors would like to recognize, first and foremost, the experience and advice of our partner and cofounder Tom Keeven. The process and technology portions of this book were built over time with the help of Tom and his many years of experience. Tom started the business that became AKF Partners. We often joke that Tom has forgotten more about architecting highly available and scalable sites than most of us will ever learn.

We further would like to recognize our colleagues and teams at Quigo, eBay, and PayPal. These are the companies at which we really started to build and test many of the approaches mentioned in the technology and process sections of this book. The list of names within these teams is quite large, but the individuals know who they are.

We'd also like to acknowledge our teams and colleagues at GE, Gateway, and Motorola. These companies provided us with hands-on engineering experience and gave us our first management and executive positions. They were our introduction to the civilian world and it is here that we started practicing leadership and management outside of the Army.

We would also like to acknowledge the US Army and United States Military Academy. Together they created a leadership lab unlike any other we can imagine.

About the Authors

Martin L. Abbott

Marty Abbott is a founding partner at the growth and scalability advisory firm AKF Partners. He was formerly COO of Quigo, an advertising technology startup sold to AOL, where he was responsible for product strategy, product management, technology development, and client services. Prior to Quigo, Marty spent nearly six years at eBay, most recently as SVP of technology and CTO and member of the executive staff. Prior to eBay, Marty held domestic and international engineering, management, and executive positions at Gateway and Motorola. Marty serves on the boards of directors for OnForce, LodgeNet Interactive (NASD:LNET), and Bullhorn; and is on the advisory boards of Rearden Commerce, Goldmail, and LiveOps. Marty has a B.S. in computer science from the United States Military Academy, an M.S. in computer engineering from the University of Florida, is a graduate of the Harvard Business School Executive Education Program, and is pursuing a doctorate in management from Case Western Reserve University.

Michael T. Fisher

Michael T. Fisher is a founding partner at the growth and scalability advisory firm AKF Partners. Michael's experience includes two years as the chief technology officer of Quigo, a startup Internet advertising company that was acquired by AOL in 2007. He also served as Quigo's president for a transition period post acquisition. Prior to Quigo, Michael served as vice president of engineering and architecture for PayPal, Inc., an eBay company, where he was responsible for the development organization of over 200 engineers. Prior to joining PayPal, Michael spent seven years at General Electric helping to develop the company's technology strategy and processes. Michael has a B.S. in computer science from the United States Military Academy, an M.S. from Hawaii Pacific University, a Ph.D. in management information systems from Kennedy Western University, and an M.B.A. from Case Western Reserve University. Michael is a certified Six Sigma Master Black Belt and is pursuing a doctorate in management from Case Western Reserve University.

Introduction

This book is about the *art* of *scale*, *scalability*, and *scaling* of technology organizations, processes, and platforms. The information contained within has been carefully designed to be appropriate for any employee, manager, or executive of an organization or company that provides technology solutions. For the nontechnical executive or product manager, this book can help you formulate the right scalability questions and focus on the right issue, whether that be people, process, or technology, in order to help prevent scalability disasters. For the technical executive, manager, or individual engineer, we address the organizational and process issues that negatively impact scale as well as provide technical models and advice to build more scalable platforms.

Our experience with scalability goes beyond academic study and research. Although we are both formally trained as engineers, we don't believe academic programs teach scalability very well. Rather, we learned about scalability from having suffered through the challenges of scaling systems for a combined thirty plus years. We have been engineers, managers, executives, and advisors for startups as well as Fortune 500 companies. The list of companies that we have worked with includes familiar names such as General Electric, Motorola, Gateway, eBay, and PayPal. The list also includes hundreds of less-known startups that need to be able to scale as they grow. Having learned the scalability lessons through thousands of hours diagnosing problems and thousands more hours of designing preventions of those problems, we want to share this combined knowledge. This was the motivation behind starting our consulting practice, AKF Partners, in 2007 and continued to be the motivation for producing this book.

Scalability: So Much More Than Just Technology

Pilots are taught and statistics show that many aircraft incidents are the result of multiple failures that snowball into total system failure and catastrophe. In aviation, these multiple failures are often called an error chain and they often start with human rather than mechanical failure. In fact, Boeing identified that 55% of the aircraft incidents with Boeing aircraft between 1995 and 2005 had human factors related causes.[1]

---

1. Boeing (May 2006), "Statistical Summary of Commercial Jet Airplane Accidents Worldwide Operations."

1

Our experience with scalability-related issues follows a similar trend. The CTO or executive responsible for scale of a technology platform may see scalability as purely a technical endeavor. This is the first, and very human, failure in the error chain. As a result, the process to identify a need to split a database into multiple databases doesn't exist: failure number two. When the user count or transaction volume exceeds a certain threshold, the entire product fails: failure number three. The team assembles to solve the problem and because it has never invested processes to troubleshoot problems such as these the team misdiagnoses the failure as "the database just needs to be tuned": failure number four. The vicious cycle goes on for days, with people focusing on different pieces of the technology stack and blaming everything from firewalls, through the application, to the database, and even pointing fingers at each other. Customers walk away, morale flat lines, and shareholders are left holding the bag.

The point here is that crises resulting from an inability to scale to end-user demands are almost never technology problems alone. In our experience as business and technology executives and advisors, scalability issues start with organizations and people and then spread to process and technology. People, being human, make ill-informed or poor choices regarding technical implementations, which in turn sometimes manifest themselves as a failure of a technology platform to scale. People also ignore the development of processes that might help them learn from past mistakes and sometimes put overly burdensome processes in place, which in turn might force the organization to make poor decisions or make decisions too late to be effective. A lack of attention to the people and processes that create and support technical decision making can lead to a vicious cycle of bad technical decisions, as depicted in the left side of Figure 0.1. This book is the first of its kind focused on creating a virtuous cycle of people and process scalability to support better, faster, and more scalable technology decisions, as depicted in the right side of Figure 0.1.

Art Versus Science

The use of the word *art* is a very deliberate choice on our part. Besides fitting nicely into the title and allowing us to associate some of Sun Tzu's teachings into our own book, Merriam-Webster's dictionary gives one definition of art as a "branch of learning."[2] Additional definitions offered by Merriam-Webster are "skill acquired by experience, study, or observation" and "an occupation requiring knowledge or skill." All of these are true of the nature of scaling platforms, processes, and organizations. But perhaps more important in our choice of *art* here are the images the word conjures up of being more fluid versus the view of science, which is more structured and

---

2. Merriam-Webster Online Dictionary. http://www.merriam-webster.com/dictionary/art.

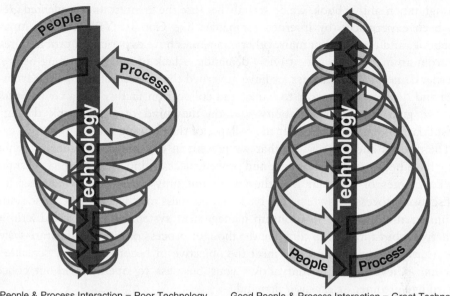

Bad People & Process Interaction = Poor Technology
Vicious Cycle

Good People & Process Interaction = Great Technology
Virtuous Cycle

Figure 0.1 *Vicious and Virtuous Technology Cycles*

static. It is this image that we are relying upon heavily within our title as our experience has taught us that there is no single approach or way to guarantee an appropriate level of scale within a platform, organization, or process. Rather, the interactions between platforms, organizations, and processes have profound impacts on the adaptation of any specific and highly structured approach. The approach to scaling must be crafted around the ecosystem created by the intersection of the current technology platform, the characteristics of the organization, and the maturity and appropriateness of the existing processes. Consistent with this use of *art*, our book focuses on providing skills and lessons regarding approaches rather than improperly teaching that a one-size-fits-all approach will solve any need.

This is not to say that we don't advocate the application of the scientific method in nearly any approach, because we absolutely do. Art here is a nod to the notion that you simply cannot take a cookie cutter approach for any potential system and expect to meet with success.

Who Needs Scalability?

Any company that continues to grow ultimately will need to figure out how to scale its systems, organizations, and processes. Although we focus on Web-centric systems through much of this book, we do so only because the greatest unprecedented growth has been experienced by Internet companies like Google, Yahoo, eBay, Amazon, Facebook, and the like. But many other companies have experienced problems resulting from an inability to scale to new demands (a lack of scalability) long before the Internet came of age. Scale issues have governed the growth of companies from airlines and defense contractors to banks and collocation facility (data center) providers. We guarantee that scalability was on the mind of every bank during the consolidation that occurred after the collapse of the banking industry.

The models and approaches that we present in our book are industry agnostic. They have been developed, tested, and proven successful in some of the fastest growing companies of our time and they work not only in front-end customer facing transaction processing systems but back-end business intelligence, enterprise resource planning, and customer relationship management systems. They don't discriminate by activity, but rather help to guide the thought process on how to separate systems, organizations, and processes to meet the objective of becoming highly scalable and reaching a level of scale that allows your business to operate without concerns regarding customer or end-user demand.

Book Organization and Structure

We've divided the book into four parts. Part I, Staffing a Scalable Organization, focuses on organization, management, and leadership. Far too often, managers and leaders are promoted based on their talents within their area of expertise. Engineering leaders and managers, for example, are very often promoted based on their technical acumen and often aren't given the time or resources to develop business, management, and leadership acumen. Although they might perform well in the architectural and technical aspects of scale, their expertise in organizational scale needs are often shallow or nonexistent. Our intent is to arm these managers and leaders with a foundation from which they can grow and prosper as managers and leaders.

Part II, Building Processes for Scale, focuses on the processes that help hypergrowth companies scale their technical platforms. We cover topics ranging from technical issue resolution to crisis management. We also discuss processes meant for governing architectural decisions and principles to help companies scale their platforms.

Part III, Architecting Scalable Solutions, focuses on the technical and architectural aspects of scale. We introduce proprietary models developed within our consulting and advisory practice of AKF Partners. These models help organizations think through their scalability needs and alternatives.

Part IV, Solving Other Issues and Challenges, discusses emerging technologies such as grid computing and cloud computing. We also address some unique problems within hyper-growth companies such as the immense growth and cost of data as well as what to consider when planning data centers and how to evolve your monitoring strategies to be closer to your customers.

The lessons in this book have not been designed in the laboratory nor are they based on unapplied theory. Rather, these lessons have been designed and implemented by engineers, technology leaders, and organizations through years of struggling to keep their dreams, businesses, and systems a float. The authors have had the great fortune to be a small part of many of these teams in many different roles—sometimes as active participants, other times as observers. We have seen how putting these lessons into practice has yielded success and the unwillingness or inability to do so has led to failure. This book will teach these lessons and hopefully put you and your team on the road to success. We believe the lessons herein are valuable for everyone from engineering staffs to product staffs including every level from the individual contributor to the CEO.

Part I

Staffing a Scalable Organization

Chapter 1

The Impact of People and Leadership on Scalability

Fighting with a large army under your command is nowise different from fighting with a small one; it is merely a question of instituting signs and signals.

—Sun Tzu

People, organizational structure, management, and leadership all have an impact on the scalability of your organization, your processes, and (as a result) the scalability of your product, platform, or systems. They are at the heart of everything you do and the core of everything you need to scale a company and a platform. Paradoxically, they are the things we overlook most often when attempting to scale large systems: Our people are overlooked and underappreciated; organization structure is a once-a-year, check-the-box exercise written in haste in PowerPoint and managed by HR; and our managers and leaders are often untrained or undertrained in the performance of their duties. In this chapter, we will explain why the people of your organization, the structure of the organization, the management, and the leadership in your organization all have an enormous impact on your ability to scale your product, platform, or services.

Introducing AllScale

Throughout *The Art of Scalability*, we will refer to a fictional company, AllScale. AllScale started out as a custom software development company, contracting individual developers out by the hour for projects. Over time, the company started to bid on special custom development projects for both back office IT systems and Web enabled Software as a Service (SaaS) platforms. As the company matured, it started developing tools for its own internal usage and then started selling these tools as a service to other companies using the SaaS model.

The tool with which AllScale has had the most traction is the human resources management (HRM) system. The tool is an employee life cycle management system, covering everything from recruiting to termination. The recruiting process is automated, with resumes held online and workflows depicting the status of each recruit and notes on the interview process. After an employee is hired, all corporate training material is performed online through the system. Employee reviews are performed within the system and tracked over time. Associated merit increases, notes from one-on-one sessions, previous jobs, and performance information are all contained within the system. When an employee leaves, is terminated, or retires, the notes from the exit interview are retained within the system as well.

AllScale is a private company with a majority ownership (51%) obtained by a single venture capital (VC) company after a B-series round. The VC firm invested in both rounds, having decided to make its initial investment after the company started building SaaS product offerings and seeing how AllScale's HRM software started to rapidly penetrate the market with viral adoption.

AllScale is an aggregation of our experience with our clients and our experience running technology organizations within Fortune 500 and startup companies. We decided to focus on one imaginary company for the sake of continuity across people, process, and technology issues. The evolution of AllScale from job shop contractor to the developer of multiple SaaS offerings also allows us to take a look at several unique challenges and how the management team might overcome them.

Why People

In our introduction, we made the statement that people are important when attempting to scale nearly anything; they are especially important when trying to scale technical platforms responsible for processing transactions under high user demand and hyper growth.

Here, we are going to go out on a limb and assert that people are the most important aspect of scale. First and foremost, without people, you couldn't possibly have developed a system that needs to scale at all (at least until such point as the HAL 9000 from *2001: A Space Odyssey* becomes a reality). Without people, who designed and implemented your system? Who runs it? Following from that, people are the source of the successes and failures that lead to whatever level of scale you have achieved and will achieve. People architect the systems, write or choose the software, and they deploy the software payloads and configure the servers, databases, firewalls, routers, and other devices. People make the tradeoffs on what pieces of the technology stack are easily horizontally scalable and which pieces are not. People design (or fail to design) the processes to identify scale concerns early on, root cause scale related availability events, drive scale related problems to closure, and report on scale needs and initiatives and their business returns. Initiatives aren't started without people and mistakes aren't made without people. People, people, people . . .

All of the greatest successes in building scalable systems have at their heart a great set of people making many great decisions and every once in awhile a few poor choices. Making the decision not to look at people as the core and most critical component of scaling anything is a very large mistake and a step in a direction that will at the very least make it very difficult for you to accomplish your objectives.

As people are at the heart of all highly scalable organizations, processes, and systems, doesn't it make sense to attract and retain the best people you can possibly get? As we will discuss in Chapter 5, Management 101, it's not just about finding the people with the right and best skills for the amount you are willing to pay. It's about ensuring that you have the right person in the right job at the right time and with the right behaviors.

The VC firm backing AllScale has a saying amongst its partners that the "fish rots from the head." Although the firm's representative on AllScale's board of directors and the remainder of the board feel that the current CEO and founder did a great job of growing the company and identifying the HRM market opportunity, they also know that the competencies necessary to run a successful SaaS company aren't always the same as those necessary to run and grow a successful consulting company. After several quarters of impressive growth in the HRM market, the board becomes concerned over stalling growth, missed numbers, and a lack of consistent focus on the HRM product. The board brings in a seasoned SaaS veteran as the new CEO, Christine E. Oberman, and moves the previous founder and CEO to the position of chief strategy officer. Christine promises to bring in and retain the best people, structure the company for success along its current and future product offerings, and focus on management and leadership excellence to supercharge and maximize shareholder wealth.

The *right person* speaks to whether the person has the right knowledge, skills, and abilities. Putting this person in the right job at the right time is about ensuring that he or she can be successful in that position and create the most shareholder value possible while tending to his or her career and offering the things that we need to feel good about and comfortable in our jobs. The *right behaviors* speaks to ensuring that the person works and plays well with others while adhering to the culture and values of the company. Bad behaviors are as good a reason for removing a person from the team as not having the requisite skills, because bad behavior in any team member creates a vicious cycle of plummeting morale and productivity.

Why Organizations

It should follow that if people are important to the scalability of a system, their organizational structure should also be important. If this isn't intuitively obvious, we offer a few things to consider regarding how organizational structure and responsibilities can positively or negatively impact your ability to scale a system.

An important concept to remember when considering organizational design as it relates to scale or any situation is that there rarely is a single right or wrong organizational structure. Once again, this is an art and not really a science. Each organizational structure carries with it pros and cons or benefits and drawbacks relative to the goals you wish to achieve. It's important when considering options on how to structure your organization to tease out the implicit and explicit benefits and drawbacks of the organizational design relative to your specific needs.

Some questions you should ask yourself when developing your organizational design are

- How easily can I add or remove people to/from this organization? Do I need to add them in groups, or can I add individual people?

- Does the organizational structure help or hinder the development of metrics that will help measure work done by the organization?

- How easily is this organization understood by the internal and external stakeholders of the organization (i.e., my customers, clients, vendors, etc.)?

- How does this organizational structure minimize the amount of work I lose on a per person basis as I add people to the organization?

- What conflicts will arise within the organizational structure as a result of the structure and how will those conflicts hinder the accomplishment of my organization's mission?

- Does work flow easily through the organization or is it easily contained within a portion of the organization?

These aren't the only questions one should ask when considering organizational structure, but each has a very real impact to the scalability of the organization. The question of how easily people are added is an obvious one as it is very difficult to significantly increase the amount of work done by an organization if your organizational structure does not allow the addition of people to perform additional or different types of work. Additionally, you want the flexibility of adding people incrementally rather than in large groups and the flexibility of easily removing people as market situations demand, such as a sudden increase in demands on the company or a market recession requiring constriction of expenses.

The question regarding metrics is important because while you often need to be able to scale an organization in size, you also want to ensure that you are measuring the output of both the organization and the individual people within the organization. An important point to remember here is that as you add people, although the total output of the team increases, the average output per person tends to go down slightly. This is the expected result of the overhead associated with communication between people to accomplish their tasks. Each person can only work so many hours in a day and certainly no more than 24. If an organization consisting of a single person were to work the maximum possible hours in a day, constrained either by law or exhaustion, doing his or her primary task and absolutely nothing else, it stands to reason that the same person when required to interface with other people will have less time to accomplish his or her primary task and as a result produce less in the same amount of time. Therefore, the more people with whom an individual needs to interface to complete any given task, the more time it will take for that person to complete that task as increasing amounts of time are spent interfacing and decreasing amounts of time are spent performing the task.

The way to envision this mathematically is that if a single person can produce 1.0 unit of work in a given timeframe, a two-person organization might produce 1.99 units of the same work in the same timeframe. Each person's output was slightly reduced and while the team produced more overall, each person produced slightly less on an individual basis. The resulting relative loss of .01 units of work in the aforementioned timeframe represents the inefficiencies caused by coordination and communication. We will cover this concept in more detail in Chapter 3, Designing Organizations, where we discuss team size and how it impacts productivity, morale, and customer relations.

If the structure of your organization is such that it disallows or makes difficult the establishment of measurements on individual performance, you will not be able to measure output. If you cannot measure the output of individuals and organizations, you can't react to sudden and rapid deteriorations in that output resulting from an increase in size of the organization or a change in organizational structure.

"How easily is this organization understood by the internal and external stakeholders of the organization" addresses the need for intuitive organizational constructs. Written another way, this question becomes "Are you aligned with your stakeholders or do you waste time getting requests from stakeholders to the right teams?" If you want an organization to scale well and easily, you don't want the external teams with which you interface (your customers, vendors, partners, etc.) to be scratching their heads trying to figuring out with whom they need to speak. Worse yet, you don't want to be spending a great deal of time trying to figure out how to parcel work out to the right groups based on some stakeholder request or need. This might mean that you need to develop teams within your organization to handle external communication or it might mean that teams are developed around stakeholder interests and needs so that each external interface only works with a single team.

We discussed the question of "How does this organization structure minimize the amount of work I lose on a per person basis as I add people to the organization?" within our explanation of our question on metrics. You might have been in organizations where you receive hundreds of internal emails a day and potentially dozens of meeting invites/requests a week. If you've been in such a situation, you've no doubt spent

Figure 1.1   *Coordination Steals Individual Productivity*

time just to eliminate the emails and requests that aren't relevant to your job responsibilities. This is a perfect example of how as you add people, the output of each individual within an organization goes down (refer back to our example of one person producing 1.0 unit of work and 2 producing 1.99 units of work). In the preceding example, as you add people, the email volume grows and time dedicated to reading and discarding irrelevant emails goes up. Figure 1.1 is a depiction of an engineering team attempting to coordinate and communicate and Table 1.1 shows the increase in overall output, but the decrease in individual output between an organization of three individuals and an organization consisting of one individual. In Table 1.1, we show an individual loss of productivity due to communication and coordination of .005, which represents 2.4 minutes a day of coordination activity in an 8-hour day. This isn't a lot of time, and most of us intuitively would expect that three people working on the same project will spend at least 2.4 minutes a day coordinating their activities even with a manager! One person on the other hand need not perform this coordination. So, as individual productivity drops, the team output still increases.

Table 1.1   *Individual Loss of Productivity as Team Size Increases*

Organization Size	Communication and Coordination Cost	Individual Productivity	Organization Productivity
1	0	1	1
3	0.005	0.995	2.985

You can offset but not completely eliminate this deterioration in a number of ways. One possibility is to add management to limit interpersonal coordination. Another possibility is to limit the interactions between individuals by creating smaller self-sufficient teams. Both of these approaches have benefits and drawbacks that we will discuss in Chapter 3. Many other approaches are possible and anything that increases individual throughput without damaging innovation should be considered.

Another important point in organizational design and structure is that anywhere you create organizational or team boundaries, you create organizational and team conflict. The question "What conflicts will arise within the organizational structure as a result of the structure and how will those conflicts hinder the accomplishment of my organization's mission?" attempts to address this problem, but there is really no way around boundaries causing friction. Your goal then should be to minimize the conflict created by organizational boundaries. The greatest conflict tends to be created when you have organizations with divergent missions, measurements, and goals, and an easy fix to this drawback is to ensure that every organization shares some set of core goals that drive their behaviors. We'll discuss this in more detail in Chapter 3 where we will cover the two basic types of organizational structures and what purposes they serve.

"Does work flow easily through the organization or is it easily contained within a portion of the organization?" is meant to focus on the suitability of your organizational design to the type of work you do. Does work flow through your organization as efficiently as a well-defined assembly line? Does the type of work you do lend itself easily to a pipeline, where one team can start its work at a predefined place marked by where another team completes its work without a lot of communication overhead? Or is the work largely custom and highly intellectual, requiring a single team to work on it from start to finish without interruption? Are the components of what you build or produce capable of operating through a well-defined interface such that two teams can work on subcomponents at the same time?

Let's take a look at our company, AllScale. AllScale recognizes that it has a need to scale the number of people within the engineering team that is supporting the HRM software in order to produce more products. Over the course of the last year, AllScale has added several engineers and now has a total of three managers and ten engineers. Each of the three managers reports to the chief technology officer (CTO) of AllScale. These engineers are broken down into the following teams:

- Two engineers responsible for the provisioning of systems, networking devices, databases, etc. for AllScale's HRM product. This is the Operations team.

- Six engineers responsible for developing the applications that make revenue for AllScale's HRM product. This is the Engineering team.

- Two engineers responsible for testing AllScale's HRM product for defects and other quality related issues. This is the QA team.

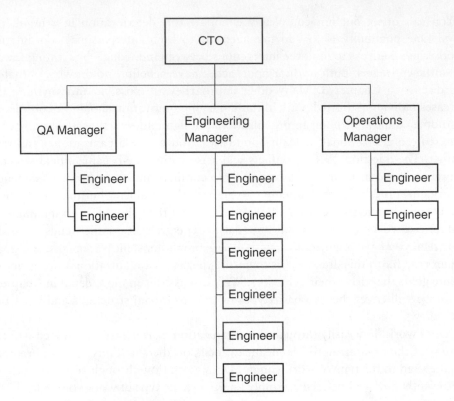

Figure 1.2 *AllScale Org Chart*

At a high level, we can intuit a few things from the structure of this organization. The designer of the organization believes that the separation into teams by skill set or functional job responsibility will not have an adverse impact on his or her ability to develop and launch new product functionality. The designer evidently sees great value in dedicating a group of people to testing the product to ensure it conforms to the company's quality standards. Benefits we would expect from such an organization are the ability to recruit top talent with focused skill sets such as software engineering in one or more programming languages, hardware/infrastructure experience, and quality/testing experience. At a high level, it appears that we should be able to relatively easily add engineers, operations/infrastructure engineers, and quality assurance engineers—at least until a manager is saturated with direct reports. This organization should be easily understood by all of the stakeholders as it is structured by relatively easily understood skills. Finally, work would seem to be able to flow easily between the organizations as we should be able to define measurable criteria that will qualify any given work product as being "ready" for the next phase of work. For instance, code might be ready for QA after it has passed a peer review and all unit testing is completed, and it might be ready for launching to the site and the Operations team after all priority one bugs are fixed and at least 90% of all other defects found in the first pass are resolved.

There are some potential drawbacks of such an organizational structure, however. For instance, how are you going to measure the throughput of the teams? Who is responsible for causing a slowdown of new initiative (feature or product) development? Will you measure your operations/infrastructure team by how many new features are launched to the site; if not, what keeps them from slowing down feature development in an attempt to increase a metric they will likely covet such as availability? When do you determine that something is "completed" for the purposes of measuring your engineering throughput? Is it when the feature launches live to site and if so, have you calculated the bug induced rework time in developing the feature?

Will the structure minimize the work loss on a per person basis as you grow the team? To know this, we probably need to dig into exactly how the software engineers are structured but we can probably also guess that coordination across teams is going to be a source of some work. Who will perform this coordination? Are the managers responsible for shepherding something from engineering to QA (Quality Assurance) and finally into the production team (Operations)? Who is responsible for setting the guidelines and criteria for when something moves from one place to another? Should you create a project management team responsible for helping to do this or should you instead reorganize your teams into self-contained teams that have all the skill sets necessary to complete any given task?

There are likely to be a great many conflicts in this proposed structure, many of them across the organizational boundaries we've defined. Operations will likely have concerns over the quality of new code or systems deployed, QA is likely to have concerns over the level of quality initially presented to them by Engineering, and Engineering will complain that Operations does not meet their needs quickly enough with respect to the creation of new systems, installation of new databases, and provisioning of new network devices. Who will be responsible for helping to resolve these conflicts, as each conflict takes time away from doing "real work."

Other, larger questions we might have of such an organizational structure might be "Who is responsible for ensuring that the product or platform has an appropriate level of scale for our needs?" or "Who is responsible for identifying and resolving issues of scale?" When considering the answer to this question, please note that a scale issue might be the result of a network capacity constraint, a database capacity constraint, or a software capacity constraint. Moreover, that constraint isn't going to be easily bucketed into one of these areas every time it comes up.

Why Management and Leadership

In our experience, relatively few managers and leaders have ever had a course on management or leadership. Few universities offer such classes, unless you happen to have been a management major or have attended an MBA program with a management curriculum. Given the lack of management and leadership courses in our universities, most people learn how to manage and how to lead informally: you watch what others do in peer positions and positions of greater responsibility and you decide what works and what doesn't. Over time, we start to develop our own "toolboxes" and add tools from our professional readings or discard tools as they age and become less relevant to our younger generations of employees. This general "life as a lab" approach is how we've developed managers for years and, although it has its benefits, it is unfortunate that the two areas don't get better treatment in structured curriculums within universities and within larger corporations.

Management and leadership either multiply or detract from your ability to scale organizations in growth environments. They are often spoken of within the same context, but they are really two very different disciplines with very different impact on scalability. Many times, the same person will perform both the functions of a leader and a manager. In most organizations, one will progress from a position of an individual contributor into a primarily management focused role; and over time with future promotions, that person will take on increasing leadership responsibilities.

In general and at a very high level, you can think of management activities as "pushing" activities and leadership as "pulling" activities. Leadership sets a destination and "waypoints" toward that destination; management gets you to that destination. Leadership would be stating "We will never have a scalability related downtime in our systems" and management would be ensuring that it never happens. You absolutely need both and if you are going to scale your organization, your processes, and your systems well and cost effectively, you need to do both well.

Far too often, we get caught up in the notion of a "management style." We might believe that a person's "management style" makes them more of a leader or more of a manager. This notion of style is our perception of an individual's bias toward the tasks that define either leadership or management. We might believe that a person is more operationally focused and is therefore more of a "manager" or more visionary and therefore more of a "leader." Although we all have a set of personality traits and skills that likely make us more comfortable or more capable with one set of activities over the other, there is no reason we can't get better at both disciplines. Recognizing that they are two distinct disciplines is a step toward isolating and developing both our management and leadership capabilities to the benefit of our shareholders.

As we have indicated, management is about "pushing." Management is about ensuring that people are assigned to the appropriate tasks and that those tasks are completed within the specified time interval and at an appropriate cost. Management is about setting individual contributor goals along the path to the greater leadership goals and helping a team to accomplish both the individual contributor and team goals. It is also about ensuring that people get performance-oriented feedback in a timely manner and that the feedback includes both praise for great performance and information regarding what they can improve. Management is about measuring and improving everything that ultimately creates shareholder value, examples of which are reducing the cost to perform an activity or increasing the throughput of an activity at the same cost. Management is communicating status early and often and clearly identifying what is on track and where help is needed. Management activities also include removing obstacles or helping the team over or around obstacles where they occur on the path to an objective. Management is important to scale as it is how you get the most out of an organization, thereby reducing cost per unit of work performed. The definition of how something is to be performed is a management responsibility and how something is performed absolutely impacts the scale of organizations, processes, and systems.

Management as it relates to people is about the practice of ensuring that we have the right person in the right job at the right time with the right behaviors. From an organizational perspective, it is about ensuring that the team operates well together and has the proper mix of skills and experiences to be successful. Management as applied to an organization's work is about ensuring that projects are on budget, on time, and meeting the expected results upon which their selection was predicated. Management means measurement and a failure to measure is a failure to manage. Failing to manage in turn is a guarantee to miss your organizational, process, and systems scalability objectives as without management, no one is ensuring that you are doing the things you need to do in the timeframe required.

Leadership has to do with all the pulling activities necessary to be successful in any endeavor. If management is the act of pushing an organization up a hill, leadership is the selection of that hill and then being first up it to encourage your organization to follow. Leadership is about inspiring people and organizations to do better and hopefully great things. Leadership is creating a vision that drives people to do the right thing for the company. Leadership is creating a mission that helps codify the aforementioned vision and creating a causal mental roadmap that helps employees understand how what they do creates value for the shareholder. Finally, leadership is about the definition of the goals on the way to an objective. Leadership is important to scale as it not only sets the direction (mission) and destination (vision) but it inspires people and organizations to achieve that destination.

Any initiative lacking leadership (including initiatives meant to increase the scalability of your company), while not doomed to certain failure, will likely only achieve success through pure dumb luck and chance. Great leaders create a culture focused on ensuring success through highly scalable organizations, processes, and products. This culture is supported by incentives structured around ensuring that the company scales cost effectively without user perceived quality of service or availability issues.

Conclusion

We've asserted that people, organizations, management, and leadership are all important to scalability. People are the most important element of scalability, as without people there are no processes and there is no technology. The effective organization of your people will either get you to where you need to be faster or hinder your efforts in producing scalable systems. Management and leadership are the push and pull, respectively, in the whole operation. Leadership serves to inspire people to greater accomplishments, and management exists to motivate them to the objective.

Key Points

- People are the most important piece of the scale puzzle.
- The right person in the right job at the right time and with the right behaviors is essential to scale organizations, processes, and systems.
- Organizational structures are rarely "right or wrong." Any structure is likely to have pros and cons relative to your needs.
- When designing your organization, consider
  - The ease with which you can add people to the organization
  - The ease with which you can measure organizational success and individual contributions over time
  - How easy the organization is to understand for an outsider
  - How the organizational structure impacts individual productivity
  - What "friction" will exist between teams within the organization
  - How easily work flows through the organization
- Adding people to organizations may increase the organizational throughput, but the average production per individual tends to go down.
- Management is about achieving goals. A lack of management is nearly certain to doom your scalability initiatives.
- Leadership is about goal definition, vision creation, and mission articulation. An absence of leadership as it relates to scale is detrimental to your objectives.

Chapter 2

Roles for the Scalable Technology Organization

> When the general is weak and without authority; when his orders are not clear and distinct; when there are no fixed duties assigned to officers and men, and the ranks are formed in a slovenly haphazard manner, the result is utter disorganization.
>
> —Sun Tzu

One of the easiest and most common ways for companies to fail in their scalability related endeavors is to not have clarity around the matter of who is responsible for what. Clearly defining high-level goals and objectives is a leadership responsibility and defining the roles and responsibilities of executives, organizations, and individual contributors is a management responsibility. A lack of clarity can be disastrous for the company and organization in a number of ways. In this chapter, we will start by taking a look at two very real examples of what might happen without role clarity and responsibility. We then will discuss the executive roles, the organizational responsibilities, individual contributor's roles, and conclude by introducing a tool that is extremely useful to ensure that initiatives have all the proper roles filled.

This chapter is meant for companies of all sizes. For large companies, it can serve as a checklist to ensure that you have covered all of the technology and executive roles and responsibilities as they relate to scale. For small companies, it can help jumpstart the process of ensuring that you have your scalability related roles properly defined. For the technology neophyte, it is a primer for how technology organizations should work, and for seasoned technology professionals, it is a reminder to review organizational structure to validate that you have your scalability related needs covered. For all companies, it clearly defines the need for individual contributors through the chief executive to be involved with the scalability of the systems, organizations, and platforms that run their company.

21

The Effects of Failure

On one end of the spectrum, a lack of clarity around roles and responsibilities may result in individuals or groups not performing a necessary task, which may in turn result in one or more failures of your product, organization, or processes. Take for instance the case where no team or individual is assigned the responsibility of capacity planning. In this context, capacity planning is the comparison of expected demand to systems capacity (supply or maximum capacity by type of request) resulting in a set of proposed actions to ensure that capacity matches demand. Expected demand is defined by the forecasted number of requests, by function, placed on the system in question. The proposed set of actions may include requesting the purchase of additional servers, requesting architectural evaluation of system components to allow systems scale to meet demand, or a requesting that systems be modified to scale more cost effectively.

The flow for this example may start with a business unit creating a demand forecast and handing it off to the person responsible for capacity analysis and planning. The capacity planner takes a look at the types of demand forecasted by the business unit and translates those into the resulting product/system/platform requests. He then also factors in the expected results of product/system changes that create new functionality and determines where the system will need modifications in order to meet new demand, new functionality, or functionality modifications. The resulting deficiencies are then passed on to someone responsible for determining what actions should be taken to correct the expected deficiencies. Those actions as previously identified may be the purchase of new systems, a change in the architecture of certain components of the platform, such as the data model or the movement of demand from one group of services to another group.

In this case, the absence of a team or person responsible for matching expected demand to existing capacity and determining appropriate actions would be disastrous in an environment where demand is growing rapidly. Nevertheless, this failure happens all the time—especially in young companies. Even companies that have a person or organization responsible for capacity planning often fail to plan for their newest system additions.

On the other end of the spectrum is a case where organizations are given similar responsibilities but are not required or incented to work together to successfully complete their objectives. If you are in a smaller company where everyone knows what everyone else is doing, this may seem a bit ridiculous to you. Unfortunately, this problem exists in many of our larger client companies and when it happens it not only wastes money and destroys shareholder value, it can create long-term resentment between organizations and destroy employee morale.

In this case, let's assume that an organization is split between an engineering organization responsible primarily for developing software and an operations organization responsible primarily for building and deploying systems, creating and managing databases, deploying networks, etc. Let's further assume that we have a relatively inexperienced CTO who has recently read a book on the value of shared goals and objectives and has decided to give both teams the responsibility of scaling the platform to meet expected customer demand. The company has a capacity planner who determines that to meet next year's demand the teams must scale the subsystem responsible for customer contact management to handle at least twice the number of transactions it is capable of handling today.

Both the engineering and operations teams have architects who have read the technology section of our book and both decide to make splits of the database supporting the customer contact management system. Both architects believe they are empowered to make the appropriate decisions without the help of the other architect as they are unaware that multiple people have been assigned the same responsibility and were not informed that they should work together. The engineering architect decides that a split along transaction boundaries (or functions of a Web site such as buying an item and viewing an item on an ecommerce site) will work best, and the operations architect decides that a split along customer boundaries makes the most sense, where groups of customers all reside in separate databases. Both go about making initial plans for the split, setting their teams about doing their work and then making requests of the other team to perform some work.

This example may sound a bit ridiculous to you, but it happens all the time. At best, the two teams stop there and resolve the issue having "only" wasted the valuable time of two architects. Unfortunately, what usually happens is that the teams polarize to waste even more time in political infighting, and the result isn't materially better after all the wasted time than if a single person or team had the responsibility to craft the best solution with the input of other teams.

Defining Roles

This section gives an example of how you might define roles to help resolve issues such as those identified in the preceding. We have given examples of how roles might be defined at the top leadership level of the company (the executive team), within classic technology organizational structures, and at an individual contributor level.

Our examples of executive, organizational, and individual contributor responsibilities are not meant to restrict you to specific job titles or organizational structure. Rather, they are to help outline the necessary roles within a company. We've chosen to define these roles by the organizations in which they have traditionally existed to make it easier to understand for a majority of our audience. For instance, you may decide that you want operations, infrastructure, engineering, and QA to exist within the same teams with each dedicated to a specific product line. You may recall from our introductory discussion on organizational structure that there is no "right or wrong" answer on the topic—simply benefits and drawbacks of any decision. The important point is to remember that you include all of the appropriate responsibilities in your organizational design and that you clearly define not only who is a responsible decision maker but also who is responsible for providing input to any decision, who should be informed of the decision and actions, and who is responsible for making the decision happen. We'll discuss this last point in a brief section on a valuable tool later in this chapter.

A Brief Note on Delegation

Before launching into the proposed division of responsibilities within an organization, we thought it important to include a brief note on delegation. In defining roles and responsibilities within organizations, you are creating a blueprint of delegation. Delegation, broadly speaking, is the act of empowering someone else to act on your behalf. For instance, by giving an architect or architecture team the responsibility to design a system, you are delegating the work of creating that architecture to that team. You may also decide to delegate the authority to make decisions to that team depending upon their capabilities, the size of your company, and so on.

Here's a very important point. You can delegate anything you would like, but you can *never* delegate the accountability for results. At best, the team or individual to whom you delegate can inherit that responsibility and you can ultimately fire, promote, or otherwise reward or punish the team for its results but you should always consider yourself responsible for the end result. Great leaders get this intuitively and they put great teams ahead of themselves in success and take public accountability for failures. Poor leaders assume that they can "pass the buck" for failures and take credit for successes.

To codify this point in your mind, let's apply "the shareholder test." Assume that you are the CEO of a company and you have decided to delegate the responsibility for one of your business units to a general manager. Can you imagine telling your board of directors or your shareholders (whom the board represents) that you will not be held accountable for the results of that business? One step removed, do you think the board will not hold you at least partially responsible if the business begins to underperform relative to expectations?

Again, this does not mean that you should make all the decisions yourself. As your company and team grow and scale, you simply won't be able to do that and in many cases might not be qualified to make the decisions. For instance, a nontechnical CEO should probably not be making architecture decisions and a CTO of a 200-person engineering organization should not be writing the most important code as he or she is needed in other executive tasks. It simply makes the point that you absolutely must have the best people possible to whom you can delegate and that you must hold those people to the highest possible standards. It also means that you should be asking the best questions possible about how someone came to his or her decisions on the most critical projects and systems.

Executive Responsibilities

The executives of a company as a team are responsible more than anyone else for imprinting the company with "scale DNA" and creating a culture of scalability as defined in our introductory chapter. Getting high-level executive responsibilities right is the easiest thing to do and also the most overlooked aspect of ensuring that organizations can scale to the need of the company and that further organizations support the need to scale the technology that makes the company money.

CEO

The CEO is the chief scalability officer of the company. As with all other matters within the company, when it comes to scale, he or she is the final decision maker and arbiter of all things related to scale. A good technology company CEO needs to be appropriately technically proficient, but that does not mean that he needs to be the technology expert or the primary technology decision maker.

It is hard to imagine that someone would rise to the position of CEO and not understand how to read a balance sheet, income statement, or statement of cash flow. That same person, unless she has an accounting background or is a former CFO, is not likely to understand the intricacies of each accounting policy nor should she need to. The CEO's job is to ask the right questions, get the right people involved, and get the right outside help or advice to arrive at the right answer.

The same holds true in the technical world—the CEO's job is to understand some of the basics (the equivalent of the financial statements mentioned above), to know which questions to ask, and to know where to get help. Here is some advice for CEOs and other managers responsible for technical organizations who have not been the chief technology officer or chief information officer of a company, do not have technical degrees, or have never been an engineer:

Ask Questions and Look for Consistency in Explanations Part of your job is to be a truth seeker, because only with the truth can you make sound and timely decisions. Although we do not think it is commonplace for teams to lie to you, it is very common for teams to have different pieces and perceptions of the truth, especially when it comes to issues of scale. When you do not understand something, or something does not seem right, ask questions. When you are unable to discern fact from perception, look for consistency in answers. If you can get over any potential ego or pride issues with asking what might seem to be ignorant questions, you will find that you not only quickly educate yourself but you will create and hone a very important skill in finding truth.

This *executive interrogation* is a key ability shared by many successful leaders. Knowing when to probe and where to probe and probing until you are satisfied with answers need not be limited to the CEO. In fact, managers and individual contributors should all hone this skill and start early in their careers.

Seek Outside Help Seek help from friends or professionals who are proficient and knowledgeable in the area of scalability. Don't bring them in and attempt to have them sort things out for you—that can be very damaging. Rather, we suggest creating a professional or personal relationship with a technically literate firm or peer. Leverage that relationship to help you ask the right questions and evaluate the answers when you need to dive deeply.

Improve Your Scalability Proficiency Create a list of your weaknesses in technology—things about which you have questions—and go get help to become smarter. You can ask questions of your team and outside professionals. Read blogs on scale related issues relevant to your company or product and attend workshops on technology for people without technical backgrounds. You probably already do this through professional reading lists on other executive topics—add technology scalability to the list. You do *not* need to learn a programming language, understand *how* an operating system or database works, or understand how "Collision Detection Multiple Access/Carrier Detect" is implemented. You just need to be able to get better at asking questions and evaluating the issues your teams bring to you. Scalability is a business issue, but to solve it, you need to at least be somewhat conversant in the technology portion of the equation.

More than likely, the CEO will decide to delegate authority to several members of his or her team including the chief financial officer (CFO), individual business unit owners (a.k.a. general managers), and the head engineering and technology executive (referred to as either the CTO or CIO in our book).

CFO

Most likely, the CEO has delegated the responsibility for budgeting to the CFO, although this may not always be the case. Budgeting is informed by capacity planning and, as we've seen in our previous example of how things can go wrong, capacity planning is a very large part of successfully scaling a system. Ensuring that the team and company have sufficient budget to scale the platform/product/system is a key portion of the budgeting officer's responsibility. The budget needs to be sufficiently large to allow the company to scale to the expected demand by purchasing or leasing servers and hiring the appropriate engineers and operations staff. That said, the budget should not be so large that the company spends money on scale long before it truly needs it because such spending dilutes near term net income for very little benefit. Purchasing and implementing "just in time" systems and solutions optimizes the company's net income and cash flow.

The CFO is also not likely to be very technical, but can benefit from asking the right questions and creating an appropriate network, just as we described with the CEO. Questions that the CFO might ask regarding scalability include asking what other scale alternatives were considered in developing the proposed budget for scale and what tradeoffs were made in deciding upon the existing approach. The intent here is to ensure that the team considered more than one option. A bad answer would be "This is the only way possible," as that is rarely the case. (We want to say it is never the case, but it is possible to have a case where only one route is possible.) A good answer might be "of the options we evaluated, this one allows us to scale horizontally at comparatively low cost while setting us up to scale even more cost effectively in the future by laying a framework whereby we can continue our horizontal scale."

Business Unit Owners, General Managers, and P&L Owners

More than any other position, the business unit general manager or owner of the company or division's profit and loss statement (also called the income statement or P&L) is responsible for forecasting the platform/product/system dependent business growth. In small- to medium-sized companies, it is very likely that the business unit owner is the CEO and that he or she might delegate this responsibility to some member of her staff. Nevertheless, demand projections are critical to the activity of determining what needs to be scaled so that the budget for scale doesn't become too large ahead of the corporate need.

Very often, we run into situations in which we hear the business unit owner claiming that demand simply can't be forecasted. Here, *demand* means the number of requests that are placed against a system or product. This is a punting of responsibility that simply should not be tolerated within any company. In essence, the lack of ownership on forecasting demand by the business gets moved to the technology organization, which in turn is very likely less capable of forecasting demand than the business unit owner. Yes, it is very likely that your forecasts will be wrong, especially in their infancy, but it is absolutely critical that you start the process early in the life cycle of the company and mature it over time.

Finally, as with other senior executive staff of the company, the business unit owner is responsible for helping to create a culture of scalability. Ensuring that he or she is asking the right questions of her peer (or subordinate) in the technology organization and trying to ensure that the technology partner receives the funding and support to properly support the business unit in question are all essential to the success of scalability within the company.

CTO/CIO

Although the CEO is the chief scalability officer of the company, the chief technology executive is the chief technology, technical process, and technology organization scalability officer. In some companies, particularly Internet companies, the chief technology executive is often titled the CTO or chief technology officer. In these companies, the CTO might be responsible for another technology executive responsible for corporate technology, or the technology that runs the back office systems of the company, and this person is often titled the CIO or chief information officer. In older companies, the chief technology executive is often titled the CIO, whereas the CTO is very often the head engineer or head architect. We will use CTO and CIO throughout this book to mean, interchangeably, the chief technology executive of the company. He or she most likely has the best background and capabilities to ensure that the company scales cost effectively ahead of the product/system or platform needs.

In essence, "the buck stops here." Although it is true that the CEO can't truly "delegate" responsibility for the success of the platform scalability initiatives, it is also true that the chief technology executive inherits that responsibility and shares it with the CEO. A failure to properly scale will likely at least result in the termination of the chief technology executive, portions of his or her organization, and potentially even the CEO.

The CTO/CIO must create the technical vision of the company overall, and for the purposes of our discussion, within a growth company that vision must include elements of scale. The chief technology executive is further responsible for setting the aggressive, measurable, and achievable goals that nest to that vision and for ensuring that his or her team is appropriately staffed to accomplish the associated scalability mission of the organization. The CTO/CIO is responsible for the development of the culture and processes surrounding scalability that will help ensure that the company is always ahead of end-user demand.

The CTO/CIO will absolutely need to delegate responsibilities for certain aspects of decision making around scalability as the company grows, but as we pointed out previously this never eliminates his or her responsibility to ensure that it is done correctly, on time, and on budget. Additionally, in hyper-growth environments where scale is critical to company survival, the CTO should never delegate the development of the vision for scale. The term "lead from the front" is never more important than here, and the vision does not need to be deeply technical.

Although the best CTOs we have seen have had technology backgrounds varying from once having been an individual contributor to having been a systems analyst or technical project manager, we have seen examples of successful CTOs without such backgrounds. When you have a nontechnical CTO/CIO, it is absolutely critical that he or she has some technical acumen and is capable of speaking the language and understanding the critical tradeoffs within technology such as the relationship of time, cost, and quality. Inserting a technology neophyte to lead a technical organization is akin to throwing a nonswimmer overboard into a lake; you may be pleased with your results assuming the person can swim, but more often than not you're going to need to find yourself a new partner in your boat.

Equally important is that the CTO have some business acumen. Unfortunately, this is as difficult to achieve as finding a chief marketing officer with a Ph.D. in electrical engineering (not that you'd necessarily want one)—they exist but they are difficult to find. Unfortunately, most technologists do not learn about business, finance, or marketing within their undergraduate or graduate courses. Although the CTO does not need to be an expert on capital markets (that's likely the job of the CFO), he should understand the fundamentals of the business in which the company operates. For example, the CTO should be able to read and understand the relationships between the income statement, balance sheet, and statement of cash flow. She should also understand marketing basics to the level of at least a community college or company sponsored course on the subject. This is not to say that the CTO needs to be an expert in any of these areas; rather, a basic understanding of these topics is critical to making the business case for scalability and to being able to communicate effectively in the business world. We'll discuss these areas in later chapters.

Organizational Responsibilities

We are going to describe roles in terms of organizational responsibilities within a traditionally constructed technology team. These usually consist of teams responsible for the overall architecture of the product (architecture), the software engineering of the product (engineering), the monitoring and production handling of the product (operations), design and deployment of hardware for the product (infrastructure engineering), and the testing of the product (quality assurance).

The choice to define these within organizations was a tradeoff. We wanted to ensure that everyone had a list of scalability related responsibilities that need to exist within any organization. This could be accomplished with a simple list of responsibilities that could be parceled out to any organizational structure. We also wanted a number of teams to be able to use the responsibilities out of the book immediately, which was best served by defining those responsibilities within the traditional organizational constructs. In no way do we mean to imply, however, that this is the only way to set up responsibilities for your organizations. You should develop the organizational structure that best serves your needs and ensure that all of the responsibilities included in the following sections are contained within one of your teams.

Architecture Responsibilities

The team responsible for architecture is responsible for ensuring that the *design* and *architecture* of the system allow for scale in the timeframe appropriate to the business. Here, we clearly indicate a difference between the intended design and the actual implementation. The team or teams responsible for architecture decisions need to think well in advance of the needs of the business and have thought through how to scale the system long before the business unit owners forecast demand exceeding the platform capacity at any given time. For instance, the architecture team may have developed an extensible data access layer (DAL) or data access object (DAO) that can allow for multiple physical databases to be accessed with varying schemas as user demand increases in any given area. The actual implementation may be such that only a single database is used, but with some cost-effective modification of the DAL/ DAO and some work creating migration scripts, additional databases can be stood up in the production environment in a matter of weeks rather than months should the need arise. The architecture team is further responsible for creating the set of architecture standards by which engineers design code and implement systems.

The architecture team, more than any other team, is responsible for designing a system and having designs ready to solve any scale related issue. In Part II, Building Processes for Scale, we identify a key process that the architecture team should adopt to help identify scale related problems across all of the technology disciplines.

Architects may also be responsible for forming information technology (IT) governance, standards, and procedures, and enforcement of those standards through such processes as the Architecture Review Board discussed in Chapter 14, Architecture Review Board. When architects perform these roles, they do so at the request of the chief technology executive. Some larger companies may create process engineering teams responsible for procedure definition and standards enforcement.

Engineering Responsibilities

This team is "where the rubber meets the road." The engineering team is the chief implementer of the scalability mission and the chief tuner of the product platform. Engineers take the architecture and create lower-level designs that they ultimately implement within code. They are responsible for adhering to the company's architectural standards. Engineering teams are one of the two or three teams most likely to truly understand the limits of the system as implemented given that they are one of the teams with the greatest daily involvement with that system. As such, they are key contributors to the process of identifying future scale issues.

Production Operations Responsibilities

The production operations team is responsible for running the hardware systems and software systems necessary to complete the mission of the company. In the Software as a Service and Web2.0 worlds, this is the team responsible for running and monitoring the systems that create the company's revenue. In a classic information technology organization, such as those that might exist in a bank, these members are responsible for running the applications and systems that handle the bank's daily transactions, and so on. In a company producing a manufactured product such as a company in the automotive industry, this team is responsible for handling all of the company's manufacturing systems, enterprise resource planning systems, and so on.

This team is part of the group of three teams with excellent insight into the limitations of the system as currently implemented. As the team interacts with how the system runs every day and as it has daily insight into system utilization data, these team members are uniquely qualified to identify bottlenecks within the system.

Often, this team is responsible for creating utilization reports, daily downtime, and activity reports, and is responsible for escalating issues and managing issues to resolution. As such, very often, capacity planning will fall onto this team, although that is not an absolute necessity. Operations personnel are also typically responsible for creating reports that show trended availability over time, bucketing root cause and corrective actions, and determining mean time to resolution and mean time to restoration for various problems.

Regardless of the composition of the team, the organization responsible for monitoring and reporting on the health of systems, applications, and quality of service plays a crucial role in helping to identify scale issues. The processes that this group employs to manage issue and problem resolution should feed information into other processes that help identify scale issues in advance of major outages. The data that the operations organization collects is incredibly valuable to those performing capacity planning as well as those responsible for designing away systemic and recurring issues such as scale related events. The architecture and engineering teams rely heavily on product operations to help them identify what should be fixed and when. We discuss some of these processes in Part II and more specifically in Chapter 8, Managing Incidents and Problems, Chapters 13, Joint Architecture Design, and Chapter 14, Architecture Review Board.

Infrastructure Responsibilities

This organization is typically comprised of database administrators, network engineers, and systems administrators. They are often responsible for defining which systems will be used, when systems should be purchased, and when systems should be retired. This group is also one of the three groups interacting with the holistic system, platform, or product on a daily basis; as such, these members are uniquely qualified to help identify where bottlenecks exist. Their primary responsibility is to identify capacity constraints on the systems, network devices, and databases that they support and to further help in identifying appropriate fixes for scale related issues.

Quality Assurance Responsibilities

In the ideal scenario, the team responsible for testing an application to ensure it is consistent with the company's product or systems requirements will also play a role in advanced testing for scale. New products, features, and functionality change the demand characteristics of a system, platform, or product. Most often, we are adding new functions that by definition create additional demand on a system. Ideally, we can profile that new demand creation to ensure that the release of our new functionality or features won't have a significant impact to the production environment. The QA organization also needs to be aware of all other changes going on around them so that it can ensure that whatever scale related testing is done gets updated in a timely fashion.

Capacity Planning Responsibilities

This organization or responsibility can reside nearly anywhere, but it needs access to up-to-date information regarding system, product, and platform performance. Capacity planning is a key to scaling efficiently and cost effectively. When performed well, the capacity planning process results in the timely purchase of equipment where systems are easily horizontally scaled, the emergency purchase of larger equipment where systems cannot yet be scaled horizontally, and the identification of systems that should be prioritized high on the list of scale related problems to correct.

You may notice that we use the word *emergency* when describing the purchase of a larger system. Many companies take the approach that "scaling up" is an effective strategy, but our position, as we will describe in Chapters 21 through 25, is that if your scaling strategy relies on faster and bigger hardware, your solution does not scale; rather, you are relying upon the scalability of your providers to allow you to scale. Stating that you scale by moving to bigger and faster hardware is like stating that you are fast by buying a bigger, faster car. You have not worked to become faster, and you are only as fast as anyone else with similar wealth. Scalability is the ability to scale independent of bigger and faster systems or the next release of an application server or database.

Individual Contributor Responsibilities and Characteristics

Having just described the scalability related roles that should be covered by different organizations within your company, we will now describe the roles of individuals that might fit within different organizations. We will cover the role of the architect, the software engineer, the operator, the infrastructure engineer, the QA analyst, and the capacity planner. These roles may not need to be staffed by a single person or a group of people if you are a small company; it is enough in small companies to have the responsibilities defined within each of the roles assigned to different individuals within your organization.

Architect

More than any other role, the architect is responsible for the availability, scalability, and technical success of the product, platform, or system design. When it comes to scalability, the great architect will have an answer for how he or she expects to scale any given component of the system and be able to explain why his or her approach is the most cost-effective solution available for that component.

The architect must know the end user, have a holistic view of the system, understand the cost of operating the system in its current design and implementation, and have a deep knowledge of all technologies employed to create the system, platform, or product. Too often, architects will work out of "ivory towers" and not really know how the product, platform, or system "really" operates. They may get too much into "markitecture," the creation of slides to impress others with their intelligence, and stray too far from the nuts and bolts of how things really work.

The architect needs to be an evangelist for the appropriate way to solve scale related issues. She needs to be aware of emerging technologies and how those might be employed to win the scalability battle. Great architects understand and have a history with both the software and the systems that comprise the production environment and facilitate the product, platform, or holistic system in question.

When it comes to scale initiatives, the architect should be measured by the true performance of the system. Has it had availability or performance related issues as a result of the architect's design?

For truly hyper-growth companies, we suggest the creation of a specialized architect focused on platform, product, or system scalability. We believe that there is sufficient specificity in technical knowledge, perspective, and focus unique to scale initiatives that companies undergoing extreme growth need someone with a focus just on scaling the system. The ideal candidate for such a position should be able to explain how to split both systems and applications along the lines we discuss in Chapters 21 through 24. Furthermore, the architect ideally comes with a resume indicating how he has performed such splits in the past. We call this unique position a *scalability architect*.

Software Engineer

A software engineer is a member of the team responsible for implementing functionality and product changes and additions in software. The software engineer is also responsible for coding any proprietary changes that allow a system to be more highly scalable.

The software engineer, more than any other role, is responsible for the scalability of his portion of the system as it is implemented. Here, we call out the difference between design and implementation as very often an implementation will not be

100% consistent with the design. For instance, if a design calls for a configurable number (max number undefined) of similarly configured *read databases*, to which all read transactions can be evenly distributed, and the software engineer implements a system capable of handling up to five read databases, he or she has implemented a system with a defined scale limit. Here, *defined scale limit* is the limitation the engineer put on how many databases can be implemented (five).

A software engineer should understand the portion of the system that she supports, maintains, or for which she creates code. He should also understand the end user and how the end user interacts with the software engineer's portion of the system. The software engineer is a contributor to many of the scalability processes we define later in Part II.

Operator

The operator is responsible for handling the daily operations of the production system, whether that system is a Web 2.0 system or a back office IT system. She is responsible for monitoring the system against specific service levels, monitoring for out of bounds conditions, alerting individuals based on service level or boundary condition failures, and tracking incidents to closure. A form of operator, sometimes called an incident manager, is responsible for managing major problems to closure and issuing root cause and corrective action reports.

Infrastructure Engineer

Infrastructure engineer is a generic term used to identify database administrators, network engineers, and systems administration professionals. The infrastructure engineer is responsible for the selection, configuration, implementation, tuning, and proper functioning of the devices or systems under his purview.

The infrastructure engineer, more than any other role, is responsible for the scalability of the systems that he supports. As such, a database analyst is responsible for identifying early when his database is going to fail based on capacity constraints and to identify potential opportunities for scaling. A systems analyst is expected to do the same for her systems and storage and a network engineer for the portions of the network that she supports.

In addition to having a deep technical understanding of his specific discipline, a skilled infrastructure engineer should understand the product he helps to support, be conversant in the "sister" disciplines within the hardware and systems community (a great systems administrator for instance should have a basic understanding of networks and a good understanding of how to troubleshoot basic database problems) in order to aid in troubleshooting, a good knowledge of competing technologies to those employed in his product or platform, and a good understanding of emerging technologies within his field. The infrastructure engineer should also understand the cost of operating his system and the opportunities to reduce that cost overtime. Finally, the best infrastructure engineers are agnostic to the technologies they employ, a point we will cover in Chapter 20, Designing for Any Technology.

QA Engineer/Analyst

The QA engineer or analyst is responsible for testing the application and the systems infrastructure to ensure that it meets the product specifications. A portion of her time should be dedicated to performance testing as it relates to scalability and as defined in Chapter 17, Performance and Stress Testing.

Capacity Planner

We've discussed the role and activity of the capacity planner in earlier sections of this chapter. Put simply, the capacity planner is responsible for matching the expected demand (typically generated by the business unit) to the current system as implemented to determine where additional changes need to be made in the system, platform, or product. The capacity planner is not responsible for defining what these changes are; rather, she outlines where changes need to occur.

In the case where a change needs to be made to a system that scales horizontally, the capacity planner may have as part of her job description the responsibility to help kick off the purchase order process to bring in new equipment. More often than not, the capacity planner is also a critical part of the process of budgeting for new systems and new initiatives to meet the business forecasted demand.

An Organizational Example

The new CEO of AllScale analyzes her team over the first 90 days. The company has had a number of scalability related incidents with its flagship HRM product and Christine determines that the current CTO (in AllScale's case, the CTO is the highest technology management position in the company) simply isn't capable of handling the development of new functionality and the stabilization of the existing platform. Christine believes that one of the issues with the executive previously in charge of technology was that he really had no business acumen and could not properly explain the need for certain purchases or projects in business terms. The former CTO simply did not understand simple business concepts like returns on investment and discounted cash flow. Furthermore, he always expected the business folks to understand the need for any of what business peers believed were his pet projects and would simply say, "We either do this or we will die." Although the technology team's budget was nearly 20% of the company's $200 million in revenue, systems still failed and the old CTO would blame unfunded projects for outages and then blame the business people for not understanding technology.

The CEO sits down with her new CTO, a person she picked from an array of candidates with graduate degrees in both business and electrical engineering or computer science, and explains that while she will delegate the responsibility for technical decisions to the CTO and empower him to make decisions within his budget limitations, she will not and cannot delegate the accountability for his results. She explains that she wants to create a culture of scalability in the company along the lines of the old manufacturing mottos of "everyone is accountable for quality." She will work to add a nod toward scalability in the corporate vision and add a corporate belief surrounding the need to cost effectively scale to customer demands without quality of service or availability (a.k.a. downtime) problems.

The new CTO, Johnny Fixer, asks for 30 days to review the organization, identify, and put in motion some quick win projects and report back with a plan to make the technology platform, organization, and processes highly scalable and highly available. He promises to keep Christine informed and communicate the issues he finds and concerns he has. They agree to talk daily on the phone, exchange emails more often, and meet personally at least once a week.

Johnny quickly identifies overlaps in jobs in certain areas and responsibilities that are completely missing from his team. For instance, no one is responsible for developing a single cohesive capacity plan. Furthermore, teams do not work together to collaborate on designs, architects are not engaged with the engineering teams and do not understand the current status of customer grief with the product, and quality defects are blamed on a QA team with no engineering ownership of bugs.

Johnny works quickly to hire a capacity planner onto his team. As it is May and the company's budgeting for the next year must be complete by October, he knows he must get good data about current system performance relative to peak theoretical capacity and start to get next year's demand projections from the business to help the CFO create his next fiscal year budget. The newly hired capacity planner starts working with the engineering team to install the appropriate monitoring systems to collect system data in order to identify capacity bottle necks and she works with finance to understand both the current budget and to help provide information to generate the next year's budget.

Although the CTO is worried about all of his technology problems, he knows that long term he is going to have to focus his teams on how they can work together and create shareholder value. He implements a tool for defining roles and responsibilities called RASCI for Responsible, Accountable, Supportive, Consulted, and Informed (this tool is defined further in the next section) and implements Joint Architecture Design and the Architecture Review Board (defined in Chapters 13 and 14) to help resolve the lack of cooperation between organizations.

Johnny walks through the past 30 days of issues and identifies that the team is not keeping track of outages, incidents, and their associated impact to the business. He makes his head of technical operations responsible for all outage tracking and indicates that together they will review all issues daily and track them to closure. He further requires that all architects attend at least one of the daily operations meetings per month to help get them closer to the customer and to better understand the pains associated with the current system. While meeting with his engineering managers, Johnny indicates that all bugs will be considered engineering and QA failures rather than just QA failure and that the company will begin tracking defects (or bugs) per feature produced with a goal to reducing all failures.

To help align his teams to the need for a more reliable and available site, Johnny implements a site uptime or availability metric and a goal to achieve greater than 99.99% availability by month within the next four months. With the CEO's advice and permission, and with the help of his architects, engineers, and infrastructure engineers, he reprioritizes some projects to attack the site outage incidents that appear (given the small amount of data) to have caused the most grief to the company.

Johnny then implements a governance council for all engineering projects consisting of the CEO, the CFO, and all of the business unit leaders. The council is responsible for prioritizing projects, including availability projects, and for additionally measuring their returns against the promised success and business metrics upon which they were based.

After the first 30 days, Johnny covers his 30-, 60-, and 90-day forward plans with the CEO and they jointly agree on a vision and set of goals for the engineering team (see Chapter 4, Leadership 101). Christine then has an "all hands" meeting with the entire company explaining that scalability and availability of the platform are of the utmost priority and that it is "everyone's job" to help ensure that the company and its services scale to meet customer demands. To help incent the company toward an appropriate culture that includes the notion of being "highly scalable," she insists that all managers have as part of their bonus compensation a scalability related goal that represents no less than 5% of their bonus. She delegates the development of those goals to her subordinates and asks to review them in the next 30 days.

A Tool for Defining Responsibilities

Many of our clients use a simple tool to help them define role clarity for any given initiative. Often when we are brought in to help with scalability in a company, we employ this tool to define who should do what, and to help eliminate wasted work and ensure complete coverage of all scalability related needs. Although technically a process, as this is a chapter on roles and responsibility, we felt compelled to include this tool here.

The tool we most often use is called RASCI. It is a responsibility assignment chart and the acronym stands for Responsible, Accountable, Supportive, Consulted, and Informed.

- R stands for Responsible. This is the person responsible for completing the project or initiative.
- A stands for Accountable. This is the person to whom R is accountable and who must approve the work before it is okay to complete. The A is sometimes referred to as the *approver* of any initiative.
- S stands for Supportive. These people provide resources to complete the project or initiative.
- C stands for Consulted. These people have data or information that can be useful in completing the project.
- I stands for Informed. These people should be notified, but do not need to be consulted or provide input to the project.

RASCI can be used in a matrix, where each activity or initiative is spelled out along the y or vertical axis of the matrix and the individual contributors or organizations are spelled out on the x-axis of the matrix. The intersection of the activity (y-axis) and the organization (x-axis) contains one of the letters R, A, S, C, or I and may include nothing if that individual or organization is not part of the initiative.

Ideally, in any case, there will be a single R and a single A for any given initiative. This helps eliminate the issue we identified earlier in this chapter of having multiple organizations or individuals feeling that they are responsible for any given initiative. By having a single person or organization responsible, you are abiding by the "one back to pat and one throat to choke" rule. A gentler way of saying this is that distributed ownership is ownership by no one.

This is not to say that others should not be allowed to provide input to the project or initiative. The RASCI model clearly allows and enforces the use of consultants or people within and outside your company who might add value to the initiative. An A should not sign off on an R's approach until such time as the R has actually consulted with all of the appropriate people to develop the right course of action. And of course if the company has the right culture, not only is the R going to want to seek those people's help, but the R is going to make them feel as if their input is valued and value added to the decision making process.

You can add as many Cs, Ss, and Is as you would like and as add value or are needed to complete any given project. That said, protect against going overboard regarding who exactly you will inform. Remember our discussion in the previous chapter about people being bogged down with email and communication that does not concern them. It is common in young companies to allow everyone to feel that they should be involved in every decision or informed of every decision. This information distribution mechanism simply does not scale and results in people reading emails rather than doing what they should be doing to create shareholder value.

A partially filled out example matrix is included in Table 2.1.

Taking some of our discussion thus far regarding different roles, let's see how we've begun to fill out this RASCI matrix.

We earlier indicated that the CEO absolutely must be responsible for the culture of scalability, or the *scale DNA* of the company. Although it is theoretically possible for her to delegate this responsibility to someone else within the company from a practical perspective, and as you will see in the chapter on leadership, she must live and walk the values associated with scaling the company and its platform. As such, even with delegation and as we are talking about how the company "acts" with respect to scale, the CEO absolutely must "own" this. Therefore, we have placed an R in the CEO's column next to the Scalability Culture initiative row. The CEO is obviously responsible to the board of directors and, as the creation of scale culture has to do with overall culture creation, we have indicated that the board of directors is the A.

Table 2.1   *RASCI Matrix*

	CEO	Business Owner	CTO	CFO	Arch	Eng	Ops	Inf	QA	Board of Directors
Scalability Culture	R									A
Technical Scalability Vision	A	C	R	C	S	S	S	S	S	I
Product Scale Design			A		R					
Software Scale Implementation			A			R	S			
Hardware Scale Implementation			A				S	R		
Database Scale Implementation			A				S	R		
Scalability Implementation Validation			A						R	

Who are the Ss of the Scalability Culture initiative? Who should be informed and who needs to be consulted? In developing your answer to this question, you are allowed to have people who are Ss of any situation also be Cs in the development of the solution. It is implied that Cs and Ss will be informed as a result of their jobs, so it is generally not necessary to include an I any place that you feel you need to communicate a decision and a result.

We've also completely filled out the row for Technical Scalability Vision. Here, as we've previously indicated, the CTO is responsible for developing the vision for scalability for the product/platform/system. The CTO's boss is very likely the CEO, so she will be responsible for approving the decision or course. Note that it is not absolutely necessary that the R's boss be the A in any given decision. It is entirely possible that the R will be performing actions on behalf of someone for whom he or she does not work. In this case, however, assuming that the CTO works for the CEO, there is very little chance that the CTO would actually have someone other than the CEO approve his or her scalability vision or scalability plan.

Consultants to the scalability vision are the CTO's peers—the people who rely on the CTO for either the availability of the product or the back office systems that run the company. These people need to be consulted because the systems that the CTO creates and runs are the lifeblood of the business units and the heart of the back office systems that the CFO needs to do his or her job.

We have indicated that the CTO's organizations (Architecture group, Engineering team, Operations team, Infrastructure team, and QA) are all supporters of the vision, but one or more of them could also be consultants to the solution. The less technical the CTO, the more he will need to rely upon his teams to develop the vision for scalability. Here, we have assumed that the CTO has the greatest technical experience on the team, which is obviously not always the case. The CTO may also want to bring in outside help in determining the scalability vision and/or plan. This outside help may be a retained advisory services firm or potentially the establishment of a technology advisory and governance board that provides for the technology team the same governance and oversight that a board of directors provides at a corporate level.

Finally, we have indicated that the board of directors needs to be Informed of the scalability vision. This might be a footnote in a board meeting or a discussion around what is possible with the current platform and how the company will need to invest to meet the scalability objectives for the coming years.

The remainder of the matrix has been partially filled out. Important points with respect to the matrix are that we have split up the tasks/initiatives to try to ensure that there aren't any overlaps in the R category. For instance, the responsibility for infrastructure tasks has been split from the responsibility for software development or architecture and design tasks. This allows for clear responsibility in line with our "one back to pat and one throat to choke" philosophy. In so doing, however, the organization might tend to move toward designing in a silo or vacuum, which is counter to what you would like to have long term. Should you structure your organization in a similar fashion, it is very important that you implement processes that require teams to design together to create the best possible solution. Matrix organized teams do not suffer from some of the silo mentality that exists within teams built in silos around functions or organizational responsibility, but they can still benefit from RASCI. You should still have a single responsible organization; but you want to ensure that collaboration happens. RASCI helps enforce that through the use of the C attribute.

Please spend time working through the rest of the matrix in Table 2.1 to get comfortable with the RASCI model. It is a very effective tool in clearly defining roles and responsibilities and can help eliminate duplicated work, unfortunate morale-deflating fights, and missed work assignments.

Conclusion

Providing role clarity is the responsibility of leaders and managers. Individuals as well as organizations need role clarity. We provided some examples of how roles might be clearly defined to help in the organization's mission of attaining higher availability. We also argued that these are but one of many examples that might be created regarding individuals and organizations and their roles. The real answer for you may vary significantly as the roles should be developed consistent with company culture and need. In attempting to create role clarity, attempt to stay away from overlapping responsibilities, as these can create wasted effort and value-destroying conflicts. Also attempt to ensure that no areas are missing, as these will result in failures.

We also introduced a tool called RASCI to help define roles and responsibilities within the organization. Feel free to use RASCI for your own organizational roles and for roles within initiatives. The use of RASCI can help eliminate duplicated work and make your organization more effective, efficient, and scalable.

Key Points

- Role clarity is critical for scale initiatives to be successful.
- Overlapping responsibility creates wasted effort and value-destroying conflicts.
- Areas missing responsibility create vacuums of activity and failed scale initiatives.
- The CEO is the chief scalability officer of the company.
- The CTO/CIO is the chief technical scale officer of the company.
- Key scale related responsibilities for any organization include

- Creation of the scalability vision for the organization
- Setting measurable scale related goals
- Staffing the team with the appropriate skill sets necessary to meet the scalability objectives
- Defining a scalable architecture
- Implementing that architecture in systems and code
- Testing the implementation against current and future user demand
- Gathering data on current platform and product utilization to determine immediate needs for scale
- Developing future demand projections and converting that demand projection into meaningful system demand
- Analyzing the demand projections against the system to determine where changes are needed
- Defining future changes based on the analysis
- Developing processes to determine when and where systems will break and prioritizing fixes for those issues

• RASCI is a tool that can help eliminate overlaps in responsibility and create clear role definition. RASCI is developed in a matrix in which

- R stands for the person Responsible for deciding what to do and running tive.
- A is Accountable or the Approver of the initiative and the results.
- S stands for Supportive, referring to anyone providing services to accomplish the initiative.
- C stands for those who should be Consulted before making a decision and regarding the results of the initiative.
- I stands for those who should be Informed of both the decision and the results.

Chapter 3

Designing Organizations

> Management of many is the same as management of few. It is a matter of organization.
>
> —Sun Tzu

In the past two chapters, we have discussed how important it is to establish the right roles within your team and to get the right people in those roles. This hopefully makes perfect sense and is in line with everything you believe: accomplishing great things starts with finding great people and getting them in the right roles. Now we have come to the organizational structure, and you are probably wondering why this has anything to do with the successful scaling of your application. The answer lies in what factors are affected by an organizational structure and in turn how important those factors are to the scalability of your application.

This chapter will highlight the factors that an organizational structure can influence and show how those are also key factors in an application's or Web service's scalability. There are two determinants of an organization: team size and team structure. If you are given the size range of the teams and how the teams are related to each other, you have a clear description of the organization. These two descriptors, size and structure, will be covered in this chapter, providing insight into the various dimensions of each, large versus small team sizes and silo versus matrix structures.

Organizational Influences That Affect Scalability

The most important factors that the organizational structure can affect are communication, efficiency, standards, quality, and ownership. Let's take each factor and examine how the organization can influence it as well as why that factor is also important to scalability. Thus, we can establish a causal relationship between the organization and scalability.

As we will see in Part II, Building Processes for Scale, which deals with processes, communication is central to all processes. Failed organizational communication is a certain guarantee for failures in the application. Not clearly communicating the proper architectural design, the extent of the outage, the customer complaints, or the changes being promoted to production can all be disastrous. If a single team has fifty people on it with no demarcation or hierarchy, the chance that everyone knows what everyone else is working on is remote. The possibility that an individual on this team of fifty people knows who to ask what questions of or who to send what information is unlikely. These breakdowns in smooth communication, on most days, may cause only minor disruptions, such as having to spam all fifty people to get a question answered. There will come a day when after being spammed for a year with questions that don't apply to her, that engineer will miss a key request for information that may prevent an outage or help to restore one quickly. Was that the engineer's fault for not being a superstar or was it the organizational structure's fault for making it impossible to communicate clearly and effectively?

The efficiency, the ratio of output produced compared to the input, of both people and entire teams can be increased when an organizational structure streamlines the workflow or decreased when projects get mired down in unnecessary organizational hierarchy. In the Agile software development methodology, product owners are often seated side-by-side engineers to ensure that product questions get answered immediately and not require long explanations via email. If the engineer arrives at a point in the development of a feature that requires clarification to continue, she has two choices. The engineer could guess which way to proceed or she could ask the product owner and wait for the answer. Until the product owner replies with an answer, that engineer is likely stuck not being able to proceed and can either try to context switch to something unrelated, which wastes a lot of time setting up environments and restudying material, or she can go to the game room and waste a few hours playing video games. Having the product owner's desk beside the engineer's desk helps maintain a high efficiency by getting those questions answered quickly and preventing the engineer from earning another high score on the video game. The problem with degrading efficiency in terms of scalability is what it does from an organizational resource perspective. As your resource pool dwindles, the tendency is to favor short-term customer facing features over longer-term scalability projects. That tendency helps meet quarterly goals at the expense of long-term platform viability.

The only standards that matter within an organization are those to which the organization adheres. An organization that does not foster the creation, distribution, and acceptance of standards in coding, documentation, specifications, and deployment is sure to decrease efficiency, reduce quality, and increase the risk of significant production issues. Take an organization that is a complete matrix, where a very few engineers, possibly only one, reside on each team along with product managers, project managers, and business owners. Without an extreme amount of diligence around communicating standards, it would be very simple for that solo engineer to stop following any guidelines that were previously established. No other engineer or manager is there to check that the solo engineer has not forgotten to submit his documentation, and the short-term gain in efficiency might seem a great tradeoff to him. The proper organization must help engineers understand and follow the established guidelines, principles, and norms that the larger group has agreed to follow. As for the potential impact of this noncompliance on scalability, imagine an engineer deciding that the architectural principle of all services must run on three or more physically different instances is not really important. When it comes time to deploy the service, this service can only run on a single server, thus increasing the likelihood of an outage of that service as well as not being able to scale the service beyond the capability of a single server.

As described earlier, an organization that does not foster adherence to norms and standards has the effect of lowering quality of the product being developed. A brief example of this would be an organization that has a solid unit test framework and process in place but is structured either through size or team composition such that it does not foster the acceptance and substantiation of this unit test framework. The solo engineer, discussed earlier, may find it too tempting to disregard the team's request to build unit tests for all features and forgo the exercise. This is very likely to lead to poorer quality code and thus an increase in major and minor defects. In turn, this can possibly lead to downtime for the application or cause other availability related issues. The resulting increase in bugs and production problems takes engineering resources away from coding new features or scalability projects, such as sharding the database. As we have seen before when resources become scarce, the tradeoff of postponing a short-term customer feature in favor of a long-term scalability project becomes much more difficult.

Longhorn

The Microsoft operating system code named Longhorn that publicly became known as Vista serves as an example of the failure of standards and quality in an organization. Ultimately, Vista became a successful product launch that achieved the ranking of being the second most widely adopted operating system, but not without significant pain for both Microsoft and their customers. The time period between the release of the previous desktop operating system XP and Vista marked the longest in the company's history between product launches.

In a front-page article on September 23, 2005, in *The Wall Street Journal*, Jim Allchin, Microsoft's copresident, admitted to telling Bill Gates that "It's not going to work," referring to Longhorn. Jim Allchin continues in the article describing the development as "crashing to the ground" due to haphazard methods by which features were introduced and integrated.[1]

---

1. Robert A Guth. "Battling Google, Microsoft Changes How It Builds Software." *Wall Street Journal*, September 23, 2005, http://online.wsj.com.

One of the factors that helped revive the doomed product was enlisting the help of senior executive Amitabh Srivastava who had a team of architects map out the operating system and established a development process that enforced high levels of code quality across the organization. Although this caused great criticism from some of the individual developers, it resulted in the recovery of a failed product.

The last major factor that the organization can affect that directly impacts the application's or service's scalability is ownership. If we take the opposite extreme of an organization from what we were using in our previous examples, and assume an organization where each team has fifty engineers and no separation or hierarchy, we may very well see many different engineers working on the same part of the code base. When lots of people work on the same code and there is no explicit or implicit hierarchy, no one feels they own the code. When this occurs, no one takes the extra steps to ensure others are following standards, building the requested functionality, or maintaining the high quality desired in the product. Thus, we see the aforementioned problems with scalability of the application that stem from issues such as less efficient use of the engineering resources, more production issues, and poor communication.

Thus, we see that the organization does affect some key factors that impact the scalability of the application. Now that we have a clear basis for caring about the organization from a scalability perspective, it is time to understand the basic determinants of all organization, size and structure.

Team Size

Before we explore the factors that influence optimal team size, first we should discuss why team size is important. Consider a team of two people; the two know each other's quirks, they always know what each other is working on, and they never forget to communicate with each other. Sounds perfect right? Well, consider that they also may not have enough engineering effort to tackle big projects, like scalability projects of splitting databases, in a timely manner; they do not have the flexibility to transfer to another team because each one probably knows stuff that no one else does; and they probably have their own coding standards that are not common among other two-person teams. Obviously, both small teams and large teams have their pros and cons. They key is to balance each to get the optimal result for your organization.

An important point is that we are looking for the optimal team size for your organization. As this implies, there is not a single magic number that is best for all teams. There are many factors that should be considered when determining the optimal size for your teams; and even among teams the sizes may vary. If forced to give a direct answer to how many team members should optimally be on a team, we would provide a range and hope that suffices for a specific enough answer. Although there are always exceptions even to this broad range of choices, our low boundary for team size is six and our upper boundary is 15. What we mean by *low boundary* is that if you have fewer than six engineers, there is probably no point in dividing them into separate teams. For the *upper boundary*, if there are more than 15 people on a single team, the size starts to hinder the management's ability to actively manage and communication between team members starts to falter. Having given this range, there are always exceptions to these guidelines; more importantly, consider the following factors as aligned with your organization, people, and goals.

The first factor to consider when determining team size is the experience level of the managers. The role of the engineering or operations manager can entail different responsibilities in different companies. Some companies require managers to meet one-on-one with every team member for at least 30 minutes each week to provide feedback, mentoring, and receive updates; others have no such requirement. Managerial responsibilities will be discussed later in this chapter as a factor by itself, but for our purposes now we will assume that managers have a base level of responsibility, which includes the three following items: ensuring engineers are assigned to projects, either self directed or by edict of management; that administrative tasks, such as resolving pay problems or passing along human resources information take place; and that managers receive status updates on projects in order to pass them along to upper management. Given this base level of responsibility, a junior manager who has just stepped from the engineering ranks into management may find that, even with a small team of six engineers, the administrative and project management tasks consume her entire day. She may have time for little else because these tasks are new to her and they require a significant amount of time and concentration compared with her more senior counterparts who can handle all these tasks for a much larger team and still have time for special projects on the side. This is perfectly normal for everyone. New tasks typically take longer and require more intense concentration than tasks that have been performed over and over again. The level of experience is a key factor to consider when determining the optimal size for a given team.

In a similar vein, the tenure of the team itself is a factor to consider when contemplating team size. A team that is very senior in tenure both at the company and in engineering will require much less overhead from both management as well as each other to perform their responsibilities. Both durations are important, time at the company and time in engineering, because they both influence different aspects of overhead required. The more time at a particular company will generally indicate that less overhead is required for the administrative and human resource tasks that inundate new people such as signing up for benefits, getting incorrect paychecks straightened out, or attending all the mandatory briefings. The more time practicing engineering the less time and overhead that will be required to explain specifications, designs, standards, frameworks, or technical problems. Of course, every individual is different and the seniority of the overall team must be considered. If a team has a well-balanced group of senior, midlevel, and junior engineers, they can probably exist in a moderate-sized team; whereas a team of all senior engineers, say on an infrastructure project, might be able to exist with twice as many individuals because they should require much less communication about nondevelopment related items and be much less distracted by more junior type questions, such as how to check out code from the repository. You should consider all of this when deciding on the optimal team size because doing so will provide a good indicator of how large the team can effectively be without causing disruption due to the overhead overwhelming the productivity.

As we mentioned earlier, each company has different expectations of the tasks that a manager should be responsible for completing. We decided that a base level of managerial responsibilities includes ensuring the following:

- Engineers are assigned to projects
- Administrative tasks take place
- Status updates are passed along

Obviously, there are many more managerial responsibilities that could be asked of the managers, including one-on-one weekly meetings with engineers, coding of features by managers themselves, reviewing specifications, project management, reviewing designs, coordinating or conducting code reviews, establishment and ensuring adherence of standards, mentoring, praising, and performance reviews. The more of these tasks that are placed upon the individual managers the smaller the team that is required in order to ensure the managers can accomplish all the assigned tasks. For example, if one-on-ones are required, and we feel they should be, an hour-long meeting with each engineer weekly for a team of ten engineers will consume 25% of a 40-hour week. The numbers can be tweaked—shorter meetings, longer work weeks—but the point remains that just speaking to each engineer on a large team can consume a very large portion of a manager's time. Speaking frequently with team members is critical to be an effective manager and leader. So obviously, the number and effort of these tasks should be considered as a major contributing factor to the size that the optimal teams should be in your organization. An interesting and perhaps enlightening exercise for upper management is to survey your front-line managers and ask how much time they spend on each task for a week. As we indicated with the one-on-one meetings, it is surprisingly deceptive how easy it is to fill up a manager's week with tasks.

The previous three factors, experience of management, tenure of team members, and managerial responsibilities, are all constraints in that they limit the size of the team based on necessity of maintaining a low enough overhead of communication and disruptions to ensure projects actually get accomplished. The next and last factor that we will discuss is one that pushes to expand the team size. This factor is the needs or requirements of the business. The business owners and product managers, in general, want to build more and larger customer facing projects in order that they continue to fend off competitors, grow the revenue stream, and increase the customer base. The two main problems with keeping team sizes small is first that large projects require, depending on the product development life cycle methodology that is employed, many more iterations or more time in development. The net result is the same, projects take longer to get delivered to the customer. The second problem is that increasing the number of engineers on staff requires increasing the number of support personnel, including managers. Engineering managers may take offense at being called support personnel but in reality that is what management should be, something that supports the teams in accomplishing their projects. The larger the teams the fewer managers are required. Obviously for those familiar with the concepts outlined in the *Mythical Man Month: Essays on Software Engineering* by Frederick P. Brooks, Jr., there is a limit to the amount a project can be subdivided in order to expedite the delivery. Even with this consideration, it is still valid that the larger the team size the faster projects can be delivered and the larger projects can be undertaken.

The preceding discussion focused on what you should consider when planning team structures, budgets, hiring plans, and product roadmaps. The four factors of management experience, team member tenure in the company and in the engineering field, managerial duties, and the needs of the business must all be taken into consideration. Returning to our example at the concocted company of AllScale, Johnny Fixer, the new CTO, had just finished briefing his 30-60-90 day plans. Among these was to analyze his organizational structure and the management team. During one of his initial meetings, Mike Softe, the VP of engineering and a direct report of Johnny's, asked for some help determining the appropriate team size for several of his teams. Johnny took the opportunity to help teach some of his concepts on team size and went to the whiteboard drawing a matrix with four factors across the top (manager experience, team member tenure, managerial duties, and business needs). He asked Mike to fill in the matrix with information about the three teams that he was concerned about. In Table 3.1, there are the three different teams that Mike is evaluating.

Table 3.1 *Team Size Analysis*

	Manager Experience	Team Member's Tenure	Managerial Duties	Business Needs
Team 1	High	High	Med	High
Team 2	Low	Low	Med	Med
Team 3	High	Low	Med	Low

For all the teams, Mike considered the managerial responsibilities to be medium and consistent across all managers. This may or may not be the case in your organization. Often, a particularly senior manager may have special projects he is responsible for, such as chairing standards meetings, and junior managers are often required to continue coding while they make the transition to management and hire their own backfill. Mike Softe's Team 1 has a very experienced manager and a long tenured team; and the business needs are high, implying either large projects are on the roadmap or they need them as soon as possible, possibly both. In this case, Johnny explains to Mike that Team 1 should be considered for a large team size, perhaps 12 to 15 engineers. Team 2 has a very inexperienced manager and team members. The business requirements on Team 2 are moderate and therefore Johnny explains that the team size should be kept relatively small, 6 to 8 members. Team 3 has a very experienced manager with a new team. The business does not require large or frequently delivered projects from this team at this time. Johnny explains that Mike should consider letting the team members on this team gain more experience at the company or in the practice of engineering and assist by keeping the team relatively small even though the manager could handle more reports. In this case, Johnny states with a smile, the manager might be a great candidate to take on an outside project that would benefit the overall organization.

Warning Signs

Now that we have discussed the factors that must be considered when determining or evaluating each team's size, we should focus on signs that the team size is incorrect. In the event that you do not have an annual or semiannual process for evaluating team sizes, some indicators of how to tell if a team is too big or too small could be helpful. If a team is too large, the indicators that you should look for are poor communication, lowered productivity, and poor morale. Poor communication could take many forms including engineers missing meetings, unresponsiveness to emails, missed specification changes, or multiple people asking the same questions.

Lowered productivity can be another sign of the team size being too large. The reason for this is that if the manager, architects, and senior engineers do not have enough time to spend with the junior engineers, these newest team members are not going to produce as many features as quickly. Without someone to mentor, guide, direct, and answer questions, the junior engineers will have to flounder longer than they normally would. The opposite is possibly the culprit as well. Senior engineers might be too busy answering questions for too many junior engineers to get their own work done, thus lowering their productivity. Some signs of lowered productivity include missing release dates, lower function or story points (if measured), and pushback on feature assignment. Function points and story points are two different methods that attempt to standardize the measurement of a piece of functionality. Function points are from the user's perspective and story points are from the engineer's perspective. Engineers by nature are typically over-optimistic in terms of what they think they can accomplish; if they are pushing back on an amount of work that they have done in the past, this might be a clear indicator that they feel at some level their productivity slipping.

Both of the preceding problems, poor communication and lowered productivity due to lack of support, can lead to the third sign of a team being too large: poor morale. When a normally healthy and satisfied team starts demonstrating poor morale, this is a clear indicator that something is wrong. Although there may be many causes for poor morale, the size of the team should not be overlooked. Similar to how you approach debugging, look for what changed last. Did the size of the team grow recently? Poor morale can be demonstrated in a variety of manners such as showing up late for work, spending more time in the game room, arguing more in meetings, and pushing back more than usual on executive level decisions. The reason for this is straightforward, as an engineer when you feel unsupported, not communicated with, or that you are not able to succeed in your tasks, it weighs heavily on you. Most engineers love a challenge, even very tough ones that will take days just to understand the nature of the problem. At the point that an engineer knows he cannot solve the problem, suddenly he falls into despair. This is especially true of junior engineers, so watch for these behaviors to occur first in the more junior team members.

Now that we have covered some of the signs to look for when a team becomes too large, we can shift our focus to the opposite extreme and look for signs when a team is too small. If the team is too small, the indicators to look for are disgruntled business partners, micromanaging managers, and overworked team members. If the team is too small, one of the first signs might be the business partners such as product managers or business development spending more time around the manager complaining that they need more products delivered. A team that is too small is just unable to quickly deliver sizable features. Another tactic that disgruntled business leaders can take is instead of complaining directly to the engineer or technology leadership, they focus their energy in a more positive manner by supporting budget requests for more engineers to be hired.

When a normally effective manager begins to micromanage team members, this is a sign to look into the root cause of this behavior. There might be lots of explanations, including the possibility that her team size is too small and she's keeping busy by hovering over her team members, second guessing their decisions, and asking for status updates about the request for a status update. If this is the case, it is the perfect opportunity to assign this manager some other tasks that will serve the organization, help professionally develop her by expanding her focus, and give her team some relief from her constant presence. Some ideas on special projects include chairing a standards committee, leading an investigation of a new software tool for bug tracking, or establishing a cross team mentoring program for engineers.

The third sign to look for when a team is too small is overworked team members. Most teams are extremely motivated by the products they are working on and believe in the mission of the company. They want to succeed and they want to do everything they can to help. This includes accepting too much work and trying to accomplish it in the expected timeframe. When the team members start to leave later and later or start to consistently work weekends, these are signs that you might want to investigate if you have enough engineers working on this particular team. This type of overworking behavior is expected and even necessary for most startup companies but working in this manner consistently month after month will eventually burn out the team causing attrition, poor morale, and poor quality. It is much better to take notice of the hours and days spent working on tasks and determine a corrective action early as opposed to waking up to the problem when your most senior engineer walks in your office to resign.

These are signs that we have seen in our teams when they were either too large or too small. Some of these symptoms of course can be caused by other things besides team size but it is often the case that managers jump to conclusions with the most cursory of investigations into the real cause and often do not even consider the organizational structure as a possible cause. Often, the most frequently blamed is the team leader and his inability to manage his team effectively or manage the customer's expectations effectively. Before you place the blame on his shoulders, be sure that the organization that you have placed them in supports them as much as possible by assisting in his success. Running a great junior leader out of management because you placed him in a team that was too large for his current skill level would be dreadful. Invest in the future of your leadership team by building the proper supporting structure around each manager, allowing his own skills and experience to develop.

Growing or Splitting Teams

For the teams that are too small, adding engineers, although not necessarily easy, is straightforward. The steps include requesting and receiving budgetary approval for hiring, writing up the job description, reviewing resumes, conducting interviews, making offers, and on boarding the new hires. Although these simple steps may take months to actually accomplish, they are generally easy to understand and fairly simple to implement. The much more difficult task is to split a team when it has become too large. Splitting a team incorrectly can have dire consequences caused by confusion of code ownership, even worse communication, and stress of working for a new manager. Every team and organization is different, so there is no perfect, standard, one-size-fits-all way of splitting teams. There are some factors to consider when undergoing this organizational surgery in order to minimize the impact and quickly get back to a productive and engaged existence among the team members.

Some of the things that you should think about when considering splitting a team include how to split the code base, who is going to be the new manager, what involvement will individual team members have, and how does this change the relationship with the business partners. The first item to concentrate on is based on the code or the work. As we will discuss in much more detail in Part III, Architecting Scalable Solutions, this might be a great opportunity to split the team as well as the code base into what we term *failure domains*. These are domains that limit the impact of failures by isolating services from one another.

The code used to be owned and assigned to a single team needs to be split between two or more teams. In the case of an engineering team, this usually revolves around the code. The old team perhaps owned all the services around the administrative part of the application, such as account creation, login, billing, and reporting. Again, there is no standard way of doing this, but a possible solution is to subdivide the services into two or more groups: one handling account creation and login, the other handling billing and reporting services. As you get deeper into the code, you will likely hit base classes that require assignment to one team or the other. In these cases, we like to assign general ownership to one team or even better to one engineer and set up alerts through the source code repository that can alert each other if anything is changed in that particular file or class, therefore everyone can be aware of changes in their sections of the code.

The next item to consider is who will be the new manager. This is an opportunity to hire someone new from the outside or promote someone internally into the position. There are pros and cons of each option. An external hire brings new ideas and experiences; whereas an internal hire provides a manager who is familiar with all the team members as well as the processes. Because of the various pros and cons of each option, this is a decision you do not want to make lightly and may want to ponder for a long time. Making a well thought out decision is absolutely the correct thing to do, but taking too much time can cause just as many problems. The stress of the unknown can be dampening to spirits and cause unrest. Make a timely decision; if that involves bringing in external candidates, do so as openly and quickly as possible. Dragging out the selection process and wavering between an internal and external candidate does nothing but cause trouble for the team.

The last of the big three items to consider when splitting a team is how the relationship with the business will be affected. If there is a one-to-one relationship between engineering team, quality assurance, product management team, and business team, this is something that will obviously change by splitting a team. A discussion with all the affected leaders should take place before a decision is reached on splitting the team. Perhaps all the counterpart teams will split simultaneously or individuals will be reassigned to interact more directly along team lines. There are many possibilities with the most important thing being an open discussion taking place beyond the engineering and beyond the technology teams.

We have covered the warning signs associated with teams that are too large and too small. We also covered the factors to consider when splitting teams. One of the major lessons that should be gleaned from this section is that the team size and changes to it can have tremendous impacts on everything from morale to productivity. Therefore, it is critical to keep in mind the team size as a major determining factor of how effective the organization is in relation to scalability of the application.

Checklist

Optimal team size checklist:

1. Determine the experience level of your managers
2. Calculate each engineer's tenure at the company
3. Look up or ask each engineer how long he or she has been in the industry
4. Estimate the total effort for managerial responsibilities
    a. Survey your managers for how much time they spend on tasks
    b. Make a list of the core managerial responsibilities that you expect managers to accomplish
5. Look for signs of disgruntled business partners and managers who are bored to indicate teams that are too small
6. Look for losses in productivity, poor communication, and degrading morale to indicate teams that are too large

Splitting a team checklist:

1. Determine how to separate the code base
    a. Split by services
    b. Divide base classes and services as evenly as possible with only one owner
    c. Set up alerts in your repository to ensure everyone knows when items are being modified
2. Determine who will be the new manager
    a. Consider internal versus external candidates
    b. Set an aggressive timeline for making the decision and stick to it
3. Analyze your team's interactions with other teams or departments
    a. Discuss the planned split with other department heads
    b. Coordinate your team's split with other teams to ensure a smoother transition
    c. Use joint announcements for all departments to help explain all the changes simultaneously

Organizational Structure

The organizational structure refers to the actual layout or how teams relate to each other within an organization. This includes the separation of employees into departments, divisions, and teams as well as the management hierarchy that is used for command and control of the forces. There are as many different structures as there are companies, but there are two basic structures from which everything else stems. These structures are functional and matrix. By understanding the pros and cons of each structure, you will be able to choose one or the other; or, perhaps a more likely scenario, create a hybrid of the two structures that best meets the needs of your company. In the ensuing paragraphs, we will cover the basic definition of each structure, the benefits and drawbacks of each, and some ideas on when to use each one. Recognize that the most important lesson is how to choose parts of one versus the other to create the organizational structure that is best for your scenario.

Functional Organization

The functional organizational structure is the original structure upon which armies and industries were based. This structure, as seen in Figure 3.1, separates departments

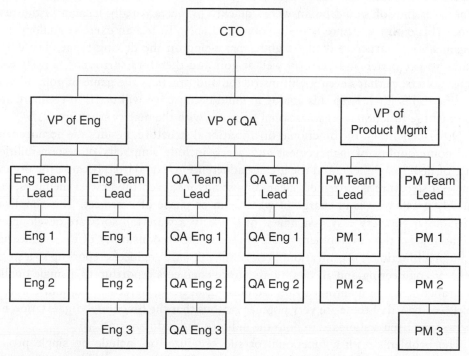

Figure 3.1 *Functional Organization Chart*

and divisions by their primary purpose or function. This was often called a silo approach because each group of people was separated from other groups just as grain or corn would be separated into silos based upon the type or grade of produce. In a technology organization, this structure would result in the creation of separate departments to house engineering, quality assurance, operations, project management, and so forth. Along with this, there would exist the management hierarchy within each department. Each would have a department head, such as the VP of engineering, and a structure into each department that was homogeneous in terms of responsibilities. Reporting into the VP of engineering would be other engineering managers such as engineering directors and reporting into them would be engineering senior managers and then engineering managers. This hierarchy was consistent in that engineering managers reported to other engineering managers and quality assurance managers reported to other quality assurance managers.

The benefits of the functional or silo organizational structure are numerous. Managers almost always were raised through the ranks; thus, even if they were not good individual performers, they at least knew what was entailed in performing the job. Unless there had been major changes in the field over the years, there was very little need to spend time explaining to bosses the more arcane or technical aspects of the job because they were well versed in it. Team members were also consistent in their expertise, engineers worked alongside engineers. Questions related to the technical aspects of the job could be answered quickly by peers usually located in the next cube. This entire structure is built along specificity. To use an exercise analogy, this organizational structure is like a golfer practicing on the driving range. The golfer wants to get better and perform well at golf and therefore surrounds himself with other golfers, perhaps even a golf instructor, and practices the game of golf, all very specific to his goal. Keep this analog in mind because we will use it to compare and contrast the functional organizational structure with the matrix structure.

Other benefits of the functional organizational structure, besides the homogeneity and commonality of management and peers, include simplicity of responsibilities, ease of task assignment, and the greater adherence to standards. Because the organizational structure is extremely clear, almost anyone, even the newest members, can quickly grasp who is in charge of what team or phase of a project. This simplicity also allows for very easy assignment of tasks. In a waterfall software development methodology, the development phase is clearly the responsibility of the engineering team in a functional organization. Because all software engineers report up to a single head of engineering and all quality assurance engineers report up to a single quality assurance head, standards can be established, decreed, agreed upon, and enforced fairly easily. All of these are very popular reasons that the functional organization has for so long been a standard in both the military and industries.

The problems with a functional or silo organization include no single project owner and poor cross-functional communication. Projects almost never reside strictly in the purview of a single functional team. Most projects always require tasks to be accomplished by multiple teams. Take a simple feature request that must have a specification drafted by the product owner, a design and coding performed by the engineers, testing performed by the quality assurance team, and deployment by the operations engineers. Responsibility for all aspects of the project does not reside with any one person in the management hierarchy until you reach the head of technology, which has responsibility over the product managers, engineering, quality assurance, and operations staffs. Obviously, this is a significant drawback having the CTO or VP of technology the lowest person responsible for the overall success of the project. When problems arise in the projects, it is not uncommon for each functional owner to place blame for delays or overspends on other departments.

As simple as the functional organization is to understand, the communication can be surprisingly difficult when attempting it across departments. As an example, a software engineer who wants to communicate to a quality assurance engineer about a specific test that must be performed to check for the proper functionality may spend the time tracking up and down the quality assurance management hierarchy looking for the manager who is assigning the testing of this feature and request that she make known who the work will be assigned in order that the information be passed along. More likely, the engineer will rely on established processes, which attempt to facilitate the passing along of such information through design and specification documents. As you can imagine, writing a line in a 20-page specification about testing is exceedingly difficult communication as compared to a one-on-one conversation between the development engineer and the testing engineer.

The benefits of the functional organization as just discussed include commonality of managers and peers, simplicity of responsibility, and adherence to standards. The drawbacks include no single project owner and poor communications. Given these pros and cons, the scenarios in which you would want to consider a functional organizational structure are ones in which the advantages of specificity outweigh the problems of overall coordination and ownership. An example of such a scenario would be a scalability project that involves sharding a database. This is a highly technical project that requires some coordination among peer departments, but the overwhelming majority of effort and tasks will be within the engineering discipline. Decisions about how to split the database, how the application will handle the lookup, and all other similar decisions will fall to the engineering team. The product management team may be requested to provide information about specific customer behavior or the cost to the business for changes to functionality, but it will not be as involved as it would be for a new product line launch.

Matrix Organization

In the 1970s, organizational behaviorists and managers began rethinking the organizational structure. As we discussed, although there are certain undeniable benefits to the functional organization, there are also certain drawbacks. Companies and even militaries began experimenting with different organizational structures. The second primary organizational structure that evolved from this was the matrix structure. The principle concept in a matrix organization is that there are two dimensions to the hierarchy. As opposed to a functional organization where each team has a single manager and thus each team member reports to a single boss, in the matrix there are at least two dimensions of management structure, whereby each team member may have two or more bosses. Each of these two bosses may have different managerial responsibilities—for instance, one (perhaps the team leader) handles administrative tasks and reviews, whereas the other (perhaps the project manager) handles the assignment of tasks and project status. In Figure 3.2, the traditional functional organization is augmented with a project management team on the side.

The right side of the organization in Figure 3.2 looks very similar to a functional structure. The big difference comes from the left side, where the project management organization resides. Notice that the Project Managers within the Project Management Organization, PMO, are shaded with members of the other teams. Project Manager 1 is shaded light gray along with Engineer 1, Engineer 2, Quality Assurance Engineer 1, Quality Assurance Engineer 2, Product Manager 1, and Product Manager 2. This light gray group of individuals comprises the project team that is working together in a matrixed fashion. The light gray team project manager might have responsibility

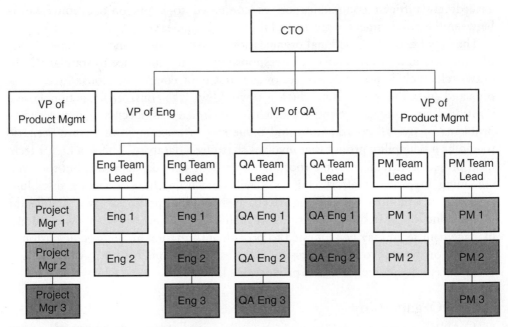

Figure 3.2 *Matrix Organization Chart*

for the assignment of tasks and the timeline. In larger and more complex matrix organizations, many members of each team can belong to project teams.

Continuing with the project team responsible for implementing the new billing feature, we can start to realize the benefits of such a structure. The two primary problems with a functional organization are no project ownership and poor cross team communication. In the matrix organization, the project team fixes both of these problems. We now have a first level manager, Project Manager 1, who owns the billing project. This project team will likely meet weekly or more and certainly have frequent email dialogues, which again solves one of the problems facing the functional organization: communication. If the software engineer wants to communicate to the QA engineer that a particular test needs to be included in the test harness, it is as simple as sending an email or mentioning it at the next team meeting, thus alleviating the need to trudge through layers of management in search of the right person.

We can pick up our golf analogy that we used in the discussion of the functional organization. You probably remember that we described a golfer who wants to get better and perform well at golf. To that end, he surrounds himself with other golfers, perhaps even a golf instructor, and practices the game of golf, all very specific to his goal. This is analogous to the functional team where we want to perform a specific function very well and so we surround ourselves with others like us and practice only that skill. What sports trainers have found out in the recent past is that specificity is excellent at developing muscle memory and basic skills but to truly excel, athletes must cross-train. This is the concept of moving away from the golf course periodically and exercising other muscles such as through weight training or running. This cross-training is similar to the matrix organization in that it doesn't replace the basic training of golf or engineering but it enhances it by layering another discipline such as running or project management. For those astute individuals who have cross-trained before, you might ask "can the cross-training actually hinder the athlete's performance?" In fact, if you are a golfer, you may have heard such talk around not playing softball because it can cause havoc with your golf swing. We will discuss this concept in the context of the drawbacks of matrix organizations.

If we have solved or at least dramatically improved the drawbacks of the functional organizational structure through the implementation of the matrix, surely there is a cost for this improvement. The truth is that while solving the problems of project ownership and communication, we introduce other problems involving multiple bosses and distraction from a person's primary discipline. Reporting to two or more people—yes, matrix structures can get complex enough to require a person to participate on multiple teams—invariably causes stressors because of differences in direction given by each boss. The engineer trapped between her engineering manager telling her to code to a standard and her project manager insisting that she finish the project on time is a setup that is asking for stress and someone not being pleased by her performance. Additionally, the project team requires overhead, as does any team in the form of meetings and email communications. This does not replace the team meetings that the engineer must attend for her engineering manager and thus takes more time away from her primary responsibility of coding.

As you can see, while solving some problems, we have introduced new ones. This really should not be too shocking because that is typically what happens and rarely are we able to solve a problem without consequences of another variety. The next question, given these pros and cons of the matrix organization, is "when would we want to use such an organizational structure?" The appropriate times to use the matrix structure are when the fate of the project is extremely important either because of the timeline or other such factor. In these cases, having a project team surrounding the project, where there is a clear owner and the team structure facilitates cross team communication, is the right answer to ensure delivery.

Unfortunately you are likely to experience challenges across your organization that are not always as straightforward as we have expressed in our simple examples. Real life, especially in a technology organization, is always more complex. Here is where the hybrid solutions become necessary. Your entire engineering organization does not need to be part of a matrix structure. Instead, teams that are focused on very cross team oriented projects may be in a matrix, but other teams working on infrastructure projects might not be. Alternatively, you could use the multidimensional nature of the matrix without actually creating the project team. An example of this would be to collocate the project team together, in the same cube row, without actually implementing the matrix. There are many other examples of how to create hybrid functional-matrix organizations. The key here is to use the organizational structure to solve your problems that exist today. There is no single right answer that is right for all companies at all times.

Conclusion

In this chapter, we highlighted the factors that an organizational structure can influence and showed how those are also key factors in an application or Web services scalability. Thus, we established a link between the organizational structure and scalability to point out that, just like hiring the right people and getting them in the right roles, building a supporting organizational structure around them is just as important. We discussed the two determinants of an organization: the team size and the structure.

In regards to the team size, we covered why size mattered—too small and you cannot accomplish enough; too large and you lose productivity and impact morale. We further covered the four factors of management experience, team member tenure in the company and in the engineering field, managerial duties, and the needs of the business. These all must be taken into consideration when determining the optimal team size for your organization. We also covered the warning signs to watch for to determine if your teams were too large or too small. For teams that were too large, we stated that poor communication, lowered productivity, and poor morale were symptoms. For teams that were too small, we stated that disgruntled business partners, micromanaging managers, and overworked team members were all symptoms. Lastly on the team size discussion, we covered what items to consider when growing or splitting teams. Growing teams was pretty straightforward but splitting up teams into smaller teams entailed much more. For splitting teams, we covered topics including how to split the code base, who is going to be the new manager, what involvement will individual team members have, and how does this change the relationship with the business partners.

The team structure discussion covered the two basic structures: functional and matrix. We described each, discussed the benefits, analyzed the drawbacks, and recommended scenarios to be used. The functional structure was the original organizational structure and essentially divided employees up by their primary function, such as engineering or quality assurance. The benefits of a functional structure include the homogeneity of management and peers, simplicity of responsibilities, ease of task assignment, and the greater adherence to standards. The drawbacks of the functional structure were no single project owner and poor cross-functional communication. These problems were specifically targeted in the matrix organizational structure and they were solved. The matrix structure started out looking very similar to the functional structure but a second dimension was added that included a new management structure. We provided examples of the matrix structure, which normally includes project managers as the secondary dimension. The strengths of the matrix organization are solving the problems of project ownership and communication but the drawbacks include multiple bosses and distraction from a person's primary discipline. We concluded the organizational structure discussion with some thoughts on how hybrid approaches are often the best because they are designed to fit the needs of your organization.

Key Points

- Organizational structure can either hinder or aid a team's ability to produce and support scalable applications.
- Team size and structure are the two key attributes with regard to organizations.
- Teams that are too small do not provide enough capacity to accomplish the priorities of the business.
- Teams that are too large can cause a loss of productivity and degrade morale.

- Two basic organizational structures are functional and matrix.
- Functional organizational structures provide benefits such as the commonality of management and peers, simplicity of responsibilities, ease of task assignment, and greater adherence to standards.
- Matrix organizational structures provide benefits such as project ownership and improved cross team communication.
- Both team size and organizational structure must be determined by the needs and capabilities of your organization.

Chapter 4

Leadership 101

A leader leads by example not by force.

—Sun Tzu

Why does a book on scalability have a chapter on leadership? The answer is pretty simple: If you can't lead, you can't scale. You can have the smartest and hardest working team in the world, but if you don't set the right vision, goals, and objectives, all of that work is going to be for naught. In our experience as executives, consultants, and advisors, a failure to lead is one of the most common reasons for a failure to scale. A failure to set the right vision, create the right culture, create the right goals and objectives, and interact with your team in the right manner are all critical ingredients to a scalability meltdown. Moreover, great leadership can create a multiplier to your organization's ability to scale your technical services or products. A great vision inspires organizations to achieve new and higher levels of performance, which in turn positively impacts the organization's ability to produce more and scale more effectively. Leading from the front and behaving morally and ethically creates an effective can-do culture, where more is done for the shareholder.

We obviously can't give you all the tools you need to make you a great leader in a single chapter. But we can arm you with some thoughts and approaches and hopefully spark your intellectual curiosity to pursue more self-driven investigation. This chapter is a mix of things you should do, things you should never do, and explanations of concepts such as vision, mission, and goals.

The most important thing that we can tell you is this: Leadership isn't a destination; it is a journey without an end and you of course are the leader of your individual journey. The journey is marked by a growth in awareness and capabilities over time. You can spend 24 hours a day, 7 days a week, 52 weeks a year for every year for the remainder of your life attempting to become a better leader and you will never "reach the end." There is always something new to discover, something new to try, and some new and difficult challenge in trying to remake who you are and how you approach leading people and organizations. The motivation behind our leadership

63

journey is to continuously improve our ability to influence people and organizations to ever increasing levels of success.

You needn't be in a position with direct reports to be a leader; everyone can and does lead from time to time, even if not put in a position of organizational responsibility to lead. When you are attempting to influence behavior to accomplish an objective, you are practicing leadership. When displaying behaviors consistent with the company culture and working diligently to solve a problem or complete a task, you are practicing a form of leadership: leadership by example. And perhaps most importantly, if you aspire to become a CEO, CTO, general manager, director, manager, or even a principal engineer, now is the time to start thinking about how to lead and developing your leadership skills.

What Is Leadership?

As we hinted at in the opening of this chapter, for the purposes of this book, we will define leadership as "influencing the behavior of an organization or a person to accomplish a specific objective." Leadership is perhaps most easily thought of along the lines of "pulling activities." The establishment of a vision that inspires an organization "pulls" that organization to the goal or objective. The setting of specific, measurable, achievable, realistic, timely goals along the way to that vision create milestones that both help "pull" the organization to the objective and help the organization correct its course along the way to ensure that it is taking the appropriate path to the destination.

Leadership applies to much more than just an individual's direct reports or organization. You can lead your peers, people in other organizations, and even your management. The definition of "influencing behavior of an organization or a person to accomplish a specific objective" does not imply that one is the "boss" of the organization. Project managers, for instance, can "lead" a project team without being the person responsible for writing the reviews of the members of that team. Role models within an organization are leaders as well. As we will see, leadership is about what you do and how you influence behaviors of those around you for the better or worse.

Leadership is very different from management and not everyone is good at both of them. That said, everyone can get better at both with practice and focus. They are both also necessary to varying degrees in the accomplishment of nearly any task. Let's take the general goal of ensuring that your product, platform, or system can scale to handle all of the user demand that has been forecasted from the business unit owner. You are obviously going to want to set a vision that exceeds that goal but that also recognizes the real-world budgetary constraints that we all face. You also want to make sure that every dollar you spend is creating shareholder value rather than destroying it, so it's not enough just to be within budget—you don't want to spend more than you need to spend in any given area before you have to spend it.

With all of these things in mind, you might develop a vision for scale that includes "a platform designed to be infinitely scalable and implemented to never have an availability or response time incident tied to scale." The indication of design versus implementation implicitly acknowledges budgetary constraints. The nod to scalability never impacting availability or response time is indeed an aggressive and potentially achievable goal.

Including goals along the way to the objective, goals that ideally are meaningful to each of the teams responsible for completing the objective, helps create a roadmap to get to the final objective.

All of that is well and good, but without someone "managing" or pushing the organization to the objective, the probability of accomplishing that objective is low. Likewise, without the establishment of the vision and goals as described, there is little sense in "managing" anything as you simply do not know where you are going.

Leaders—Born or Made?

No discussion of leadership, even in a brief chapter, would be complete without at least addressing the topic of whether leaders are born or made. Our answer to this is that the question is really irrelevant when you consider our conceptual model, described next.

A person's ability to lead is a direct result of his ability to influence behavior in individuals and organizations. That ability to influence behavior is a result of several things, some of which are traits with which a person is born, some are a result of his environment and some are easily modified tools and approaches the person has developed over time.

When people say that someone is a "born leader," they are probably talking about the person's charisma and presence and potentially his looks. The latter (good looks) is unfortunate in many respects (especially given the appearance of the authors), but it is an absolute truth that most people would rather be around "good looking" people. That's why there aren't a whole lot of ugly politicians (remember, we're talking about looks here and not political views). The former—charisma, personality, and presence—are all things that have developed over time and are very hard to change. They are things we typically believe that people are "born with," but those characteristics are probably a result of not only genetics but also our environments. Regardless, we pin those characteristics on the person as if it's his birthright. We then jump to the conclusion that a leader must be born because having good looks, a good personality, great presence, and great charisma absolutely help when influencing the behaviors of others.

But looks, charisma, presence, charm, and personality are just a few of the components of leadership; and although they help, there are other components that are just as important. As we will discuss in the next section, many attributes of leadership can and should be constantly worked at to gain proficiency and improve consistently.

Leadership—A Conceptual Model

Let's first discuss a model we can use to describe leadership in order to make it easier for us to highlight components of leadership and how they impact scale. We believe that the ability to lead or influence the behaviors of a person or organization to a goal is a function of several characteristics and perceptions. This function can be thought of producing a score that's indicative of a person's ability to affect change and influence behaviors. This isn't the only way to think about leadership, but it's an effective conceptual model to help illustrate how improvements in any given area can not only improve your ability to lead, but also offset things that you may not be able to change.

Some of these characteristics are things that the person "has." Potentially, the person has been born with them, like good looks. It's unlikely, without significant time under a surgeon's scalpel, that you are going to change the way you look, so we usually discount spending much time or thought on the matter.

Some of these characteristics are likely products of a person's upbringing or environmental issues. Examples of these might be charm, charisma, personality, and presence. These characteristics and attributes can and should be addressed, but they are difficult and tend to need constant attention to make significant and lasting change. For instance, a person whose personality makes her prone to disruptive temper tantrums probably needs to find ways to hold her temper in check. A person who is incapable of displaying anger toward failure probably needs to at least learn to "act" upset from time to time, as the power of showing displeasure in a generally happy person has a huge benefit within an organization. By way of example, you've probably at least once said something like, "I don't think I've ever seen John mad like that," and more than likely it made a point to you that stuck for quite some time and helped influence your actions.

Some aspects of leadership have to do with what you can create through either innovation or perseverance. Are you innovative enough to create a compelling vision or can you persevere to make enough attempts to create a compelling vision (assuming that you are consulting with someone to try it out on them)? Innovation here speaks to the ability to come up with a vision on the fly, whereas the perseverance and intelligence to continue trying will take longer but can come up with exactly the same result. In this case, we gave an example of both something with which you are likely born (innovation) and something that you can absolutely improve upon regardless of your natural tendencies (perseverance).

Some characteristics of leadership have to do with how you are perceived by others. Are you perceived to be a giver or a taker? Are you selfish or selfless? Are you perceived to be a very ethical person or morally bankrupt? There are two important points here: one is the issue of perception and the other is the effect of that perception on the team you are leading.

Everyone has probably heard the statement "Perception is reality," and you have more than likely heard the statement "Leaders are under a microscope." Everyone is watching you all of the time and they will see you in your weakest moment and form an opinion of you based on that. Get used to it. It's not fair, but it's the way things work. If someone sees you accept tickets to the Super Bowl from a vendor, he is very likely to jump to the conclusion that you are morally bankrupt or at the very least that you have questionable ethics. Why, after all, would you accept tickets from a vendor who is obviously trying to influence you to purchase his products? Someone is going to catch you doing something at a low point in your day, and that something might not even be "bad" but simply taken out of context. The only thing you can do is be aware of this and attempt the best you can to limit the number of "low points" that you have in any given day.

As to the effect of perception, we think the answer is pretty clear. Taking the example of the Super Bowl tickets, it's pretty simple to see that the perception that you are willing to allow vendors to influence your decisions is going to have a negative impact on your ability to influence behaviors. Every vendor discussion you have with your team is likely going to be tainted. After a meeting in which you indicate you want to include the vendor with whom you went to the Super Bowl in some discussion, just imagine the team's comments when you depart! You may have desired the inclusion of that vendor for all the right reasons, but it just doesn't matter. You've caused significant damage to your ability to lead the team to the right answers.

The point of describing leadership as an equation is to drive home the view that although there are some things you may not be able to change, you can definitely work on many other things to become a better leader. More importantly, there is no maximum boundary to the equation! You can work your whole life to become a better leader and reap the benefits along the way. Make life your leadership lab and become a lifelong student. By being a better leader, you will get more out of your organizations and your organizations will make decisions consistent with your vision and mission. The result is greater scalability, more benefit with less work (or rework), and happier shareholders.

Taking Stock of Who You Are

Most people are not as good a leader as they think. We make this assertion from our personal experience, and while relying on the Dunning-Kruger effect. Through their studies, David Dunning and Justin Kruger witnessed that we often overestimate our abilities and that the overestimation is most severe where we lack experience or have a high degree of ignorance.[1] With very little formal leadership training available in our universities or workplaces, we believe that leadership ignorance abounds and that as a result, many people overestimate their leadership skills.

Few people are formally trained in how to be leaders. Most people have seen so many poor leaders get promoted for all the wrong reasons that they emulate the very behaviors they despise. Think we have it wrong? How many times in your career have you found yourself saying, "I will never do what he did just now if I have his job"? Now think through whether anyone in your organization is saying that about you and whether it is something you've said before in a similar position. The answer is almost definitely "Yes." It's happened to us, it will likely continue to happen to us over time, and we can almost guarantee that it is happening to you.

But that's not the end of it. You can lead entirely the wrong way and be successful and then mistakenly associate that success with your leadership approach. Sometimes, this happens by chance; your team just happened to accomplish the right things in spite of your approach. Sometimes, this happens because you get great performance out of individuals for a short period of time by treating them poorly, but ultimately your behaviors result in high turnover and an inability to attract and retain the best people that you need to accomplish your mission.

At the end of the day, to reap the scalability benefits that great leadership can offer, you need to measure where you are today. In their book *Resonant Leadership*, Richard Boyatzis and Annie McKee discuss the three components necessary for change in individuals as mindfulness, hope, and compassion.[2] Mindfulness here is the knowledge of one's self, including feelings and capabilities, whereas hope and compassion help to generate the vision and drivers for change. Unfortunately, as the Dunning-Kruger effect would argue, you probably aren't the best person to evaluate where you are today. All of us have a tendency to inflate certain self-perceived strengths and potentially even misdiagnose weaknesses.

Elite military units strip a potential leader down to absolutely nothing and force him to know his limits. They deprive the person of sleep and food and force the person to live in harsh climates all to get the person to truly understand his strengths, weaknesses, and limitations. You likely don't have time to go through such a process, nor

1. Kruger, Justin and David Dunning (1999). "Unskilled and Unaware of It: How Difficulties in Recognizing One's Own Incompetence Lead to Inflated Self-Assessments." *Journal of Personality and Social Psychology*. 77 (6): 1121–34. doi:10.1037/0022-3514.77.6.1121. PMID 10626367.

Dunning, David and Kerri Johnson, Joyce Ehrlinger, and Justin Kruger (2003). "Why people fail to recognize their own incompetence." *Current Directions in Psychological Science*. 12 (3): 83–87.

2. Boyatzis, Richard and Annie McKee (2005). *Resonant Leadership*. Harvard Business School Press.

do the demands of your job likely require that you have that level of self-awareness. Your best option is a good review by your boss, your peers, and most importantly your subordinates! This process is often referred to as a *360-degree* review process.

Ouch! An employee review sounds like a painful process, doesn't it? But if you want to know what you can do to get better at influencing the behavior of your team, what better place to go than to your team to ask that question? Your boss will have some insights, as will your peers. But the only people who can tell you definitively how you can improve their performance and results are the people whom you are trying to influence. Moreover, if you want good information, the process is going to need to be anonymous. People's input tends to be swayed if they believe that there is the potential that you will get upset at them or potentially hold their input against them. Finally, if you are really willing to go this far (and you should), you need to act on the information. Sitting down with your team and saying, "Thanks for the input and here's what I have heard on how I can improve," will go a long way to creating respect. Adding the very necessary step of saying, "And here is how I am going to take action to improve myself," will go even further.

It should go without saying that a self-evaluation that does not result in a plan for improvement is a waste of both your time and the time of your organization and management. If leadership is a journey, the review process described helps set your starting point. Now you need a personal destination and a plan (or route) to get there. A number of books will suggest that you rely upon and build your strengths. Others suggest that you eliminate or mitigate your weaknesses. We think that your plan should include both a reliance and strengthening of your strengths and the mitigation of your weaknesses. Few people fail in their objectives because of their strengths and few people win as a result of their weaknesses. We must reduce the dilutive aspects of our leadership by mitigating weaknesses and increase our accretive aspects by multiplying and building upon our strengths.

Having discussed a model for leadership, and the need to be mindful of your strengths and weaknesses, we will now look at several characteristics shared by some of the greatest leaders with whom we've had the pleasure of working. These characteristics include setting the example, leading without ego, driving hard to accomplish the mission while being mindful and compassionate about the needs of the organization, timely decision making, team empowerment, and shareholder alignment.

Leading from the Front

We've all heard the phrase "Set the example," and if you are a manager you may even have used it during performance counseling sessions. But what does "Set the example" really mean, how do you do it, and how does it impact scalability?

We think most people would agree that employees with an optimal work environment or culture will produce much more than a company with a less than desirable work environment or culture. Producing more with a similar number of employees is an element of scale as the company producing more at a comparable cost structure is inherently more "scalable." Terrible cultures can rob employees of productivity; employees gather around the water cooler and discuss the recent misdeeds of the boss or complain about how the boss abuses her position.

Evaluate the cultural norms that you expect of your team and determine once again whether you are behaving consistently with these cultural norms. Do you expect your organization to be above the temptations of vendors? If so, you had best not take any tickets to a Super Bowl or any other event. Do you expect your organization to react quickly to events and resolve them quickly? If so, you should display that same behavior. If a person is up all night working on a problem for the betterment of the organization and the company, do you still expect them at work the next day? If so, you had better pull a few all-nighters yourself.

It's not enough to say that you wouldn't have your team do anything you haven't done. When it comes to behaviors, you should show your team that you aren't asking them to do anything that you don't do now! People who are perceived to be great leaders don't abuse their position and they don't assume that their progression to their position allows them certain luxuries not afforded to the rest of the organization. You likely already get paid more and that's your compensation.

Having your administrative assistant get your car washed or pick your kids up from school may seem to be an appropriate job related perk to you, but to the rest of the company it may appear to be an abuse of your position. You may not care about such perceptions, but they destroy your credibility with your team and impact the result of the leadership equation we previously discussed. This destruction of the leadership equation causes employees to waste time discussing perceived abuses and moreover may make them think it's acceptable to abuse their positions similarly, which wastes time and money and reduces organizational scale. If such activities are voted on by the board of directors or decided upon by your management as part of your compensation, you should request that they be paid for separately and not rely upon company employees to perform the functions.

The key here is that everyone can increase the value of their leadership score by "leading from the front." Act and behave ethically and do not take advantage of your position of authority. Behave exactly as you expect your organization to behave. By abiding by these rules, you will likely notice that your employees emulate your behaviors and that their individual output increases, thereby increasing overall scale of the organization.

Checking Your Ego at the Door

There is simply no place for a big ego in any position within any company. It is true that there is a high degree of correlation between passionate inspirational leaders and people who have a need to talk about how great, intelligent, or successful they are. But we argue that it is also true that those people would be that much more successful if they kept their need for publicity or public recognition to themselves. The concept isn't new and is embodied in Jim Collins' concept of Level 5 Leadership within his wonderful book *Good to Great*.

CTOs who need to talk about being the "smartest person in the room" and CEOs who say "I'm right more often than I'm wrong" simply have no place in a high performing team. As a matter of fact, they are working as hard as they can to destroy the team by making such statements. Focusing on an individual rather than the team, regardless of who that individual is, is the antithesis of scale; scale is about growing cost effectively, and a focus on the one rather than the many is clearly a focus on constraints rather than scale. Such statements alienate the rest of a team and very often push the very highest performing individuals—those actually getting stuff done—out of the team and out of the company. These actions and statements run counter to building the best team and over time will serve to destroy shareholder value. The best leaders give of themselves selflessly in an ethical pursuit of creating shareholder value. The right way to approach your job as a leader and a manager is to figure out how to get the most out of your team in order to maximize shareholder wealth. You are really only a critical portion of that long-term wealth creation cycle if your actions evolve around being a leader of the team rather than an individual. Take some time and evaluate yourself and your statements through the course of a week. Identify how many times you reference yourself or your accomplishments during the course of your daily discussions. If you find that you are doing it often, take some time to step back and redirect your thoughts and your statements to things that are more team oriented than self oriented.

It is not easy to make this type of change. There are people all around us who appear to be rewarded for being egoists and narcissists, and it is easy to come to the conclusion that humility is a character trait embodied by the unsuccessful business person. But all you need to do is reflect on your career and identify the boss to whom you had the greatest loyalty and for whom you would do nearly anything; that boss most likely put the shareholders first and the team always. Be the type of person who thinks first about how to create shareholder value rather than personal value and you will succeed!

Mission First, People Always

As young leaders serving in the Army, we were introduced to an important concept in both leadership and management: Leaders and managers accomplish their missions through their people. Neither getting the job done at all cost nor caring about your people makes a great leader; great leaders know how to do both even in light of their apparent contradictions. Broadly speaking, as public company executives, managers, or individual contributors, "Getting our jobs done" means maximizing shareholder value. We'll discuss maximizing shareholder value in the section on vision and mission.

Effective leaders and managers get the mission accomplished—great leaders and managers do so by creating a culture and environment in which people feel appreciated and respected and wherein performance related feedback is honest and timely. The difference here is that the latter leader—the one who creates a long-term nurturing and caring environment—is leading for the future and will enjoy the benefits of greater retention, loyalty, and long-term performance. Caring about people means giving thought to the careers and interests of your employees; giving timely feedback on performance and in so doing recognizing that even stellar employees need feedback regarding infrequent poor performance (how else can they improve). Great leaders ensure that those creating the most value are compensated most aggressively and they ensure that people get the time off that they deserve for performance above and beyond the call of their individual positions.

Caring about people does *not* mean creating a sense of entitlement or lifetime employment within your organization. We will discuss this more in the management chapter. Caring also does *not* mean setting easy goals, as in so doing you would not be accomplishing your mission of creating shareholder value.

It is very easy to identify Mission First leaders because they are the ones who are getting the job done even in the face of adversity. It is not so easy to identify Mission First, People Always leaders because it takes a long time to test whether the individual leader has created a culture that inspires people and makes high performance individuals want to follow the person from job to job because they are a caring individual. The easiest People Always test to apply for a seasoned leader is to find out how many direct reports have followed them consistently from position to position within successful organizations. Mission First, Me Always leaders find that their direct reports will seldom work for them in more than one or two organizations or companies, whereas Mission First, People Always seldom have problems in getting their direct reports to follow them through their careers.

Mission First, Me Always leaders climb a ladder with rungs made of their employees, stepping on them as they climb to the top. Mission First, People Always leaders build ladders upon which all of the stellar performers can climb.

Making Timely, Sound, and Morally Correct Decisions

Your team expects you to help resolve major issues quickly and with proper judgment. Rest assured that you are going to make mistakes overtime. Welcome to humanity. But on average, you should move quickly to make the best decision possible with the proper input without wasting a lot of time. Be courageous and make decisions. That's what being a leader is entirely about.

Why did we add "morally correct" in this point? Few things destroy shareholder value or scale faster than issues with your personal ethics. We earlier asserted that you are always under a microscope and that you are doubtlessly going to be caught or seen doing things you wish you hadn't done. Our hope is that those things are nodding off at your desk because you've been working too hard, or running out to your car to perform a personal errand during work hours because you work too late at night to perform it. Hopefully, it does not include things like accepting tickets for major sporting events for the reasons we've previously indicated. We also hope that it doesn't include allowing others within your team to do the same.

One of our favorite quotes goes something like "What you allow you teach and what you teach becomes your standard." Here, *allowance* means either yourself or others. Nowhere does that ring more true than with ethical violations large and small. We're not sure how issues like Tyco or Enron ultimately start. Nor are we certain how a Ponzi scheme as large as Bernie Madoff's, which destroyed billions of dollars of wealth, can possibly exist for so many years. We do know, however, that they could have been stopped long before the problems grew to legendary sizes and that each of these events destroyed the size and scale of the companies in question along with a great deal of shareholder value

We don't believe that people start out plotting billion dollar Ponzi schemes and we don't believe that people start off by misstating tens or hundreds of millions of dollars of revenue or embezzling tens of millions of dollars of money from a company. We're fairly certain that it starts small and slowly progresses. People get closer and closer to a line they shouldn't cross and then they take smaller and smaller steps into the abyss of moral bankruptcy until it is just too late to do anything.

Our answer is to never start. Don't take company pens, don't take favors from vendors who wish to sway your decision, and don't use the company plane for personal business unless it is authorized by the board of directors as part of your compensation package. Few things will destroy your internal credibility and therefore your ability to influence an organization as the perception of impropriety. There is no way you can align lying, cheating, or stealing with the creation of shareholder wealth.

Empowering Teams and Scalability

Perhaps no leadership activity or action impacts an organization's ability to scale more than the concept of team empowerment. Empowerment is the distribution of certain actions, accountability, and ownership. Empowerment may include giving some or all components of both leadership and management to an individual or an organization.

The leadership aspects of empowerment come from the boost individuals, teams, leaders, and managers get out of the feeling and associated pride of ownership. Individuals who believe they are empowered to make decisions and own a process in general are more productive than those who believe they are following orders. Mechanically, the leader truly practicing empowerment multiplies his organization's throughput as he or she is no longer the bottleneck for all activities.

When empowerment happens in statement only, such as when a leader continues to review all decisions for a certain project or initiative that has been given to an empowered team, the effect is disastrous. The leader may indicate that he is empowering people, but in actuality he is constraining the organizational throughput by creating a chokepoint of activity. The teams immediately see through this and rather than owning the solution, they feel as though they are merely consultants to the process. Worse yet, they may feel absolutely no ownership and as a result neither gain the gratitude that comes with owning a solution or division nor feel the obligation to ensure that the solution is implemented properly or the division run well. The net result is that morale, throughput, and trust are destroyed.

This is not to say that in empowering individuals and teams the leader is no longer responsible for the results, because although a leader can distribute ownership she can never abdicate her responsibility to achieve results for shareholders. When delegating and empowering teams, one should be clear as to what the team is empowered to do. The trick is to give the team or individual enough room to maneuver, learn, and create value while still providing a safety net and opportunities to learn. For instance, a small corporation is likely to limit budgetary decisions for managers to no more than several thousand dollars, whereas a division chief of a Fortune 500 company may have latitude within his budget up a few million dollars. These limitations should not come as a surprise in the empowerment discussions, as most boards or directors require that large capital expenditures be approved by the board.

Alignment with Shareholder Value

Everything you do as a leader and manager needs to be aligned with shareholder value. Although we probably shouldn't absolutely need to say this, we've found in our practice that this concept isn't raised enough within companies. Put simply, if you are in a for-profit business, your job is to create shareholder wealth. More importantly, it is to maximize shareholder wealth. You probably get to keep your job if your actions and the actions of your team make your shareholders wealthier. You are the best if you make shareholders more money than anyone else. Even if you are in a not-for-profit company, you are still responsible for creating a type of wealth. The wealth in these companies is more often the emotional wealth creation of the people who donate to the company if you are a charity, or the other type of "good" that you do for the people who pay you if you are something other than a charity. Whatever the reason, if you aren't attempting to maximize the type of wealth the company sets out to make, you shouldn't be in the job.

As we discuss things like vision, mission, and goals, a test that you should apply is "How does this create and maximize shareholder wealth?" You should be able to explain this in relatively simple terms; later in this chapter, we will discuss something that we call the "causal roadmap" and its impact to individuals within nearly any job. Moreover, you should find ways to ask the shareholder-wealth-creation question in other aspects of your job. Why would you ever do anything in your job that doesn't somehow help create shareholder wealth or keep natural forces like growth and the resulting instability of your systems from destroying it? Why would you ever hire a person who isn't committed to creating shareholder wealth? Why would you ever assign a task not related to the creation of shareholder wealth?

Vision

It is our experience that, in general, leaders don't spend enough time on vision and mission. Both of these tend to be something that gets done as a result of a yearly planning session and the leader or the leader and her team might spend an hour or two discussing it together. Think about that for a minute: You spend an hour or two talking about the thing that is going to be the guiding light for your company or organization? Does that sound right? Your vision is your destination; it's something that should inspire people within your company, attract outside talent, help retain the best of your current talent, and help people understand what they should be doing in the absence of a manager standing over their shoulders. You probably spend more time planning your next vacation than you do the destination for your entire company. Hopefully, we've convinced you that the creation and communication of a compelling vision is something that's incredibly important to the success of your company and nearly any initiative.

Vision is your description of a destination for a company, an organization, or an initiative. It is a vivid description of the ideal future; the desired state or outcome clearly defined, measurable, and easily committed to memory. Ideally, it is inspirational to the team and can stand alone as a beacon of where to go and what to do in the absence of further leadership or management. It should be measurable and testable, meaning that there is an easy way to determine whether you are actually at that point when you get there. It should also incorporate some portion of your beliefs so that it has meaning to the organization.

U.S. Pledge

By way of example, the U.S. Pledge of Allegiance has such an inspirational destination or vision as one of its components. "One Nation under God, indivisible, with Liberty and Justice for all" is a vivid description of an ideal future.

The pledge is certainly testable at any given point in time by dividing it into its subcomponents and determining whether they have been met. Are we one nation—apparently as we are still governed by a single government and the attempt during the Civil War to split the country was not successful? Are we "under God"? This is debatable but certainly not everyone believes in God if that were the intent of the passage and we'll discuss this portion of the pledge in the next paragraph. Do we have liberty and justice for all? We have laws, and everyone is theoretically governed by those laws and given some set of what we call "inalienable rights." Of course, there is a great amount of debate as to whether the laws are effective and whether we apply them equally based on color, sex, beliefs, and so on but the system in general appears to work as well as any system anywhere else. At the very least, you can agree that there is a test set up in this vision statement—the debate would be about whether everyone who applies the test is going to come up with the same answer.

An interesting side note here is that the phrase "under God" was added in the 1950s after years of lobbying by the Knights of Columbus and other religious orders. Regardless of your religious beliefs, the modification of the pledge of allegiance serves to stand that visions can be modified over time to more clearly define the end goal. Vision, then, can be modified as the desired outcome of the company, organization, or initiative changes. It does not need to be static, but should not be so fluid that it gets modified constantly.

The entire pledge hints at a shared belief structure; elements such as the unity of the nation, a nod toward religious belief, and the equal distribution of "Liberty" and "Justice." As to value creation, the value created here is really in supporting the shared values of the members or citizens of the United States. Although not universally true even at the time of the creation of the pledge, most people within the United States agree that equality in liberty and justice is value creation in and of itself.

The U.S. Declaration of Independence is an example of vision, though a majority of the document describes the vision in terms of the things we do not want to be. A majority of the document spends time on things the King of Britain had done, which were not desirable in the ideal future. Although such an approach can certainly be inspirational and effective in motivating organizations, it simply takes too much time to define an end state by what the end state is not. For this reason, we suggest that vision be brief and that it define what an end state is.

The beginning of the Preamble of the U.S. Constitution is another example of a vision statement. It reads as follows: "We the People of the United States, in Order to form a more perfect Union." Although certainly a description of an ideal future, it is difficult to determine whether you can really "know" that you are there when you reach that future. What exactly is a "perfect union"? How do you test "perfection"? Perfection certainly would create value as who wouldn't want to live in and contribute to a "perfect union"? The preamble gets high marks for inspiration, memorization, and value creation, but relatively low marks for measurability. It's hard to describe how vivid it is, because it is difficult to determine how you would know you are truly there. Finally, the Preamble hints at certain beliefs but does not explicitly incorporate them.

Perhaps the easiest way to envision a vision statement is to view it within the context of giving someone directions. One of the things you are likely to do when giving someone directions is to give them criteria to determine whether their journey to the destination was a success. Let's assume that someone is asking us to give them directions to a department store where they can find nearly anything they need at a reasonable price for their new apartment. We decide that the best place to send them is the local Walmart store. Let's further assume that the people we are directing have never been to a Walmart store (maybe they are space aliens or perhaps they just emerged from a religious cult's underground bomb shelter).

One of the first things we are likely to do in this case is give these rather strange people an indication of how they know they are successful in their journey. Maybe we say something like "The best place for you to go is Walmart as it has the lowest prices within the 10 miles surrounding this area and I know you don't want to travel far. The local Walmart is a big white building with blue trim and huge letters on the top that spell out WALMART. The address is 111 Sam Walton Street. The parking lot is huge and within the parking lot you will find several other stores such as a McDonald's and a gas station. Across the street you will see two more gas stations and a strip mall." Such a description is not only vivid but it outlines a set of tests that will indicate to our travelers exactly when they have arrived at their destination.

We've accomplished everything we wanted to do in creating our vision statement. We gave our travelers an inspiration—"lowest prices within the 10 miles surrounding this area" is inspiring because it meets their needs of being inexpensive and it is not too distant. We've provided a vivid description of the ideal state—arriving at Walmart and giving the travelers an indication of what it will look like when they arrive there. We gave our travelers a set of tests to validate that their initiative was successful in the vivid description and the beliefs were implicitly identified in the need for low prices. The vision is easily committed to memory. The travelers can look at the street address and determine for certain that they've definitely arrived at the appropriate location.

We suggest that you research other statements of vision and use the rules we have identified before creating your own. Apply these rules or tests and figure out which ones work for you. Simply put, and as a reminder, a vision statement should be

- Vivid description of an ideal future
- Important to value creation
- Measurable
- Inspirational
- Incorporate elements of your beliefs
- Mostly static, but modifiable as the need presents itself
- Easily remembered

Mission

If vision is the vivid description of the ideal future or the end point of our journey, mission is the general path or actions that will get us to that destination. The mission statement focuses more on the present state of the company as that present state is important to get *to* the desired state or "vision" of the company. The mission statement should incorporate a sense of purpose, a sense of what needs to be done *today*, and a general direction regarding how to get to that vision. As with a vision statement, the mission statement should be testable. The test for the mission statement should include the determination of whether, if properly executed, the mission statement will help drive the initiative, organization, or company toward the vision of the company.

Let's return to our analysis of the Preamble of the U.S. Constitution to see if we can find a mission statement. ". . . establish Justice, ensure domestic Tranquility, provide for the common defence, promote the general Welfare, and secure the Blessings of Liberty to ourselves and our Posterity, do ordain and establish this Constitution for the United States of America" appears to us to be the mission statement of the preamble. The entire remainder of the quoted passage serves to implicitly establish an existing state. By the need to "establish" these things, the founding fathers are indicating that they do not exist today. The purpose of the United States is also explicitly called out in the establishment of these things. These actions also serve to attempt to identify the creation of the vision: a "perfect Union." Testability, however, is weak and suffers from the subjective analysis necessary to test any of the points. Have we for instance ensured domestic tranquility after over 200 years of existence? We still suffer from domestic strife along the boundaries of race, belief structure, and sex. We have certainly spent a lot of money on defense and in general have probably performed well relative to other nations, but have we truly met the initial goals? What about general welfare? Does our rising cost of health care somehow play into that? By now, you've probably gotten the point.

Now, we return to the directions that we were giving our rather strange travelers who have never seen a Walmart. After providing the vision statement describing where they need to go, and consistent with our definition of a mission statement, we need to give them general directions or approach on how to get there. We need to indicate present state, a sense of purpose, and a general direction. The mission statement could then simply be "To get to Walmart from here, drive mostly SW roughly 7 miles."

That's it; we've accomplished everything within a single sentence. We've given the travelers purpose by stating "To get to Walmart." We've given the travelers an indication of current position "from here" and we've given them a general direction to the vision "drive mostly SW roughly 7 miles." The whole mission is testable, as they can clearly see where they are (though most mission statements should be a bit more descriptive), they already know how to understand their destination, and they have a direction and limit to determine when they are out of bounds.

As a review, a mission statement should

- Be descriptive of the present state and actions
- Incorporate a sense of purpose
- Be measurable
- Include a general direction or path toward the vision

Now you might state, "But that doesn't really get them to where they need to go!" You are correct, and that's a perfect segue into a discussion on goals.

Goals

If vision is our description of where we are going and mission is a general direction on how to get there, goals are the guideposts or mile markers to ensure that we are on track during our journey. In our minds, the best goals are achieved through the SMART acronym.

SMART goals are

- Specific
- Measurable
- Attainable (but aggressive)

- Realistic
- Timely (or contain a component of time)

Going back to the Constitution, we can look at many of the amendments as goals that Congress desired to achieve en route to its vision. Let's take the abolition of slavery in the 13th Amendment. This amendment was obviously meant as a goal en route to the equality promised within the vision of a perfect union and the mission of securing the blessings of liberty. The text of this amendment is as follows:

> **Section 1.** Neither slavery nor involuntary servitude, except as a punishment for crime where of the party shall have been duly convicted, shall exist within the United States, or any place subject to their jurisdiction.
>
> **Section 2.** Congress shall have the power to enforce this article by appropriate legislation.

It is specific in terms of who, what, and where, and it implies a "when." Congress has the power to enforce the article, and everyone is subject to the article's rule. The "where" is the United States and the "what" is slavery or any involuntary servitude except as punishment for crimes.

The article is measurable in its effect as the presence of slavery is binary: it either exists or it does not. The result is attainable as slavery is abolished, though from time to time strange pockets pop up and are handled by law enforcement personnel. The goal is realistic and it was time bounded as the amendment took immediate effect.

Returning now to our example of guiding our friends to their Walmart destination, we look at how we might provide them with goals. Remember that goals don't tell someone *how* to do something but rather they give them an indication that they are on track. You might remember that we defined a vision or ideal end state for them, which was the local Walmart store. We also gave them a mission, or a general direction to get there: "To get to Walmart from here, drive mostly SW roughly 7 miles." Now we need to give them goals to ensure that they are on track in their destination.

We might give them two goals: one identifying the end state or vision and an interim goal to help them on their way. The first goal might look like this: "Regardless of your path, you should be in the center of town as identified by the only traffic light within 10 minutes of leaving here. That is roughly halfway to Walmart." This goal is specific, describing where you should be. It is measurable in that you can easily tell that you have achieved it. It is both attainable and realistic because if we expect them to move at an average of 30 miles per hour and travel 7 miles, they should be able to travel a mile every 2 minutes and anything over 10 minutes (5 miles) would put them somewhere other than where they should be. The inclusion of a 10-minute time interval means that our goal is time bounded.

The last goal we give them will deal with the end vision itself. It is also a simple goal as we've already described the location. "You should arrive at Walmart located at 111 Sam Walton St. in no more than 20 minutes." We are specific, measurable, achievable, realistic, and time bounded. Bingo!

Have we given the travelers everything they need to be successful? Are we missing anything? You are probably wondering why we haven't given them directions. What do you think the answer to this is? Okay, we won't make you wait. You might recall our definition of leadership versus management, where leadership is a "pulling" activity and management is a "pushing" activity. Explaining or defining a path to a goal or vision is a management activity and we'll discuss that in the next chapter.

Putting Vision, Mission, and Goals Together

We've now spent several pages describing vision, mission, and goals. You might again be asking yourself what exactly this has to do with scalability. Our answer is that it has everything to do with scalability. If you don't define where you are going and you don't provide a general direction to get there and a set of goals to help identify that your team is on the right path, you are absolutely doomed. Yes, we took a bit of time defining leadership, some characteristics of a good leader, and some things to consider, but all of those things were absolutely important to the success of any initiative, and we felt obliged to discuss them if even only at a high level.

Now that we've done so, let's see how we can put these things to use in the development of a vision, mission, and set of goals for a generic scalability plan and initiative for a fictitious company. As an example, we will return to AllScale's new CTO Johnny Fixer.

Johnny decides to focus first on the vision of his organization. After all, what difference does it matter what direction you travel if you have absolutely no idea where you are going and where you are today? Additionally, when defining a vision, it's really not necessary to take stock of where you are.

As you recall, AllScale is a company that has grown up from a consulting business into a provider of SaaS services. The primary product today is a human resources management (HRM) module with functionality that extends from recruiting services to employee development software. Johnny is responsible for all aspects of engineering from hardware acquisition and deployment to software engineering and QA across all current and future projects supporting existing and future applications and platforms.

The company is just starting to experience another phase of rapid growth for the HRM product. The company's HRM product offering has always grown well, but has suffered lately from availability and scalability issues resulting from a failure to focus on properly architecting and maintaining the platform. In addition, several new product launches including a customer resource management module have been delayed as a result of existing problems in the HRM module. Both Johnny and Christine (the CEO) believe that these growing pains stem from a lack of focus on scalability and result in impact to the company's availability or "uptime." Christine brought

Johnny in as a scale expert and is willing to listen to him and support him in his endeavor to ensure that the company can live up to its name. The CEO makes Johnny the "R," the person Responsible, in all things related to technology scale.

As part of your planning for your first 30, 60, and 90 days, Johnny decides to perform a SWOT (strengths, weaknesses, opportunities, and threats) analysis and determines that the greatest current threat is the lack of scale of the platform. As such, he decides to define a catalyzing vision that can help move the company in the right direction. Johnny recalls that the components of vision are

- Vivid description of an ideal future
- Important to shareholder value creation
- Measurable
- Inspirational
- Incorporate elements of your beliefs
- Mostly static, but modifiable as the need presents itself
- Easily remembered

Johnny knows that he needs to make the vision short and to the point for it to be memorable. After all, people don't act on what they can't recall. He also figures that he can't really "create" value as much as ensure that value isn't "destroyed," and he decides that to keep from destroying value he must ensure that the system is available as much as possible for end users. Furthermore, Johnny is of the belief that it is possible with the right diligence and effort to ensure that issues of scale never cause a problem with uptime or availability. Johnny decides to "keep it simple" and asks Christine to review the following:

> AllScale products will all achieve 99.999% availability. Our people, processes, and technology will all be capable of handling at least double our current transactions without issue and planning to ten times our current need.

Christine loves it and Johnny moves on to figuring out the mission. Johnny recalls that a mission statement should

- Be descriptive of the present state and actions
- Incorporate a sense of purpose
- Be measurable
- Include a general direction or path toward the vision

Johnny decides to make the mission statement easily memorized. Ultimately, he wants each of his employees to have the organization's vision, mission, and goals pinned up in their cubes next to the pictures of their families so that they serve as a constant reminder of what they should be doing. He decides that he wants to remind people of the dire straits in which the company finds itself while it quickly moves toward a position of strength. Johnny develops the following mission:

> To move from crisis to our vision of a highly available and scalable environment within 11 months.

While not pretty, it's descriptive of the current state (crisis), is measurable, and clearly moves to the vision. The sense of purpose is implied. We leave it to you to try to refine this mission as an exercise.

Now that Johnny's defined his organization's vision, and the general direction he wants to move, it's time to give the team some goals. Johnny decides to give each of the teams a few goals along the way. He remembers the SMART acronym; recall that it stands for

- Specific
- Measurable
- Attainable (but aggressive)
- Realistic
- Timely (or contain a component of time)

Johnny decides to "stem the bleeding" within the production systems—those systems that actually handle customer demands. Johnny believes that that there is some low hanging fruit in early identification of system over utilization that could yield huge results. He recalls that goals are really guideposts along the way to a vision and consistent with the stated mission. He decides to give the operations team goals that increase monthly. Johnny's analysis leads him to believe he can reduce his monthly downtime (currently more than one hour per month) in half simply by catching issues sooner. He gives the operations team the goal of taking three minutes of downtime off per month. The first goal might be "Reduce scalability related downtime to no more than 57 minutes in month 1, no more than 54 minutes in month 2, and so on."

Johnny remembers that the objective of a goal isn't to define how something should happen, but rather what the end result should be. He believes this new goal is attainable and realistic, that it is time bounded (in month 1), and that it is very specific and measurable. Johnny might get into a debate with the operations leader on the topic but believes strongly that any goal related negotiation should never stand as a reason for not creating shareholder value. Johnny makes the operations head the "R" for determining how to accomplish the goal. He believes the operations team can accomplish the goal on its own and additionally makes the operations team the "S." He defines the engineering team as the "C" to ensure that they have input on the approach. The rest of the operations goals are left as an exercise for the reader.

Johnny knows that he must make architectural changes, but that those architectural changes will take some time to implement. Johnny suspects that the intellectual isolation of the architecture team from daily operations is a major reason for some of the poor decisions made in the past. He decides to make the architecture team accountable for some implementations and issues three goals to the architecture team.

The first goal has to do with the leadership of the team. Johnny wants the manager of the architecture team to develop a process to help eliminate new and future scale issues within two months. Done! This hits all of the SMART elements in one brief section.

Johnny also wants the architects to eliminate the largest cause of downtime within the current system. The data in this area is a little sketchy and Johnny makes a note to give the operations team another goal to create better incident tracking data. Anecdotally, the issues appear to stem from login and registration services. All users from all companies and organizations reside in a single monolithic database, and Johnny knows that isn't healthy long term. Johnny tells the architects that he wants a plan to resolve this issue in 30 days as goal 2 and that he wants that plan implemented within 4 months, which is goal 3.

Johnny's on his way to turning things around! He has set a vision, a mission, and some goals. Now Johnny just has to complete the creation of goals, ensure that roles are appropriately defined, lead from the front, take care of his people, and check his ego at the door! He will also need to create a causal roadmap to success, make timely and morally correct decisions, and manage his people.

The Causal Roadmap to Success

One of the best and easiest things you can do as a leader to help ensure success within an organization is help people understand how what they do every day contributes to the vision of the organization and as a result the creation of shareholder value. We call this creation of understanding the *causal roadmap to success* and our guess is that you've never sat down with any of your employees and explained it to them.

There is an old management maxim that goes something like "People join companies and leave managers." We think that's true in general and we've seen a lot of it in our time as managers, executives, and advisors within and to companies. But we've also seen a lot of good people leave because they feel that they lack purpose; their job doesn't meet the need they have to add value to someone or something. Loosely speaking, if the person otherwise appreciates her manager, she is still leaving her manager because the manager didn't give her that sense of purpose.

The causal roadmap is pretty easy to create for people, and if it isn't, there is a good reason to question whether the job should exist. We'll start with a position within a company that might otherwise be pretty difficult to dream up and then end with some of the traditional positions within a technology organization.

As an extreme case of showing the causal roadmap to success, let's first take the example of a janitor employed by AllScale. AllScale has decided to hire employee janitors rather than outsource the job. Unfortunately, we can't disclose this very good reason due to a binding fictional nondisclosure agreement with our fictitious company. AllScale has had a hard time keeping the best and brightest janitors—many of them leaving the company for jobs in outsourced janitorial firms. What's really strange here is that AllScale offers its janitors something that few other companies offer: stock options! After interviewing the janitors, we find that they are leaving because they don't feel they add value to the company. They believe that everyone has jobs that contribute to the shareholders except for them. Not true!

The chief janitorial officer (CJO) begins to work with the janitors to help them understand how they create shareholder value. First, he explains that while the janitors are paid market rates and as much as they would be paid anywhere else, the company saves money because it doesn't have to pay the management overhead associated with maintaining a team of janitors. This in turn contributes to the bottom line of the company (profitability), which in turn is a piece most shareholders deem critical in calculating the valuation of the company. The greater the profits and the greater the future expected profit growth, the more a shareholder is likely to pay for a piece of the equity within the company.

But that's not it, explains the CJO. Because the janitors create a clean and safe workplace, fewer germs are transmitted between the engineers, accountants, marketing professionals, and so on. This comparatively germ-free environment results in more time spent at work and more things getting done. Moreover, the cleanliness is done at lower cost than having the other professionals worry about cleaning common areas, and so on. Finally, sensitive documents are shredded by the proprietary janitorial team and as a result fewer trade secrets are lost thereby increasing barriers to entry for competitors. The janitors now have purpose in life and they are significantly happier with their jobs.

If we can develop a causal roadmap for janitors, it stands to reason that teams that are closer to the creation of value should be even easier. For instance, an engineer writes and designs the code that creates the product upon which your revenue is predicated. An engineer working within a classic back office IT group is responsible for writing code and developing systems that allow people to be more productive for each hour that they spend at work, thereby decreasing unit cost of work produced and either reducing the total cost structure of the organization or alternatively increasing the throughput at similar cost. Either way, the bottom line is affected beneficially, profits go up, and shareholders are willing to pay more for equity. The increase in equity price creates shareholder value.

Operations teams are responsible for ensuring that systems are available when they should be available in order to keep the company from experiencing lost opportunity with their systems. Doing that well also contributes to shareholder value by maximizing productivity or revenue, thereby increasing the bottom line either through increasing the top line or reducing cost. Again, increasing the bottom line (net income or profits) increases the price shareholders would be willing to pay and increases shareholder value.

Quality assurance teams help reduce lost opportunity associated with the deployment of a product *and* the cost of developing that product. By ensuring that the product meets predefined requirements, scalability needs, and so on of a product, the organization manages the risk and as a result the potential lost revenue associated with deploying a product with issues. Furthermore, because the team is dedicated to testing tasks, it frees up engineers who would otherwise need to spend valuable engineering hours (typically at a higher cost than QA) testing to perform engineering tasks. This refocusing of engineering time results in a lower cost per unit of product produced, thereby reducing the company's cost structure and increasing net income.

Although we've painted some of the pictures here of how the causal roadmap works in general, it is (and should be) a little more complicated than just blurting out a paragraph of how an organization impacts the company's profitability. The discussion should be conducted one-on-one between a leader and each member of their team individually. We do not mean that a CEO should talk to each of the 5,231 people in her company, but rather that a manager of individual contributors should speak to each and every one of her employees. The director in turn should speak to each of her managers, the VP to her directors, and so on. The conversation is meant to be personal and tailored to the individual. The underlying reasons will not change, but the message should be tailored to exactly what that individual does.

Furthermore, people need to be reminded of what they do and how it impacts the maximization of shareholder wealth. This isn't a one-time conversation. It's not as much about performance feedback, though you can certainly work that in, as ensuring that the person has purpose and meaning within his job. The impact to retention is meaningful and it can potentially also help employees produce more. A happy employee, after all, is a productive employee. And a productive employee is producing more to help you scale more!

Conclusion

We discussed what leadership is, a mental model for thinking of leadership, the composition of leaders, and how leadership impacts scalability of organizations and teams. Leadership is the influencing of an organization or person to accomplish a specific objective. Our model is a function consisting of personal characteristics, skills, experiences, and actions. We also reviewed how to become a better leader and argued that it all starts with knowing where you are weak and where you are strong within our leadership function.

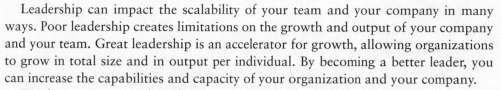

Leadership can impact the scalability of your team and your company in many ways. Poor leadership creates limitations on the growth and output of your company and your team. Great leadership is an accelerator for growth, allowing organizations to grow in total size and in output per individual. By becoming a better leader, you can increase the capabilities and capacity of your organization and your company.

We then went on to describe several aspects of successful leaders. These include leading by example, leaving your ego at the door, leading selflessly, and accomplishing the mission while taking care of your team. We concluded by arguing that you should always be thinking of how to lead ethically and that everything you do should be aligned with shareholder value.

We described the components of vision, mission, and goals and suggested an acronym (SMART) to be used in the creation of your scalability goals. Finally, we introduced what we call the causal roadmap to success, which is the notion of helping your organization to tie everything that it does back to what is important to the company: the maximization of shareholder value.

Key Points

- Leadership is influencing the behavior of an organization or a person to accomplish a specific objective.

- Leaders, whether born or made, can get better and the pursuit of getting better should be a lifelong goal.

- Leadership can be viewed as a function consisting of personal characteristics, skills, experiences, actions, and approaches. Increasing any aspect increases your leadership "quotient."

- The first step in getting better as a leader is to know where you stand. Get a 360-degree review from employees, peers, and your manager.

- Lead as you would have people follow—abide by the culture you wish to create.

- There is no place for ego when leading teams. Check your ego at the door.

- Leadership should be a selfless endeavor.

- Mission First, People Always. Get the job done on time, but ensure you are doing it while taking care of your people.

- Be morally straight always. What you allow you teach and what you teach becomes your standard.

- Align everything you do with shareholder value. Don't do things that don't create shareholder value.

- Vision is a vivid description of an ideal future. The components of vision are
  - Vivid description of an ideal future
  - Important to shareholder value creation

- Measurable
- Inspirational
- Incorporate elements of your beliefs
- Mostly static, but modifiable as the need presents itself
- Easily remembered

- Mission is the general path or actions that will get us to our vision. The components of mission are
  - Descriptive of the present state and actions
  - A sense of purpose
  - Measurable
  - General direction or path toward the vision

- Goals are the guideposts to your vision and are consistent with the path of your mission. SMART goals are
  - Specific
  - Measurable
  - Attainable (but aggressive)
  - Realistic
  - Timely (or contain a component of time)

- The causal roadmap to success will help you frame your vision, mission, and goals and help employees understand how they contribute to those goals and how the employee aids in the creation of shareholder value.

Chapter 5

Management 101

Why does a book on scalability have a chapter on management? Similar to our answer in Chapter 4, Leadership 101, if you can't direct your teams to the lofty goals and vision you created as a leader, you are not likely to get to your destination. Recall that we've set an inspirational and vivid description of the ideal future (our vision), a general path to get to that vision (our mission), and a number of mileposts along the way (our goals). Along with our behaviors, these provide the "pulling" activity that will get us to our scalability objectives. But now, we need to plot the path that will actually get there and to "push" or drive the organization to get there as quickly as possible. We will undoubtedly stumble across unexpected barriers to our success and, without the action of directing the team to the goal line, we would be relying solely upon luck and providence to get there.

A team without management focused on achieving specific objectives is a team without direction. A team without direction is dilutive to shareholder value. And as we've stated throughout this book thus far, our jobs are to maximize—not destroy—shareholder value. In this chapter, we will give our definition of management and define some elements and characteristics of great managers. From there, we will move on to describe the need for focusing on and continually improving and upgrading one's team, and to provide a conceptual framework to accomplish that task. We'll then move to a description of the importance of measurements and metrics within management and provide a tool for your consideration to tie metrics to the creation of shareholder wealth (the ultimate metric). We end this chapter with the need for management to remove obstacles for teams so that they can reach their objectives.

What Is Management?

Merriam-Webster defines management as "the conducting or supervising of something" and as the "judicious use of means to accomplish an end." We'll make a minor modification to this and add ethics to the mix ending with "the judicious and ethical use of means to accomplish an end." Why ethics? Today, more than ever, we need managers and actions that show concern for the wealth of the shareholders of our companies. How can ethics negatively influence scalability? When intellectual property is pirated, licenses for third-party products duped, or erroneous public and private statements about the scalability of a platform made, ethics are involved. Ethics play a role in how we treat our people, how we incent them, and how we accomplish our mission. If we tell an under-performer that he is performing acceptable work, we are not behaving ethically; we are both cheating the shareholders by not giving critical performance related feedback to someone who needs it and cheating the employee because he deserves to know how he is performing. The way in which a mission is accomplished is every bit as important as the actual accomplishment of that mission.

As we've previously stated, management and leadership differ in many ways, but both are important. If leadership is a promise, management is action. If leadership is a destination, management is the directions. If leadership is inspiration, management is motivation. If leadership is a painting, management is the brush. Leadership is the pulling activities and management the pushing activities. Both are necessary to be successful in maximizing shareholder wealth.

Management includes the activities of measuring, goal evaluation, and metric creation. It also includes the personnel responsibilities of staffing, personnel evaluation, and team construction (including skills, etc.). Finally, management includes all the activities one might typically consider "project management" including driving the team to work completion, aggressive dates, and so on.

What Makes a Good Manager?

Leadership and management are so significantly different that it is rare to find someone really good at both disciplines. The people who are good at both were likely good at one and worked at becoming good at both. As with leadership, the ability to manage projects, people, and organizations to a series of goals is truly a function of multiple criteria. Some variables within this function are similar to those of the leadership function. Having a great personality, for instance, is useful, as it can help influence individuals and organizations to get tasks done.

But many things that make truly great managers have little to do with the leadership equation. The best managers have an eye for detail and are incredibly task and goal oriented. The best managers are the ones that, upon given a task or goal, immediately start to break down that task or goal into everything that needs to happen for it to be successful. This activity consists of so much more than just the actions; it includes the communication, organizational structure and compensation, logistics, and capital to be successful. Very often, this detail orientation is at odds with the innovative qualities that allow people to generate compelling visions. Again, people can adjust themselves to do both, but it takes effort and time.

Great managers also develop a variety of people interaction skills that help them get the most out of the people within their organizations. The very best of these managers don't describe themselves as having a specific "style" but rather understand that they might need to employ any number of approaches to motivate certain individuals. Some people respond best to terse descriptions and matter-of-fact approaches, whereas others prefer a bit of nurturing and emotional support. Some people need a task master and still others a den mother.

Finally, the very best managers recognize the need for continual improvement and realize that the only way to improve things is to measure them. "Measurement, measurement, measurement" is the phrase by which they live. They measure the availability of their systems, the output of their organizations, and the efficiency of everything.

Project and Task Management

Good managers get projects done on time, on budget, and meet the expectations of shareholder value creation in the completion of their projects. Great managers do the same thing even in the face of adversity. Both accomplish those tasks based on a decomposition of goals into the component parts necessary to accomplish those goals. They then enlist the appropriate help both within and outside of the organization and measure progress along the path to goal accomplishment. Although this isn't a book on project management, and we will not be going into great detail on how to effectively manage scale projects, it is important to understand the necessary actions in those projects to be successful.

Tom Harde is the operations and infrastructure director within AllScale, and Johnny Fixer has given him the goal of reducing scalability related downtime incidents to no more than 57 minutes in a month. Tom decides that some component tasks of this goal are to identify the root causes of incidents, categorize them, determine the cost and time to fix each, and implement a solution. Initially, he believes there is a finish-to-start relationship between the identification of the incidents and all other activities, meaning that he must identify the incidents to categorize all of them, assign times and costs, and implement solutions. As Tom thinks more deeply about the problem though, he realizes that he could identify a series of issues without truly completing this step and move immediately to solution implementation. Given that he thinks he needs to identify something within two weeks to be able to affect a change in the first month, Tom decides to spend no more time than one calendar week trying to identify the largest causes of issues, and he will further focus on those that have happened just within the last two months.

Tom organizes his team and employs RASCI to ensure that everyone has clearly defined goals and objectives. One team consists of the folks responsible for logging and tracking all incidents within the product, and Tom assigns them the tasks of identifying issues from the last two months. Tom works closely with them, monitoring their progress daily so that he can identify any quick hits that can be pulled out and immediately worked. Within two days, Tom and the team identify one such candidate, the constant restarting of a group of application servers that are negatively impacting the company's ability to process all requests during peak demand. Leaving the team to continue to focus on the categorization of the remainder of incidents for future work, Tom moves on to work on this issue.

Tom quickly realizes that the fix for this solution will require more than just the systems administrators, operators, network engineers, and database administrators under Tom's direct control, and asks Johnny Fixer for assistance. Tom presents his business case, showing that he can shave about eight minutes of downtime a month off with some configuration changes that will allow more database communication threads to be opened during peak demand. Tom believes the changes could be made within a week or so with the right focus, and Johnny assigns Tom an architect and two engineers to focus on this for the next two weeks.

Working with the architect and engineers, Tom develops three potential solutions for solving the restarts, two of which he would not have developed on his own. The simplest approach appears to be to rate limit the requests within the application rather than queuing those requests internally. This will require additional application servers to be deployed, but with a slight increase in capital and a small modification to code, a significant downtime savings can be realized. Tom creates a project plan with responsibilities for deploying infrastructure assets, making code changes, and testing all the changes together with daily milestones given the need for speed on this project. Tom also decides to have a daily project status meeting to track the project to completion. Additionally, Tom creates daily management meeting notes that include the desired end state of the project, current status, and risks to completion.

As small issues arise that need immediate resolution, they are either raised in the project status meeting or handled immediately on an exception basis. Tom communicates daily with Johnny so that Johnny can help Tom resolve any major roadblocks.

Here, we've attempted to show you, through a story, how management is a very active discipline. The decomposition of goals into tasks, the active management of those tasks, the measurement of completion of those tasks, and the communication of progress are all necessary to successfully manage a project to completion.

Building Teams—A Sports Analogy

Professional football team coaches and management know that having the right team to accomplish the mission is critical to reaching the Super Bowl in any given season. Furthermore, they understand that the right team today might not be the right team for next season; rookie players enter the sport stronger and faster than ever before; offensive strategies and needs change; injuries plague certain players; and salary caps create downward pressure on the total value of talent that can exist within any team in any year.

Managing team skill sets and skill levels in professional sports is a constant job requiring the upgrading of talent, moving personnel to different positions, management of depth and bench strength, selection of team captains, recruiting new talent, and coaching individual high performance players.

Imagine a coach or general manager faced with the difficult task of needing to bring in a new player at a high salary to fill a specific weakness in his team. That coach is likely already at or near the team's salary cap. The choices are to remove an existing player, renegotiate one or more players' salaries to make room for the new player's salary, or not hire the necessary player into the critical position. What do you think would happen to the coach who decides to take no action and not hire the new player? If his owners find out, they would likely remove him and if they didn't find out sooner or later, the team would atrophy and consistently turn out substandard seasons resulting in lower ticket sales and unhappy shareholders (owners).

Our jobs as managers and executives are really no different than the jobs of the coaches of professional football teams. Our salary caps are the budgets that are developed by the executive management team and are reviewed and approved by our boards of directors. In order to ensure that we are cost effectively doing our jobs with the highest possible throughput and an appropriate level of quality, we too must constantly look for the best talent available at a price that we can afford. Yet most of us don't actively manage the skills, people, and composition of our teams, which in turn means that we aren't doing the right thing for our company and our shareholders. Scalability in professional sports means scaling the output of individuals; professional football, for instance, will not allow you to add a twelfth player. In your organization, scaling individuals might mean the same thing. The output of your organization is dependent both on the output of any individual as well as the size of your team. Efficiency in output, another component of scale (or at least scaling cost effectively), is a measurement of getting more for the same amount of money or (better yet) more for less money. Scaling with people then is a function both of the individual people, the number of people, and the organization of people.

Now think about a coach who refused to spend time improving his players. Can you imagine such a coach keeping her job? Similarly, can you imagine walking into your next board of directors meeting and stating that part of your job is *not* to grow and maintain the best team possible? Think about that last point for a minute. In our last chapter on leadership, we made the case that everything you do needs to be focused on shareholder value creation. Here, we have just identified a test to help you know when you are not creating shareholder value. For any major action that you make, would you go in and present it to the board of directors as something that *must* be done? Remember that a decision to *not* do something is the same as deciding to do something. Further, ignoring something that should be done is a decision not to do it. If you have not spent time with the members of your team for weeks on end, you have *decided* not to spend time with them and that is absolutely inexcusable and not something that you would likely feel comfortable discussing with your board of directors.

The parallels in professional sports to the responsibilities of team building for corporate executives are clear but all too commonly ignored. To get our jobs done, we must have the best talent (the best people) possible for our board authorized budgets. We must constantly evaluate and coach our team to ensure that each member is adding value appropriate to his level of compensation, find new and higher performing talent, and coach the great talent that we have to even higher levels of performance.

Upgrading Teams—A Garden Analogy

Even a novice gardener knows that gardening is about more than just raking some soil, throwing some seeds, and praying for rain. Unfortunately, if you are like most managers, rake, throw, and pray is probably exactly what you do with your team. Our team is a garden and our garden expects more of us than having manure spread upon it at times convenient to us. As importantly, the scalability of our organization as we described in our last metaphor is largely tied to how great our talent is on a per person basis and how consistent their behaviors are with our corporate culture.

Gardens should be designed and so should our teams. Designing our teams means finding the right talent that matches the needs of our vision and mission. Before planting our garden or inserting new seeds or seedlings in our garden, we evaluate how the different plants and flowers will interact. We should do the same with our teams. Will certain team members steal too many nutrients? Will the soil (our culture) properly support their needs? Should the garden be full of only bright and brilliant flowers or will it be more pleasing with robust and healthy foliage to support the flowers?

Managers in hyper-growth companies often spend a lot of time interviewing and selecting candidates but usually not much time on a per candidate basis. Worst still, these managers often don't take the time to determine where they've gone wrong with past hiring decisions and what they've done well in certain decisions. Finding the right individual for your job requires paying attention to and correcting your past failures and repeating your past hiring successes. We might interview for skills but overlook critical items like cultural or team fit. Why have you had to remove people? Why have people decided to leave?

Candidate selection also requires paying attention to the needs of the organization from a productivity and quality perspective. Do you really need another engineer or product manager, or do your pipeline inefficiencies indicate additional process definition needs, tools engineers, or quality assurance personnel?

Too often, we try to make hiring decisions after we've spent 30 to 60 minutes with a candidate. We encourage you to spend as much time as possible with the candidate and try to make a good hire the first time. Seek help in interviewing by adding people whom you trust and who have great interviewing skills to your interview team. Call previous managers and peers and be mindful to ask and prod for weaknesses of individuals in your background checks. Pay attention to more than just the skills and determine whether you and your team will like spending a lot of time with the individual. Interview the person to make certain that she will be a fit with your cultures and that her behaviors are consistent with the behavioral expectations of the company.

The Cultural Interview

One of the most commonly overlooked components of any interview is interviewing a candidate to ensure that he is a cultural and behavioral fit for your company. We recommend picking up a book or taking a class on behavioral interviewing, but here are some things that you can do in your next interview to find the right cultural and behavior fit for your company:

- Make a list of your company's beliefs regarding people. They may be on the back of your identification badge or on your intranet. Identify questions around these beliefs and distribute them to interview members.

- Identify interviewers who are both high performers within your team and a good match with the cultures, beliefs, and behaviors of your company (or the behaviors to which your company aspires).

- Gather after the interview and discuss the responses to the questions and the feelings of the team.

It is as important to make the right cultural hire as it is to hire the right talent and experience. Can you spend 9 to 12 hours a day with this person? Can the team do the same? Can you learn from him? Will the candidate allow the team to teach him?

Feeding your garden means spending time growing your team. Of all the practices in tending to your team, this is the one that is most often overlooked for lack of time. We might spend time picking new flowers (though not enough on a per flower basis), but we often forget about the existing flowers needing nourishment within our garden.

The intent of feeding is to help grow the members of your team who are producing to the expectations of your shareholders. Feeding consists of coaching, praising, correcting technique or approach, adjusting compensation and equity, and anything else that creates a stronger and more productive employee.

Feeding your garden also means taking individuals who might not be performing well in one position and putting them into positions where they can perform well. However, if you find yourself moving an employee more than once, it is likely that you are avoiding the appropriate action of weeding.

Finally, feeding your garden means raising the bar on the team overall and helping employees achieve greater levels of success. Great teams enjoy aggressive but achievable challenges, and it is your job as a manager to challenge them to be the best they can be.

Although you should invest as much as possible in seeding and feeding, we all know that underperforming and nonperforming individuals choke team productivity just as surely as weeds steal vital nutrients from the flowers within your garden. The nutrients in this case are the time that you spend attempting to coach underperforming individuals to an acceptable performance level and the time your team spends compensating for an underperforming individual's poor results. Weeding our gardens is often the most painful activity for most managers and executives, and as a result it is often the one to which we tend last.

Although you must abide by your company's practices regarding the removal of people who are not performing (these practices vary not only by country but by state as well), it is vital that you find ways to quickly remove personnel who are keeping you and the rest of your team from achieving your objectives. The sooner you remove them, the sooner you can find an appropriate replacement and get your team where it needs to be.

When considering performance as a reason for termination, one should always include an evaluation of the person's behaviors. It is possible to have an individual within an organization who creates more and gets more done than any other team member, but whose actions and behaviors bring the total output of the team down. This is typically pretty obvious in the case of an employee creating a hostile work environment, but it can also be the case for an employee who simply does not work well with others. For instance, you might have an employee who gets a lot done, but does so in a manner that absolutely no one wants to work with him. The result might be that you spend a great deal of time soothing hurt feelings or finding out how to assign the employee work that does not require teamwork. If the employee's actions are such that she limits the output of the team, that limitation is by definition a scale limitation and one upon which you should immediately act.

We've found that it's often useful to use the concept of a two-dimensional axis with defined actions such as in Figure 5.1. The x-axis here is the behavior of the employee and the y-axis is the employee's performance. Many employee reviews, when done properly, identify the actions on the y-axis. But many such reviews do not consider the impact of the behavioral x-axis. The idea here is that the employees you want to keep are in the upper-right portion of our graph. Those that should be immediately "weeded" are in the bottom-left portion of the graph. You should coach those individuals in the upper-left and lower-right portion of the graph, but be prepared to weed them should they not respond to coaching. And of course, you want all of your seeds or new employees to be targeted in the upper-right portion of the graph.

One thing that we have learned over time is that you will always wish you had acted earlier in removing underperformers. There are a number of reasons why you just can't act quickly enough, including company travel, competing requests, meetings, and so on. You shouldn't waste time agonizing over whether you are acting too quickly—that never happens. You will always wish you had acted even sooner when you have completed the termination.

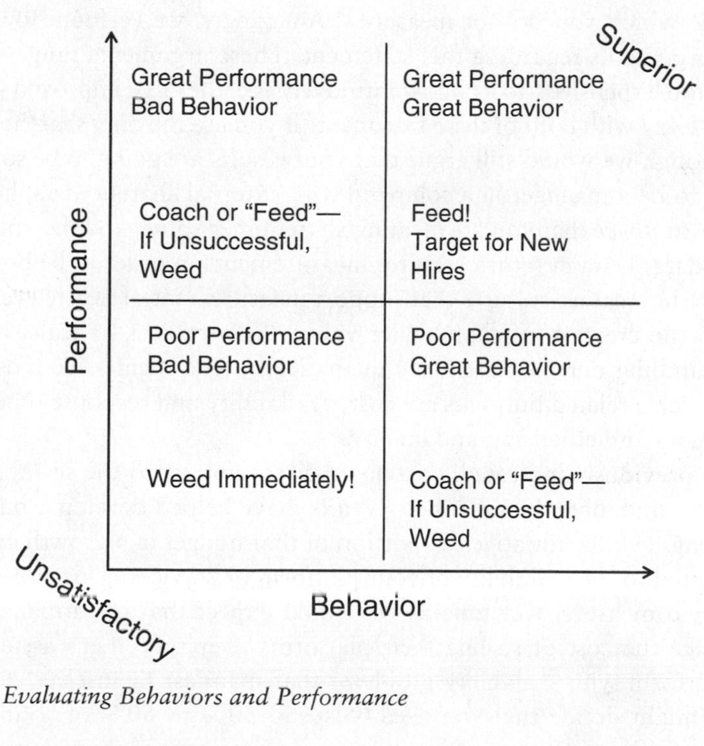

Great Performance Bad Behavior	Great Performance Great Behavior
Coach or "Feed"— If Unsuccessful, Weed	Feed! Target for New Hires
Poor Performance Bad Behavior	Poor Performance Great Behavior
Weed Immediately!	Coach or "Feed"— If Unsuccessful, Weed

Performance (y-axis, from Unsatisfactory to Superior) · Behavior (x-axis)

Figure 5.1 *Evaluating Behaviors and Performance*

Seed, Feed, and Weed to Succeed

To continually upgrade or improve our team's performance, we need to perpetually perform three individual activities:

- *Seeding* is the addition of new and better talent to our organization.
- *Feeding* is the development of the people within our organization we want to retain.
- *Weeding* is the removal of underperforming individuals within our organization.

As managers, we often spend too little time interviewing and selecting our new employees, too little time developing and coaching our high performing employees, and act too late to remove employees who do not display behaviors consistent with our culture or have the drive and motivation to create shareholder wealth.

Measurement, Metrics, and Goal Evaluation

We're not certain who first said it, but one of our favorite sayings is "You can't improve that which you do not measure." Amazingly, we've found ourselves in a number of arguments regarding this statement. These arguments range from "Measurement is too expensive" to "I know intuitively whether I've improved something." You can get away with both of these statements if you are the only shareholder of your company, though we would still argue that your results are going to be suboptimal. If you happen to be a manager in a company with external shareholders, however, you must be able to *prove* that you are creating shareholder value, and the only way to do that is with data. Data in return requires measurements in order to be produced.

We believe in creating cultures that support measurement of nearly everything that is related to the creation of shareholder value. With respect to scale, however, we believe in bundling our measurements thematically. The themes we most often recommend for scale related purposes are cost, availability and response times, engineering productivity and efficiency, and quality.

As we've previously indicated, cost has a direct impact to the scalability of your platform. You undoubtedly are either given or have helped develop a budget for the company's engineering initiatives. A portion of that budget in a growth company ideally is dedicated to the scalability of your platform or services. This alone is an interesting value to measure over time as we would expect that good managers will be able to reduce the cost of scaling their platforms over time. Let's assume that you inherit a platform with scalability problems that manifest themselves as availability issues. You might decide that you need to spend 30% to 50% of your engineering time and a significant amount of capital to fix a majority of these issues in the first two to 24 months of your job. However, something is wrong if you can't slowly start giving more time back to the business for business initiatives (customer features) over time. We recommend measuring the *cost of scale* as both a percentage of total engineering spending and as a cost per transaction.

Cost of scale as a percentage of engineering time should go down over time. But it's easy to "game" this number. If in year 1 you have a team of 20 engineers and dedicate 10 to scalability initiatives, you are spending 50% of your engineering headcount related budget on scalability. If in year 2 you hire 10 more engineers but still only dedicate the original 10 to scale, you are now spending only 33% of your budget. Although it would appear that you've reduced the cost of scale, you've really kept it constant, which could argue for measuring and reporting on the relative and absolute cost of scale.

Rather than reporting the absolute cost of scale (10 engineers, or $1.2M per annum), we often recommend normalizing the value by the activities that create shareholder value. If you are a Software as a Service platform (SaaS) provider and make money on a per transaction basis, either through advertising or the charging of transaction fees, this might be accomplished by reporting the cost of scale on a per transaction basis. For instance, if you have 1.2 million transactions a year and spend 1.2 million in headcount on scale initiatives, your cost of scale would be $1/transaction. Ouch! That's really painful if you don't make at least a dollar a transaction!

Availability is another obvious choice when figuring out what to measure. If you see a primary goal of scalability initiatives as eliminating scalability related downtime, you must measure availability and report on how much of your downtime is associated with scalability problems within your platforms or systems. The intent here is to eliminate lost opportunity associated with users not being able to complete their transactions. In the Internet world, this most often is a real impact to revenue; whereas in the back office information technology world, it might result in a greater cost of operations as people are required to work overtime to complete jobs when systems become available again.

Closely related to measuring availability for the purposes of scalability is measuring response time of your systems. In most systems, increasing user perceived response times often escalate to *brownouts* followed by *blackouts* or downtime for the system. Brownouts are typically caused by systems performing so slowly that most users will abandon their efforts, whereas blackouts are a result of a system that completely fails under high demand. The measurement of response times should be against an absolute service level agreement (SLA), even if that agreement isn't published to the end users. Ideally, the measurement is performed using actual end-user transactions rather than proxies for their interaction. In addition to the absolute measurement against internal or external service levels, relative measurement against past month values should be tracked over time for critical transactions. This data can later be used to justify projects if a slowing of any given critical transaction is proven to be tightly correlated with revenue associated with that transaction, abandon rates, and so on.

Engineering productivity and efficiency is another important measurement when considering scalability. Your first reaction may be that these two things have absolutely nothing to do with the scalability of a platform. Consider an organization that measures and improves the productivity of its engineers over time versus that of an organization that has no such measurements. You would expect that the former will start to produce more products and complete more initiatives at an equivalent cost to the latter or that they would start to produce the same at a lower cost. Either of these will help us in our scalability initiatives because if we produce more, by allocating an equivalent percentage of our engineering team, we can get more done more quickly and thereby reduce future scale demands on our engineering team. And if we can produce the same at lower cost, we are increasing shareholder value as the net decrease in cost structure to produce a scalable platform means greater profitability for the company.

The real trick in figuring out how to measure engineering productivity and efficiency is to split it up into at least two component parts. The first part has to do with whether your engineering teams are using as much of the available engineering days as possible for engineering related tasks. To do this, assume that an engineer is available for 200 days/year minus your company's sick time, vacation time, training time, and so on. Maybe your company has 15 days of paid time off a year and expects engineers to be in 10 days of training a year resulting in 175 engineering days/engineer. This becomes the denominator within our equation. Then, subtract from this denominator all of the hours and days spent "blocked" on issues related to unavailable build environments, nonworking test environments, broken tools or build environments, missing source code or documentation, and so on. It shouldn't surprise you if you haven't measured such value destroyers in the past to find out that you are only getting to make use of 60% to 70% of your engineering days.

The second component part of engineering productivity and efficiency is to measure how much you get out of each of your engineering days. This is a much harder exercise as it requires you to choose among a set of unattractive options. These options range from measuring thousands of lines of code (KLOC) produced by an engineer, to stories produced, function points produced, or use cases produced. The options are unattractive as they all have "failures" within their implementation. For instance, you may produce 100 lines of code per engineer per day, but what if you really only need to write 10 to get the same job done? Function points on the other hand are difficult and costly to calculate. Stories and use cases don't really contain a measure of complexity within their evaluation or use. As such, they all sound like bad options. But a worse option is to decide not to measure this area at all. Training programs, after all, are intended to help increase individual output, and without some sort of measurement of their effectiveness, there is no way to prove to a shareholder that the money spent on training was well spent.

Quality rounds out our scalability management measurement suite. Quality has a positive or negative impact on many of the other measurements. Poor product quality can cause scalability issues in the production environment and as a result can increase downtime and decrease availability. Poor product quality causes an increase in cost and a reduction in productivity and efficiency as rework is needed to meet the appropriate scalability needs. Although you obviously need to look at such typical metrics as bugs KLOC in production and per release, absolute bug numbers for your entire product, and the cost of your product quality initiatives, we also recommend further breaking these out into the issues that affect scale. How many defects cause scalability (response time or availability) problems for your team? How many do you release per major or minor release of your code and how are you getting these to trend down over time? How many do you catch in your quality assurance initiatives versus those that are found in production, and so on?

The Goal Tree

One easy way to map organizational goals to company goals is through a *goal tree*. A goal tree takes as its root one or more company or organizational goals and breaks it down into the subordinate goals to achieve that major goal. Here, we will use the computer science inverted view of a tree, where the root is at the top of the tree rather than the bottom. For instance, AllScale may have a goal to "Achieve Profitability by Q1." As you can see in Figure 5.2, this company goal is at the "root" of the tree. Johnny Fixer decides that the two ways he can increase profitability is by creating more monetization opportunities and creating greater revenue at a reduced cost base.

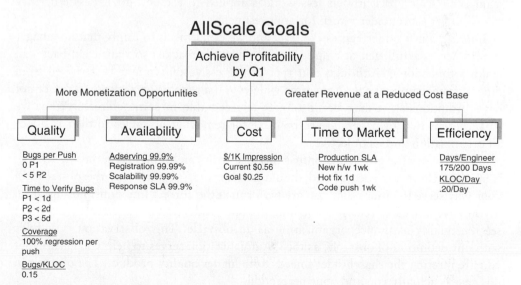

Figure 5.2 *Example Goal Tree for AllScale Networks*

Johnny determines that quality and availability affect the opportunity to monetize AllScale's platform and adds a number of quality and availability goals. One availability goal has to do with scalability (no more than .01% downtime for the quarter due to scalability), and he also adds a 99.9% adherence to the internal response time SLAs for the platform. Quality goals are to reduce the number of bugs per push (with measurable amounts), reduce the time to verify bugs, increase test suite coverage for regression tests, and have fewer than .15 bugs/KLOC outstanding in production.

From a cost perspective, Johnny desires to reduce the cost per thousand pages delivered by over 50%. Johnny also wants to impact time to market (TTM), thereby decreasing the cost of delivery, and has specific goals for that. Finally, he desires to increase his engineering productivity and decides to count both used man days versus available man days and KLOC produced per day.

Paving the Path for Success

So far, we've painted the picture of a manager as being equal parts task master, tactician, gardener, and measurement guru. But a manager's job isn't done there. Besides being responsible for ensuring the team is up to the job, deciding on the path to take to a goal, and measuring progress, a manager is also responsible for ensuring that the path to that goal is bulldozed and paved. A manager who allows a team to struggle unnecessarily over rough terrain on the way to an objective when he can easily pave the way means reducing the output of the team. This reduction in output means the team can't scale efficiently, as less work is applied to the end goal. Less efficiency means lower shareholder return for an investment.

Bulldozed is a rather aggressive term and we don't mean to imply that a manager should act as a fullback attempting to lay out a linebacker so that a halfback can make a touchdown. Although that type of aggressive play might be required from time to time, employing it all the time will get you a reputation that you'd rather not have. Additionally, it may be absolutely unacceptable in some cultures. What we mean here is that managers are responsible for removing obstacles to the success of an organization and its objectives.

It is very easy for people to confuse this idea with "anything that stands in my way is an obstacle to my success and should be removed." Sometimes, the obstacles in your way serve to ensure that you are performing the correct functions. For instance, if you have a need to release something to your production environment, you might see the quality assurance organization as an obstacle. This observation is at odds with our definition of obstacle, as the QA organization serves to help you ensure that you are meeting the shareholder's needs for a higher quality product. The obstacle in this case is actually you and your perception.

Obstacles are issues that arise and for which the team is not equipped to handle. Examples might be a failure of a partner to deliver software or hardware in a time consistent with your needs or issues in getting testing support or capital to be freed up for a project. The team isn't working *for* you but rather *with* you. You may be the captain of the team, but you are still a critical part of its success. Great managers actually get their hands dirty and "help" the team accomplish its goals.

Conclusion

Management is about execution and all of the activities necessary to reach goals, objectives, and vision, while adhering to the mission of the company. It should be thought of as a "judicious and ethical use of means to accomplish an end." Being good at management, as is the case with leadership, requires a focus and commitment to learning and growing as a manager. Management requires a focus on tasks, people, and measurements to accomplish the desired goals.

Project and task management is essential to successful management. It includes the disaggregation of goals into their associated projects and tasks, the assignment of individuals and organizations to those tasks, the measurement of progress, communication of status, and resolution of issues. In larger projects, it will include the relationship of tasks to each other in order to determine which tasks should happen when and to help determine timelines.

People management has to do with the composition and development of organizations and the hiring, firing, and development of individuals. We often spend too much time with our underperformers and wait too long to eliminate them from the team. The result is that we don't spend enough time growing the folks who are truly adding value. In general, we need to spend more time giving timely feedback to the individuals on our team to ensure that they have an opportunity to create greater shareholder value. We also spend a great deal of time interviewing new candidates in total, but often not enough on a per candidate basis. Too often, our new team members have spent 30 minutes to an hour with six to seven people before a hiring decision is made. Spend enough time with people to be comfortable with welcoming them into your family.

Measurement is critical to management success. Without measurements and metrics, we cannot hope to improve, and if there is no hope for improvement, why employ people as managers? We gave a number of measurement suggestions in "Measurement, Metrics, and Goal Evaluation," and we highly recommend a review of these from time to time as you develop your scalability program.

Managers need to help their team complete its tasks. This means ensuring that issues are resolved in a timely fashion and helping to ensure that issues don't arise whenever possible. Good managers will work to immediately remove barriers to success and great managers keep them from arising in the first place.

Key Points

- Management is the judicious and ethical use of means to accomplish an end.

- As with leadership, the pursuit of management excellence is a lifelong goal and as much a journey as it is a definition.

- As with leadership, management can be viewed as a function consisting of personal characteristics, skills, experiences, actions, and approaches. Increasing any aspect increases your management "quotient."

- Project and task management are critical to successful management. They require the ability to decompose a goal into component parts, determine relationships of those parts, assignment of ownership with dates, and the measurement of progress to those dates.

- People and organization management is broken into "seeding, feeding, and weeding:"

  - Seeding is the hiring of people into an organization with the goal of getting better and better people. Most managers spend too little time on the interview process and don't aim high enough. Cultural and behavioral interviewing should be included when looking to seed new employees.

  - Feeding is the development of people within an organization. We can never spend enough time giving good performance related feedback to our employees.

  - Weeding is the elimination of underperforming people within an organization. It is almost impossible to do this "soon enough," though we should feel obligated to give someone performance related feedback first.

- We can't improve that which we do not measure. Scalability measurements should include measurements of availability, response time, engineering productivity and efficiency, cost, and quality.

- Goal trees are an effective way to map organizational goals to company goals and help form the "causal roadmap to success."

- Managers are responsible for paving the path to success. The most successful managers see themselves as critical parts of their teams working toward a common goal.

Chapter 6

Making the Business Case

In war, the general receives his command from the sovereign.

—Sun Tzu

So far in Part I, Staffing a Scalable Organization, we have talked about how important it is to choose the right people, get them in the right roles, exercise great leadership and management, and finally establish the right organization size and structure. To pull this all together, we need to talk about the final link in the scalable organization chain. This is how to make the business case for hiring resources, allocating resources, and staying focused on scalability as a business initiative. In this chapter, we are going to cover these topics and explain some of the reasons that many companies and their executive teams are so reluctant to listen to the lamentations of their technology staff until it is too late. Most importantly we will give you some tips on how to turn these problems around and become successful at making the proper business case for scalability.

Understanding the Experiential Chasm

It is our belief that a great deal of the problem existing between many general managers and their technical teams is a result of a huge and widening chasm in education and experience that causes a type of "destructive interference" in communication. The education of the two individuals are often very different with the technical executive likely having taken an increasingly difficult and complex engineering curriculum in college, whereas the general manager might have had a less math intensive liberal arts undergraduate degree. The behaviors of the two executives may vary with the technical executive likely having been promoted rightly or wrongly based on his focused, somewhat introverted behavior ("put him in a dark room alone and he can get anything done") and with the general manager being much more extroverted, friendly, and "sales-person like." The work experience likely varies with the general manager having been promoted to her position through closing deals, selling proposals, and making connections. The technical executive might have been promoted either based on technical brilliance or the ability to get product complete and potentially shipped on time.

This mismatch in education and experience causes difficulty in communication for several reasons. First, with very little in common, there is often little reason outside of work specific tasks for the two people to communicate or have a relationship. They might not enjoy the same activities and might not know the same people. Without this common bond outside of work, the only way to build trust between the two individuals is through mutual success at work. Success may in the end create a bond that kindles a relationship that can last through hard times, but when mutual success has not yet been achieved, the spark that occurs kindles the opposite of trust; and without trust, the team is doomed.

Second, without some previous relationship, communication does not happen on mutual footing. Questions are often rightfully asked from a business perspective, and the answers are often given in technical terms. The general manager may for instance ask, "When can we ship the Maxim 360 Gateway for revenue release?" to which the technical executive may respond, "We are having problems with the RF modulation and power consumption and we are not sure if it is a software potentiometer or a hardware rheostat. That said, I do not think we are off more than two weeks of the original delivery schedule to QA." Although the technical executive here gave a full and complete response, it probably only frustrated the general manager as she likely has no idea what a soft-pot or a rheostat is and may not even know what RF is. The information came so fast and was intermixed with so many important, but to her meaningless pieces of information that it just became confusing.

This resulting mismatch in communication actually quite often gives way to a more destructive form of communication, which we call *destructive interference*. Questions begin to be asked in a finger-pointing fashion—for example, "What are you doing to keep this on track?" or "How did you let it slip a week?"—rather than in a fashion meant to resolve issues early—such as, "Let us see if together we cannot work to find out how we can get the project back on the timeline." This is not to say that you should not keep and hold high expectations of your management team, but doing so should *not* create a destructive team dynamic. It is possible to both have high standards and actually be a participative, supporting, and helpful leader and executive.

Why the Business Executive Might Be the Problem

Some questions can be asked to determine if the likely culprit of poor communication is the business executive. Do not fret; we will give a similar set of questions to point the blame at the technology executive. The most likely result is that some amount of

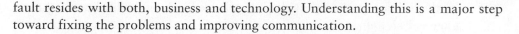

fault resides with both, business and technology. Understanding this is a major step toward fixing the problems and improving communication.

- Has the head of technology been replaced more than once?
- Do different people in the technology team give the business the same explanations but they are still not believed?
- Do business leaders spend as much time attempting to understand technology as they have spent learning to read financial statements?
- Do the business leaders understand how to ask questions to know whether dates are both aggressive and achievable?
- Does the business spend time in the beginning of a product life cycle figuring out how to measure success?
- Do business leaders lead by example or do they point fingers?

Chances are that at least one, and likely several, of the preceding points hits home. We do not mean to imply that the business leaders are the *only* problem. However, if they absolutely refuse to accept culpability in the problem, this is a huge warning sign. The best leaders accept that they are at least part of the problem, and we believe that the very best leaders believe that they are the source of most problems. It absolutely may be the case, and often is the case, that other people need to be fired in order to get the problem fixed. But if the business is constantly hiring and firing technology leaders, at the very least, they owe it to the shareholders to consider themselves part of the problem.

To get back on point, however, note how many of the preceding questions can be easily traced back to education and experience. For instance, if you are getting consistent answers throughout from your team, maybe it is the case that you just do not understand what they are saying. There are two ways to resolve that: You can either gain a better understanding of what it is they are telling you, or you can work with them to speak a language that you better understand. Better yet, do both!

Why the Technology Executive Might Be the Problem

For nearly all of the reasons that the business executives are responsible for their own frustration with the technology teams, so is the technical executive responsible. She is standing on the opposite side of the chasm and is participating in the "staring game." Each is looking at the other and attempting to find ways to communicate effectively, each ultimately falling into the mode of destructive interference that destroys trust and organizations.

As promised, here are the questions to ask your technology leadership to see how much of the communication problem it is responsible for.

- Does the technology team provide you early feedback on the likelihood of making key dates?

- Is that feedback consistently incorrect?

- Is the business experiencing the same problems over and over, either in production or in product schedules?

- Does the technology team measure themselves against metrics that are meaningful?

- Are the technology choices couched in terms of technical merit rather than business benefit and cost?

- Does the technology team understand what drives your business, who your competitors are, and how your business will be successful?

- Does the technology team understand the business challenges, risks, obstacles, and strategy?

Just as the business executives have not spent as much time understanding how to run technical projects or how to "speak tech" as the technology leaders have spent learning to read financial statements, it is also likely that the technical executive has not spent a lot of time learning what truly drives your business. To be sure, he probably believes he knows. A good test is to have him define the technology metrics in terms of things that are important to your business: revenue, profit, time to market, barriers to entry, customer retention, and so on. It is critical for the technology executive to understand how the business makes money, the drivers of that revenue equation, the current financial reality within the business, and the current year's financial goals for the business.

In AllScale, as discussed in Chapter 2, Roles for the Scalable Technology Organization, the previous CTO was promoted based on his technical acumen. As the CEO Christine quickly learned, the previous CTO had no business acumen and could not properly explain the need for purchases or projects in business terms. This frustrated the remainder of the company's executives as technology initiatives were never tied to business goals or needs. When other departments were cutting travel to save money, the old CTO was buying extra terabytes of storage area network (SAN) space costing hundreds of thousands of dollars that no one could explain the need for. The old CTO would rely on the threat of "we either do this or we will die" to get all the other executives in line. Although this worked for the short term, it left all the other executives feeling that something was not right with the decision that had to be forced on them. Christine quickly saw this situation and put an end to it. She brought on board the new CTO, Johnny Fixer, who understands both technology and business. Johnny in only his first couple of months has been able to put metrics in place that represent the business goals and can explain all of his team's initiatives in terms of revenue generation or cost cutting. He has definitely been a welcome relief to the executive team.

Defeating the Corporate Mindset

Lots of companies claim that technology is a key differentiator, critical to the business, or in military lingo, a force multiplier, but the reality is that many of them, including Software as a Service (SaaS) companies, treat technology as a support service. There are two basic forms that a technology organization can take within a business. One is to be a support service where technology supports the business processes of manufacturing, sales, or any number of other business lines. The other form that technology can take within a business is to be the product for the business, such as with SaaS, infrastructure as a service (IaaS), hardware product companies, or Web 2.0 companies.

Being a support service and supporting other key business processes is a fine calling. As a technologist, being the product that the business is founded around, while often more stressful, is great as well. The terms usually applied to these are *cost center* for the support service and *profit center* for the product development organizations. Cost center, as the name implies, is a center or organization that adds cost to the income statement of a business usually at the Selling General and Administrative expense line. A profit center is an organization that derives revenue for the business. The problem arises when one type of company thinks of itself, or worse acts as if, it were the other type. To understand this more, we need to dive into the two forms deeper. All different types of organizations require technology support to ensure their processes are efficient and consistent. Today's manufacturing would be lost without technology from computer numerical control (CNC) machines to ladder logic. These types of companies and technology departments are hopefully upfront and aware of how technology is viewed. It is a support service or cost center that will likely always be viewed as a cost line item in the budget. No matter how scalable, artful, impressive, or on time the tech is, the best these technology systems and projects can strive for is a reduction of cost or improvement in efficiency for the business. We label this view of technology as the "corporate mindset" because most very large corporations whose primary business is not technology, Corporate America, have this view.

On the other hand, businesses that were founded on the technology as the product hopefully see things quite differently. In companies such as eBay, PayPal, Amazon, and Google, one would expect that executives view technology as being directly correlated with the revenue and treat them as a profit center. If a new feature is requested for the system or platform, that feature should be predicated on a change in revenue and a return on investment. These companies should understand in their DNA that the technology is the business. This should not, however, give the technology team carte blanche to spend any amount or not relate technology projects into business terms; in fact, the opposite is true. These technology leaders owe it to the business to justify and explain themselves just as thoroughly.

If you are in Corporate America and the business has a corporate mindset about technology, as it does with all other support functions such as human resources and finance (assuming it is not an HR or CPA services company), the problems are much more straightforward. If you want a technology project approved, you know you need to cost justify it through cost cutting explanations. Although the problem is clear cut, you will certainly have a more difficult challenge convincing your business partners that improving the scalability of a particular platform is necessary. In this case, you should pay particular attention to the next section where we will provide some mechanisms to help you justify the projects.

The real challenges with corporate mindset come when it exists in a SaaS or Web 2.0 company. When the primary business of the company is selling the technology product or service, yet the business leaders think the technology team simply supports their brilliant product ideas or sales initiatives, we have real problems. These business executives are the ones who, if they were willing to answer, would answer "yes" to all the questions in the preceding subsection "Why the Business Executives Might Be the Problem." Unfortunately, these executives are also probably not insightful or self-reflective enough to think they could be part of the problem and therefore need to be fixed. Having worked in a few and having been a spectator to many of these types of environments, our first reaction is to run away. And if you are lucky enough during the interview process to catch a vibe of this, our recommendation is to run away. These are uphill battles that we are getting ready to describe and if you can avoid the confrontation, you are probably better off. We know, however, that this is not always an option for any of us. Sometimes, you find yourself committed before you recognize this problem and you are faced with confronting and fixing it rather than turning your back on it.

To solve the corporate mindset problem, we have seven ideas that you should consider implementing. These are all things that as a technology leader are in your control. Waiting for your colleagues to wake up and realize their deficiencies will not work. Take responsibility into your own hands and make the organization the type of place that you want it to be. Here is the list of ideas:

1. Form relationships
2. Set the example
3. Educate other executives
4. Use the RASCI model
5. Speak in business terms
6. Get them involved
7. Scare the executive team with facts

Forming Relationships

One of the best ways to start changing the business executives is to begin forming a relationship with them. As discussed in the section "Understanding the Experiential Chasm" of this chapter, a relationship is the key to communication. Start building those relationships today. Schedule monthly lunches with each member of the executive staff. Spend time over a meal getting to know these team members, their careers, their families, their business challenges. Pay attention and get to know them on multiple levels. Open up and share your background as well; let them get to know you. The best teams in the world spend *thousands* of hours training with each other and maybe even living together. When you think of great teams, you probably think of professional sports teams or Navy SEALS or Delta Force. The one thing all of these organizations have in common is a set of shared experiences and shared trials created over thousands and thousands of hours of training time. You aren't likely to spend as much time creating relationships through shared experiences in your entire career as these teams spend in a single year. The lesson here is that you need to force yourself to create relationships with the people who are your peers and your boss.

Setting the Example

There may be finger pointing or, worse, backstabbing, politics, or gamesmanship already existing on the executive staff or between departments. Avoid getting pulled into this. Be the better person and set the example for how you want to see people interact. Instead of jumping to defend your team, ask the person or group how can we work together to solve this and learn from it. Pulling a concept from emotional intelligence, start by asking if they are willing to accept that there is a better way. This is supposed to be a very disarming question that opens people up to discussing alternatives.

It surely will be tempting for most to jump in and start playing the games, setting each other up for failure, and defending your actions. Avoid this if at all possible, but remain on strong footing by looking for solutions. The worse case is that you are not able to change the culture and you are eventually another technology executive that pays the price for the business's incompetence. Although this seems dire for you and your career, leaving or being asked to leave a no-win scenario is better in the long run than sticking it out and ultimately having the business fail, which is a likely outcome.

Educating Other Executives

One of the best things that you can do for your colleagues is to educate them about technology and the role it plays in the business. There are many ways that you can accomplish this. Some of them are covered below in the section below entitled "The Business Case for Scale." Some other ways include teaching classes on technology.

This can be brownbag sessions over lunch or asking for 15 minutes each staff meeting to discuss a technology subject. The more they understand how things work, how complicated, and how different parts affect customers, the more likely they are to being sympathetic and understanding when it comes to discussions about technology.

Another creative way to educate business executives is to invite them for a "technology ride-along." This concept is similar to what police departments have set up for private citizens to ride along with them on patrol. Usually, the citizens walk away from this with a renewed respect for the police officers and the incredibly stressful and tough job that they perform. Hopefully, this is what the business executives will take away from the evening as well. To most business executives outside of technology, what the technology team and system does is black magic and most likely they are afraid to ask for fear of looking stupid. Get over this by reaching out to them and inviting them to spend the night alongside you as you release the next version of the product or patch bug fixes. As they come in the next morning from being up late, they will likely appreciate the many late nights and intellectually challenging problems that you and your team face on a daily and weekly basis.

Using the RASCI Model

As we have covered in Chapter 2, we highly recommend the use of the RASCI model for helping define role clarity for initiatives. As a quick review, R is Responsible, A is Accountable, S is Supportive, C is Consulted, and I is Informed. The I is often given lip service but generally not followed up on as intensely as the other roles. For helping to solve the corporate mindset, we recommend reconsidering the importance of the I. Technology initiatives are a great way to involve other business executives by adding them to the list of those to keep informed about a particular project. Weekly emails, monthly report outs, whatever manner your team deems necessary to keep this group informed will aid in your initiative to fix the corporate mindset problem.

Speaking in Business Terms

Just because the business has not bothered to learn your native tongue, the language of technology, does not mean that you should not try to speak in a language that they can understand. If you have ever traveled internationally and you ran across native people who attempted to speak English in order to make you feel more comfortable and understood, you can relate to how your business counterparts will feel when you start explaining things in their language. By making the effort to speak the universal language of business, you will earn the gratitude and respect of your business counterparts.

Remember our points regarding the maximization of shareholder value. If you hold a technology management or executive position, you are first and foremost a manager or executive of that business. You must learn to speak the language of business and you must also learn what drives your business. You cannot possibly maximize shareholder value if you do not understand the concepts that drive all businesses at a macro level and equally important your business at a micro level.

Translate projects, goals, and initiatives to business metrics such as revenue, customer acquisition, customer retention, and so on. When providing an update on an initiative, instead of describing the project as "the initiative to shard the database by mod of customer_id," try describing it as "the database project that will allow the business to double revenue over the next year as the growth projections indicate." The last description will get them a lot more excited and help them understand it a lot better.

Getting Them Involved

Even better than keeping the business executives informed about major technology initiatives, get them involved. Moving them from no involvement to owning projects is probably not going to happen overnight, but you can start by getting them involved. Ask for members from their teams as Cs. The idea is that the more stakes they have in the projects the more they will be interested and support you.

Another way to get the business executives involved is asking them to mentor your top folks. It is always great for technologists to learn about the business, so this should not be seen as unreasonable. The dual benefit is that while your key staff members get exposure and education from the business leaders, your team members are teaching the business leaders about technology and keeping them updated on projects. It is a great win-win situation.

Scaring the Executive Team with Facts

Our last idea, when all else has failed and your business colleagues continue to not give you support for necessary scalability projects, is to use the next outage as an example of what will happen without a consistent and focused support on scalability. The reality is that if you are not focused on continuous improvements and the scalability of your applications, there will be a downtime event. Crisis is a catalyst for change. It is easier to get people's attention and get their support for change if they have witnessed or experienced a calamity.

Note that this should never be your first choice and in most organizations should truly be seen as a failure for the executive team to make the right calls. The only time this is an appropriate approach is if all other options have failed. The only way this approach will work is if you can show the case over time you've been attempting to make for the need for scale. Additionally, this approach will only work one time. If you are consistently using the "scared straight" method over and over to get your way, you are in effect Chicken Little claiming that the sky is falling. You are either in the wrong company or you are the wrong person for the job.

That concludes the list of ideas that you should consider when attempting to remedy the corporate mindset problem. Take notice that these are all actionable and put you in control. Do not wait for your colleagues to wake up and realize they are part of the problem. Be proactive, take responsibility, and make the organization what you want it to be.

The Business Case for Scale

So far in this chapter, we have covered why there may be a communication breakdown between you and your business colleagues, perhaps even your boss. Next, we covered the corporate mindset and why this may be a big problem for your business. Lastly, we provided some ideas on how to change the corporate mindset and get your business colleagues involved and supportive of your scalability projects. Now that you have a clear understanding of why a problem might exist, how this problem can negatively affect your efforts to build a scalable platform, and what to do about it, it is time to focus on the last piece of the puzzle: the business case for scale. After you have your boss' and colleagues' attention and support, wrap the whole thing up by explaining in clear business related terminology the need for scalability. In this section, we are going to cover some ideas on how to accomplish this.

Your business is unique and therefore your business case will need to be tailored for your platform or application. Through these examples, you should hopefully see the pattern and how you should be able to relate almost any aspect of your application to metrics and goals that the business cares about. The most straightforward concept is that downtime equals lost revenue, assuming you are past the early stage of giving away your product and are actually generating revenue. When the site is not available, the company does not make money. Simply take the projected revenue for the quarter or month and calculate what that is per hour or minute. This is the amount associated with the downtime. There are way more complicated methods of doing this if you are so inclined, but a simple straight line projection is useful to get the point across.

For a more accurate example of downtime cost calculation, you can use the graph of your site's normal daily and weekly traffic. Take last week's traffic graph, assuming last week was a normal week, and put over top of it the traffic graph depicting the outage. The amount of area between the two lines should be considered the percentage of downtime. This method is particularly useful for partial outages, which you should have if you follow our advice in Chapter 21, Creating Fault Isolative Architectural Structures.

In Figure 6.1, AllScale's HRM Outage Graph, the solid gray line is AllScale's normal day's traffic and the dashed black line is the traffic from yesterday when there

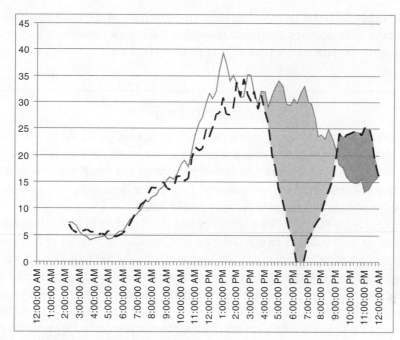

Figure 6.1 *AllScale's HRM Outage Graph*

was an outage of the HRM SaaS system. Johnny, the CTO, has requested that his operations team pull this graph together in order that they understand the exact customer impact of downtime. The outage began at 4:00 PM and lasted until approximately 9:00 PM when the site was fully recovered. The area between the lines from 4:00 to 9:00 PM would be considered the outage percentage and could be used in the calculation of downtime and cost associated with it. However, notice the dashed line from 9:00 PM to 12:00 AM goes much higher than the normal traffic in solid. This is typical of sites for consumer user bases where there is a pent-up demand for the service and a spike usually occurs afterward. Unfortunately, this is a busy time of the year for AllScale's HRM system. A lot of its customer base is performing annual evaluations and have tight deadlines for getting their evaluations in the system. There were likely many managers that needed to get personnel files uploaded and had to stay up late to get their work done. To most accurately account for the cost of the downtime, this area, highlighted in dark gray, must be added back into the outage percentage, because it was recovered revenue or recovered service depending on the actual business model. In this example, the area under the solid gray line is 100% of the daily traffic; the area between the solid gray line and dashed black line during the outage, highlighted in light gray, is approximately 27%. The dark gray highlighted area is approximately 9%. The percentage of missed traffic and potential revenue due to the outage would be 27% – 9% = 18% of the daily total. Johnny can now take this percentage and use it to calculate the cost or impact of the outage, although this does not take into account the frustration that AllScale's customers had to put up with having the system unavailable during peak work hours.

Amazon Outage

As an extreme example of how downtime translates into revenue dollars, let us take a service such as Amazon and see what its downtime costs are. Now, we do not mean to single Amazon out in any negative way because it typically has great uptime and almost any other large Internet service has seen equal or more downtime. But Amazon does make a great case study because it is so large and is a public company (NASD: AMZN).

According to the *New York Times* technology blog "Bits," on June 6, 2008, Amazon experienced over an hour outage of its site. Using the expected revenue from Q2 of $4 billion, this calculates as a straight line projection to $1.8 million in lost sales per hour. One can make the argument that customers who could not purchase during that hour will come back, but it is also likely that they made their purchases elsewhere. Even if the company only ultimately lost 50% or 25% of that revenue, it is still a significant amount. This lost revenue calculation is what you should be doing for your outages, not only to drive home to your technology team the importance of keeping the system available but also as a fact to help explain to your business counterparts the cost of not investing in the proper people and projects to keep the site available and scaling properly.

Another approach to capturing platform issues in terms of business metrics is to relate it to customer acquisition cost. If your business spends marketing dollars to attract users to visit the site or sign up, most likely there is a cost associated with each customer acquired. This way, the marketing team can determine which media offers the lowest cost per user. When the site is down, the marketing spend does not stop—usually these campaigns cannot be started and stopped immediately and very rarely do people think about this until after the fact. Because the marketing continues, users are still being lured to the site even though they cannot experience the wonders of the service. When this occurs, it is very unlikely that a customer will ever show back-up when their first experience was terrible. Downtime can be directly responsible for the lost customers during the outage. Extending beyond this, if you keep track of returning users, another metric to look at is how many users stop returning after an outage. If you have 35% of your users returning to the site once per month, watch this metric post outage. If the numbers drop, you may have just lost those users permanently.

The last idea for describing the outages or potential for outages in business terms is to translate it to cost within the organization. This can be in terms of operations staff, engineers, or customer support staff, the last being the most immediately noticeable by the business. When downtime occurs and engineers and operations staff must attend to it, they are not working on other projects such as customer features. A dollar amount can be associated to this by determining the total engineering budget for salaries and support and associate the number of engineers and time spent on the outage as a percentage of the total budget. As noted previously, the factor closest to the business would be customer support staff that are either not able to work due to the support tools being unavailable during the outage or having to handle extra customer complaints during the outage and for hours afterward. For companies with large support staffs, this amount of work can add up to significant amounts of money.

Although determining the actual cost of an outage may be a painful exercise for the technology staff, it serves several purposes. The first is that it puts in real dollar values what downtime costs the business. This should be helpful in your arguments for needing support and staffing for scalability projects. The second purpose is that it helps educate the technology staff to what it really costs the business to not have the platform available. This can be a huge motivator to engineers when they understand how profitability, bonuses, budgets, hiring plans, and so on are all tied together dependent on the platform.

Conclusion

In this chapter, we wrapped up Part I by pulling together the final link in the scalable organization chain: how to make the business case for hiring resources, allocating resources, and staying focused on scalability as a business initiative. We covered the experiential chasm that exists between most technologists and their business counterparts, including most likely the CTO's boss, and we explored the idea of a business having a "corporate mindset." We have given some ideas on how to cross the chasm and undo the corporate mindset in order that the business be receptive to the need to focus on scalability, especially from a people and organizational perspective, which include hiring the right people, putting them in the right roles, demonstrating the necessary leadership and management, as well as building the proper organizational structure around the teams.

Key Points

- There is an experiential chasm between technologists and other business leaders due to education and experiences that are missing from most nontechnology executive's careers.

- Technologists must take responsibility for crossing over into the business in order to bridge the chasm.

- In order to garner support and understanding scaling, initiatives must be put in terms the business leaders can understand.

- Calculating the cost of outages and downtime can be an effective method of demonstrating the need for a business culture focused on scalability.

Part II

Building Processes
for Scale

Chapter 7

Understanding Why Processes Are Critical to Scale

After that, comes tactical maneuvering, than which there is nothing more difficult. The difficulty of tactical maneuvering consists in turning the devious into the direct, and misfortune into gain.

—Sun Tzu

In Part II, Building Processes for Scale, we are going to spend some time discussing processes. As with Part I, Staffing a Scalable Organization, you may be asking yourself, "What do processes have to do with scalability?" The same answer applies here as it did with our focus on people, "Process has a lot to do with scalability." Admittedly, we started with people because we think people are the most important aspect to building and sustaining a scalable system. Do not think that you can hire great people and forget about everything else. Undervalue process at the peril of your team, your system, and yourself.

Great people can only accomplish a limited amount as an individual; they need to be part of teams in order to accomplish goals beyond what a single individual can achieve. Working in teams dictates the use of processes that govern, control, suggest, guide, teach, and advise team members.

In Part II, we are going to spend time explaining various essential processes and the roles they should play in your organizations, depending on the size, maturity, culture, and duration of your business. We will cover this in much more detail but we believe there is a right time and right place for processes and not every process should be a part of every organization. Some of the processes that we will cover in Part II include

- How to properly control change in your production environment
- What to do when things go wrong or when there is a crisis
- How to design scalability into your products from the beginning
- How to understand and manage risk

- When to build and when to buy
- How to determine the amount of scale in your systems
- When to go forward with a release and when not to
- When to roll back and how to prepare for that eventuality

Before we dive into the individual processes that will constitute the remaining chapters in Part II, we will cover, in this chapter, how processes affect scalability, both positively and negatively. We are going to look first at what is the purpose of processes in general, and then discuss the importance of coordinating the right amount of process rigor or repeatability to the right time in an organization's life cycle, and wrap up our focus on the generalities of process with a look at what happens when the wrong process is implemented. By focusing on these topics, we will derive a causal link between the ability of an organization to scale to the processes that support it.

The Purpose of Process

As defined by Wikipedia, a business process is a "collection of related, structured activities or tasks that produce a specific service or product (serve a particular goal) for a particular customer or customers."[1] These processes can be directly related to providing a customer with a product or service, such as manufacturing, or can be a supporting process, such as accounting. The Software Engineering Institute defines process as what holds together three critical dimensions of organizations: people, methods, and tools. In their published Capability Maturity Model for Development v. 1.2, the Software Engineering Institute states that processes ". . . allow you to address scalability and provide a way to incorporate knowledge of how to do things better." Processes allow your teams to react quickly to crisis, determine the root cause of failures, determine capacity of systems, analyze scalability needs, implement scalability projects, and many more fundamental needs for a scalable system. These are vital if you want your system to scale with your growth. As an example, if you rely on an ad hoc response to restore your service when an outage occurs, you are going to experience much more downtime than if you have a clear set of steps that your team should take to respond, communicate, debug, and restore services.

As we discussed in Chapter 5, Management 101, managing is a critical function for teams to perform efficiently and effectively, which in turn allows them to focus on the most critical scalability projects as well as properly prioritize work. As important as managers are, they cannot stand around all day waiting for someone to have a question about what to do in a certain situation, such as when an engineer is checking in code to the source code repository and unsure of the proper branch. Although

---

1. Wikipedia: http://en.wikipedia.org/wiki/Business_process.

it might be helpful to have this sort of management for the engineer, it is not cost efficient. Instead, perhaps the engineering team can decide that bug fixes go into the maintenance branch and new features go into the main branch. To make sure everyone on the team knows this, someone might write it up and send it around to the team, post it on their wiki, or tell everyone about it at their next all-hands meeting. Congratulations, the team just developed a process. And, that is one of the principle purposes of processes, to manage people when the manager is not available or it is not cost-effective for the manager to spend time providing the same guidance to the team over and over for the same task. Good process supplements management and augments its reach.

Back to our example of an engineer checking in code to the source code repository: What would happen if the engineer did not have a process to reference, could not find her manager, and did not have a process established for dealing with procedural uncertainties? Assuming she checked all the logical manager hangouts like the game room, kitchen, and water cooler, she would have to make a decision for herself. Today, she decides that she should check her bug fix into the maintenance branch. This seems pretty logical because the branch is called "maintenance" and the bug fix is maintaining the application. A couple days later, long enough for her to forget about her decision of where to check in the bug fix, she has been assigned another bug to fix. She quickly identifies the problem and makes the correction. All ready to check in the fix, she has the same question: which branch? She again looks for her manager and cannot find him; he must have a very clever hiding spot in which to watch his favorite game show. She also cannot seem to remember what she did last time in this situation. She does remember hearing that code is being promoted from the main branch tonight and it seems logical that the product team and her boss would want this fix in as soon as possible. Therefore, she checks in her bug fix to the main branch and proceeds with her new feature development. See the problem? Yes, without a clear process, there is room for everyone to make their own decisions about how to accomplish certain tasks. In some cases, this might be the right thing for organizations; we'll talk about too much process later in this chapter. But in most cases that deal with recurring tasks that everyone should repeat in the same manner, a process is just the ticket. Two key reasons that we create and maintain processes are the standardization of how to perform tasks and what to do in the event of procedural uncertainty.

In our consulting practice, we are often faced with teams that mistakenly believe that the establishment of processes will stifle creativity. The reality is quite different; in fact, well-placed processes can have just the opposite effect and foster creativity among team members. For those with little experience working in an environment where someone has done a great job identifying the proper tasks suitable for processes, selecting the proper granularity and rigidness of the process, and effectively documenting and disseminating the steps, this may come as a completely counterintuitive statement. Let us explain. There is only so much time in each work day and only so many tasks that your engineers can concentrate on. Equally important, people tend to only have a limited amount of creativity within them before they must "recharge their batteries." If an engineer has to spend time and some amount of creative thought on menial tasks, we lose that time and creative power that could be spent on the really important tasks, like designing your new user interface. A well-structured environment of processes can take away the distractions and leave the engineer time and energy to focus on being creative.

Now that we have covered the purpose of process, we can focus on how to determine what is the right process or amount of process for a particular task in your particular organization. Although processes do help augment management and standardize repetitive or unclear tasks, not all organizations need or can tolerate the same amount of process. Just as some organizations are not as efficient, productive, or able to produce as high of quality products as other organizations, not all organizations are able to handle levels of process and rigor.

CMMI

The origin of the Capability Maturity Model (CMM) in software engineering can be traced back to a military funded research project at Carnegie-Mellon Software Engineering Institute for a method of evaluating software subcontractors. Founded as a pure software engineering model, many CMMs were later developed as a general assessment of the process capability maturity of many different technology arenas such as systems engineering, information technology, and acquisitions. The propagation of CMMs gave birth to the Capability Maturity Model Integration (CMMI) project with the intent of creating a general CMM framework. This framework supports "constellations," which are collections of CMMI components. There are currently three constellations: CMMI for Development, CMMI for Services, and CMMI for Acquisitions.

CMMI uses levels to describe an evolutionary path of process improvement described as either a "capability level" for organizations utilizing continuous improvement or "maturity level" for those using a staged representation. These levels are shown in Figure 7.1 and described in Tables 7.1 and 7.2.

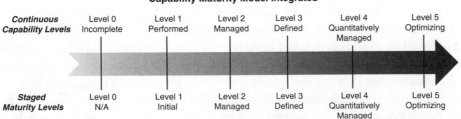

Figure 7.1 *CMMI Levels*

Table 7.1 *Capability Levels*

Level Number	Capability Level	Description
0.	Incomplete	When a process is not completed or is only partially completed
1.	Performed	When a process is performed that satisfies the stated goal of the process
2.	Managed	When processes that have basic infrastructure to support and are retained during times of stress
3.	Defined	When the standards and procedures are consistent and described rigorously
4.	Quantitatively Managed	When a process is controlled using statistical or other quantitative techniques
5.	Optimizing	When processes are improved through incremental and innovative improvements

Table 7.2 *Maturity Levels*

Level Number	Maturity Level	Description
1.	Initial	This first level consists of processes that are characterized as being reactive and chaotic.
2.	Managed	In this level, project management has been established and some amount of process discipline exists.
3.	Defined	In the third level, processes have been documented and institutionalized.
4.	Quantitatively Managed	The penultimate level is characterized by the quantitative measurements of processes that are used for improvements.
5.	Optimization	This level is where processes are continuously improved based on incremental and innovative advances.

Right Time, Right Process

All organizations are comprised of different people, with different backgrounds, different experiences, different relationships with each other, and different environments. Therefore, all organizations are different. Even if you left your old job for a terrific new position and brought all your old buddies with you, you won't be able to transport your previous company's culture. You are all somewhat older now, have had new experiences in and out of work, have new business peers, and a new office environment. Regardless of whether you left your old job, even that organization is forever in flux. People quit, new people get hired, the business climate changes, people get promoted, and so on. The same organization two years ago compared to today is different. There is no stopping the change that is forever taking place.

If all organizations are different and all organizations are in a constant state of change, what does this mean for an organization's processes? The answer is that there is no single right answer when it comes to processes. Each and every process must be evaluated first for general fit within the organization in terms of its rigor or repeatability and then specifically for what steps are right for your particular team in terms of complexity. As an example, when you first founded your company and it was you and one other engineer with very few customers, the crisis management process would have simply been that you get out of bed in the middle of the night and reboot the server. If you missed the alert, you would reboot it the morning because there were likely no customers wanting to use your service in the middle of the night. Using that same process when your team is 50 engineers and you have thousands of customers would result in pure chaos and lost revenue. You now need to have a process that spells out to everyone the necessary steps to take when a significant incident arises and that process needs to be consistently repeatable.

How Much Rigor

As a guideline for discussing the rigor or repeatability of a process, we like to refer to the capability and maturity levels from the Capability Maturity Model Integrated (CMMI) framework. This section is in no way a full or complete explanation of the CMMI framework, much more information can be found at the Software Engineering Institute's site, http://www.sei.cmu.edu. We are introducing this framework as a way to simply standardize terminology for process improvement and repeatability. The CMMI levels are an excellent way to express how processes can exist in a number of states from ill-defined to one that uses quantitative information to make improvements. These extreme states are marked in Figure 7.2 with the O and the X points along the gradient depicting the capability and maturity levels.

As introduced in the CMMI sidebar, the levels are used to describe an evolutionary path of process improvement described as either a "capability level" for organizations utilizing continuous improvement or "maturity level" for those using a staged representation. Although it may be idyllic to have all level 5 processes in your business, it is unlikely, especially at a startup, that you will have enough resources to focus on establishing, managing, documenting, measuring, and improving processes to accomplish this. It is much more reasonable that you should periodically focus on

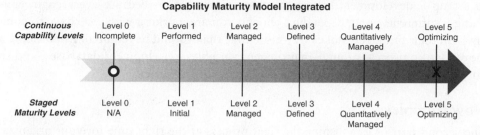

Figure 7.2 *Extremes of Possible Process Levels*

evaluating your process level of maturity and determine if this can and should be improved given your competing priorities.

To answer the question of where should you focus on process improvement, we could ask the employees or managers involved whether they need a more repeatable process, but it is often difficult to know without some yardstick against which to measure your current behavior or performance. We feel there are some warning signs or guidelines that you can use to help decide whether the existing capability or maturity level of process is working for your organization or if you should consider improving the process. These signs are derived from the three purposes of processes.

The first is if there is repetitive management of the same task. Recall that processes augment the management of our teams and employees; therefore, a sure sign that a process could be effective is if you or your managers are constantly managing people through certain tasks. Observe your managers to see if they are spending an inordinate amount of time assisting people in determining which source code repository branch to check their code into or what steps to take during and after an incident with the production environment. If they or you are spending time on these again and again, this is a good sign that you could use some amount of process.

Another sign of the impending need for process improvement is if every engineer seems to be doing the same task differently. For instance, if one engineer checks bug fixes into the main branch and another checks them into the maintenance branch and still others don't bother checking it in but build packages on their local machine, this is probably a great place for a process. If you need to standardize people's behaviors or actions, consider improving the process as a means to achieve this.

The third sign that you might need some process in your organization is if employees are being overly burdened by mundane stuff. These distractions take away from their time, energy, and creativity. Some ways that this might manifest itself would be first complaining from your teams. Engineers generally are not the type of person to keep quiet if they feel hindered from performing their jobs or if they feel they have a better idea of how to accomplish something. Another way this warning sign might appear would be rushed or poorer quality designs. Having to reinvent the proper way to set up a development environment for every sprint—because every engineer is doing it differently and, depending on who you are working with, you have to comply with their practices—takes way more time than should be required. Establishing a more mature process around environment variables, development databases, and so on would save a lot of engineering time and energy.

How Complex

The second part of establishing the right process at the right time for your organization is the level of complexity of the process. As we discussed previously, organizations are constantly changing, new employees are added, others leave, people mature, people learn lessons, and sometimes they forget lessons. Choosing the right level of process complexity is not a matter of determining it forever, but rather choosing the right level of complexity for today. Tomorrow, this might need to be reevaluated. To restate the problem statement, you need to determine the right amount of process complexity for your organization at this time.

We have two suggestions for ways to determine the right amount of process complexity. Before we explore these two methods, let's provide an example of the differences in complexity of processes. In Figure 7.3, we see another gradient, this time it is depicting complexity from simple to complex with two examples of a process for incident management. The first one on the left depicts the very simple three-step process that is most applicable for a small startup with just the couple of engineers. The process on the right is a much more complex process that is more applicable to a larger organization that has a staffed operations team. As depicted by the gradient, there can be a large variety of levels of complexity for a given process.

Now that we understand how there can be many different variations on the same process, we need to explore some methods of how to determine which of these multi-

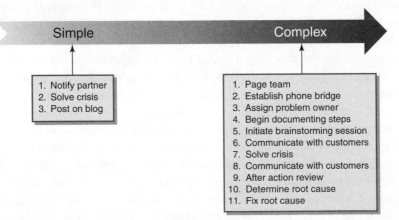

Figure 7.3 *Process Complexity*

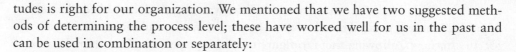

tudes is right for our organization. We mentioned that we have two suggested methods of determining the process level; these have worked well for us in the past and can be used in combination or separately:

- The first is to start with the smallest amount of process complexity and iteratively move to the more complex and sophisticated processes periodically. The advantage of this is that there is very little chance of overwhelming the team with the new process because it is likely to be much simpler than what is required or that they can tolerate (remember culture is a factor in how much process should exist on a team). The disadvantages of this approach are that it takes time to narrow in on the optimal amount of process, it requires that you remember to revisit the process periodically, and it requires you to change the process that people are used to on a frequent basis. If these disadvantages are too much, you may consider using our second method.

- The second method of narrowing in on the optimal process for your organization is to let the team decide for itself. This approach can either be democratic, where everyone gets a voice, or representative, where a chosen few speak for the group. Either way, this approach will get you closer to the optimal amount of process much quicker than the preceding small to large approach. It also has the advantage that it makes the team feel a sense of ownership making the adoption of the process much easier.

You can choose to implement one method or the other to find your optimal process, or you can mix them together. In a mixed method, you could have the team decide on the process and then step it down slightly in order to ensure the adoption is even quicker. If the team feels they need a very strict branching process, you could suggest that to start you would like them to ease up just slightly and allow for some flexibility on the naming convention and timing of pulling branches just until everyone is familiar with the process. After the process is fully established, after a release or two, modify the process and adopt the original suggestions for naming conventions and timing.

Johnny Fixer, the new CTO at AllScale, was facing a process problem with his operations staff headed up by the Director of Infrastructure and Operations, Tom Harde. Tom had been around since the early days of AllScale and had provisioned and racked many of the original servers himself. As Tom brought on board other systems administrators to help with the work load, he didn't revisit the provisioning process for getting servers ready to load the HRM software. Still today with four systems administrators, this work is done ad hoc with no defined tasks or established policies. This has caused numerous problems from missing deadlines for having hardware ready for deployment to bad configurations that took hours of engineering time to debug. Johnny asked Tom to fix this process and explained the two approaches that had worked best for him in the past, either start with the smallest process that meets the goals or let the team decide. Tom was skeptical but liked the second approach best and decided that he would gather the systems administrators in a room for an afternoon, allowing them to figure out the best process. Tom thought at least one of the systems administrators would derail the meeting with a rant about hating process. To his surprise, the senior systems administrator was completely on board and as soon as he threw his vote behind the establishment of a standard process, everyone else was eager to help. Within a few short hours, they had decided on a set of standard steps that they would all adhere to for provisioning equipment. Although the steps were well defined, they provided enough leeway to allow the administrators to continue using some of their favorite scripts as long as the goals were met.

When Good Processes Go Bad

Until this point, we have discussed all the noble attributes of processes and, as much as we would like to believe that there is no downside, the reality is that processes can cause issues themselves. Similar to how a poorly designed monitoring system can cause downtime on the production site due to load issues, processes can, when the complexity and level of rigor are not carefully considered, cause issues within the organization. These challenges are generally not the fault of the processes themselves, or even due to having a process; rather, they are due to the fit between the process and the team. You see this often with technology, designs, and architectures. There are almost no purely wrong technologies: flat network (sure, we can find a use for that), stateful apps (yes, even that can have a purpose), singletons (yes, they have a place in our world). But use these in the wrong place and you're sure to have problems.

One of the biggest problems with a bad fitted process is the culture clash. When a Wild West culture meets a very complex hundred-step process, sparks are sure to fly. The result is that the teams will either ignore the process, in which case it is actually causing more problems than it is helping, or they will spend a lot of time complaining about the process. Both of these results are probably worse than not having the process at all. If you witness this on your teams, you must act quickly—the process is not only hurting the team in the short term but it is likely causing even more of a buildup in the resistance to process or change, which will make implementing any process in the future more difficult.

Another of the big problems associated with poor fit between the organization and the process is the dreaded "b" word: bureaucracy. This term is defined by the Merriam-Webster Online Dictionary as "a system of administration marked by officialism, red tape, and proliferation." The last thing we want to do with process is create red tape or officialism. The result of bureaucracy as you might expect is lowered productivity and poorer morale. As we mentioned before, engineers love challenges and thrive on being asked to do difficult things. When they are so hindered as to be unable to succeed, it is easy for engineers to become demoralized. This is why engineers are typically so ready to speak out about things that hinder their ability to perform their jobs effectively. The challenge for you as a manager and leader is to decide when the complaining is just a matter of not liking change or an engineer being a curmudgeon instead of a real problem that needs to be addressed. The best way to tell the difference is to know the team and how it generally reacts.

To prevent the culture clash and bureaucracy, or in the event that you already have them, there are three key areas to focus on. The first is listening to your teams. When you have learned the nuances of each team member's personality, including those of your managers if you have a multilayered organization, you will be able to tell when something is really bothering them versus when something is just a mild disturbance.

The second is implementing the process using one of the two methods we described earlier. Either move small to large on the process continuum or let the team decide what the right amount of process is to establish. Either or both of these, if you elect to use them in conjunction with each other, should result in a good fit between the team and their processes.

The third area to focus on is performing periodic maintenance on your processes. As we have repeatedly stated, there is no right or wrong process, just right processes for the right organization at the right time. And, organizations change over time. This implies that as the organization changes, processes must be reevaluated to ensure they are still the optimal process. Performing periodic maintenance on the process is critical to ensure it does not turn into a culture clash or start to become bureaucratic.

Conclusion

We have covered quite a bit about processes in general in this chapter. We started by looking at the purpose of processes and determined that they serve three general purposes: they augment the management of our teams and employees, they standardize employee's actions while performing repetitive tasks, and they free employees up from daily mundane decisions to concentrate on grander, more creative ideas. Without processes such as crisis management or capacity planning and without them fitting our teams well in terms of complexity and repeatability, we cannot scale our systems effectively.

We then took a look at how there are many variations in terms of complexity and process maturity that exist. We also concluded that organizations are all different and they are even different from themselves over time because they change as people get hired or leave or mature or learn. The real challenge is fitting the right amount of the right process to the organization at the right time. We offered two suggestions on how to ensure you achieve this goal. The first idea was to start off with a very low amount of process and then slowly start increasing the granularity and stricter definitions around the process. This manner of wading into the process can be effective for easing one's way into the world of processes. The other manner is to let the team decide what the right process is for a given task. Assign either one person to figure this out or ask the entire team to sit in a room for a couple hours to make the decision.

We finished off the chapter by discussing the problems that can arise for ill-fitting processes. These include culture clashes and bureaucracy. We gave some warning signs to look for to identify these problems and some corrective actions to take to resolve them. We also provided some ideas on how to avoid these problems through periodic maintenance of your processes. Reviewing the fit for each process on an annual basis or as the organization undergoes a significant change such as a large amount of new hires will help ensure you have the right process for the organization at the right time.

The rest of Part II of this book is going to deal with the details of specific processes that we feel are very important for scalability. For each one of these, you should remember the lessons learned in this chapter and think about how this would affect the way to introduce and implement each process.

Key Points

- Processes, such as application design or problem resolution, are a critical part of scaling an application.

- Processes assist in management tasks and standardization, and free employees up to focus on more creative endeavors.

- There is a multitude of process variations that exist to choose from for almost any given process.

- Determining to implement any process at all is the first step. After that has been decided, next is deciding the optimal amount of process to implement.

- There are two suggested methods for determining the optimal amount of process: migrating from small to large through periodic changes or let the teams decide on the right amount.

- A bad fit between a process and an organization can result in culture clashes or bureaucracy.

- Avoid problems between processes and organizations by letting the team determine the right amount of process, or start slowly and ramp up over time.

- Maintenance of processes is also critical to ensure organizations do not outgrow processes.

Chapter 8

Managing Incidents and Problems

> Again, if the campaign is protracted, the resources of the State will not be equal to the strain.
>
> —Sun Tzu

The management of issues and problems is critical to creating a highly scalable platform or system. This chapter describes the bare minimum processes that all companies must have to help correctly resolve production incidents and minimize the rate at which they reoccur. Recurring incidents are the enemy of scalability. Each time we allow an incident with the same root cause to recur in our production environments, we steal time away from our teams that would be better used developing systems and features that maximize shareholder value. This theft of engineering time runs counter to our scalability goals as we are increasing the cost of producing our service or product when the goal of scalability is to produce more with less.

Our past performance is the best indicator we have of our future performance, and our past performance is best described by the incidents we've experienced and the underlying problems causing those incidents. To the extent that we currently have problems scaling our systems to meet end-user demand, or concerns about our ability to scale these systems in the future, our recent incidents and problems are very likely great indications of our current and future limitations. By defining appropriate processes to capture and resolve incidents and processes, we can significantly improve our ability to scale. Failing to recognize and resolve our past failures means a failure to learn from our past mistakes in architecture, engineering, and operations. Failing to recognize past mistakes and learn from them with the intent of ensuring that we do not repeat them is disastrous in any field or discipline. For that reason, we've dedicated a chapter to incident and problem management.

Throughout this chapter, we will rely upon the United Kingdom's Office of Government Commerce (OGC) Information Technology Infrastructure Library (ITIL) for definitions of certain words and processes. The ITIL and the Control Objectives for

Information and related Technology (COBIT) created by the Information Systems Audit and Control Association are the two most commonly used frameworks for developing and maturing processes related to managing the software, systems, and organizations within information technology. This chapter is not meant to be a comprehensive review or endorsement of either the ITIL or COBIT. Rather, we try to summarize some of the most important aspects of the parts of these systems as they relate to managing incidents and their associated problems and identify the portions that you absolutely must have regardless of the size or complexity of your organization or company.

Whether you are a large company expecting to complete a full implementation of either the ITIL or COBIT or a small company looking for a fast and lean process to help identify and eliminate recurring scalability related issues, the following are absolutely necessary:

- Recognize the difference between incidents and problems and track them accordingly.

- Follow an incident management life cycle (such as DRIER identified shortly) to properly catalog, close, report on, and track incidents.

- Develop a problem management tracking system and life cycle to ensure you are appropriately closing and reacting to scalability related problems.

- Implement a daily incident and problem review to support your incident and problem management processes.

- Implement a quarterly incident review to learn from past mistakes and help identify issues repeatedly impacting your ability to scale.

- Implement a robust postmortem process to get to the heart of all problems.

What Is an Incident?

The ITIL definition of an incident is "Any event which is not part of the standard operation of a service and which causes, or may cause, an interruption to, or a reduction in, the quality of that service." That definition has a bit of "government speak" in it. Let's give it a more easily understood meaning of "Any event that reduces the quality of our service."[1] An incident here then could be a downtime related event, an event that causes slowness in response time to end users, or an event that causes incorrect or unexpected results to be returned to end users.

Issue management, as defined by the ITIL, is "to restore normal operations as quickly as possible with the least possible impact on either the business or the user, at

---

1. ITIL Open Guide, Incident Management portion. http://www.itilibrary.org/index.php?page= incident_management.

a cost-effective price." Thus, management of an issue really becomes the management of the impact of the issue. We love this definition and love the approach as it separates cause from impact. We want to resolve an issue as quickly as possible, but that does not necessarily mean understanding its root cause. Therefore, rapidly resolving an incident is critical to the perception of scale, as once a scalability related incident occurs, it starts to cause the perception (and of course the reality) of a lack of scalability.

Now that we understand that an incident is an unwanted event in our system that impacts our availability or service levels and that incident management has to do with the timely and cost-effective resolution of incidents to force the system into perceived normal behavior, let's discuss problems and problem management.

What Is a Problem?

The ITIL defines a problem as "the unknown cause of one or more incidents, often identified as a result of multiple similar incidents." The ITIL further defines a "known error" as an identified root cause of a problem. Finally, "The objective of Problem Management is to minimize the impact of problems on the organization."[2]

Again, we can see the purposeful separation of events (incidents) and their causes (problems). This simple separation of definition in incident and problem helps us in our everyday lives by forcing us to think about their resolution differently. If for every incident we attempt to find root cause before restoring service, we will very likely have lower availability than if we separate the restoration of service from the identification of cause. Furthermore, the skills necessary to restore service and manage a system back to proper operation may very well be different from those necessary to identify root cause of any given incident. If that is the case, serializing the two processes not only wastes engineering time but further destroys shareholder value.

Take, for example, the case that a Web site makes use of a monolithic database structure and is unavailable in the event that the database fails. This Web site has a database failure where the database simply crashes and all processes running the database die and produce varying core files during its peak traffic period from 11 AM to 1 PM. One very conservative approach to this problem may be to say that you never restart your database until you know why it failed. This could take hours and maybe even days while you go through log and core files and bring in your database vendor to help you analyze everything. The intent is obvious—you don't want to cause any data corruption in restarting the database.

But most databases these days can recover from nearly any crash without significant data hazards. A quick examination could tell you that no processes are running, that you have several core and log files, and that a restart of the database may actually

---

2. ITIL OPEN Library. http://www.itilibrary.org/index.php?page=problem_management.

help you understand what type of problem you are experiencing. Maybe you start up the database and run a few quick "health checks" like the insertion and updating of some dummy data to verify that things are likely to work well, then put the database back into service. Obviously, this approach, assuming the database will restart, is likely to result in less downtime associated with scalability related events than serializing the management of the problem (identifying root cause) and the management of the incident (restoration of service).

We've just highlighted a very real conflict between these two processes that we'll address later in this chapter. Specifically, this problem is that incident management (the restoration of service) and problem management (the identification and resolution of root cause) are often in conflict with each other. The rapid restoration of service often conflicts with the forensic data gathering necessary for problem management. Maybe the restart of servers or services causes the destruction of critical data. We'll discuss how to handle this later. For now, recognize that there is a benefit in thinking about the differences in actions for the restoration of service and the resolution of problems.

The Components of Incident Management

The ITIL defines the activities essential to the incident management process as

- Incident detection and recording
- Classification and initial support
- Investigation and diagnosis
- Resolution and recovery
- Incident closure
- Incident ownership, monitoring, tracking, and communication

Implicit to this list is an ordering such that nothing can happen before incident detection, classification comes before investigation and diagnosis, resolution and recovery must happen only after initial investigation, and so on. We completely agree with this list of necessary actions, but if you are not an organization strictly governed by the OGC and you do not require any OGC related certification, there are some simple changes you can make to this order that will speed issue recovery. First, we wish to create our own simplified definitions of the preceding activities.

Incident detection and recording is the activity of identifying that there is an incident affecting users or the operation of the system and then recording it. Both of these are very important, and many companies have quite a bit they can do to make both actions better and faster. Incident detection is all about the monitoring of your systems. Do you have customer experience monitors in place to identify problems before the first customer complaint? Do they measure the same things customers do? It is very important in our experience to perform actual customer transactions within your system and measure them over time both for the expected results (are they returning the right data?) and for the expected response times (are they operating as quickly as you would expect?).

A Framework for Maturing Monitoring

Far too often, we see clients attempting to implement monitoring solutions intended to tell them the root cause of any potential problem they might be facing. This sounds great, but this monitoring panacea rarely works and the failures are largely attributed to two issues:

- The systems they are attempting to monitor aren't designed to be monitored.
- The company does not approach monitoring in a planned, methodical evolutionary (or iterative) fashion.

You should not expect a monitoring system (or incident identification system) to correctly identify the faults within your platform if you did not design your platform to be monitored. The best designed systems build the monitoring and notification of incidents into their code and systems. As an example, world class real-time monitoring solutions have the capability to log the times and errors for each internal call to a service. Here, the service may be a call to a data store or another Web service that exposes account information, and so on. The resulting times, rates, and types of errors might be plotted in real time in a statistical process control chart (SPC) with out-of-bound conditions highlighted as an alert on some sort of monitoring panel.

Designing a system to be monitored is necessary but not sufficient to identify and resolve incidents quickly. You also need a system that identifies issues from the perspective of your customer and helps to identify the underlying system causing that problem.

Far too many companies bypass the step of monitoring their systems from a customer perspective. Build or incorporate a real time system that interacts with your platform in the same fashion as your customers and performs the most critical transactions. Throw an alert when the system is outside of internally generated service levels for response time and availability.

Next, implement something to help identify which system is causing the incident. In the ideal world, you will have developed a fault isolative architecture to create *failure domains* that will isolate failures and help you determine where the fault is occurring (we discuss failure domains and fault isolative architectures in Chapter 21, Creating Fault Isolative Architectural Structures). Failing that, you need monitoring that can help indicate the rough areas of concern. These are typically aggregated system statistics such as load, CPU, or memory utilization.

Note that our first step here is not only issue identification but also the recording of the issues. Many companies that correctly identify issues don't immediately record them before taking other actions or don't have systems implemented that will record the problems. The best answer is to have an automated system that will immediately record the issue and its timestamp, leaving operators free to handle the rest of the process.

The ITIL identifies classification and initial support as the next step, but we believe that in many companies this can really just be the step of "getting the right people involved." Classification is an activity that can happen in hindsight in our estimation—after the issue is resolved.

Investigation and diagnosis is followed by resolution and recovery. Put simply, these are the steps of identifying what has failed and then taking the appropriate steps to put that service back into proper working order. As an example, they may be the steps that determine that application server 5 is not responding (investigation and diagnosis), at which point we immediately attempt a reboot (a resolution step) and the system recovers (recovery).

Incident closure is the logging of all information associated with the incident. The final steps include assigning an owner for follow-up, communication, tracking, and monitoring.

We often recommend an easily remembered acronym when implementing incident management (see Figure 8.1). Our acronym, although not supported by the ITIL, supports ITIL implementations and for smaller companies can be adopted with or without an ITIL implementation. The acronym is DRIER and it stands for

- Detect an incident through monitoring or customer contact
- Report the incident, or log it into the system responsible for tracking all incidents, failures, etc.
- Investigate the incident to determine what should be done

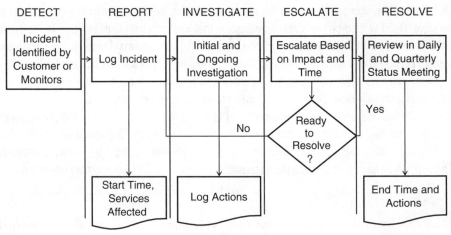

Figure 8.1 *DRIER Process*

- Escalate the incident if not solved in a timely fashion
- Resolve the incident by restoring end-user functionality and log all information for follow up

In developing DRIER, we've attempted to make it easier for our clients to understand how issue management can be effectively implemented. Note that although we've removed the classification of issues from our acronym, we still expect that these activities are being performed in order to develop data from the system and help inform other processes. We recommend that the classification of issues happens within the Daily Incident Management meeting identified later in this chapter.

The Components of Problem Management

The ITIL defined components of problem management are a little more difficult to navigate than those for incident management. The ITIL definitions define a number of processes that control other processes and in anything but a large organization this can be a bit cumbersome. We attempt to highlight steps that will help in the resolution of problems within this section without the deep treatment of all of the supporting processes. Remember that problems are the causes of incidents and as such, within the context of scalability, they are likely to be the reasons you are not scaling to meet end customer demand, are not scaling cost effectively, or will not scale easily in the future.

Problems in our model start concurrent with an issue and last until the root cause of an incident is identified. As such, most problems last longer than most incidents, though a problem can be the cause of many incidents.

Just as with incidents, we need a type of workflow that supports our problem resolutions. We need a system or place to keep all of the open problems and ensure that they can be associated with the incidents they cause. We also need to be able to track these problems to closure identified in the ideal world by the fix being applied to whatever system is experiencing the incident. Our reasoning for this definition of "closure" is that a problem exists until it no longer causes incidents. This meaning is the meaning holding the most value for our shareholders as they have a very high expectation of us and our teams in the maximization of their value.

In our mind, problems are either small enough to be handled by a single person or large enough that they require a team to resolve them. Both are similar in that the workflow and closure criteria remain the same, but they differ in the amount of involvement both from individual contributors and management. Small problems can be handed to a single person, and when ready for closure, they can go through whatever QA and testing criteria is appropriate and then validated as closed by the appropriate management or owner of the system experiencing the incidents and problems.

Larger problems are more complex and need specialized processes to help ensure rapid resolution. A large problem may be the subject of a postmortem (described later in this chapter), which in turn will drive another of investigative or resolution action items to individuals. The outcome of these action items should be reviewed on a periodic basis, either by a dedicated team of project managers responsible for problem resolution, by a manager with responsibility for tracking problem resolution, or within the confines of a meeting dedicated to handling incident tracking and problem resolution such as our recommended daily incident meeting.

Resolving Conflicts Between Incident and Problem Management

We previously mentioned an obvious and very real tension between incident management and problem management. Very often, it is the case that the actions necessary to restore a system to service will potentially destroy evidence necessary to determine root cause (problem resolution). Our experience is that incident resolution (the restoration of service) should always trump root cause identification unless an incident has a high frequency of recurrence without root cause and problem resolution.

That said, we also believe it is important to have thought your approach through before you are in the position of needing to make calls on when to restore service and when to continue root cause analysis. We have some suggestions:

- Determine what needs to be collected by the system before system restoration.
- Determine how long you are willing to collect diagnostic information before restoration.
- Determine how many times you will allow a system to fail before you require that root cause analysis is more important than system restoration.
- Determine who should make the decision as to when systems should be restored if there is a conflict (who is the R and who is the A).

If an incident occurs and you don't get a good root cause from it during the problem management process, it is wise to determine the preceding for that incident in addition to ensuring that you clearly identify all of the people who should be involved the next time the incident happens to get better diagnostics about the incident more quickly.

Incident and Problem Life Cycles

There is an implied life cycle and relationship between incidents and problems. An incident is open or ongoing until the system is restored. This restoration of the system may cause the incident to be closed in some life cycles, or it may move the incident to "resolved" in other life cycles. Problems are related to incidents and are likely opened at the time that an incident happens, potentially "resolved" after root cause is determined, and "closed" after the problem is corrected and verified within the production environment. Depending upon your approach, incidents might be closed after service is restored, or several incidents associated with a single problem might not be finally closed until their associated problems are fixed.

Regardless of what words you associate to the life cycles, we often recommend the following simple phases be tracked in order to collect good data about incidents, problems, and what they cost you in production:

Incident Life Cycle

Open   Upon an incident or when an event happens in production

Resolved   When service is restored

Closed   When the associated problems have been closed in production

Problem Life Cycle

Open   When associated to an incident

Identified When a root cause of the problem is known

Closed   When the problem has been "fixed" in production

Our approach here is to ensure that incidents remain open until the problems that cause them have root causes identified and fixed in the production environment. Note these life cycles don't address the other data we like to see associated with incidents and problems, such as the classifications we recommend adding in the Daily Incident Meeting that follows.

We recommend against reopening incidents as it makes it more difficult to query your incident tracking system to identify how often an incident reoccurs. That said, having a way to "reopen" a problem is useful as long as you can determine how often you reopen the problem. Having a problem reoccur after it was thought to be closed is an indication that you are not truly finding root cause and is an important data point to any organization. Consistent failure to correctly identify root cause results in continued incidents and is disastrous to your scalability initiatives as it steals time away from your organization, causes repeated failures for your customers and is dilutive to shareholder wealth and all other initiatives having to do with high availability and an appropriate quality of service for your end users.

Implementing the Daily Incident Meeting

We previously discussed the Daily Incident Meeting or Daily Incident Management Meeting. This is a meeting and process we encourage all of our clients to use and adopt as quickly as possible. This meeting occurs daily in most high transaction and rapid growth companies and serves to tie together the incident management process and the problem management process.

All incidents from the previous day are reviewed during this meeting to assign ownership of problem management to an individual, or if necessary a group. The frequency with which a problem occurs as well as its resulting impact serves to prioritize the problems to be root caused and fixed. We recommend that incidents be given classifications meaningful to the company within this meeting. Classifications may include severity, systems affected, customers affected, and so on. Ultimately, the classification system employed should be meaningful in future reviews of incidents to determine impact and areas of the system causing the company the greatest pain. This last point is especially important to identify scalability related issues throughout the system.

Additionally, the open problems are reviewed. Open problems are problems associated with incidents that may be in the open or identified state but not completely closed (problem not root caused and fixed in the production environment). The problems are reviewed to ensure that they are prioritized appropriately, that progress is being made in identifying their cause, and that no help is required of the owners assigned the problems. It may not be possible to review all problems in a single day; if that is the case, a rotating review of problems should start with the highest priority problems (those with the greatest impact) being reviewed most frequently. Problems should also be classified in this meeting in a manner consistent with business need and indicative of type of problem (e.g., internal versus vendor-related), subsystem (e.g., storage, server, database, login application, buying application, and so on) and type of impact (e.g., scalability, availability, response time, and so on). This last classification is especially important to be able to pull out meaningful data to help inform our scale efforts in processes and meanings described later in this portion of the book. Problems should inherit the impact determined by their incidents, including the aggregate downtime, response time issues, and so on.

Let's pause to review the amount of workflow we've discussed thus far in this section. We've identified the need to associate incidents with systems and other classifications, the need to associate problems with incidents and still more classifications, and the need to review data over time. Furthermore, owners need to be assigned at least to problems and potentially to incidents and status needs to be maintained for everything. Most readers have probably figured out that a system to aid in this collection of information would be really useful. Most open source and third-party "problem ticketing" solutions have a majority of this functionality enabled with some small configuration right out of the box. We don't think you should wait to implement an incident management process, a problem management process, and a daily meeting until you have a tracking system. However, it will certainly help if you work to put a tracking system in place shortly after the implementation of these processes.

Implementing the Quarterly Incident Review

No set of incident and problem management processes would be complete without a process of reviewing their effectiveness and ensuring that they are successful in eliminating recurring incidents and problems.

We mentioned earlier in "Incident and Problem Life Cycles" that you may find yourself incorrectly identifying root cause for some problems. This is almost guaranteed to happen to you at some point and you need to have a way for determining when it is happening. Is the same person incorrectly identifying root cause? This may require some coaching of the individual, a change in the person's responsibilities, or the removal of the person from the organization. Is the same subsystem consistently being misdiagnosed? If so, perhaps you have insufficient training or documentation on how the system really behaves. Are you consistently having problems with a single partner or vendor? If so, you may need to implement a vendor scorecard process or give the vendor other performance related feedback.

Additionally, to ensure that your scalability efforts are applied to the right systems, you need to review past system performance and evaluate the frequency and impact of past events on a per system or subsystem basis. This evaluation helps to inform the prioritization for future architectural work and becomes an input to processes such as the Headroom Process or 10x process that we describe in Chapter 11, Determining Headroom for Applications.

The output of the quarterly incident review also gives you the data that you need to define the business case for scalability investments in Chapter 6, Making the Business Case. Being able to show the business where you are going to put your effort and why, prioritized by impact, is a powerful way of securing the resources necessary to run your systems and maximize shareholder wealth. Furthermore, using that data to paint the story of how your efforts are resulting in fewer scalability associated outages and response time issues makes the case that past investments are paying dividends and helps give you the credibility you need to continue doing a good job.

The Postmortem Process

Earlier in this chapter, we identified that some large problems require a special approach to help resolve them. Most often, these large problems will require a cross-functional brainstorming meeting, often referred to as a *postmortem* or *after action review meeting*. Although the postmortem meeting is valuable in helping to identify root cause for a problem, if run properly, it can also help identify issues related to process and training. It should not be used as a forum for finger pointing.

The first step in developing a postmortem process is to determine for what size of an incident or group of incidents a postmortem should be required. Postmortems are very useful but costly events as you are taking several people away from their assigned tasks and putting them on the special duty of helping to determine what failed and what can work better within a system, process, or organization. When thinking back to our section on metrics and measurements within Chapter 5, Management 101, the use of people in a postmortem would reduce our engineering efficiency metric as they would be spending hours away from creating product and scaling systems. We want to use the postmortem on items that have hugely and negatively impacted us, but not on every single incident we face (unless those incidents are all large).

The input to the postmortem process is a timeline that includes data and time-stamps leading up to the end-user incident, the time of the actual customer incident, all times and actions taken during the incident, and everything that happened up until the time of the postmortem. Ideally, all actions and their associated timestamps have been logged in a system during the restoration of the service, and all other actions have been logged either in the same system or other places to cover what has been done to collect diagnostics and fix the root cause. Logs should be parsed to grab all meaningful data leading up to the incidents with timestamps associated to the collected data.

The attendees of the postmortem should consist of a cross-functional team from software engineering, systems administration, database administration, network engineering, operations, and all other technical organizations that could have valuable input like capacity planning. A manager trained in facilitating meetings and who also has some technical background should be assigned to run the meeting. Figure 8.2 introduces the process that the team should cover during the postmortem meeting.

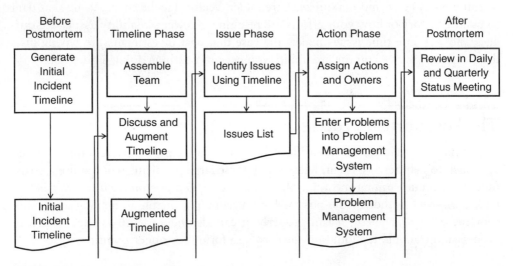

Figure 8.2 *Example Postmortem Process*

The first step in the postmortem process is to cover the initial timeline and ensure that it is complete. We call this the Timeline Phase of the postmortem. Attendees of the postmortem might identify that critical dates, times, and actions are missing. For instance, the team might identify that an alert from an application was thrown and not acted upon two hours before the first item identified in the initial incident time-line. Note that during this phase of the process only times, actions, and events should be recorded. No problems or issues should be identified or debated.

The next step in the postmortem meeting is to cover the timeline and identify issues, mistakes, problems, or areas where additional data would be useful. We call this phase the Issue Phase. Each of these areas is logged as an issue, but no discussion over what should happen to fix the issue happens until the entire timeline is discussed and all of the issues are identified. The facilitator of the meeting needs to ensure that she is creating an environment in which all ideas and concerns over what might be issues are encouraged without concern for retribution or retaliation. She should also ensure that no reference to ownership is made. For instance, it is inappropriate in a postmortem to say, "John ran the wrong command there." Instead, the reference should be "at 10:12 AM, command A was incorrectly issued." Ownership can be identified later by management if there is an issue with someone violating company policy, repeatedly making the same mistake, or simply needing some coaching. The postmortem is not meant to be a public flogging of an individual and if it is used as such a forum, the efficacy of the process will be destroyed.

After a first run through the timeline is made and an issues list generated, a second pass through the timeline should be made with an eye toward whether actions were taken in a timely manner. For instance, let's consider the case where a system starts to exhibit high CPU utilization at 10 AM and no action is taken. At noon, customers start to complain of slow response times. A second pass through the timeline might result in someone indicating that the early indication of CPU might be correlated with slow response times later and an issue generated indicating as such.

After a complete list of issues is generated from at least one and preferably two passes through the timeline, we are ready to begin the creation of the task list. This final phase is called the Action Phase of the postmortem. The task list is generated from the issues list with at least one task identified for each issue. Where a specific action to fix some issue can't be agreed upon by the team, an analysis task can be created to identify additional tasks to solve the issue.

After the task list is created, owners should be assigned for each task. Where necessary, use the RASCI methodology outlined earlier to clearly identify who is responsible for completing the task and who is the Approver of the task, and so on. Attempt to use the SMART criteria for the tasks, making them specific, measurable, aggressive/attainable, realistic, and timely. Though initially intended for goals, the SMART acronym can also help ensure that we are putting time limits on our tasks. Ideally, these items are logged into a problem management system or database for future follow-up.

Putting It All Together

Putting the components of issue management, process management, the daily incident management meeting, and the quarterly incident review together along with a well-defined postmortem process and a system to track and report on all systems and problems will give us a good foundation for identifying, reporting, prioritizing, and taking action against past scalability issues.

Any given incident will follow our DRIER process of detecting the issue, reporting upon the issue, investigating the issue, escalating the issue, and resolving the issue. The issue is immediately entered into a system we've developed to track incidents and problems. Investigation leads to a set of immediate actions and if help is needed, we escalate according to our escalation processes. Resolving the issue changes the issue status to "resolved" but does not close the incident until root cause is identified and fixed within our production environment.

The problem is assigned to an individual or organization during our daily status review unless it is of the size that it needs immediate assignment. During that daily review, we also review incidents and their status from the previous day and the high priority problems that remain open in the system. We also validate the closure of problems and assign categories for both incidents and problems in our daily meeting.

Problems, when assigned, get worked by the team or individual assigned to them in priority order. After root cause is determined, the problem moves to the "identified" status, and when fixed and validated in production, it moves to "closed." Large problems go through a well-defined postmortem process with the focus being the identification of all possible issues within the process and technology stacks. Problems are tracked within the same system and reviewed in our daily meeting.

Quarterly, we review incidents and problems to determine whether our processes are correctly closing problems and to determine the most common occurrences of incidents. This data is collected and used to prioritize architectural, organizational, and process changes to aid in our mission of increasing scalability. Additional data is collected to determine where we are doing well in reducing scale related problems and to help create the business case for scale initiatives.

Let's look at how Johnny and his team employ these processes by following an incident through its life cycle. Late one Tuesday evening, the network operations center is notified of an event by the customer support organization that is characterized by several customers complaining that they cannot get access to some professional training documents within the HRM product offering. The issue has now been detected within the DRIER process, so the operations team logs (or reports) it into the incident management system. The company uses an open source ticket system to track incidents through their life cycle. The network operations team can't immediately identify the root cause of the problem, even though they suspect a recent change, so pursuant to company policy for an incident of this size (medium) after

Investigating for 10 minutes, they escalate to the next level of support. The team logs all of their investigations and opens up a chat room for communication as well as a phone line/conference bridge for coordination.

Level two support, consisting of software engineers, systems administrators, and database administrators, work the problem for the next 20 minutes and identify that a network attached storage device containing the training documents identified by the complaining customers has had several training documents renamed. The team identifies the appropriate names for the documents and changes the names. Working with customer support, the team determines that the problem is resolved by renaming the documents. They close the incident knowing that the problem will remain open until after the morning incident review.

The next morning, during the daily incident review, as Johnny Fixer is reviewing the previous day's problems and all open issues with his team, he determines that the size of the previous night's document incident is large enough to demand a postmortem. Johnny requires postmortems for any incident impacting more than 10% of his customer base for 15 minutes or more. He assigns ownership for running the postmortem to his infrastructure and operations manager, Tom Harde.

Tom and his team generate an initial timeline for the postmortem from items in the incident management system that were logged by the operations team and the team attempting to resolve the problem. Additionally, they identify that there were application errors being thrown two hours prior to the first customer contact and that customer support did not contact the operations center for two hours after the first customer contact was received. Additionally, they find several changes logged against the network attached storage device in question. They schedule the postmortem with members of the level two support team, the teams logging the changes, and customer support representatives.

Stepping through the postmortem process, the team covers the timeline. Several members attempt to jump to adding issues but Tom focuses the team initially on completing the timeline. Several data points are added to the timeline before moving along to the next part of the postmortem. During the second phase of the postmortem, Tom and the team identify issues. Again, team members attempt to jump to actions but Tom focuses them on just identifying issues. The delays between the first alerts from the software and the first customer contact and the delay from first customer contact to first report are included in the issues. The team also identifies a process issue with one of the changes that caused the files to be improperly changed. In the next phase of the postmortem, they identify actions and owners.

One month later, during Johnny Fixer's quarterly incident review, Johnny notes with his team that the issues with files apparently missing on the network attached storage devices happen at least twice a quarter and sometimes even more than that. Although several root causes have been identified, the problem continues to happen. Johnny assigns Tom to look into the issue and starts to track it again in the morning incident reviews with the hope of finding the true root cause.

Conclusion

We have focused on one of the most important processes within any technology organization: the process of resolving, tracking, and reporting on incidents and problems. We learned that incident resolution and problem management should be thought of as two separate and sometimes competing processes. We also discussed the need for some sort of system to help us manage the relationships and the data associated with these processes.

We gave examples of how a few simple meetings can help meld the incident and problem management processes. The daily incident management meeting helps manage incident and problem resolution and status, whereas the quarterly incident review helps to create a continual process improvement cycle. Finally, we discussed supportive processes such as the postmortem process to help drive major problem resolution.

Key Points

- Incidents are issues in our production environment and incident management is the process focused on timely and cost-effective restoration of service in the production environment.

- Problems are the cause of incidents and problem management is the process focused on determining root cause of and correcting problems.

- Incidents can be managed using the acronym DRIER, standing for detect, report, investigate, escalate, and resolve.

- There is a natural tension between incident and problem management. Rapid restoration of service may cause some forensic information to be lost that would otherwise be useful in problem management. Thinking through how much time should be allowed to collect data and what data should be collected will help ease this tension for any given incident.

- Incidents and problems should have defined life cycles. An example is for an incident to be open, resolved, and closed, whereas a problem is open, identified, and closed.

- A daily incident meeting should be organized to review incidents and problem status, assign owners, and assign meaningful business categorizations.

- A quarterly incident review should look back at past incidents and problems in order to validate proper first-time closure of problems and thematically analyze both problems and incidents to help prioritize scalability related architecture, process, and organization work.

- The postmortem process is a brainstorming process used for large incidents and problems to help drive closure and identify supporting tasks.

Chapter 9

Managing Crisis and Escalations

A crisis is an incident on steroids. If not handled properly and if approached in the same fashion you would approach smaller incidents, a crisis will drive your customers away and tear your organization and company apart. Crisis situations, if handled properly, including ensuring that you learn from them and that they never happen again, can redefine a company and help set it on the right track. Assuming that the crisis was not a result of a gross lack of judgment and assuming that the company lives through it, it can serve to galvanize the company and become a source of strength. In this chapter, we discuss how to handle major crises and more specifically crises related to scalability. We will show you how to go up, over, around, or if necessary through the brick wall of scale.

What Is a Crisis?

We prefer the medical definitions of crisis from Merriam-Webster's dictionary: "the turning point for better or worse in an acute disease or fever" and "a paroxysmal attack of pain, distress or disordered function." Wow! In our experience, these two definitions define a crisis of scale better than any we know.

The first definition offered by Merriam-Webster is our favorite as it is so true of our personal experiences. A crisis can be both cathartic and galvanizing. It can be your Nietzsche event, allowing you to rise from the ashes like the mythical Phoenix. It can in one fell swoop fix many of the things we described in Chapter 6, Making the Business Case, and force the company to focus on scale. Ideally, you will have gotten the company interested in fixing the problems before the crisis occurs. More importantly, we hope you've led ethically and not landed at this crisis to prove a point to peers or management, as that would be the epitome of the wrong thing to do! But if you've arrived here and take the right actions, you can become significantly better.

The actual definition of a crisis that is relevant to your business is based on business impact and impact to the competitive landscape. It might be the case that a 30- to 60-minute failure between 1 AM and 1:30 AM is not really a crisis situation for your company, whereas a three-minute failure at noon is a major crisis. Your business may be such that you make 30% of your annual revenue during the three weeks surrounding Christmas. As such, downtime during this three-week period may be an order of magnitude more costly than downtime during the remainder of the year. In this case, a crisis situation for you may be any downtime between the first and third weeks of December, whereas at any other point during the year you are willing to tolerate 30-minute outages. Your business may rely upon a data warehouse supporting hundreds of analysts between the hours of 8 AM and 7 PM and with nearly no usage after 7 PM in the evening and during weekends. A crisis for you in this case may be any outage during working hours that would idle the expensive time of your analysts.

That's not to say that all crises are equal, and obviously not everything should be treated as a crisis. Certainly, a brownout of activity on your Web site for three minutes Monday through Friday during "prime time" (peak utilization) is more of a crisis than a single 30-minute event during relatively low user activity levels. Our point here is that after you determine what the *crisis threshold* is for your company, everything that exceeds that should be treated the same way. Losing a leg is absolutely worse than losing a finger, but both require immediate medical attention. The same is true with crises; after the predefined crisis threshold is passed, they should all be approached the same way.

You may recall from Chapter 8, Managing Incidents and Problems, that recurring problems (those problems that occur more than once) rob you of time and therefore destroy your ability to scale your services and scale your organization. Crises also ruin scale as they steal even more resources; and allowing the root cause of a crisis to surface more than once will not only steal vast resources and keep you from scaling your organization and services, it has the possibility of destroying your business.

Why Differentiate a Crisis from Any Other Incident?

You can't treat a crisis as any normal incident because it won't treat you the way an incident would treat you. This is the time to pull out all of the stops during *and* after the end of the crisis. This is the time to fix the problem faster than you've ever fixed a problem before, and then continue working the real root causes to remove every bit of cholesterol that has clogged your scalability arteries and caused this technology heart attack. When the operation is done, it's time to change your life—including the technical, process, and organizational equivalent of exercise, diet, and discipline to ensure that you never have a crisis again.

Although we are generally believers that there is a point at which adding resources to a project has diminishing returns, in a crisis, you are looking for the shortest possible time to resolution rather than the efficiency or return on those resources. While in a crisis, it is not the time to think about future product delivery as such thoughts and their resulting actions will only increase the duration of the crisis. As a matter of fact, you need to lead by example and be at the scene of the crisis for as long as it is humanly possible and eliminate all other distractions from your schedule. Every minute that the crisis continues is another minute that destroys shareholder value.

Your job is to stop the crisis from causing a negative trend within your business. If you can't fix it quickly by getting enough people on the problem to ensure that you have appropriate coverage, two things are going to happen. The first is that the crisis will perpetuate: Events will happen again and again and you will lose customers, revenue, and maybe your business. The second is that in allowing the crisis to continue to take precious time out of your organization over a prolonged period, you will eventually lose traction on other projects anyway. The very thing you were trying to avoid by not putting "all hands on deck" happens anyway *and* you allowed the problem to go on longer than necessary.

How Crises Can Change a Company

Perhaps you now agree that not all incidents are created equal and that some incidents actually have the possibility through duration or frequency to potentially kill a company. You may be wondering how any of that can be good. How is it possible that something that bad might actually turn out to benefit the company?

The answer is that it only benefits the company if the crisis, or series of crises, serves to change the direction, culture, organization, processes, and technology of the company. It's not like you are going to wake up three days after the crisis and everything will magically be better. As a matter of fact, the resolution of the crisis is going to pale in comparison to the blood, sweat, and tears you will shed trying to change everything. But the crisis or series of crises can serve as the catalyst for change. It will serve to focus shareholders, directors, executives, and managers on the horrors of failing to meet the scalability needs of the company.

Again, we can't urge you enough to manage and lead in such a way that such a crisis can be avoided. The pain of such an event is incredible and it can cost shareholders millions (or more) in market capitalization. Steering a company toward a crisis as a method of changing culture is like putting a gun to your head to solve a headache. It's just not the right thing to do.

The eBay Scalability Crisis

As proof that a crisis can change a company, consider eBay in 1999. In its early days, eBay was the darling of the Internet and up to the summer of 1999, few if any companies had experienced its exponential growth in users, revenue, and profits. Through the summer of 1999, eBay experienced many outages including a 20-plus hour outage in June of 1999. These outages were at least partially responsible for the reduction in stock price from a high in the mid $20s the week of April 26, 1999, to a low of $10.42 the week of August 2, 1999.

The cause of the outages isn't really as important as what happened within the company *after* the outages. Additional executives were brought in to ensure that the engineering organization, the engineering processes, and the technology they produced could scale to the demand placed on them by the eBay community. Initially, additional capital was deployed to purchase systems and equipment (though eBay was successful in actually lowering both its technology expense and capital on an absolute basis well into 2001). Processes were put in place to help the company design systems that were more scalable, and the engineering team was augmented with engineers experienced in high availability and scalable designs and architectures. Most importantly, the company created a culture of scalability. The lessons from the summer of pain are still discussed at eBay, and scalability has become part of eBay's DNA.

eBay continued to experience crises from time to time, but these crises were smaller in terms of their impact and shorter in terms of their duration as compared to the summer of 1999. The culture of scalability netted architectural changes, people changes, and process changes. One such change was eBay's focus on managing each and every crisis in the fashion described in this chapter.

Order Out of Chaos

Bringing in and managing several different organizations within a crisis situation is difficult at best. Most organizations have their own unique subculture and oftentimes, even within a technology organization, those subcultures don't even truly speak the same language. It is entirely possible that an application developer will use terms with which a systems engineer is not familiar, and vice versa.

Moreover, if not managed, the attendance of many people and multiple organizations within a crisis situation will create chaos. This chaos will feed on itself creating a vicious cycle that can actually prolong the crisis or worse yet aggravate the damage done in the crisis through someone taking an ill-advised action. Indeed, if you cannot effectively manage the force you throw at a crisis, you are better off using fewer people.

Your company may have a crisis management process that consists of both phone and chat (instant messaging or IRC) communications. If you listen on the phone or follow the chat session, you are very likely to see an unguided set of discussions and statements as different people and organizations go about troubleshooting or trying different activities in the hopes of finding something that will work. You may have questions asked that go unanswered or requests to try something that go without authorization. You might as well be witnessing a grade school recess, with different groups of children running around doing different things with absolutely no coordination of effort. But a crisis situation isn't a recess; it's a war, and in war such a lack of coordination results in an increase in the rate of friendly casualties through "friendly fire." In a technology crisis, these friendly casualties are manifested through prolonged outages, lost data, and increased customer impact.

What you really want to see in such a situation is some level of control applied to the chaos. Rather than a grade school recess, you hope to see a high school football game. Don't get us wrong, you aren't going to see an NFL style performance, but you do hope that you witness a group of professionals being led with confidence to identify a path to restoration and a path to identification of root cause.

Different groups should have specific objectives and guidelines unique to their expertise. There should be an expectation that they are reporting their progress clearly and succinctly in regular time intervals. Hypotheses should be generated, quickly debated, and either prioritized for analysis or eliminated as good initial candidates. These hypotheses should then be quickly restated as the tasks necessary to determine validity and handed out to the appropriate groups to work them with times for results clearly communicated.

Someone on the call or in the crisis resolution meeting should be in charge, and that someone should be able to paint an accurate picture of the impact, what has been tried, the best hypotheses being considered and the tasks associated with those hypotheses, and the timeline for completion of the current set of actions, as well as the development of the next set of actions. Other members should be managers of the technical teams assembled to help solve the crisis and one of the experienced (described in organizations as senior, principal, or lead) technical people from each manager's teams. We will now describe these roles and positions in greater detail. Other engineers should be gathered in organizational or cross-functional groups to deeply investigate domain areas or services within the platform undergoing a crisis.

The Role of the "Problem Manager"

The preceding paragraphs have been leading up to a position definition. We can think of lots of names for such a position: outage commander, problem manager, incident manager, crisis commando, crisis manager, issue manager, and from the military, battle captain. Whatever you call the person, you had better have someone capable of taking charge on the phone. Unfortunately, not everyone can fill this kind of a role. We aren't arguing that you need to hire someone just to manage your major production incidents to resolution, though if you have enough of them you might consider that; rather, ensure you have at least one person on your staff who has the skills to manage such a chaotic environment.

The characteristics of someone capable of successfully managing chaotic environments are rather unique. As with leadership, some people are born with them and some people nurture them over time. The person absolutely needs to be technically literate but not necessarily the most technical person in the room. He should be able to use his technical base to form questions and evaluate answers relevant to the crisis at hand. He does not need to be the chief problem solver, but he needs to effectively manage the process of the chief problem solvers gathered within the crisis. The person also needs to be incredibly calm "inside" but be persuasive "outside." This might mean that he has the type of presence to which people naturally are attracted or it may mean that he isn't afraid to yell to get people's attention within the room or on the conference call.

The crisis manager needs to be able to speak and think in business terms. She needs to be conversant enough with the business model to make decisions in the absence of higher guidance on when to force incident resolution over attempting to collect data that might be destroyed and would be useful in problem resolution (remember the differences in definitions from Chapter 8). The crisis manager also needs to be able to create succinct business relevant summaries from the technical chaos that is going on around her in order to keep the remainder of the business informed.

In the absence of administrative help to document everything said or done during the crisis, the crisis manager is responsible for ensuring that the actions and discussions are represented in a written state for future analysis. This means that the crisis manager will need to keep a history of the crisis as well as help ensure that others are keeping histories to be merged. A shared chat room with timestamps enabled is an excellent choice for this.

In terms of *Star Trek* characters and financial gurus, the person is 1/3 Scotty, 1/3 Captain Kirk, and 1/3 Warren Buffet. He is 1/3 engineer, 1/3 manager, and 1/3 business manager. He has a combat arms military background, an M.B.A., and a Ph.D. in some engineering discipline. Hopefully, by now, we've indicated how difficult it is to find someone with the experience, charisma, and business acumen to perform such a function. To make the task even harder, when you find the person, she probably isn't going to want the job as it is a bottomless pool of stress. You will either need to incent the person with the right merit based performance package or you will need to clearly articulate how it is that they have a future beyond managing crises in your organization. However you approach it, if you are lucky enough to be successful in finding such an individual, you should do everything possible to keep him or her for the "long term."

Although we flippantly suggested the M.B.A., Ph.D., and military combat arms background, we were only half kidding. Such people actually do exist! As we mentioned earlier, the military has a role that they put such people in to manage their battles or what most of us would view as crises. The military combat arms branches attract many leaders and managers who thrive on chaos and are trained and have the personalities to handle such environments. Although not all former military officers have the right personalities, the percentage within this class of individual who have the right personalities are significantly higher than the rest of the general population. Moreover, they have life experiences consistent with your needs and specialized training on how to handle such situations. Finally, as a group, they tend to be highly educated, with many of them having at least one and sometimes multiple graduate degrees. Ideally, you would want one who has been out of the military for awhile and running engineering teams to give him the proper experience.

The Role of Team Managers

Within a crisis situation, a team manager is responsible for passing along action items to her teams and reporting progress, ideas, hypotheses, and summaries back to the crisis manager. Depending upon the type of organization, the team manager may also be the "senior" or "lead" engineer on the call for her discipline or domain.

A team manager functioning solely in a management capacity is expected to manage his team through the crisis resolution process. A majority of his team is going to be somewhere other than the crisis resolution (or "war") room or on a call other than the crisis resolution call if a phone is being used. This means that the team manager must communicate and monitor the progress of his team as well as interacting with the crisis manager. Although this may sound odd, the hierarchical structure with multiple communication channels is exactly what gives this process so much scale. This structured hierarchy affects scale in the following way: If every manager can communicate and control 10 or more subordinate managers or individual contributors, the capability in terms of manpower grows by one or more orders of magnitude. The alternative is to have everyone communicating in a single room or in a single channel, which obviously doesn't scale well as communication becomes difficult and coordination of people becomes near impossible. People and teams would quickly drown each other out in their debates, discussions, and chatter. Very little would get done in such a crowded environment.

Furthermore, this approach to having managers listen and communicate on two channels has been very effective for many years in the military. Company commanders listen to and interact with their battalion commanders on one channel and issue orders and respond to multiple platoon leaders on another channel (the company commander is at the upper-left of Figure 9.1). The platoon leaders then do the same with their platoons; each platoon leader speaks to multiple squads on a frequency

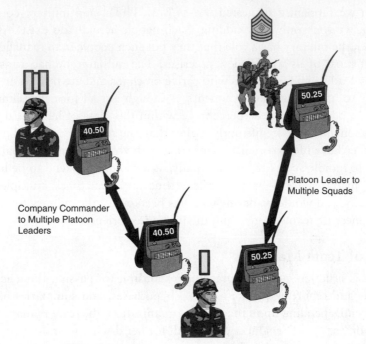

Figure 9.1 *Military Communication*

dedicated to the platoon in question (see the center of Figure 9.1 speaking to squads shown in upper-right). So although it may seem a bit awkward to have someone listening to two different calls or being in a room and while issuing directions over the phone or in a chat room, the concept has worked well in the military since the advent of the radio and we have employed it successfully in several companies. It is not uncommon for military pilots to listen to four different radios at one time while flying the aircraft: two tactical channels and two air traffic control channels.

The Role of Engineering Leads

The role of a senior engineering professional on the phone can be filled by a deeply technical manager. Each engineering discipline or engineering team necessary to resolve the crisis should have someone capable of both managing that team and answering technical questions within the higher level crisis management team. This person is the lead individual investigator for her domain experience on the crisis management call and is responsible for helping the higher-level team vet information, clear and prioritize hypotheses, and so on. This person can also be on both the calls of the organization she represents and the crisis management call or conference, but her primary responsibility is to interact with the other senior engineers and the crisis manager to help formulate appropriate actions to end the crisis.

The Role of Individual Contributors

Individual contributors within the teams assigned to the crisis management call or conference communicate on separate chat and phone conferences or reside in separate conference rooms. They are responsible for generating and running down leads within their teams and work with the lead or senior engineer and their manager on the crisis management team. Here, an individual contributor isn't just responsible for doing work assigned by the crisis management team. The individual contributor and his teams are additionally responsible for brainstorming potential problems causing the incident, communicating them, generating hypotheses, and quickly proving or disproving those hypotheses. The teams should be able to communicate with the other domains' teams either through the crisis management team or directly. All status, however, should be communicated to the team manager who is responsible for communicating it to the crisis management team.

Communications and Control

Shared communication channels are a must for effective and rapid crisis resolution. Ideally, the teams are moved to be located near each other at the beginning of a crisis. That means that the lead crisis management team is in the same room and that each of the individual teams supporting the crisis resolution effort are located with each other to facilitate rapid brainstorming, hypothesis resolution, distribution of work, and status reporting. Too often, however, crises happen when people are away from work; because of this, both synchronous voice communication conferences (such as conference bridges on a phone) and asynchronous chat rooms should be employed.

The voice channel should be used to issue commands, stop harmful activity, and gain the attention of the appropriate team. It is absolutely essential that someone from each of the teams be on the crisis resolution voice channel and be capable of controlling her team. In many cases, two representatives, the manager and the senior (or lead) engineer, should be present from each team on such a call. This is the command and control channel in the absence of everyone being in the same room. All shots are called from here, and it serves as the temporary change control authority and system for the company. The authority to do anything other than perform nondestructive "read" activities like investigating logs is first "OK'd" within this voice channel or conference room to ensure that two activities do not compete with each other and either cause system damage or result in an inability to determine what action "fixed" the system.

The chat or IRC channel is used to document all conversations and easily pass around commands to be executed so that time isn't wasted in communication. Commands that are passed around can be cut and pasted for accuracy. Additionally, the timestamps within the IRC or chat can be used in follow-up postmortems. The crisis manager is responsible for ensuring that he is not only putting his notes in the chat room and writing his decisions in the chat room for clarification, but for ensuring that status updates, summaries, hypotheses, and associated actions are put into the chat room.

It is absolutely essential in our minds that both the synchronous voice and asynchronous chat channels are open and available for any crisis. The asynchronous nature of chat allows activities to go on without interruption and allows individuals to monitor overall group activities between the tasks within their own assigned duties. Through this asynchronous method, scale is achieved while the voice allows for immediate command and control of different groups for immediate activities. Should everyone be in one room, there is no need for a phone call or conference call other than to facilitate experts who might not be on site and updates for the business managers. But even with everyone in one room, a chat room should be opened and shared by all parties. In the case where a command is misunderstood, it can be buddy checked by all other crisis participants and even "cut and pasted" into the shared chat room for validation. The chat room allows actual system or application results to be shared in real time with the remainder of the group and an immediate log with timestamps is generated when such results are cut and pasted into the chat.

The War Room

Phone conferences are a poor but sometimes necessary substitute for the "war room" or crisis conference room we had previously mentioned. So much more can be communicated when people are in a room together, as body language and facial expressions can actually be meaningful in a discussion. How many times have you heard someone say something, but when you read or look at the person's face you realize he is not convinced of the validity of his statement? That isn't to say that the person is lying, but rather that he is passing along something that he does not wholly believe. For instance, someone might say, "The team believes that the problem could be with the login code," but she has a scowl on her face that shows that something is wrong. A phone conversation would not pick that up, but you have the presence of mind in person to say, "What's wrong, Sue?" Sue might answer that she doesn't believe it's possible given that the login code hasn't changed in months, which may lower the priority for investigation. Sue might also respond by saying, "We just changed that damn thing yesterday," which would increase the prioritization for investigation.

In the ideal case, the war room is equipped with phones, a shared desk, terminals capable of accessing systems that might be involved in the crisis, plenty of work space, projectors capable of displaying key operating metrics or any person's terminal, and lots of whiteboard space. Although the inclusion of a white board might initially appear to be at odds with the need to log everything in a chat room, it actually supports chat activities by allowing graphics, symbols, and ideas best expressed in pictures to be drawn quickly and shared. Then, such things can be reduced to words and placed in chat, or a picture of the whiteboard can be taken and sent to the chat members. Many new whiteboards even have systems capable of reducing their contents to pictures immediately. Should you have an operations center, the war room should be close to that to allow easy access from one area to the next.

You may think that creating such a war room would be a very expensive proposition. "We can't possibly afford to dedicate space to a crisis," you might say. Our answer is that the war room need not be expensive or dedicated to crisis situations. It simply needs to be given a priority to any crisis and as such any conference room equipped with at least one and preferably two lines or more will do. Individual managers can use cell phones to communicate with their teams if need be, but in this case, you should consider the inclusion of low-cost cell phone chargers within the room. There are lots of low-cost whiteboard options available including special paint that "acts" like a whiteboard and is easily cleanable, and windows make a fine whiteboard in a pinch.

Moreover, the war room is useful for the "ride along" situation we described in Chapter 6. If you want to make a good case for why you should invest in creating a scalable organization, scalable processes, and a scalable technology platform, invite some business executives into a well-run war room to witness the work necessary to fix scale problems that result in a crisis. One word of caution here: If you can't run a crisis well and make order out of its chaos, do not invite people into the conference. Instead, focus your time on finding a leader and manager who can run such a crisis and then invite other executives into it.

Tips for a Successful War Room

A good war room has the following:

- Plenty of white board space
- Computers and monitors with access to the production systems and real-time data
- A projector for sharing information
- Phones for communication to teams outside the war room
- Access to IRC or chat
- Workspace for the number of people who will occupy the room

War rooms tend to get loud, and the crisis manager must maintain control within the room to ensure that communication is concise and effective. Brainstorming can and should be used, but limit communication during discussion to one individual at a time.

Escalations

Escalations during crisis events are critical for several reasons. The first and most obvious is that the company's job in maximizing shareholder value is to ensure that it isn't destroyed in these events. As such, the CTO, CEO, and other execs need to hear quickly of issues that are likely to take significant time or have significant negative customer impact. In a public company, it's all that much more important that the senior execs know what is going on as shareholders demand that they know about such things, and it is possible that public facing statements will need to be made. Moreover, executives have a better chance at helping to marshal *all* of the resources necessary to bring a crisis to resolution, including customer communications, vendor, and partner relationships, and so on.

The natural tendency for engineering teams is to feel that they can solve the problem without outside help or help from their management teams. That may be true, but solving the problem isn't enough—it needs to be resolved the quickest and most cost-effective way possible. Often, that will require more than the engineering team can muster on their own, especially if third-party providers are at all to blame for some of the incident. Moreover, communication throughout the company is important as your systems are either supporting critical portions of the company or in the case of Web companies they *are* the company. Someone needs to communicate to shareholders, partners, customers, and maybe even the press. That job is best handled by people who aren't involved in fighting the fire.

Think through your escalation policies and get buy-in from senior executives *before* you have a major crisis. It is the crisis manager's job to adhere to those escalation policies and get the right people involved at the time defined in the policies regardless of how quickly the problem is likely to be solved after the escalation.

Status Communications

Status communications should happen at predefined intervals throughout the crisis and should be posted or communicated in a somewhat secure fashion such that the organizations needing information on resolution time can get the information they need to take the appropriate actions. Status is different than escalation. Escalation is made to bring in additional help as time drags on during a crisis, and status communications are made to keep people informed. Using the RASCI framework, you escalate to Rs, As, Ss, and Cs, and you post status communication to Is.

A status should include start time, a general update of actions since the start time, and the expected resolution time if known. This resolution time is important for several reasons. Maybe you support a manufacturing center and the manufacturing

---

To: Crisis Manager Escalation List

Subject: September 22 Login Failures

Issue: 100% of internet logins from our customers started failing at 9:00 AM on Thursday, 22 September. Customers who were already logged in could continue to work unless they signed out or closed their browsers.

Cause: Unknown at this time, but likely related to the 8:59 AM code push.

Impact: User activity metrics are off by 20% as compared to last week, and 100% of all logins from 9 AM have failed.

Update: We have isolated potential causes to one of three candidates within the code and we expect to find the culprit within the next 30 minutes.

Time to Restoration: We expect to isolate root cause in the code, build the new code and roll out to the site within 60 minutes.

Fallback Plan: If we are not live with a fix within 90 minutes we will roll the code back to the previous version within 75 minutes.

Johnny Onthespot
Crisis Manager
AllScale Networks

Figure 9.2 *Status Communication*

manager needs to know if she should send home her hourly employees. Potentially, you provide sales or customer support software in a SaaS fashion, and those companies need to be able to figure out what to do with their sales and customer support staff.

Your crisis process should clearly define who is responsible for communicating to whom, but it is the crisis manager's job to ensure that the timeline for communications is followed and that the appropriate communicators are properly informed. A sample status email is shown in Figure 9.2.

Crises Postmortems

Just as a crisis is an incident on steroids, so is a crisis postmortem a juiced-up postmortem. Treat this postmortem with extra special care. Bring in people outside of technology because you never know where you are going to get advice critical to making the whole process better. Remember, the systems that you helped create and manage have just caused a *huge* problem for a lot of people. This isn't the time to get defensive; this is the time to be reborn. This is the meeting that will fulfill or destroy the process of turning around your team, setting up the right culture, and fixing your processes.

Absolutely everything should be evaluated. The very first crisis postmortem is referred to as the "master postmortem" and its primary task is to identify subordinate postmortems. It is not to resolve or identify all of the issues leading to the incident; it is meant to identify the areas for which subordinate postmortems should be responsible. You might have postmortems focused on technology, process, and organization failures. You might have several postmortems on technology covering different aspects—one on your communication process, one on your crisis management process, and one on why certain organizations didn't contribute appropriately early on in the postmortem.

Follow the same timeline process as the postmortem described in Chapter 8, but focus on creating other postmortems and tracking them to completion. The same timeline should be used, but rather than identifying tasks and owners, you should identify subordinate postmortems and leaders associated with them. You should still assign dates as you normally would, but rather than tracking these in the morning incident meeting, you should set up a weekly recurring meeting to track progress. It is critically important that executives lead from the front and be at these weekly meetings. Again, we need to change our culture or, should we have the right culture, ensure that it is properly supported through this process.

Crises Follow-up and Communication

Just as you had a communication plan during your crisis, so must you have a communication plan until all postmortems are complete and all problems identified and solved. Keep all members of the RASCI chart updated and allow them to update their organizations and constituents. This is a time to be completely transparent. Explain, in business terms, everything that went wrong and provide aggressive but achievable dates in your action plan to resolve all problems. Follow up with communication in your staff meeting, your boss' staff meeting, and/or the company board meeting. Communicate with everyone else via email or whatever communication channel is appropriate for your company. For very large events where morale might be impacted, consider using a company all hands meeting followed by weekly updates via email or on a blog.

A Note on Customer Apologies

When you communicate to your customers, buck the recent trend of apologizing without actually apologizing and try sincerity. Actually *mean* that you are sorry that you disrupted their businesses, their work, and their lives! Too many companies use the passive voice, point the fingers in other directions, or otherwise misdirect customers as to true root cause. If you find yourself writing something like "Can'tScale, Inc. experienced a brief 6-hour downtime last week and we apologize for any inconvenience that this may have caused you," stop right there and try again. Try the first person "I" instead of "we," drop the "may" and "brief," try acknowledging that you messed up what your customers were planning on doing with your application, and try getting this posted immediately not "last week."

It is very likely that you have significantly negatively impacted your customers. Moreover, this negative customer impact is not likely to have been the fault of the customer. Acknowledge your mistakes and be clear as to what you are going to do to ensure that it does not happen again. Your customers will appreciate it, and assuming that you can make good on your promises, you are more likely to have a happy and satisfied customer.

Conclusion

We've discussed how not every incident is created equally and how some incidents require significantly more time to truly identify and solve all of the underlying problems. We call these incidents crisis and you should have a plan to handle them from inception to end. We define the end of this crisis management process as the point at which all problems identified through postmortems have been resolved.

We discussed the roles of the technology team in responding to, resolving, and handling the problem management aspects of a crisis. These roles include the problem manager/crisis manager, engineering managers, senior engineers/lead engineers, and individual contributor engineers from each of the technology organizations.

We explained the four types of communication necessary in crisis resolution and closure, including internal communications, escalations, and status reports during and after the crisis. We also discussed some handy tools for crisis resolution such as conference bridges, chat rooms, and the war room concept.

Key Points

- Crises are incidents on steroids and can either make your company stronger or kill your business. Crisis, if not managed aggressively, will destroy your ability to scale your customers, your organization, and your technology platform and services.

- To resolve crises as quickly and cost effectively as possible, you must contain the chaos with some measure of order.

- The leaders most effective in crises are calm on the inside but are capable of forcing and maintaining order through those crises. They must have business acumen and technical experience and be calm leaders under pressure.

- The crisis resolution team consists of the crisis manager, engineering managers, and senior engineers. In addition, teams of engineers reporting to the engineering managers are employed.

- The role of the crisis manager is to maintain order and follow the crisis resolution, escalation, and communication processes.

- The role of the engineering manager is to manage her team and provide status to the crisis resolution team.

- The role of the senior engineer from each engineering team is to help the crisis resolution team create and vet hypotheses regarding cause and help determine rapid resolution approaches.

- The role of the individual contributor engineer is to participate in his team and identify rapid resolution approaches, create and evaluate hypotheses on cause, and provide status to his manager on the crisis resolution team.

- Communication between crisis resolution team members should happen face to face in a crisis resolution or war room; or when face-to-face communication isn't available, the team should use a conference bridge on a phone. A chat room should also be employed.

- War rooms, ideally adjacent to operations centers, should be developed to help resolve crisis situations.

- Escalations and status communications should be defined during a crisis. After a crisis, the crisis process should define status updates at periodic intervals until all root causes are identified and fixed.

- Crisis postmortems should be strict and employed to identify and manage a series of follow-ups on postmortems that thematically attack all issues identified in the master postmortem.

Chapter 10

Controlling Change in Production Environments

> If you know neither the enemy nor yourself, you will succumb in every battle.
>
> —Sun Tzu

In engineering and chemistry circles, the word *stability* is a resistance to deterioration or constancy in makeup and composition. Something is "highly instable" if its composition changes regardless of the actual rate of activity within the system, and it is "stable" if its composition remains constant and it does not disintegrate or deteriorate. In the hosted services world, and with enterprise systems, one way to create a stabile service is simply to not allow activity on it and to limit the number of changes made to the system. *Change*, in the previous sentence, is an indication of activities that an engineering team might take on a system, such as modifying configuration files or updating a revision of code on the system. Unfortunately for many of us, the elimination of changes within a system, while potentially accomplishing stability, will limit the ability of our business to grow. Therefore, we must allow and enable changes with the intent of limiting impact and managing risk, thereby creating a stabile platform or service.

If unmanaged, a high rate of change will cause you significant problems and will result in the more modern definition of instability within software: something that does not work or is not reliable consistently. The service will deteriorate or disintegrate (that is, become unavailable) with unmanaged and undocumented change. A high rate of change, if not managed, will cause the events of Chapters 8, Managing Incidents and Problems, and 9, Managing Crisis and Escalations, to happen as a result of your actions. And, as we discussed in Chapters 8 and 9, incidents and crises run counter to your scalability objectives. It follows that you must manage change to ensure that you have a scalable service and happy customers.

In our experience, one of the greatest consumers of scalability is change, especially when a change includes the implementation of new functionality. An implementation that supports two times the current user demand on Tuesday may be in the position of barely handling all the user requests after a release that includes a series of new features is made on Wednesday. Some of the impact may be a result of poorly tuned queries or bugs, and some may just be a result of unexpected user demand after the release of the new functionality. Whatever the reason, you've now put yourself in a very desperate situation for which there may be no easy and immediate solution.

Similarly, infrastructure changes can have significant and negative impact to your ability to handle user demand, and this presents yet another scalability concern. Perhaps you implement a new tier of firewalls and as a result all customer transactions take an additional 10 milliseconds to complete. Maybe that doesn't sound like a lot to you, but if your departure rate of the requests now taking an additional 10 milliseconds to complete is significantly less than the arrival rate of those requests, you are going to have an increasingly slow system that may eventually fail altogether. If the terms departure rate and arrival rate are confusing to you, think of departure rate as the rate (requests over time) that your system completes end-user requests and arrival rate is the rate (requests over time) at which new requests arrive. A reduction in departure rate resulting from an increase in processing time might then mean that you have fewer requests completing within a given timeframe than you have arriving. Such a situation will cause a backlog of requests and should such a backlog continue to grow over time, your systems might appear to end users to stop responding to new requests.

If your scalability goals include both increasing your availability and increasing the percentage of time that you adhere to internally or externally published service levels for critical functions, having processes that help you manage the effect of your changes are critical to your success. The absence of any process to help manage the risk associated with change is a surefire way to cause both you and your customers a great deal of heartache. Thinking back to our "shareholder" test, can you really see yourself walking up to one of your largest shareholders and saying, "We will never log our changes or attempt to manage them as it is a complete waste of time"? The chances are you would make such a statement and if you wouldn't make such a statement, then you agree that the need to monitor and manage change is important to your success.

What Is a Change?

Sometimes, we define a change as any action that has the possibility of breaking something. There are two problems with this definition in our experience. The first is that it is too "subjective" and allows too many actions to be excluded such as giving people the luxury of saying that "this action wouldn't possibly cause a problem."

The second issue is that it is sometimes too inclusive as it is pretty simple to make the case that all customer transactions could cause a problem if they encounter a bug. This latter choice is often cited as a reason not to log changes. The argument is that there are too many activities that induce "change" and therefore it simply isn't worth trying to capture them all.

We are going to assume that you understand that all businesses have some amount of risk. By virtue of being in business, you have already accepted that you are willing to take the risk of allowing customers to interact with your systems for the purpose of generating revenue. In the case of back office IT systems, we are going to assume that you are willing to take the risk of stakeholder interactions in order to reduce cost within your company or increase employee productivity.

Although you wish to manage the risk of customer or stakeholder interactions causing incidents, we assume that you manage that risk through appropriate testing, inspections, and audits. Further, we are going to assume that you want to manage the risk of interacting with your system, platform, or product in a fashion for which it is not designed. In our experience, such interactions are more likely to cause incidents than the "planned" interactions that your system is designed to handle. The intent of managing such interactions then is to reduce the number and duration of incidents associated with the interactions. We will call this last set of interactions "changes." A change then is any action you take to modify the system or data outside normal customer or stakeholder interactions provided by that system.

Changes include modifications in configuration, such as modifying values used during startup or run time of your operating systems, databases, proprietary applications, firewalls, network devices, and so on. Changes also include any modifications to code, additions of hardware, removal of hardware, connection of network cables to network devices, and powering on and off systems. As a general rule, any time any one of your employees needs to touch, twiddle, prod, or poke any piece of hardware, software, or firmware, it is a change.

What If I Have a Small Company?

Every company needs to have some level of process around managing and documenting change. Even a company of a single individual likely has a process of identifying what has changed, even if only as a result of that one individual having a great memory and being able to instinctively understand the relationship of the systems she has created in order to manage her risk of changes.

The real question here is how much process you need and how much needs to be documented. The answer to that is the same answer as with any process: You should implement exactly enough to maximize the benefit of the process. This in turn means that the process should return more to you in benefit than you spend in time to document and adhere to the process.

A small company with few employees and few services or systems interactions might get away with only change identification. A large company with a completely segmented services oriented architecture and moderate level of change might also only need change identification, or maybe it implements a very lightweight change management process. A large company with a complex system with several dependencies and interactions in a hosted SaaS environment likely needs complex change identification and change management.

Change Identification

The very first thing you should do to limit the impact of changes is to ensure that each and every change that goes into your production environment gets logged with

- Exact time and date of the change
- System undergoing change
- Actual change
- Expected results of the change
- Contact information of person making the change

An example of the minimum necessary information for a change log is included in Table 10.1.

To understand why you should include all of the information from these five bullets, let's examine an event at AllScale. The HRM system login functionality starts to fail and all attempted logins result in a "website not found" error. The AllScale definition of a crisis is that any rate of failure above a 10% failure rate for any critical component (login is considered to be critical) is a crisis. The crisis manager is paged, and she starts to assemble the crisis management team with the composition that we discussed in Chapter 9. When everyone is assembled in a room or on a telephonic

Table 10.1 *Example Excerpt from AllScale Change Log*

Date	Time	System	Change	Expected Results	Performed By
1/31/09	00:52	search02	Add watchdog.sh to init.d	Watchdog daemon starts on startup	mabbott
1/31/09	02:55	login01	Restart login01	Hung system restored to service	mfisher
1/31/09	12:10	db01	Add @autoextend to config.db	Tables automatically extend when out of space	tkeeven
1/31/09	14:20	lb02	Run syncmaster	Sync state from master load balancer	hbrooks

conference bridge, what do you think should be the first question out of the crisis manager's mouth?

We often get answers to this question ranging from "What is going on right now?" to "How many customers are impacted?" and "What are the customers experiencing?" All of these are good questions and absolutely should be asked, but they are not the question most likely to reduce the time and amount of impact of your current incident. The question you should ask first is "What most recently changed?" In our experience, more than any other reason, changes are the cause of most incidents in production environments. It is possible that you have an unusual environment where some piece of faulty equipment fails daily, but after that type of incident is fixed, you are most likely to experience that your interaction with your system causes more customer impact issues than any other situation.

Asking "What most recently changed?" gets people thinking about what they did that might have caused the problem at hand. It gets your team focused on attempting to quickly undo anything that is correlated in time to the beginning of the incident. In our experience, it is the best opening question for any discussion around any ongoing incident from a small customer impact to a crisis. It is a question focused on restoration or service rather than problem resolution.

One of the most humorous answers we encounter time and again after asking "What most recently changed?" goes like this: "We just changed the configuration of the (insert system or software name here) but *that can't possibly be the cause of this problem!*" Collectively, we've heard this phrase hundreds if not thousands of times in our career and we can almost guarantee you that if you ever hear that phrase you will know *exactly* what the problem is. Stop right there! Cease all work! Focus on the action identified in the (insert system or software name here) portion of the answer and "undo" the change! In our experience, the person might as well have said "I caused this—sorry!" We're not sure why there is such a high correlation between *"that can't possibly be the cause of this problem"* and the actual cause of the problem, but it probably has something to do with our subconscious knowing that it is the cause of the problem while our conscious mind hopes that it isn't the case. Okay, back to more serious matters.

It is not likely that when you ask "What most recently changed?" that you will have everyone who performed all changes on the phone or in the room with you unless you are a very small company. And even if you are a small company of say three engineers, it is entirely possible that you'd be asking the question of yourself in the middle of the night while your partners are sound asleep. As such, you really need a place to easily collect the information identified earlier. The system that stores this information does not need to be an expensive, third-party change management and logging tool. It can easily be a shared email folder, with all changes identified in the subject line and sent to the folder at the time of the actual change by the person making the change. Larger companies probably need more functionality including a way to query the system by the subsystem being affected, type of change, and so on. But *all* companies need a place to log changes in order to quickly recover from those that have an adverse customer or stakeholder impact.

Change Management

Change identification is a component of a much larger and more complex process called *change management*. The intent of change identification is to limit the impact of any change by being able to determine its correlation in time to the start of an event and thereby its probability of causing that event; this limitation of impact increases your ability to scale as less time is spent working on value destroying incidents. The intent of change management is to limit the probability of changes causing production incidents by controlling them through their release into the production environment and logging them as they are introduced to production. Great companies implement change management not to reduce the rate of change, but rather to allow the rate of change to increase while decreasing the number of change related incidents and their impact on shareholder wealth creation. Increasing the velocity and quantity of change while decreasing the impact and probability of change related incidents is how change management increases the scalability of your organization, service, or platform.

Change Management and Air Traffic Control

Sometimes, it is easiest to view change management as the same type of function as the Federal Aviation Administration (FAA) provides for aircraft at busy airports. Air Traffic Control (ATC) exists to reduce and ideally eliminate the frequency and impact of aircraft accidents during takeoff and landing at airports just as change management exists to reduce the frequency and impact of changes within your platform, product, or system.

ATC works to order aircraft landings and takeoffs based on the availability of the aircraft, its personal needs (does the aircraft have a declared emergency, is it low on fuel, and so on), and its order in the queue for takeoffs and landings. Queue order may be changed for a number of reasons including the aforementioned declaration of emergencies.

Just as ATC orders aircraft for safety, so does the change management process order changes for safety. Change management considers the expected delivery date of a change, its business benefit to help indicate ordering, the risk associated with the change, and its relationship with other changes to attempt to deliver the fewest accidents possible.

Change identification is a point-in-time action, where someone indicates a change has been made and moves on to other activities. Change management is a life cycle process whereby changes are

- Proposed
- Approved
- Scheduled
- Implemented and logged
- Validated as successful
- Reviewed and reported on over time

The change management process may start as early as when a project is going through its business validation (or return on investment analysis) or it may start as late as when a project is ready to be moved into the production environment. Change management also includes a process of continual process improvement whereby metrics regarding incidents and resulting impact are collected in order to improve the change management process.

Change Management and ITIL

The Information Technology Infrastructure Library (ITIL) defines the goal of change management as follows:

> The goal of the Change Management Process is to ensure that standardized methods and procedures are used for efficient and prompt handling of all changes, in order to minimize the impact of change-related incidents upon service quality, and consequently improve the day-to-day operations of the organization.

Change management is responsible for managing change process involving

- Hardware
- Communications equipment and software
- System software
- All documentation and procedures associated with the running, support, and maintenance of live systems

The ITIL is a great source of information should you decide to implement a robust change management process as defined by a recognized industry standard. For our purposes, we are going to describe a lightweight change management process that should be considered for any medium-sized enterprise.

Change Proposal

As described, the proposal of a change can occur anywhere in your cycle. The IT Service Management (ITSM) and ITIL frameworks hint at identification occurring as early in the cycle as the business analysis for a change. Within these frameworks, the change proposal is called a *request for change*. Opponents to ITSM actually cite the inclusion of business/benefit analysis within the change process as one of the reasons that the ITSM and ITIL are not good frameworks. These opponents state that the business benefit analysis and feature/product selection steps have nothing to do with managing change. Although we agree that these are two separate processes, we also believe that a business benefit analysis should be performed somewhere. If business benefit analysis isn't conducted as part of another process, including it within the change management process is a good first step. That said, this is a book on scalability and not product and feature selection, so we will leave it that a benefit analysis should occur.

The most important thing to remember regarding a change proposal is that it kicks off all other activities. Ideally, it will occur early enough to allow some evaluation as to the impact of the change and its relationship with other changes. For the change to actually be "managed," we need to know certain things about the proposed change:

- The system, subsystem, and component being changed
- Expected result of the change
- Some information regarding how the change is to be performed
- Known risks associated with the change
- Relationship of the change to other systems, recent or planned changes

You may decide to track significantly more information than this, but we consider this the minimum information necessary to properly plan change schedules.

The system undergoing change is important as we hope to limit the number of changes to a given system during a single time interval. Consider that a system is the equivalent of a runway at an airport. We don't want two changes colliding in time on the same system because if there is a problem during the change, we won't immediately know which change caused it. As such, we need to know the item being changed down to the granularity of what is actually being modified. For instance, if this is a software change and there is a single large executable or script that contains 100% of the code for that subsystem, we need only identify that we are changing out that executable or script. On the other hand, if we are modifying one of several hundred configuration files, we should identify which exact file is being modified. If we are changing a file, configuration, or software on an entire pool of servers with similar functionality, the pool is the most granular thing being changed and should be identified here; the steps of the change including rolling to each of the systems in the pool would be identified in information regarding how the change will be performed.

Architecture here plays a huge role in helping us increase change velocity. If we have a technology platform comprised of a number of noncommunicating services, we increase the number of airports or runways for which we are managing traffic; as a result, we can have many more "landings" or changes. If the services communicate asynchronously, we would have a few more concerns, but we are also likely more willing to take risks. On the other hand, if the services all communicate synchronously with each other, there isn't much more fault tolerance than with a monolithic system (see Chapter 21, Creating Fault Isolative Architectural Structures) and we are back to managing a single runway at a single airport.

The expected result of the change is important as we want to be able to verify later that the change was successful. For instance, if a change is being made to a Web server and that change is to allow more threads of execution in the Web server, we should state that as the expected result. If we are making a modification to our proprietary code to correct an error where the capital letter Q shows up as its hex value 51, we should indicate such.

Information regarding how the change is to be performed will vary with your organization and system. You may need to indicate precise steps if the change will take some time or requires a lot of work. For instance, if a server needs to be stopped and rebooted, that might impact what other changes can be going on at the same time. The larger and more complex the steps for the change in production, the more you should consider requiring those steps to be clearly outlined.

Identifying the known risks of the change is an often overlooked step. Very often, requesters of a change will quickly type in a commonly used risk to speed through the change request process. A little time spent in this area could pay huge dividends in avoiding a crisis. If there is the risk that should a certain database table not be "clean" or truncated prior to the change that data corruption may occur, that should be pointed out during the change. The more risks that are identified, the more likely it is that the change will receive the proper management oversight and risk mitigation and the higher the probability of success for the change. We will cover risk identification and management in a future chapter in much more detail.

Complacency often sets in quickly with these processes and teams are quick to feel that identifying risks is simply a "check the box" exercise. A great way to incent the appropriate behaviors and to get your team to analyze risks is to reward those that identify and avoid risks and to counsel those who have incidents occur outside of the risk identification. This isn't a new technique, but rather the application of tried and true management techniques. Reminding the team that a little time spent managing risks can save a lot of time in managing incidents and even showing the team data from your environment as to how that is true is a great tactic.

Finally, identifying the relationship to other systems and changes is a critical step. For instance, take the case that a requested change requires a modification to the login service of AllScale's site and that this change is dependent upon another change to the account services module in order for the login service to function properly. The requester of the change should identify this dependency in her request. Ideally, the requester will identify that if the account services module is not changed, the login service will not work or will corrupt data or whatever the case might be given the dependency.

Depending upon the process that you ultimately develop, you may or may not decide to include a required or suggested date for your change to take place. We highly recommend developing a process that allows individuals to suggest a date; however, the approving and scheduling authorities should be responsible for deciding on the final date based on all other changes, business priorities, and risks.

Change Approval

Change approval is a simple portion of the change management process. Your approval process may simply be a validation that all of the required information necessary to "request" the change is indeed present, that the change proposal has all required fields filled out appropriately. To the extent that you've implemented some form of the RASCI model, you may also decide to require that the appropriate A, or owner of the system in question, has signed off on the change and is aware of it. The primary reason for the inclusion of this step in the change control process is to validate that everything that should happen prior to the change occurring has in fact happened. This is also the place at which changes may be questioned with respect to their priority relative to other changes.

An approval here is not a validation that the change will have the expected results; it simply means that everything has been discussed and that the change has met with the appropriate approvals in all other processes prior to rolling out to your system, product, or platform. Bug fixes, for instance, may have an abbreviated approval process compared to a complete reimplementation of your entire product, platform, or system. The former is addressing a current issue and might not require the approval of any organization other than QA, whereas the latter might require the final sign-off of the CEO.

Change Scheduling

The process of scheduling changes is where most of the additional benefit of change management occurs over the benefit you get when you implement change identification. This is the point where the real work of the "air traffic controllers" comes in. Here, a group tasked with the responsibility of ensuring that changes do not collide or conflict applies a set of rules identified by its management team to maximize change benefit while minimizing change risk.

The business rules very likely will include limiting changes during peak utilization of your platform or system. If you have the heaviest utilization between 10 AM and 2 PM and 7 PM and 9 PM, it probably doesn't make sense to be making your largest and most disrupting changes during this timeframe. You might limit or eliminate altogether changes during this timeframe if your risk tolerance is low. The same might hold true for specific times of the year. Sometimes though, as in very high volume change environments, we simply don't have the luxury of disallowing changes during certain portions of the day and we need to find ways to manage our change risks elsewhere.

The Business Change Calendar

Many businesses, from large to small, put the next three to six months and maybe even the next year's worth of proposed changes into a shared calendar for internal viewing. This concept helps communicate changes to various organizations and often helps reduce the risks of changes as teams start requesting dates that are not full of changes already. Consider the Change Calendar concept as part of your change management system. In very small companies, a change calendar may be the only thing you need to implement (along with change identification).

This set of business rules might also include an analysis of risk of a type discussed in Chapter 16, Determining Risk. We are not arguing for an intensive analysis of risk or even indicating that your process absolutely needs to have risk analysis. Rather, we are stating that if you can develop a high level and easy risk analysis for the change, your change management process will be more robust and likely yield better results. Each change might include a risk profile of say high, medium, and low during the change proposal portion of the process. The company then may decide that it wants no more than three high risk changes happening in a week, six medium risk changes, and 20 low risk changes. Obviously, as the amount of change requests increase over time, the company's willingness to accept more risk on any given day within any given category will need to go up or changes will back up in the queue and the time to market to implement any change will increase. One way to help both limit risk associated with change and increase change velocity is to implement fault isolative architectures as we describe in Chapter 21.

Another consideration during the change scheduling portion of the process might be the beneficial business impact of the change. This analysis ideally is done in some other process, rather than being done first for the benefit of change. Someone, somewhere decided that the initiative requiring the change was of benefit to the company, and if you can represent that analysis in a lightweight way within the change process, you will likely benefit from it. If the risk analysis measures the product of the probability of failure multiplied by the effect of failure, benefit would then analyze the probability of success with the impact of success. The company would be incented to move as many high value activities to the front of the queue as possible while being wary not to starve lower value changes.

An even better process would be to implement both processes with each recognizing the other in the form of a cost-benefit analysis. Risk and reward might offset each other to create some value the company comes up with and with guidelines to implement changes in any given day with a risk-reward tradeoff between two values. We'll cover the concepts of risk and benefit analysis in Chapter 16.

Key Aspects of Change Scheduling

Change scheduling is intended to minimize conflicts and reduce change related incidents. Key aspects of most scheduling processes are

- Change blackout times/dates during peak utilization or revenue generation
- Analysis of risk versus reward to determine priority of changes
- Analysis of relationships of changes for dependencies and conflicts
- Determination and management of maximum risk per time period or number of changes per time period to minimize probability of incidents

Change scheduling need not be burdensome, it can be contained within another meeting and in small companies can be quick and easy to implement without additional headcount.

Change Implementation and Logging

Change implementation and logging is basically the function of implementing the change in a production environment in accordance with the steps identified within the change proposal and consistent with the limitations, restrictions, or requests identified within the change scheduling phase. This phase consists of two steps: starting and logging the start time of the change and completing and logging the completion time of the change. This is slightly more robust than the change identification process identified earlier in the chapter, but also will yield greater results in a high change environment. If the change proposal does not include the name of the individual performing the change, the change implementation and logging steps should name the individuals associated with the change.

Change Validation

No process should be complete without verification that you accomplished what you expected to accomplish. While this should seem intuitively obvious to the casual observer, how often have you asked yourself "Why the heck didn't Sue check that before she said she was done?" That question follows us outside of the technology world and into everything in our life: The electrical contractor completes the work on your new home, but you find several circuits that don't work; your significant other says that his portion of the grocery shopping is done but you find five items missing; the systems administrator claims that he is done with rebooting and repairing a faulty system but your application doesn't work.

Our point here is that you shouldn't perform a change unless you know what you expect to get from that change. And it stands to reason that should you not get that expected result, you should consider undoing the change and rolling back or at least pausing and discussing the alternatives. Maybe you made it halfway to where you want to be if it was a tuning change to help with scalability and that's good enough for now.

Validation becomes especially important in high scalability environments. If you are a hyper-growth company, we highly recommend adding a *scalability validation* to every significant change. Did you change the load, CPU utilization, or memory utilization for worse on any critical systems as a result or your change? If so, does that put you in a dangerous position during peak utilization/demand periods? The result of validation should either be an entry as to when validation was complete by the person making the change, a rollback to the change if it did not meet the validation criteria, or an escalation to resolve the question of whether to roll back the change.

Change Review

The change management process should include a periodic review of its effectiveness. Looking back and remembering Chapter 5, Management 101, you simply cannot improve that which you do not measure. Key metrics to analyze during the change review are

- Number of change proposals submitted
- Number of successful change proposals (without incidents)
- Number of failed change proposals (without incidents but change unsuccessful and didn't make it to validation phase)
- Number of incidents resulting from change proposals
- Number of aborted changes or changes rolled back due to failure to validate
- Average time to implement a proposal from submission

Obviously, we are looking for data indicating the effectiveness of our process. If we have a high rate of change but also a high percentage of failures and incidents, something is definitely wrong with our change management process and something is likely wrong with other processes, our organization, and maybe our architecture. Aborted changes on one hand should be a source of pride for the organization that the validation step is finding issues and keeping incidents from happening; on the other hand, it is a source for future corrections to process or architecture as the primary goal should be to have a successful change.

The Change Control Meeting

We've several times referred to a meeting wherein changes are approved and scheduled. The ITIL and ITSM refer to such meetings and gatherings of people as the Change Control Board or Change Approval Board. Whatever you decide to call it, we recommend a regularly scheduled meeting with a consistent set of people. It is absolutely okay for this to be an additional responsibility for several individual contributors and/or managers within your organization; oftentimes, having a diverse group of folks from each of your technical teams and even some of the business teams helps to make the most effective reviewing authority possible.

Depending upon your rate of change, you should consider a meeting once a day, once a week, or once a month. Attendees ideally will include representatives of each of your technical organizations and hopefully at least one team outside of technology that can represent the business or customer needs. Typically, we see the head of the infrastructure or operations teams "chairing" the meeting as he most often has the tools to be able to review change proposals and completed or failed changes.

The team should have access to the database wherein the change proposals and completed changes are stored. The team should also have a set of guidelines by which it analyzes changes and attempts to schedule them for production. Some of these guidelines were discussed previously in this chapter.

Part of the change control meetings, on a somewhat periodic basis, should include a review of the change control process using the metrics we've identified. It is absolutely acceptable to augment these metrics. Where necessary, postmortems should be scheduled to analyze failures of the change control process. These postmortems should be run consistently with the postmortem process we identified in Chapter 8. The output of the postmortems should be tasks to correct issues associated with the change control process, or feed into requests for architecture changes or changes to other processes.

Continuous Process Improvement

Besides the periodic internal review of the change control process identified within the preceding "Change Control Meeting" section, you should implement a quarterly or annual review of the change control process. Are changes taking too long to implement as a result of the process? Are change related incidents increasing or decreasing as a percentage of total incidents? Are risks being properly identified? Are validations consistently performed and consistently correct? As with any other process, the change control process should not be assumed to be correct. Although it might work well for a year or two given some rate of change within your environment, as you grow in complexity, rate of change, and rate of transactions, it very likely will need tweaking to continue to meet your needs. As we discussed in Chapter 7, Understanding Why Processes Are Critical to Scale, no process is right for every stage of your company.

Change Management Checklist

Your change management process has, at a minimum, the following phases:

- Change Proposal (the ITIL Request for Change or RFC)
- Change Approval
- Change Scheduling
- Change Implementation and Logging
- Change Validation
- Change Review

Your change management meeting should be comprised of representatives from all teams within technology and members of the business responsible for working with your customers or stakeholders.

Your change management process should have a continual process improvement loop that helps drive changes to the change management process as your company and needs mature and also drives changes to other processes, organizations, and architectures as they are identified with change metrics.

Conclusion

We've discussed two separate change processes for two very different companies. Change identification is a very lightweight process for very young and small companies. It is powerful in that it can help limit the customer impact of changes when they go badly. However, as companies grow and their rate of change grows, they often need a much more robust process that more closely approximates our air traffic control system.

Change management is a process whereby a company attempts to take control of its changes. Change management processes can vary from lightweight processes that simply attempt to schedule changes and avoid change related conflicts to very mature processes that attempt to manage the total risk and reward tradeoff on any given day or hour within a system. As your company grows and as your needs to manage change associated risks grows, you will likely move from a simple change identification process to a very mature change management process that takes into consideration risk, reward, timing, and system dependencies.

Key Points

- A change happens any time any one of your employees needs to touch, twiddle, prod or poke any piece of hardware, software, or firmware.

- Change identification is an easy process for young or small companies focused on being able to find recent changes and roll them back in the event of an incident.

- At a minimum, an effective change identification process should include the exact time and date of the change, the system undergoing change, the expected results of the change, and the contact information of the person making the change.

- The intent of change management is to limit the impact of changes by controlling them through their release into the production environment and logging them as they are introduced to production.

- Change management consists of the following phases or components: change proposal, change approval, change scheduling, change implementation and logging, change validation, and change efficacy review.

- The change proposal kicks off the process and should contain as a minimum the following information: system or subsystem being changed, expected result of the change, information on how the change is to be performed, known risks, known dependencies, and relationships to other changes or subsystems.

- The change proposal in more advanced processes may also contain information regarding risk, reward, and suggested or proposed dates for the change.

- The change approval step validates that all information is correct and that the person requesting the change has the authorization to make the change.

- The change scheduling step is the process of limiting risk by analyzing dependencies, rates of changes on subsystems and components, and attempting to minimize the risk of an incident. Mature processes will include an analysis of risk and reward.

- The change implementation step is similar to the change identification lightweight process, but it includes the logging of start and completion times within the changes database.

- The change validation step is responsible for ensuring that the change had the expected result. A failure here might trigger a rollback of the change, or an escalation if partial benefit is achieved.

- The change review step is the change management team's internal review of the change process and the results. It looks at data relating to rates of changes, failure rates, impact to time to market, and so on.

- The change control meeting is the meeting in which changes are approved, scheduled, and reviewed after implementation. It is typically chaired by the head of operations and/or infrastructure and has as its members participants from each engineering team and customer facing business teams.

- The change management process should be reviewed by teams outside the change management team to determine its efficacy. A quarterly or annual review is appropriate and should be performed by the CTO/CIO and members of the executive staff of the company.

Chapter 11

Determining Headroom for Applications

Knowing the place and the time of the coming battle, we may concentrate
from the greatest distances in order to fight.

—Sun Tzu

If you were blindfolded and dropped off in the middle of the woods with a map and compass, what is the first thing you would do? If you are an experienced outdoors person or even better an orienteering expert, you would probably try to determine your exact location. You might accomplish this by looking around you at the terrain such as mountains, streams, or roads and trying to match that to a position on the map that has similar terrain elements depicted. If there is a stream to your east and a mountain to your north, you look on the map for streams and find where a likely position is along that stream where you would have a mountain to the north. The reason you do this is that in order to have a better chance at navigating your way out of the woods, you need to know the point from which you are starting.

Scalability is like the preceding scenario. You need to know where you are starting from in order to move confidently to a better place. In scalability terms, this means understanding your application's headroom. We use the term *headroom* to mean the amount of free capacity that exists within your system before you start having problems such as a degradation of performance or an outage. Because your application is a system that involves many different components such as databases, firewalls, and application servers, in order to truly understand headroom, you need to first understand the headroom for each of these. There are many scenarios in which you will need to determine the headroom of an application. Your company might have acquired another company and now you have responsibility for an application that you know nothing about. Or, you are designing a brand-new system that you need to be able to scale because of an expected influx of traffic. Or, you have an existing application that is starting to have outages and you need to determine how to scale the application. Most commonly, you will make several changes to your existing application such that it no longer looks or behaves like the previous version for which you determined headroom. All of these and many more are scenarios that you may encounter that will require you to determine the headroom of an application in order for it to scale.

This chapter will walk you through the process of determining headroom for your application. We will start with a brief discussion of the purpose of headroom and where it is used. Then, we will talk about how to determine the headroom of some common components found in systems. Lastly, we will discuss the ideal conditions that you want to look for in your components in terms of loads or performance.

Purpose of the Process

The purpose of determining the headroom of your application, as we started to discuss, is to understand where your system stands in terms of its capability to continue to serve the needs of your customers as that customer base grows or the demands for the service grows. If you do not plot out where you are in terms of capacity usage and determine what your growth path looks like, you are likely to be blindsided by a surge in capacity from any number of sources. There are a number of different places within the product development life cycle where you will find a good use for your headroom calculations or projections.

One of the very earliest places that you will probably use your headroom projections is when planning an annual budget. If you are planning on capital investments or expense expenditures for increased capacity in the form of application servers, database servers, network gear, or network bandwidth, you need a good idea of your application's headroom in all those various areas. If you don't have a good handle on what amount of headroom you have, you are just guessing when it comes to a budget of how much you will need to spend next year. It is unfortunate if you approach budgeting this way, but you are not alone; and we will show you a better way. Many organizations do a rough, back-of-the-envelope calculation by saying, for example, they grew x% this year and spent $y, so therefore if they expect to grow x% again next year, they should spend $y again. Although this passes as a planned budget in many organizations, it is guaranteed to be wrong. Not taking into account different types of growth, existing headroom capacity, and optimizations, there is no way your projections could be accurate other than by pure luck.

Another area very early in the planning process where you will need headroom projections is when putting together a hiring plan. Determining how many engineers versus network engineers versus database administrators can either be left to the squeaky wheel method or actually planned out based on probable workloads. We prefer putting a little bit of science behind the plan. If you understand that you have plenty of headroom on your application servers and on your database but you are bumping up against the bandwidth capacity of your firewalls and load balancers, you may want to add another network engineer to the hiring plan instead of another systems administrator.

As you design and plan for new features during your product development life cycle, you should be considering very early what hardware implications the new features will cause. If you are building a brand-new service, you will likely want to run it on its own pool of servers. If this feature is an enhancement of another service, you should consider what ramifications it will have on the headroom of the current servers. Will the new feature require the use of more memory, larger log files, intensive CPU operations, the storage of external files, or more SQL calls? Any of these can impact the headroom projections for your entire application from network to database to application servers.

The last area that you can and should use your headroom projections for is prioritization of headroom or scalability projects. As you establish the processes outlined in this book, you will begin to amass a list of projects to improve and maintain your scalability. Without a way to prioritize this list, the projects that people like the most or that are someone's pet project are the ones that will get worked on. The proper way of selecting the project priority is to use a cost-and-benefits analysis. The cost is the estimated time in engineering and operations effort to complete the project. The benefit is the increase in headroom or scale that the projects will bring. After reading through the chapter on risk management, you may want to add a third comparison, and that is risk. How risky is the project in terms of impact to customers, completion within the timeline, or impact to future feature development?

Those are the four principle areas that you should consider using headroom projections when planning. Budgets, headcount, feature development, and scalability projects all can benefit from the introduction of headroom calculations. Using headroom data, you will start making much more data driven decisions and become much better at planning and predicting.

Structure of the Process

The process of determining your application's headroom is straightforward but not simple. It requires research, insight, and calculations. The more attention to detail that you pay during each step of the process the better and more accurate your headroom projections will be. There will be enough ambiguity in the numbers already, but if you cut corners when you should spend the time to find the right answer, you will ensure that the variability will be so large as to make the numbers worthless. You already have to account for unknown user behavior, undetermined future features, and many more variables that are not easy to pin down. Do not add more variation by not doing the homework or legwork in some cases.

The very first step in the headroom process is to identify the major components of the system. Typically, there are items such as application servers, database servers, network infrastructure that should be broken down even further if at all possible. If you have a Service Oriented Architecture and different services reside on different servers, treat each pool separately. A sample list might look like this:

- Account management service application servers
- Reports and configuration services application servers
- Firewalls
- Load balancers
- Bandwidth
- Oracle database cluster

After you have the major component list of your system, assign responsibility to the appropriate party to determine the actual usage over time, preferably the past year, and the maximum capacity in whatever is the appropriate measurement. For most of the components, there will be multiple measurements. The database, for example, would include the number of SQL transactions (based on the current query mix), the storage, and the server loads. These assignees should be the people responsible for the health and welfare of these components whenever possible. The database administrators are most likely the best candidates for the database analysis, the systems administrators for the application servers.

The next step can be done by a manager, CTO, product manager, project manager, or anyone with insight into the business plans for the next 12 or more months. This person should determine the growth rate of the business. This growth rate is made up of many parts. The first rate of growth is the natural or intrinsic growth. This is how much growth would occur if nothing else was done to the system or by the business (no deals, no marketing, no advertising, and so on) except basic maintenance. This would include the rate of walkup users that occur naturally and the increase or decrease usage by existing users. The second growth rate is the expected increase in growth caused by business activities such as developing new or better features, marketing, or signing deals that bring more customers or activities.

The natural growth rate can be determined by analyzing periods of growth without any business activity explanations. For instance, if in June the application has a 5% increase in traffic and there was no big signed deal in the prior month nor release of customer facing features to explain the increase, this could be taken as a natural monthly growth rate. Determining the business activity growth rate requires knowledge of the planned feature initiatives, business department growth goals, marketing campaigns, increases in advertising budgets, and any other similar metric or goal that may influence how quickly the application usage will grow. In most businesses, the business profit and loss (P&L), general manager, or business development team is assigned a goal to meet for the upcoming year in terms of customer acquisition, revenue, usage, or any combination. To meet these goals, they put together plans that include signing deals with customers for distribution, developing products to entice more users or increased usage, or marketing campaigns to get the word out about their fabulous products. These plans should have some correlation to their business goals and can be the background for determining how these will affect the application in terms of usage and growth.

After you have a very solid projection of natural and man-made growth projections, you can move on to understanding the seasonality effect. Some retailers see 75% of their revenue in the last 45 days of the year due to the holiday season. Some see the summer doldrums as people spend more time on vacations and less time browsing sites or purchasing books. Whatever is the case for your application, you should take this into account in order to understand what point of the seasonality curve you are on and how much you can expect this curve to raise or lower the demand. If you have at least one year's worth of data, you can begin projecting seasonal differences. The way to accomplish this is to strip out the average growth rate from the numbers and see how the traffic or usage changed from month to month. You are looking for a sine wave or something similar to Figure 11.1.

Now that you have seasonality data, growth data, and actual usage data, you need to determine how much headroom you are likely to retrieve through your scalability initiatives next year. Similar to the way we used the business growth rates for customer facing features, you need to determine an amount of headroom that you will gain by developing *infrastructure features*, or *scalability projects*, as these are sometimes called. These infrastructure features could be projects such as splitting a database or adding a caching layer. For this, you can use various approaches such as historic

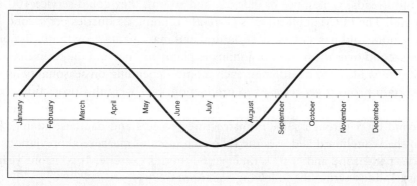

Figure 11.1 *Seasonality Trend*

gains from similar projects or multiple estimations by several architects as you would for an estimated effort for story points. When organized into a timeline, these projects will give you a projected increase in headroom throughout the year. Sometimes, projects have not been identified for the entire next 12 months; in that case, you would use an estimation process similar to what you would do for business driven growth. Use historic data to provide the most likely outcome of future projects weighted with an amount of expert insight from your architects or chief engineers who best understand the system.

The last step is to bring all the data together to calculate the headroom. The formula for doing this is shown in Figure 11.2.

$$\text{Headroom} = (\text{Ideal Usage Percentage} \times \text{Maximum Capacity}) - \text{Current Usage}$$
$$- \sum_{t=1}^{12} (\text{Growth}(t) - \text{Optimization Projects}(t))$$

Figure 11.2 *Headroom Equation*

This equation states that the headroom of a particular component of your system is equal to the ideal usage percentage of the maximum capacity minus the current usage minus the sum over a time period (here it is 12 months) of the growth rate minus the optimization. We will cover the ideal usage percentage in the next section of this chapter; for now, let's use 50% as the number.

If the headroom number is positive, you have enough headroom for the period of time used in the equation. If it is negative, you do not. Let's return to our team at AllScale and follow them through a headroom calculation to illustrate this and what it means. Tom Harde, the director of infrastructure and operations, had never performed a headroom analysis, so Johnny Fixer, the CTO, has offered to guide Tom and his team through the steps. The exercise was to calculate the headroom of the HRM database in terms of SQL queries. Tom's DBA stated that assuming a similar query mix (reads, writes, use of indexes, and so on), they could service 100 queries per second. The HRM application is currently running 25 queries per second on this database node and has a combined (natural and man-made) growth of 10 more queries per second over the next year. Johnny explains to Tom and the team that the real growth rate is likely to be different each month depending on seasonality as well as when certain projects get released to production, but using this projection is a good estimate. Continuing with the exercise, Tom expects that they can reduce the queries per second by 5 through some infrastructure projects and database tuning. Johnny goes to the whiteboard and uses the following units of measure abbreviations: "q/s" is queries per second and "t p" is time period (in this exercise, "t p" is one year or 12 months). Johnny writes the following equation:

$$\text{Headroom}_{q/s} = 0.5 \times 100_{q/s} - 25_{q/s} - (10 - 5)_{q/s/t\,p} \times 1_{t\,p}$$

And then Johnny begins solving the equation, resulting in the following:

$$\text{Headroom}_{q/s} = 50_{q/s} - 25_{q/s} - 5_{q/s} = 20_{q/s}$$

Johnny explains that because the number is positive, they have enough headroom to make it through the next 12 months; this was the time period that the growth, seasonality, and optimization covered.

Tom raised the question that was on most of his team members' minds: What does the headroom number $20_{q/s}$ mean? Johnny explained that strictly speaking this means that the HRM application has 20 queries per second of spare capacity. Additionally, this number when combined with the summation clause (growth, seasonality, and optimization over the time period) tells the team how much time it has before the application runs out of headroom. Johnny goes back to the whiteboard and writes the equation for this, as shown in Figure 11.3.

$$\text{Headroom Time} = \text{Headroom} / \sum_{t=1}^{12} (\text{Growth}(t) - \text{Optimization Projects})$$

Figure 11.3   *Headroom Time Equation*

Johnny continues with the exercise stating that they have Headroom Time = $20_{q/s}$ / $5_{q/s/t\,p}$ = $4.0_{t\,p}$. Because the time period is 12 months or one year, Johnny states that if their projected growth rates continue as predicted for the first 12 months, they have four years of headroom remaining on this database server. Tom and his team are pretty impressed with not only this answer but the entire process of calculating headroom and are excited to try it on their own for some other components in the HRM system. Johnny cautions them that although this is a great way to determine how much longer an application can grow on a particular set of hardware, it involves lots of estimates and those should be rechecked periodically.

Ideal Usage Percentage

If you recall, we used a variable in our headroom calculations that we called the ideal usage percentage. This is a pretty fancy name, but its definition is really simple. We are describing the amount of capacity for a particular component that should be planned for usage. Why not 100% of capacity, you ask? Well, there are several reasons for not wanting to plan on using every spare bit of capacity that you have in a component, whether that is a database server or load balancer. The first reason is that you might be wrong. I know it's hard to believe, but you and your fine team of engineers and database architects might be wrong about the actual maximum capacity because stress testing is not always equal to real-world testing. We'll cover the issues with stress testing in Chapter 17, Performance and Stress Testing. The other way you might be wrong is that your projections could be off. Either way, you should leave some amount of room in the plan for being off in your estimates.

The second reason that you do not want to use 100% of your capacity is that as you approach maximum usage, unpredictable things start happening, such as thrashing, which is the excessive swapping of data or program instructions in and out of memory. Unpredictability in our hardware and software, when discussed as a theoretical concept, is entertaining, but when it occurs in the real world, there is nothing entertaining about it. Sporadic behavior is a factor that makes a problem incredibly hard to diagnose.

Thrashing

As one example of unpredictable behavior, let's look at thrashing or excessive swapping. You are probably familiar with the concept, but as a quick review, almost all operating systems have the ability to swap programs or data in and out of memory if the program or data that is being run is larger than the allocated physical memory. Some operating systems divide memory into pages, and these pages are swapped out and written to disk. This capability to swap is very important for two reasons: the first being that some items used by a program during startup are used very infrequently and should be removed from active memory. Secondly, when the program or dataset is larger than the physical memory, swapping the needed parts into memory makes the execution much faster. This speed difference between disk and memory is actually what causes problems. Memory is accessed in nanoseconds, whereas disk access is typically in milliseconds. The difference is thousands of times slower.

Thrashing occurs when a page is swapped out to disk but is soon needed and must be swapped back in. After it is in memory, it gets swapped back out in order to let something else have the freed memory. The reading and writing of pages to disk is very slow compared to memory; therefore, the entire execution begins to slow down while processes wait for pages to land back in memory. There are lots of factors that influence thrashing, but closing in on the limits of capacity on a machine is a very likely cause.

What is the ideal percentage of capacity to use for a particular component? As with most things, the answer is that it depends. It depends on a number of variables, one of the most important being the type of component. Certain components, most notably networking gear, are notoriously predictable as demand ramps. Application servers are in general much less predictable, not because of the hardware being inferior, but because of their general use nature. They can and usually do run a wide variety of processes, even when dedicated to single services. Therefore, you may decide to use a higher percentage in the headroom equation for your load balancer than you do on your application server.

As a general rule of thumb, we like to start at 50% as the ideal usage percentage and work up from there as the arguments dictate. Your app servers are probably your most variable component so someone could make arguments that the servers dedicated to API traffic are less variable and therefore could run higher toward the true maximum usage, perhaps 60%. And then there is the networking gear that we discussed earlier that you may feel comfortable running as high as 75% of maximum. We're open to these changes, but as a guideline, we recommend starting at 50% and having your teams or yourself make the arguments why you should feel comfortable running at a higher percentage. We would not recommend going above 75% because you have to still account for error in your estimates of growth.

Another way that you can arrive at the usage percentage or how close you can run to the maximum capacity of a component is by using statistics. The concept is to figure out how much variability resides in your services running on the particular component and then use that as a guide to buffer away from the maximum capacity. If you are planning on using this method, you should consider revisiting these numbers often, especially after releases with major features because the performance of services can change dramatically based on user behavior or new code. For this method, we look at weeks' or months' worth of performance data such as load on a server and then calculate the standard deviation of that data. We then subtract 3 × the standard deviation from the maximum capacity and use that in the headroom equation as the substitute for the Ideal Usage Percentage × Maximum Capacity.

In Table 11.1, Load Averages, we have three weeks worth of maximum load values on our application servers. The standard deviation for this sample data set is 1.49. If we take 3× that amount, 4.48, and subtract the maximum load capacity that we have established for this server class, we then have the amount of load capacity that we can plan to use up to but not exceed. In this case, our systems administrators believe that 15 is the maximum, therefore 15 − 4.48 = 10.5 is the maximum amount we can plan for. This is the number that we would use in the headroom equation to replace the Ideal Usage Percentage × Maximum Capacity.

Table 11.1 *Load Averages*

Mon	Tue	Wed	Thu	Fri	Sat	Sun
5.64	8.58	9.48	5.22	8.28	9.36	4.92
8.1	9.24	6.18	5.64	6.12	7.08	8.76
7.62	8.58	5.6	9.02	8.89	7.74	6.61

Headroom Calculation Checklist

These are the major steps that should be followed when completing a headroom calculation:

1. Identify major components.

2. Assign responsibility for determining actual usage and maximum capacity.

3. Determine intrinsic or natural growth rate.

4. Determine business activity based growth rates.

5. Determine peak seasonality affects.

6. Estimate headroom or capacity reclaimed by infrastructure projects.

7. Make headroom calculation:

- If positive, you have capacity for the timeframe analyzed.

- If negative, you do *not* have capacity over the specified timeframe.

8. Divide headroom by the (growth rate + seasonality – optimizations) to get the amount of time remaining to use up the capacity.

Conclusion

In this chapter, we started our discussion by investigating the purpose of the headroom process. We decided that there are four principle areas where you should consider using headroom projections when planning: budgets, headcount, feature development, and scalability projects.

We then covered the basic structure of the headroom process. This process consists of many steps, which are detail oriented, but overall the process is very straightforward. The steps include identifying major components, assigning responsible parties for determining actual usage and maximum capacity for those components, determining the intrinsic growth rate as well as the growth rate caused by business activities, accounting for seasonality, making estimates for improvement in usage based on infrastructure projects, and then performing the calculations.

The last topic we covered in this chapter was the ideal usage percentage for components. We stipulated that in general we prefer to use a simple 50% as the amount of maximum capacity that should be planned on using. The reason is that this accounts for variability or mistakes in determining the maximum capacity as well as errors in the growth projects. We capitulated that we could be convinced to increase this percentage if the administrators or engineers could make sound and reasonable

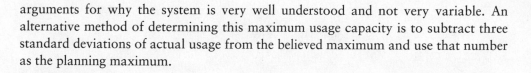

arguments for why the system is very well understood and not very variable. An alternative method of determining this maximum usage capacity is to subtract three standard deviations of actual usage from the believed maximum and use that number as the planning maximum.

Key Points

- The reason that you should want to know your headroom for various components is that you need this information for budgets, hiring plans, release planning, and scalability project prioritization.

- Headroom should be calculated for each major component within the system such as each pool of application servers, networking gear, bandwidth usage, and database servers.

- Without a sound and factually based argument for deviating, we recommend not planning on using more than 50% of the maximum capacity on any one component.

Chapter 12

Exploring Architectural Principles

He wins his battles by making no mistakes. Making no mistakes is what establishes the certainty of victory, for it means conquering an enemy that is already defeated.

—Sun Tzu

If your company has been around for awhile, there is a good chance that you have signs posted about the company and Web pages devoted to things like "core values" or "beliefs." These are intended to remind people of the desired culture and oftentimes when they resonate with the employees you will see them printed off from the corporate intranet site and pinned up in cubicles or framed in offices. Sometimes, they are even printed on the back of employee badges as reminders of how the company hopes to operate or as an embodiment of what the corporation holds dear. We can't attest to the effectiveness of such materials, but it certainly "feels" like one of those things that you should do and that can only help create and support the culture the company desires.

In this chapter, we present an analog to these corporate values or beliefs; one that is inherently more testable and not only can be embodied within framed materials and Web pages but that can actually help drive and be the heart of your scalability initiatives. We call this analog *architectural principles*, and they are to your scalability initiatives what core beliefs are to a company's culture. The primary difference is that they are also a critical portion of several processes we will discuss later in Chapter 13, Joint Architecture Design, and Chapter 14, Architecture Review Board. Moreover, if implemented properly, they truly become part of your everyday engineering life and over the long term can support the culture of scale necessary to be successful in any hyper-growth company.

Principles and Goals

Let's review the high-level goal tree we defined in Chapter 5, Management 101, presented in Figure 12.1.

You might recall that the tree indicates two general themes: the creation of more monetization opportunities and greater revenue at a reduced cost base. These general themes were further broken out into thematic leafs such as quality, availability, cost, time to market, and efficiency. Johnny Fixer, the CTO of AllScale, wants to develop a set of principles by which his team will design and implement systems to support these overall themes. Recognizing the goals might change, he wants to take his time and develop principles that will be supportive of increasingly aggressive and potentially ever broadening goals and initiatives.

In so doing, Johnny decides that he will group the principles thematically to support the goals identified in his goal tree. Further, given the current issues facing AllScale, although he has goals surrounding both time to market and efficiency, he really wants his teams focusing their architectural efforts on reducing cost, increasing availability, and increasing scalability. Johnny believes that many of those efforts are likely to decrease time to market as well, but he believes that the time to market issue is a project management and management issue more than it is an architectural issue.

Having developed themes for our architectural principles, Johnny schedules a two-day offsite with his architects, senior engineers, and managers from each of the engineering teams. On day one of the offsite, they begin to brainstorm the set of princi-

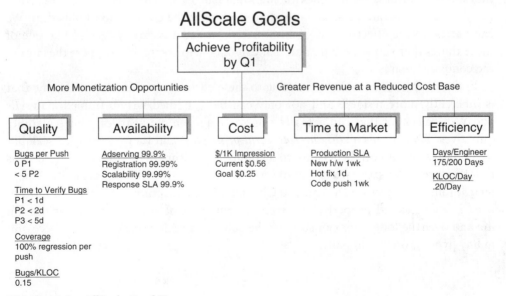

Figure 12.1 *AllScale Goal Tree*

ples that will best enable their teams' future efforts from a scalability, availability, and cost perspective. As a framework, Johnny starts with the goal tree and explains his reasoning for selecting cost, scalability, and availability as the goals. Johnny tells the team that because he believes some of the principles are likely to affect two or more of the themes (e.g., cost and scalability or availability and scalability), he decided to represent the principles in a Venn diagram as depicted in Figure 12.2.

Johnny places large depictions of the Venn diagram around the room and breaks the assembled group of people into teams of three or four individuals. Each team has representation from software engineering, quality assurance, and at least one of the infrastructure disciplines. Architects are spread among the teams, but some teams do not have architects. Johnny gives each team several sticky notes on which they are to write the team's choices for architectural principles to guide future development. The teams are then to affix the sticky notes on their own copy of the Venn diagrams placed around the room. At the end of several hours, each of the teams presents their Venn diagram for several minutes, each including the reasons for choosing each of the principles and for choosing what "theme" they support within the Venn diagram.

Because Johnny wants the resulting architectural principles to be easily remembered for the maximum opportunity to truly guide behavior, he decides that each team can choose no more than twelve principles. Johnny also doesn't want to spend time discussing reasons why other themes should be present so he asks that any other comments be written in a "parking lot," or whiteboard outside of the team's areas. Johnny tells the teams that the entire group can discuss other themes for principles at the end of the meeting and that he is open to adding themes but that he is also absolutely certain that scalability, cost, and availability are the most important themes to discuss today.

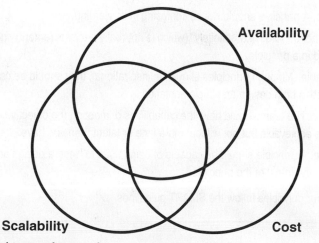

Figure 12.2 *Architectural Principles Venn Diagram*

Finally, Johnny reminds the teams that he wants the principles to embody as many of the SMART characteristics discussed in Chapter 4, Leadership 101, as possible. Although he realizes a principle can't really be "time bounded" or timely, you do believe that principles can be specific, measurable, attainable, and realistic. Most importantly, Johnny really wants them to be "testable" and usable in discussions around future and current implementations. Johnny does not wish to have any principles that are so lofty and nebulous that you cannot test a design against the principle.

As an example, Johnny tells the team that he doesn't want a principle that says something to the effect of "infinitely scalable." Infinitely scalable is a goal of a group of principles but on its own isn't truly measurable, isn't specific, and can't be used to test any given design effectively. The principles should be meaningful and easily applied in everyday use both to test whether something meets the intended criteria and to help guide decision making. Instead, Johnny tells them that he hopes for the goals to be similar to "scale out not up." In this case, Johnny explains, the principle is easy to test. Something is either designed to run and work on multiple systems at once or it requires larger and faster hardware as demands grow on the system. Johnny's team spends the better part of the day broken into smaller teams and then joins together at the end of the day for the team presentations.

Good Principles Are . . .

Principles should help influence the behavior and the culture of the team. They should help guide designs and be capable of being used to determine if designs meet the goals and needs of the company. Ideally, principles are tightly aligned with goals, vision, and mission to be effective. A good principle is

- Specific. A principle should not be confusing in its wording.
- Measurable. Words like "infinitely" (which is not really a measurement) should not be included in a principle.
- Achievable. Although principles should be inspirational, they should be capable of being achieved in both design and implementation.
- Realistic. The team should have the capabilities of meeting the objective. Some principles are achievable but not without more time or talent than you have.
- Testable. A principle should be capable of being used to "test" a design and validate that it meets the intent of the principle.

Make sure your principles follow the SMART guidelines.

Principle Selection

On day two of Johnny's team offsite, Johnny gives each team an opportunity to refine its principles. Each team then does a short presentation summarizing yesterday's principles presentation and any changes that were made during the morning session. Amazingly, many of the principles start to converge and many of the team's Venn diagrams start to look alike.

In the afternoon session, Johnny mediates a session that starts with identifying and ranking the principles based on the number of times they occur in each of the team's presentations. After the morning session, there are now six common principles that are present in each of the team's presentations, and everyone agrees that these should be adopted outright. There are approximately twenty other principles represented among all of the teams and at least eight of these are present in more than one team's presentations.

Johnny writes each of the remaining twenty principles on the whiteboard and asks everyone to come up and vote for exactly six principles, giving the team a total of twelve. After the votes, Johnny ranks the principles and draws a line after the sixth principle on the list. Of the twenty remaining principles, six did not get votes, leaving fourteen with one or more votes. Now Johnny decides to allow debates between the top ten principles receiving votes and asks representatives for each of the eight principles receiving votes below the six receiving the most votes to come and explain why one of those should displace the top six. After a few hours of debate, the team votes to accept twelve principles consisting of the six identified within each of the original presentations and then another six developed through voting, ranking debating, and a final ranking. Amazingly, the twelve principles look much like the twelve principles we most often recommend to our clients that we will share with you next.

Engendering Ownership of Principles

You want the team to "own" the architectural principles that guide your scalability initiatives. The best way to do this is to have them intimately involved with the development of the principles and to mediate the process. A good process to follow in principle development is to

- Ensure representation from all parties that would apply the principles.
- Provide context for the principles by tying them into the vision, mission, and goals of the organization and the company. Create that *causal map to success*.
- Develop *themes* or buckets for the principles. Venn diagrams are useful to show overlap of principles within different themes.
- Break the larger team into smaller teams to propose principles. Although principles will likely be worded differently, you will be surprised at how much overlap occurs.

- Bring the team together for small presentations and then break them back up into smaller teams to modify their principles.
- Perform another round of presentations and then select the overlap of principles.
- Place the remaining principles on the wall and allow individuals to vote on them.
- Rank order the principles and make the cut line at some easily remembered number of principles (six to twelve) consisting of the overlap from earlier and the next N highest ranking principles equaling your preferred number.
- Allow debate on the remaining principles and then perform a final rank ordering and ask the team to "ratify" the principles.

Be sure to apply RASCI to the process of development as you don't want the team thinking that there isn't a final decision maker in the process. Failing to include key team members and having only architects develop principles may create the perception an "ivory tower" architecture culture wherein engineers do not believe that architects are appropriately connected to the needs of the clients and architects feel that engineers are not owning and abiding by architectural standards.

AKF's Twelve Architectural Principles

In this section, we introduce twelve architectural principles. Many times after engagements, we will "seed" the architectural principle gardens of our clients with our twelve principles and then ask them to run their own process, taking as many of ours as they would like, discarding any that do not work for them, and adding as many as they would like. We only ask that they let us know what they are considering so that we can modify our principles over time if they come up with an especially ingenious or useful principle. The Venn diagram shown in Figure 12.3 depicts our principles as they relate to scalability, availability, and cost. We will discuss each of the principles at a high level and then dig more deeply into those that are identified as having an impact on scalability.

N+1 Design

Simply stated, this principle is the need to ensure that anything you develop has at least one additional instance of that system in the event of failure. Apply the *rule of three* that we will discuss in Chapter 32, Planning Data Centers, or what we sometimes call *ensuring that you build one for you, one for the customer, and one to fail.* This principle holds true for everything from large data center design to Web Services implementations.

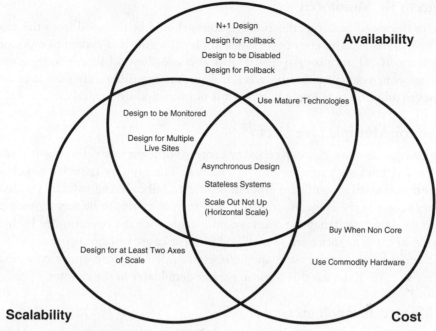

Figure 12.3 *AKF Architecture Principles*

Design for Rollback

This is a critical principle for Web services, Web 2.0, or Software as a Service (SaaS) companies. Whatever you build, ensure that it is backward compatible. Make sure that you can roll it back if you find yourself in a position of spending too much time "fixing forward." Some companies will indicate that they can roll back within a specific window of time, say the first couple of hours. Unfortunately, some of the worst and most disastrous failures don't show up for a few days, especially when those failures have to do with customer data corruption. In the ideal case, you will also design to allow something to be rolled, pushed, or deployed while your product or platform is still "live." The rollback process will be covered in more detail in Chapter 18, Barrier Conditions and Rollback.

Design to Be Disabled

When designing systems, especially very risky systems that communicate to other systems or services, design them to be capable of being "marked down" or disabled. This may give you additional time to "fix forward" or ensure that you don't go down as a result of a bug that introduces strange out of bounds demand characteristics on your system.

Design to Be Monitored

As we've discussed earlier in this book, systems should be designed from the ground up to be monitored. This goes beyond just applying agents to a system to monitor the utilization of CPU, memory, or disk I/O. It also goes beyond simply logging errors. You want your system to identify when it is performing differently than it normally operates in addition to telling you when it is not functioning properly.

Design for Multiple Live Sites

Many companies have disaster recovery centers with systems sitting mostly idle or used for QA until such time as they are needed. The primary issue with such solutions is that it takes a significant amount of time to fail over and validate the disaster recovery center in the event of a disaster. A better solution is to be serving traffic out of both sites live, such that the team is comfortable with the operation of both sites. Our rule of three applies here as well and in most cases you can operate three sites live at equal to or lower cost than the operation of a hot site and a cold disaster recovery site. We'll discuss this topic in greater detail later in the chapter.

Use Mature Technologies

When you are buying technology, use technology that is proven and that has already had the bugs worked out of it. There are many cases where you might be willing or interested in the vendor promised competitive edge that some new technology offers. Be careful here, because if you become an early adopter of software or systems, you will also be on the leading edge of finding all the bugs with that software or system. If availability and reliability are important to you and your customers, try to be an early majority or late majority adopter of those systems that are critical to the operations of your service, product, or platform.

Asynchronous Design

Whenever possible, systems should communicate in an asynchronous fashion. Asynchronous systems tend to be more fault tolerant to extreme load and do not easily fall prey to the multiplicative effects of failure that characterize synchronous systems. We will discuss the reasons for this in greater detail in the next section of this chapter.

Stateless Systems

Although some systems need state, state has a cost in terms of availability, scalability, and overall cost of your system. When you store state, you do so at a cost of memory or disk space and maybe the cost of databases. This results in additional calls that are often made in synchronous fashion, which in turn reduces availability. As state is often costly compared to stateless systems, it increases the *per unit cost* of scaling your site. Try to avoid state whenever possible.

Scale Out Not Up

This is the principle that addresses the need to scale horizontally rather than vertically. Whenever you base the viability of your business on faster, bigger, and more expensive hardware, you define a limit on the growth of your business. That limit may change with time as larger scalable multiprocessor systems or vendor supported distributed systems become available, but you are still implicitly stating that you will grow governed by third-party technologies. When it comes to ensuring that you can meet your shareholder needs, design your systems to be able to be horizontally split in terms of data, transactions, and customers.

Design for at Least Two Axes of Scale

Whenever you design a major system, you should ensure that it is capable of being split on at least two axes of the cube that we introduce in Chapter 22, Introduction to the AKF Scale Cube, to ensure that you have plenty of room for "surprise" demand. This does not mean that you need to implement those splits on day one, but rather that they are thought through and at least architected so that the long lead time of rearchitecting a system is avoided.

Buy When Non Core

We will discuss this a bit more in Chapter 15, Focus on Core Competencies: Build Versus Buy. Although we have this identified as a cost initiative, we can make arguments that it affects scalability and availability as well as productivity even though productivity isn't a theme within our principles. The basic premise is that regardless of how smart you and your team are, you simply aren't the best at everything. Furthermore, your shareholders really expect you to focus on the things that *really* create competitive differentiation and therefore shareholder value. So only build things when you are really good at it *and* it makes a significant difference in your product, platform, or system.

Use Commodity Hardware

We often get a lot of pushback on this one, but it fits in well with the rest of the principles we've outlined. It is similar to our principle of using mature technologies. Hardware, especially servers, moves at a rapid pace toward commoditization characterized by the market buying predominately based on cost. If you can develop your architecture such that you can scale horizontally easily, you should be buying the cheapest hardware you can get your hands on, assuming that the cost of ownership of that hardware (including the cost of handling higher failure rates) is lower than higher end hardware.

Scalability Principles In Depth

Now that we've had an overview of our suggested principles, let's dig deeper into the ones that we believe support scalability the most.

Design to Be Monitored

Monitoring, when done well, goes beyond the typical actions of identifying services that are alive or dead, examining or polling log files, collecting system related data over time, and evaluating end-user response times. When done well, applications and systems are designed from the ground up to be if not self-healing then at least self-diagnosing. If a system is designed to be monitored and logs the correct information, you can more easily determine the headroom remaining for the system and take the appropriate action to correct scalability problems earlier.

For instance, you know at the time of design of any system what services and systems it will need to interact with. Maybe the service in question repeatedly makes use of a database or some other data store. Potentially, the service makes a call, preferably asynchronously, to another service. You also know that from time to time you will be writing diagnostic information and potentially errors to some sort of volatile or stable storage system. All of this knowledge can be used to design a system that can give you more information about future scale needs and increase your availability.

People by their very nature are self diagnosing. In examples where we clearly have problems such as running a fever or breaking a leg, we are likely to seek immediate help. In the systems world, this would be similar to throwing "hard errors" and crying for help immediately. But how about when we just appear to be working slower than before over a period of time? Maybe we feel that we are consistently forgetting more names, losing our appetite, or taking longer to digest our food. It would be difficult and costly to develop after the fact monitoring agents for such illnesses if we didn't subconsciously keep track of such things in our minds.

We argue that you should build systems that help you identify potential or future issues. Going back to our system and its calls to a database, we should log the response time of that database over time, the amount of data, and maybe the rate of errors. Rather than just reporting on that data, our system could be designed to show "out of bounds" conditions plotted from a mean of the last thirty Tuesdays (assuming today is Tuesday) for our five-minute time of day. Significant standard deviations from the mean could be "alerted" for future or immediate action depending upon the value. This approach leverages a control chart from statistical process control.

We could do the same with our rates of errors, the response time from other services, and so on. The information could then feed into our capacity planning process to help us determine where we might start to have demand versus supply problems such that we can know which systems we should focus on for future architectural changes.

Design for Multiple Live Sites

As previously indicated, having multiple sites is a must to assure your shareholders that you can weather any geographically isolated disaster or crisis. The time to start thinking about how to run data center strategies isn't when you are attempting to deploy your services, but rather when you are designing them. There are all sorts of design tradeoffs that will impact whether you can easily serve data out of more than one geographically dispersed data center while you are live. Does your application need or expect that all data will exist in a monolithic database? Does your application expect that all reads and writes will occur within the same database structures? Must all customers reside in the same data structures? Are other services called in synchronous fashion and are they intolerant to latency?

Ensuring that your system's designs can be hosted nearly anywhere and operate independently from other sites if need be is critical to being able to deploy new systems rapidly without the constraints of space or power in a single facility. You may have an incredibly scalable application and platform, but if your physical environment and your operating contracts keep you from scaling quickly as demand grows, you are just as handicapped as the company with nearly infinite space and a platform that needs to be rearchitected for scale. Scalability is about much more than just ensuring that the system is designed to allow for scale; it is about ensuring that the environment in which you operate, including your contracts, partners, and facilities will allow you to scale. Therefore, your architecture must allow you to make use of several facilities (both existing and potentially new facilities) on an on-demand basis.

Asynchronous Design

Systems designed to interact synchronously have a higher failure rate than those designed to act asynchronously. In addition, their ability to scale is tied directly to the slowest system in the chain of communications. If one system or service slows, the entire chain prior to that system slows, and as a result output occurs less frequently and throughput is lowered. Thus, synchronous systems are more difficult to scale in real time.

Asynchronous systems are more tolerant of such slowdowns. Let's take the case that a system can serve 40 simultaneous requests synchronously. When all 40 requests are in flight, no more can be handled until at least one completes. Asynchronous systems handle the request and do not block for the response. Rather, they have a service that waits for the response while handling the next request. Although throughput is roughly the same, they are more tolerant to slowness as requests can continue to be processed. Responses are slowed, but the entire system does not grind to a halt. Thus, if you only have a periodic slowness, it allows you to work through that slowness without stopping the entire system. This approach may buy you several days in order to "fix" a scale bottleneck as compared to a synchronous system.

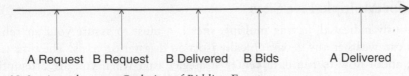

Figure 12.4   *Asynchronous Ordering of Bidding Events*

There are many places where you are seemingly "forced" to use a synchronous system. For instance, many database calls would be hampered and the results potentially flawed if subjected to an asynchronous passing of messages. Imagine two servers requesting similar data from a database, both of them asking for the current bid price on a car, as in Figure 12.4.

System A makes a request followed by system B making a request. B receives the data first and then makes a bid on the car thereby changing the car's price. A then receives data that is out of date. Although this seems undesirable, we can make a minor change to our logic that allows this to happen without significant impact to the entire process.

We only need to change the case where A subsequently makes a bid. If the bid value by A is less than the bid made by B, we simply indicate that the value of the car has changed and display the now current value. A can then make up her mind as to whether she wants to continue bidding. We have taken something most people would argue needs to be synchronous and made it asynchronous.

Stateless Systems

Stateful systems are those in which operations are performed within the context of previous and subsequent operations. As such, information on the past operations of any given thread of execution or series of requests must be maintained somewhere. In maintaining state for a series of transactions, engineering teams typically start to gather and keep a great deal of information about the requests. State costs money, processing power, availability, and scalability. Although there are many cases where state is valuable, it should always be closely evaluated for return on investment. State often implies the need for additional systems and sometimes synchronous calls that would not exist in a stateless system. It also makes designing for multiple live data centers more difficult—how can you possibly handle a transaction with state stored in data center X in data center Y without replicating that state between data centers? The replication of that data would not only need to occur in near real time, implying that the data centers need to be relatively close, but it represents a doubling of space necessary to store relatively transient data.

Whenever possible, *stateful* applications should be avoided in engineering applications for extreme scale. Where it is necessary, consider attempting to store state with the end user rather than within your system. If that is not possible, consider a centralized state caching mechanism that keeps state off of the application servers and allows for distribution across multiple servers. Where state needs to be *multitenant* for any reason, attempt to segment the state by customer or transaction class to allow distribution across multiple data centers and try to maintain persistency for that customer or class of transaction within a single data center with only the data that is necessary for failover being replicated.

Scale Out Not Up

A good portion of this book is about the need to be able to scale horizontally. If you want to achieve near infinite scale, you must disaggregate your systems, organization, and processes to allow for that scale. Forcing transactions through a single person, computer, or process is a recipe for disaster. Many companies rely upon Moore's law for their scale and as a result continue to force requests into single system (or sometimes two systems to eliminate single points of failures), relying upon faster and faster systems to scale. Moore's law isn't so much a law as it is a prediction that the number of transistors that can be placed on an integrated circuit will double roughly every two years. The expected result is that the speed and capacity of these transistors (in our case, a CPU and memory) will double within the same time period. But what if your company grows faster than this, as did eBay, Yahoo, Google, Facebook, MySpace, and so on? Do you really want to become the company that is limited in growth when Moore's Law no longer holds true?

Could Google, Amazon, Yahoo, or eBay run on a single system? Could any of them possibly run on a single database? Many of them started out that way, but the technology of the day simply could not keep up with the demands that their users placed on them. Some of them faced crises of scale associated with attempting to rely upon bigger, faster systems. All of them would have faced those crises had they not started to scale out rather than up.

Design for at Least Two Axes of Scale

Leaders, managers, and architects are paid to think into the future. You are designing not just for today, but attempting to piece together a system that can be used, with some modification, for some time to come. As such, we believe that you should always consider how you will perform your next set of horizontal splits even before the need arrives.

"Scaling out not up" speaks to the implementation of the first set of splits. Perhaps you are splitting transaction volume across cloned systems. You may have five application servers with five duplicate read only caches consisting of startup information and nonvolatile customer information. With this configuration, you might be able to scale to 1 million transactions an hour across 1,000 customers and service 100% of all your transactions from login to logout and everything in between. But what will you do when you have 75 million customers? Will startup times of the application suffer? Will memory access times begin to degrade or can you even keep all of the customer information within memory?

For any service, you should consider how you will perform your next type of split. In this case, you might divide your customers into N separate groups and service customers out of N separate pools of systems with each pool handling 1/Nth of your customers. Or maybe you move some of the transactions (like login and logout or updating account information) to separate pools if that will lower the number of startup records necessary within the cache. Whatever you do, for major systems implementations, you should think about it during the initial design even if you only implement one axis of scale.

Twelve Architectural Principles

The twelve principles we most often recommend are

1. N+1 Design. Never less than two of anything, and remember the rule of three.
2. Design for Rollback. Ensure you can roll back any release of functionality.
3. Design to Be Disabled. Be able to turn off anything you release.
4. Design to Be Monitored. Think about monitoring during design, not after.
5. Design for Multiple Live Sites. Don't box yourself into one-site solutions.
6. Use Mature Technologies. Use things you know work well.
7. Asynchronous Design. Communicate synchronously only when absolutely necessary.
8. Stateless Systems. Use state only when the business return justifies it.
9. Scale Out Not Up. Never rely on bigger, faster systems.
10. Design for at Least Two Axes. Think one step ahead of your scale needs.
11. Buy When Non Core. If you aren't the best at building it and it doesn't offer competitive differentiation, buy it.
12. Commodity Hardware. Cheaper is better most of the time.

Conclusion

In this chapter, we discussed architectural principles and how they impact the culture of your organization. Principles should be aligned with the vision, mission, and goals of your organization. They should be developed with your team to ensure that the team feels ownership over the principles and they should be the foundation for your scalability focused processes such as the Joint Architecture Design process and the Architecture Review Board.

Key Points

- Principles should be developed from your goals and be aligned to your vision and mission.

- Principles should be broad enough that they are not continually revised but should also be SMART and thematically bundled or grouped.

- To ensure ownership and acceptance of your principles, consider having your team help you develop them.

- Ensure that your team understands the RASCI of principle development and modification.

- Keep your principles to a number that is easily memorized by the team to increase utilization of the principles. We suggest having no more than twelve principles.

Chapter 13

Joint Architecture Design

> Thus it is that in war the victorious strategist only seeks battle after the victory has been won, whereas he who is destined to defeat first fights and afterwards looks for victory.
>
> —Sun Tzu

So far in Part II, Building Processes for Scale, we have focused on many reactionary processes such as managing issues, crisis management, and determining headroom. In this chapter and the next, we are going to introduce two processes that are proactive, not reactive. We are going to shift from reaction (what to do when something goes wrong) to discuss how to build the application in a scalable manner in the first place. These two processes are cross functional and are interwoven within the product development life cycle. They are the Joint Architecture Design (JAD) and the Architecture Review Board (ARB). In this chapter, we are going to focus on JAD, which comes earlier in the product development life cycle than does ARB and sets the stage for designing a system that scales.

Using a very simple sport analogy of running, JAD would be equivalent to the training or preparation for the race. ARB, continuing the analogy, would be the actual race. JAD is a collaborative design process wherein all engineering assets necessary to develop some new major functionality work together to define a design consistent with the architectural principles of the organization. ARB Board is a review board of select architects from each of the functional or business areas, whose job is to ensure that prior to final sign-off of a design, all company architectural principles have been incorporated, and that best practices have been applied.

Fixing Organizational Dysfunction

In the introduction, we mentioned that the JAD process was cross functional. In dysfunctional organizations, the implementation of JAD is challenging but absolutely necessary to help cure the dysfunction. If you are part of one of those organizations where engineers do not trust operations staff and vice versa, unfortunately you are among the majority. It is sad but common to have distrust and even animosity between teams. Before we can figure out how we can overcome this dysfunction and start building scalable applications through the use of cross-functional teams, we need to understand why this problem exists.

In most software development shops, it is not too difficult to find an engineer who feels that the architects and the operations staff, database administrators, systems administrators, and network engineers are either not knowledgeable about coding or don't fully understand the software development process. The reverse distrust is also prevalent where operations staff or architects feel that software engineers only know how to code and do not understand higher level design or total systems concepts. Even worse, each believes that the other's job is in direct opposition to accomplishing his own goals. Operations staff can often be heard mumbling that "they could keep the servers up if the developers would stop putting code on them" and developers mumble back that "they could develop and debug much faster if they didn't have operations making them follow silly policies." This set of perceptions and misgivings is destructive to the scalability of the application and organization. They also show how the "experiential chasm," which we discussed in Chapter 6, Making the Business Case, can exist among technology teams as easily as it can between the business and technology teams.

As a brief refresher on the experiential chasm, we proposed that the differences in education and experience between the two groups of people cause a type of *destructive interference* in communication. The formal education of a software developer and a systems administrator at an undergraduate level may be very similar—same computer science degree—or they may vary significantly—computer science versus computer engineering. The on-the-job education is where the really large differences begin to emerge. Systems administrators or database administrators typically get mentored by more senior administrators for several years until they become proficient with a specific technology, ever increasing their specialization in that field. Software engineers typically follow a similar path but are focused on a particular programming language. What server the application runs on or what database the application calls is for the most part abstracted away for the software engineers so they can concentrate on feature development.

With the experiential chasm as the starting point between the two groups, when we add differing and sometimes opposing goals, these groups start becoming so far apart they see no common ground. Most organizations do not share goals across teams. This is problematic if the intent is to get these teams working together instead of fighting each other. The operations team usually is saddled with the goal of uptime or availability for the site. Any downtime gets taken out of their bonuses. The development team is usually given the goal of feature delivery. A missed delivery date results in lower bonuses for them. At the CTO level, the CTO thinks that all of his goals are being handled by one of his teams and therefore everything is covered. The reality is that separating goals like this actually causes strife among his teams.

The development goal of feature delivery pushes them to want to get code out fast, and if it breaks, they figure they can fix it on-the-fly. This is by far the fastest way to achieve initial delivery of code, which is usually all that is measured. In the long run, this approach actually takes more time because fixing problems takes a lot of time to find, fix, and redeploy. As we mentioned earlier, this post-delivery time is usually never measured and therefore is missed as being part of the delivery goal.

The operations team wants to keep the site up and increase the availability as per its goal. It is therefore motivated to keep changes out of production because changes are the primary cause of issues. It decides that the fewer code pushes or changes made to the production environment the more likely the team is able to meet its goal. Whether consciously or not, the team is suddenly not so motivated to get code pushed out and in fact will start to find any reason for delays.

As you can hopefully see by now, you have two or more groups that have incredibly valuable knowledge about how systems and architectures work in general and specific knowledge about how your system operates, but they are naturally weary of each other and are likely being incented to not work together. How can you fix this? The JAD process is a great place to start. As we'll discuss in the next section of this chapter, JAD is a collaborative process that pulls cross-functional team members together with a common goal. The JAD team either succeeds or fails together and this reflects on its organizations and its leadership team.

The basic process of JAD is to assign a major feature to not only a software engineer but also to an architect, at least one operations engineer (database administrator, systems administrator, or network engineer), and optionally a product manager, project manager, and quality assurance engineer as needed for this specific feature. The responsibility of this team is to come up with a design that follows the established architecture principles of the organization that will allow the system to continue to scale, that allows the feature to meet the product requirements, and that will be able to pass the ARB. This team is comprised of the people who will ultimately present the design to the ARB, which we will discuss in the next chapter is made up of peers and managers who get to decide if this design satisfies the exit criteria. Fortunately, this collusion does not just stop at the design; because these individuals have put their credentials on the line with this feature, they are now motivated to watch it through the entire life cycle to ensure it is a success. Engineers are now being held responsible for the design and how it performs in production. The database administrators are being held accountable for designing this feature to not only scale but to also meet the business requirements. Now we have the developers, architects, and operations staff working together, jointly, with a shared goal.

Designing for Scale Cross Functionally

We discussed briefly the structure and mechanism of JAD. Now, we can get into more detail. JAD is a collaborative design process wherein all engineering assets necessary to develop some new major functionality or architectural modification work together to define a design consistent with the architectural principles and best practices of the company to implement the business unit requirements. This group of engineering assets is comprised of the software engineer responsible for ultimately coding the feature, an architect, at least one but possibly multiple operations staff, and, as needed based on the feature, the product manager, a project manager, and a quality assurance engineer. As mentioned earlier, each brings unique knowledge, perspectives, experiences, and goals that augment each other as well as counter-balance each other. Although the operations engineer now has the goal of designing a feature that meets the business requirements, she also still has the goal from her organization of maintaining availability. This helps ensure that she is vigilant as ever about what goes into production.

Involving each of the technology groups, tradeoffs between hardware, software, middleware, and build versus buy approaches can help shave time to market, cost of development and cost of operations, and increase overall quality. The software engineer has typically been abstracted from the hardware by the services of the operations team. So trying to have the software engineer design a feature for image storage—see the "Image Storage Feature" sidebar for the complete example—without knowledge of the storage device that can and should be used is asking to fail in meeting the requirements, fail in the cost-effectiveness, or fail in the scalability of the system. Shared goal of scalability ensures the culture is pervasive; when there are issues or crises, all hands are on deck because of shared ownership.

This JAD approach is not limited to waterfall development methodologies where one phase of product development must take place before the other. JAD can and has been successfully used in conjunction with all types of development methodologies such as iterative or agile, in which specifications, designs, and development evolve as greater insights are gained about the product feature. Each time a design is being modified or appended to, a JAD can be called to help with it. The type of architecture does not preclude the use of JAD either. Whether it is a traditional three-tier Web architecture, Service Oriented Architecture, or simply a monolithic application, the collaboration of engineering, operations, and architects to arrive at a better design is simply taking advantage of the fact that solutions arrived at by teams are better than individuals. The more diverse the background of the team members, the more holistic the solution is likely to be.

The actual structure of the JAD is very informal. After the team has been assigned to the feature, one person takes the lead on coordinating the design sessions; this is typically the software engineer or the project manager, if assigned. There are usually multiple design sessions that can last between one and several hours depending on people's schedules. For very complex features, multiple design sessions for various components of the feature should be scheduled. For example, a session focused on the database should be set up, and then another one on the cache servers should be set up separately.

Typically, the sessions start with a discussion covering the background of the feature and the business requirements. During this phase, it is a good idea to have the product manager present and then on call for any clarifications as questions come up. After the product requirements have been discussed, a review of the architectural principles that relate to this area of the design is usually a good idea. Following this, the teams brainstorm about various solutions and typically arrive at a few different possible solutions. These are written up at the end of the meeting and sent around for people to ponder over until the next session. Usually only a session or two are required to come to an agreement on the best approach for the design of the feature. The final design is written down and documented for presentation at that ARB.

Image Storage Feature

At our fictional company AllScale, a feature for the human resource management (HRM) application has been requested that will allow for the storage of pictures of personnel to be displayed in their personnel folders that the HR and hiring managers bring up to conduct reviews, salary adjustments, and so on. The software engineer, Sam Codur, who has been assigned to this feature, has very little idea of the hardware or storage devices that are used in production. He has overheard the operations folks talk about a SAN or NAS but he is really clueless about the differences. Furthermore, he has never even heard of different classes of storage and has never given a single minute of thought to backup and recovery of storage in the event of data corruption, hardware failure, or natural disasters. Figure 13.1 depicts Sam trying to decide on all the nuances of hardware, software, and network devices alone without any other experts to aid him

Figure 13.1 *Software Engineer Pondering Classes of Storage*

The product manager has specified for this feature that any standard image format be acceptable, that all past profile images be available, and that the size be less than 500KB per image. To Sam, the software engineer, this seems reasonable and instead of soliciting guidance from the operations staff, he decides that he can code the feature and let ops worry about how and where the images actually get stored. The result, after ten days of coding and another five days of quality assurance testing, is the feature gets noticed in the notes for the upcoming release by Tom Harde, VP of operations. Tom sends a set of questions to Mike Softe, VP of engineering, asking how this feature was designed, the response time requirements, and the storage estimates per year. After this email gets passed back and forth several times, it eventually gets escalated to Johnny Fixer, the CTO, with both sides demanding that the other is being unreasonable. Johnny now has to get involved and make some hard decisions to either delay the release in order that the feature be redeveloped to meet the operation team's standards (images less than 100KB, no multiple images, timeouts coded for response times greater than 200msec, no guarantee of image storage, etc.) or push the feature out as developed and worry about it causing issues across the site.

Johnny decides to pull the feature from the release, which requires some retesting to be performed and the delay of a day for the release date. Instead of just fixing this single feature, Johnny decides that he needs to fix the process to make sure there are not more features like this one in the future. Johnny gathers Mike and Tom to introduce the Joint Architecture Design process. He explains that when an engineer is developing a feature and it is either part of the core modules/services of the HRM system or it is estimated to take more than five days of development, then a JAD must take place. The participants will be the engineer developing the feature, a systems architect, and an operations staff member assigned by Tom or his managers. Johnny continues to explain that this team of individuals own the design and will be held accountable for the success or failure of the feature in terms of its performance, availability, and scalability. Tom and Mike see this process as a way to achieve a win-win situation and depart quickly to explain it to their teams.

JAD Checklist

Here is a quick checklist for how to conduct the JAD sessions to ensure you do not skip any of the most important steps. As you feel more comfortable with this process, feel free to modify this and create your own JAD checklist for your organization to follow:

1. Assign participants.
2. Mandatory. Software engineer, architect, operations engineer (database administrator, systems administrator, and/or network engineer).
3. Optional. Product manager, project manager, quality assurance engineer.
4. Schedule one or more sessions. Divide sessions by component if possible: database, server, cache, storage, etc.

5. Start the session by covering the specifications.

6. Review the architectural principles related to this session's component.

7. Brainstorm approaches. No need for complete detail.

8. List pros and cons of each approach.

9. If multiple sessions are needed, have someone write down all the ideas and send around to the group.

10. Arrive at consensus for the design. Use voting, rating, ranking, or any other decision technique that everyone can support.

11. Create the final documentation of the design in preparation for the ARB.

Don't be afraid to modify this checklist as necessary for your organization.

Entry and Exit Criteria

With the JAD process, we recommend that specific criteria must be met before a feature can begin the JAD process. Likewise, certain criteria must be met in order for that feature to move out of JAD. By holding fast to these entrance and exit criteria, you will preserve the integrity of the JAD process and not weaken it. Some examples of how allowing these criteria to be bypassed are introducing features that aren't large enough to require a team effort to design or allowing a feature without an operations engineer on the team to start JAD because the operations team is swamped handling a crisis. Giving in to these one off requests will ultimately devalue the JAD and participants will believe that they can stop attending meetings or that they are not being held accountable for the outcome. Do not even start down this slippery slope; make the entrance and exit criteria rigorous and unwavering, no exceptions.

The entrance criteria for JAD are the following:

- *Feature Significance.* The feature must be significant enough to require the focus of a cross-functional team. The exact nature of significance can be debated. We suggest measuring this in three ways:

  1. The first is size. For size, we use the amount of effort to develop as the measurement. Features requiring more than 10 days of total effort are considered significant. To calculate this for features that have multiple engineers assigned to them, sum all engineering days estimated for the feature.

  2. The second is potential impact on the overall application or system. If the feature touches many of the core components of the system, this should be considered significant enough to design cross functionally.

3. The third is complexity of the feature. If the feature requires components that are not typically involved in features such as caching or storage, it should go through JAD. A feature that runs on the same type of application server as the rest of the site and retrieves data from the database is not complex enough to meet this requirement.

- *Established Team.* The feature must have representatives assigned and present from engineering, architecture, and operations (database and system admin, possibly network). If needed, members from quality assurance, project management, and product management should be assigned. If these required team members are not assigned and made available to attend the meetings, the feature should not be allowed to participate in JAD.

- *Product Requirements.* The feature must have product requirements and a business case in order to participate. The reason is that tradeoffs are likely to be made based on different architectural solutions, and the team will need to know the critical requirements from the nice-to-have ones. Also understanding the revenue generated by this feature will help when deciding how much investment should be considered for different solutions.

- *Empowered.* The JAD team must be empowered to make decisions that will not be second-guessed by other engineers or architects. The only team that can approve or deny the JAD design is the ARB, who gets final review of the architecture. In RASCI terminology, the JAD team is the R (Responsible) for the design and the ARB is the A (Accountable).

The exit criteria for a feature coming out of JAD are the following:

- *Architectural Principles.* The final design of the feature must follow all architectural principles that have been established in the organization. If there are exceptions to this rule, they should be documented and expected to be questioned in ARB, resulting in a possible rejection of the design. We will talk more about the ARB process in the next chapter.

- *Consensus.* The entire team should be in agreement and support the final design. Time for dissention is during the team meetings and not afterward. If someone from the JAD team begins second-guessing team decisions, this should be grounds for requiring the JAD to be conducted again and any development on the feature should be stopped immediately.

- *Tradeoffs Documented.* If there were any significant tradeoffs made in the design with respect to the requirements, cost, or principles, these should be spelled out and documented for the ARB to review and for any other team member to reference when reviewing the design of the feature.

- *Final Design Documented.* The final design must be documented and posted for reference. The design may or may not be reviewed by ARB, but the design must be made available for all teams to review and reference in the future. These designs will soon become system documentation as well as design patterns that engineers, architects, and operations folks can reference when they are participating in future JADs.

- *ARB.* The final step in the JAD process is to decide whether the feature needs to go to ARB for final review and approval. We will talk in more detail in the next chapter about what features should be considered for ARB but here are our basic recommendations. If this feature meets any of the following, it should proceed through ARB:

  1. Noncompliance with architectural principles. If any of the architectural principles were violated, this feature should go through ARB.

  2. Projects that cannot reach consensus on design. If the team fails to reach consensus, it can either be reassigned to a new JAD team or it can be sent to ARB for a final decision on the competing designs.

  3. Significant tradeoffs made. If tradeoffs had to be made in terms of product requirements, cost, or other nonarchitectural principles, this should flag a feature to proceed to ARB.

  4. High risk features. We will discuss how to assess risk in much more detail in Chapter 16, Determining Risk, but if the feature is considered a high risk feature, it should go through ARB. A quick way of determining if this is high risk is to look at how many core components the feature touches or how different it is from other features. The more core components that are touched or the greater the difference from other features, the higher the risk.

Conclusion

In this chapter, we covered the Joint Architecture Design (JAD) process. We started by understanding the dysfunction in technology organizations that causes features to be designed in silos. We revisited the experiential chasm as it played a role in this dysfunction. We also saw how differing goals among different technology teams can add to this problem. The fix is forcing the teams to work together for a shared goal. This occurs with the JAD process.

We then covered in detail the JAD process, including who were mandatory participants in the process and who were some of the optional team members. We described how the design meetings should be structured based on components and how important it was to start by making sure every team member was familiar with the business requirements of the feature as well as the applicable architecture principles of the organization.

We shared with you a JAD checklist that will be useful to get you and your organization started quickly with the JAD process. Our recommendation for using this was to start with our standard steps but fill it out as necessary to make it part of your organization. And then of course document the process so it becomes fixed in your organization's culture and processes.

We closed the chapter with the entry and exit criteria of JAD. The entry criteria are focused on the preparation to ensure the JAD will be successful and to ensure that the integrity of the process remains. Letting features slip into a JAD without all the required team members is a sure way to cause the process to lose focus and not be as effective as it should be. The exit criteria are focused on ensuring that the feature design has been agreed upon by all members of the team and that if necessary it is prepared to be presented in the Architecture Review Board (ARB), which we will discuss in the next chapter.

Key Points

- Designing applications in a vacuum leads to problems; the best designs are done involving multiple groups offering different perspectives.

- The JAD is the best way to involve a cross-functional team that may not be incented to work together.

- The JAD team must include members from engineering, architecture, and operations (database administrators, systems administrators, or network engineers).

- The optional members of the JAD team include project management, product management, and quality assurance. These people should be added to the team as required by the feature.

- JAD is most successful when the integrity of the process is respected and entry and exit criteria are rigorously upheld.

Chapter 14

Architecture Review Board

> We shall be unable to turn natural advantage to account unless we make use of local guides.
>
> —Sun Tzu

We started the last chapter by explaining our shifting focus from reactive processes, such as what we do when things go wrong, to proactive processes, such as how we design features to have fewer problems. The first proactive process that we introduced was the Joint Architecture Design (JAD) process. JAD ensures the design of features, and projects are conducted in a cross-functional manner, bringing the best of all technology knowledge to work on the problem. We concluded with the mention of a review process for certain JAD projects. This review process is known as the Architecture Review Board (ARB). The ARB has many purposes, but the primary goal is to validate the design of the JAD.

We used a very simple sport analogy of running to provide a high-level idea of the difference between JAD and ARB. If you will recall in our analogy, JAD was the equivalent to the training and ARB was the actual race. JAD can take place over several days or weeks, whereas ARB is generally a single meeting that provides a focused discussion on the outcome of the JAD, including not only the design but the tradeoffs as well. ARB is by our definition a review board of select architects and leaders from each of the functional or business areas, whose job is to ensure that all company architectural principles have been incorporated and that best practices have been applied. ARB is also one of the barrier condition processes that we will discuss within Chapter 18, Barrier Conditions and Rollback.

Ensuring Scale Through Review

We have asked you repeatedly through this book how a certain process or focus might have an impact on scalability. It shouldn't come as any surprise that the answer

221

is generally the same: the people and processes within your organization will make or break the scalability of your application. Chances are nil that you will luck into an architecture that scales as required by your business and supports itself without the proper team in place and with that team following the proper processes. As we discussed in the last chapter, having a cross-functional team design the application ensures that people with different knowledge work together to find the best solution. Additionally, these people now have a combined goal of making this feature a success. Without those two critical pieces in place, the missing knowledge and *experiential chasm* prevalent in most organizations ensure that periodically features will fail and cause availability and scalability issues for your business.

The JAD process is an excellent major step in guaranteeing that you have designed a feature that takes into account all the various technology aspects as well as one that helps to break down the cross team barriers that typically exist. The second step in this process is to make certain that there is some oversight and governance on the JAD teams as well as provide a check to ensure consistency across the JAD teams. This oversight and consistency check comes in the form of the ARB.

Architectural principles are similar to coding standards; if they are documented and taught to all engineers, they should be consistently followed. But if you don't follow up and check on your engineers, some of them, even those with the best intentions, may cut some corners with the intention of fixing things later. Unfortunately, with competing demands for engineers' time, the likelihood is that they won't fix those corners that were cut, no matter how well intentioned they are. If standards are not reviewed by peers or managers, they will slip. Unfortunately, it is a natural phenomenon among almost every team. We will discuss this more in Chapter 19, Fast or Right? when we cover whether to do things quickly or correctly. In a perfect world, there would be no other pressures on the engineers except to get the projects done correctly, but that is rarely the case. There are almost always additional pressures that must be balanced. The other factor with standards is that someone will likely misinterpret even the clearest of them. Especially as you have new engineers coming on to the team, you need to ensure that they all properly understand the standards and can implement them. Discussion on hypothetical examples and even testing can be good predictors, but validating with real-world examples is always the best way to ensure the standards are truly understood.

Validation of the use and interpretation of architectural principles is the primary purpose of the ARB. By reviewing certain JAD designs, you will ensure that teams stay focused on performing the best designs possible, not cutting corners, and that across all the teams there is a consistent understanding and implementation of the principles. Through a continuous use of the architectural principles, you will guarantee that your application is designed from the start to scale. This is the direct correlation between architecture principles and scalability that we talked about in Chapter 12,

Exploring Architectural Principles. JAD is used to set the standard that these principles should consistently be followed and ARB is the check to make sure this is done.

Board Constituency

There are certain people or roles that you will want on the ARB, but more importantly are the traits that these people need to display. Let's talk about these traits first and then we will discuss the roles. Hopefully, these two spheres overlap completely and all the proper roles are filled with people who display all the proper attributes. To start with, you want people who are respected in the organization. They may be respected because of their position, their tenure, or possibly because of their expertise in a particular area of technology or business.

People who hold a particular position can be important to the ARB in order to provide the gravitas to uphold their decisions. You do not want the JAD team to be asked by ARB to redesign something only to have them petition to the CTO or VP of engineering to have that decision overthrown. The ARB needs to be comprised of the right people to make the right decision and to be given the final authority of that decision. If this requires VPs to be on the ARB, they should be. If the VPs delegate the ARB to managers or architects, the VPs need to support them and not second-guess them. The ARB, in these matters, would be considered the A (Accountable) within our RASCI process.

There are always leaders in an organization that are not in the management ranks. These can be senior engineers or architects, anyone who demonstrates leadership in some manner. These are the people that the team looks to in meetings to sway opinions and provide guidance. These people are the ones we describe in our chapter on leadership as naturally gifted in understanding people and how to motivate them, or they have worked very hard to become good at that. Either way, the trait of leadership is one that you want to look for when selecting people to place on the ARB.

Expertise, whether in engineering disciplines, architecture, or business, is a characteristic that people should display if they are participants on the ARB. These people usually are in roles such as architects, senior engineers, or business analysts but can be found in lots of other places as well. They are the type of people that get sought out when there is a tough question to answer or a crisis to be solved. Their expertise comes in a variety of subjects and could include expertise on the platform itself because of a long tenure working with the product or perhaps with a specific technology such as caching or even with a specific large customer of the business.

To summarize, the traits or characteristics that we want to look for in ARB members are leaders who are respected and who have domain expertise. Some members may have a greater amount of one characteristic than another. For instance, a senior director of engineering may be well respected and display great leadership but may not have true domain expertise. This senior director may still be an excellent candidate for the review board. Here are some roles within the organization that you should consider looking at as possible candidates as members of the ARB.

- Chief architects
- Scalability architects
- Infrastructure architects
- VP or directors of engineering
- VP or directors of operations or infrastructure
- Senior systems administrators, database administrators, or network engineers
- Senior engineers
- CTO or CIO
- General manager of business unit
- Business analysts

This list is not inclusive but should provide you with an idea of where to look for members who display our three key traits of respectability, leadership, and domain expertise. As with most topics that we have discussed, the real test is whether it works for and within your organization. The number of members of the ARB can vary depending on the organization, the number of people available, and the variety of skill sets required. We recommend the board consist of between four and eight members.

Membership on the ARB should be considered an additional responsibility to an individual's current role. It is always considered voluntary, so if necessary a member can ask to be excused. We ideally would like to see the ARB team remain in place for a significant period of time so that it can establish tenure in terms of assessing projects and designs. There are many ways that you can modify the permanent or nonpermanent nature of this membership and several factors that you may want to consider when deciding on who should be a permanent member and who should be rotational.

One factor to start considering is how many suitable members do you have in your organization? If there are only four people who display the traits that we mention previously as necessary for serving on this board, you will probably have to insist that these be permanent positions. Another factor that will determine how permanent, semipermanent, or rotational this role should be is how often you have features that need to proceed through ARB. If you have enough engineers and enough JAD projects that you are meeting more than once per week, you may need to rotate people or even consider having two different ARB teams that can alternate. A third factor, besides the quantity of candidates and quantity of ARB meetings, is specificity of expertise. If there are multiple technologies or technology stacks or separate applications, you should consider rotating people in and out of the board depending on the feature being discussed.

There are various methods of rotation for the ARB positions. One straightforward method is to change the constituency of the board every quarter of the year. Depending on how many people are fit for this service, they could rotate on the board every six months or once each year or even beyond. Another method for rotation of ARB members is to leave some members permanent, such as the architects, and rotate the management (VP of engineering, VP of operations, CTO, etc.) and the team members (senior engineer, senior systems administrator, senior network engineer, etc). Any of these methods will work fine as long as there is consistency in how each team approaches its decisions and is given the authority of approving or rejecting the JAD proposals.

Conducting the Meeting

The ARB meeting can be as formal or informal as your organizational culture feels that it is necessary. Our experience is that these meetings can be very intimidating for line engineers, database administrators, and other JAD members; therefore, a very informal setting is our preference. The formality should come from the fact that there will be a go or no-go decision made on the architecture of the feature; that should be enough to establish the need for a well thought out and well-presented design by the JAD team.

Regardless of how formal or informal you determine the meeting should be, they should all include the following steps:

1. *Introduction.* Some members of the JAD may not know members of the ARB if the engineering organization is large.

2. *State Purpose.* Someone on the ARB should state the purpose of the meeting so that everyone understands what the goal of the meeting is. We suggest you point out that the ARB will be making a judgment on the proposed architecture and not people on the JAD team. If the design is sent back with major or minor revisions requested, the decision should not be taken as a personal attack. Everyone in the organization should have as their agenda to ensure the proper governance of the IT systems and ensure the scalability of the system.

3. *Architecture Presentation.* The JAD team should present to the ARB its proposed design. A well-structured presentation should walk the ARB members through the thought process starting with the business requirements; follow this

with the tradeoffs, alternative designs, and finally the recommended design with strengths and weaknesses.

4. *Q&A*. The ARB should spend some time asking questions about the design to clarify any points that were vague from the presentation.

5. *Deliberation*. The ARB members should dismiss the JAD team and deliberate on the merits of the proposed design. This can be in many forms, such as cast an initial vote to weigh where each member stands or choose someone to lead the discussion point by point through the pros and cons of the design before casting ballots.

6. *Vote*. The ARB should have an established process for determining when product features get approved and when they get rejected. We have often seen ARBs that reject a design if a single member votes Nay. You may want to adopt a 3/4 rule if you believe getting a 100% agreement will be unlikely and unproductively arduous. If this is the case, we recommend that you reconsider who makes up the constituency of the board. Members should most highly consider what is best for the company. Someone who abuses his power and consistently hassles JAD teams is not looking out for the company and should be replaced on the ARB team.

7. *Conclusion*. When a decision is made, the ARB should call back in the JAD and explain its decision. This decision could be one of four courses:

   - *Approval*. The first decision could be an approval to move forward as outlined in the proposal.

   - *Rejection*. The second decision could be a rejection of the design and a request for a completely new design to be constructed. This second choice is an absolute rarity. Almost always there is something from the proposed design that can be salvaged.

   - *Conditional Approval*. The third option is an approval to move forward but with some changes. This would indicate that the team does not need to resubmit to ARB but can proceed under its own guidance.

   - *Rejection of Components*. The fourth choice is a rejection of the proposed design but with specific requests for either more information or redesigned components. This fourth option is the most common form of rejection and the specific request for more information or a change in the design usually comes from specific members of the ARB. This fourth decision does require a resubmission to ARB for final approval prior to beginning development on the feature.

These steps can be modified as necessary to accommodate your team size, expertise, and culture. The most important item to remember (and you should remind the team of) is that it should first and foremost put what is best for the company before personal likes, distastes, or agendas, such as something causing more work for their team. And, what is best for the company is to get more products in front of the customers while ensuring the scalability of the system.

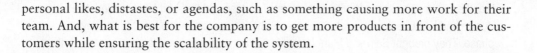

Image Storage Feature

At our fictional company AllScale, a feature for the human resource management (HRM) application that allows for the storage of pictures of personnel had been developed. The software engineer, Sam Codur, was not knowledgeable about storage hardware and designed the feature without any input from the operations team. When it was time to deploy the feature, the VP of operations, Tom Harde, had some tough questions that could not be answered in terms of the system level requirements of the storage such as SLAs, retrieval time, and so on. After lots of discussion with the VP of engineering, Mike Softe, the issue was escalated to Johnny Fixer, the CTO. He decided to pull the feature from the release and redesign it properly. As part of the after action review or postmortem of this issue, Johnny decided to introduce the teams to the concept of Joint Architecture Design. Both the engineering and operations teams embraced this process as a way to improve the product features being developed as well as strengthen the working relationships between the teams.

Johnny was very pleased with how the teams had really taken to the JAD process. He knew there was more that he could do and thought now was the time to continue improving his teams' processes. Johnny asked Tom and Mike to join him for lunch and introduced the idea of an Architectural Review Board. The idea, he explained, was to allow us, the leadership team, as well as our senior technical folks, a chance to review all of the large or riskier features. With both the teams having availability and scalability as goals, which affected their bonuses, both Tom and Mike were anxious to implement a process that would allow them to have a direct say in the design and architecture of key features. The three of them worked the rest of the afternoon to rough out the process, including who should be permanent members of the board (the three of them) and who should be revolving (the engineering architects and operations directors).

After introducing the new ARB process to their teams, it was decided that the first feature that would go through the ARB process was the image storage feature that had been the inspiration for the JAD process. Sam Codur, the engineer responsible for the image storage feature, and Mark Admeen, the operations systems administrator, assigned the responsibility of participating in the JAD, worked on their presentation of the feature's design. They were a bit nervous when it came time for the meeting, but Johnny, Tom, Mike, and the other board members present quickly put them at ease by asking questions and taking up the conversation themselves to discuss the merits of various approaches. Sam and Mark concluded their presentation and were asked to wait outside for a few minutes while the board discussed the matter.

After the door closed, Johnny began by asking each member in turn his or her opinion of the design. Knowing that this was his or her chance to sign off or reject the proposed design, each person started quite cautiously. By the end of the discussion, all members had agreed that they were impressed with the level of detail and thought that had been put into the feature design and had unanimously voted to approve the feature to move forward to the development phase. They brought Sam and Mark back into the room and shared the good news with them, congratulating them on being the first to present to the ARB and on being the first to pass the ARB with flying colors.

Entry and Exit Criteria

Similar to the JAD process, we recommend that specific criteria must be met before a product feature can begin the ARB process. As such, certain criteria must be met in order for that feature to move out of ARB and for development to begin. These criteria should be held up as strict standards to ensure that the ARB process is respected and decisions emanating from the board are adhered. Failure to do so results in a weak process that wastes everyone's time and is eventually bypassed in favor of quicker routes to design and development.

The entry criteria for a feature coming out of JAD into ARB are the following:

- *Established Board*. The Architecture Review Board must be established based upon the criteria mentioned earlier in terms of roles and behaviors that the members should demonstrate.

- *JAD Complete*. The feature should meet the exit criteria outlined in the last chapter for JAD. This includes the following:

  ○ *Consensus*. The JAD team should be in agreement and all members should support the final design. If this is absolutely not possible, a feature may be submitted to ARB with this fact acknowledged and the two or more proposed designs each presented.

  ○ *Tradeoffs Documented*. If there were any significant tradeoffs made in the design with respect to the requirements, cost, or principles, these should be documented.

  ○ *Final Design Documented*. The final design must be documented and posted for reference.

- *Feature Selection*. The feature having completed JAD should be considered as a candidate for ARB. If this feature meets any of the following, it should proceed through ARB:

  ○ *Noncompliance with architectural principles*. If any of the architectural principles were violated, this feature should go through ARB.

  ○ *Projects that cannot reach consensus on design*. If the team fails to reach consensus, it can either be reassigned to a new JAD team or it can be sent to ARB for a final decision on the competing designs.

○ *Significant tradeoffs made.* If tradeoffs had to be made in terms of product requirements, cost, or other nonarchitectural principles, this should flag a feature to proceed to ARB.

○ *High risk features.* We will discuss how to assess risk in much more detail in a future chapter, but if the feature is considered a high risk feature, it should go through ARB. A quick way of determining if this is high risk is to look at how many core components the feature touches or how different it is from other features. Either of these will result in an increase amount of risk.

Depending on the decision made by the ARB, there are different exit criteria for a feature. Here are the four decisions and what must be done following the ARB session:

- *Approval.* Congratulations, nothing more, required of the team from ARB. Now the tough part begins by having to actually develop and implement the project as it has been designed.

- *Rejection.* If the design is completely rejected, the ARB provides a number of reasons for its decision. In this case, the same JAD team may be asked to redesign the feature or a new team may be formed to do this second design. The team should remain in place to provide the design if the current team has the right expertise and if it is still motivated to succeed.

- *Conditional Approval.* If the ARB has conditionally approved the design, the team should incorporate the conditions into its design and begin to produce the feature. The team may return to the ARB in person or via email if there are any questions or feel it needs further guidance.

- *Rejection of Components.* If the ARB rejects the design of certain components, the same JAD team should come up with alternative designs for these components. Because ARB is most often treated as a discussion, the JAD team should have a good idea of why each component was rejected and what would be needed to satisfy the board. In this case, the JAD team does need to reschedule with the ARB to receive final signoff on its design.

Checklist—Keys for ARB Success

The following is a checklist of key attributes or actions that you should follow to ensure your ARB is a success:

- Proper board composition
- Successfully complete JAD with the feature
- Ensure the right features get sent to ARB
- Do not allow political pressures to bypass features from ARB

- Ensure everyone understands the purpose of ARB—improved scalability through rigorous design

- JAD team should be well prepared for its presentation and Q&A session

- Establish ahead of time the ARB criteria for passing (100% of members is recommended)

- No petitions allowed on the board's decisions

By following this checklist, you should be able to ensure the success and proper outcome of the ARB process.

Conclusion

In this chapter, we covered the Architecture Review Board in detail. We started by discussing why it is important to review the outputs of processes such as designs from JAD or code from development. Without review, it is too common for people with the best of intentions to allow the standards to slip, inadvertently misunderstand the standards, or misapply them. Review solves both of these problems and does not create an overly burdensome process step.

We then talked about the ARB constituency. We detailed the three behaviors or traits that we felt were essential for members of the ARB regardless of their positions. These behaviors are respect, leadership, and expertise. We offered some suggestions on specific roles that individuals may hold within your organization who would likely meet these criteria. Lastly in this section, we discussed whether the ARB membership should be a rotational role or a permanent one. Either way, the ARB position should be in addition to one's primary job in the organization.

Next, there was an outline of how the ARB meeting should be conducted. The amount of formality in the ARB is dependent on the culture of the organization, but we recommended for as much informality as possible in order for it not to be too intimidating and to foster a discussion about the design.

We concluded this chapter with the entry and exit criteria for ARB. The entry criteria are focused on ensuring that the right feature is being sent through ARB, that the right ARB team is formed, and that the feature is as prepared as possible to proceed through ARB. Selecting the right feature is not always easy; therefore, we recommended four tests for whether a feature should proceed through ARB. These were noncompliance with architectural principles, significant tradeoffs having to be made to the business requirements, inability of the JAD team to reach consensus, and high risk features.

Through the proper establishment of ARB, adherence to the criteria, and following the proper process steps, your organization can be ensured of better designs that are purposefully made for improving your scalability.

Key Points

- A final review of the application's architecture ensures buy-in and acknowledgement as well as prevents finger pointing.

- The proper constituency of the ARB is critical for it to uphold the purpose of a final architecture signoff as well as for the decisions to be respected.

- Members of the ARB should be seen as leaders, well respected, and have expertise in some area of the application or architecture.

- ARB membership can be on a rotational basis but the position is always seen as incremental to current duties.

- The ARB should be as informal as possible as long as it is taken seriously and the decisions are understood to be final.

- All ARBs should start with a discussion of the purpose of the ARB—to ensure designs that support the business needs including scalability.

- Entry into an ARB should only be granted to features that are sufficiently prepared.

- Decisions by the ARB should be considered final. Some organizations may include an appeals process if it is deemed necessary.

Chapter 15

Focus on Core Competencies: Build Versus Buy

Thus far, we've made the case that if you are truly undergoing hyper growth and need to scale indefinitely, you need to take charge of your architecture; relying on third-party solutions alone is a recipe for disaster. This is not to say that third-party solutions are evil; in fact, we believe just the opposite. The point we make in this chapter is that you should absolutely purchase software and systems where you are not the best qualified to build such software and systems, but you should *not* rely upon them as the means for your scalability. In the extreme case, you cannot possibly subject your shareholders to restricting the growth of your business until after the next release of some partner's software or hardware. In past chapters, we have offered suggestions on how to make the business case for scalability initiatives (Chapter 6, Making the Business Case) and to measure and increase your productivity to allow for scalability initiatives (Chapter 5, Management 101). We also added, as one of our suggested architectural principles, Buying When Non Core. Although we did not specifically indicate Buying When Non Core as a scalability principle, your build and purchase will absolutely have an indirect impact on your scalability. In this chapter, we are going to discuss when you should build and when you should buy systems and software. Although the concepts apply to all of your decisions within technology, we are going to put a special emphasis on scalability.

Building Versus Buying, and Scalability

As a rule, when you decide to build something that is commercially available, it has two impacts to your organization and your company. The first is that the item you build typically ends up costing more after you factor in engineering time to support and maintain the system that you've built. The second, and in many cases more important, point is that you have finite development resources and anything you build uses some of that development capacity. Obviously, if you were to build everything from your computers to your operating systems and databases, you would find yourself with little to no capacity remaining to work on the application that makes your company money.

How does this impact scalability? The more time that you spend architecting and implementing supportive components of your site the less time you have in architecting and implementing an overall architecture that allows the entire platform, product, or system to scale. As we will discuss in Chapter 20, Designing for Any Technology, building scalable architectures is about architecting solutions that grow horizontally as user demand increases for any given system or service. When architectures are built to scale horizontally and agnostically, the question of whether to build or buy something becomes one of competitive differentiation and cost rather than religion and capabilities.

When you have created an agnostic architecture, you further reduce the value and minimize the returns associated with dedicating internal and expensive resources to any piece of your architecture. Building a database now has very low shareholder value as compared to the alternative of using several commodity databases. Need more database power? Design your application to make use of any number of databases rather than spending incredible amounts of time developing your own super fast database. Need encryption capabilities? Determine the additional value of your encryption software versus the next best solution available to the public.

Any time you can buy something rather than build it, you free up engineering resources that can be applied to business projects and projects focused on allowing your platform to scale. You don't have an infinite number of resources, so why would you ever want to focus them on things that do not create shareholder value?

You may recall from past education or even some of our discussions within this book that shareholder value is most closely associated with the profits of the company. Rising profits often result in changes to dividends, increases in stock prices, or both. Profits, in turn, are a direct result of revenues minus costs. As such, we are going to focus our build versus buy discussions along the paths of decreasing cost and increasing revenue through focusing on strategy and competitive differentiation.

Focusing on Cost

Cost focused approaches center on lowering the total cost to the company for any build versus buy analysis. These approaches range from a straight analysis of total capital employed over time to a discounted cash flow analysis that factors in the cost of capital over time. Your finance department likely has a preferred method for helping to decide how to determine the lowest cost approach of any number of approaches.

Our experience in this area is that most technology organizations have a bias toward building components. This bias most often shows up in an incorrect or incomplete analysis showing that building a certain system is actually less expensive to a company than purchasing the same component. The most common mistakes in this analysis are an underestimation of the initial cost of building the component, and missing or underestimating future costs of maintenance and support. It is not uncommon for a company to underestimate the cost of support by an order of magnitude as it does not have the history or DNA to know how to truly develop or support critical infrastructure on a 24×7 basis.

If you adopt a cost focused strategy to determine build versus buy of any system, a good way to test whether your strategy is working is to evaluate how often the process results in a build decision. Your decision process is probably spot on if nearly all decisions result in a buy decision. The exception to this rule is in the areas where your company produces the product in question. Obviously, you are in business to make money and to make money you must produce something or provide a service to someone.

A major weakness of cost focused strategies is that they do not focus on strategic alignment or competitive differentiation. The focus is purely to reduce or limit the cost incurred by the company for anything that is needed from a technology perspective. Very often, this strategy is employed by groups implementing back office information technology systems. Focusing on cost alone though can lead to decisions to build something when a commercial off the shelf (COTS) or vendor provided system will be more than adequate.

Focusing on Strategy

Strategy focused approaches look at build versus buy from a perspective of alignment to the vision, mission, supporting strategy, and goals of the company. In most cases, there is a two-part question involved with the strategy focused approach:

- Are we the best or among the best (top two or three) providers or builders of the technology in question?
- Does building or providing the technology in question provide sustainable competitive differentiation?

To be able to answer the first question, you need to be convinced that you have the right and best talent to be the best at what you are doing. Unfortunately, here again, we find that too many technology organizations believe that they are the best at providing, well, *you name it*! Counter to the way some parents have decided to raise their children, not everyone can be the best, not everyone deserves a trophy, and not everyone deserves to feel good about their accomplishments. In the real world, there are only two or three providers of anything with the claim of being the best or at least in the top two to three. Given the number of candidates out there for nearly any service, unless you are the first provider of some service, the chances are slim that your team really is the best. It can be good, but it probably is not the best. Your team is definitely not the best if you haven't been applying the management principles of "seed, feed, and weed" from Chapter 5.

Being the Best

The only people unbiased enough to really make a determination of whether you can be the best provider of anything are those that start from the position of belief that you are not the best provider. No one gets to be the best at anything without proving it, and proving it requires at least some work toward the achievement of a goal. Stating something emphatically is not proof enough of anything but your belief. Against whom or what are you comparing yourself or your team? Just because this is the best group of people you have ever worked with does not justify the title. What are the metrics and measurements that you are using?

And being the best does not necessarily mean having the best technology. You have to win the entire game, from technology to marketing to partnerships that will make you successful. Beta was arguably a better technology than VHS, yet it still lost. Apple's Macintosh had a more intuitive interface than the PC, yet the PC won based on the ecosystem of providers and tools available for it.

To be able to answer the second question, you really need to be able to explain how, by building the system in question, you are raising switching costs, lowering barriers to exit, increasing barriers to entry, and the like. How is it that you are making it harder for your competitors to compete against you? How does this help you to win new clients, keep existing clients, and operate more cost effectively than any of your competitors? What keeps them from copying what you are doing in very short order?

"Not Built Here" Phenomenon

If we seem a little negative in this chapter, it is because we are. We see a lot of value destroyed in a lot of companies from executives and technology teams deciding that they should build something based on incorrect information or biased approaches. We very often find ourselves in discussions on why a company absolutely has to build this or that, when the thing being discussed has absolutely nothing to do with how they make money. We've used the examples of databases and encryption methodologies and we weren't talking about the use of open source databases (we completely support the use of those). In our consulting practice at AKF Partners, we've had clients running commerce sites who built their own databases from the ground up! We've also seen proprietary load balancers, entity and object caches, heavily modified and sometimes nearly entirely proprietary operating systems, and so on. Most often, the argument is "we can build it better and we need something better, so we built it" followed closely by "it was cheaper for us to build it than to buy it."

We call this the "Not Built Here" phenomenon and not only is it dangerous from the perspective of scalability, it is crippling from a shareholder perspective. When applied to very small things that take only a portion of your development capacity, it is just an annoyance. When applied to critical infrastructure, it very often becomes the source of the company's scalability crisis. Too much time is spent managing the proprietary system that provides "incredible shareholder value" and too little making and creating business functionality and working to really scale the platform.

To clarify this point, let's take a well known real-world example like eBay. If eBay had a culture that eschewed the use of third-party or COTS products, it might focus on building critical pieces of its software infrastructure such as application servers. Application servers are a commodity and can typically be acquired and implemented at very little cost. Assuming that eBay spends 6% to 8% of its revenue on building applications critical to the buying and selling experience, a portion of that 6% to 8% will now be spent building and maintaining its proprietary application server. This means that either less new product functionality will be created for that 6% to 8% or it will need to spend more than 6% to 8% in order to both maintain its current product roadmap and build its proprietary application server. Either way, shareholders suffer. eBay, by the way, does not have such a culture and in fact has a very robust build versus buy analysis process to keep just such a problem from happening.

Although the application server scenario might seem a bit ridiculous to you, the scenario happens all the time in our advisory practice. We see customers focused on building proprietary databases, proprietary encryption programs, proprietary application servers, and even proprietary load balancing programs. In almost every case, it's a result of the team feeling it can build something that's better without a focus on whether "better" truly adds any shareholder value. In most cases, in our experience, these approaches destroy shareholder value.

Merging Cost and Strategy

Now that we've presented the two most common approaches to analyzing build versus buy decisions, we'd like to present what we believe to be the most appropriate solution. Cost centric approaches miss the questions of how a potential build decision supports the company's objectives and do not consider the lost opportunity of development associated with applying finite resources to noncompetitive differentiating technologies. Strategy centric approaches fail to completely appreciate the cost of such a decision and as such may end up being dilutive to shareholder value.

The right approach is to merge the two approaches and develop a set of tests that can be applied to nearly any build versus buy decision. We also want to acknowledge a team and a company's natural bias to build and we want to protect against that at all costs. We've developed a very simple, non-time-intensive, four-part test to help decide whether you should build or buy the "thing" you are considering.

Does This Component Create Strategic Competitive Differentiation?

This is one of the most important questions within the build versus buy analysis process. At the heart of this question is the notion of shareholder value. If you are not creating competitive differentiation, thereby making it more difficult for your competition to win deals or steal customers, why would you possibly want to build the object in question? Building something that makes your system "faster" or reduces customer perceived response time by 200 milliseconds may sound like a great argument for building the component in question, but how easy is it for your competitors to get to the same place? Does 200 milliseconds really make a big difference in customer experience?

Are you increasing switching costs for your customers or making it harder for them to leave your product or platform? Are you increasing the switching costs for your suppliers? Are you changing the likelihood that your customers or suppliers will use substitutes rather than you or a competitor? Are you decreasing exit barriers for the competition or making it harder for new competitors to compete against you? Does this create new economies of scale for you? These are but some of the questions you should be able to answer to be comfortable with a build over a buy decision. In answering these questions, or going through a more formal analysis, recognize your natural bias toward believing that you can create competitive differentiation. You should answer "No" more often than "Yes" to this question and stop your analysis in its tracks. There is no reason to incur the lost opportunity associated with dedicating engineers to something that is not going to make you significantly better than your competition.

Are We the Best Owners of This Component or Asset?

Simply stated, do you really have the right team to develop and maintain this? Do you have the support staff to give yourself the support you need when the system breaks? Can you ensure that you are always covered? Very often, a good question to truly test this is "If you are the best owners of this asset, should you consider selling it?" Think long and hard about this follow-up question because many people get the answer wrong or at best half right. It may be enough to be the best, or potentially in the top two or three, but there is rarely a good justification for being "one of the top 10" providers of anything, especially if it is not closely aligned with your core business.

If you answer "No, because it creates differentiation for us and we want to win with our primary product," you are only half right. A fully correct answer would also include "and it won't make us more money than we make with our primary product," or "the value in selling it does not offset the cost of attempting to sell it," or something along those lines.

Here's something else to consider: Given that there can only be one best at any given "thing," how likely is it that your team can be the best at both what you do to make money and the new component you are considering building? If you are a small company, the answer is nearly none. If it was statistically unlikely you are the best at the thing you started on, how can it be more probable that you are the best at both that old thing and this new thing?

If you are an online commerce company, it's entirely possible that you are the best at logistics planning or the best at presenting users what they are most likely to buy. It is not very likely at all that you can be the best at one of those things *and* be the best developer of databases for your internal needs or the best at developing your special firewall or your awesome load balancer. More than likely someone else is doing it better.

What Is the Competition to This Component?

If you have gotten this far in the questionnaire, you already believe that the component you are building creates competitive differentiation and that you are the best owners and developers of the component. Now the question is how much differentiation can you truly create? To answer this, you really need to dig in and find out who is doing what in this space and ensure that you are so sufficiently different from them as to justify using your valuable engineering resources. Recognize that over time most technologies that are sold become commodities, meaning that the feature set converges with very little differentiation from year to year and that buyers purchase mostly on price. How long do you have before a competing builder of this technology, who also specializes in this technology, can offer it to your primary competitors at a lower cost than you need to maintain your proprietary system?

Can We Build This Component Cost Effectively?

And our last question is about cost. We hinted at the cost component within the analysis of the existing competition for our new component, but here we are talking about the full fledged analysis of cost over time. Ensure that you properly identify all of the maintenance costs that you will incur. Remember that you need at least two engineers to maintain anything, even if at least part time, as you need to ensure that someone is around to fix problems when the other person is on vacation. Evaluate your past project delivery schedules and make sure you adjust for the likelihood that you are overly aggressive in your commitments. Are you generally off by 10% or 100%? Factor that into the cost analysis.

Make sure you treat the analysis as you would a profit and loss statement. If you are dedicating engineers to this project, what projects are they not working and what revenue are you deferring as a result, or which scalability projects won't get done and how will that impact your business?

Checklist—Four Simple Questions

Use this simple checklist of four questions to help you in your build versus buy decisions:

- Does this component create strategic competitive differentiation? Are we going to have long-term sustainable differentiation as a result of this in switching costs, barriers to entry, etc.?

- Are we the best owners of this component or asset? Are we the best equipped to build it and why? Should we sell it if we build it?

- What is the competition to this component? How soon until the competition catches up to us and offers similar functionality?

- Can we build this component cost effectively? Are we reducing our cost and creating additional shareholder value and are we avoiding lost opportunity in revenue?

Remember that you are always likely to be biased toward building so do your best to protect against that bias. The odds are against you that you can build a better product than those already available and you should tune your bias toward continuing to do what you do well today—your primary business.

AllScale's Build or Buy Dilemma

AllScale decides to expand its services beyond the HRM platform and begins to build a customer relationship management (CRM) system focused initially at staffing and recruiting companies. After the product has been defined at a business level, a team of engineers, architects, and product managers begin to work on the high-level architecture of the platform that will support the CRM functionality. One piece of functionality within the system will be the capability for companies to extend the system by adding their own functionality. A debate soon begins over whether AllScale should build an interpreter for a proprietary AllScale scripting language that customers would need to learn and use.

The engineers think the project to build such an interpreter would be very exciting and quickly they set about defining why the interpreter should be proprietary rather than using one of the many existing interpreters ranging from Visual Basic to Python or PERL. The engineers all believe that they can make an interpreter specific to the needs of AllScale's needs and as a result the interpreter dubbed ScaleTalk will run faster and more efficiently than any interpreted language they would otherwise implement. Johnny Fixer, CTO, on the other hand, is concerned about the time it would take to develop such an interpreted language and is dubious regarding the potential returns of such a system. Christine E. Oberman, CEO, is always talking about how they should think in terms of shareholder value creation, so Johnny decides to discuss the opportunity with her.

Together, Johnny and Christine walk through the four-part build versus buy checklist. They decide that using a proprietary language increases the switching costs for customers because for a customer to leave AllScale for another provider of CRM technology, AllScale would need to rewrite its ScaleTalk scripts. The barriers to entry are also raised, as other companies adopting readily available interpreters for similar functionality would lack some of the functionality specific to the AllScale product. They agree that there is a strong business case for creating strategic competitive differentiation through an interpreter that customers can use to extend and modify the functionality of the AllScale CRM product.

Johnny and Christine disagree on whether they are the best builders and owners of the asset. Although they agree that it can create shareholder value, Christine doubts that the engineers they have today have the best skills to build such an interpreter. Christine pushes Johnny to experienced help in interpreters should they decide to move forward and build ScaleTalk. Johnny reluctantly agrees to do so.

Christine and Johnny agree that there is little direct competition to ScaleTalk as it is defined. There are lots of substitutes that would offer 60% of the intended functionality, but nothing that would allow them to give customers the flexibility and power of ScaleTalk within the AllScale CRM system. Johnny believes that it could take years for someone else to build an interpreter for their own platforms, but Christine pushes back indicating that it would probably take less time for a competitor to copy AllScale's solution than for AllScale to build it. Her reasoning is that the competitor needn't innovate but rather copy nearly wholesale the features and functionality of AllScale's intended interpreted language. Johnny decides that she has a good point but indicates that AllScale would continue to innovate and give customers additional language functionality over time.

Christine asks Johnny to estimate how long it would take to build the interpreter for ScaleTalk and to determine how much they would save in license fees, support fees, and other costs of the system over the course of five years. Johnny does a back-of-the-envelope calculation indicating that five engineers over seven months should be able to create the interpreter for a net headcount of expense of roughly $300,000.00. He further indicates that the company will need to dedicate one engineer full time for the life of the system to maintain it for an ongoing expense of $80,000.00 per year. He believes the company will save about $60,000.00 per year in license and support fees for a similar product and about $200,000.00 in initial purchase costs. That leaves a $100,000.00 gap in initial development costs and an ongoing deficit of $20,000.00

per year. Johnny believes both of these will be made up in three years by needing fewer systems to support a similar number of transactions and in faster time to market.

Although not a perfect scenario, Christine and Johnny jointly decide that ScaleTalk for the AllScale CRM application is worth pursuing. Christine asks to be kept in the loop regarding development timeframe and issues as she is concerned about cost overruns. Johnny agrees and makes a note to clearly call out ScaleTalk progress in his weekly status meetings and monthly product updates. Christine makes a note to create a slide or two for the upcoming board of directors meetings to discuss the ScaleTalk decision.

Conclusion

Build versus buy decisions have an incredible capability to destroy shareholder value if not approached carefully. Incorrect decisions can steal resources to scale your platform, increase your cost of operations, steal resources away from critical customer facing and revenue producing functionality, and destroy shareholder value. We noted that there is a natural bias toward building over buying and we urged you to guard strongly against that bias.

We presented the two most common approaches, cost centric and strategy centric. We offered a third approach that merges the benefits of both approaches and avoids most of the problems each approach has individually. Finally, we offered a four-part checklist for your build versus buy decisions to help you make the right choice.

Key Points

- Making poor build versus buy choices can destroy your capability to scale cost effectively and can destroy shareholder value.

- Cost centric approaches to build versus buy focus on reducing overall cost but suffer from a lack of focus on lost opportunity and strategic alignment of the component being built.

- Strategy centric approaches to build versus buy focus on aligning the decision with the long-term needs of the corporation but do not account for total cost.

- Merging the two approaches results in a four-part test that has the advantages of both approaches but eliminates the disadvantages.

- To reach a "buy" decision, you should be able to answer the following:

  ○ Does this component create strategic competitive differentiation?

  ○ Are we the best owners of this asset?

  ○ What is the competition to the component?

  ○ Can we build the component cost effectively?

Chapter 16

Determining Risk

Hence in the wise leader's plans, considerations of advantage and disadvantage will be blended together.

—Sun Tzu

In the previous 15 chapters, we have often mentioned risk management or suggested that you analyze the amount of risk, but we have not given you a detailed explanation of what we mean by these phrases and terminology. This chapter is going to be all about how to determine the amount of risk in a feature, release, bug fix, configuration change, or other technology related action. Managing risk is one of the most fundamentally important aspects of increasing and maintaining availability and scalability. To manage risk, you first must know how to calculate risk and determine how much risk exists in some action or lack of action.

In this chapter, we will first discuss why risk plays such a large part in scalability. This discussion will build upon all the other times so far in the book that we have mentioned risk management and its importance. After we have clearly articulated the importance of risk management, we will discuss how to measure the amount of risk and finally how to manage the overall risk in a system. Here, the use of system means not only the application, but the entire product development life cycle, technology organization, and all the processes that make these up. There are many different ways of calculating the amount of risk, and we will cover some of the best ones that we have seen, including the pros and cons of each method.

At the end of this chapter, you will have a much better grasp of risk and understand how to determine the amount of risk involved in something, as well as how to manage the overall level of risk that the business is willing to take. These are fundamental skills that need to exist in the organization at almost every level to ensure that the scalability of the system is not impaired by improper decisions and behaviors.

Importance of Risk Management to Scale

Why is the ability to manage risk so important to scalability? The answer to this question lies in the fact that business is inherently a risky endeavor. For example, the risk that customers will not want products that you offer, that the tradeoffs made between speed and quality don't exceed the threshold for customers, that skipped steps for cost savings don't result in catastrophic failure, the risk that the business model will ever work, and so on and so on. To be in business, at least for any amount of time, you must be able to identify and balance the risks with the rewards. It is risky to demo for a potential huge customer your newest untested product, but if it works that customer might sign up; is that a risk worth taking? The capability to balance risk and reward are essential to survive as a business, especially a startup. This balance of risk and reward is exactly what entrepreneurs do every day and what technologists in companies must do. Pushing the new release has inherent risks, but it should also have expected rewards. Knowing how to determine the amount of risk that exists allows you to solve this risk–reward equation and make the right decisions about when to take the risk in turn for rewards.

If risk is an inherent part of any business, especially a hyper-growth SaaS Web 2.0 company, are the successful companies necessarily great at managing risk? The answer is probably not, but they probably have either someone who innately manages risk or they have been extremely lucky so far and will likely run out of luck at some point. There are certain people who can naturally feel and manage risk; we'll talk more about this in the section of this chapter about ways to measure risk. These people may have developed this skill from years of working around technology and having an acute sense of when things are likely to go wrong. They also might just have an inborn ability to sense risk. It's great if you have someone like this, but even in that case you want the rest of the organization to be able to identify risk and not have to rely on a single individual as the human risk meter. Remember that singletons, especially if that singleton is a person, do not scale well. If you are one of the lucky organizations who have been successful without any focus or understanding of risk, you should be even more worried. You could argue that risk demonstrates a Markov property, meaning that the future states are determined by the present state and are independent of past states. We would argue that risk is cumulative to some degree, perhaps with an exponential decay but still additive. A risky event today can result in failures in the future, either because of direct correlation such as today's change breaks something else in the future, or via indirect methods such as an increased risk tolerance by the organization leading to riskier behaviors in the future. Either way, actions can have near- and long-term consequences.

Because risk management is important to scalability, we need to understand the components and steps of the risk management process. We'll cover this in more detail in this chapter but a high-level overview of the risk management process entails first and foremost as accurately as possible determining the risk of a particular action. There are many ways to go about trying to accurately determine risk, some more involved than others and some often more accurate than others. The important thing is to select the right process for your organization, which means balancing the rigor and required accuracy to what makes sense for your organization. After the amount of risk has been determined or estimated, you must actively manage the amount of risk both acutely and overall within the system. *Acute risk* is the amount of risk associated with a particular action, such as changing a configuration on a server. *Overall risk* is the amount that is cumulative within the system because of all the actions that have taken place over the previous days, weeks, or possibly even months.

Measuring Risk

The first step in being able to manage risk is the ability to as accurately as *necessary* determine what amount of risk is involved in a particular action. The reason we use the term *necessary* and not *possible* is that you may be able to more accurately determine risk, but it might not be necessary given the current state of your product or your organization. For example, a product in beta, where customers are expecting some glitches, may dictate that a sophisticated risk assessment is not necessary and that a cursory analysis is sufficient at this point. There are many different ways to analyze, assess, or estimate risk. The more of these that are in your tool belt, the more likely you will use the most appropriate one for the appropriate time and activity. We are going to cover three methods of determining risk. With each of these, we will discuss the advantages and disadvantages as well as the accuracy.

The first assessment method is the *gut feel* method. This is when someone either because of his position, VP of operations, or because of his innate ability to *feel* risk, is given the job of making go/no-go decisions on actions. As we mentioned earlier, some people inherently have this ability and it is great to have someone like this in the organization. However, we would caution you on two very important concerns. First, does this person really have the ability to understand risk at a subconscious level or do you just wish he did? In other words, have you tracked this person's accuracy? If you haven't, you should before you consider this as anything more than a method of guessing. Secondly, if indeed this person has some degree of accuracy with regard to determining risk, you do not want your organization to be dependent on one person. You need multiple people in your organization to understand how to assess risk. Ideally, everyone in the organization is familiar with the significance of risk and the methodologies that exist for assessing and managing it.

As an example of the gut feel method, let us say that the VP of operations, Tom Harde, for our fictitious company AllScale is revered for his ability to make on-the-spot decisions about problems and go/no-go decisions. As far as anyone can remember, his decisions have never been questioned and have always been correct, at least that is what the team recalls. The team has just finished preparing a release to go to production for the HRM application and has asked Tom for permission to push the code this evening. This Wednesday evening between 10 PM and midnight has in the past been designated as a maintenance window; not for down time, but because of the low traffic, it is a suitable time to perform the higher risk actions. Tonight, there is a database split taking place during this window that has already been planned and approved. Tom decides, without explanation to the engineering team, that they cannot push code tonight and should expect to be allowed to push it the next night. The team accepts this decision because even though they are engineers and skeptical by nature, no one has ever questioned a go/no-go decision from Tom. Later that night, the database split goes disastrously wrong and the team is forced to work late into the morning rolling back the changes. The engineering team hears about this in the morning and is very glad for the no-go decision last night.

The advantages of the gut feel method of risk assessment is that it is very fast. A true expert who fundamentally understands the amount of risk inherent in certain tasks can make decisions in a matter of a few seconds. The disadvantages of the gut feel method are, as we discussed, the person might not have this ability but may be fooled into thinking he does because of a few key saves. The other disadvantage is that this method is rarely replicable. People tend to develop this ability over years of working in the industry and honing their expertise, not something that can be taught in an hour-long class. Another disadvantage of this method is that it leaves a lot of decision making up to the whim of one person as opposed to a team or group that can question each others' data and conclusions. The accuracy of this method is highly variable depending on the person, the action, and a host of other variables. This week a person might be very good at assessing the risk and next week strike out completely.

The second method that we are going to cover is the *traffic light* method. In this method, you determine the risk of an action by breaking down the action into the smallest components and assigning a risk level to them of green, yellow, or red. The smallest component could be a feature in a release or a configuration change in a list of maintenance steps, the granularity depends on several factors including the time available and the amount of practice the team has in performing these assessments. After each component has been assigned a color of risk, there are two ways of arriving at the overall risk of the action. The first method is to assign a risk value to each color, count the number of each color, and multiply the count by the risk value. Then, sum these multiplied values and divide by the total count of items or actions. Whatever risk value this is closest to gets assigned the overall color. Figure 16.1 depicts the risk rating of three features that provides a cumulative risk of the overall release.

The assessment of risk for the individual items in the action, release, or maintenance is done by someone very familiar with the low-level component and they

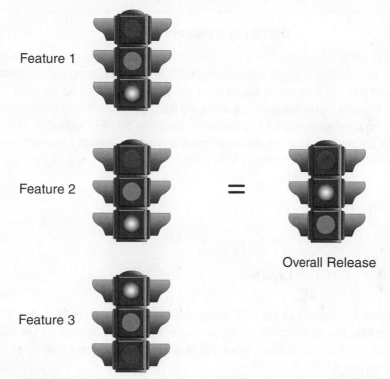

Feature 1

Feature 2 = Overall Release

Feature 3

Figure 16.1 *Traffic Light Method of Risk Assessment*

decide on green, yellow, or red by analyzing various factor such as the difficulty of the task, the amount of effort required for the task (the more effort generally the higher the risk), the interaction of this component with others (the more connected or centralized this item is the higher the risk), and so on. Table 16.1 shows some of the most common attributes and their associated risk factors that can be used by engineers or other experts to gauge the risk of a particular feature or granular item in the overall list.

Table 16.1 *Risk-Attribute Correlation*

Attribute	Risk
Effort	Low = Green; High = Red
Difficulty	Low = Green; High = Red
Complexity	Low = Green; High = Red
Connectivity to other components	Low = Green; High = Red
Likelihood of errors	Low = Green; High = Red
Ability to detect issues	High = Green; Low = Red

Traffic Light Release Example

Mike Softe, VP of engineering at AllScale, has adopted the traffic light method of risk assessment. He has decided to assign numeric equivalents to the colors, assigning 1 to green, 3 to yellow, and 9 to red. Mike knows that he could use any arbitrary scale but he prefer this one because it causes higher risk items to dramatically stand out, which is very conservative. Mike is producing a risk assessment for an upcoming release for the HRM application. He has four items that are green, two that are yellow, and one that is red; the math for calculating the overall risk number/color is depicted in Figure 16.2.

$$4 \times 1 + 2 \times 3 + 1 = 19$$

$$\frac{19}{(4 + 2 + 1)} = 2.7$$

Figure 16.2   *Traffic Light Equation*

Therefore, our total risk for the HRM release is 2.7, which is closest to 3 or yellow. We'll discuss what Mike should do with this number or color in the next section when we talk about how to manage risk. For now, we are satisfied that Mike has performed some level of risk assessment on the action.

One large advantage of the traffic light method is that it begins to become methodical, which implies that it is repeatable, able to be documented, and able to be trained. Many people can conduct the risk assessment so you are no longer dependent on a single individual. Again, because many people can perform the assessment, there can be discussion about the decisions that people arrive at and as a group they can decide whether someone's argument has merit. The disadvantages of this method is that it does take more time than the gut feel method and it is an extra step in the process. Another disadvantage is that it relies on each expert to choose which attributes she will use to assess the risk of individual components. Because of this possible variance among the experts, the accuracy of this risk assessment is mediocre. If the experts are very knowledgeable and have a clear understanding of what constitutes risky attributes for their particular area, this method can be fairly accurate. If they do not have a clear understanding about what attributes are important to look at when performing the assessment, the risk level may be off quite a bit. We will see in the next risk assessment methodology how this potential variance is fixed allowing the assessments to be more accurate.

The third method of assessing the amount of risk in a particular action is known as the Failure Mode and Effects Analysis (FMEA). This methodology was originally developed for use by the military in the late 1940s.[1] Since then, it has been used in a multitude of industries including automotive, manufacturing, aerospace, and software development. The method of performing the assessment is similar to the traffic light method in that components are broken up into the smallest parts that can be assessed for risk; for a release, this could be features, tasks, or modules. Each of these components is then identified with one or more possible failure modes. Each failure mode has an effect that describes the impact if this particular failure occurred.

For example, a signup feature may fail by not storing the new user's information properly in the database or by assigning the wrong set of privileges to the new user or a variety of other failure scenarios. The effect would be the user not being registered or having the ability to see data she was not authorized to see. These failure scenarios are scored on three factors: likelihood of failure, severity of that failure, and the ability to detect if that failure occurs. Again, we choose to use a scoring scale of 1, 3, and 9 because it allows us to be very conservative and differentiate items with high risk factors well above those with medium or low risks. The *likelihood* of failure is essentially the probability of this particular failure scenario coming true. The *severity* of the failure is the total impact to the customer and the business if this occurs. This can be in monetary terms or in reputation (good will) or any other business related measurement. The *ability to detect the failure* is rating whether you will be likely to notice the failure if it occurs. As you can imagine, a very likely failure that has disastrous consequences that is practically undetectable is the worst possible of all three.

After the individual failure modes and effects have been scored, the scores are multiplied to provide a Total Risk Score that is equal to the Likelihood Score × Severity Score × Ability to Detect Score. This score shows the overall risk that a particular component has within the overall action. The next step in the FMEA process is to determine mitigation steps that you can perform or put in place that will lower the risk of a particular factor. For instance, if a component of a feature had a very high ability to detect score, meaning that it would be hard to notice if the event occurred, the team might decide ahead of time to write some queries to check the database every hour post-release for signs of this failure, such as missing data or wrong data. This mitigation step has a lowering effect on this risk factor of the component and should then indicate what the risk was lowered to.

In Table 16.2, there are two features that the AllScale team is planning on releasing as part of its HRM application. One is a new signup flow for its customers and the other is changing to a new credit card processor. Each of the features has several

---

1. Procedure for performing a failure mode effect and criticality analysis. November 9, 1949. United States Military Procedure, MIL-P-1629.

failure modes identified. Walking through one as an example, let's look at the Credit Card Payment feature and focus on the Credit Card billed incorrectly failure mode with the effect of either a payment too large or too small being charged to the card. The engineering expert, Sam Codur, has ranked this as very unlikely to occur, probably because Mike Softe, VP of engineering at AllScale, has ensured that this feature received extensive code review and quality assurance testing due to the fact that it was dealing with credit cards. The engineer, Sam, gave the failure mode a 1 for likelihood. Sam also scored this failure mode as having disastrous severity, giving it a 9. This seems reasonable because a wrongly billed credit card would result in customers being very upset, charge backs, which cost money, and probably refunds, which cost more money. Should this failure occur, Sam feels that it will be somewhat hard to detect but not impossible so he gave it a score of 3. The Total Risk score for this failure mode is 27, arrived at by multiplying 1×3×9. Sam also identified the fact that if this new payment processor were rolled out in beta for a limited customer set, the severity would be much lower because only a few select customers would be impacted and if anything went wrong the overall monetary and publicity amounts would be limited. If this remediation action is taken, the risk would be lowered to a 3 for severity and the Revised Risk Score would be only a 9, much better than before.

The advantage of the FMEA as a risk assessment process is that it is very methodical, which allows it to be documented, trained, evaluated, and modified. Another advantage is the accuracy. Especially over time as your team becomes better at identifying failure scenarios and accurately assessing the risk, this will become the most accurate way for you to determine risk. The disadvantage of the FMEA method is that it takes time and thought. The more time and effort put into this yields better and more accurate results. This method is very similar to test-driven development. Failure modes can often be determined up front from the specification, and the more identified the better understanding you will have of the feature and how it should be designed to minimize the risk of these failures.

As we will discuss in the next section, these scores, especially ones from a FMEA can be used to manage the amount of risk in a system across any time interval or in any one release/action. The next step in the risk assessment is to have someone or a team of people review the assessment for accuracy and to question any decision. This is the great part about using a methodical approach such as the FMEA: Everyone can be trained on and thus can police each other to ensure the highest quality assessment is performed. The last step in the assessment process is to revisit the assessment after the action has taken place to see how accurate you and the experts were in determining the right failure modes and in assessing their factors. If a problem arose that was not identified as possible, have that expert review the situation in detail and provide a reason this was not identified ahead of time and a warning to other experts to watch out for this type of failure.

Table 16.2 *Failure Mode and Effect Analysis Example*

Feature	Failure Mode	Effect	Likelihood of Failure Occurring (1 = Low, 3 = Medium, 9 = High)	Severity if Failure Occurs (1 = Minimal, 3 = Significant, 9 = Extreme)	Ability to Detect Should Failure Occur (1 = Easy, 3 = Medium, 9 = Difficult)	Total Risk Score	Remediation Actions	Revised Risk Score
Sign Up	User data not inserted into the database properly	Users not registered	3	3	3	27	• Test all registration paths (reduce likelihood score to 1) • Write queries to use post-launch for data validation (reduce detection to 1)	3
	Users given the wrong set of privileges	Users have access to other users' information	1	9	3	27	• Write a query to run every hour post-launch to check for new registrants with unusual privileges (reduce detection score to 1)	9
	Users not sent passwords	Users unable to login	3	1	1	3	N/A	3
Credit Card	Credit card billed incorrectly	Charges to credit cards are too much or too little	1	9	3	27	• Roll credit card feature out in beta for limited customers (reduce severity score to 3)	9
	Authorization number not stored	Unable to recharge credit card without reentering number	1	1	1	1	N/A	1
	Credit card numbers not encrypted	Allows possibility of someone grabbing credit card numbers	1	9	1	9	N/A	9

Risk Assessment Steps

If you are planning on using any methodical approach to risk assessment, these are the steps for a proper risk assessment. These steps are appropriate for the traffic light method or the FMEA method that were discussed:

1. Determine the proper level of granularity to assess the risk.

2. Choose a method that you can reproduce.

3. Train the individuals who will be performing the risk assessment.

4. Have someone review each assessment or a team can review the entire assessment.

5. Choose an appropriate scoring scale (1, 3, 9) that takes into account how conservative you need to be.

6. Review the risk assessments after the action, release, or maintenance has occurred to determine how good the risk assessment was at identifying the types of failures as well as how likely, severe, and detectable they were.

Whether you are using the traffic light method, the FMEA, or another risk assessment methodology, be sure to follow these steps to ensure a successful risk assessment that can be used in the overall management of risk.

Managing Risk

As we discussed earlier in this chapter we fundamentally believe that risk is cumulative. As you take more risky actions or pile on risky changes, there will come a point where the risk is realized and there will be problems in the system. In our practice at AKF Partners, we teach our clients to manage both acute and overall risk in a system. The acute risk is how much risk exists from a single change or combination of changes in a release. The overall level of risk comes from the accumulation of risk over hours, days, or weeks of performing risky actions on the system. Either type of risk, acute or overall, can result in a crisis scenario in the system. We will discuss how to manage both these types of risk to ensure you are making good decisions about what should and what should not be allowed to change within your system at any given point in time.

Acute risk is managed by monitoring the risk assessments performed on proposed changes to the system such as releases. You may want to establish ahead of time some limits to the amount of risk that any one concurrent action can have or that you are willing to allow at a particular time of day or customer volume. For instance, you may decide that any single action that contains a risk above 50 points, as calculated through the FMEA methodology, must be remediated below this amount or split into two separate actions. Or, you may want only actions below 25 points taking place on the system before midnight, everything higher must occur after midnight. Even though this is a discussion about the acute risk of a single action, this too is cumulative in that the more risky items contained in a risk, the higher the likelihood of a problem and the more difficult the detection or determination of the cause because so many things changed.

As a thought experiment, imagine a release with one feature that has two failure modes identified compared to a release with 50 features, each with two or more failure modes. Firstly it is way more likely for a problem to occur because of the number of opportunities. As an analog consider flipping 50 pennies at the same time. While each coin is an independent probability of landing on heads, you are more likely to have at least one head in the total results. Secondly, with 50 features, the likelihood of changes affecting each other or touching the same component, class, or method in an unexpected way is higher. Therefore, both from a cumulative opportunity as well as from a cumulative probability of negative interactions, there is an increased likelihood of a problem occurring. If a problem arises after these releases, it is also a lot easier to determine the cause of the problem when the release contains one feature than when it contains 50, assuming that all the features are somewhat proportional in complexity and size.

For managing acute risk, we recommend that you determine a chart such as the one in Table 16.3 that outlines all the rules and associated risk levels that are acceptable. This way, it is clear cut. You should also decide on an exceptions policy such as anything outside of these rules must be approved by the VP of engineering *and* the VP of operations *or* the CTO alone.

For managing the overall risk amount, there are two factors that can cause issues. The first is the cumulative amount of changes that have taken place in the system and the corresponding increase in the amount of risk associated with each of these changes. Just as we discussed in the earlier section on acute risks, combinations of

Table 16.3 *Acute Risk Management Rules*

Rules	Risk Level
New feature release	< 150 pts
Bug fix release	< 50 pts
6 AM – 10 PM	< 25 pts
10 PM – 6 AM	< 200 pts
Maintenance patches	< 25 pts
Configuration changes	< 50 pts

actions can have unwanted interactions as well. The more releases or database splits or configuration changes that are made, the more likely one will cause a problem or the interaction of them will cause a problem. If the development team has been working in a development environment with a single database and two days before the release the database is split into a master and read host, it's pretty likely that the next release is going to have a problem unless there has been a ton of coordination and remediation work done.

The second factor that should be considered in the overall risk analysis is the human factor. As people perform riskier and riskier activities, their level of risk tolerance goes up. This human conditioning can work for us very well when we need to become adapted to a new environment, but when it comes to controlling risk in a system, this can lead us astray. If a sabre-toothed tiger has moved into the neighborhood and you still have to leave your cave each day to hunt, the ability to adapt to the new risk in your life is critical to your survival. Otherwise, you might stay in your cave all day and starve. Pushing more and more changes to your production environment because you haven't been burnt yet and you feel somewhat invincible is a good way to cause serious issues.

We recommend that to manage the overall amount of risk in a system, you adopt a set of rules such as in Table 16.4, which lays out the amount of risk, as determined by at FMEA, for specific time periods. If you are using a different methodology than FMEA, you need to adjust the risk level column with some scale that makes sense, such as instead of < 150 pts you could use < 5 green or 3 yellow actions. Like the acute risk management process, you will need to account for objections and overrides. You should plan ahead and have an escalation process established. An idea would be that a director can grant an extra 50 points to any risk level, a VP can grant 100 points, and the CTO can grant 250 points, but not cumulative. Any way you decide to set this up, it matters most that it makes sense for your organization and that it is documented and adhered to strictly.

Table 16.4 *Overall Risk Management Rules*

Rules	Risk Level
6-hour period	< 150 pts
12-hour period	< 250 pts
24-hour period	< 350 pts
72-hour period	< 500 pts
7-day period	< 750 pts
14-day period	< 1200 pts

Conclusion

In this chapter, we have focused on risk. Our discussions started with the purpose of risk management and how that related to scalability. We concluded that risk is prevalent in all businesses, especially startups. To be successful, you have to take risks in the business world. In the Web 2.0 and SaaS world, scalability is part of this risk/reward structure. You must take risks in terms of your system's scalability or else you will overbuild your system and not deliver products that will make the business successful. By actively managing your risk, you will increase the availability and scalability of your system.

Our next discussion in this chapter was focused on how to assess risk. Although there are many different approaches used for this, we offered three different ones. The first was the gut feeling, which we abdicated that some are naturally gifted at but many others are credited for but actually lack the ability and are simply mislabeled.

The second method was the traffic light, which assessed components as low risk (green), medium risk (yellow), or high risk (red). The combination of all components in an action, release, change, or maintenance was the overall risk level. We provided some examples of how this overall number could be calculated.

The third and our recommended approach is the Failure Mode and Effect Analysis methodology. In this method, experts are asked to assess the risk of components by identifying the failure modes that are possible with each component or feature and the impending effect that this failure would cause. An example given was a credit card payment feature that could fail by charging a wrong amount to the credit card, the effect being a charge that was too large or too small to the customer. These failure modes and effects were scored by their likelihood of occurrence, the severity if they were to occur, and the ability to detect if it did occur. These were multiplied for a total risk score. The experts would then recommend remediation steps that would reduce the risk of one or more of the factors and thus reduce the overall risk score.

After the risk assessment was completed, the management of risk needed to begin. We broke this up into the management of acute risk and the management of overall risk. The acute risk dealt with single actions, releases, maintenances, and so on, whereas the overall risk dealt with all changes over periods of time such as hours, days, or weeks. For both acute and overall, we recommended the adoption of rules that specified predetermined amounts of risk that would be tolerated for each action or time period. Additionally, in preparation for objections, we recommended an escalation path be established ahead of time so that the first crisis does not create its own path without thought and proper input from all parties.

As with most processes, the most important aspect of both the risk assessment and the risk management is the fit within your organization at this particular time. As your organization grows and matures, there may be a need to modify or augment these processes. For risk management to be effective, it must be used, and in order for it to be used, it needs to be a good fit for your team.

Key Points

- Business is inherently risky; the changes that we make to improve scalability of our systems can be risky as well.

- Managing the amount of risk in a system is key to availability and ensuring the system can scale.

- Risk is cumulative with some degree of degradation over time.

- For best results, use a method of risk assessment that is repeatable and measureable.

- Risk assessments like other processes can be improved over time.

- There are advantages and disadvantages to various risk assessment approaches.

- There is a great deal of difference in the accuracy of various risk assessment approaches.

- Risk management can be viewed as both acute and overall.

- Acute risk management deals with single instances of change such as a release or a maintenance procedure.

- Overall risk management is about watching and administering the total level of risk in the system at any point in time.

- For the risk management process to be effective, it must be used and followed.

- The best way to ensure a process is adhered to is to make sure it is a good fit for the organization.

Chapter 17

Performance and Stress Testing

> If you know neither the enemy nor yourself, you will succumb in every battle.
>
> —Sun Tzu

After peripherally mentioning performance and stress testing in previous chapters, we now turn our attention to these tests and discuss how they differ in purpose and output and how they impact scalability. Your organization may currently be using neither, one, or both of these tests. Either way, this chapter should give you some fresh perspectives on the purpose and viability of testing that you can use to either revamp or initiate a testing process in your organization.

An important thing to remember up front is that no matter how good your testing is, including performance and stress testing, nothing will replace good design and proper development in terms of a quality and scalable product. Just as you cannot test quality into a product, you cannot load test scalability into one either. You need to establish very early in the product development life cycle that there will be a focus on scalability and quality from the start. This doesn't mean that you should skip performance testing any more than you should skip quality testing; they are both essential, but they are verification and validation steps that ensure the proper work was done up front. You should not expect to build the required quality or scalability in at the end of the life cycle.

Performing Performance Testing

Performance testing, by definition, according to Wikipedia, covers a broad range of engineering evaluations, where the emphasis is on the final measurable performance characteristics instead of the actual material or product.[1] With respect to computer

---

1. This definition is from Wikipedia: http://en.wikipedia.org/wiki/Performance_testing.

science, performance testing is focused on determining the speed, throughput, or effectiveness of a device or piece of software. Performance testing is often called load testing and to us the terms are interchangeable. Some professionals will argue that performance testing and load testing have different goals but similar techniques. To avoid a pedantic argument, we will use a broader goal for defining performance testing in order that it incorporates both.

By our definition, the goal of performance testing is to identify, document, and, where possible, eliminate bottlenecks in the system. This is done through a strict controlled process of measurement and analysis. Load testing is utilized as a method in this process.

Handling the Load with Load Testing

Load testing is the process of putting load or user demand on a system to measure its response and stability, the purpose of which is to verify that the application can meet the desired performance objectives often specified as a service level agreement (SLA). A load test measures such things as response time, throughput, and resource utilization. It is not intended to identify the system's breaking point unless this point occurs below the peak load condition that is expected by the specifications, requirements, or normal operating conditions. If that should occur, you have a serious issue that must be addressed prior to release.

Example load tests include

- Test a mail server with the load of the expected number of users' email accounts.

- Test the same mail server with the expected load of email messages.

- Test a SaaS application by sending many and varied simulated user requests to the application over an extended period of time—the more like production traffic the better.

- Test a load balanced pair of app servers with a scaled down load of user traffic.

Criteria

Before we can begin our performance testing to identify bottlenecks, we must first clearly identify the specifications of the system. This is the first step in performance testing, establishing the success criteria. For Web 2.0 and SaaS systems, this is often based on the concurrent usage and response time metrics. Unless this is the very time conducting performance testing, these specifications will have already been established. The first time you conducted performance testing, hopefully prior to the first release, you should have increased the load until the application either stopped responding or responded in an unpredictable manner—at which point, you would have established a benchmark for the performance of the application.

There are other ways that you can establish these benchmarks or requirements, such as having specifications detailed ahead of time for the particular project. This is often the case when developing a replacement system or doing a complete redesign. The old system may have handled a certain number of concurrent users and in order to not have to purchase more hardware, the project has a major requirement of maintaining or improving this metric. Other times, the business is growing beyond the current system and a decision is made to completely redesign the system from the ground up. In this case, the usage and response time requirements generally go way up based on the amount of investment necessary to completely redevelop the system.

Environment

After you have these benchmarks, the second step is to establish your environment. The environment encapsulates the network, servers, operating system, and third-party software that the application is running on. It is typical to have separate environments for development, quality assurance testing, performance testing, staging, and production. The environment is important because you need a stable, consistent environment to conduct the test repeatedly over some extended duration. There are a wide variety of tests that we will discuss in the next step of defining the test; for now, know that there can be many tests to test the breadth of components. Additionally, some of these tests need to be run over certain time periods, such as 24 hours, to produce the load expected for batch routines. The other reason that the environment is important is that for the tests results to be accurate and meaningful, the environment must mirror production as much as possible.

The reason it is important that the performance testing environment mimic production as much as possible is because environmental settings, configurations, different hardware, different firewall rules, and much more can all dramatically affect test results. Even different patch versions of the operating system, which seems trivial, can have dramatically different performance characteristics for applications. This does not mean that you need a full copy of your production environment; although that would be nice, few companies can afford such a luxury. Instead, make wise tradeoffs but stick to the same basic architecture and implementation as possible. For example, pools of servers that in production have 40 servers in them can be scaled down in a test environment to only two or three servers. Databases are often very difficult to scale down because the amount of data affects the query performance. In some cases, you can "trick" the database into believing it has the same amount of data as the production database in order to ensure the queries execute with the same query plans. Spend some time deciding on a performance testing environment and discuss the tradeoffs that you are making. Balance the cost with the effectiveness and you will be able to make the best decisions in terms of what the environment should look like and how accurate the results will be.

Define Tests

The third step in performance planning is to define the tests. As mentioned earlier, there are a multitude of tests that can be performed on all the various services and features. If you try to run all of them, you may never release any products. The key is to use the Pareto Distribution or Rule of 80/20. Find the 20% of the tests that will provide you with 80% of the information. System's tests almost always follow some similar distribution when it comes to the amount or value of information provided. This is because the features are not all used equally, and some are more critical than others. A feature handling user payments is more important than one handling a user's search for friends, and thus can be tested more vigorously.

Vilfredo Pareto

Vilfredo Federico Damaso Pareto was an Italian economist who lived from 1848 to 1923 and was responsible for contributing several important advances to economics. One of the most notable insights that almost everyone has heard of today is the Pareto Distribution. Fascinated by power and wealth distribution in societies, he studied the property ownership in Italy and observed in his 1909 publication that 20% of the population owned 80% of the land, thus giving rise to his Pareto Distribution.

Technically, the Pareto Distribution is a power law of probability distribution, meaning that it has a special relationship between the frequency of an observed event and the size of the event. Another power law is Kleiber's Law of metabolism, which states that the metabolic rate of an animal scales to the 3/4 power of the mass. As an example, a horse that is 50 times larger than a rabbit will have a metabolism 18.8 times greater than the rabbit.

There are lots of other rules of thumb that you can use, but the Pareto Distribution is very useful, when it applies, for getting the majority of a result without the majority of the effort. The caution of course is to make sure the probability distribution applies before using it. If you have a scenario where the information is one for one with the action, you cannot get 80% of it by only performing 20% of the action; you will have to perform the percentage work that you need to achieve the equivalent percentage information.

When you do define the tests, be sure to include tests of various types. Some types or categories of tests include endurance, load, most used, most visible, and component (app, network, database, cache, and storage). The endurance test is used to ensure that a standard load experienced over a prolonged period of time does not have any adverse effects due to such problems as memory leaks, data storage, log file creation, or batch jobs. A normal user load with as realistic traffic patterns and activities as possible is used here. It is often difficult to come up with actual or close to actual user traffic. A minimum substitute for this is a series of actions such as a sign up process followed by a picture upload, a search for friends, and a log out, written into a script that can be executed over and over. More of an ideal scenario is to gather actual users' traffic from a network device or app server and replay these in the exact same order varying the time period. At first, you can run the test over the same time period that the users generated the traffic, and then you can increase the speed and ensure the application performs as expected with the increased throughput.

Execute Tests

The load test is essentially putting a user load on the system up to the expected or required level to ensure the application is stable and responsive according to internal or external service level agreements. A most used test scenario is testing the most common path that users take through the application. In contrast, a most visible test scenario is testing the part of the application that is seen the most such as the home page or a new landing page. The component test category is a broad set of tests that are designed to test individual components in the system. One such test might be to exercise a particularly long running query on the database to ensure it can handle the prescribed amount of traffic. Similarly, traffic requests through a load balancer or firewall are other component tests that you might consider.

After you have finalized your test plan based on the size of the system, the relative value of the information that you will gain from each test, the amount of time that you have available, and the amount of risk that the organization is willing to accept, you are ready to move on to step four, which is to actually execute the tests. In this step, you work through the test plan executing the tests methodically in the environment established for this testing and begin recording various measurements such as transaction times, response times, outputs, and behavior. All available data is gathered; data is your friend in performance testing, and you really can't have too much. It is important to keep this data from release to release. As we will talk about in the next step, comparison between various releases is critical to understanding the data and determining if the data indicates normal operating ranges or if there could be a problem.

Analyze Data

Step five in the performance testing process is to analyze the data gathered. This analysis can be done in a variety of manners depending on such things as the expertise of the analyst, the expectations of thoroughness, the acceptable risk level, and the time allotted. Perhaps the simplest analysis is a comparison of this candidate release with past releases. A query that can only execute 25 times per second without increased response time compared to last release when it could execute 50 times per second with no noticeable degradation in performance indicates a potential problem. The fun begins in the next step trying to figure out why this change has occurred. Although decreases in capacity of throughput or increases in response time are clearly things that should be noted for further investigation, the opposite is true as well. A sudden dramatic increase in capacity might indicate that a particular code path has been dropped or SQL conditionals have been lost and should be noted as well for explanation. We hope that in these scenarios an engineer has refactored and improved the performance, but it is best to note this and ask the questions.

A more detailed analysis involves graphing the data for visual reference. Sometimes, it is much easier when data is graphed on line, bar, or pie charts to recognize anomalies or differences. Although these may or may not be truly significant, they are generally quick ways of making judgments about the release candidate. A further detailed analysis involves performing statistical analysis on the data. There is a multitude of statistical tests that can be used, such as control charts, t-tests, factor analysis, main effects plot, analysis of variance, and interaction plots. The general purpose of conducting any of this analysis is to determine what factors are causing the observed behavior, is it statistically significantly different from other releases, and will it meet the service level agreements that are in place.

Report to Engineers

The sixth step in the performance testing process is to report the results to the engineering team responsible for the release. This is generally done in an informal manner and can be done either at one time with all parties present or in smaller teams. The goal of the meeting is to have each item that gets raised as a possible anomaly handled in one of three ways. The first case would be that the anomaly gets explained away by the engineer. In this case, the engineer must make a good enough argument for why the results of the test are different than expected to make the tester as well as the engineering leadership feel comfortable passing this test without investigating further. The second case is for a bug to be filed against the engineer in order that he investigate the issue further and either fix it or explain it. The third option is for the engineering team to ask for additional tests with the expectation that more data will help narrow down the actual problem.

Repeat Tests and Analysis

The last step in the performance process is to repeat the testing and reanalyze the data. This can either be because a fix was provided for a bug that was logged in step six or because there is additional time, and the code base is likely always changing due to functional bug fixes. If there are time and resources available, these tests should definitely be repeated to ensure the results have not changed dramatically from one build to another for the candidate release and to continue probing for potential anomalies.

Summary of Performance Testing Steps

When conducting performance testing, the following steps are the critical steps to completing it properly. You can add steps as necessary to fit your organization's needs, but these are the ones you must have to ensure you achieve the results that you expect.

1. *Criteria.* Establish what criteria are expected from the application, component, device, or system that is being tested.

2. *Environment.* Make sure your testing environment is as close to production as possible to ensure that your test results are accurate.

3. *Define tests.* There are many different categories of tests that you should consider for inclusion in the performance test. These include endurance, load, most used, most visible, and component.

4. *Execute tests.* This step is where the tests are actually being executed in the environment established in Step 2.

5. *Analyze data.* Analyzing the data can take many forms—some as simple as comparing to previous releases, others include stochastic models.

6. *Report to engineers.* Provide the analysis to the engineers and facilitate a discussion about the relevant points.

7. *Repeat tests & analysis.* As necessary to validate bug fixes or as time and resources permit, continue testing and analyzing the data.

Follow these seven steps and any others that you need to add for your specific situations and organization. The key to a successful process is making it fit the organization.

Performance testing covers a broad range of testing evaluations, but they share the focus on the necessary characteristics of the system rather than the individual materials, hardware, or code. Staying focused on ensuring the software meets or exceeds the specified requirements or service level agreements is what performance testing is all about. We covered the seven steps of a successful performance testing process and identified that the key to this, as with all processes, is a good fit within the organization. Additional important aspects of performance testing include a methodical approach from the very beginning of establishing the benchmarks and success criteria to the very end of repeating the tests as often as possible for validation purposes. Because there are always necessary tradeoffs between testing, time, and monetary investments, a methodical, scientific approach is the way to ensure success with performance testing.

Don't Stress Over Stress Testing

Stress testing is a process that is used to determine an application's stability when subjected to above normal loads. As opposed to load testing, where the load is only as much as specified or normal operations require, stress testing goes well beyond these, often to the breaking point of the application, in order to observe the behaviors. There are different methods of stress testing, the two most common are positive testing and negative testing. *Positive testing* is where the load is progressively increased to overwhelm the system's resources. *Negative testing* takes away resources such as memory, threads, or connections. Besides determining the exact point of demise or in some instances the degradation curve of the application, the other purpose is to drive the application beyond its capacity to make sure that when it fails it can recover gracefully. This is testing the application's recoverability.

As an example, let's revisit our fictitious AllScale human resources management (HRM) application again. The application has a service that provides searching functionality for managers to find employees. This is particularly useful for HR managers who might have hundreds of employees that they are responsible for in terms of HRM. Kevin Qualman, the director of quality assurance, has asked his team to develop a stress test for this service. One method that Kevin's team has come up with is to subject the service to an increasing number of simultaneous requests. At each progressive step, the team would want to monitor and record response time, returned results, and the behavior of various components such as the buffer pool of the database or the freshness of a caching layer. When the team gets to a point that response time begins to degrade beyond the specifications, it makes note of this and continues to monitor specifically to ensure that the system degrades nicely. Kevin's team members do not want the service to topple over and stop serving any requests. If this is the case, there is a problem in the system that should be fixed. Instead, they want to see the system handle this inability to service incoming requests in some acceptable manner such as reject requests that exceed its capacity or queue them to be serviced later. At this point in the test, they should begin tapering off the requests back to an acceptable and manageable level for the service. They should expect to see that as the requests are tapered off the system will clean up the queued or rejected requests and continue processing. This is the recoverability that they expect in the service.

Identify Objectives

We have identified eight separate steps in a basic stress test. You may choose to add to this as required by the needs of your organization, but this basic outline will get you started or help refine your process if it exists already. The first step is to identify what you want to achieve with the test. As with all projects, time and resources are limited; therefore, by identifying up front the goals, you can narrow the field of tests that you will perform. This is crucial to saving a great deal of time or worse, executing the tests and then having the data not tell you want you need to know about the application or service.

There are four categories of goals that a stress test can provide results for analysis. These categories are establishing a baseline, testing failure and recoverability, negative testing, and system interactions. The goal of establishing baseline behavior of a service is usually the goal when you have never done stress testing and you need to establish the peak utilization possible or degradation curve. The second category of goals for stress testing is to test the service's behavior during failure and then its subsequent recoverability. The service may have been modified or enhanced and you want to ensure it still behaves properly during periods of extreme stress. These two goals involve positive stress testing because you are putting a continually increasing positive load on the service. The third category of goals that you might have for a stress test is negative testing. In this case, you are interested in determining what happens should you lose cache or have a memory leak or any other resource becomes limited or restricted. The final category of goals that you may have for your stress test is testing the interactivity of the system's services. Here, you are trying to ensure that some given functionality continues to work when one or more other services are overloaded. Between these four categories of goals, you should be able to define specifically the purpose of your stress test.

Identify Key Services

After you have identified the goal or objective of your stress test, the second step is to identify the services that you will be testing. Again, we have limited time and resources and must choose which services are to be tested to ensure we achieve our goals established in the first step. Some factors that you should consider are criticality to the overall system, ones most likely to affect performance, and those identified through load testing as bottlenecks. Let's talk about each one individually. The first factor to use in determining which services should be selected for stress testing is the criticality of each service to the overall system performance. If there is a central service such as a data abstract layer (DAL) or user authorization, this should be included as a candidate for stress testing because the stability of the entire application depends on this service. If you have architected your application into fault tolerant "swim lanes," which will be discussed in Chapter 21, Creating Fault Isolative Architectural Structures, you still likely have core services that have been replicated across the lanes. The second consideration for determining services to stress test is the likelihood that a service affects performance. This decision will be influenced by knowledgeable engineers but should also be somewhat scientific. You can rank services by the usage of things such as synchronous calls, I/O, caching, locking, and so on. The more of these higher risk processes that are included in the service the more likely they will have an effect on performance. The third factor for selecting services to be stress tested is those services identified during load testing as a bottleneck. Hopefully, if a service has been identified as a bottleneck, this constraint will have already been fixed but you should recheck them during stress testing. These three factors should provide you with strong guidelines for selecting the services on which you should focus your time and resources to ensure you get the most out of your stress testing.

Determine Load

The third step in stress testing is to determine how much load is actually necessary. Determining the load is important for a variety of reasons. First, it is helpful to know at approximately what load the application will start exhibiting strange behaviors so that you don't waste time on much lower loads. Second, you need to understand if you have enough capacity on your test systems to generate the required load. The load that you decide to place upon a particular service should stress it sufficiently beyond the breaking point in order to enable you to observe the behavior and consequences of the stress. One way to accomplish this is to identify the load under which the service begins to exhibit poor behavior, and incrementally increase the load beyond this point. The important thing is to be methodical, record as much data as possible, and create a significant failure of the service. Stress can be placed upon the service in a variety of manners, such as increasing the requests, shortening any delays, or reducing the hardware capacity. An important factor to remember is that loads, whether identified in production or in load testing, should always be scaled to the appropriate level based on the differences in hardware between the environments.

Environment

As with performance testing, establishing the appropriate environment is critical. This is the fourth step in stress testing. The environment must be stable, consistent, and as close to production as possible. This last item might be hard to accomplish unless you have an unlimited budget. If you are one of the less fortunate technology managers, constrained by a budget like the rest of us, you will have to scale this down. Large pools of servers in production can be scaled down to small pools of two or three servers, but the fact that there are multiple servers load balanced behind the same rules is important. The class of servers should be the same if at all possible or a scale factor must be introduced. A production environment with 7.2K rpm SATA disks and a test environment with 5.4K rpm SATA disks may cause the application to have different performance characteristics and different load capacities. It is important to spend some time deciding on a stress testing environment, just as you did for your performance testing environment. Understand the tradeoffs that you are making with each difference between your production and testing environment. Balance the risk and rewards to make the best decisions in terms of what the environment should look like and how useful the tests will be.

Identify Monitors

The fifth step in the stress testing process is to identify what needs to be monitored or what data needs to be collected. It is as equally important to identify what needs to be monitored and captured as it is to properly choose the service, load, and tests. You certainly do not want to go to the trouble of performing the tests only to find that you did not capture the data that you needed to perform a proper analysis. Some things that might be important to consider as potential data points are the results or behavior of the service, the response time, CPU load, memory usage, disk usage, thread deadlocks, SQL count, transactions failed, and so on. The results of the service are important in the event that the application provide erroneous results. Comparison of the expected and actual results should be considered as a very good measure of the behavior of the service under load.

Create Load

The next step in the process is to create the simulated load. This sixth step is important because this often takes more work than running the actual tests. Creating sufficient load to stress the service may be very difficult if you have services that have been well architected to handle especially high loads. The best loads are those that are replicated from real user traffic. Sometimes, it is possible to gather this from application or load balancer logs. If this is possible and the source of your load data, it is likely that you will need to coordinate other parts of the system such as the database to coincide with the load data. For example, if you are testing a signup service and plan on replaying actual user registrations from your production logs, you will need to not only extract the registration requests from your logs but also have the data in the test database set to a point before the user registrations began. The reason for this is that if the user is already registered in the database, it will cause a different code path to be executed than normal for a user registration. This difference will significantly skew your testing results and is not an accurate test. If you cannot get real user traffic to simulate your load, you can revert to writing scripts that simulate a series of steps that exercise the service as close to normal user traffic as possible.

Execute Tests

After you have finalized your test objectives, identified the key services to be tested, determined the load necessary, set up your environment, identified what needs to be monitored, and created the simulated load that will be used, you are ready for the seventh step, which is to actually execute the tests. In this step, you will methodically progress through your identified services performing the stress tests under the loads determined and methodically record the data that you identified as being important to perform a proper analysis. Like with performance testing, you should keep data from release to release. Comparison between various releases is a great way to quickly understand the changes that have taken place from one release to another.

Analyze Data

The last step in stress testing is to perform the analysis on the data gathered during the tests. The analysis for the stress test data is similar to that done for the performance tests in that a variety of methods can be implemented depending on factors such as the amount of time allocated, the skills of the analyst, the acceptable amount of risk, and the level of details expected. The other significant determinant in how the data should be analyzed is the objectives or goals determined in Step 1. If the object is to establish a baseline, little analysis needs to be done, perhaps just to validate that the data accurately depicts the baseline, that it is statistically significant, and that it only has common cause variation. If the object is to identify the failure behavior, the analysis should focus on comparing results from when the load was below the breaking point and above it. This will help identify warning signs of an impending problem as well as if there is a problem or inappropriate behavior of the system at certain loads. If the objective is to test for the behavior when the resource is removed completely from the system, the analysis will probably want to include a comparison of response times and other system metrics between various resource-constrained scenarios and post-load to ensure that the system has recovered as expected. For the interactivity objective, the data from many different services may have to be looked at together. This type of examination may include multivariate analysis such as principal component or factor analysis. The objective identified in the very first step will be the guidepost for the analysis. A successful analysis will meet the objectives set forth for the tests. If a gap in the data or missing test scenario prevents you from completing the analysis, you should reexamine your steps and ensure you have accurately followed the eight-step process outlined earlier.

Summary of Stress Testing Steps

When performing stress testing, the following steps are the critical steps to completing it properly. As with performance testing, you can add additional steps as necessary to fit your organization's needs.

1. *Identify objectives.* Identify why you are performing the test. These goals usually fall into one of four categories: establish a baseline, identify behavior during failure and recovery, identify behavior during loss of resources, and determine how the failure of one service will affect the entire system.

2. *Identify key services.* Time and resources are limited so you must select only the most important services to test.

3. *Determine load.* Calculate or estimate the amount of load that will be required to stress the application to the breaking point.

4. *Environment.* The environment should mimic production as much as possible to ensure the validity of the tests.

5. *Identify monitors.* You don't want to execute tests and then realize you are missing data. Plan ahead by using the objectives identified in Step 1 as criteria for what must be monitored.

6. *Create load.* Create the actual load data, preferably from user data.

7. *Execute tests.* This step is where the tests are actually being executed in the environment established previously.

8. *Analyze data.* The last step is to analyze the data.

Follow these eight steps and any others that you need to add for your specific situations and organization. Ensure the process fits the needs of the organization.

We need to take a break in our description and praise of the stress testing process to discuss the downside. Although we encourage the use of stress testing, it is admittedly one of the hardest types of testing to perform properly; and if you don't perform it properly, the effort is almost always wasted. As we discussed in Step 4 about setting up the proper environment, if you switch classes of storage or processor speeds, these can completely throw off the validity of the test results. Unfortunately, the environment is relatively easy to get correct, especially when compared to the sixth step, creating the load. This is by far the hardest and most likely place that you or your team will mess up the process and cause erroneous or inaccurate results. It is very, very difficult to accurately capture and replay real user behavior. As we discussed, this often necessitates the synchronization of data within caches and stores, such as database or files, because inconsistencies will exercise different code paths and render inaccurate results. Additionally, creating a very large load itself can often be problematic from a capacity standpoint, especially when trying to test the interactivity of multiple services. For reasons such as these, we caution the use of stress testing as your only safety net. As we will discuss in the next chapter on go/no-go decisions and rollback, you must have multiple relief valves in the event problems arise or disaster strikes. We will also cover this subject more in Part III, Architecting Scalable Solutions, with the discussion of how to use swim lanes and other application splitting methods to improve scalability and stability.

As we stated in the beginning, the purpose of stress testing is to determine an application's stability when subjected to above normal loads. Differentiated from load testing, where the load is only as much as specified, in stress testing we go well beyond this to the breaking point and watch the failure and the recovery of the service or application. To more thoroughly understand the stress testing process, we covered an eight-step process starting with defining objectives and ending with analyzing the data. Each step in the process is critical to ensuring a successful test yielding the results that you desire. As with our other processes, we recommend starting with this one intact and adding to it as necessary for your organization's needs.

Performance and Stress Testing for Scalability

We usually lead off our chapters with the rhetorical question of how a particular process could possibly have anything to do with scalability. This time, we've waited until we covered the processes in depth to have this discussion; hopefully, as a result, you can already start listing the reasons that performance testing and stress testing have a great place among the multitude of factors that affect scalability. The three areas that we are going to focus on for exploring the relationship are the headroom, change control, and managing risk.

As we discussed in Chapter 11, Determining Headroom for Applications, it is critical to scalability that you know where you are in terms of capacity for a particular service within your system. This is for you to calculate how much time and growth you have left to scale. This is fundamental for planning headroom or infrastructure projects, splitting databases/applications, and making budgets. The way to ensure your calculations remain accurate is to conduct performance testing on all your releases to ensure you are not introducing unexpected load increases. It is not uncommon for an organization to implement a maximum load increase allowed per release. As you start to become more sophisticated in capacity planning, you will come to see the load added by new features and functionality as a cost that must be accounted for in the cost/benefit analysis. Additionally, stress testing is necessary to ensure that the expected breakpoint or degradation curve is still at the same point as previously identified. It is possible to leave the normal usage load unchanged but decrease the total load capacity through new code paths or changes in logic. For instance, an increase in a data structure lookup of 90 milliseconds would likely be unnoticed in total response time for a user's request, but if this service is tied synchronously to other services, as the load builds, hundreds or thousands of 90-millisecond delays adds up to decrease the peak capacity that services can handle.

When we talk about change management, as defined in Chapter 10, Controlling Change in Production Environments, we are really discussing more than the lightweight change identification process for small startup companies, but instead the fuller featured process by which a company is attempting to actively manage the changes that occur in their production environment. We defined change management as consisting of the following components: change proposal, change approval, change scheduling, change implementation and logging, change validation, and change efficacy review. Performance testing and stress testing augment this change management process by providing a practice implementation and most importantly a validation of the change. You would never expect to make a change without verifying that it actually affected the system the way that you think it should, such as fix a bug or provide a new piece of functionality. As part of performance and stress testing, we validate the expected results in a controlled environment prior to production. This is an additional step in ensuring that when the change is made in production it will also work as it did during testing under varying loads.

The most significant factor that we should consider when relating performance testing and stress testing to scalability is the management of risk. As outlined in Chapter 16, Determining Risk, risk management is one the most important processes when it comes to ensuring your systems will scale. The precursor to risk management is risk analysis, which attempts to calculate an amount of risk in various actions or components. Performance testing and stress testing are two methods that can significantly decrease the risk associated with a particular service change. For example, if we were using a failure mode and effects analysis tool and identified a failure mode of a particular feature to be the increase in query time, the mitigation recommended could be to test this feature under actual load conditions, as with a performance test, to determine the actual behavior. This could also be done with extreme load conditions as with a stress test to observe behavior above normal conditions. Both of these would provide much more information with regard to the actual performance of the feature and therefore would lower the amount of risk. These two testing processes are powerful tools when it comes to reducing and thus managing the amount of risk within the release or the overall system.

From these three areas, headroom, change control, and risk management, we can see the inherent relationship between successful scalability of your system and the adoption of the performance and stress testing processes. As we cautioned previously in the discussion of the stress test, the creation of the test load is not easy, and if done poorly can lead to erroneous data. However, this does not mean that it is not worth pursuing the understanding, implementation, and (ultimately) mastery of these processes.

Conclusion

In this chapter, we discussed in detail the performance testing and stress testing processes. We also discussed how these processes related to scalability for the system. For the performance testing process, we defined a seven-step process. The key to the process is to be methodical and scientific about the testing.

For the stress testing process, we defined an eight-step process. These were the basic steps we felt necessary to have a successful process. It was suggested that other steps be added as necessary for the proper fit within your organization.

We concluded this chapter with a discussion on how performance testing and stress testing fit with scalability. We concluded that based on the relationship between these testing processes and three factors (headroom, change control, and risk management), that have already been established as being causal to scalability, these processes too are directly responsible for scalability.

Key Points

- Performance testing covers a broad range of engineering evaluations where the emphasis is on the final measurable performance characteristic.
- The goal of performance testing is to identify, document, and where possible eliminate bottlenecks in the system.
- Load testing is a process used in performance testing.
- Load testing is the process of putting load or user demand on a system in order to measure its response and stability.
- The purpose of load testing is to verify that the application can meet a desired performance objective often specified as a service level agreement (SLA).
- Load and performance testing are not substitutes for proper architecture.
- The seven steps of performance testing are as follows:
    1. Establish the criteria expected from the application.
    2. Establish the proper testing environment.
    3. Define the right test to perform.
    4. Execute the tests.
    5. Analyze the data.
    6. Report to the engineers.
    7. Repeat as necessary.
- Stress testing is a process that is used to determine an application's stability when subjected to above normal loads.
- Stress testing, as opposed to load testing, goes well beyond the normal traffic, often to the breaking point of the application, in order to observe the behaviors.
- The eight steps of stress testing are as follows:
    1. Identify the objectives of the test.
    2. Choose the key services for testing.
    3. Determine how much load is required.
    4. Establish the proper test environment.
    5. Identify what must be monitored.
    6. Actually create the test load.
    7. Execute the tests.
    8. Analyze the data.
- Performance testing and stress testing impact scalability through the areas of headroom, change control, and risk management.

Chapter 18

Barrier Conditions and Rollback

He will conquer who has learned the artifice of deviation. Such is the art of maneuvering.

—Sun Tzu

Whether you develop with an agile methodology, a classic waterfall methodology, or some hybrid, good processes for the promotion of systems into your production environment have the capability of protecting you from significant failures; whereas poor processes may end up damning you to near certain technical death. Checkpoints and barrier conditions within your product development life cycle can increase quality and reduce the cost of developing your product by detecting early when you are off course. But processes alone are not always enough. Even the best of teams, with the best processes and great technology make mistakes and incorrectly analyze the results of certain tests or reviews. If your platform implements a service, either Software as a Service play or a traditional back office IT system, you need to be able to quickly roll back significant releases to keep scale related events from creating availability incidents.

Developing effective go/no-go processes or *barrier conditions*, ideally within a fault isolative infrastructure, and coupling them with a process and capability to roll back production changes, are necessary components within any highly available service and are critical to the success of your scalability goals. The companies focused most intensely on cost effectively scaling their systems while guaranteeing high availability create several checkpoints in their development processes. These checkpoints are an attempt to guarantee the lowest probability of a scalability related event and to minimize the impact of that event should it occur. They also make sure that they can quickly get out of any event created through recent changes by ensuring that they can always roll back from any major change.

273

Barrier Conditions

You might read this heading and immediately assume that we are proposing that waterfall development cycles are the key to success within highly scalable environments. Very often, barrier conditions or entry and exit criteria are associated with the phases of waterfall development and sometimes identified as a reason for the inflexibility of a waterfall development model. Our intent here is not to promote the waterfall methodology, but rather to discuss the need for standards and protective measures regardless of your approach to development. For the purposes of this discussion, assume that a barrier condition is a standard against which you measure success or failure within your development life cycle. Ideally, you want to have these conditions or checkpoints established within your cycle to help you decide whether you are indeed on the right path for the product or enhancements that you are developing. Remember our discussion on goals in Chapters 4, Leadership 101, and 5, Management 101, and the need to establish and measure these goals. Barrier conditions are static goals within a development at regular "heartbeats" to ensure that what you are developing aligns with your vision and need. Barrier conditions for scalability might include *desk checking* a design against your architectural principles within an Architecture Review Board before the design is implemented, code reviewing the implementation to ensure it is consistent with the design, or performance testing an implementation within QA and then measuring the impact to scalability upon release to the production environment.

Example Scalability Barrier Conditions

We often recommend that the following barrier conditions be inserted into your development methodology or life cycle. Each has a purpose to try to limit the probability of occurrence and resulting impact of any scalability issues within your production environment:

1. *Architecture Review Board.* From Chapter 14, Architecture Review Board, the ARB exists to ensure that designs are consistent with architectural principles. Architectural principles, in turn, ideally address one or more key scalability tenets within your platform. The intent of this barrier is to ensure that time isn't wasted implementing or developing systems that are difficult or impossible to scale to your needs.

2. *Code Reviews.* Modifying what is hopefully an existing and robust code review process to include ensuring that architectural principles are followed within the implementation of the system in question is critical to ensuring that code can be fixed for scalability problems before being identified within QA and being required to be fixed later.

3. *Performance Testing*: From Chapter 17, Performance and Stress Testing, performance testing helps you identify potential issues of scale before introducing the system into a production environment and potentially impacting your customers with a scalability related issue.

4. *Production Monitoring and Measurement*. Ideally, your system has been designed to be monitored as discussed within Chapter 12, Exploring Architectural Principles. Even if it is not, capturing key performance data from both a user perspective, application perspective, and system perspective after release and comparing it to previous releases can help you identify potential scalability related issues early before they impact your customers.

Your processes may include additional barrier conditions that you've found useful over time, but we consider these to be the bare minimum to help manage the risk of releasing systems that negatively impact customers due to scalability related problems.

Barrier Conditions and Agile Development

In our practice, we have found that many of our clients have a mistaken perception that the including or defining standards, constraints, or processes in agile processes, is a violation of the agile mindset. The very notion that process runs counter to agile methodologies is flawed from the outset as any agile method is itself a process. Most often, we find the Agile Manifesto quoted out of context as a reason for eschewing any process or standard.[1] As a review, and from the Agile Manifesto, agile methodologies value

- Individuals and interactions over processes and tools
- Working software over comprehensive documentation
- Customer collaboration over contract negotiation
- Responding to change over following a plan

Organizations often take the "Individuals and interactions over processes and tools" out of context without reading the line that follows these bullets, which states, "That is, while there is value in the items from the right, we value the items on the left more."[2] It is clear with this line that processes add value, but that people and interactions should take precedent over them where we need to make choices. We absolutely agree with this approach and prefer to inject process into agile development most often as barrier conditions to test for an appropriate level of quality, scalability, and availability, or to help ensure that engineers are properly evaluated and taught over time. Let's examine how some key barrier conditions enhance our agile method.

---

1. This information is from the Agile Manifesto at www.agilemanifesto.org.
2. Ibid.

We'll first start with valuing working software over comprehensive documentation. None of the suggestions we've made from ARB and code reviews to performance testing and production measurement violate this rule. The barrier conditions represented by ARB and Joint Architecture Design (JAD) are used within agile methods to ensure that the product under development can scale appropriately. ARB and JAD can be performed orally in a group and with limited documentation and therefore are all consistent with the agile method.

The inclusion of barrier conditions and standards to help ensure that systems and products work properly in production actually supports the development of working software. We have not defined comprehensive documentation as necessary in any of our proposed activities, although it is likely that the results of these activities will be logged somewhere. Remember, we are interested in improving our processes over time so logging performance results for instance will help us determine how often we are making mistakes in our development process that result in failed performance tests in QA or scalability issues within production.

The processes we've suggested also do not in any way hinder customer collaboration or support contract negotiation over customer collaboration. In fact, one might argue that they foster a better working environment with the end customer in that by inserting scalability barrier conditions you are actually looking out for your customer's needs. Your customer is not likely capable of performing the type of design evaluation, reviews, testing, or measuring that is necessary to determine if your product will scale to its needs. Your customer does, however, expect that you are delivering a product or service that will meet not only its business objectives but its scalability needs as well. Collaborating to develop tests and measurements that will help ensure that your product meets customer needs and to insert those tests and measurements into your development process is a great way to take care of your customers and create shareholder value.

Finally, the inclusion of the barrier conditions we've suggested helps us to respond to change by helping us identify when that change is occurring. The failure of a barrier condition is an early alert to issues that we need to address immediately. Identifying that a component is incapable of being scaled horizontally (scale out not up from our recommended architectural principles) in an ARB session is a good indication of potential issues for our customer. Although we may make the executive decision to launch the feature, product, or service, we had better ensure that future agile cycles are used to fix the issue we've identified. However, if the need for scale is so dramatic that a failure to scale out will keep us from being successful, should we not respond immediately to that issue and fix it? Without such a process and series of checks, how would we ensure that we are meeting our customer's needs?

Hopefully, we've convinced you that the addition of criteria against which you can evaluate the success of your scalability objectives is a good idea within your agile implementation. If we haven't, please remember our "board of directors" test within

Chapter 5, Management 101. Would you feel comfortable stating that you absolutely would not develop processes within your development life cycle to ensure that your products and services could scale? Imagine yourself saying, "In no way, shape, or form will we ever implement barrier conditions or criteria to ensure that we don't release products with scalability problems!" How long do you think you would have a job?

Cowboy Coding

Development without any process, without any plans, and without measurements to ensure that the results meet the needs of the business is what we often refer to as *cowboy coding*. The complete lack of process in cowboy-like environments is a significant barrier to success for any scalability initiatives.

Often, we find that teams attempt to claim that cowboy implementations are "agile." This simply isn't true. The agile methodology is a defined life cycle that is tailored to be adaptive to your needs over time, versus other models that tend to be more predictive. The absence of processes, such as any cowboy implementation, is neither adaptive nor predictive. Agile methodologies are not arguments against measurement or management. They are methodologies tuned to release small components or subsets of functionality quickly. They were developed to help control chaos through managing small, easily managed components rather than trying to repeatedly fail at attempting to predict and control very large complex projects.

Do not allow yourself or your team to fall prey to the misconception that agile methodologies should not be measured or managed. Using a metric such as velocity to improve the estimation ability of engineers but not to beat them up over, is a fundamental part of the agile methodology. A lack of measuring dooms you to never improving and a lack of managing dooms you to getting lost en route to your goals and vision. Being a cowboy when it comes to designing highly scalable solutions is a sure way to get thrown off of the bucking scalability bronco!

Barrier Conditions and Waterfall Development

The inclusion of barrier conditions within waterfall models is not a new concept. Most waterfall implementations include a concept of entry criteria and exit criteria for each phase of development. For instance, in a strict waterfall model, design may not start until the requirements phase is completed. The exit criteria for the requirements phase in turn may include a signoff by key stakeholders and a review of requirements by the internal customer (or an external representative) and a review by the organizations responsible for producing those requirements. In modified, overlapping, or hybrid waterfall models, requirements may need to be complete for the systems to be developed first but may not be complete for the entire product or system. If prototyping is employed, potentially those requirements need to be mocked up in a prototype before major design starts.

For our purposes, we need only inject the four processes we identified earlier into the existing barrier conditions. The Architecture Review Board lines up nicely as an exit criterion for the design phase of our project. Code reviews, including a review consistent with our architectural principles, might create exit criteria for our coding or implementation phase. Performance testing should be performed during the validation or testing phase with requirements being that no more than a specific percentage change be present for any critical system resources. Production measurements being defined and implemented should be the entry criteria for the maintenance phase and significant increases in any measured area if not expected should trigger work to reduce the impact of the implementation or changes in architecture to allow for more cost-effective scalability.

Barrier Conditions and Hybrid Models

Many companies have developed models that merge agile and waterfall methodologies, and some continue to follow the predecessor to agile methods known as rapid application development (RAD). For instance, some companies may be required to develop software consistent with contracts and predefined requirements, such as those that interact with governmental organizations. These companies may wish to have some of the predictability of dates associated with a waterfall model, but desire to implement chunks of functionality quickly as in agile approaches.

The question for these models is where to place the barrier conditions for the greatest benefit. To answer that question, we need to return to the objectives of the barrier conditions. Our intent with any barrier condition is to ensure that we catch problems or issues early in our development so that we reduce the amount of rework to meet our objectives. It costs us less in time and work, for instance, to catch a problem in our QA organization than it does in our production environment. Similarly, it costs us less to catch an issue in ARB than to allow it to be implemented and caught in a code review.

The answer to the question of where to place the barrier conditions, then, is to place the barrier conditions where they add the most value and incur the least cost to our processes. Code reviews should be placed at the completion of each coding cycle or at the completion of chunks of functionality. The architectural review should occur prior to the beginning of implementation, production metrics obviously need to occur within the production environment, and performance testing should happen prior to the release of a system into the production environment.

Rollback Capabilities

You might argue that an effective set of barrier conditions in your development process should obviate the need for being able to roll back major changes within your production environment. We can't really argue with that thought or approach as technically it is correct. However, arguing against the capability to roll back is really an argument against having an insurance policy. You may believe, for instance, that you don't have a need for health insurance because you are a healthy individual and fairly wealthy. Or, you may argue against automobile insurance because you are, in the words of Dustin Hoffman in *Rain Man*, "an excellent driver." But what happens when you contract a treatable cancer and don't have the funds for the treatment, or someone runs into your vehicle and doesn't have liability insurance? If you are like most people, your view of whether you need (or needed) this insurance changes immediately when it would become useful. The same holds true when you find yourself in a situation where fixing forward is going to take quite a bit of time and have quite an adverse impact on your clients.

Rollback Window Requirements

Rollback requirements differ significantly by business. The question to ask yourself in determining how to establish your specific rollback needs, at least from the perspective of scalability, is to decide by when you will have enough information regarding performance to determine if you need to undo your recent changes. For many companies, the bare minimum is to allow a weekly business day peak utilization period to have great confidence in the results of your analysis. This bare minimum may be enough for modifications to existing functionality, but when new functionality is added, it may not be enough.

New functions or features often have adoption curves that take more than one day to get enough traffic through that feature to determine its resulting impact on system performance. The amount of data gathered over time within any new feature may also have an adverse performance impact and as a result negatively impact your scalability.

Let's return to Johnny Fixer and the HRM application at AllScale. Johnny's team has been busy implementing a "degrees of separation" feature into the resume tracking portion of the system. The idea is that the system will identify people within the company who either know a potential candidate personally or who might know people who know the candidate with the intent being to enable background checking through individual's relationships. The feature takes as inputs all companies at which current employees have worked and the list of companies for any given candidate. Johnny's team initially figures that a linear search should be appropriate as the list of potential companies and resulting overlaps are likely to be small.

The new feature is released and starts to compute relationship maps over the course of the next few weeks. Initially, all goes well and Johnny's team is happy with the results and the runtime of the application. However, as the list of candidates grows, so does the list of companies for which the candidates have worked. Additionally, given the growth of AllScale, the number of employees has grown as have their first and second order relationship trees. Soon, many of the processes relying upon the degrees of separation function start timing out and customers are getting aggravated.

The crisis management process kicks in and Johnny's team quickly identifies the culprit as the degrees of separation functionality. Working with the entire team, Johnny feels that the team can make a change to this feature to perform a more cost-effective search algorithm within a day and get it tested and rolled out to the site within 30 hours. Christine, the CEO, is concerned that the company will see a significant departure in user base if the problem is not fixed within a few hours.

If Johnny had followed our advice and made sure that he could roll back his last release, he could simply roll the code back and then roll it back out when the fix is made, assuming that his rollback process allowed him to roll back code released three days ago. Although this may cause some user confusion, proper messaging could help control that and within two days, Johnny could have the new code out and functioning properly without impact to his current scalability. If Johnny didn't take our advice, or Johnny's rollback process only allowed rolling back within the first six hours of a release, our guess is that Johnny would be a convert to ensuring he always has a rollback insurance policy to meet his needs.

The last major consideration for returning your rollback window size deals with the frequency of your releases and how many releases you need to be capable of rolling back. Maybe you have a release process that has you releasing new functionality to your site several times a week. In this case, you may need to roll back more than one release if the adoption rate of any new functionality extends into the next release cycle. If this is the case, your process needs to be slightly more robust, as you are concerned about multiple changes and multiple releases rather than just one release to the next.

Rollback Window Requirements Checklist

To determine your timeframe necessary to perform a rollback, you should consider the following things:

- How long between your release and the first heavy traffic period for your product?
- Is this a modification of existing functionality or a new feature?
- If this is a new feature, what is the adoption curve for this new feature?
- For how many releases do I need to consider rolling back based on my release frequency? We call this the rollback version number requirement.

Your rollback window should allow you to roll back after significant adoption of a new feature (say up to 50% adoption) and after or during your first time period of peak utilization.

Rollback Technology Considerations

We often hear during our discussions around the *rollback insurance policy* that clients in general agree that being able to roll back would be great but that it is technically not feasible for them. Our answer to this is that it is almost always possible; it just may not be possible with your current team, processes, or architecture.

The most commonly cited reason for an inability to roll back in Web enabled platforms and back office IT systems is database schema incompatibility. The argument usually goes that for any major development effort, there may be significant changes to the schema resulting in an incompatibility with the way old and new data is stored. This modification may result in table relationships changing, candidate keys changing, table columns changing, tables added, tables merged, tables disaggregated, and tables removed.

The key to fixing these database issues is to grow your schema over time and keep old database relationships and entities for at least as long as it would require you to roll back to them should you run into significant performance issues. In the case where you need to move data to create schemas of varying normal forms, either for functionality reasons or performance reasons, consider using data movement programs potentially started by a database trigger or using a data movement daemon or third-party replication technology. This data movement can cease whenever you have met or exceeded your *rollback version number* limit identified during your requirements. Ideally, you can turn off such data movement systems within a week or two after implementation and validation that you do not need to roll back.

Ideally, you will limit such data movement, and instead populate new data in new tables or columns while leaving old data in its original columns and tables. In many cases, this is sufficient to accomplish your needs. In the case where you are reorganizing data, simply move the data from the new to old positions for the period of time necessary to perform the rollback. If you need to change the name of a column or its meaning within an application, you must first make the change in the application leaving the database alone and then come back in a future release and change the database. This is an example of the general rollback principle of making the change in the application in release one and making the change in the database in a later release.

Cost Considerations of Rollback

If you've gotten to this point and determined that designing and implementing a rollback insurance policy has a cost, you are absolutely right! For some releases, the cost can be significant, adding as much as 10% or 20% to the cost of the release. In most cases and for most releases, we believe that you can implement an effective rollback strategy for less than 1% of the cost or time of the release as very often you are really just talking about different ways to store data within a database or other storage system. Insurance isn't free, but it exists for a reason.

Many of our clients have implemented procedures that allow them to violate the rollback architectural principle as long as several other risk mitigation steps or processes are in place. We typically suggest that the CEO or general manager of the product or service in question sign off on the risk and review the risk mitigation plan (see Chapter 16, Determining Risk) before agreeing to violating the rollback architectural principle. In the ideal scenario, the principle is only violated with very small, very low risk releases where the cost of being able to roll back exceeds the value of the rollback given the size and impact of the release. Unfortunately, what typically happens is that the rollback principle is violated for very large and complex releases in order to hit time to market constraints. The problem with this approach is that these large complex releases are often the ones for which you need rollback capability the most.

Challenge your team whenever it indicates that the cost or difficulty to implement a rollback strategy for a particular release is too high. Often, there are simple solutions, such as implementing short lived data movement scripts, to help mitigate the cost and increase the possibility of implementing the rollback strategy. Sometimes, the risk of a release can be significantly mitigated by implementing markdown logic for complex features rather than needing to ensure that the release can be rolled back. In our consulting practice at AKF Partners, we have seen many team members who start by saying, "we cannot possibly roll back." After they accept the fact that it is possible, they are then able to come up with creative solutions for almost any challenge.

Markdown Functionality—Design to Be Disabled

Another of our architectural principles from Chapter 12 was designing a feature to be disabled. This differs from rolling back features in at least two ways. The first is that, if implemented properly, it is typically faster to turn a feature off than it is to replace it with the previous version or release of the system. When done well, the application may listen to a dedicated communication channel for instructions to disallow or disable certain features. Other approaches may require the restart of the application to pick up new configuration files. Either way, it is typically much faster to disable functions causing scalability problems than it is to replace the system with the previous release.

Another way functionality disabling differs from rolling back is that it might allow all of the other functions within any given release, both modified and new, to continue to function as normal. If in our example of our dating site we had released both the "has he dated a friend of mine" search and another feature that allowed the rating of any given date, we would only need to disable our search feature until it is fixed rather than rolling back and in effect turning off both features. This obviously gives us an advantage in releases containing multiple fixes, modified and new functionality.

Designing all features to be disabled, however, can sometimes add an even more significant cost than designing to roll any given release back. The ideal case is that the cost is low for both designing to be disabled and rolling back and the company chooses to do both for all new and modified features. Most likely, you will identify features that are high risk, using a Failure Mode and Effects Analysis described in Chapter 16, to determine which features should have mark down functionality enabled. Code reuse or a shared service that is called asynchronously may help to significantly reduce the cost of implementing functions that can be disabled on demand. Implementing both rollback and feature disabling helps enable agile methods by creating an adaptive and flexible production environment rather than relying on predictive methods such as extensive, costly, and often low return performance testing.

If implemented properly, designing to be disabled and designing for rollbacks can actually decrease your time to market by allowing you to take some risks in production that you would not take in their absence. Although not a replacement for load and performance testing, it allows you to perform such testing much more quickly in recognition of the fact that you can easily move back from implementations once released.

The Barrier Condition, Rollback, and Markdown Checklist

Do you have the following?

- Something to block bad scalability designs from proceeding to implementation?
- Reviews to ensure that code is consistent with a scalable design or principles?
- A way to test the impact of an implementation before it goes to production?
- Ways to measure the impact of production releases immediately?
- A way to roll back a major release that impacts your ability to scale?
- A way to disable functionality that impacts your ability to scale?

Answering yes to all of these puts you on a path to identifying scale issues early and being able to recover from them quickly when they happen.

Conclusion

This chapter covered topics such as barrier conditions, rollback capabilities, and markdown capabilities that help companies manage the risk associated with scalability incidents and recover quickly from them if and when they happen. Barrier conditions (a.k.a. go/no-go processes) focus on identifying and eliminating risks to future scalability early within a development process, thereby lowering the cost of identifying the issue and eliminating the threat of it in production. Rollback capabilities allow for the immediate removal of any scalability related threat, thereby limiting its impact to customers and shareholders. Markdown and disabling capabilities allow features impacting scalability to be disabled on a per feature basis, removing them as threats when they cause problems.

Ideally, you will consider implementing all of these. Sometimes, on a per release basis, the cost of implementing either rollback or markdown capabilities are exceptionally high. In these cases, we recommend a thorough review of the risks and all of the risk mitigation steps possible to help minimize the impact to your customers and shareholders. In the event of high cost of both markdown and rollback, consider implementing at least one unless the feature is small and not complex. Should you decide to forego implementing both markdown and rollback, ensure that you perform adequate load and performance testing and that you have all of the necessary resources available during product launch to monitor and recover from any incidents quickly.

Key Points

- Barrier conditions or go/no-go processes exist to isolate faults early in your development life cycle.

- Barrier conditions can work with any development life cycle. They do not need to be document intensive, though data should be collected to learn from past mistakes.

- Architecture Review Board, code reviews, performance testing, and production measurements can all be considered examples of barrier conditions if the result of a failure of one of these conditions is to rework the system in question.

- Designing the capability to roll back into an application helps limit the scalability impact of any given release. Consider it an insurance policy for your business, shareholders, and customers.

- Designing to disable, or markdown, features complements designing by rollback and adds the flexibility of keeping the most recent release in production while eliminating the impact of offending features or functionality.

Chapter 19

Fast or Right?

Thus, though we have heard of stupid haste in war, cleverness has never been seen associated with long delays.

—Sun Tzu

You have undoubtedly heard that from the choices of speed, cost, and quality, we can only ever choose two. This is the classic refrain when it comes to business and technology. Imagine a product feature where the business sponsor has given your team the requirements of delivery by a very aggressive date assuming the use of all of your team, a quality standard consisting of absolutely zero defects, and the constraint of only being able to use one engineer. Although this particular example is somewhat silly, the time cost and quality constraints are omnipresent and very serious. There is always a budget for hiring; even in the fastest growing companies, there is always an expectation of quality, whether in terms of feature completion or bugs; and there is always a need to deliver by aggressive deadlines.

In this chapter, we will discuss the general tradeoffs made in business and specifically the product development life cycle. We will also discuss how these tradeoffs relate to scalability and availability. Finally, we will provide a framework for thinking through these decisions on how to balance these three objectives or constraints, depending on how you view them. This will give you a guide by which you can assess situations in the future and hopefully make the best decision possible.

Tradeoffs in Business

The speed, quality, and cost triumvirate is often referred to as the *project triangle* as it provides a good visual for how these three are inextricably connected and how you cannot have all of them. There are several variations on this that also include scope as a fourth element. This can be represented by putting quality in the middle and defining the three legs of the triangle as speed, scope, and cost. We prefer to use the traditional speed/cost/quality project triangle and define scope as the size of the trian-

Figure 19.1   *Project Triangle*

gle. This is represented in Figure 19.1, where the legs are speed, cost, and quality, whereas the area of the triangle is the scope of the project. If the triangle is small, the scope of the project is small and thus the cost, time, and quality elements are proportional. The representation is less important than the reminder that there is a balance necessary between these four factors in order to develop products.

Ignoring any one of legs of the triangle will cause you to deliver a poor product. If you ignore the quality of the product, it will result in either a feature without the desired or required characteristics and functionality or it will be so buggy as to render it unusable. If you choose to ignore the speed, your competitors are likely to beat you to market and you will lose first mover advantage and your perception as an innovator rather than a follower. The larger the scope of the project, the higher the cost, the slower the speed to market, and the more effort required to achieve a quality standard. Any of these scenarios should be worrisome enough for you to seriously consider how you and your organization actively balance these constraints.

To completely understand why these tradeoffs exist and how to manage them, you must first understand each of their definitions. We will define cost as any related expense or capital investment that is utilized by or needed for the project. Costs will include such direct charges as the number of engineers working on the project, the number of servers required to host the new service, and the marketing campaign for the new service. It will also include indirect cost such as an additional database administrator necessary to handle the increased workload caused by another set of databases or the additional bandwidth utilized by customers of the feature. You will probably ask why such costs would be included in the proverbial bucket of costs associated to the feature, and the answer is that if you spend more time on the feature, you are very much more likely to figure out ways to shrink the cost of new hardware, additional bandwidth, and all the other miscellaneous charges. Thus, there is automatically a tradeoff between the amount of time spent on something and the ultimate cost associated with it.

For the definition of quality, we will include not only the often thought of bugs that mark poor quality, but also the fullness of the functionality. A feature launched with half of the specified functionality is not likely to generate as much interest nor revenue from customers as one with all the functionality intact. Thus, the tradeoff from launching a feature quickly can often result in lower quality in terms of functionality. The same is true for utilizing fewer engineers on a project or assigning only the most junior engineers on a project that requires senior engineers. As you would expect, quality also includes the amount of time and resources provided during quality assurance. Resources within quality assurance can include not only testing engineers but also proper environments and testing tools. Organizations that skimp on tools for testing cannot as efficiently utilize their testing engineers.

For the definition of speed, we will use the amount of time that a feature or project takes to move from the initial step in the product development life cycle to release in production. We know that the life cycle doesn't end with the release to production, and in fact continues through support and eventually deprecation, but those phases of the feature's life are typically a result of the decisions made much earlier. For example, a feature that is rushed through the life cycle without the ample time in quality assurance or design will significantly increase the amount of time that a feature will need to be supported once in production. Features that are not given enough or ample time to be designed properly, possibly in a Joint Architecture Design process and then reviewed at an Architecture Review Board, are destined to be of lower quality or higher cost or possibly both.

For the definition of scope, we will consider the amount of product features being developed as well as the level of effort required for the development of each product feature. Often, the scope of a feature can be changed dramatically depending on the requirements that are deemed necessary in order to achieve the business goals that have been established for that feature. For example, take a particular feature that is a new customer signup flow. The goal of this feature is to increase customer signup completion by 10%, meaning that 10% more of the people who start the signup process complete it. The initial scope of this feature might specify the requirement of integration with another service provider's single signon. The team might decide through user testing that this functionality is not required and thus the scope of this feature would be dramatically reduced.

We use the Project Triangle to represent the equality in importance of these constraints. As with Figure 19.2, change the emphasis of the project as well as the scope. The two diagrams represent different focuses for different projects. The project on the left has a clear predilection for faster speed and higher quality at the necessary increase in cost. This project might be something that is critical to block a competitor. Thus, it needs to be launched by the end of the month and be full featured in an attempt to beat a competitor to market with a similar product. The cost of adding more engineers, possibly more senior engineers and more testing engineers, is worth the advantage in the marketplace with your customers.

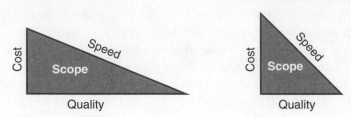

Figure 19.2   *Project Triangle Choices*

The project on the right in Figure 19.2 has a focus on increased speed to market with a lower cost point at the expense of reduced quality. This project might be something necessary for compliance where it is essential to meet a deadline to avoid penalties. There are likely no revenue generating benefits for the feature; therefore, it is essential to keep the costs as low as possible. This project might be the equivalent to a Y2K bug where the fix does not need to be full functioned but just needs to perform the basic functionality by the specified date with minimal cost.

For anyone who has been in business for any amount of time, it should not come as a surprise that there are tradeoffs that must be made. It is expected in business that leaders make decisions everyday about how to allocate their precious resources, be they engineers, dollars, or time. Often, these decisions are made with a well thought out process in order to understand the pros and cons of giving more or less time, money, or people to certain projects. As we will discuss later in this chapter, there are several processes that you can use to analyze these decisions, some more formal than others. Knowing that business is almost a constant tradeoff that the product development life cycle is part of, this is to be expected. Decisions must be made on allocating engineers to features, cutting out functionality when estimates prove not to be accurate, and deciding go/no-go criteria in terms of open bugs that remain in the candidate release.

The cost, quality, speed, and scope constraints that comprise the Project Triangle are all equally important overall but may vary significantly from project to project in terms of their importance and effort to manage. Projects that require higher quality may or may not be easier to achieve higher quality than other projects. Also, just because it cost more to achieve, does not make it necessarily required. So, just because we need higher quality in our project does not mean that the cost of this is a linear relationship. A 1% improvement in quality might cost 5%, but once you are past a 20% improvement in quality, this cost might go up to 10%. This is why each project uses its own Allocation Circle placed over the Project Triangle that designates where the focus should be for this project. You can create this diagram for every project as part of the specification if you feel it provides valuable information for everyone involved in the project, or you can just do the tradeoff analysis without the diagram.

Relation to Scalability

How can these tradeoffs between cost, quality, speed, and scope affect a system's scalability? As hinted at in the last chapter, it can be a very straightforward relationship of tradeoffs made directly for scalability or infrastructure projects. Another more indirect way that scalability is affected by the tradeoffs made between these constraints is that decisions made on feature projects can in the long term affect the scalability of that feature as well as of the entire system.

A scalability project that needs to split the primary database, just like a feature development release, will have to balance the four constraints. Will you take your most senior engineers off feature development for this? Will you give the team six months or eighteen months to complete the project? Will you include the built-in functionality to allow further database splits as necessary, or will you cut the project short and have it only provide a single split? All of these questions are ones that you will have to make over the course of the project and are a balance of the speed, cost, quality, and scope Project Triangle.

These constraints can also affect scalability indirectly. Let's take for example a payment feature at AllScale where the focus is placed more heavily on the side of speed. This feature must be released by the end of the month in order to be ready for the end-of-month billing cycle. Missing this date would result in days of manual work to process the payments, which would introduce many more errors resulting in charge backs and lost revenue. The engineering manager, Mike Softe, pulls three senior engineers off another project to place them on this payment project in order to get it done on time. All goes well and the feature is released the weekend before month-end allowing it to process the billing as planned.

Six months later, the AllScale HRM site's volume has increased over 100% and an even larger percentage of users are participating in the end-of-month billing cycle producing a total increase in load on the billing feature of close to 150% from when it was launched. Thus far, it has held up stoically with processing times of no more than 12 hours. However, this month's increase in users put it over the edge and the processing time jumps to over 38 hours. Designed as an add-on feature to a singleton application, this service cannot be run on multiple servers. Now the consequences of decisions made six months ago start to be seen. The AllScale operations team must reallocate a much larger server, planned to be used as a database server, for this application in order to get through next month's processing cycle. Of course, this negatively affects the hardware budget. The operations team also has to spend a lot of time monitoring, provisioning, configuring, and testing the server for this move. Engineers and quality assurance engineers are likely brought in to this project to provide advice on changes as well as final validation that the application works on the new hardware. This new hardware project has to take place during a maintenance window because of the high risk to the users and takes up a good portion of the risk allocation that is authorized for the system this particular week. The database split project has to be postponed because new hardware has to be ordered, which adds more risk of problems arising from the database being overloaded.

As you can see from our example, the decisions made during initial feature development can have many unseen affects on scalability of the entire system. Does this mean that the decisions and tradeoffs were incorrect? No, in fact, even with the benefit of hindsight, you might still feel the decision to push to quickly get the feature into production was the right decision, and we probably agree in this scenario. The important learning here is not that one decision is right or wrong but rather that the decisions have short- and long-term ramifications that you may not be able to ever completely understand.

How to Think About the Decision

Now that we have described how these tradeoffs are being made every day in your organization and how these can affect the scalability of the individual features as well as the overall system, it is time for us to discuss how to properly make these decisions. There are a variety of methods to choose from when you need to determine the proper tradeoff. You can choose to rely on one of these methods or you can learn them all in order that you use them each in the most appropriate manner. Unfortunately, no decision process is going to be able to guarantee that you reach a *correct* decision because often there is no *correct* decision; rather, there are just ones that have different pros and cons than others. Just as with risk management, managing tradeoffs or risk or even people is an ongoing process that keeps managers on their toes. Today's seemingly straightforward decision becomes a quagmire tomorrow with the addition of one more factor. A bug fix identified as low risk suddenly becomes high risk as the engineer digs into the code and realizes that a complete rewrite of a base class is necessary. A great idea to rush a payments feature into production today becomes a mess when headroom calculations predict that it will outgrow the payment server in two months.

Our goal here is to arm you with several methodologies that won't always give you the *correct* answer, because that can be elusive, but rather will help you rigorously process the information that you do have in order for you to make the *best* decision based on the information that you have today. There are three general methods that we have seen used. The first one is essentially the same *gut feel* method that we described in Chapter 16, Determining Risk. The second method is a list of pros and cons for each constraint. The third is what we call a *decision matrix* and involves constructing a well thought out analysis of what factors are important, both short and long term, ranking these factors compared to each other, defining the actual tradeoffs being considered, and determining how directly the tradeoffs impact the factors. If that last one sounds confusing, don't worry; we'll go through it in more detail in a few paragraphs.

First, let's discuss the gut feel method for making tradeoffs. As we discussed with regards to risk, there are some people who have an innate ability or well-honed skill to determine the pros and cons of decisions. This is great, but as we pointed out before, this method is not scalable and not accurate. That doesn't mean that you need to abandon this method; in fact, you probably already use this method the most of any other method and you probably do it on a daily basis. We use the gut method every time we decide to walk the ten blocks to the market instead of getting a cab, allocating more to the cost saving constraint and less on the speed to market constraint. You use this in business everyday as well. You decide to hire one person who will require slightly more salary but will hopefully produce faster and higher quality work. It's doubtful that you conduct a formal analysis about each hire that is a couple percentage points over the budgeted salary; it is more likely that you are like other managers who have become used to conducting quick tradeoff analysis in their heads or relying on their "guts" to help them make the best decisions given the information that they have at the time.

The second and more formal method of tradeoff analysis is the comparison of pros and cons. In this method, you would either by yourself or with a team of individuals knowledgeable about the project gather your thoughts on paper. The goal is to list out the pros and cons of each tradeoff that you are making. For example, at AllScale, when Mike Softe was deciding to rush the payment feature into production by reallocating three engineers who were working on other projects, he could list out as many tradeoffs as he could come up with. Then, Mike would identify the pros and cons of each tradeoff, which would look something like this:

1. Engineers reallocated
   - Pros: Faster payment feature development; better feature design
   - Cons: Other features suffer from reallocation; cost allocated to feature increases
2. Speed feature into production
   - Pros: Fulfill business need for no more manual processing
   - Cons: Possibly weaker design; fewer contingencies thought through; increased cost in hardware
3. Reduce quality testing
   - Pros: Meet business timeline
   - Cons: More bugs

After the tradeoffs that are being considered have been identified and the pros and cons of each listed, Mike is ready to move to the next step. This step is to analyze the pros and cons to determine which ones outweigh the others for each tradeoff. Mike can do this by simply examining them or by allocating a score to them in terms of how bad or good they are. For instance, with the reduce quality testing tradeoff, the pros and cons can simply be looked at and a determination made that the pros outweigh the cons in this case. With the tradeoff of reallocating the engineers, the pros and cons would probably have to be analyzed in order to make the decision. In this case, Mike may feel that the features the engineers have been pulled from were all low-to-medium priority and can be postponed or handed off to more junior engineers. In the event that Mike decides to let more junior engineers work on the features, he can mitigate the risk by having an architect review the design and mark this feature for a code review. Because he can mitigate the risk and the benefit is so great, he would likely decide to proceed with this tradeoff. This process of listing out the tradeoffs, determining pros and cons, and then analyzing each one is the second method of performing a tradeoff analysis.

The third method of tradeoff analysis is a more formal process. In this process, you will take the tradeoffs identified and add to them factors that are important in accomplishing the project. What you will have at the end of the analysis is a score that you can use to judge each tradeoff based on the most important metrics to you. As stated earlier, this cannot guarantee that you will make a correct decision, because factors that may impact you in the future might not be known at this point. However, this method will help you be assured that you have made a decision based on data and it is the best decision you can make at this time.

Let us continue the example that we were using with the AllScale payment feature. The tradeoffs that Mike Softe, VP of engineering, had decided on for the payment feature were reallocating engineers, speeding the feature to production, and reducing the quality of testing. He now needs to identify the factors that are most important to him while accomplishing this project. This list can be generated by one person or with a group of people familiar with the project and general needs of the business and technology organizations. For our example, Mike has composed the following list of important factors:

- Meet the business goals of launching by the EOM
- Maintain availability of the entire system at 99.99%
- The feature should scale to 10x growth
- The other product releases should not be pushed off track by this
- We want to follow established processes as much as possible

He then needs to rank order these to find out what factors are the most important. Mike considers the preceding order stated as the order of importance. In Figure 19.3, you can see that Mike has listed the tradeoffs down the left column and placed the

Tradeoffs	Factors	Meet Business Goal of Launch by EOM	Maintain Availability at 99.99%	Feature Scales to 10x	Keep Other Releases on Track	Follow Established Processes	Total
	Weight	5	4	3	2	1	
Engineers Reallocated		9	1	9	−3	−3	67
Speed Feature to Production		9	−3	−3	3	−3	27
Reduce Quality of Testing		1	−3	−1	9	−9	−1

Scale
−9 Highly Unsupportive
−3 Very Unsupportive
−1 Unsupportive
1 Supportive
3 Very Supportive
9 Highly Supportive

Figure 19.3 *Decision Matrix*

factors across the top of the matrix. These factors are sorted and he has added a *weight* below each factor. For simplicity, Mike used 1 through 5, as there are five factors. For more elaborate matrixes, you can use a variety of scales, such as 1, 3, 9, or allocation out of a 100 value sum, where you have 100 points to allocate among the factors (one may get 25, whereas others may get 3).

After the matrix is created, you need to fill in the middle, which is the strength of support that a tradeoff has on a factor. Mike is using a scale from −9 to 9, with increments of 1, 3, −3, and −1. If a tradeoff fully supports a factor, it would receive a score of 9. If it somewhat supports, it gets a 3. If it is unsupportive of the factor, and in which case it would cause the opposite of the factor, it gets a negative score; the higher the more it is unsupportive. For example, the tradeoff of Reduce the Quality Testing for the feature has a −9 score for Follow Established Processes because it clearly does not follow established processes of testing. After the matrix is filled out, Mike can perform the calculations on them. The formula is to multiply each score in the body of the matrix by the weight of each factor and then sum these products for each tradeoff producing the total score. Using the Engineers Reallocated tradeoff, Mike has a formula as depicted in Figure 19.4.

The total score for this tradeoff in the equation in Figure 19.4 is 67. This formula is calculated for each tradeoff. With this final score, Mike and his team can analyze each tradeoff individually as well as all the tradeoffs collectively. From this sample analysis, Mike has decided to find a way to allow more time spent in quality testing while proceeding with reallocating engineers and expediting the feature into production.

$$\text{Total} = (9 \times 5) + (1 \times 4) + (9 \times 3) + (-3 \times 2) + (-3 \times 1)$$

Figure 19.4 *Total Calculation*

Fast or Right Checklist

- What does your gut tell you about the tradeoff?

- What are the pros and cons of each alternative?

- Is a more formal analysis required because of the risk or magnitude of the decision?

- If a more formal analysis is required:

  What are the most important factors? In Six Sigma parlance, these are critical to quality indicators.

  How do these factors rank compared to each other—that is, what is the most important one of these factors?

  What are the actual tradeoffs being discussed?

  How do these tradeoffs affect the factors?

- Would you feel comfortable standing in front of your board explaining your decision based on the information you have today?

We have given you three methods of analyzing the tradeoffs from balancing the cost, quality, and speed constraints. It is completely appropriate to use all three of these methods at different times or in increasing order of formality until you believe that you have achieved a sufficiently rigorous decision. The two factors that you may consider when deciding which method to use are the risk of the project and the magnitude of the decision. The risk should be calculated by one of the methods described in Chapter 16. There is not an exact level of risk that corresponds to a particular analysis methodology. Using the traffic light risk method, projects that would be considered green could be analyzed by gut feeling, whereas yellow projects should at least have the pros and cons compared as described in the pro and con comparison process earlier. Examples of these tradeoff rules are shown in Table 19.1. Of course, red projects should be candidates for a fully rigorous decision matrix. This is another great intersection of processes where a set of rules to work by would be an excellent addition to your documentation.

Table 19.1 *Risk and Tradeoff Rules*

Risk Traffic Light	Risk FMEA	Tradeoff Analysis Rule
Green	< 100 pts	No formal analysis required
Yellow	< 150 pts	Compare pros/cons
Red	> 150 pts	Fill out decision matrix

Conclusion

In this chapter, we tackled the tough and ever present balancing act between cost, quality, speed, and scope. The Project Triangle is used to show how each of these constraints are equally important to pay attention to. Each project will have a different predilection for satisfying one or more of these constraints. Some projects need to more satisfy the need to reduce cost; in others, it is imperative that the quality of the feature be maintained at the detriment of cost, speed, and scope.

We first looked at the definitions of cost, quality, speed, and scope. We determined that the cost of a feature or project included the direct and indirect costs. This can become fairly exhaustive to attempt to allocate all costs with a particular feature, and this exercise is generally not necessary. It is sufficient to be aware that there are many levels of cost and these occur over both short and long terms. For quality, we used a definition that included both the amount of bugs in the feature but also the amount of full functionality. A feature that did not have all the functions specified is of poorer quality than one that has all the specified features. For speed, we defined this term as the time to market or the pace in which the feature moves through the product development life cycle into production but not beyond. Post-production support was a special case that was more a cause of the cost, quality, speed tradeoff, rather than a part of it.

Armed with the definitions, we concluded that as business leaders and technology managers, we are constantly making tradeoff decisions between the three constraints of cost, quality, and speed. Some of these decisions we are aware of and others we are not. Some occur consciously, whereas others are subconscious analyses that are done in a matter of seconds.

We then discussed how the tradeoffs were related to scalability. We concluded that there was a direct relationship when these constraints were made for infrastructure or scalability projects. There was also an indirect relationship when decisions made for features affect the overall scalability of the system many months or years later because of predictable and in some cases unforeseen factors.

Because there is a very strong relationship with decisions made in these tradeoffs to scalability, it is important to make the best decision possible. To help you make these decisions, we provided three methods for decision analysis. These methods were the gut feel method first introduced in our earlier discussion on risk, a pro and con comparison, and finally a rigorous decision matrix that involved formulas for us to calculate scores for each tradeoff. Although we conceded that there is no *correct* answer possible due to the unknowable factors, there are best answers that can be achieved through rigorous analysis and data driven decisions.

As we consider the actual decisions made on the tradeoffs to balance cost, quality, speed, and scope as well as the method of analysis used to arrive at those decisions, the fit within your organization at this particular time is most important. As your organization grows and matures, there may be a need to modify or augment these processes, make them more formal, document them further, or add steps that customize it more for your needs. For any process to be effective, it must be used, and for it to be used, it needs to be a good fit for your team.

Key Points

- There is a classic balance between cost, quality, and speed in almost all business decisions.

- Technology decisions, especially in the product development life cycle, must balance these three constraints daily.

- Each project or feature can have a different allocation across cost, quality, and speed.

- Cost, quality, and speed are known as the Project Triangle because a triangle represents the equal importance of all three constraints.

- We describe a circle that cannot quite fit over the entire Project Triangle as the Allocation Circle. This demonstrates the challenge of having to select equal weighting to all but not complete coverage of any, or a skewed allocation heavily geared toward one or the other constraints.

- There are short- and long-term ramifications of decisions and tradeoffs made during feature development.

- These tradeoffs made on individual features can affect the overall scalability of the entire system.

- Technologists and managers must understand and be able to make the right decisions in the classic tradeoff between speed, quality, and cost.

- There are at least three methods of performing a tradeoff analysis. These are gut feel, pro/con comparison, and decision matrix.

- The risk of the project should help decide which method of tradeoff analysis should be performed.

- A set of rules to govern which analysis method should be used when would be extremely useful for your organization.

Part III

Architecting Scalable Solutions

Chapter 20

Designing for Any Technology

Success in warfare is gained by carefully accommodating ourselves to the enemy's purpose.

—Sun Tzu

Have you ever heard someone describe a design or platform architecture by using the names of the third-party or open source systems used to implement that platform or architecture? The discussion starts with a question, "How are you architected?" and ends with a statement like,

> We use ACME Web servers running on Platinum computers connected to our own internal application running on Ace application servers. We use Bestco databases running on Fastco SMP servers to maintain state and store information. The Fastco servers are connected to a Bestsan storage area network. All of our network gear is Fastgcar and Datasafe provides our firewalls.

Nice product plugs. Each of the speaker's vendors and partners no doubt love how he described his implementation. And yes, we meant to say implementation because the preceding statement is neither a design nor an architecture. The implementation speech sounds like one long product plug covering multiple vendors and might be fine if the company is getting paid by the reference, but that is not likely the case. Describing architectures through implementation is akin to constructing a picture of your current or desired soulmate from pictures cut out of *US* Magazine; the result may paint a good picture of what you have or want, but it in no way describes how it is that the soulmate will meet your current or future needs.

This chapter describes the difference between architecture and implementation. We further make the argument that the best architectures are not accomplished through vendor partnerships but rather through vendor and technology agnostic "boxes" and descriptions.

An Implementation Is Not an Architecture

Sometimes it is easiest, albeit indirect, to describe what something *is* by defining that something by what it *is not*. For instance, in attempting to teach a child what a dog is, you might be required from time to time to explain that a cat is not a dog and that a dog is not a cat. This approach is especially useful when two things are often confused in popular speech and literature. An example of such a popular confusion exists within the definition of an implementation and an architecture.

Put simply, and with the "bottom line up front," an implementation is not an architecture nor is an architecture an implementation. The best architects of buildings and houses do not describe trusses, beams, and supports using the vendor's name, but describe them in terms of size, load capacity, and so on. This is because the architect realizes that in most cases the items in question are commodities and that the vendor solution will likely be selected based on price, reputation, and quality. In essence, the house architect intuitively or as a result of education understands that describing something with a vendor's name is an implementation, whereas describing something through specifications and requirements is an architecture. Similarly, electrical design engineers do not typically reference vendor names when describing a design; they are more likely to reference a resistor and its level of resistance rather than indicating a specific vendor and part number.

Implementations define what you are today and represent the choices you have made due to cost considerations, build versus buy decisions, returns on investment, skill sets within your team, and so on. The use of C++ or Java or PHP as a coding language is not indicative of your architecture; they are choices of tools and materials to implement components of your architecture. The choice of a Microsoft database over Sybase or Oracle as a database is not an architecture, but rather an implementation of a database component of your architecture. The decision to go open source versus a vendor provided solution is another example of an implementation decision, as is the decision to use a Microsoft operating system over using some variant of UNIX.

Technology Agnostic Design

Mature organizations looking to produce the most highly scalable and reliable systems, platforms, and products understand that there is a very big difference between architecture and implementation. The architecture of a platform describes how something works in generic terms with specific requirements, and the implementation describes the specific technologies or vendor components employed. Physical architectures tend to describe the components performing the work, whereas logical architectures tend to define the activities and functions necessary to do the work. We like to discuss architectures from a system's perspective, where the logical architecture is mapped to its physical components such that both can be evaluated in the same view to the extent possible.

The implementation is a snapshot of the architecture and may not even be consistent with the end or desired state of any given architecture. For instance, take an architecture that has a write database as a subcomponent of the system, to which all writes and updates go, and several read databases, from which all reads occur, in a load balanced fashion. For a very small site, it may make sense for a single database to accomplish all of these things (with an additional database for high availability of course). The implementation in this case would be a single database, whereas the site is potentially architected for more than one. Further consider the case where the architecture calls for nearly any database to be used with the application connecting through an abstracted data access layer (DAL) or data access object (DAO). The specific implementation at a point in time might be a database from Microsoft, but with some modifications to the DAL/DAO could ultimately become an open source database or database from IBM, Oracle, or Sybase.

The aim of technology agnostic design (TAD) and technology agnostic architecture (TAA) is to separate design and architecture from the technology employed and the specific implementation. This separation decreases both cost and risk while increasing scalability and availability of your product, system, or platform. Some of our clients even incorporate TAD or TAA into their architectural principles.

TAD and Cost

As we mentioned earlier, architects of houses and buildings rarely describe their work through the names of the vendors providing materials. Certain components, such as 2×4s may have similar characteristics, but many finishing components that differentiate houses do not, such as cabinetry, sinks, toilets, and kitchen appliances. For these components, architects often attempt to describe them in terms of "fit and finish," giving dimensions and design characteristics. These architects understand that if they architect something appropriately, they open up several opportunities for negotiations among competing providers of the aforementioned materials. These negotiations in turn help drive down the cost of building (or implementing) the house. Each vendor is subject to a competitive bidding process, where price, quality, and reputation all come into play.

Technology solutions, much like building materials, suffer the effects of commoditization over time. A good idea or implementation that becomes successful in an industry is bound to attract competitors. The competitors within the solution space initially compete on differences in functionality and service, but over time, these differences decrease as useful feature sets get adopted by all competitors. In an attempt to forestall the effects of commoditization through increased switching costs, providers of systems and software try to produce proprietary solutions or tools that interact specifically and exclusively with their systems.

Avoiding getting trapped by extensive modification of any provider's solution or adoption of tightly integrated provider tools allows you the flexibility of leveraging the effects of commoditization. As competitors within a solution space begin to converge on functionality and compete on price, you remain free to choose the lowest cost of ownership for any given solution. This flexibility results in capital outlay, which minimizes the impact to cash flow and lowers amortized costs, which positively impacts profits on a net income basis. The more your architecture allows you to bring in competing providers or partners, the lower your overall cost structure.

Several times within your career, you are likely to find a provider of technology that is far superior in terms of features and functionality to other providers. You may determine that the cost of implementing this technology is lower than the other providers because you have to build less to implement the product. In making such a decision, you should feel comfortable that the "lock in" opportunity cost of choosing such a provider exceeds the option cost of switching to another provider in the future. In other words, recognize that other providers will move quickly to close the functionality gap and do your best to ensure that the integration of the service in question can be replaced with other providers down the road.

TAD and Risk

In 2009, several American institutions suddenly collapsed; only five years earlier, those institutions would have been considered indestructible. Most independent investment banks that long led the storied march of American capitalism collapsed in a matter of weeks or were devoured by larger banks. Many people started to question the futures of Citibank and Bank of America as the government moved to prop them up with federal funds. Fannie Mae and Freddie Mac both received government funds and became the object of additional government legislation. Other industries, perennially teetering on the edge of disaster, such as the American automobile industry, struggled to find ways to remake themselves.

Imagine that you have built a wonderful business producing specialty vans for handicapped people from Ford vehicles. One hundred percent of your business is built around the Ford Econoline Van, and you can't easily retool your factory for another van given the degree of specialization, your tools, the types of parts necessary to perform your conversions, and your deep relationship with Ford. What do you do if Ford goes out of business? What happens if Ford stays in business but increases its prices, significantly changes the Econoline Van family, or increases the interest rate on the loans you use to purchase and customize the vans?

Now, apply a similar set of questions to your implementation (again, not an architecture) should you choose to become tightly integrated in design and implementation with a database or application server provider. Maybe you have used a proprietary set of APIs for some specific asynchronous functionality unique to the database in question or maybe you have leveraged a proprietary set of libraries unique to the application server you've chosen. What do you do when one or both of those providers go out of business? What if the provider of either technology finds itself being sued for some portion of its solution? What if the viability and maintenance of the product relies upon the genius of a handful of people within the company of the provider and those people leave? What if the solution suddenly starts to suffer from quality problems that aren't easily fixed?

Technology agnostic design reduces all of these risks by increasing your ability to quickly move to other providers. By reducing your switching costs, you not only have reduced your cost, but you have reduced the risk to your customers and shareholders as well.

TAD and Scalability

TAD aids scalability in two ways. The first way is that it forces your company and organization to create disciplines around scale that are not dependent upon any single provider or service. This discipline allows you to scale in multiple dimensions through multiple potential partners, the result of which is a more predictable scalable system independent of any single solution provider. As stated earlier, your risks and costs of scalability are decreased.

A common misperception is that by implementing a certain solution, you are reliant upon that solution. Just because you use Rapidware's database replication technology does not mean that you are dependent upon it alone for scale. True, on any given day, you rely upon the application to work for proper functioning of your site, but that is not the same as saying that the architecture relies upon it for scale. Again, we separate architecture from implementation. Architecture is a design and should not rely upon any given vendor for implementation. Implementation is a point-in-time description of how the architecture works on that day and at that moment. The proper architecture in this replication scenario would call for a replication mechanism with requirements that can be fulfilled by a number of vendors, of which Rapidware is one. If you have done a thorough analysis of the provider landscape and know that you can either switch databases or replication technology providers easily (again, not without some work), you have a scalable solution that is independent of the provider.

You should not get caught in the trap of saying that you must personally build all components to be truly independently scalable. Remember our discussion in Chapter 15, Focus on Core Competencies: Build Versus Buy. Scalable design allows you to drop in commodity solutions to achieve an implementation. Furthermore, nearly all technologies ultimately move toward commoditization or attract open source alternatives. The result is that you rarely need to build most things that you will need outside of those things that truly differentiate your product or platform.

Review of the Four Simple Questions from Chapter 15

These are the four questions from Chapter 15 that we recommend be used to guide any build versus buy decision:

- Does this component create strategic competitive differentiation? Are we going to have long-term sustainable differentiation as a result of this in switching costs, barriers to entry, and so on?

- Are we the best owners of this component or asset? Are we the best equipped to build it and why? Should we sell it if we build it?

- What is the competition to this component? How soon until the competition catches up to us and offers similar functionality?

- Can we build this component cost effectively? Are we reducing our cost and creating additional shareholder value and are we avoiding lost opportunity in revenue?

Remember that you are always likely to be biased toward building so do your best to protect against that bias. The odds are against you that you can build a better product than those already available and you should tune your bias toward continuing to do what you do well today—your primary business.

The second way that TAD supports scalability is actually embedded within the four questions from Chapter 15. Can you see it? Let's ask two questions to get to the answer. Do you believe there will be a rapid convergence of the functionality in question? Do you need to deeply integrate the solution in question to leverage it? If you believe that competitors will rapidly converge on functionality and you do not need deep integration to the selected provider's solution, you should consider using the solution. In doing so, you avoid the cost of building the solution over the long term. The key, as hinted at by the second question, is to keep away from deep integration. You should not be building logic deep within your system to benefit from a providers solution. Building such logic ties you into the solution provider and makes it more difficult for you to benefit from commoditization.

We argue that deep integration of a third-party solution provider is almost never critical to scale if you've properly architected your system, platform, or product. In our experience, we have never come across such a situation that absolutely demands that a company be deeply tied with a third-party provider in order to scale to the company's needs. In most cases, this misconception is fueled by a poor decision somewhere else in the architecture. You may, however, find yourself in a situation where it is faster to resolve a pending or existing crisis by leveraging unique functionality provided by a third party. Should you find yourself in that situation, we recommend the following course of action:

1. Abstract the integration into a service so that future changes to eliminate the integration are limited to the service and not deeply integrated with your systems. Such an abstraction will limit the switching costs after your crisis is over.

2. Make a commitment to resolve the dependency as soon as possible after the crisis.

To illustrate our first point, the abstraction of a service, let's consider AllScale's selection of a database within its technology stack. AllScale desires to leverage a feature from BaseData's new database offering that allows the database to be immediately replicated to multiple locations without replication delay and further allows any replicated database to be the primary database of record for all writes to the database. At the time of the decision, no other database provider or open source alternative has this capability, and in implementing the BaseData's offering, the AllScale team believes it can save more than one hundred thousand dollars in internal development costs for similar functionality. Time to market is key here, so Johnny, Christine, and the technology team decide to purchase the database and quickly implement it.

Christine insists that the team protect the company from being locked into Base-Data's offerings. She does not want BaseData to put a gun to AllScale's head for long-term licensing and maintenance fees. Johnny and the team decide to abstract the database access into a service or "layer" of the architecture. By structuring all database access within a single layer or object, they limit the amount of work necessary to change the database at a future date. Although some functions are unique to Base-Data, the team believes it can simply modify or rewrite this single layer without extensive code modifications throughout the AllScale HRM system. Only a certain number of developers are allowed to write code that will ultimately access the database, and the rest of the development team is required to use a developer API to request data objects from the database.

Resolving Build Versus Buy and TAD Conflicts

Don't be confused with the apparent conflicts between a build versus buy decision and designing agnostically; the two are actually complementary when viewed properly. We've stated that you should own and have core competencies within your team around architecting your platform, service, or product to scale. This does not mean that you need to build each discrete component of your architecture. Architecture and design are completely separate disciplines from development and implementation. Build versus buy is an implementation or development decision and TAD/TAA are design and architecture decisions.

A proper architecture allows for many choices within the build versus buy decision, and the build versus buy decision should only result in buying if sustainable competitive advantage can be created.

TAD and Availability

TAD and TAA affects availability in a number of ways, but the most obvious is the way in which it supports the ability to switch providers of technology when one provider has significantly greater availability or quality than other providers. Often, this leadership position changes over time between providers of services, and you are best positioned to take advantage of that leadership position by being agnostic as to the provider. Again, agnosticism in design and architecture leads to benefits to customers and shareholders.

The TAD Approach

Now that we've discussed the reasons for TAD and TAA, let's discuss how to approach TAD and TAA. Implementing TAD/TAA is fairly simple and straightforward. At its core, it means designing and architecting platforms using concepts rather than solutions. Pieces of the architecture are labeled with their generic system type (database, router, firewall, payment gateway, and so on) and potentially further described with characteristics or specific requirements (gigabit throughput, 5 terabytes of storage, ETL cloud, and so on).

The approach for TAD is straightforward and consists of three easily remembered rules. The first is to think and draw only "boxes," as in what you might find in a wire diagram. For a physical architecture, these boxes depict the type of system employed but never the brand or model. Router, switch, server, storage, database, and so on are all appropriate boxes to be employed in a physical architecture. Logical architectures define the activities, functions, and processes of the system and should also avoid the inclusion of vendor names. For this step, it does not matter that your company might have contracts with specific providers or have an approved provider list. This step is just about ensuring that the design is agnostic, and contracts and approved providers are all implementation related issues.

We hinted at the second step in the first step. Scrub and remove all references to providers, models, or requirements that demand either a provider or model. It's appropriate to indicate requirements in a design, such as a switch that is capable of 10 gigabit throughput; but it is not appropriate to indicate a switch capable of running a Cisco proprietary protocol. Again, interface requirements have to do with implementation. If you have something running in your production environment that requires the same brand of system in other places, you have already locked yourself into a vendor and violated the TAD approach.

The final step is to describe any requirements specific to your design in agnostic terms. Use SQL transactions per second instead of a proprietary vendor database term. Use storage in terms of bytes, spindles, or speeds rather than anything specific to any given vendor like a proprietary storage replication system, and so on. When in doubt, ask yourself whether your design has forced you into a vendor for any given reason, or whether the description of the design is biased by any given vendor or open source solution.

The TAD Approach—Three Simple Steps

Here are three simple steps to help guide you in TAD designs:

- In the design itself, think in terms of boxes and wire diagrams rather than prose. Leave the detail of the boxes to the next step.
- In defining boxes and flows, use generic terms. Application server, Web server, RDBMS, and so on. Don't use vendor names.
- Describe requirements in industry standards. Stay away from proprietary terms specific to a vendor.

Allow your instinct to help guide you. Should you "feel" as though you are being pulled toward a vendor in a description or design statement, attempt to "loosen" that statement to make it agnostic.

A very simple test to determine if you are violating a technology agnostic design is to check whether any component of your architecture is identified with the name of a vendor. Data flows, systems, transfers, and software that are specifically labeled as coming from a specific provider should be questioned. Ideally, even if for some reason a single provider must be used (remember our arguments that this should never be the case), the provider's name should be eliminated. You simply do not want to give any provider a belief that you have already chosen its solution or you handicap yourself in negotiations.

Technology agnosticism is as much about culture as it is a process or principle during design. Engineers and administrators tend to be very biased toward specific programming languages, operating systems, databases, and networking devices. This bias is very often a result of past experiences and familiarity. An engineer who knows C++ better than Java, for instance, is obviously going to be biased toward developing something within C++. An engineer who understands and has worked with Cisco networking equipment her entire career is obviously going to prefer Cisco over a competitor. This bias is simply human nature, and it is difficult to overcome. As such, it is imperative that the engineers and architects understand the reasons for agnosticism. Bright, talented, and motivated individuals who understand the causality between agnosticism and the maximization of flexibility within scalability and the maximization of shareholder wealth will ultimately begin parroting the need for agnosticism.

Conclusion

This chapter made the case for technology agnostic design and architecture. Technology agnostic design (TAD) lowers cost, decreases risk, and increases both scalability and availability. If implemented properly, TAD complements a build versus buy decision process.

TAD is as much of a cultural initiative as it is a process or principle. The biggest barrier to implementing TAD will likely be the natural biases of the engineers and architects for or against certain providers. Ensuring that the organization understands the benefits and reasons for TAD will help overcome these biases. Review the section in Chapter 4, Leadership 101, covering the causal roadmap to success.

Key Points

- The most scalable architectures are not implementations and should not be described as implementations. Vendors, brand names, or open source identifications should be avoided in describing architectures as these are descriptions of implementations.
- TAD and TAA reduce cost by increasing the number of options and competitors within a competitive selection process.
- TAD and TAA reduce risk by lowering switching costs and increasing the speed with which providers or solutions can be replaced in the event of intellectual property issues or issues associated with business viability of your providers.
- TAD and TAA increase scalability through the reduction of cost to scale and the reduction of risk associated with scale. Where technology solutions are likely to converge, TAD and TAA can help you achieve rapid and cost-effective scale by buying rather than building a solution yourself.
- TAD and TAA increase availability by allowing you to select the highest quality provider and the provider with the best availability at any point in time.
- TAD and TAA are as much cultural initiatives as they are processes or principles. To effectively implement them, you need to overcome the natural human bias for and against technologies with which we are more or less conversant, respectively.

Chapter 21

Creating Fault Isolative Architectural Structures

> The natural formation of the country is the soldier's best ally.
>
> —Sun Tzu

Part III, Architecting Scalable Solutions, focuses on the technology aspects of scale. If you purchased this book and flipped immediately to Part III, we entreat you to review the introduction and Parts I, Staffing a Scalable Organization, and II, Building Processes for Scale, of this book. The ties between technology and architecture and scalability are obvious, but where companies most often go wrong is in also addressing the issues of process and organization. In our minds, a failure to treat the issues within your process and organization is akin to treating acquired diabetes with insulin and not addressing exercise and diet as well.

This chapter focuses on architecting to isolate and limit the effects of failure within any system. In the days before full duplex and 10 gigabit Ethernet, when repeaters and hubs were used within CSMA/CD (carrier sense multiple access with collision detection) networks, collisions among transmissions were common. Collisions reduced the speed and effectiveness of the network as collided packets would likely not be delivered on their first attempt. Although the Ethernet protocol (then an implementation of CSMA/CD) used collision detection and binary exponential back off to protect against congestion in such networks, network engineers additionally developed the practice of segmenting networks to allow for fewer collisions and a faster overall network. This segmentation into multiple collision domains also created a fault isolative infrastructure wherein a bad or congested network segment would not necessarily propagate its problems to each and every other peer or sibling network segment. With this approach, collisions were reduced, overall speed of delivery in most cases was increased, and failures in any given segment would not bring the entire network down.

This same general approach can be applied to not just networks, but every other component of your system's architecture. When we use the term system's architecture, we are referring to the way in which your holistic product or platform works. The platform is composed of several entities or subcomponents: a network, proprietary software, servers, databases, operating systems, firewalls, third-party software, application servers, Web servers, and so on. The concept of creating a fault isolative architecture can be applied to each of these individual components and to the system's architecture as a whole.

Fault Isolative Architecture Terms

In our practice, we often refer to fault isolative architectures as *swim lanes*. Although we did not coin the term, we believe it to be a great metaphor for what it is we want to create within architectures. For swimmers, the swim lane represents both a barrier and a guide. The barrier exists to ensure that the swimmer does not cross over into another lane and interfere with another swimmer. In a race, this helps to ensure that no interference happens to unduly influence the probability that any given swimmer will win the race. In practice, or in exercise pools, the barriers exist to ensure that novice swimmers do not interfere with swimmers of greater capabilities. Additionally, the lanes help guide the swimmer toward her objective with minimal effort on the part of the swimmer; in strokes requiring the submersion of a swimmer's head, she can see the lanes as the head is turned or raised for air.

Swim lanes in architecture protect your systems operations similarly to how swim lanes protect swimmers and ensure safe and efficient operation of a pool. Operations of a set of systems within a swim lane are meant to stay within the guide ropes of that swim lane and not cross into the operations of other swim lanes. Furthermore, swim lanes provide guides for architects and engineers designing new functionality to help them decide what set of functionality should be placed in what type of swim lane for progress toward the architectural goal of high scalability.

The term *swim lane*, however, is not the only fault isolative term used within the technical community. Terms like a *pod* are often used to define fault isolative domains representing a group of customers or set of functionality. *Podding* is the act of splitting some set of data and functionality into several groups of fault isolation. Sometimes pods are used to represent groups of services and sometimes they are used to represent separation of data. Thinking back to our definition of fault isolation as applied to either components or systems, the separation of data or services alone would be fault isolation at a component level only. Although this has benefits to the overall system, it is not a complete fault isolation domain from a systems perspective and as such only protects you for the component in question.

Shard is yet another term that is often used within the technical community. Most often, it describes a database structure or storage subsystem. *Sharding* is the splitting of these systems into failure domains with the failure of a single shard not bringing the remainder of the system down as a whole. A storage system comprised of 100 shards may have a single failure that allows the other 99 shards to continue to operate. As with pods, however, this does not mean that the systems addressing those remaining 99 shards will function properly. We will discuss this concept in more detail later in this chapter.

Slivers, chunks, and pools are also terms with which we have become familiar over time. *Slivers* are often used as a replacement for shards. *Chunks* often are used as a synonym for pods. *Pools* most often reference a group of servers that perform similar tasks, this is a fault isolation term but not in the same fashion as swim lanes as we'll discuss later. Most often, these are application servers or Web servers performing some portion of functionality for your platform. All of these terms most often represent components of your overall system design, though the term can easily be extended to mean the entire system or platform rather than just its subcomponent.

Ultimately, there is no single "right" answer regarding what you should call your fault isolative architecture. Choose whatever word you like the most or make up your own descriptive word. There is, however, a "right" approach and that's to design to allow for scale and graceful failure under extremely high demand.

Common Fault Isolation Terms

Swim lane is most often used to describe a fault isolative architecture from a platform or complete system perspective.

Pod is most often used as a replacement for swim lane, especially when fault isolation is performed on a customer or geographic basis.

Shard is a fault isolation term most often used when referencing the splitting of databases or storage subcomponents.

Sliver is a synonym for pod, often also used for storage and database subcomponents.

Chunk is a synonym for pods.

Pool is a fault isolation term commonly applied to software services but is not necessarily a swim lane in implementation.

Benefits of Fault Isolation

Fault isolative architectures offer many benefits within a platform or product. These benefits range from the obvious benefits of increased availability and scalability to the less obvious benefits of decreased time to market and cost of development. Companies find it easier to roll back releases, as we described in Chapter 18, Barrier Conditions and Rollback, and push out new functionality while the site, platform, or product is "live" and serving customers.

Fault Isolation and Availability—Limiting Impact

As the name would seem to imply, fault isolation greatly benefits the availability of your platform or product. When a fault isolation domain or swim lane fails at the platform or systems architecture level, you only lose the functionality, geography, or set of customers that the swim lane serves. Of course, this assumes that you have architected your swim lane properly and that other swim lanes are not making calls to the swim lane in question. Of course, the choice of a swim lane in this case can result in having no net benefit to your availability, so the architecting of swim lanes becomes very important. To explain this, let's look at a swim lane architecture that supports high availability and contrast it with a poorly architected swim lane architecture.

Our fictitious company AllScale, which we have been using to provide examples for various topics, is at it again. The AllScale team decides to apply the concept of creating swim lanes to both the newly developed customer relationship management (CRM) and the existing human resources management (HRM) system. Both are SaaS (Software as a Service) platforms. Johnny Fixer, CTO, and his team develop the CRM platform from scratch to allow for multitenancy at a company level, meaning that multiple companies can reside within the same physical database to reduce your overall cost and make the most efficient use of your capital. The AllScale architects also recognize the need for scalability long term as their customer base grows over time. As such, they decide that they will split the application and databases along customer boundaries for both the newly developed CRM solution and the existing HRM solution. Johnny and the AllScale team decide that the smallest customer segment they will ever need to split upon is a division within a company. The AllScale architects also decide to run multiple live data centers throughout the United States.

The AllScale architects select a swim lane, or fault isolative architecture, that places somewhere between a very large company division and several smaller companies into a single data center with all of the services necessary to run those customers out of that data center. The swim lane construction is depicted in Figure 21.1. The data center location is selected based on proximity to the corporate headquarters of the companies the data center will serve. No services are allowed to communicate between data centers. As a result, when any set of components from the database to

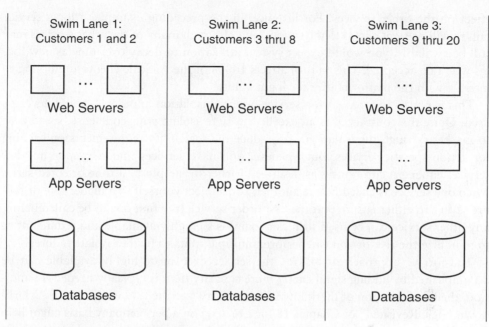

Figure 21.1 *Swim Lane by Customer*

the border routers fail within a data center, only the customers contained within that data center are impacted for the period of outage or service degradation.

The AllScale architects further identify a way to scale with fault isolation within a data center. With virtual local area network segmentation and multiple databases, more than one division or group of companies can be placed into one of many fault isolation domains within the data center. This allows for fault isolation of systems and services below the internal router and inclusive of network LANs, databases, application servers, and so on. Again, services are not allowed to communicate across these fault isolation domains. Here too, the result is that any equipment failure other than shared network components such as routers and border routers will be isolated to the customers within a single zone or domain within the data center. In implementation, the design exceeds expectations and allows the company to roll beta products to isolated customer segments, thereby further decreasing risk.

Contrast the preceding approach with an approach where fault isolation domains are created on a services level. Let's imagine that the AllScale team created fault isolative structures along the boundaries of services rather than customer boundaries. In this case, the team might create a swim lane for the login service, one for the population and updating of leads, one for the reading of leads, one for reporting on lead metrics, and so on. This initially seems like an appropriate approach to achieve some level of scale within the system and isolate faults. The issue with this approach is that the failure of at least one of these services is going to have an unintended downstream effect on the other services. For instance, in the preceding example, a login service failure will prevent access to the system, and although many of the other services may still be available, you would expect system utilization to decay over time as new logins won't be accepted. This in turn affects 100% of the AllScale clients attempting to interact with the platform after the login failure.

This is not to say that such a service-oriented isolation approach should never be used. Quite the contrary, it is an excellent way to isolate your code base, speed time to market through the isolation, and reduce the scalability requirements on caching for action specific services. But whenever you have services that rely upon another service, either synchronously as described earlier or simply in a time oriented series when one service is called before another, you subject yourself to a higher rate of failure. You can either ensure that the first order service (the first one to be called before any other service can be used such as a login) is so highly available and redundant as to minimize the risk or you can perform multiple splits to further isolate failures.

The former approach of making the service even more highly available can be accomplished by adding significantly more capacity than is typically needed. In addition, the incorporation of markdown functionality (see the following sidebar "Markdown Logic Revisited" or Chapter 18 for a review) on a per company basis might help us isolate certain problems. Forcing a small percentage of customers through a specialized login pool service for new login code might reduce AllScale's risk with new rollouts, and establishing connection limits on the servers might help them keep some customers logging in properly when they have slowdowns in service for some reason.

Markdown Logic Revisited

You may recall from Chapter 18 that we provided an implementation of the architectural principle Design to be Disabled in what we called *markdown functionality*. Markdown functionality enables certain features within a product to be turned off without affecting other features. The typical reason companies invest in markdown functionality is to limit the negative impact of new feature releases on either availability or scalability.

Proper markdown functionality allows a new release to remain in a production environment while the offending code or system is fixed and without rolling the entire release back. The offending code or system is simply taken offline typically through a software "toggle" and is brought back online after the cause of unintended behavior is rectified.

The latter approach of performing multiple splits to isolate failures is our preferred method of addressing both scalability and availability. In this method, AllScale could combine the splits of services and splits of customers on a per company basis.

AllScale could have the services oriented split of logins be the primary method of split and isolation by implementing a login service swim lane and then make a customer oriented split with swim lanes by companies within the services swim lane. Alternatively, AllScale could swap the approach and create a customer pod (or swim lane) for groups of companies; within that pod, it could break out its services by swim lanes, one of which would be a login service. Either method is fine, though most companies find that the customer oriented split is a little more intuitive. We will discuss these types of splits in greater detail in Chapters 22, Introduction to the AKF Scale Cube, 23, Splitting Applications for Scale, and 24, Splitting Databases for Scale, where we address the AKF Scale Cube and how to apply it to services, databases, and storage structures.

Fault Isolation and Availability—Incident Detection and Resolution

Fault isolation also increases availability because incidents are easier to detect, identify, and resolve. If you have several swim lanes, each dedicated to a group of customers, and only a single swim lane goes down, you know quite a bit about the failure immediately; it is limited to a set of customers. As a result, your questions to resolve the incident are nearly immediately narrowed. More than likely, the issue is a result of systems or services that are servicing that set of customers alone. Maybe it's a database unique to that customer swim lane. You might ask, "Did we just roll code out to that swim lane or pod?" or more generally, "What were the most recent changes to that swim lane or pod?" As the name implies, fault isolation has incredible benefits to incident detection and resolution. Not only does fault isolation isolate the incident from propagation throughout your platform, it focuses your incident resolution process like a laser and shaves critical time off the restoration of service.

Fault Isolation and Scalability

This is a book on scalability and it should be no surprise, given that we've included fault isolation as a topic, that it somehow benefits your scalability initiatives. The subject of exactly how fault isolation affects scalability has to do with how you split your services, as we'll discuss in Chapters 22 through 24, and has to do with the architectural principle of scaling out rather than up. The most important thing to remember is that to have a swim lane it must not communicate synchronously into any other swim lane. It can make asynchronous calls with the appropriate timeouts and discard mechanisms to other swim lanes, but you cannot have a connection oriented communication to any other service outside of the swim lane. We'll discuss how to construct and test swim lanes later in this chapter.

Fault Isolation and Time to Market

Creating architectures that allow you to isolate code into service oriented or resource oriented systems gives you the flexibility of focus and the ability to dedicate engineers to those services. When you are a small company, this probably doesn't make much sense. But as your company grows, the lines of code, number of servers, and overall complexity of your system will grow. To handle this growth in complexity, you will need to focus your engineering staff. Failing to specialize and focus your staff will result in too many engineers having too little information on the entire system to be effective.

If you run a commerce site, you might have code, objects, methods, modules, servers, and databases focused on checkout, finding, comparing, browsing, shipping, inventory management, and so on. By dedicating teams to these areas, each team will become an expert on a codebase that is itself complex, challenging, and growing. The resulting specialization will allow for faster new feature development and a faster time to resolve known or current incidents and problems. All of this increase in speed to delivery may result in a faster time to market for bug fixes, incident resolution, and new feature development.

Additionally, this isolation of development and ideally isolation of systems or services will reduce the merge conflicts that would happen within monolithic systems development. Here, we use the term monolithic systems development to identify source that is shared across all set of functions, objects, procedures, and methods within a given product. Duplicate checkouts for a complex system across many engineers will result in an increase in merge conflicts and errors. Specializing the code and the engineering teams reduce these conflicts.

This is not to say that code reuse should not be a focus for the organization; it absolutely should be a focus. Shared libraries should be developed, and potentially you should consider a dedicated team responsible for shared library development and oversight. These libraries can be implemented as services to services, as shared dynamically loadable libraries, or compiled and/or linked during the build of the product. Our preferred approach, however, would be to have shared libraries dedicated to a team, and should a nonshared library team develop a useful and potentially sharable component, that component should be moved to the shared library team.

Recognizing that engineers like to continue to be challenged, you might be concerned that engineers will not want to spend a great deal of time on a specific area of your site. You can slowly rotate engineers to get them a better understanding of the entire system and in so doing stretch and develop them over time. Additionally, you start to develop potential future architects with a breadth of knowledge regarding your system or fast reaction SWAT team members that can easily get into and resolve incidents and problems.

Fault Isolation and Cost

In the same ways and for the same reason that fault isolation reduces time to market, it can also reduce cost. One way to look at it is as you get greater throughput for each hour and day spent on a per engineer basis, your per unit cost goes down. For instance, if it normally took you 5 engineering days to produce the average story or use-case in a complex monolithic system, it might now take you 4.5 engineering days to produce the average story or use-case in a disaggregated system with swim lanes. The average per unit cost of your engineering endeavors was just reduced by 10%!

You can do one of two things with this per unit cost reduction, both of which impact net income and as a result shareholder wealth. You might decide to reduce your engineering staff by 10% and produce exactly the same amount of product enhancements, changes, and bug fixes at a lower absolute cost than before. This reduction in cost increases net income without an increase in revenue.

Alternatively, you might decide that you are going to keep your current cost structure and attempt to develop more products at the same cost. The thought here is that you will make great product choices that increase your revenue. If you are successful, you also increase net income and as a result your shareholders will become wealthier.

You may correctly believe that additional sites usually end up costing more capital than running out of a single site and that operational expenses may increase. Although this is true, most companies aspire to have products capable of weathering geographically isolated disasters and invest to varying levels in disaster recovery initiatives that help mitigate the effects of such disasters. As we will discuss in Chapter 32, Planning Data Centers, assuming you have an appropriately fault isolated architecture, the capital and expense associated with running three or four properly fault isolated data centers can be significantly less than two completely redundant data centers.

Another consideration in justifying fault isolation is the effect that it has on revenue. Referring back to Chapter 6, Making the Business Case, you can attempt to calculate the lost opportunity (lost revenue) over some period of time. Typically, this will be the easily measured loss of a number of transactions on your system added to the future loss of a higher than expected customer departure rate and the resulting reduction in revenue. This loss of current and future revenue can be used to determine if the cost of implementing a fault isolated architecture is warranted. In our experience, some measure of fault isolation is easily justified through the increase in availability and the resulting decrease in lost opportunity.

How to Approach Fault Isolation

The most fault isolative systems are those that make absolutely no calls and have no interaction with anything outside of their functional or data boundaries. The best way to envision this is to think of a group of lead lined, concrete structures, each with a single door. Each door opens into a long isolated hallway that has a single door at each end; one door accesses the lead lined concrete structure and one door accesses a shared room with an infinite number of desks and people. In each of these concrete structures is a piece of information that one of the people sitting at the many desks might want. To get that information, he has to travel the long hallway dedicated to the room with the information he needs and then walk back to his desk. After that journey, he may decide to get a second piece of information from the room he just entered, or travel down another hallway to another room. It is impossible for a person to cross from one room to the next; he must always make the long journey. If too many people get caught up attempting to get to the same room down the same hallway, it will be immediately apparent to everyone in the room and they can either decide to travel to another room or simply wait.

In this example, we've not only illustrated how to think about fault isolative design, but we've demonstrated two benefits of such a design. The first benefit is that a failure in capacity of the hallway does not keep anyone from moving on to another room. The second benefit is that everyone knows immediately which room has the capacity problem. Contrast this with an example where each of the rooms is connected to a shared hallway and there is but one entrance to this shared hallway from our rather large room. Although each of the rooms is isolated, should he back up into the hallway, it becomes both difficult to determine which room is at fault and impossible to travel to the other rooms. This example also illustrates our first principle of fault isolative architecture.

Principle 1: Nothing Is Shared

The first principle of fault isolative design or architecture is that absolutely nothing is shared. Of course, this is an extreme and may not be financially feasible in some companies, but it is nevertheless the starting point for fault isolative design. If you want to ensure that capacity or system failure does not cause problems for multiple systems, you need to isolate system components. This may be very difficult in several areas, like border or gateway routers. That said, and recognizing both the financial and technical barriers in some cases, the more thoroughly you apply the principle, the better your results.

One often overlooked area is URIs/URLs. For instance, consider using different subdomains for different groups. If grouping by customers, consider cust1.allscale.com to custN.allscale.com. If grouping by services, maybe view.allscale.com, update.allscale.com, input.allscale.com, and so on. The domain grouping ideally also references isolated Web and app servers as well as databases and storage unique to that URI/URL. If financing allows and demand is appropriate, dedicated load balancers, DNS, and access switches should be used.

If you identify two swim lanes and have them communicate to a shared database, they are the same swim lane in the big picture. You may have two smaller fault isolation zones from a service's perspective (for instance, the application servers), which will help when one application server fails; but should the database fail, it will bring down both of these service swim lanes.

Principle 2: Nothing Crosses a Swim Lane Boundary

This is another important principle in designing fault isolative systems. If you have systems communicating synchronously and even asynchronously, they can cause a potential fault. Although it is true that asynchronous systems are less likely to cause such a fault, they have caused plenty of issues in extremely high demand scenarios when timeouts aren't aggressive enough to bump unlikely to complete processes.

You cannot build a fault isolation zone and have that zone communicate to anything outside of the zone. Think back to our concrete room analogy: the room and its hallway were the fault isolation zone or domain. The large shared room was the Internet. There was no way to move from one room to the next without travelling back to the area of the desk (our browser) and then starting down another path. As a result, we know exactly where bottlenecks or problems are immediately and we can figure out how to handle those problems.

Any communication between zones, or paths between rooms in our scenario, can cause problems with our fault isolation. A backup of people in one hallway may be the cause of the hallway connected to that room or any of a series of rooms connected by other hallways. How can we tell easily without a thorough diagnosis? Conversely, a backup in any room may have an unintended effect in some other room; as a result, our room availability goes down.

Principle 3: Transactions Occur Along Swim Lanes

Given the name and the previous principle, this principle should go without saying; but we learned long ago not to assume anything. In technology, assumption is the mother of catastrophe. Have you ever seen swimmers line up facing the length of a pool, but seen the swim lane ropes running widthwise? Of course not, but the resulting water obstacle course would probably be great fun to watch.

The same is true for technical swim lanes. It is incorrect to say that you've created a swim lane of databases, for instance. How would transactions get to the databases? Communication would have to happen across the swim lane; and per Principle 2, that should never happen. In this case, you may well have created a pool, but because transactions cross a line, it is not a swim lane as we define it.

When to Implement Fault Isolation

If only money grew on trees . . . . Fault isolation isn't free and it is not even cheap. Although it has a number of benefits, attempting to design every single function of your platform to be fault isolative would likely be cost prohibitive. Moreover, the shareholder return just wouldn't be there. And that's the answer to the preceding heading. After twenty and a half chapters, you probably can sense where we are going.

You should implement just the right amount of fault isolation in your system to generate a positive shareholder return. "OK, thanks, how about telling me how to do that?" you might ask.

The answer, unfortunately, is going to depend on your particular needs, the rate of growth and unavailability and causes of unavailability in your system, customer expectation with respect to availability, contractual availability commitments, and a whole host of things that result in a combinatorial explosion, which make it impossible for us to describe for you what you need to do in your environment.

That said, there are some simple rules to apply to increase your scalability and availability. We present some of the most useful here to help you in your fault isolation endeavors.

Approach 1: Swim Lane the Money-Maker

Whatever you do, always make sure that the thing that is most closely related to making money is appropriately isolated from the failures and demand limitations of other systems. If you are a commerce site, this might be your purchase flow from the "buy" button and checkout process through the processing of credit cards. If you are a content site and you make your money through proprietary advertising, ensure that the advertising system functions separately from everything else. If you are a recurring registration fee based site, ensure that the processes from registration to billing are appropriately fault isolated.

It stands to reason that you might have some subordinate flows that are closely tied to the money making functions of your site and you should consider these for swim lanes as well. For instance, in a commerce site, the search and browse functionality might need to be in swim lanes. In content sites, the most heavily trafficked areas might need to be in their own swim lanes or several swim lanes to help with demand and capacity projections. Social networking sites may create swim lanes for the most commonly hit profiles or segment profile utilization by class.

Approach 2: Swim Lane the Biggest Sources of Incidents

If in your recurring quarterly incident review (Chapter 8, Managing Incidents and Problems), you identify that certain components of your site are repeatedly causing other incidents, you should absolutely consider these for future headroom projects (Chapter 11, Determining Headroom for Applications) and isolate these areas. The whole purpose of the quarterly incident review is to learn from our past mistakes, and if demand related issues are causing availability problems on a recurring basis, we should isolate those areas from impacting the rest of our product or platform.

Approach 3: Swim Lane Along Natural Barriers

This is especially useful in multitenant SaaS systems and most often relies upon the z-axis of scale discussed later in Chapters 22 to 24. The sites and platforms needing the greatest scalability often have to rely on segmentation along the z-axis, which is most often implemented on customer boundaries. Although this split is often first accomplished along the storage or database tier of architecture, it follows that we should create an entire swim lane from request to data storage or database and back.

Very often, *multitenant* indicates that you are attempting to get cost efficiencies from common utilization. In many cases, this approach means that you can design the system to run one or many "tenants" in a single swim lane. If this is true for your platform, you should make use of it. If you have a tenant that is very busy, assign it a swim lane. A majority of your tenants have very low utilization? Assign them all to a single swim lane. You get the idea.

Fault Isolation Design Checklist

The design principles for fault isolative architectures are

- *Principle 1: Nothing Is Shared (a.k.a. share as little as possible).* The less that is shared within a swim lane, the more fault isolative the swim lane becomes.

- *Principle 2: Nothing Crosses a Swim Lane Boundary.* Communication never crosses a swim lane boundary or the boundary is drawn incorrectly.

- *Principle 3: Transactions Occur with Swim Lanes.* You can't create a swim lane of services as the communication to those services would violate Principle 2.

The approaches for fault isolative architectures are

- *Approach 1: Swim Lane the Money-Maker.* Never allow your cash register to be compromised by other systems.

- *Approach 2: Swim Lane the Biggest Sources of Incidents.* Identify the recurring causes of pain and isolate them.

- *Approach 3: Swim Lane Natural Barriers.* Customer boundaries make good swim lanes.

Although there are a number of approaches, these will go a long way to increasing your scalability while not giving your CFO a heart attack.

How to Test Fault Isolative Designs

The easiest way to test a fault isolative design is to draw your platform at a high level on a whiteboard. Draw a dotted line for any communication between systems, and a solid line for where you believe your swim lanes exist or should exist. Anywhere a dotted line crosses a solid line, you have a violation of a swim lane. From a purist perspective, it does not matter if that communication is synchronous or asynchronous, though synchronous transactions and communications are a more egregious violation from both a scalability and an availability perspective. This test will test against the first and second principles of fault isolative designs and architectures.

To test the third principle, simply draw an arrow from the user to the last system on your whiteboard. The arrow should not cross any lines for any swim lane; if it does, you have violated the third principle.

Conclusion

In this chapter, we discussed the need for fault isolative architectures, principles of implementation, approaches for implementation, and finally a design test. We most commonly use swim lanes to identify a completely fault isolative component of an architecture, though terms like pods and slivers are often used to mean the same thing.

Fault isolative designs increase availability by ensuring that subsets of functionality do not hamper the overall functionality of your entire product or platform. They further aid in increasing availability by allowing for immediate detection of the areas causing problems within the system. They lower both time to market and cost by allowing for dedicated, deeply experienced resources to focus on the swim lanes and by reducing merge conflicts and other barriers and costs to rapid development. Scalability is increased by allowing for scale in multiple dimensions as discussed in Chapters 22 through 24.

The principles of swim lane construction include a principle addressing sharing, one addressing swim lane boundaries, and one addressing swim lane direction. The fewer things that are shared within a swim lane, the more isolative and beneficial that swim lane becomes to both scalability and availability. Swim lane boundaries should never have lines of communication drawn across them. Swim lanes always move in the direction of communication and customer transactions and never across them.

Always address the transactions making the company money first when considering swim lane implementation. Then, move functions causing repetitive problems into swim lanes. Finally, consider the natural layout or topology of the site for opportunities to swim lane, such as customer boundaries in a multitenant SaaS environment.

Key Points

- Swim lane is a term used to describe a fault isolative architecture construct in which a failure in the swim lane is not propagated and does not affect other platform functionality.

- Pods, shards, and chunks are often used in place of the term swim lane, but often they do not represent a "full system" view of functionality and fault isolation.

- Fault isolation increases availability and scalability while decreasing time to market and cost of development.

- The less you share in a swim lane, the greater its benefit to availability and scalability.

- No communication or transaction should ever cross a swim lane boundary.

- Swim lanes go in the direction of and never across transaction flow.

- Swim lane the functions that directly impact revenue, followed by those that cause the most problems and any natural boundaries that can be defined for your product.

Chapter 22

Introduction to the AKF Scale Cube

Ponder and deliberate before you make a move.

—Sun Tzu

Chapter 21, Creating Fault Isolative Architectural Structures, focused on making things more fault isolative so that when something failed, either as a result of incredible demand or technical glitches, our entire product or service didn't go away. There, we referred several times to the AKF Scale Cube to highlight methods by which components of our architecture might be split into swim lanes or failure domains. In this chapter, we are going to reintroduce the AKF Scale Cube. We developed the scale cube to help our clients think about how to split services, data, and transactions, and to a lesser degree as outlined in the introduction, teams and processes. As with our principles, we gave the AKF Scale Cube to our clients as a way to think about scale. Feel free to use it within your own company or for your own purposes.

Concepts Versus Rules and Tools

Before we reintroduce the cube, we thought it important to discuss why we developed the AKF Scale Cube versus a set of steps, rules, or tools that one might employ. The reason for the development of the cube has its roots in our beliefs regarding the difference between engineers and technicians. Engineers are taught *why* something works and this understanding typically starts at a level much lower than the specific discipline of engineering in question. Most engineers spend nearly two years learning the building blocks that they will later apply in the latter two years of a four-year degree. Often, the engineer really doesn't understand why she is learning something, and unfortunately professors don't create the causal roadmap to success between what is learned during freshman calculus and how it will ultimately apply to say

Faraday's law and the calculation of electromagnetic force (EMF) in a sophomore physics class or a junior core electrical engineering class. Nevertheless, concepts and building blocks are stressed first, and to graduate to the application of these concepts, one must first master the concepts themselves.

Technicians, on the other hand, are often handed a set of rules and equations and given a rote course focused on understanding the rough interrelationships and are taught how something works. How is predicated on a set of rules that does not require understanding why those rules exist or the method by which one would prove the rules work. Why doesn't start at the level of the rules, but rather deep below those rules with the physics and chemistry that ultimately become the building blocks for those rules.

Electricians are not in the business of deriving the equations they apply; their expertise is in knowing a set of rules that explains how something works. They are experts in applying those rules and coming up with an action. Electricians are great at planning electrical infrastructure for projects requiring the application of the same set of tools and the same set of products or components. It is rare, however, to find an electrician or a technician who is going to create a paradigm shift based on the understanding of the whys for any given system when they haven't been taught the reasons for the whys. More likely, when looking for major changes to the way something operates and to allow that something to achieve new and higher levels of performance, you are going to need an engineer.

As such, we developed a cube that consists of concepts rather than rules. The cube on its own serves as a way to think about the whys of scale and helps create a bridge to the hows. The cube also serves to facilitate a common language for discussing different strategies, just as physics and math serve as the underlying languages for engineering discussions.

Introducing the AKF Scale Cube

Imagine first, if you will, a Rubik's cube or classic colored children's building block. Hold this imaginary block directly in from of you, or stare down directly at it so that you can only see a single face of the six faces. At this point, the cube is nothing more than a two-dimensional square, similar to the square seen in Figure 22.1.

Figure 22.1 *Starting Point of the AKF Scale Cube*

Now take the cube in your hand and rotate it one-eighth of a turn to the left, such that the face to the right of the cube is visible and roughly the same size as the original face you had viewed of the cube. Note that you should not yet see the top or bottom of the cube or block in your hand, but rather two roughly equal faces, each of them moving at a 45-degree angle away from you to the right and to the left.

Now for one last turn. Turn the cube roughly one-eighth a turn down. To accomplish this, you want to take the lower point of the edge created between the two sides that you can currently see and rotate it downward or to the 6 o'clock position. The result is that you should now see roughly three sides of the cube: the original face, which is now one-eighth of a turn to your left and pointing off at roughly a 45-degree angle away from you, the right face, which was exposed in the first rotation to the left, and the top of the cube, which was exposed in the last rotation. The result should look something like in the cube show in Figure 22.2.

On its own, this cube doesn't offer us much, so we need to add reference points to help us in our future discussion. To do this, we will add the traditional three-dimensional axes. Adding an x-axis moving from left to right, a y-axis moving up and down the page, and a z-axis that points out directly behind the cube gives us something that looks like Figure 22.3.

We will call the point of intersection of our three axes the *initial point*, as referenced by the values x = 0, y = 0, and z = 0.

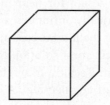

Figure 22.2 *AKF Scale Cube Without Axes*

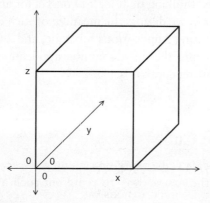

Figure 22.3 *AKF Scale Cube with Axes*

Meaning of the Cube

The initial point, with coordinates of (0,0,0), is the point of least scalability within any system. It consists of a single monolithic application and storage retrieval system likely running on a single physical system. It might scale "up" (which would violate one of our principles of scale as defined in Chapter 12, Exploring Architectural Principles) with larger and faster hardware, but it won't scale "out"; as a result, it will limit your growth to the growth allowed by the hardware and software available in open source or through third-party providers.

As you move along any axis, making modifications, the scalability of your system is increased. One axis might benefit certain scale characteristics more than others. For instance, a split along the x-axis might allow transaction growth to scale very well but not materially impact your ability to store, retrieve, and search through customer, account, or catalog information. To address such a storage or memory constraint, you might need to consider a y-axis implementation or split. Y-axis splits, on the other hand, might allow you to split information for the purposes of searching through it faster, but may hinder your efforts when the joining of information is required, and for this you might need to consider z-axis splits.

The use of one axis does not preclude you from making use of other axes. In the ideal case where financial considerations and the need to ensure profitability did not impact our decisions, we would design for near infinite splits along all three axes. Doing so would give us theoretically infinite scale from a design perspective. In implementation, we could choose the lowest cost approach to meeting our real-time scalability needs by selecting the cheapest solution from a split in the x-, y-, or z-axis. Of course, designing for near infinite scale, although cheaper than implementing such a design, still has costs in terms of engineering and architecture time spent and lost opportunity of revenue associated with the delay in time to market. Furthermore, only the fastest growing of hyper-growth platforms really need to consider such a move, which is why we suggested thinking of at least two axes for any given implementation.

In the following sections, we discuss the meaning of each of the axes at a very high level. In Chapters 23, Splitting Applications for Scale, and 24, Splitting Databases for Scale, we will dig deeper into the most common applications of each of these axes: splitting services and splitting databases.

The X-Axis of the Cube

The x-axis of the AKF Scale Cube represents cloning of services and data with absolutely no bias. Perhaps the easiest way to represent such a split is to think first in terms of people and organizations. Let's first consider the days in which typing pools handled the typing of meeting minutes, letters, internal memos, and so on. Note the use of the term *pool* as far back as 50 or more years identifying a service distributed among several entities (in this case people). Work would be sent to the typing pool largely without a bias as to what individual typist performed the work. Some typists might be faster than others and as a result would get more work sent their way and accomplish more work within the course of a day, but ideally it would not matter where any individual piece of work went within the pool. Everyone could type and everyone was capable of typing one of the set of internal memos, external letters, or meeting minutes. In effect, other than the speed of the hardware (typewriter) used and the speed of the person, everyone was a clone and capable of doing the work. This distribution of work among clones is a perfect example of x-axis scalability.

Another people example to illustrate our point might be within the accounts receivable or accounts payable portion of your company's finance organization. Initially, for small to medium companies, and assuming that the work is not outsourced, the groups might be comprised of a few people, each of whom can perform all of the tasks within his area. The accounts payable staff can all receive bills and generate checks based on a set of processes and send those checks out or get them countersigned depending upon the value of the check written. The accounts receivable staff is capable of generating invoices from data within the system, receiving checks, making appropriate journal entries, and depositing the checks. Each person can do all of the tasks, and it docs not matter to whom the work goes.

All three of these examples illustrate the basic concept of the x-axis, which is the unbiased distribution of work across clones. Each clone can do the work of the other clones and there is no bias with respect to where the work travels (other than individual efficiency). Each clone has the tools and resources to get the work done and will perform the work given to it as quickly as possible.

The x-axis seems great! When we need to perform more work, we just add more clones. Is the number of memorandums exceeding your current typing capacity? Simply add more typists! Is your business booming and there are too many invoices to make and payments coming in? Add more accounts receivable clerks! Why would we ever need any more axes? Let's return to our typing pool first to answer this question.

Let's assume that in order to write some of our memorandums, external letters, and notes a typist needs to have certain knowledge to complete them. Let's say that as the company grows, the services offered by the typing pool increases. The pool now performs some 100 different types and formats of services and the work is not evenly distributed across these types of services. External client letters have several different formats that vary by the type of content included within the message, memorandums vary by content and intent, and meeting notes vary by the type of meeting, and so on. Now an individual typist may get some work done very fast (the work that is most prevalent throughout the pool) but be required to spend time looking up the less frequent formatting, which in turn slows down the entire pipeline of work. As the type of work increases for any given service, more time may be spent trying to get work of varying sizes done; and the instruction set to accomplish this work may not be easily kept in any given typist's head. These are all examples of problems associated with the x-axis of scale; it simply does not scale well with an increase in data, either as instruction sets or reference data. The same holds true if the work varies by the sender or receiver. For instance, maybe vice presidents and above get special formatting or are allowed to send different types of communication than directors of the company. Perhaps special letterhead or stock is used that varies by the sender. Maybe the receiver of the message causes a variation in tone of communication or paper stock. Account delinquent letters may require a special tone not referenced within the notes to be typed, for instance.

As another example, consider again our accounts receivable group. This group obviously performs a very wide range of tasks from the invoicing of clients to the receipt of bills, the processing of delinquent accounts, and finally the deposit of funds into our bank account(s). The processes for each of these grows as the company grows and our controller is going to want some specific process controls to exist so that money doesn't errantly find its way out of the accounts receivable group and into one of our employees pockets before payday! This is another place where scaling for transaction growth alone is not likely to allow us to scale cost effectively into a multibillion dollar company! We will likely need to perform splits based on the services this group performs and/or the clients or types of clients they serve. These splits are addressed by the y- and z-axes of our cube, respectively.

The x-axis split tends to be easy to understand and implement and fairly inexpensive in terms of capital and time. Little additional process or training is necessary, and managers find it easy to distribute the work. Our people analogy holds true for systems as well, which we will see in Chapters 23 and 24. The x-axis works well when the distribution of a high volume of transactions or work is all that we need to do.

Summarizing the X-Axis

The x-axis of the AKF Scale Cube represents the cloning of services or data such that work can easily be distributed across instances with absolutely no bias.

X-axis implementations tend to be easy to conceptualize and typically can be implemented at relatively low cost.

X-axis implementations are limited by growth in instructions to accomplish tasks and growth in data necessary to accomplish tasks.

The Y-Axis of the Cube

The y-axis of the cube of scale represents a separation of work responsibility by either the type of data, the type of work performed for a transaction, or a combination of both; one way to view these splits is a split by responsibility for an action. We often refer to these as *service or resource oriented splits*. In a y-axis split, the work for any specific action or set of actions, as well as the information and data necessary to perform that action, is split away from other types of actions. This type of split is the first split that addresses the monolithic nature of work and the separation of the same into either pipelined work flows or parallel processing flows. Whereas the x-axis is simply the distribution of work among several clones, the y-axis represents more of an industrial revolution for work; we move from a "job shop" mentality to a system of greater specialization, just as Henry Ford did with his automobile manufacturing. Rather than having 100 people creating 100 unique automobiles, with each person doing 100% of the tasks, we now have 100 unique individuals performing subtasks such as engine installation, painting, windshield installation, and so on.

Let's return to our previous example of a typing service pool. In our x-axis example, we identified that the total output of our pool might be hampered as the number and diversity of tasks grew. Specialized information might be necessary based on the type of typing work performed: an internal memorandum might take on a significantly different look than a memo meant for external readers, and meeting notes might vary by the type of meeting, and so on. The vast majority of the work may be letters to clients of a certain format and typed on a specific type of letterhead and bond. When someone is presented with one of the 100 or so formats that only represent about 10% to 20% of the total work, they may stop and have to look up the appropriate format, grab the appropriate letterhead and/or bond, and so on. One approach to this might be to create much smaller pools specializing in some of the more common requests within this 10% to 20% of the total work and a third pool that handles the small minority of the remainder of the common requests. Both of these new service pools could be sized appropriate to the work.

The expected benefit of such an approach would be a significant increase in the throughput of the large pool representing a vast majority of the requests. This pool would no longer "stall" on a per typist basis based on a unique request. Furthermore, for the next largest pool of typists, some specialization would happen for the next most common set of requests, and the output expectations would be the same; for those sets of requests typists would be familiar with them and capable of handling them much more quickly than before. The remaining set of requests that represent a majority of formats but a minority of request volume would be handled by the third pool and although throughput would suffer comparatively, it would be isolated to a smaller set of people who might also at least have some degree of specialization and knowledge. The overall benefit should be that throughput should go up significantly. Notice that in creating these pools, we have also created a measure of fault isolation as identified within Chapter 21. Should one pool stall due to paper issues and such, the entire "typing factory" does not come to a halt.

It is easy to see how the separation of responsibilities would be performed within our running example of the accounts receivable department. Each unique action could become its own service. Invoicing might be split off into its own team or pool, as might payment receiving/journaling and deposits. We might further split late payments into its own special group that handles collections and bad debt. Each of these functions has a unique set of tasks that require unique data, experience, and instructions or processes. By splitting them, we reduce the amount of information any specific person needs to perform his job, and the resulting specialization should allow us to perform processing faster. The y-axis industrial revolution has saved us!

Although the benefits of the y-axis are compelling, y-axis splits tend to cost more than the simpler x-axis splits. The reason for the increase in cost is that very often to perform the y-axis split there needs to be some rework or redesign of process, rules, software, and the supporting data models or information delivery system. Most of us don't think about splitting up the responsibilities of our teams or software when we are a three-person company or a Web site running on a single server. Additionally, the splits themselves create some resource underutilization initially that manifests itself as an initial increase in operational cost.

The benefits are numerous, however. Although y-axis splits help with the growth in transactions, they also help to scale what something needs to know to perform those transactions. The data that is being operated upon as well as the instruction set to operate that data decreases, which means that people and systems can be more specialized, resulting in higher throughput on a per person or per system basis.

Summarizing the Y-Axis

The y-axis of the AKF Scale Cube represents separation of work by responsibility, action, or data.

Y-axis splits are easy to conceptualize but typically come at a slightly higher cost than the x-axis splits.

Y-axis splits aid in scaling not only transactions, but instruction size and data necessary to perform any given transaction.

The Z-Axis of the Cube

The z-axis of the cube is a split biased most often by the requestor or customer. The bias here is focused on data and actions that are unique to the person or system performing the request, or alternatively the person or system for which the request is being performed. Z-axis splits may or may not address the monolithic nature of instructions, processes, or code, but they very often do address the monolithic nature of the data necessary to perform these instructions, processes, or code.

To perform a z-axis split of our typing service pool, we may look at both the people who request work and the people to whom the work is being distributed. In analyzing the request work, we can look at segments or classes of groups that might require unique work or represent exceptional work volume. It's likely the case that executives represent a small portion of our total employee base but also represent a majority or supermajority of the work for internal distribution. Furthermore, the work for these types of individuals might be somewhat unique in that executives are allowed to request more types of work to be performed. Maybe we limit internal memorandums to executive requests, or personal customer notes might only be requested from an executive. This unique volume of work and type of work might be best served by a specialist pool of typists. We may also dedicate one or more typists to the CEO of the company who likely has the greatest number and variety of requests. All of these are examples of z-axis splits.

In our accounts receivable department, we might decide that some customers require specialized billing, payment terms, and interaction unique to the volume of business they do with us. We might dedicate a group of our best financial account representatives and even a special manager to one or more of these customers to handle their unique demands. In so doing, we would reduce the amount of knowledge necessary to perform a vast majority of our billing functions for a majority of our customers while creating account specialists for our most valuable customers. We would expect these actions to increase the throughput of our standard accounts group as they need not worry about special terms, and the relative throughput for special accounts should also go up as these individuals specialize in that area and are familiar with the special processes and payment terms.

Z-axis splits are very often the most costly for companies to implement, but the returns (especially from a scalability perspective) can be phenomenal. Specialized training in the previous examples represent a new cost to the company, and this training is an analog to the specialized set of services one might need to create within a systems platform. Data separation can become costly for some companies, but when performed can be amortized over the life of the platform or the system.

An additional benefit that z-axis splits create is the ability to separate services by geography. Want to have your accounts receivable group closer to the accounts they support to decrease mail delays? Easy to do! Want your typing pool close to the executives and people they support to limit interoffice mail delivery (remember these are the days before email)? Also simple to do!

Summarizing the Z-Axis

The z-axis of the AKF Scale Cube represents separation of work by customer or requestor.

As with x- and y-axis splits, the z-axis is easy to conceptualize, but very often is the most difficult and costly to implement for companies.

Z-axis splits aid in scaling transactions and data and may aid in scaling instruction sets and processes if implemented properly.

Putting It All Together

Why would we ever need more than one, or maybe two, axes of scale within our platform or organizations? The answer is that your needs will vary by your current size and expected annual growth. If you expect to stay small and grow slowly, you may never need more than one axis of scale. If you grow quickly, however, or growth is unexpected and violent, you are better off having planned for that growth in advance. Figure 22.4 depicts our cube, the axes of the cube, and the appropriate labels for each of the axes.

The x-axis of scale is very useful and easy to implement, especially if you have stayed away from creating state within your system or team. You simply clone the activity among several participants. But scaling along the x-axis starts to fail when

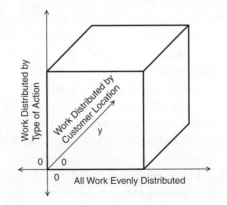

Figure 22.4 *AKF Scale Cube*

you have a lot of different tasks requiring significantly different information from many potential sources. Fast transactions start to run at the speed of slow transactions and everything starts to work suboptimally.

State Within Applications and the X-Axis

You may recall from Chapter 12 that we briefly defined stateful systems as "those in which operations are performed within the context of previous and subsequent operations." We indicated that state very often drives up the cost of the operations of systems as most often the state (previous and subsequent calls) is maintained within the application or a database associated with the application. The associated data often drives up memory utilization, storage utilization, and potentially database usage and licenses.

Stateless systems often allow us to break affinity between a single user and a single server. Because subsequent requests can go to any server clone, the x-axis becomes even easier to implement. No affinity between customer and server means that we need not design systems specific to any type of customer and so forth. Systems are now free to be more uniform in composition. This topic will be covered in more detail in Chapter 26, Asynchronous Design for Scale.

The y-axis helps to solve that by isolating transaction type and speed to systems and people specializing in that area of data or service. Slower transactions are now bunched together, but because the data set has been reduced relative to the X only example, they run faster than they had previously. Fast transactions are also sped up as they are no longer competing with resources for the slower transactions and their data set has also been reduced. Monolithic systems are reduced to components that operate more efficiently and can scale for data and transaction needs.

The z-axis helps us scale not only transactions and data, but may also help with monolithic system deconstruction. Furthermore, we can now move teams and systems around geographically and start to gain benefits from this geographic dispersion, such as disaster recovery.

Looking at our pool of typists, we can separate the types of work that they perform by the actions. We might create a customer focused team responsible for general customer communication letters, an internal memos team, and team focused on meeting minutes—all of these are examples of the y-axis. Each team is likely to have duplication to allow for growth in transactions within that team, which is an example of x-axis scale. Finally, we might specialize some members of the team relevant to specific customers or requestors such as an executive group. Although this is a z-axis split, these teams may also have specialization by task (y-axis) and duplication of team members (x-axis). Aha! We've put all three axes together.

For our accounts receivable department we have split them by invoicing, receiving, and deposits, all of which are y-axis splits. Each group has multiple members performing the same task, which is an x-axis split. We have created special separation of these teams focused on major accounts and recurring delinquent accounts and each of these specialized teams (a z-axis split) has further splits by function (y-axis) and duplication of individuals (x-axis).

AKF Scale Cube Summary

Here is a summary of the three axes of scale:

- The x-axis represents the distribution of the same work or mirroring of data across multiple entities.
- The y-axis represents the distribution and separation of work responsibilities or data meaning among multiple entities.
- The z-axis represents distribution and segmentation of work by customer, customer need, location, or value.

Hence, x-axis splits are mirror images of functions or data, y-axis splits separate data based on data type or type of work, and z-axis splits separate work by customer, location, or some value specific identifier (like a hash or modulus).

When and Where to Use the Cube

We will discuss the topic of where and when to use the AKF Scale Cube in Chapters 23, Splitting Applications for Scale, and 24, Splitting Databases for Scale. That said, the cube is a tool and reference point for nearly any discussion around scalability. You might make a representation of it within your scalability, 10x, or headroom meetings—a process that was discussed in Chapter 11, Determining Headroom for Applications. The AKF Scale Cube should also be presented during Architecture Review Board (ARB) meetings, as discussed in Chapter 14, Architecture Review Board, especially if you adopt a principle requiring the design of more than one axis of scale for any major architectural effort. It can serve as a basis for nearly any conversation around scale as it helps to create a common language among the engineers of an organization. Rather than talking about specific approaches, teams can focus on concepts that might evolve into any number of approaches.

You may consider requiring footnotes or light documentation indicating the type of scale for any major design within Joint Architecture Design (JAD) introduced in

Chapter 13, Joint Architecture Design. The AKF Scale Cube can also come into play during problem resolution and postmortems in identifying how intended approaches to scale did or did not work as expected and how to fix them in future endeavors.

The AKF Scale Cube is a tool best worn on your tool belt rather than placed in your tool box. It should be carried at all times as it is lightweight and can add significant value to you and your team. If referenced repeatedly, it can help to change your culture from one that focuses on specific fixes and instead discusses approaches and concepts to help identify the best potential fix. It can switch an organization from thinking like technicians to acting like engineers.

Conclusion

This chapter reintroduced the concept of the AKF Scale Cube. Our cube has three axes, each of which focused on a different approach toward scalability. Organizational construction was used as an analogy for systems to help better reinforce the approach of each of the three axes of scale. The cube is constructed such that the initial point (x = 0, y = 0, z = 0) is a monolithic system or organization (single person) performing all tasks with no bias based on the task, customer, or requestor.

Growth in people or systems performing the same tasks represents an increase in the x-axis. This axis of scale is easy to implement and typically comes at the lowest cost but suffers when the number of types of tasks or data necessary to perform those tasks increases.

A separation of responsibilities based on data or the activity being performed is growth along the y-axis of our cube. This approach tends to come at a slightly higher cost than x-axis growth but also benefits from a reduction in the data necessary to perform a task. Other benefits of such an approach include some fault isolation and an increase in throughput for each of the new pools based on the reduction of data or instruction set.

A separation of responsibility biased on customer or requestor is growth along the z-axis of scale. Such separation may allow for reduction in the instruction set for some pools and almost always reduces the amount of data necessary to perform a task. The result is that throughput is often increased, as is fault isolation. Cost of z-axis splits tends to be the highest of the three approaches in most organizations, though the return is also huge. The z-axis split also allows for geographic dispersion of responsibility.

Not all companies need all three axes of scale to survive. Some companies may do just fine with implementing the x-axis. Extremely high growth companies should plan for at least two axes of scale and potentially all three. Remember that planning (or designing) and implementing are two separate functions.

Ideally the AKF Scale Cube, or a construct of your own design, will become part of your daily toolset. Using such a model helps reduce conflict by focusing on concepts and approaches rather than specific implementations. If added to JAD, ARB, and headroom meetings, it helps focus the conversation and discussion on the important aspects and approaches to growing your technology platform.

Key Points

- The AKF Scale Cube offers a structured approach and concept to discussing and solving scale. The results are often superior to a set of rules or implementation based tools.

- The x-axis of the AKF Scale Cube represents the cloning of entities or data and an equal unbiased distribution of work across them.

- The x-axis tends to be the least costly to implement, but suffers from constraints in instruction size and dataset.

- The y-axis of the AKF Scale Cube represents separation of work biased by activity or data.

- The y-axis tends to be more costly than the x-axis but solves issues related to instruction size and data set in addition to creating some fault isolation.

- The z-axis of the AKF Scale Cube represents separation of work biased by the requestor or person for whom the work is being performed.

- The z-axis of the AKF Scale Cube tends to be the most costly to implement but very often offers the greatest scale. It resolves issues associated with dataset and may or may not solve instruction set issues. It also allows for global distribution of services.

- The AKF Scale Cube can be an everyday tool used to focus scalability related discussions and processes on concepts. These discussions result in approaches and implementations.

- ARB, JAD, and headroom are all process examples where the AKF Scale Cube might be useful.

Chapter 23

Splitting Applications for Scale

> Whether to concentrate or to divide your troops must be decided by circumstances.
>
> —Sun Tzu

The previous chapter introduced the model by which we describe splits to allow for nearly infinite scale. Now we're going to apply the concepts we discussed within Chapter 22, Introduction to the AKF Scale Cube, to our realworld technology platform needs. To do this, we will separate the platform into pieces that address our application and service offerings (covered in this chapter) and the splits necessary to allow our storage and databases to scale (covered in the next chapter). The same model and set of principles hold true for both approaches, but the implementation varies enough that it makes sense for us to address them in two separate chapters.

The AKF Scale Cube for Applications

The underlying meaning of the AKF Scale Cube really doesn't change when discussing either databases or applications. However, given that we are now going to use this tool to accomplish a specific purpose, we are going to add more specificity to the axes. These new descriptions, although remaining absolutely true to our original definitions, will make it more useful for us to apply the AKF Scale Cube to the architecting of applications to allow for greater scalability. Let's first start with the AKF Scale Cube from the end of Chapter 22.

In Chapter 22, we defined the x-axis of our cube as the cloning of services and data with absolutely no bias. In the x-axis approach to scale, the only thing that is different between one system and 100 systems is that the transactions are evenly split between those 100 systems as if each of them was a single instance capable of handling 100% of the original requests rather than the 1% that they actually handle. We will rename our x-axis to Horizontal Duplication/Cloning of Services to make it more obvious how we will apply this to our architecture efforts.

The y-axis from Chapter 22 was described as a separation of work responsibility by either the type of data, the type of work performed for a transaction, or a combination of both. We most often describe this as a service oriented split within an application and as such we will now label this axis as a split by function or service. Here, function and service are indicative of the actions performed by your platform, but they can just as easily be resource oriented splits such as the article upon which an action is being taken. A function or service oriented split should be thought of as being split along action or "verb" boundaries, whereas a resource oriented split is most often split along "noun" boundaries. We'll describe these splits later in this chapter.

The z-axis from Chapter 22 was described as being focused on data and actions that are unique to the person or system performing the request, or alternatively the person or system for which the request is being performed. In other words, these are requests that are split by the person or system making a request or split based on the person or system for whom the data is intended. We also often refer to the z-axis as being a "lookup oriented" split in applications. The lookup here is an indication that users or data are subject to a non action oriented bias that is represented somewhere else within the system. We store the relationships of users to their appropriate split or service somewhere, or determine an algorithm such as a hash or modulus of user_id that will reliably and consistently send us to the right location set of systems to get the answers for the set of users in question.

The new AKF Scale Cube for applications now looks like Figure 23.1.

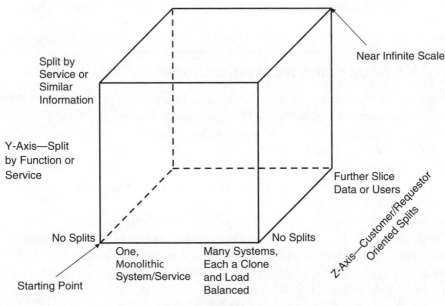

Figure 23.1 *AKF Application Scale Cube*

The X-Axis of the AKF Application Scale Cube

The x-axis of the AKF Application Scale Cube represents cloning of services with absolutely no bias. As described previously, if we have a service or platform that is scaled using the x-axis alone and consisting of N systems, each of the N systems can respond to any request and will give exactly the same answer as the other (N-1) systems. There is no bias to service performed, customer, or any other data element. Login functionality exists in the same location and application as shopping cart, checkout, catalog, and search functionality. Regardless of the request, it is sent to one of the N systems that comprise our x-axis split.

The x-axis approach is simple to implement in most cases. You simply take exactly the same code that existed in a single instance implementation and put it on multiple servers. If your application is not "stateful," meaning per our previous definitions that you are not using a user's previous transactions to inform future decisions, simply load balance all of the inbound requests to any of the N systems. If you are maintaining data associated with user state or otherwise are requiring persistence from a user to an application or Web server, both of which increase the cost of implementation for a number of reasons, the implementation is slightly more difficult, but the same basic approach is used. In the cases where persistency or state is necessary (or persistency resulting from the need for state), a series of transactions from a single user is simply pegged to one of the N instances of the x-axis split. This can be accomplished with session cookies from a load balancer. Additionally, as we will discuss more in Chapter 26, Asynchronous Design for Scale, there are methods of centralizing session management to still allow any of N systems to respond to an individual user's request without requiring persistency to that system.

The x-axis split has several benefits and drawbacks. As a benefit, this split is relatively simple to envision and implement. Other benefits include that it allows for near infinite scale from a number of transactions perspectives and when hosting your applications or services it does not increase the complexity of your hosting environment. Drawbacks of the x-axis approach include the inability of this split to address scalability from a data/cache perspective or instruction complexity perspective.

As just stated, x-axis splits are easy to envision and implement. As such, when put in a position of needing a quick solution to any scale initiative, x-axis splits should be one of the first that you consider. Because it is generally easy to clone services, the impact to cost in terms of design expense and implementation expense is low. Furthermore, the impact to time to market to release functionality with an x-axis split is generally low compared to other implementations as you are, after all, merely cloning the services in question.

X-axis splits also allow us to easily scale our platforms with the number of inbound transactions or requests. If you have a single user or small number of users who grow from making 10 requests per second to 1000 requests per second, you need only add roughly 100 times the number of systems or cloned services to handle the increase in requests. There isn't a lot of engineering magic involved—simply input the demand increase and a spreadsheet can tell you how many systems to buy and when.

Finally, the team responsible for managing the services of your platform does not need to worry about a vast number of uniquely configured systems or servers. Every system performing an x-axis split is roughly equivalent to every other system performing the same split. Configuration management of all servers is relatively easy to perform and new service implementation is as easy as cloning an existing system or generating a new system from a "jumpstart server" and assigning it a unique name or address. Configuration files do not vary and the only thing the operations group needs to be concerned about is the total number of systems in an x-axis implementation and that each is getting an appropriate amount of traffic.

Although x-axis splits scale well with increased transaction volumes, they do not address the problems incurred by increasing amounts of data. If your system requires that you cache a great deal of data to serve client requests, as that data grows, your time to serve any given request will likely increase, which is obviously bad for the customer experience. Additionally, you might find yourself constrained on the server or application itself if your data gets too unwieldy. Even if you don't need to cache any data, searching through data on other storage or database systems will likely increase as your customer base and/or product catalog increases in size.

X-axis splits also don't address the complexity of the software implementing your system, platform, or product. Everything in an x-axis split alone is assumed to be monolithic in nature; as a result, applications will likely start to slow down as servers page instruction/execution pages in and out of memory to perform different functions. As your product becomes more feature rich, monolithic applications slow down and become more costly and less easily scaled either as a result of this instruction complexity or the data complexity mentioned earlier.

Summarizing the Application X-Axis

The x-axis of the AKF Application Scale Cube represents the cloning of an application or service such that work can easily be distributed across instances with absolutely no bias.

X-axis implementations tend to be easy to conceptualize and typically can be implemented at relatively low cost. They are the most cost-effective way of scaling transaction growth. They can be easily cloned within your production environment from existing systems or "jumpstarted" from "golden master" copies of systems. They do not tend to increase the complexity of your operations or production environment.

X-axis implementations are limited by the growth of a monolithic application, which tends to slow down the processing of transactions. They do not scale well with increases in data or application size.

The Y-Axis of the AKF Application Scale Cube

The y-axis of the cube of scale represents a separation of work responsibility within your application. When discussing application scale, we most frequently think of this in terms of functions, methods, or services within an application. The y-axis split addresses the monolithic nature of an application by separating that application into parallel or pipelined processing flows. A pure x-axis split would have 100 instances of the exact same application performing exactly the same work on each of the N transactions that a site received over T time. Each of the 100 instances would receive N/100 of the work. In a y-axis split, we might take a single monolithic application and split it up into 100 distinct services such as login, logout, read profile, update profile, search profiles, browse profiles, checkout, display similar items, and so on.

Y-axis splits are a bit more complicated to implement than x-axis splits. At a very high level, it is possible to implement a y-axis split in production without actually splitting the code base itself. You can do this by cloning a monolithic application and setting it on multiple physical or virtual servers. Let's assume that you want to have four unique y-axis split servers, each serving 1/4th of the total number of functions within your site. One server might serve login and logout functionality, another read and update profile, another server handles "contact individual" and "receive contacts," and the last server handles all of the other functions of your platform. You may assign a unique URL or URI to each of these servers, such as login.allscale.com and contacts.allscale.com, and ensure that any of the functions within the appropriate grouping always get directed to the server in question. This is a good, first approach to performing a split and helps work out the operational kinks associated with splitting applications. Unfortunately, it doesn't give you all of the benefits of a full y-axis split made within the codebase itself.

Y-axis splits are most commonly implemented to address the issues associated with a code base and dataset that have grown significantly in complexity or size. They also help scale transaction volume, as in performing the splits you must add virtual or physical servers. To get most of the benefits of a y-axis split, the code base itself needs to be split up from a monolithic structure to the services that comprise the entire platform.

Operationally, y-axis splits help reduce the time necessary to process any given transaction as the data and instruction sets that are being executed or searched are smaller. Architecturally, y-axis splits allow you to grow beyond the limitations that systems place on the absolute size of software or data. Y-axis splits also aid in fault isolation as identified within Chapter 21, Creating Fault Isolative Architectural Structures; a failure of a given service does not bring down all of the functionality of your platform.

From an engineering perspective, y-axis splits allow you to grow your team more easily by focusing teams on specific services or functions within your product. You can dedicate a person or a team to searching and browsing, a team toward the development of an advertising platform, a team to account functionality, and so on. New engineers come up to speed faster as they are dedicated to a specific section of functionality within your system. More experienced engineers become experts at a given system and as a result can produce functionality within that system faster. The data elements upon which any y-axis split works will likely be a subset of the total data on the site; as such, engineers better understand the data with which they are working and are more likely to make better choices in creating data models.

Y-axis splits also have drawbacks. They tend to be more costly to implement in engineering time than x-axis splits because engineers either need to rewrite or at the very least disaggregate services from the monolithic application. The operations and infrastructure teams will now need to support more than one configuration of server. This in turn might mean that there is more than one class or size of server in the operations environment to get the most cost-efficient systems for each type of transaction. When caching is involved, data might be cached differently in different systems, but we highly recommend that a standard approach to caching be shared across all of the splits. URL/URI structures will grow, and when referencing other services, engineers will need to understand the current structure and layout of the site or platform to address each of the services.

Summarizing the Application Y-Axis

The y-axis of the AKF Application Scale Cube represents separation of work by service or function within the application.

Y-axis splits are meant to address the issues associated with growth and complexity in code base and datasets. The intent is to create both fault isolation as well as reduction in response times for y-axis split transactions.

Y-axis splits can scale transactions, data sizes, and code base sizes. They are most effective in scaling the size and complexity of your code base. They tend to cost a bit more than x-axis splits as the engineering team either needs to rewrite services or at the very least disaggregate them from the original monolithic application.

The Z-Axis of the AKF Application Scale Cube

The z-axis of the Application Scale Cube is a split based on a value that is "looked up" or determined at the time of the transaction; most often, this split is based on the requestor or customer of the transaction. The requestor and the customer may be completely different people. The requestor, as the name implies, is the person submitting a request to the product or platform, whereas the customer is the person who will receive the response or benefit of the request. Note that these are the most common implementations of the z-axis, but not the only possible implementation. For In order for the z-axis split to be valuable, it must help partition not only transactions, but the data necessary to operate on those transactions. A y-axis split helps us reduce data and complexity by reducing instructions and data necessary to perform a service; a z-axis split attempts to do the same thing through nonservice oriented segmentation.

To perform a z-axis split, we look for similarities among groups of transactions across several services. If a z-axis split is performed in isolation of the x- and y-axis, each split will be a monolithic code base. If N unique splits are identified, it is possible that each of the N instances will be the same exact code base, but this does not necessarily need to be the case. We may, for example, decide that we will allow some number of our N servers to have greater functionality than the remainder of the servers. This might be the case if we have a "free" section of our services and a "paid" section of our services. Our paying customers may get greater functionality and as a result be sent to a separate server or set of servers. The paying code base may then be a super set of the free code base.

How do we get benefits in a z-axis split if we have the same monolithic code base across all instances? The answer lay in the activities of the individuals interacting with those servers and the data necessary to complete those transactions. So many applications and sites today require extensive caching that it becomes nearly impossible to cache all the necessary data for all potential transactions. Just as the y-axis split helped us cache some of this data for unique services, so does the z-axis split help us cache data for specific groups or classes of transactions biased by user characteristics.

Let's take AllScale's customer resource manager (CRM) solution as an example. It would make a lot of sense that a set of sales personnel within a given company would have a lot in common and as a result that we might get considerable benefit from caching data unique to that company within a z-axis split. In the event that a company is so small that it doesn't warrant having a single system dedicated to it, we implement multitenancy and allow multiple small companies to exist on a single server. We gain the benefit of caching unique to the companies in question while also leveraging the cost benefits of a multitenant system. Furthermore, we don't subject the larger companies to cache misses resulting from infrequent accesses from small companies that force the larger company data out of the cache.

We also gain the benefit of fault isolation first identified in Chapter 21. When one of our servers fails, we only impact a portion of our customers. Moreover, we now have a benefit that allows us to roll out code to a portion of our customer base whenever we are releasing new features. This, in turn, allows us to performance test the code, validate that the code does not create any significant user incidents, and ensure that the expected benefits of the release are achieved before we roll or push to the remainder of our clients.

Because we are splitting transactions across multiple systems, in this particular case identified by companies, we can achieve a transactional scale similar to that within the x-axis. Unfortunately, as with the y-axis, we increase our operational complexity somewhat as we now have pools of services performing similar functions for different clients, requesters, or destinations. And unlike the y-axis, we don't likely get the benefit of splitting up our architecture in a service oriented fashion; our engineers do not necessarily become more proficient with areas of the code just as a result of a z-axis split. Finally, there is some software cost associated with z-axis splits in that the code must be able to recognize that requests are not all equivalent for any given service. Very often, an algorithm to determine where the request should be sent is created, or a "lookup" service is created that can determine to what system or pod a request should be sent.

The benefits of a z-axis split then are that we increase fault isolation, increase transactional scalability, and increase the cache-ability of objects necessary to complete our transactions. You might also offer different levels of service to different customers, though to do so you might need to implement a y-axis split within a z-axis split. The end results we would expect from these are higher availability, greater scalability, and faster transaction processing times.

The z-axis, however, does not help us as much with code complexity, nor does it help with time to market. We also add some operational complexity to our production environment; we now need to monitor several different systems with similar code bases performing similar functions for different clients. Configuration files may differ as a result and systems may not be easily moved once configured depending upon your implementation.

Because we are leveraging characteristics unique to a group of transactions, we can also improve our disaster recovery plans by geographically dispersing our services. We can, for instance, locate services closer to the clients using or requesting those services. Thinking back to our sales lead system, we could put several small companies in one geographic area on a server close to those companies; and for a large company with several sales offices, we might split that company into several sales office systems spread across the company and placed near the offices in question.

Summarizing the Application Z-Axis

The z-axis of the AKF Application Scale Cube represents separation of work based on attributes that are looked up or determined at the time of the transaction. Most often, these are implemented as splits by requestor, customer, or client.

Z-axis splits tend to be the most costly implementation of the three types of splits. Although software does not necessarily need to be disaggregated into services, it does need to be written such that unique pods can be implemented. Very often, a lookup service or deterministic algorithm will need to be written for these types of splits.

Z-axis splits aid in scaling transaction growth, may aid in scaling instruction sets, and aids in decreasing processing time by limiting the data necessary to perform any transaction. The z-axis is most effective at scaling growth in customers or clients.

Putting It All Together

We haven't really modified our original AKF Scale Cube from the introduction within this chapter, but we have attempted to clarify it from an application perspective. We did not redefine the axes, but rather focused the previous meaning to the context of splitting applications for scale.

The observant reader has probably also figured out by now that we are going to explain why you need multiple axes of scale. To mix things up a bit, we will work backward through the axes and first explain the problems with implementing them in isolation.

A z-axis only implementation has several problems when implemented in isolation. Let's assume the previous case where you make N splits of your customer base in a sales lead tracking system. Because we are only implementing the z-axis here, each instance is a single virtual or physical server. If it fails for hardware or software reasons, the services for that customer or set of customers have become completely unavailable. That availability problem alone is reason enough for us to implement an x-axis split for each of our z-axis splits. If we split our customer base N ways along the z-axis, with each of the N splits having at least 1/Nth of our customers initially, we would put at least two "cloned" or x-axis servers in each of the N splits. This ensures that should a server fail we still service the customers in that pod. Reference Figure 23.2 as we discuss this implementation further.

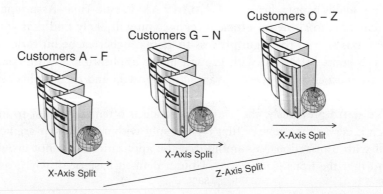

Figure 23.2 *Z- and X-Axis Split*

It is likely more costly for us to perform continued customer oriented splits to scale our transactions than it is to simply add servers within one of our customer oriented splits. Operationally, it should be pretty simple, assuming that we do not have a great deal of state enabled to simply add a cloned system to our service for any given customer. Therefore, in an effort to reduce overall cost of scale, we will probably implement a z-axis split with an x-axis split within each z-axis split. We can also now perform x-axis scale within each of our N number of z-axis pods. If a customer grows significantly in transactions, we can perform a cost-effective x-axis split (the addition of more cloned servers) within that customer's pod.

Finally, as we have previously mentioned, the z-axis split really does not help us with code complexity. As our functionality increases and the size of our application grows, performing x-and z-axis splits alone will not allow us to focus and gain experience on specific features or services. Our time to market will likely suffer. We may also find that the large monolithic z- and x-axis splits will not help us enough for all of the functions that need cached data. A single, very active customer, focused on many of his own clients within our application, may find that a monolithic application is just too slow. This would force us to focus more on y-axis splits as well.

The y-axis split has its own set of problems when implemented in isolation. The first is similar to the problem of the x-axis split in that a single server focused on a subset of functionality results in the functionality being unavailable when the server fails. As with the z-axis split, we are going to want to increase our availability by adding another cloned or x-axis server for each of our functions. We also save money by adding servers in an x-axis fashion for each of our y-axis splits versus continuing to split along the y-axis. Rather than modifying the code and further deconstructing it, we simply add servers into each of our y-axis splits and bypass the cost of further code modification.

The y-axis split also does not scale as well with customer growth as the z-axis split. Y-axis splits focus more on the cache-ability of similar functions and work well when we have an application growing in size and complexity. Imagine, however, that you have decided to perform a y-axis split of your login functionality and that many of your client logins happen between 6 AM to 9 AM Pacific Time. Assuming that you need to cache data to allow for efficient logins, you will likely find that you need to perform a z-axis split of the login process to gain a higher cache hit ratio. As stated before, y-axis splits help most with growth in the application and functionality, x-axis splits are most cost-effective for transaction growth, and z-axis splits aid most in the growth of customers and users.

As we've stated previously, the x-axis approach is often the easiest to implement and as such is very often the very first type of split within systems or applications. It scales well with transactions, assuming that the application does not grow in complexity and that the transactions come from a defined base of slowly growing customers. As your product becomes more feature rich, you are forced to start looking at ways to make the system respond more quickly to user requests. You do not want, for instance, long searches to slow down the average response time of short duration activities such as logins. To resolve average response time issues caused by competing functions, you need to implement a y-axis split.

The x-axis also does not handle a growth in customer base elegantly. As your customers increase and as the data elements necessary to support them within an application increases, you need to find ways to segment these data elements to allow for maximum cost effective scale such as with y- or z-axis splits.

AKF Application Scale Cube Summary

Here is a summary of the three axes of scale:

- The x-axis represents the distribution of the same work or mirroring of an application across multiple entities. It is useful for scaling transaction volume cost effectively, but does not scale well with data volume growth.

- The y-axis represents the distribution and separation of work responsibilities by verb or action across multiple entities. The y-axis can benefit development time as services are now implemented separately. It also helps with transaction growth and fault isolation. It helps to scale data specific to features and functions, but does not greatly benefit customer data growth.

- The z-axis represents distribution and segmentation of work by customer, customer need, location, or value. It can create fault isolation and scale along customer boundaries. It does not aid in the growth of data specific to features or functions nor does it aid in reducing time to market.

Hence, x-axis splits are mirror images of functions, y-axis splits separate applications based on the work performed, and z-axis splits separate work by customer, location, or some value specific identifier (like a hash or modulus).

Practical Use of the Application Cube

Let's examine the practical use of our application cube for three unique purposes. The first business we will discuss is an ecommerce auction site, the second is AllScale's human resources management (HRM) solution, and the third is AllScale's back office IT implementation.

Ecommerce Implementation

The engineering team at AllScale has been hard at work developing ecommerce functionality in addition to its CRM and HRM functionality. The new platform provides functionality to sell goods, which range from argyle sweaters to ZZ Top CDs. AllScale intends to sell it all, and it also allows other folks to list their goods for sale on its site. AllScale's platform has all the functionality you can imagine, including searching, browsing, shopping carts, checkout, account and order status functionality, and so on. The platform also offers multiple buying formats from auctions to fixed price sales.

The AllScale architects ultimately decide that the system is going to be constrained in three dimensions: transaction growth, functionality growth, and the third dimension consisting of both catalog growth and customer growth. As such, they are going to need to rely on all three axes of the AKF Application Scale Cube.

The architects decide that it makes most sense to split the application primarily by the functions of the site. Most of the major functions that don't directly rely on customer information will get a swim lane of functionality (see Chapter 21). Browsing, searching, catalog upload, inventory management, and so on and every other verb that can be performed without needing to know specific information about a particular customer becomes a branch of functionality within the site and its own code base. These splits allow these services to grow with transaction volume regardless of customer growth as the number of customers isn't important when delivering the results of a search, or a catalog upload, and so on.

All applications regarding customers will be split into N pods, where N is a configurable number. Each of these pods will host roughly 1/Nth of our customers. This is a z-axis split of our customer base. Within each of these z-axis splits, the architects are going to perform y-axis splits of the code base. Login/logout will be its own function, checkout will be its own function, account status and summary will be its own function, and so on. Note that AllScale doesn't have $N \times M$ (where M is the number of y-axis splits and N is the number of z-axis splits) separate code bases here; it is simply replicating the M code bases across N pods for a total of M new code splits for customer functionality. In deciding to split by both the y- and z-axis in this case, AllScale can scale its number of customers and the amount of code functionality dedicated to them independently. No single y-lane will need to know about more than 1/Nth the customers; as a result, caching for things like login information will be much more lightweight and much faster. The resulting splits are shown in Figure 23.3.

Finally, AllScale will apply x-axis splits everywhere to scale the number of transactions through any given segmentation. Search is an area about which we are concerned, as AllScale wants very fast searches and is concerned about the response times. This, however, is more of a data scaling issue, so we will address this in Chapter 24, Splitting Databases for Scale.

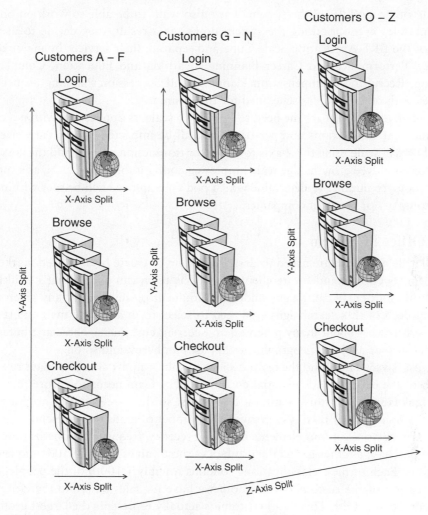

Figure 23.3 *Three Axis Split Example*

Human Resources ERP Implementation

Recall the AllScale HRM solution, which does absolutely everything for HR organizations including recruiting, training, career progression counseling, performance reviews, succession planning, compensation analysis, termination automation, and so on. If an HR professional needs it, AllScale does it, all in a SaaS environment. AllScale's largest customer happens to be the largest company in the world, FullScale Oil, and its smallest client is a 20-person startup in New York City, FullScale Attitude.

The architects decide that what they want to build appears to be one large application to their customers but with each module capable of growing in complexity without affecting other modules in the system. They also want to be able to work on one or more modules without taking the system down; as a result, they decide to use the y-axis of the AKF Application Scale Cube and separate their services by major functionality. Performance and Career Planning, Learning and Education, Compliance Tracking, Recruiting, Compensation Planning, and Succession Planning all become modules with other modules scheduled for the future.

The team also recognizes the need to be able to scale its application within a company and that transactions and personnel will all be impacted by company size. As such, they will scale using the x-axis to allow for transaction growth and the z-axis to allow for employee growth. The team employs a configurable number, N, as a modulus to employee number to determine which pod an employee will be sent within any given company or group of companies.

Back Office IT System

The AllScale architects are asked to design a system to create personalized marketing emails for its current and future client bases. The team can expect that it will have several different email campaigns under development or shipping at any given time and that each of these campaigns will need to select from a diverse mailing list that includes attributes about many potential and current customers. These attributes are elements such as age, sex, geographic area, past purchases, and so on.

The list is very large, and the team decides to split it up by classes of data relevant to each of the existing and potential customers. The team needs to ensure that mail campaigns launch and finish within a few hours, so they are going to need a fairly aggressive split of their mail system given the number of mails that we send.

The architects select four elements including recency, frequency, monetization, and class of purchase as criteria, and the product of these values result in 100 unique classifications. Each of these classifications contains roughly 1/100th of the people, with the exception of the customers for whom we have no sales data and therefore just represent a contact list. This set of customers actually represents the largest group by population, and for them the team simply splits on contact_id, which is a unique key within the system. The AllScale architects select a configurable number N for this split and set N initially to 100. As such, it has 199 unique Z splits: 100 splits for customers who have yet purchased anything from AllScale and for whom we have no data, and 99 splits for all other customers split by a product of their recency, frequency, monetization (aggregate value), and classification of purchases. These splits correspond primarily to the mail and tracking farms (described in the following section) but also to the data repositories that we will describe in further detail in Chapter 24.

The y-axis splits then become the functions of the AllScale marketing system. The team will need a creative development system, a mail sending system, a mail viewing system, a mail reporting system, and a customer tracking system to view the efficacy of its campaigns and a data warehouse to handle all past campaign reporting. These are all y-axis splits to give the system additional scale in transactions and to allow the team to modify components independent of each other.

Most systems will have at least one extra system for availability, but some will have multiple clones such as the mail sending system within each of the Z splits.

Observations

You may have noticed that while we use each of the axes in the preceding examples, the distribution of the axes appears to change by company or implementation. In one example, the z-axis may be more predominant and in others the Y appears to be the most predominant split. This is all part of the "Art of Scalability." Referring back to the introduction, the determination in the absence of data about where you start in your scalability initiatives are as much about gut feel as anything else. As you grow and collect data, you will ultimately, hopefully, determine in advance where you made incorrect assumptions.

Where to draw the line with y-axis splits is not always easy. If you have tens of thousands of features or "verbs," it doesn't make sense to have tens of thousands splits. You want to have manageable sizes of code bases in each of your splits but not so many splits that the absolute number itself becomes unmanageable. You also want your cache sizes in your production environment to be manageable. Both of these become considerations for determining where you should perform splits and how many you should have.

Z-axis splits are a little easier from a design perspective. Ideally, you will simply design a system that has flexibility built into it. We previously mentioned a configurable number N in both the ecommerce and back office IT systems. This number is what allows us to start splitting application flows by customer within the system. As we grow, we simply increase N to allow for greater segmentation and to help smooth load across our production systems. Of course, there is potentially some work in data storage (where those customers live) that we will discuss in Chapter 24, but we expect that you can develop tools to help you manage that. The y-axis, unfortunately, is not so easy to design flexibility into the system.

As always, the x-axis is relatively easy to split and handle because it is always just a duplicate of its peers. In all of our previous cases, the x-axis is always subordinate to the y- and z-axis. This is almost always the case when you perform y- and z-axis splits. To the point, the x-axis becomes relevant *within* either a y- or z-axis split. Sometimes, the y- or z-axis, as was the case in more than one of the examples, is subordinate to the other, but in nearly all cases, the x-axis is subordinate to either y or z whenever the y or z or both are employed.

What do you do if and when your business contracts? If you've split to allow for aggressive hyper growth and the economy presents your business with a downward cycle not largely under your control, what do you do? X-axis splits are easy to unwind as you simply remove the systems you do not need. If those systems are fully depreciated, you can simply power them off for future use when your business rebounds. Y-axis splits might be hosted on a smaller number of systems, potentially leveraging virtual machine software to carve a set of physical servers into multiple servers. Z-axis splits should also be capable of being collapsed onto similar systems either through the use of virtual machine software or just by changing the boundaries that indicate which customers reside on which systems.

Conclusion

This chapter discussed the employment of the AKF Scale Cube to applications within a product, service, or platform. We modified the AKF Scale Cube slightly, narrowing the scope and definition of each of the axes so that it became more meaningful to application and systems architecture and the production deployment of applications.

Our x-axis still addresses the growth in transactions or work performed by any platform or system. Although the x-axis handles the growth in transaction volume well, it suffers when application complexity increases significantly (as measured through the growth in functions and features) or when the number of customers with cacheable data needs grows significantly.

The y-axis addresses application complexity and growth. As we grow our product to become more feature rich, it requires more resources. Furthermore, transactions that would otherwise complete quickly start to slow down as demand laden systems mix both fast and slow transactions. Our ability to cache data for all features starts to drop as we run into system constraints. The y-axis helps address all of these while simultaneously benefiting our production teams. Engineering teams get to focus on smaller portions of our complex code base. As a result, defect rates decrease, new engineers come up to speed faster, and expert engineers can develop software faster. Because all axes address transaction scale as well, the y-axis also benefits us as we grow the transactions against our system, but it is not as easily scaled in this dimension as the x-axis.

The z-axis addresses growth in customer base. As we will see in Chapter 24, it can also help us address growth in other data elements such as product catalogs and so forth. As transactions and customers grow, and potentially as transactions *per* customer grow, we will find ourselves in a position that we might need to address the specific needs of a class of customer. This might be solely because each customer has an equal need for some small cache space, but it might be that the elements you cache by customer are distinct by some predefined customer class. Either way, segmenting by requester, customer, or client helps us solve that problem. It also helps us scale along the transaction growth path, though not as easily as with the x-axis.

As indicated in Chapter 22, not all companies need all three axes of scale to survive. When more than one axis is employed, the x-axis is almost subordinate to the other axes. You might for instance have multiple x-axis splits, each occurring within a y- or z-axis split. When employing y-and z-axis splits together (typically with an x-axis split), either split can become the "primary" means of splitting. If you split first by customer, you can still make y-axis functionality implementations within each of your z-axis splits. These would be clones of each other such that login in z-axis customer split 1 looks exactly like login for z-axis customer split N. The same is true for a y-axis primary split; the z-axis implementations within each functionality split would be similar or clones of each other.

Key Points

- X-axis application splits scale linearly with transaction growth. They do not help with the growth in code complexity, customers, or data. X-axis splits are "clones" of each other.

- The x-axis tends to be the least costly to implement, but suffers from constraints in instruction size and dataset.

- Y-axis application splits help scale code complexity as well as transaction growth. They are mostly meant for code scale because as they are not as efficient as x-axis in transaction growth.

- Y-axis application splits also aid in reducing cache sizes where caches sizes scale with function growth.

- Y-axis splits tend to be more costly to implement than x-axis splits as a result of engineering time necessary to separate monolithic code bases.

- Y-axis splits aid in fault isolation.

- Y-axis splits can be performed without code modification, but you might not get the benefit of cache size reduction and you will not get the benefit of decreasing code complexity.

- Z-axis application splits help scale customer growth, some elements of data growth (as we will see in Chapter 24), and transaction growth.

- Z-axis application splits can help reduce cache sizes where caches scale in relation to the growth in users or other data elements.

- As with y-axis splits, z-axis splits aid in fault isolation. They too can be implemented without code changes but may not gain the benefit of cache size reduction without some code modification.

- The choice of when to use what method or axis of scale is both art and science. Intuition is typically the initial guiding force, whereas production data should be used over time to help inform the decision.

Chapter 24

Splitting Databases for Scale

> So in war, the way is to avoid what is strong and to strike at what is weak.
>
> —Sun Tzu

Chapter 22, Introduction to the AKF Scale Cube, introduced the scale cube and described the concepts by applying them to organizational structures. Chapter 23, Splitting Applications for Scale, showed how the cube could be applied to applications and systems. In this chapter, we are going to focus the AKF Scale Cube on databases and persistent storage systems. By the end of the chapter, you will have all the concepts necessary to apply the cube to the needs of your own business. Armed with Chapters 21, Creating Fault Isolative Architectural Structures, through 24, you should be able to create a fault isolative architecture capable of nearly infinite scale, thereby increasing customer satisfaction and shareholder returns.

The AKF Scale Cube for Databases

As we discussed in Chapter 23, the AKF Scale Cube really doesn't change when applied to databases and other persistent storage systems. We will, however, want to focus the names and themes of the axes to make them more easily used as a tool to help us scale our data. As with our application focused descriptions, these new descriptions won't deviate from the original cube but will rather enable them with greater meaning when applied to databases and data. For the following discussion, please reference Figure 22.4 (in Chapter 22) and Figure 24.1.

The x-axis, as you will recall from Chapter 22, focuses on the cloning of services and data with absolutely no bias. Each x-axis implementation requires the complete cloning or duplication of an entire data set. We will rename our x-axis to be called Horizontal Duplication/Cloning of Data to make it more obvious how we will apply this to our data scalability efforts.

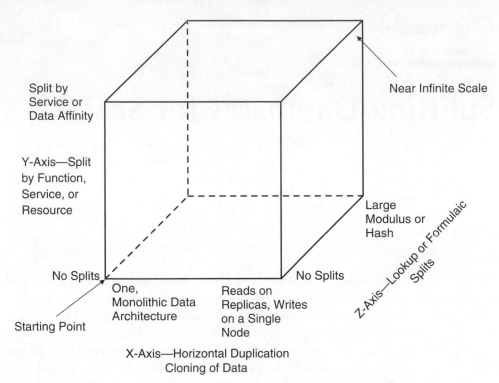

Figure 24.1   *AKF Database Scale Cube*

The y-axis was described as a separation of work responsibility by either the type of data, the type of work performed for a transaction, or a combination of both. When applied to data, this definition remains completely true. Y-axis data splits either focus on splitting data thematically with a bias to the type of data being split or with a bias toward the work that is performed on that data. This latter definition is a services oriented split similar to those discussed in Chapter 23.

The z-axis of our database cube continues to have a customer or requestor bias. When applied to databases and data, the z-axis very often requires the implementation of a lookup service or lookup algorithm. We store the relationships of user data to their appropriate split within a service or a database, or we calculate the location based on an algorithm such as a hash, modulus, or other deterministic means.

The new AKF Scale Cube for databases now looks like Figure 24.1.

The X-Axis of the AKF Database Scale Cube

The x-axis of the AKF Database Scale Cube represents cloning of data with absolutely no bias. If we have a data tier scaled using the x-axis alone and consisting of N systems, each of the N databases will have exactly the same data as other (N-1) systems, with some minor differences resulting from replication delay. There is no bias to the transactions performed on this data, or to customer or any other data element; customer metadata and account information exists alongside product catalog data, inventory information, contact information, and so on. A request for data can be served from any of the N databases or storage implementations. Typically, writes are made to a single node within the replicated copies of data, primarily to reduce read and write contention on the nodes that make up this data tier.

As with the application cube, the x-axis approach is simple to implement in most cases. Typically, you will implement some sort of replication system that allows for the near real-time replication of data within the database or storage systems across some scalable and configurable number N replicated databases or persistent storage systems. Your database likely has this replication capability built into it natively, but you can also likely find third-party tools to allow you to perform the replication.

Replication Delay Concerns

Many companies with which we work initially display some level of concern when we bring up the topic of *replication delay*. The most common theme within this concern is the perceived need to be able to immediately access the most current data element for any write. In the most extreme case, we've had clients immediately read a piece of datum out of a database to validate that what was just written was in fact correct.

In most cases, we are successful in helping our clients identify a large portion of their data that need only be current within the last single digit number of seconds. Database native and third-party replication tools within a single data center, even under high volume, can typically keep replicated copies of databases in synch with a master within five seconds, and sometimes even within a second of the master copy. Geographically distant data centers can often be synchronized in less than 10 seconds.

The tests and questions that we most often recommend in determining if replicated data is sufficient include the following:

- How often is this particular data element updated? If the ratio of views to updates is high, replication delay is probably acceptable. If updates are frequent and views are infrequent or very low in number, there is little benefit in replication.

- Will the element that is read be used in a calculation for a future write? If so, replication delays might not be acceptable.

- What is the difference in value for decision making purposes? If, for instance, the newest update changes a value insignificantly will it really make a difference in a resulting decision on the part of the person viewing the data?

When considering database replication options, look first for functionality native to your database. It almost never makes sense to build replication functionality yourself, and with most databases having replication built-in, there is seldom a need to purchase third-party software.

Writes typically happen to a single node within the replicated x-axis data tier. By writing to a single node, we reduce the read and write conflicts across all nodes and force a single node to do the work of ensuring the ACID properties (Atomicity, Consistency, Isolation, and Durability) of the database or to ensure that the storage subsystem can be optimized for writes or reads only. Many times, the "write" copy of the storage tier is used only to write, but sometimes a small number of reads is scheduled to that node if the time sensitivity of the read in question will not allow for the minor delay inherent to replication.

We often teach that distributed object caches and other database related caches, at least those intended to reduce load on a database, can be examples of x-axis splits. Some might argue that if the data is represented in a format intended to be more easily consumed by service that they are examples of y-axis splits. Rather than discussing either in this chapter, we will have a broad treatment of caches in Chapter 25, Caching for Performance and Scale.

The x-axis split has several benefits and drawbacks. Consistent with Chapters 22 and 23, this split is easy to envision and implement. Many databases have native replication technologies that allow for "write and read only" copies or "master and slave" copies of a database. These native replication engines usually allow for multiple read or "slave" copies of the database. Another x-axis implementation is clustering. Most open source or licensed relational database management systems have this capability. By clustering we mean two or more physically separated databases that appear to the application as a single instance.

Should a storage system without a database be the target of this technique, there are many logical and physical replication systems existing in both open source and third-party supported systems. The system allows for linear scale with transactions, but most replication processes have limits to the number of targets or read only nodes allowed. While this approach allows for linear transaction growth, it does not address data growth and the impact of that data growth on request processing time or the impact of that data growth to addressable storage within any given storage subsystem.

Because x-axis splits are easy to envision and implement, they should typically be your first approach to scale any system when the number of transactions is the primary driver of growth. The impact to cost in terms of loss opportunity associated with engineering effort is low and although the first time setup cost to implement the additional datasets and begin replication is not trivial, it is still low relative to the other methods of data scalability. As with the application x-axis split, the impact to time to market to release functionality is generally low, as typically you are implementing a third-party, native, or open source replication technology.

X-axis splits also allow us to easily scale our data with the number of inbound transactions or requests. As request growth increases, we simply add more read nodes. Capacity planning is easy as well because each of our nodes, if served from similar hardware, can likely handle a similar number of requests. There is likely a limit to the number of systems that can be employed and this limit will normally drive us to other methods of scale as our transaction growth continues to increase. Sometimes, we cannot even achieve the vendor or system supported limit due to the increase in replication time delays because additional read only nodes are deployed. Usually, each node has some small impact to the time that it takes to replicate data from the write node. In some implementations, this impact may not manifest itself as a delay to all nodes but rather a consistently unacceptable delay to one of the nodes within the cluster as we start to reach our maximum target. As such, we cannot simply rely on the x-axis for scale even in systems of relatively low data growth if transaction growth is going to accelerate over time.

One final benefit of the x-axis is that the team managing the infrastructure of your platform does not need to worry about a vast number of uniquely configured schemas or storage systems. Every system performing an x-axis split is exactly equivalent to every other system performing the same split, with the exception of a single system dedicated to "writing." Configuration management of all nodes is relatively easy to perform and new service implementation is as easy as replicating the data within an existing system. Your application, when written to read from a "read service" and write to a "write service," should scale without further involvement from your engineering team. Ideally, the multiple read systems are addressed through a third-party load balancing system rather than the alternative of having your team write even a small routine to "load balance" or evenly apportion the reads.

There are two primary drivers that move us away from scaling along the x-axis alone. The first was discussed while addressing the limitations of existing replication technology. The second driver is that x-axis scale techniques do not address the scale issues inherent to an increase in the size or amount of data. As with the caching concern in Chapter 23, when you increase the size of data within a database, the response times even in indexed tables increase. This increase is not a linear relationship if you are properly using an index, but it represents a cost in response time and processing time nonetheless. This increase in response time may ultimately drive you to other splits. In nondatabase storage systems, the complexity of storage relationships for very large volumes of data will likely drive you to segmentation for ease of maintenance and operations.

Another drawback to x-axis replication is the cost of replicating large amounts of data. Typically, x-axis implementations are complete clones of a primary database, which in turn means that we might be moving lots of data that is seldom read relative to data within the same replication set that is read frequently. A solution to this concern is to select only the data for replication that has a high volume of reads associated with it. Many of the replication technologies for databases allow such a selection to occur on a by table basis, but to our knowledge few, if any, allow columns within a table to be selected.

Other drawbacks include data currency concerns, data consistency concerns, and the reliance on third parties to scale. We addressed data currency in our earlier sidebar "Replication Delay Concerns." Consistency is typically managed by the native or third-party product that you choose to perform your replication and seldom in our experience does it create a problem even in the highest request volume products. More often, we see that the consistency manager stops replication due to some concern, which in turn creates a larger data currency issue. These issues are usually able to be solved in a relatively short time frame. As for scaling through third parties, as long as you are designing your solution such that any replication technology can support your needs, you can always switch an underperforming partner out for another commodity solution.

Summarizing the Database X-Axis

The x-axis of the AKF Database Scale Cube represents the replication of data such that work can easily be distributed across nodes with absolutely no bias.

X-axis implementations tend to be easy to conceptualize and typically can be implemented at relatively low cost. They are the most cost-effective way of scaling transaction growth, though they usually have limitations in the number of nodes that can be employed. They can be easily created from a monolithic database or storage system, though there typically is an upfront cost to do so. They do not tend to significantly increase the complexity of your operations or production environment.

X-axis implementations are limited by the aforementioned replication technology limitations and the size of data that is being replicated. In general, x-axis implementations do not scale well with data size and growth.

The Y-Axis of the AKF Database Scale Cube

The y-axis of the AKF Database Scale Cube represents a separation of data meaning within your database schema or data storage system. When discussing database scale, we are usually aligning data with a predetermined application y-axis split. The y-axis split addresses the monolithic nature of the data architecture by separating the data into schemas that have meaning relative to the applications performing work on that data or reading from that data. A pure x-axis split might have 100 instances of the exact same data with one write and 99 read instances. In a y-axis split, we might split the data into the same "chunks" as we split our application in Chapter 23. These might be exactly the data necessary to perform such separate functions as login, logout, read profile, update profile, search profiles, browse profiles, checkout, display similar items, and so on. Obviously, there might be overlap in the data such as customer specific data present in the login/logout functionality, as well as the update profile functionality. We'll address ways to handle this later.

You might also consider splitting data from a "noun" perspective, rather than leading with the y-axis services based split first. The difference here is that we think of how we might partition our data in a resource oriented fashion rather than in a service (or verb) oriented fashion as in our application example. This change in approach might lead us to put customer data in one spot, product data in another, user generated content in a third, and so on. This approach has the benefit of leveraging the affinity data elements often have with each other and leveraging the talents of database architects who are familiar with entity relationships within relational databases. The drawback of this approach is that we must either change our approach for splitting applications to also be resource based (that is, "all services that interact with customer data in one application") or suffer the consequences of not having a swim lane based application and as a result non fault isolative architecture. More to the point, if we split our data along resource meaningful boundaries and split our application along service meaningful boundaries, we will almost certainly have services talking to several resources. As we discussed in Chapter 21, this will absolutely lower our availability, which likely runs counter to our overall company objectives. For this reason, we strongly suggest sticking with resource oriented or services oriented splits for both your application and your data.

Consistent with our past explanations of split complexities in Chapters 22 and 23, y-axis data splits are more complex than x-axis data splits. You can lower some of the initial cost and prove your concepts by performing splits of virtual data storage or databases without an actual physical split. In a database, this might be implemented by moving tables and data to a different schema or even to another database instance within the same physical hardware. Although this move saves you the initial capital expense of purchasing additional equipment, it unfortunately does not allow you to forego the engineering cost of changing your code to address different storage implementations or databases. For the physical split you can, temporarily, use tools that link the separate physical databases together so that if your engineers missed any tables being moved they have the opportunity to fix the code before breaking the application. After you are sure that the application is properly accessing the moved tables, you should remove these links because they can cause a chain reaction of degraded performance in some instances.

Y-axis splits are most commonly implemented to address the issues associated with a dataset that has grown significantly in complexity or size and which is likely to continue to grow. These splits also help scale transaction volumes because as you perform the splits you are moving requests to multiple physical or logical systems and in turn decreasing logical and/or physical contention for the data. Ultimately, in hyper-growth environments where both the data and transaction volume grows, the splits need to happen to separate physical instances of a database or storage on separate hardware instances.

Operationally, y-axis splits help reduce the time necessary to process any given transaction as the data being searched and very likely retrieved is smaller and tailored to the service performing the transaction. Conceptually, y-axis splits allow you to better understand vast amounts of data by thematically bundling that data, rather than lumping everything into the same "storage" container. Y-axis splits also aid in fault isolation as identified within Chapter 21; a failure of a given data element does not bring down all of the functionality of your platform (assuming that you have properly implemented the swim lane concept).

When bundled with similar splits at an application level, y-axis splits allow you to grow your team more easily by focusing teams on specific services or functions within your product and the data relevant to those functions and services. As discussed in Chapter 23, you can dedicate a person or a team to searching and browsing, a team toward the development of an advertising platform, a team to account functionality, and so on. All of the engineering benefits including "on boarding" and the application of experience to a problem set discussed in Chapter 23 are realized when both the data and the services acting on that data are split together.

Y-axis splits also have drawbacks. They are absolutely more costly to implement in engineering time than x-axis splits. Not only do services need to be rewritten to address different data storage systems and databases, but the actual data likely needs to be moved if you have a product that has already launched. The operations and infrastructure teams will now need to support more than one schema. This in turn might mean that there is more than one class or size of server in the operations environment to get the most cost-efficient systems for each type of transaction.

Summarizing the Database Y-Axis

The y-axis of the AKF Database Scale Cube represents separation of data meaning, often by service, resource, or data affinity.

Y-axis splits are meant to address the issues associated with growth and complexity in data size and its impact to requests or operations on that data. If implemented and architected to be consistent with an application y-axis split, it can create fault isolation as described in Chapter 21.

Y-axis splits can scale with both the growth in number of transactions and the size of data. They tend to cost more than x-axis splits as the engineering team needs to rewrite services and determine how to move data between separate schemas and systems

The Z-Axis of the AKF Database Scale Cube

As with the Application Scale Cube, the z-axis of the AKF Database Scale Cube consists of splits based on values that are "looked up" or determined at the time of the transaction. This split is most commonly performed by looking up or determining the location of data based on a reference to the customer or requestor. However, it can also be applied to any split of data within a resource or service where that split is done without a bias to affinity or theme. Examples would be a modulus or hash of product number if that modulus or hash was not indicative of the product type. For instance, if an ecommerce company sold jewelry and decided to split its data into groups such as watches, rings, bracelets, and necklaces, such splits would not be z-axis splits; such splits are actually y-axis splits as they are splits relevant to themes or affinity of the resource in question. On the other hand, if the company decided to split its product catalog by a modulus (say mod 10) of the unique product number for each item, and the resulting databases storing the items each had a roughly equal quantity of watches, rings, necklaces, and so on, the item would be a z-axis split.

The easiest way to think of the difference between y- and z-axis splits is to differentiate between things that we know before a request happens and things we must look up or determine at the time of the transaction. For instance, if we were to split watches from our jewelry retailer into their own database, we know that any call for watches goes to the watches database. On the other hand, if we split watches across several databases and combine them with other pieces of jewelry by performing a modulus of the product id, we must look at the product id sent in the request, perform our modulus on that product id, and determine the database in which the watch is located.

A similar relationship can be made to customer information. Let's consider the case where we split customers by geography. Technically speaking, if we predetermine the geographic location of a customer and that customer is always guaranteed to be in the Northwest U.S. database and we make that determination prior to the request (say through a URL), that split is a y-axis split. However, if we make that determination at the time of the request by looking up the username and determining the password or performing a geo-location test of the requestor IP address, we have performed a z-axis split. For the sake of simplicity, we usually just reduce this to the most common case that all customer based splits are z-axis splits.

As with the Application Scale Cube, for the z-axis split to be valuable, it must help us scale our transactions and the data upon which those transactions are performed.

A z-axis split attempts to accomplish the benefits of a y-axis split without a bias to the action (service) or resource itself. In doing so, it also tends to offer a more balanced demand across all of your data than a y-axis split in isolation. If you assume that each datum has a relatively equal opportunity to be in high demand, average demand, or low demand, and if you apply a deterministic and unbiased algorithm to store and locate such data, you will likely get a relatively equal distribution of demand across all of your databases or storage systems. This is not true for the y-axis split, which may cause certain systems to have unique demand spikes based on their contents. For instance, the rings database may have incredibly high utilization relative to the watches database during the peak wedding month of August, whereas a z-axis split that implemented a modulus would spread that peak demand for rings across all of the databases. There might in fact be one ring with very high demand, but the more likely case is that a few rings would exhibit high demand and those would have a good chance of being on different databases.

Because we are splitting our data and as a result our transactions across multiple systems, we can achieve a transactional scale similar to that within the x-axis. Furthermore, we aren't inhibited to the replication constraints of the x-axis because in a z-axis only split we are not replicating any data. Unfortunately, as with the y-axis, we increase our operational complexity somewhat as we now have many unique databases or data storage systems; the schema or setup of these databases is similar, but the data is unique. Unlike the y-axis, we don't likely get the benefit of splitting up our architecture in a service or resource oriented fashion. Schemas or setups are monolithic in z-axis only implementations, though the data is segmented as with the y-axis split. Finally, there is some software cost associated with z-axis splits in that the code must be able to recognize that requests are not all equivalent. As with our application splits, very often an algorithm to determine where the request should be sent is created, or a lookup service is created that can determine to what system or pod a request should be sent.

The benefits of a z-axis split are that we increase fault isolation, increase transactional scalability, increase data scalability, and increase our ability to adequately predict demand across multiple databases as our load will likely be fairly evenly distributed. The end results we would expect from these are higher availability, greater scalability, faster transaction processing times, and a better capacity planning function within our organization.

The z-axis, however, is more costly given the need to develop new code. We also add some operational complexity to our production environment; we now need to monitor several different systems with similar code bases performing similar functions for different clients. Configuration files may differ as a result and systems may not be easily moved when configured depending upon your implementation.

As stated in Chapter 23, because we are leveraging characteristics unique to a group of transactions, we can also improve our disaster recovery plans by geographically dispersing our services.

Summarizing the Database Z-Axis

The z-axis of the AKF Database Scale Cube represents separation of work based on attributes that are looked up or determined at the time of the transaction. Most often, these are implemented as splits by requestor, customer, or client, though they can also be splits within a product catalog and determined by product id or any other split that is determined and looked up at the time of the request.

Z-axis splits are often the most costly implementation of the three types of splits. Software needs to be modified to determine where to find, operate on, and store information. Very often, a lookup service or deterministic algorithm will need to be written for these types of splits.

Z-axis splits aid in scaling transaction growth, aid in decreasing processing time by limiting the data necessary to perform any transaction, and aid the capacity planning function by more evenly distributing demand across systems. The z-axis is most effective at evenly scaling growth in customers, clients, requesters, or other data elements that can be evenly distributed.

Putting It All Together

You may have noticed that Chapters 22, 23, and 24 have all had similar messages with very little deviation. That's because the AKF Scale Cube is a very powerful and flexible tool. Of all the tools we've used in our consulting practice, our clients have found it to be the most useful in figuring out how to scale their systems, databases, and even their organizations. Because it represents a common framework and language, little energy is wasted in defining what is meant by different approaches. Groups can now argue over the relative merits of an approach rather than spending time trying to understand how something is being split. Furthermore, teams can rather easily and quickly start applying the concepts within any of their meetings rather than struggle with the options on how to scale something. As with Chapter 23, in this section, we will discuss how the cube can be applied to create near infinite scalability within your databases and storage systems.

A z-axis only implementation of the AKF Database Scale Cube has several problems when implemented in isolation. Let's assume the previous case where you make N splits of your customer base in a jewelry ecommerce platform. Because we are only implementing the z-axis here, each instance is a single virtual or physical server. If it fails for hardware or software reasons, the services for that customer or set of customers have become completely unavailable. That availability problem alone is reason enough for us to implement an x-axis split for each of our z-axis splits. At the very least, we should have one additional database that we can use in the event that our primary database for any given set of customers fails. The same holds true if the z-axis is used to split our product catalog. If we split our customer base or product catalog N ways along the z-axis, with each of the N splits having at least 1/Nth of our customers initially, we would put at least two "cloned" or x-axis servers in each of the N splits. This ensures that should a server fail we still service the customers in that pod.

It is likely more costly for us to perform continued customer or product catalog oriented splits to scale our transactions than it is to simply add databases within one of our customer or product oriented splits. The reason for this is that each time we perform a split, we need to update our code to recognize where the split information is or at the very least update a configuration file giving the new modulus or hash values. Additionally, we need to create programs or scripts to move the data to the expected positions within the newly split database or storage infrastructure. Therefore, in an effort to reduce overall cost of scale, we will probably implement a z-axis split with an x-axis split within each z-axis split. We can also now perform x-axis scale within each of our z-axis splits. If a customer grows significantly in transactions, we can perform a cost-effective x-axis split (the addition of more replicated databases) within that customer's pod.

Y-axis splits, in conjunction with z-axis splits can help us create fault isolation. If we led an architectural split by splitting customers first, we could then create fault isolative swim lanes by function or resource within each of the z-axis splits. We might have product information in each of the z-axis splits separate from customer account information and so on.

The y-axis split has its own set of problems when implemented in isolation. The first is similar to the problem of the z-axis split in that a single database focused on a subset of functionality results in the functionality being unavailable when the server fails. As with the z-axis split, we are going to want to increase our availability by adding at least another cloned or x-axis server for each of our functions. We also save money by adding servers in an x-axis fashion for each of our y-axis splits versus continuing to split along the y-axis. As with our z-axis split, it costs us engineering time to continue to split off functionality or resources, and we likely want to spend as much of that time on new product functionality as possible. Rather than modifying the code and further deconstructing our databases, we simply add replicated databases into each of our y-axis splits and bypass the cost of further code modification. Of course, this assumes that we've already written the code to write to a single database and read from multiple databases.

The y-axis split also does not scale as well with customer growth, product growth, or some other data elements as the z-axis split. Y-axis splits in databases help us disaggregate data, but they have a finite number of splits determined by the affinity of data and your application architecture. Take the case that you split all product information off from the rest of your data. You now have your entire product catalog separated from everything else within your data architecture. You may be able to perform several y-axis splits in this area similar to our previous discussion in this chapter of splitting watches from rings, necklaces, and so on. But what happens when the number of rings available grows to a point that it becomes difficult for you to further split them by categories? What if the demand on a subset of rings is such that you need to be careful about which hardware serves them? A z-axis split can help out quite a bit here by allowing the rings to exist across several databases without regard to the type of ring. As we've previously indicated, the load will likely also be relatively uniformly distributed.

As we've stated previously, the x-axis approach is often the easiest to implement and as such is very often the very first type of split within data architectures. It scales well with transactions, but very often has a limit to the number of nodes to which you can scale. As your transaction volume grows and the amount of data that you serve grows, you will need to implement another axis of scale. The x-axis is very often the first axis of scale implemented by most companies, but as the product and transaction base grows, it typically becomes subordinate to either the y- or z-axis.

Ideally, as we indicated in Chapter 12, Exploring Architectural Principles, you will plan for at least two axes of scale even if you only implement a single axis. Planning for y or z in addition to initially implementing an x-axis of scale is a good approach. If you find yourself in a hyper-growth situation, you will want to plan for all three. In this situation, you should determine a primary implementation (say a z-axis by customer), a secondary (a y-axis by functionality), and an x-axis for redundancy and transaction growth. Then, apply a fault isolative swim lane per Chapter 21 and even a swim lane within a swim lane concept. You may swim lane your customers in a z-axis, and then swim lane each of the functions within each z-axis in a y-axis fashion. The x-axis then exists for redundancy and transaction scale. Voila! You are both highly available and highly scalable.

AKF Database Scale Cube Summary

Here is a summary of the three axes of scale:

- The x-axis represents the distribution of the same data or mirroring of data across multiple entities. It typically relies upon replication and has a limit to how many nodes can be employed.

- The y-axis represents the distribution and separation of the meaning of data by service, resource, or data affinity.

- The z-axis represents distribution and segmentation of data by attributes that are looked up or determined at the time of request processing.

Hence, x-axis splits are mirror images of data, y-axis splits separate data thematically, and z-axis splits separate data by a lookup or modulus. Often, z-axis splits happen by customer, but may also happen by product id or some other value.

Practical Use of the Database Cube

Let's examine the practical use of our application cube for three unique purposes. We will look at the same implementations as we discussed in Chapter 23, continuing with our fictitious company AllScale.

Ecommerce Implementation

The AllScale data architects ultimately decide that the data architecture is going to be impacted along three dimensions: transaction growth upon the databases, decisions made in Chapter 23 to scale the application, and growth in customers and products. As such, they are going to need to rely on all three axes of our AKF Application Scale Cube.

In Chapter 23, the team decided to split functionality of the site to allow for growth and complexity in the application. You may recall that browsing, searching, catalog upload, inventory management, and so on, and every other verb that can be performed without needing to know specific information about a particular customer, became a branch of functionality within the site and its own code base. Applying the principles of Chapter 21, the team decides to make these swim lanes; each swim lane needs to have data relevant to the needs of the application. The team recognizes that in so doing it is changing the normal form of its data architecture and there will be elements of data replicated throughout the architecture. It is very important that the team ensures that for any given data element there is a single "point of truth" that holds the most current and up-to-date value for this data. Ideally, the team limits the updates to one lane, with some form of asynchronous updates happening outside of the customer transactions to update the elements in other portions of their architecture.

Per our decisions in Chapter 23, all customer information will be split into N pods, where N is a configurable number. Each of these pods will host roughly 1/Nth of our customers. This is a z-axis split of the customer base. Within each of these z-axis splits, the team is going to perform y-axis splits of the code base and the data necessary to handle those splits. Login/logout will be its own function, checkout will be own function, account status and summary will be its own function, and the data necessary to support each of these will be split appropriately with the application. No single Y lane will need to know about more than 1/Nth the customers; as a result, caching for things like login information will be much more lightweight and much faster.

Finally, the team applies x-axis splits everywhere to scale the number of transactions through any given segmentation.

Search causes the AllScale data and software architects some concern, so they ultimately decide to focus a bit of attention on this area. They are going to leverage the x-, y-, and z-axes of the scale cube to address the search needs and to make search results very fast for their end customers. Splitting search off alone is a y-axis split so we will focus on the x- and z-axes next. Please reference Figure 24.2 for the discussion in the following paragraphs.

The team decides to use an aggregator concept to help it make search requests speedy. The aggregators are responsible for growth in the number of transactions and each is a clone of the others, creating an x-axis implementation. They ultimately make requests of systems that have 1/Nth of the total items for sale in a modulus of the product catalog, where N is the modulus applied to the product catalog. This N way split is a z-axis split along the product id. Additionally, each N-way z-axis split has M replicated datasets further allowing transaction growth.

A search request is load balanced across any one of the aggregators. That aggregator in turn makes N separate requests, one to each of our N tiers of product databases. Each of these has 1/Nth the data (product id mod N). Each tier in turn has M

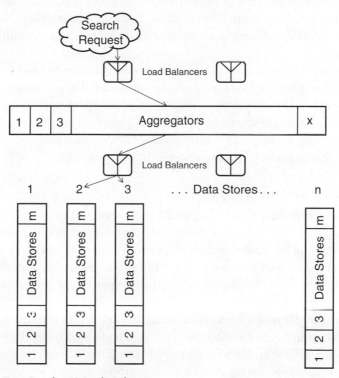

Figure 24.2   *Fast Read or Search Subsystem*

replicated copies of the 1/Nth the data and the request to that tier is load balanced to one of the M copies. As each N tier returns a result, the aggregator compiles the complete list of elements and when complete returns the ordered list to the requester.

Returns from each of the N z-axis splits are very fast as the data can be kept in memory and each database is searching only 1/Nth the data. The system is completely redundant given the multiple aggregators and the M x-axis copies of each of the N z-axis splits. The system scales easily with transactions by adding more aggregators and x-axis copies of the data. If necessary, aggregators of aggregators can be added should the aggregators need to talk to too many z-axis splits at once.

Human Resources ERP Implementation

The AllScale HRM database architecture needs to support the decisions the team made in Chapter 23. In Chapter 23, the architects decided that they wanted to build what appeared to be one large application to their customers but with each module capable of growing in complexity without affecting other modules in the system. The service separations or y-axis splits in Chapter 23 need to have data that supports them so the architects will split our data up accordingly. The architects remember our advice to ensure that there is only one updated copy of any piece of data, with asynchronous updates to all copies in other tiers of data. Performance and Career Planning, Learning and Education, Compliance Tracking, Recruiting, Compensation Planning, and Succession Planning all become modules with other modules scheduled for the future.

Each company has its own database, which is a z-axis split of the product, and additionally the architects allow for employee splits within a company split. As such, companies are split in z fashion, data supporting products are split in a y fashion, and employees within those products are split in a z fashion. This follows the architect's code decisions from Chapter 23. Additionally, the AllScale architects employ read databases where necessary, which is an x-axis implementation.

Back Office IT System

Remember the system defined in Chapter 23 that is focused on developing personalized marketing emails for AllScale's current and future client base. The team decided to split the system up by classes of data relevant to each of the existing and potential customers. The team needs to ensure that mail campaigns launch and finish within a few hours so it is going to need a fairly aggressive split of the mail system given the number of mails that it sends.

The team's first split was a z-axis split defined by the recency, frequency, monetization, and class of purchase as a criterion. The team had an additional split for all people for whom it has data and who did not purchase from AllScale. All told, the team had 199 unique splits consisting of 99 unique customer splits and 100 potential customer splits. The data for these needs to be split consistent with the z-axis splits for the AllScale services.

In Chapter 23, the team created y-axis functional splits of its application consistent with the functions of the marketing system. Creative development, mail sending, mail viewing, bounce reporting, and so on all became separate Y splits within the end customer oriented Z splits and as such the team will need to have the data relevant to these functions split within their databases.

The team needs to ensure that each of the databases is highly available so at the very least it will make a single x-axis split or replicated copy of each of the databases identified earlier.

Observations

We've twice now discussed when to use which axis of scale. We discussed it first in the "Observations" section of Chapter 23 and again earlier in this chapter after we discussed each of the axes. The next obvious question you are probably asking is "When do I decide to allow the application considerations to lead my architectural decisions and when do I decide to allow the data concerns to drive my decisions?"

The answer to that question is not an easy one, and again we refer back to the "Art" portion of our title. In some situations, the decision is easier to make, such as the decision within data warehousing discussions. Data warehouses are most often split by data concerns, though this is not always the case. The real question to ask is "What portion of my architecture most limits my scale?"

You may have a low transaction, low data growth environment, but an application that is very complex. An example may be encryption or cipher breaking systems. Here, the application likely needs to be broken up into services to allow specialists to develop the systems in question effectively. Alternatively, you may have a system such as a content site where the data itself (the content) is the thing that drives most of your scale concerns, and as such you would likely design your architecture around the data concerns.

If you are a site with transaction growth, complexity growth, and growth in data, you will probably switch between application leading design and database leading design to meet your needs. You choose the one that is most limiting for any given area and allow it to lead your architectural efforts. The most mature teams see them as one holistic system.

Timeline Considerations

One of the most common questions we get asked is, "When do I perform an x-axis split, and when should I consider y- and z-axis splits?" Put simply, the question really addresses whether there is an engineered maturity to the process of the AKF Scale Cube. In theory, there is no general timeline for these splits, but in implementation, most companies follow a similar path.

Ideally, a technology or architecture team would select the right axes of scale for its data and transaction growth needs and implement them in a cost-effective manner. Systems with high transaction rates, low data needs, and a high read to write ratio are probably most cost effectively addressed with an x-axis split. Such a system or component may never need more than simple replication in both the data tier and the systems tier. Where customer data growth, complex functionality, and high transaction growth intersect, a company may need to perform all three axes.

In practice, what typically happens is that a technology team will find itself in a bind and need to do something quickly. Most often, x-axis splits are easiest to implement in terms of time and overall cost. The team will rush to this implementation, and then start to look for other paths. Y- and z-axis splits tend to follow, with y implementations tending to be more common as a second step than z implementations, due to the conceptual ease of splitting functions within an application.

Our recommendation is to design your systems with all of the axes in mind. At the very least, make sure that you are not making decisions that will preclude you from easily splitting customers or functions in the future. Attempt to implement your product with x-axis splits for both the application and the database and have designs available to split the application and data by both functions and customers. In this fashion, you can rapidly scale should demand take off without struggling to keep up with the needs of your end users.

Conclusion

This chapter discussed the employment of the AKF Scale Cube to databases and data architectures within a product, service, or platform. We modified the AKF Scale Cube slightly, narrowing the scope and definition of each of the axes so that it became more meaningful to databases and data architecture.

Our x-axis still addresses the growth in transactions or work performed by any platform or system. Although the x-axis handles the growth in transaction volume well, it suffers by the limitations of replication technology and does not handle data growth well.

The y-axis addresses data growth as well as transaction growth. Unfortunately, it does not distribute demand well across databases as it focuses on data affinity. As such, we will often get irregular demand characteristics, which might make capacity modeling difficult and will likely result in x- or z-axis splits.

The z-axis addresses growth in data and is most often related to customer growth or inventory element (product) growth. Z-axis splits have the ability to more evenly distribute demand (or load) across a group of systems.

Not all companies need all three axes of scale to survive. When more than one axis is employed, the x-axis is almost subordinate to the other axes. You might, for instance, have multiple x-axis splits, each occurring within a y- or z-axis split. Ideally, all such splits occur in relationship to application splits with either the application or the data being the reason for making a split.

Key Points

- X-axis database splits scale linearly with transaction growth but usually have predetermined limits as to the number of splits allowed. They do not help with the growth in customers or data. X-axis splits are mirrors of each other.
- The x-axis tends to be the least costly to implement.
- Y-axis database splits help scale data as transaction growth. They are mostly meant for data scale because in isolation they are not as effective as the x-axis in transaction growth.
- Y-axis splits tend to be more costly to implement than x-axis splits as a result of engineering time necessary to separate monolithic databases.
- Y-axis splits aid in fault isolation.
- Z-axis application splits help scale transaction and data growth.
- Z-axis splits allow for more even demand or load distribution than most y-axis splits.
- As with y-axis splits, z-axis splits aid in fault isolation.
- The choice of when to use what method or axis of scale is both art and science as is the decision of when to use an application leading architecture split or a data leading architecture split.

Chapter 25

Caching for Performance and Scale

What the ancients called a clever fighter is one who not only wins, but excels in winning with ease.

—Sun Tzu

What is the best way to handle large volumes of traffic? This is, of course, a trick question and at this point in the book hopefully you answered something like "establish the right organization, implement the right processes, and follow the right architectural principles to ensure the system can scale." That's a great answer, but we think the absolute best way to handle large traffic volumes and user requests is to not have to handle it at all. That probably sounds too good to be true but there is a way to achieve this. Although not an actual architectural principle, the guideline of "don't handle the traffic if you don't have to" should be a mantra of your architects. The key to achieving this is through the pervasive use of something called a cache.

In this chapter, we are going to cover caching and how it can be one of the best tools in your tool box for scalability. There are numerous forms of caching already present in our environments, ranging from CPU cache to DNS cache to Web browser cache. Covering all forms of caching is beyond the scope of this book, but this should not dissuade you from pursuing a further study of all types of caching. Understanding these various caches will allow you to take better advantage of them in your applications and services. We are going to stick to three levels of caching that are most under your control from an architectural perspective. These are caching at the object, application, and content delivery network (CDN) levels. We will start with a simple primer on caching and then discuss each of these levels of caching in order that you understand their fundamental purposes and you begin considering how to leverage them for your system.

Caching Defined

Cache is an allocation of memory by a device or application for the temporary storage of data that is likely to be used again. The term was first used in 1967 in the publication *IBM Systems Journal* to label a memory improvement described as a high-speed buffer.[1] Don't be confused by this point; caches and buffers have similar functionality but are different in purpose. Both buffers and caches are allocations of memory and have similar structures. A buffer is memory that is used temporarily for access requirements, such as when data from disk must be moved into memory in order for processor instructions to utilize it. Buffers can also be used for performance, such as when reordering of data is required before writing to disk. A cache, on the other hand, is used for the temporary storage of data that is likely to be accessed again, such as when the same data is read over and over without the data changing.

The structure of a cache is very similar to data structures, such as arrays with key-value pairs. In a cache, these tuples or entries are called *tags* and *datum*. The tag specifies the identity of the datum, and the datum is the actual data being stored. The data stored in the datum is an exact copy of the data stored in either a persistent storage device, such as a database or as calculated by an executable application. The tag is the identifier that allows the requesting application or user to find the datum or determine that it is not present in the cache. In Table 25.1, the cache has three items cached from the database, items with tags 3, 4, and 0. The cache can have its own index that could be based on recent usage or other indexing mechanism to speed up the reading of data.

Table 25.1   *Cache Structure*

(a) *Database*

Index	Data
0	$3.99
1	$5.25
2	$7.49
3	$1.15
4	$4.45
5	$9.99

(b) *Cache*

Index	Tag	Datum
0	3	$1.15
1	4	$4.45
2	0	$3.99

---

1. According to the caching article in Wikipedia: http://en.wikipedia.org/wiki/Cache.

When the requesting application or user finds the data that it is asking for in the cache, this is called a *cache-hit*. When the data is not present in the cache, the application must go to the primary source to retrieve the data. Not finding the data in the cache is called a *cache-miss*. The number of hits to requests is called a *cache ratio* or *hit ratio*. This ratio is important to understand how effective the cache is being in offsetting load from the primary storage or executable. If the ratio is low, meaning there are very few hits, there may be a serious degradation in performance due to the overhead of first checking a cache that does not have the data being requested.

There are a couple methods of updating or refreshing data in a cache. The first is an offline process that periodically reads data from the primary source and completely updates the datum in the cache. There are a variety of uses for such a refresh method. One of the most common situations when this method would be utilized are upon startup when the cache is empty and when the data is recalculated or restored on a fixed schedule, such as through batch jobs.

Batch Cache Refresh

As an example, let's assume there is a batch job in the AllScale system called price_recalc. Part of AllScale's human resources management (HRM) service is acting as a reseller of online tutorials provided by third parties. These tutorials are used by customers for training their staff or employees on tasks such as interviewing and performance counseling. This batch job calculates the new price of a tutorial based on input from the vendors who sometimes change their prices daily or monthly as they run specials on their products. Instead of running a pricing calculation on demand, it has been determined that based on the business rules, it is sufficient to calculate this every 20 minutes.

Although we have saved a lot of resources by not dynamically calculating the price, we still do not want the other services to request it continuously from the primary data source, the database. Instead, we need a cache that stores the most frequently used items and prices. In this case, it does not make sense to dynamically refresh the cache because price_recalc runs every 20 minutes. It makes much more sense to refresh the cache on the same schedule that the batch job runs.

Another method of updating or refreshing data in a cache is when a cache-miss occurs, the application or service requesting the data retrieves it from the primary data source and then stores it in the cache. Assuming the cache is filled, meaning that all memory allocated for the cache is full of datum, storing the newly retrieved data requires some other piece of data to be ejected from the cache. The decision on which piece of data to eject is an entire field of study. The algorithms that are used to make this determination are known as caching algorithms. One of the most common algorithms used in caching is the least recently used (LRU) heuristic which removes the data that has been accessed furthest in the past.

In Figure 25.1, the service has requested Item #2 (step 1), which is not present in the cache and results in a cache-miss. The request is reiterated to the primary source, the database (step 2), where it is retrieved (step 3). The application then must update the cache (step 4), which it does, creating the new cache by ejecting the least recently used item (index 2 tag 0 datum $3.99). This is a sample of a cache-miss with update based on the least recently used algorithm.

Another algorithm is the exact opposite of LRU and is the most recently used (MRU). LRU is pretty commonsensical in that it generally makes sense that something not being used should be expunged to make room for something needed right now. The MRU at first take seems nonsensical, but in fact it has a use. If the likelihood that a piece of data will be accessed again is most remote when it first has been read, MRU works best. Let's take our AllScale price_recalc batch job example again. This time, we don't have room in our cache to store all the item prices, and the application accessing the price cache is a search engine bot. After the search engine bot has accessed the page to retrieve the price, it marks it off the list and is not likely to revisit this page or price again until all others have been accessed. Here, the MRU algorithm is the most appropriate. As we mentioned earlier, there is an entire field of study ded-

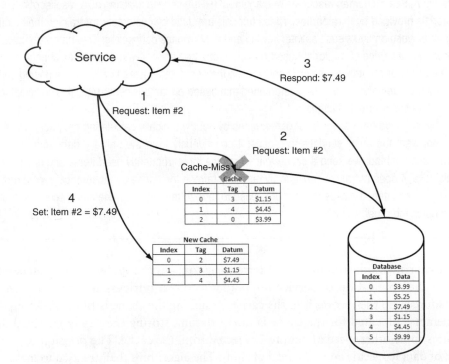

Figure 25.1   *Cache-Miss LRU*

icated to caching algorithms. Some very sophisticated algorithms take factors, such as differences in retrieval time, size of data, and user intent, into account when determining what data stays and what data goes.

Thus far, we've focused on reading the data from the cache and we've assumed that only reads were being performed on the data. What happens when that data is manipulated and must be updated to ensure that if it is accessed again it is correct? In this case, we need to write data into the cache and ultimately get the data in the original data store updated as well. There are a variety of ways to achieve this. One of the most popular methods is a write-through policy. This is when the application manipulating the data writes it into the cache and into the data store. The application has responsibility for ensuring integrity between the stores. Another method is known as write-back, where the cache stores the updated data until a certain point in the future. In this case, the data is marked as *dirty* in order that it be identified and understood that it has changed from the primary data source. Often, the future event that causes the write-back is the data being ejected from the cache. The way this would work is the data is retrieved by a service and is changed. This changed data is placed back into the cache and marked as dirty. When there is no longer room in the cache for this piece of data, it is expelled from the cache and written to the primary data store. Obviously, this write-back method relieves the burden of writing to two locations from the service, but as you can imagine, this increases the complexity of many situations, such as when shutting down or restoring the cache.

In this brief overview of caching, we have covered the tag-datum structure of caches; the concepts of cache-hit, cache-miss, and hit-ratio; the cache refreshing methodologies of batch and upon cache-miss; caching algorithms such as LRU and MRU; and write-through versus write-back methods of manipulating the data stored in cache. Armed with this brief tutorial, we are going to begin our discussion of three types of caches: object, application, and CDN.

Object Caches

Object caches are used to store objects for the application to be reused. These objects usually come from either a database or have been generated by calculations or manipulations of the application. The objects are almost always serialized objects, which are marshaled or deflated into a serialized format that minimizes the memory footprint. When retrieved, they must be inflated or unmarshalled to be converted into its original data type. *Marshalling* is the process of transforming the memory representation of an object into a byte-stream or sequence of bytes in order that it be stored or transmitted. *Unmarshalling* is the process of decoding from the byte representation into the original object form. For object caches to be used, the application must be aware of them and have implemented methods to manipulate the cache.

The basic methods of manipulation of a cache include a way to add data into the cache, a way to retrieve it, and a way to update the data. These are typically called *set* for adding data, *get* for retrieving data, and *replace* for updating data. Depending on the particular cache that is chosen, many programming languages already have built-in support for the most popular caches. Memcached is one of the most popular caches in use today. It is a "high-performance, distributed memory object caching system, generic in nature, but intended for use in speeding up dynamic web applications by alleviating database load."[2] This particular cache is very fast-using non-blocking network input/output (I/O) and its own slab allocator to prevent memory fragmentation guaranteeing allocations to be O(1) or able to be computed in constant time and thus not bound by the size of the data.

As indicated in the description of memcached, it is primarily designed to speed up Web applications by alleviating requests to the database. This makes sense because the database is almost always the slowest retrieval device in the application tiers. The overhead of implementing ACID (Atomicity, Consistency, Isolation, and Durability) properties in a relational database management system is larger, especially when data has to be written and read from disk. However, it is completely normal and advisable in some cases to use an object caching layer between other tiers of the system.

The way that an object cache fits into a typical two- or three-tier architecture is to place it in front of the database tier. As indicated earlier, this is because it is usually the slowest overall performing tier and also it is often the most expensive tier to expand. In Figure 25.2, there is a typical three-tier system stack depicted with a Web server tier, an application server tier, and a database tier. Instead of just one object cache, there are two. One cache is in between the application servers and the database, and one is between the Web servers and the application servers. This makes sense if the application server is performing a great deal of calculations or manipulations that are cacheable. This prevents the application servers from having to constantly recalculate the same data and instead allows it to be cached and relieve the load on the application servers. Just as with the database, this caching layer can help scale the tier without additional hardware. It is very likely that the objects being cached are a subset of the total data set from either the database or the application servers. For example, it is possible that the application code on the Web servers make use of the cache for user permission objects but not for transaction amounts, because user permissions are rarely changed and are accessed frequently; whereas a transaction amount is likely to be different with each transaction and accessed only once.

---

2. The description of memcached from the Web site http://www.danga.com/memcached/.

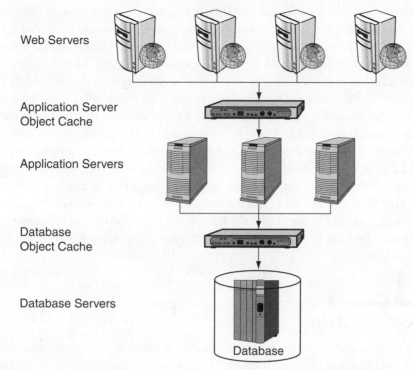

Figure 25.2 *Object Cache Architecture*

ACID Properties of a Database

Atomicity, Consistency, Isolation, and Durability (ACID) are properties that a database management system employ to ensure that transactions are considered completely reliable.

Atomicity is a property of a database management system to guarantee that all tasks of a transaction are completely performed or the entire transaction is rolled back. Failures of hardware or software will not result in half-completed transactions.

Consistency is the property that ensures that the database remains in a steady state before and after a transaction. If a transaction is successful, it moves the database from one state to another that is "consistent" with the rules.

Isolation is the property that prevents another transaction from accessing a piece of data while another transaction is acting on it. Most database management systems use locks to ensure this.

Durability is the property that after the system has marked the transaction as successful, it will remain completed and not be rolled back. All consistency checks must be completed prior to the transaction being considered complete.

The use of an object cache makes sense if you have a piece of data either in the database or in the application server that gets accessed frequently but is updated infrequently. The database is the first place to look to offset load because it is generally the slowest and most expensive of your application tiers. However, don't stop there; consider other tiers or pools of servers in your system for an object cache. Another very likely candidate for an object cache is as a centralized session management cache. If you make use of session data, we recommend you first eliminate session data as much as possible. Completely do away with sessions if you can as they are costly within your infrastructure and architecture. If you cannot, we encourage you to consider a centralized session management system that allows requests to come to any Web server and the session be moved from one to another without disruption. This way, you can make more efficient use of the Web servers through a load balanced solution, and in the event of a failure, users can be moved to another server with minimal disruption. Continue to look at your application for more candidates for object caches.

Application Caches

The next level of caching that we need to discuss is what we call application caching. There are two varieties of application caching: *proxy caching* and *reverse proxy caching*. Before we dive into the details of each, let's cover the concepts behind application caching in general. The basic premise is that you want to either speed up perceived performance or minimize the resources used. What do we mean by speeding up perceived performance? End users interacting with a Web based application or service don't care how fast the Web server actually is returning their request or how many requests per second each server can handle. All end users care about is how fast the application appears to respond in their browser. The use of smoke and mirrors is not only allowed but encouraged if it doesn't degrade the experience and improves performance. The smoke and mirror that people use is known as application caching. The same logic is applied to minimizing resources utilized. As long as end users have the same experience, they don't care if you utilize 100% of the available system resources or if you utilize 1%; they just want the pages to load quickly and accurately.

Proxy Caches

How do you speed up response time and minimize resource utilization? The way to achieve this is not to have the application or Web servers actually handle the requests. Let's start out by looking at *proxy caches*. These types of caches are usually implemented by Internet service providers, universities, schools, or corporations. The terms *forward proxy cache* or *proxy server* are sometimes used to be more descriptive. The idea is that instead of the Internet service provider (ISP) having to transmit an end user's request through its network to a peer network to a server for the URL requested, the ISP can proxy these requests and return them from a cache without ever going to the URL's actual servers. Of course, this saves a lot of resources on the ISP's network from being used as well as speeds up the processing. The caching is done without the end user knowing that it has occurred; to her, the return page looks and behaves as if the actual site had returned her request.

Figure 25.3 shows an implementation of a proxy cache at an ISP. The ISP has implemented a proxy cache that handles requests from a limited set of users for an unlimited number of applications or Web sites. The limited number of users can be their entire subscriber population or more than likely subsets of subscribers who are geographically collocated. All of these grouped users make requests through the cache; if the data is present, it is returned automatically; if the data is not present, the authoritative site is requested and the data is potentially stored in cache in case some other subscriber requests it. The caching algorithm that determines whether a page or piece of data gets updated/replaced can be customized for the subset of users that are using the cache. It may make sense for caching to only occur if a minimum number of requests for that piece of data are seen over a period of time. This way, the most requested data is cached and sporadic requests for unique data does not replace the most viewed data.

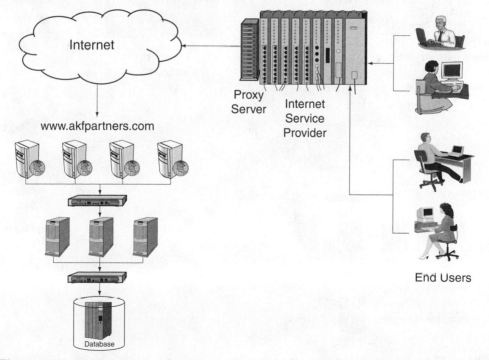

Figure 25.3 *Proxy Server Implementation*

Reverse Proxy Cache

The other type of application caching is the reverse proxy cache. With proxy caching, the cache handles the requests from a limited number of users for a potentially unlimited number of sites or applications. A reverse proxy cache is opposite in that it caches for an unlimited number of users or requestors and for a limited number of sites or applications. Another term used for reverse proxy caches is *gateway caches*. These are most often implemented by system owners themselves in order to off load the requests on their Web servers. Instead of every single request coming to the Web server, another tier is added for all or part of the set of available requests in front of the Web servers. Requests that are being cached can be returned immediately to the requestor without processing on the Web or application servers. The cached item can be anything from entire static pages to static images to parts of dynamic pages. The configuration of the specific application will determine what can be cached. Just because your service or application is dynamic does not mean that you cannot take advantage of application caching. Even on the most dynamic sites, many items can be cached.

Figure 25.4 shows an implementation of a reverse proxy cache in front of a site's Web servers. The reverse proxy server handles some or all of the requests until the

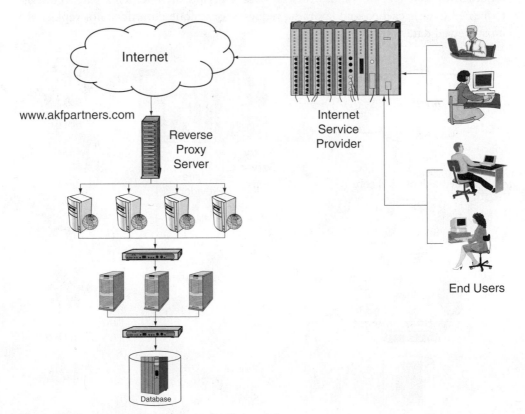

Figure 25.4 *Reverse Proxy Server Implementation*

pages or data that is stored in them is out of date or until the server receives a request for which it does not have data (a cache miss). When this occurs, the request is passed through to a Web server to fulfill the request and to refresh the cache. Any users that have access to make the requests for the application can be serviced by the cache. This is why a reverse proxy cache is considered the opposite of the proxy cache. A reverse proxy cache handles any number of users for a limited number of sites.

HTML Headers and Meta Tags

Many developers believe that they can control the caching of a page by placing meta tags, such as Pragma: no-cache, in the <HEAD> element of the page. This is only partially true. Meta tags in the HTML can be used to recommend how a page should be treated by browser cache, but most browsers do not honor these tags. Because proxy caches rarely even inspect the HTML, they do not abide by these tags.

HTTP headers, on the other hand, give much more control over caching, especially with regard to proxy caches. These headers cannot be seen in the HTML and are generated by the Web server. You can control them by configurations on the server. A typical HTTP response header could look like this:

```
HTTP/1.x 200 OK
Date: Tue, 24 Feb 2009 19:52:41 GMT
Server: Apache/2.2.3 (CentOS)
Last-Modified: Mon, 26 Jan 2009 23:03:35 GMT
Etag: "1189c0-249a-bf8d9fc0"
Accept-Ranges: bytes
Content-Length: 9370
p3p: policyref="/w3c/p3p.xml",
CP="ALL DSP COR PSAa PSDa OUR NOR ONL UNI COM NAV"
Connection: close
Cache-Control: no-cache
Content-Type: image/gif
```

Notice the Cache-Control header identifying no-cache. In accordance with the Request For Comments (RFC) 2616 Section 14 defining the HTTP 1.1 protocol, this header *must* be obeyed by all caching mechanisms along the request/response chain.

Another header that is useful in managing caching is the Etag and Last-Modified tags. These are used to validate the freshness of the page by the caching mechanisms.

Understanding the request and response HTTP headers will allow you to more fully control the caching of your pages. This is an exercise that is well worth doing to ensure your pages are being handled properly by all the caching layers between your site and the end users.

Caching Software

Adequately covering even a portion of the caching software that is available both from vendors and the open source communities is beyond the scope of this chapter. However, there are some points that should be covered to guide you in your search for the right caching software for your company's needs. The first point is that you should thoroughly understand your application and user demands. Running a site with multiple GB per second of traffic requires a much more robust and enterprise-class caching solution than does a small site serving 10MB per second of traffic. Are you projecting a doubling of requests or users or traffic every month? Are you introducing a brand-new video product line that is going to completely change that type and need for caching? These are the types of questions you need to ask yourself before you start shopping the Web for a solution, or you could easily fall into the trap of making your problem fit the solution.

The second point addresses the difference between add-on features and purpose-built solutions and is applicable to both hardware and software solutions. To understand the difference, let's discuss the life cycle of a typical technology product. A product usually starts out as a unique technology that sells and gains traction, or is adopted in the case of open source, as a result of its innovation and benefit within its target market. Over time, this product becomes less unique and eventually commoditized, meaning everyone sells essentially the same product with the primary differentiation being price. High tech companies generally don't like selling commodity products because the profit margins continue to get squeezed each year. And open source communities are usually passionate about their software and want to see it continue to serve a purpose. The way to prevent the margin squeeze or the move into the history books is to add features to the product. The more "value" the vendor adds the more the vendor can keep the price high. The problem with this is that these add-on features are almost always inferior to purpose-built products designed to solve this one specific problem.

An example of this can be seen in comparing the performance of mod_cache in Apache as an add-on feature with that of the purpose-built product memcached. This is not to belittle or take away anything from Apache, which is a very common open source Web server that is developed and maintained by an open community of developers known as the Apache Software Foundation. The application is available for a wide variety of operating systems and has been the most popular Web server on the World Wide Web since 1996. The Apache module, mod_cache, implements an HTTP content cache that can be used to cache either local or proxied content. This module is one of hundreds available for Apache, and it absolutely serves a purpose, but when you need an object cache that is distributed and fault tolerant, there are better solutions such as memcached.

Application caches are extensive in their types, implementations, and configurations. You should first become familiar with the current and future requirements of

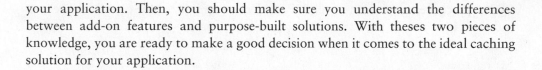

your application. Then, you should make sure you understand the differences between add-on features and purpose-built solutions. With theses two pieces of knowledge, you are ready to make a good decision when it comes to the ideal caching solution for your application.

Content Delivery Networks

The last type of caching that we are going to cover in this chapter is the content delivery networks (CDNs). This level of caching is used to push any of your content that is cacheable closer to the end user. The benefits of this include faster response time and fewer requests on your servers. The implementation of a CDN is varied but most generically can be thought of as a network of gateway caches located in many different geographical areas and residing on many different Internet peering networks. Many CDNs use the Internet as their backbone and offer their servers to host your content. Others, to provide higher availability and differentiate themselves, have built their own network point to point between their hosting locations.

The advantages of CDNs are that they speed up response time, off load requests from your application's origin servers, and possibly lower delivery cost, although this is not always the case. The concept is that the total capacity of the CDN's strategically placed servers can yield a higher capacity and availability than the network backbone. The reason for this is that if there is a network constraint or bottleneck, the total throughput is limited. When these are eliminated by placing CDN servers on the edge of the network, the total capacity is increased and overall availability increases as well. The way this works is that you place the CDN's domain as an alias for your server by using a canonical name (CNAME) in your DNS entry. A sample entry might look like this:

```
ads.akfpartners.com          CNAME          ads.akfpartners.akfcdn.net
```

Here, we have our CDN, akfcdn.net, as an alias for our subdomain ads.akfpartners.com. The CDN alias could then be requested by the application, and as long as the cache was valid, it would be served from the CDN and not our origin servers for our system. The CDN gateway servers would periodically make requests to our application origin servers to ensure that the data, content, or Web pages that they have in cache is up-to-date. If the cache is out-of-date, the new content is distributed through the CDN to their edge servers.

Today, CDNs offer a wide variety of services in addition to the primary service of caching your content closer to the end user. These services include DNS replacement, geo-load balancing, which is serving content to users based on their geographical location, and even application monitoring. All of these services are becoming more commoditized as more providers enter into the market. In addition to commercial

CDNs, there are more peer-to-peer P2P services being utilized for content delivery to end users to minimize the bandwidth and server utilization from providers.

Conclusion

In this chapter, we started off by explaining the concept that the best way to handle large amounts of traffic is to avoid handling them in the first place. You can best do this by utilizing caching. In this manner, caching can be one of the best tools in your tool box for ensuring scalability. We identified that there are numerous forms of caching already present in our environments, ranging from CPU cache to DNS cache to Web browser caches. In this chapter, we wanted to focus primarily on three levels of caching that are most under your control from an architectural perspective. These are caching at the object, application, and content delivery network levels.

We started with a primer on caching in general and covered the tag-datum structure of caches and how they are similar to buffers. We also covered the terminology of cache-hit, cache-miss, and hit-ratio. We discussed the various refreshing methodologies of batch and upon cache-miss as well as caching algorithms such as LRU and MRU. We finished the introductory section with a comparison of write-through versus write-back methods of manipulating the data stored in cache.

The first type of cache that we discussed was the object cache. These are caches used to store objects for the application to be reused. Objects stored within the cache usually come from either a database or have been generated by the application. These objects are serialized to be placed into cache. For object caches to be used, the application must be aware of them and have implemented methods to manipulate the cache. The database is the first place to look to offset load through the use of an object cache, because it is generally the slowest and most expensive of your application tiers; but the application tier is often a target as well.

The next type of cache that we discussed was the application cache. We covered two varieties of application caching: proxy caching and reverse proxy caching. The basic premise of application caching is that you desire to speed up performance or minimize resources used. Proxy caching is used for a limited number of users requesting an unlimited number of Web pages. This type of caching is often employed by Internet service providers or local area networks such as in schools and corporations. The other type of application caching we covered was the reverse proxy cache. A reverse proxy cache is used for an unlimited number of users or requestors and for a limited number of sites or applications. These are most often implemented by system owners in order to off load the requests on their application origin servers.

The last type of caching that we covered was the content delivery networks (CDNs). The general principle of this level of caching is to push content that is cacheable closer to the end user. The benefits include faster response time and fewer requests on the origin servers. CDNs are implemented as a network of gateway caches in different geographical areas utilizing different ISPs.

No matter what type of service or application you provide, it is important to understand the various methods of caching in order that you choose the right type of cache. There is almost always a caching type or level that makes sense with Web 2.0 and SaaS systems.

Key Points

- The most easily scalable traffic is the type that never touches the application because it is serviced by cache.

- There are many layers to consider adding caching, each with pros and cons.

- Buffers are similar to caches and can be used for performance, such as when reordering of data is required before writing to disk.

- The structure of a cache is very similar to data structures, such as arrays with key-value pairs. In a cache, these tuples or entries are called *tags* and *datum*.

- A cache is used for the temporary storage of data that is likely to be accessed again, such as when the same data is read over and over without the data changing.

- When the requesting application or user finds the data that it is asking for in the cache this is called a *cache-hit*.

- When the data is not present in the cache, the application must go to the primary source to retrieve the data. Not finding the data in the cache is called a *cache-miss*.

- The number of hits to requests is called a *cache ratio* or *hit ratio*.

- The use of an object cache makes sense if you have a piece of data either in the database or in the application server that gets accessed frequently but is updated infrequently.

- The database is the first place to look to offset load because it is generally the slowest and most expensive of your application tiers.

- A reverse proxy cache is opposite in that it caches for an unlimited number of users or requestors and for a limited number of sites or applications.

- Another term used for reverse proxy caches is *gateway caches*.

- Reverse proxy caches are most often implemented by system owners themselves in order to off load the requests on their Web servers.

- Many CDNs use the Internet as their backbone and offer their servers to host your content.

- Others, in order to provide higher availability and differentiate themselves, have built their own network point to point between their hosting locations.
- The advantages of CDNs are that they lower delivery cost, speed up response time, and off load requests from your application's origin servers.

Chapter 26

Asynchronous Design for Scale

> In all fighting, the direct method may be used for joining battle,
> but indirect methods will be needed in order to secure victory.
>
> —Sun Tzu

This last chapter in Part III, Architecting Scalable Solutions, will address an often overlooked problem when developing services or product—that is, overlooked until it becomes a noticeable and costly inhibitor to scaling. This problem is the use of synchronous calls in the application. We will explore the reasons that most developers overlook asynchronous calls as a scaling principle and how converting synchronous calls to asynchronous ones can greatly improve the scalability and availability of the system.

We will explore the use of state in applications including why it is used, how it is often used, why it can be problematic, and how to make the best of it when necessary. Examining the need for state and eliminating it where possible will pay huge dividends within your architecture if it is not already a problem. If it already is a problem in your system, this chapter will give you some tools to fix it.

Synching Up on Synchronization

Let's start our discussion by covering some of the basics of synchronization, starting with a definition and some different types of synchronization methods. The process of synchronization refers to the use and coordination of simultaneously executed threads or processes that are part of an overall task. These processes must run in the correct order to avoid a race condition or erroneous results. Stated another way, synchronization is when two or more pieces of work must be in a specific order to accomplish a task. An example is a login task. First, the user's password must be encrypted; then it must be compared against the encrypted version in the database; then the session data must be updated marking the user as authenticated; then the welcome page must be generated; and finally the welcome page must be presented. If any of those pieces of work are done out of order, the task of logging the user in fails to get accomplished.

There are many types of synchronization processes that take place in programming. One that all developers should be familiar with is the mutex or mutual exclusion. Mutex refers to how global resources are protected from concurrently running processes to ensure only one process is updating or accessing the resource at a time. This is often accomplished through semaphores, which is kind of a fancy flag. Semaphores are variables or data types that mark or flag a resource as being in use or free. Another classic synchronization method is known as thread join. Thread join is when a process is blocked from executing until a thread terminates. After the thread terminates, the other process is free to continue. An example would be for a parent process, such as a "look up," to start executing. The parent process kicks off a child process to retrieve the location of the data that it is going to look up, and this child thread is "joined." This means that the parent process cannot complete until the child process terminates.

Dining Philosophers Problem

This analogy is credited to Sir Charles Anthony Richard Hoare (a.k.a. Tony Hoare), as in the person who invented the Quicksort algorithm. This analogy is used as an illustrative example of resource contention and deadlock. The story goes that there were five philosophers sitting around a table with a bowl of spaghetti in the middle. Each philosopher had a fork to his left, and therefore each had one to his right. The philosophers could either think or eat, but not both. Additionally, in order to serve and eat the spaghetti, each philosopher required the use of two forks. Without any coordination, it is possible that all the philosophers pick up their forks simultaneously and therefore no one has two forks in which to serve or eat.

This analogy is used to show that without synchronization the five philosophers could remain stalled indefinitely and starve just as five computer processes waiting for a resource could all enter into a deadlocked state. There are many ways to solve such a dilemma. One is to have a rule that each philosopher when reaching a deadlock state will place his fork down, freeing up a resource, and think for a random time. If this solution sounds familiar, it might be because it is the basic idea of retransmission that takes place in the Transmission Control Protocol (TCP). When no acknowledgement for data is received, a timer is started to wait for a retry. The amount of time is adjusted by the smoothed round trip time algorithm and doubled after each unsuccessful retry.

As you might expect, there are many other types of synchronization processes and methods that are employed in programming. We're not presenting an exhaustive list but rather attempting to give you an overall understanding that synchronization is used throughout programming in many different ways. Eliminating synchronization is not possible, nor would it be advisable. It is, however, prudent to understand the purpose and cost of synchronization so that when you use it you do so wisely.

Synchronous Versus Asynchronous Calls

Now that we have a basic definition and some examples of synchronization, we can move on to a broader discussion of synchronous versus asynchronous calls within the application. Synchronous calls perform their action completely by the time the call returns. If a method is called and control is given to this method to execute, the point in the application that made the call is not given control back until the method has completed its execution and returned either successfully or with an error. In other words, synchronous methods are called, they execute, and when they finish, you get control back. As an example of a synchronous method, let's look at a method called query_exec from AllScale's human resource management (HRM) service. This method is used to build and execute a dynamic database query. One step in the query_exec method is to establish a database connection. The query_exec method does not continue executing without explicit acknowledgement of successful completion of this database connection task. Doing so would be a waste of resources and time. If the database is not available, the application should not waste time creating the query and waiting for it to become available. Indeed, if the database is not available, the team should reread Chapter 24, Splitting Databases for Scale, on how to scale the database so that there is improved availability. Nevertheless, this is an example of how synchronous calls work. The originating call is halted and not allowed to complete until the invoked process returns.

A nontechnical example of synchronicity is communication between two individuals either in a face-to-face fashion or over a phone line. If both individuals are engaged in meaningful conversation, there is not likely to be any other action going on. One individual cannot easily start another conversation with another individual without first stopping the conversation with the first person. Phone lines are held open until one or both callers terminate the call.

Contrast the synchronous methods or threads with an asynchronous method. With an asynchronous method call, the method is called to execute in a new thread, and it immediately returns control back to the thread that called it. The design pattern that describes the asynchronous method call is known as the asynchronous design, or the asynchronous method invocation (AMI). The asynchronous call continues to execute in another thread and terminates either successfully or with error without further interaction with the initiating thread. Let's turn back to our AllScale example with the query_exec method. After calling synchronously for the database connection, the method needs to prepare and execute the query. In the HRM system, AllScale has a monitoring framework that allows them to note the duration and success of all queries by asynchronously calling a method for start_query_time and end_query_time. These methods store a system time in memory and wait for the end call to be placed in order to calculate duration. The duration is then stored in a monitoring database that can be queried to understand how well the system is performing in terms of query run time. Monitoring the query performance is important but not as important as actually servicing the users' requests. Therefore, the calls to the monitoring methods of start_query_time and end_query_time are done asynchronously. If they succeed and return, great—AllScale's operations and engineering teams get the query time in the monitoring database. If the monitoring calls fail or get delayed for 20 seconds waiting on the monitoring database connection, they don't care. The user query continues on without any concern over the asynchronous calls.

Returning to our communication example, email is a great example of asynchronous communication. You write an email and send it, immediately moving on to another task, which may be another email, a round of golf, or whatever. When the response comes in, at an appropriate time, you read the response and potentially issue yet another email in response. The communication chain blocks neither the sender nor receiver for anything but the time to process the communication and issue a response.

Scaling Synchronously or Asynchronously

Now we understand the difference between synchronous and asynchronous calls. Why does this matter? The answer lies in scalability. Synchronous calls, if used excessively or incorrectly, cause undue burden on the system and prevent it from scaling. Let's continue with our query_exec example where we were trying to execute a user's query. If we had implemented the two monitoring calls synchronously using the rationale that (1) monitoring is important, (2) the monitoring methods are very quick, and (3) even if we slow down a user query what's the worst that could happen. These are all good intentions, but they are wrong. As we stated earlier, monitoring is important but it is not more important than returning a user's query. The monitoring methods might be very quick, when the monitoring database is operational, but what happens when it has a hardware failure and is inaccessible? The monitoring queries back up waiting to time out. This means the users' queries are blocked waiting for completion of the monitoring queries and are in turn backed up. When the user queries are slowed down or temporarily halted waiting for a time out, it is still taking up a database connection on the user database and is still consuming memory on the application server trying to execute this thread. As more and more user threads start stalling waiting for their monitoring calls to time out, the user database might run out of connections preventing other nonmonitored queries from executing, and the threads on the app servers get written to disk to free up memory, which causes swapping on the app servers. This swapping in turn slows down all processing and may result in the TCP stack of the app server reaching some maximum limit and refusing subsequent connections. Ultimately, new user requests are not processed and users sit waiting for browser or application timeouts. Your application or platform is essentially "down." As you see, this ugly chain of events can quite easily occur because of a simple oversight on whether a call should be synchronous or asynchronous. The worst thing about this scenario is the root cause can be elusive. As we step through the chain it is relatively easy to follow but when the symptoms of a problem are that your system's Web pages start loading slowly and over the next 15 minutes this continues to get worse and worse until finally the entire system grinds to a halt, diagnosing the problem can be very difficult. Hopefully, you have sufficient monitoring in place to help you diagnose these types of problems, but these extended chains of events can be very daunting to unravel when your site is down and you are frantic to get it back into service.

Despite the fact that synchronous calls can be problematic if used incorrectly or excessively, method calls are very often done synchronously. Why is this? The answer is that synchronous calls are simpler than asynchronous calls. "But wait!" you say. "Yes, they are simpler but often times our methods require that the other methods invoked do successfully complete and therefore we can't put a bunch of asynchronous calls in our system." Ah, yes; good point. There are many times when you do need an invoked method to complete and you need to know the status of that in order to continue along your thread. We are not going to tell you that all synchronous calls are bad; in fact, many are necessary and make the developer's life a thousand times less complicated. However, there are times when asynchronous calls can and should be used in place of synchronous calls, even when there is dependency as described earlier. If the main thread could care less whether the invoked thread finishes, such as with the monitoring calls, a simple asynchronous call is all that is required. If, however, you require some information from the invoked thread, but you don't want to stop the primary thread from executing, there are ways to use callbacks to retrieve this information. An in-depth discussion of callbacks are beyond the scope of this chapter. An example of callback functionality is interrupt handlers in operating systems that report on hardware conditions.

Asynchronous Coordination

Asynchronous coordination and communication between the original method and the invoked method requires a mechanism that the original method determines when or if a called method has completed executing. Callbacks are methods passed as an argument to other methods and allow for the decoupling of different layers in the code.

In C/C++, this is done through function pointers; in Java, it is done through object references. There are many design patterns that use callbacks, such as the delegate design pattern and the observer design pattern. The higher level process acts as a client of the lower level and calls the lower level method by passing it by reference. An example of what a callback method might be invoked for would be an asynchronous event like file system changes.

In the .NET Framework, the asynchronous communication is characterized by the use of `BeginBlah`, where `Blah` is the name of the synchronous version of the method. There are four ways to determine if an asynchronous call has been completed: first is polling (the `IsCompleted` property), second is a callback `Delegate`, third is the `AsyncWaitHandle` to wait on the call to complete, and fourth the `EndBlah`, which waits on the call to complete.

Different languages offer different solutions to the asynchronous communication and coordination problem. Understand what your language and frameworks offer so that you can implement them when needed.

In the preceding paragraph, we said that synchronous calls are simpler than asynchronous calls and therefore they get used an awful lot more often. Although this is completely true, it is only part of the reason that engineers don't pay enough attention to the impact of synchronous calls. The second part of the problem is that developers typically only see a small portion of the application. Very few people in the organization get the advantage of viewing the application in total from a higher level perspective. Your architects should certainly be looking at this level, as should some of your management team. These are the people that you will have to rely on to help challenge and explain how synchronization might cause scaling issues.

Example Asynchronous Systems

To fully understand how synchronous calls can cause scaling issues and how you can either design from the start or convert a system in place to use asynchronous calls, we shall invoke an example system that we can explore. The system that we are going to discuss is taken from an actual client implementation that we reviewed in our advisory practice at AKF Partners, but obviously it is obfuscated to protect privacy and simplified to derive the relevant teaching points quickly.

The client had a system, we'll call it MailScale, that allowed subscribed users to email groups of other users with special notices, newsletters, and coupons (see Figure 26.1). The volume of emails sent in a single campaign could be very large, as many as several hundred thousand recipients. These jobs were obviously done asynchronously from the main site. When a subscribed user was finished creating or uploading the email notice, he submitted the email job to process. Because processing tens of thousands of emails can take several minutes, it really would be ridiculous to hold up the user's done page with a synchronous call while the job actually processes. So far, so

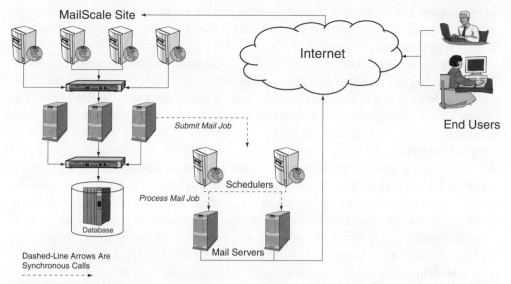

Figure 26.1 *MailScale Example*

good; we have email batch jobs that are performed asynchronously from the main user site.

The problem was that behind the main site there were schedulers that queued the email jobs and parsed them out to available email servers when they became available. These schedulers were the service that received the email job from the main site when submitted by the user. This was done synchronously: a user clicked Send, the call was placed to the scheduler to receive the email job, and a confirmation was returned that the job was received and queued. This makes sense that you don't want this submission to fail without the user knowing it and the call takes a couple hundred milliseconds usually, so this is just a simple synchronous method invocation. However, the engineer who made this decision did not know that the schedulers were placing synchronous calls to the mail servers.

When a scheduler received a job, it queued it up until a mail server became available. Then, the scheduler would establish a synchronous stream of communication between itself and the mail server to pass all the information about the job and monitor the job while it completed. When all the mail servers were running under maximum capacity, and there were the proper number of schedulers for the number of mail servers, everything worked fine. When mail slowed down because of an excessive number of bounce back emails or an ISP mail server was slow receiving the outbound emails, the MailScale email servers could slow down and get backed up. This in turn backed up the schedulers because they relied on a synchronous communication channel for monitoring the status of the jobs. When the schedulers slowed down and became unresponsive, this backed up into the main site, making the application servers trying to synchronously insert and schedule email jobs to slow down. The entire site became slow and unresponsive, all because of a chain of synchronous calls that no single person was aware of.

The fix for this problem was to break the synchronous communication into asynchronous calls, preferably at both the app to scheduler and scheduler to email servers, but at least at one of those places. There are a few lessons to be learned here. The first and most important is that synchronous calls can cause problems in your system in unexpected places. One call can lead to another call to another, which can get very complicated with all the interactions and multitude of independent code paths through most systems, often referred to as the *cyclomatic complexity* of a program. The next lesson that we can take from this is that engineers usually do not have the overall architecture vision, and this can cause them to make decisions that daisy chain processes together. This is the reason that architects and managers are critical to help with designs, constantly teach engineers about the larger system, and oversee implementations in an attempt to avoid these problems. The last lesson that we can take from this example is the complexity in debugging problems of this nature. Depending on the monitoring system, it is likely that the first alert comes from the slowdown of the site and not the mail servers. If that occurs, it is natural that everyone start looking at why the site is slowing down the mail servers instead of the other way around. These problems can take a while to unravel and decipher.

Another reason to analyze and remove synchronous calls is the multiplicative effect of failure. If you are old enough, you might remember the old Christmas tree lights. These were strings of lights where if you had a single bulb out in the entire string of lights, it caused every other bulb to be out. These lights were wired in series, and should any single light fail, the entire string would fail. As a result, the "availability" of the string of lights was the product of the availability (1—the probability of failure) of all the lights. If any light had a 99.999% availability or a 0.001% chance of failure and there were 100 lights in the string, the theoretical availability of the string of lights was 0.99999^{100} or 0.999, reduced from 5-nine availability to 3-nine availability. In a year's time, 5-nine availability, 99.999%, has just over five minutes of downtime, bulbs out, whereas a 3-nine availability, 99.9%, has over 500 minutes of downtime. This equates to increasing the chance of failure from 0.001% to 0.1%. No wonder our parents hated putting up those lights!

Systems that rely upon each other for information in a series and in synchronous fashion are subject to the same rates of failure as the Christmas tree lights of yore. Synchronous calls cause the same types of problems as lights wired in series. If one fails, it is going to cause problems within the line of communication back to the end customer. The more calls we make, the higher the probability of failure. The higher the probability of failure, the more likely it is that we hold open connections and refuse future customer requests. The easiest fix to this is to make these calls asynchronous and ensure that they have a chance to recover gracefully with timeouts should they not receive responses in a timely fashion. If you've waited two seconds and a response hasn't come back, simply discard the request and return a friendly error message to the customer.

This entire discussion of synchronous and asynchronous calls is one of the often missed but necessary topics that must be discussed, debated, and taught to organizations. Skipping over this is asking for problems down the road when loads start to grow, servers start reaching maximum capacity, or services get added. Adopting principles, standards, and coding practices now will save a lot of downtime and wasted resources on tracking down and fixing these problems in the future.

Defining State

Another oft ignored engineering topic is stateful versus stateless applications. An application that uses state is called *stateful* and it relies on the current condition of execution as a determinant of the next action to be performed. An application or protocol that doesn't use state is referred to as *stateless*. Hyper Text Transfer Protocol (HTTP) is a stateless protocol because it doesn't need any information about the previous request to know everything necessary to fulfill the next request. An example of the use of state would be in a monitoring program that first identifies that a query was requested instead of a cache request and then, based on that information, it calculates a duration time for the query. In a stateless implementation of the same program, it would receive all the information that it required to calculate the duration at the time of request. If it was a duration calculation for a query, this information would be passed to it upon invocation.

You may recall from a computer science computational theory class the description of Mealy and Moore machines, which are known as state machines or finite state machines. A state machine is an abstract model of states and actions that is used to model behavior; these can be implemented in the real world in either hardware or software. There are other ways to model or describe behavior of an application, but the state machine is one of the most common.

Mealy Moore Machines

A Mealy machine is a finite state machine that generates output based on the input and the current state of the machine. A Moore machine, on the other hand, is a finite state machine that generates output based solely on the current state. A very simple example of a Moore machine is a turn signal that alternates on and off. The output is the light being turned on or off and is completely determined by the current state. If it is on, it gets turned off. If it is off, it gets turned on.

Another very simple example, this time of a Mealy machine, is a traffic signal. Assume that the traffic signal has a switch to determine whether a car is present. The output is the traffic light red, yellow, or green. The input is a car at the intersection waiting on the light. The output is determined by the current state of the light as well as the input. If a car is waiting and the current state is red, the signal gets turned to green. Obviously, these are both overly simplified examples, but you get the point that there are different ways of modeling behavior using states, inputs, outputs, and actions.

Given that finite state machines are one of the fundamental aspects of theoretical computer science as mathematically modeled by automatons, it is no wonder why this is a fundamental structure of our system designs. But why exactly do we see state in almost all of our programs, and are there alternatives? The reason that most applications rely on state is that the languages used for Web based or Software as a Service (SaaS) development are almost all imperative based. Imperative programming is the use of statements to describe how to change the state of a program. Declarative programming is the opposite and uses statements to describe what changes need to take place. Procedural, structured, and object-oriented programming all are imperative-based programming methodologies. Example languages include Pascal, C/C++ and Java. Functional or logical programming is declarative and therefore does not make use of the state of the program. Standard Query Language (SQL) is a common example of a logical language that is stateless.

Now that we have explored the definition of state and understand why state is fundamental to most of our systems, we can start to explore how this can cause problems when we need to scale our applications. Having an application run as a single instance on a single server, the state of the machine is known and easy to manage. All users run on the one server, so knowing that a particular user has logged in allows the application to use this state of being logged in and whatever input arrives, such as clicking a link, to determine what the resulting output should be. The complexity of this comes when we begin to scale our application along the X-axis by adding servers. If a user arrives on one server for this request and on another server for the next request, how would each machine know the current state of the user? If your application is split along the Y-axis and the login service is running in a completely different pool than the report service, how does each of these services know the state of the other? These are all questions that arise when trying to scale applications that require state. These are not insurmountable, but they do require some thought, hopefully before you are in a bind with your current capacity and have to rush out a new server or split the services.

One of the most common implementations of state is the user session. Just because an application is stateful does not mean that it must have a user sessions. The opposite is true also. An application or service that implements a session may do so as a stateless manner; consider the stateless session beans in enterprise java beans. A user session is an established communication between the client, typically the user's browser, and the server that gets maintained during the life of the session for that user. There are lots of things that developers store in user sessions, perhaps the most common is the fact that the user is logged in and has certain privileges. This obviously is important unless you want to continue validating the user's authentication at each page request. Other items typically stored in session include account attributes such as preferences for first seen reports, layout, or default settings. Again, having these retrieved once from the database and then kept with the user during the session can be the most economical thing to do.

As we laid out in the previous paragraph, there are lots of things that you may want to store in a user's session, but storing this information can be problematic in terms of increased complexity for scaling. It makes great sense to not have to constantly communicate with the database to retrieve a user's preferences as they bounce around your site, but this improved performance makes it difficult when there is a pool of servers handling user requests. Another complexity of keeping session is that if you are not careful the amount of information stored there will become unwieldy. Although not common, sometimes an individual user's session data reaches or exceeds hundreds of kilobytes. Of course, this is excessive, but we've seen clients fail to manage their session data and the result is a Frankenstein's monster in terms of both size and complexity. Every engineer wants his information to be quickly and easily available, so he sticks his data in the session. After you've stepped back and looked at the size and the obvious problems of keeping all these user sessions in memory or transmitting them back and forth between the user's browser and the server, this situation needs to be remedied quickly.

If you have managed to keep the user sessions to a reasonable size, what methods are available for saving state or keeping sessions in environments with multiple servers? There are three basic approaches: avoid, centralize, and decentralize. Similar to our approach with caching, the best way to solve a user session scaling issue is to avoid having the issue. You can achieve this by either removing session data from your application or making it stateless. The other way to achieve avoidance is to make sure each user is only placed on a single server. This way, the session data can remain in memory on the server because that user will always come back to that server for requests; other users will go to other servers in the pool. You can accomplish this manually in the code by performing a z-axis split (modulus or lookup) and put all users with usernames A through M on one server and all users with usernames N through Z on another server. If DNS pushes a user with username jackal to the second server, it just redirects her to the first server to process her request. Another solution to this is to use session cookies on the load balancer. These cookies assign all users to a particular server for the duration of the session. This way, every request that comes through from a particular user will land on the same server. Almost all load balancer solutions offer some sort of session cookie that provides this functionality. There are several solutions for avoiding the problem all together.

Let's assume that for some reason none of these solutions work. The next method of solving the complexities of keeping session on a myriad of servers when scaling is decentralization of session storage. The way that this can be accomplished is by storing session in a cookie on the user's browser. There are many implementations of this, such as serializing the session data and then storing all of it in a cookie. This session data must be transferred back and forth, marshalled/unmarshalled, and manipulated by the application, which can add up to lots of time required for this. Remember that marshalling and unmarshalling are processes where the object is transformed into a data format suitable for transmitting or storing and converted back again. Another twist to this is to store a very little amount of information in the session cookie and use it as a reference index to a list of objects in a session database or file that contain all the session information about each user. This way, the transmission and marshalling costs are minimized.

The third method of solving the session problem with scaling systems is centralization. This is where all user session data is stored centrally in a cache system and all Web or app servers can access his data. This way, if a user lands on Web server 1 for the login and then on Web server 3 for a report, both servers can access the central cache and see that the user is logged in and what that user's preferences are. A centralized cache system such as memcached that we discussed in Chapter 25, Caching for Performance and Scale, would work well in this situation for storing user session data. Some systems have success using session databases, but the overhead of connections and queries seem too much when there are other solutions such as caches for roughly the same cost in hardware and software. The issue to watch for with session caching is that the cache hit ratio needs to be very high or the user experience will be awful. If the cache expires a session because it doesn't have enough room to keep all the user sessions, the user who gets kicked out of cache will have to log back in. As you can imagine, if this is happening 25% of the time, it is going to be extremely annoying.

Three Solutions to Scaling with Sessions

There are three basic approaches to solving the complexities of scaling an application that uses session data: avoidance, decentralization, and centralization.

- Avoidance

  Remove session data completely

  Modulus users to a particular server via the code

  Stick users on a particular server per session with session cookies from the load balancer

- Decentralization

  Store session cookies with all information in the browser's cookie.

  Store session cookies as an index to session objects in a database or file system with all the information stored there.

- Centralization

  Store sessions in a centralized session cache like memcached.

  Databases can be used as well but are not recommended.

There are many creative methods of solving the session complexities when scaling applications. Depending on the specific needs and parameters of your application, one or more of these might work better for you than others.

Whether you decide to design your application to be stateful or stateless and whether you use session data or not are decisions that must be made on an application by application basis. In general, it is easier to scale applications that are stateless and do not care about sessions. Although this may aid in scaling, it may be unrealistic in the complexities that it causes for the application development. When you do require the use of state—in particular, session state—consider how you are going to scale your application in all three axes of the AKF Scale Cube before you need to do so. Scrambling to figure out the easiest or quickest way to fix a session issue across multiple servers might lead to poor long-term decisions. These on the spot architectural decisions should be avoided as much as possible.

Conclusion

In this last chapter of Part III, we dealt with synchronous versus asynchronous calls. This topic is often overlooked when developing services or products until it becomes a noticeable inhibitor to scaling. We started our discussion exploring synchronization. The process of synchronization refers to the use and coordination of simultaneously executed threads or processes that are part of an overall task. We defined synchronization as the situation when two or more pieces of work must be done to accomplish a task. One example of synchronization that we covered was a mutex or mutual exclusion. Mutex was a process of protecting global resources from concurrently running processes, often accomplished through the use of semaphores.

After we covered synchronization, we tackled the topics of synchronous and asynchronous calls. We discussed synchronous methods as ones that, when they are called, execute, and when they finish, the calling method gets control back. This was contrasted with the asynchronous methods calls where the method is called to execute in a new thread and it immediately returns control back to the thread that called it. The design pattern that describes the asynchronous method call is known as the asynchronous method invocation (AMI). With the general definitions under our belt, we continued with an analysis of why synchronous calls can become problematic for scaling. We gave some examples of how an unsuspecting synchronous call can actually cause severe problems across the entire system. Although we did not encourage the complete elimination of synchronous calls, we did express the recommendation that you thoroughly understand how to convert synchronous calls to asynchronous ones. Additionally, we discussed why it is important to have individuals like architects and managers overseeing the entire system design to help point out to engineers when asynchronous calls could be warranted.

Another topic that we covered in this chapter was the use of state in an application. We started with what is state within application development. We then dove into a discussion in computational theory on finite state machines and concluded with a distinction between imperative and declarative languages. We finished the stateful versus stateless conversation with one of the most commonly used implementations of state: that being the session state. Session as we defined it was an established communication between the client, typically the user's browser, and the server, that gets maintained during the life of the session for that user. We noted that keeping track of session data can become laborious and complex, especially when dealing with scaling an application on any of the axes from the AKF Scale Cube. We covered three broad classes of solutions—avoidance, centralization, and decentralization—and gave specific examples and alternatives for each.

The overall lesson that this chapter should impart on the reader is that there are reasons that we see engineers use synchronous calls and write stateful applications, some due to carefully considered reasons and others because of the nature of modern computational theory and languages. The important point is that you should spend the time up front discussing these so that there are more, carefully considered decisions about the uses of these rather than finding yourself needing to scale an application and finding out that there are designs that prevent you from doing so.

Key Points

- Synchronization is when two or more pieces of work must be done in order to accomplish a task.
- Mutex is a synchronization method that defines how global resources are protected from concurrently running processes.
- Synchronous calls perform their action completely by the time the call returns.
- With an asynchronous method call, the method is called to execute in a new thread and it immediately returns control back to the thread that called it.

- The design pattern that describes the asynchronous method call is known as the asynchronous design and alternatively as the asynchronous method invocation (AMI).

- Synchronous calls can, if used excessively or incorrectly, cause undue burden on the system and prevent it from scaling.

- Synchronous calls are simpler than asynchronous calls.

- The second part of the problem of synchronous calls is that developers typically only see a small portion of the application.

- An application that uses state is called stateful and it relies on the current state of execution as a determinant of the next action to be performed.

- An application or protocol that doesn't use state is referred to as stateless.

- Hyper Text Transfer Protocol (HTTP) is a stateless protocol because it doesn't need any information about the previous request to know everything necessary to fulfill the next request.

- A state machine is an abstract model of states and actions that is used to model behavior; these can be implemented in the real world in either hardware or software.

- The reason that most applications rely on state is that the languages used for Web based or SaaS development are almost all imperative based.

- Imperative programming is the use of statements to describe how to change the state of a program.

- Declarative programming is the opposite and uses statements to describe what changes need to take place.

- One of the most common implementations of state is the user session.

- Choosing wisely between synchronous/asynchronous as well as stateful/stateless is critical for scalable applications.

- Have discussions and make decisions early, when standards, practices, and principles can be followed.

Part IV

Solving Other Issues and Challenges

Chapter 27

Too Much Data

The skillful soldier does not raise a second levy, nor are his supply wagons loaded more than once.

—Sun Tzu

Hyper growth, or even slow steady growth over time, presents some unique scalability problems with data retention and storage. We might log information relevant at the time of a transaction, insert information relevant to a purchase, or keep track of user account changes. We may log all customer contacts or allow users to store data ranging from pictures to videos. This size, as we will discuss later, has significant cost implications to our business and can negatively affect our ability to scale, or at least scale cost effectively.

Time also affects the value of our data in most systems. Although not universally true, in many systems, the value of data decreases over time. Old customer contact information, although potentially valuable, probably isn't as valuable as the most recent contact information. Old photos and videos aren't likely accessed as often and old log messages that we've made probably aren't as relevant to us today. So as our costs increase with all of the additional data being stored, the value on a per data unit stored decreases, presenting unique challenges for most businesses.

The size of data alone can present issues for your business. Assuming that not all elements of the data are valuable to all requests or actions against that data, we need to find ways to process and store this data quickly and cost effectively.

This chapter is all about data size or the amount of data that you store. How do we handle it, process it, and keep our business from being overly burdened by it? What data do we get rid of and how do we store data in a tiered fashion that allows all data to be accretive to shareholder value?

The Cost of Data

Data is costly. Your first response to this might be that the costs of mass storage devices have decreased steadily over time and with the introduction of cloud storage services, storage has become "nearly free." But free and nearly free obviously aren't the same thing as a whole lot of something that is nearly free actually turns out to be quite expensive. As the price of storage decreases over time, we tend to care less about how much we use and as a result our usage typically increases significantly. Prices might drop by 50% and rather than passing that 50% reduction in price off to shareholders as a reduction in our cost of operations, we may very likely allow the size of our storage to double because it is "cheap."

But the initial cost of this storage is not the only cost you incur with every piece of data you store on it. The more storage you have, the more storage management you need. This might be the overhead of systems administrators to handle the data, or capacity planners to plan for the growth, or maybe even software licenses that allow you to "virtualize" your storage environment and manage it more easily. As your storage grows, so does the complexity of managing that storage.

Furthermore, as your storage increases, the power and space costs of handling that storage increases as well. You might argue here that the advent of Massive Array of Idle Disks (MAID) has offset those costs, or maybe you are thinking of even less costly solutions such as cloud storage services. We applaud you if you have put your infrequently accessed data on such a storage infrastructure. But the fact of the matter is that if you run one massive array, it will cost you less than 10 massive arrays, and less storage in the cloud will cost you less than more storage in the cloud. In the case of MAID solutions, those disks spin from time to time, and they take power just to ensure that they are "functioning." Furthermore, you either paid for the power distribution units (power sockets) into which they are plugged or you pay a monthly or annual fee in the case of a collocation provider to have the plug and power available. Finally, you either paid to build an infrastructure capable of some maximum power utilization likely driven by a percentage of those drives being active or you pay someone else (again in the case of collocation) to handle that for you. And of course, if you aren't using MAID drives, the cost of your power to run systems that are always spinning is even higher. If you are using cloud services, you still need the staff and processes to understand where that storage is located and to ensure that you can properly access it.

And that's not it! If this data resides in a database upon which you are performing transactions for end users, each query of that data increases with the size of the data being queried. We're not talking about the cost of the physical storage at this point, but rather the time to complete the query. Although it's true that if you are querying upon a properly balanced index that the time to query that data is not linear (it is more likely $\log_2 N$ where N is the number of elements), it nevertheless increases with an increase in the size of the data. Sixteen elements in binary tree will not cost twice as much to traverse and find an element as eight elements—but it will still cost more. This increase in steps to traverse data elements takes more processor time per user query, which in turn means that fewer things can be processed within any given amount of time. Let's say that we have eight elements and it takes us on average 1.5 steps to find our item with a query. Let's then say that with 16 elements it takes us on average two steps to find our item. This is a 33% increase in processing time to handle 16 elements versus the eight. Although this seems like a good leverage scaling method, it is still taking more time. It doesn't just cost more time on the database. This increase in time, even if performed asynchronously, is probably time that an app server is waiting for the query to finish, the Web server is waiting for the app server to return the data, and the time your customer is waiting for a page to load.

Let's now consider our peak utilization time of say 1 to 2 PM in the afternoon. If each query takes us 33% more time on average to complete and we want to run at 100% utilization during our peak traffic period, we might need as many as 33% more systems to handle twice the data (16 elements) versus the original eight elements if we do not want the user response time adversely impacted. In other words, we either let each of the queries take 33% more time to complete and affect the user experience as new queries get backed up waiting for longer running queries to complete given constrained capacity, or we add capacity to try to limit the impact to the users. At some point of course, without disaggregation of the data similar to the trick we performed with search in Chapter 24, Splitting Databases for Scale, user experience will begin to suffer. Although you can argue that faster processors, better caching, and faster storage will help the user experience, none of these really affect the fact that more data costs you more in processing time than less data with similar systems.

If you think that's the end of your costs relative to storage, you are probably wrong again. You undoubtedly back up your storage from time to time, potentially to an offsite storage facility. As your data grows, the amount of work you do to perform a "full backup" grows as well. Not only that, but you do that work over and over again with each full backup. Much of your data probably isn't changing, but you are nevertheless rewriting it time and again. Although incremental backups (backing up only the changed data) helps with this concern, you more than likely perform a periodic full backup to forego the cost of needing to apply a multitude of incremental backups to a single full backup that might be years old. If you did only a single full and then relied on incremental backups alone to recover some section of your storage infrastructure, your recovery time objective (the amount of time to recover from a storage failure) would be long indeed!

Hopefully, we've disabused you of the notion that storage is free. Storage prices may be falling, but they are only a portion of your true cost to store information, data, and knowledge.

The Six Costs of Data

As the amount of data that you store increases, the following costs increase:

- Storage costs to store the data
- People and software to manage the storage
- Power and space to make the storage work
- Capital to ensure the proper power infrastructure
- Processing power to traverse the data
- Backup time and costs

Data isn't just about the physical storage, and sometimes the other costs identified here can even eclipse the actual cost of storage.

The Value of Data and the Cost-Value Dilemma

All data is not created equally in terms of its value to our business. In many businesses, time negatively impacts the value that we can get from any specific data element. For instance, old data in most data warehouses is less likely to be useful in modeling business transactions. Old data regarding a given customer's interaction with your ecommerce platform might be useful to you, but it's not likely as useful as the most current data that you have. Detail call records for the phone company from years ago aren't as valuable to the users as new call records, and old banking transactions from three years ago probably aren't as useful as the ones that occurred in the last couple of weeks. Old photos and videos might be referenced from time to time, but they aren't likely accessed as often as the most recent uploads. Although we won't argue that as a law older data is less valuable than new data, we believe it holds true often enough in most businesses to call it generally true and directionally correct.

If the value of data decreases over time and the cost of keeping it increases over time, why do we so very often keep so darn much of it? We call this question the *Cost-Value Data Dilemma*. In our experience, most companies simply do not pay attention to the deteriorating value of data and the increasing cost of data retention over time. Often, new or faster technologies allow us to store the same data for lower cost or store more data for the same cost. As the per unit cost of storage drops, our willingness to keep more of it increases.

Moreover, many companies point to the *option value* of data. How can you possibly know what you might use that data for in the future? It might become at some point in the company's future incredibly valuable. Nearly everyone can point to a case at some point in her career where we have said, "if only we had kept that data." We use that experience or set of experiences to drive decisions about all future data; if we needed one or a few pieces of data once and didn't have it, that becomes a reason to keep all other data for all time.

Another common reason is *strategic advantage*. Very often, this reason is couched as, "We keep this data because our competition doesn't keep it." That becomes reason enough as it is most often decided by the general manager or CEO and a number of surveys support its implementation. In fact, it might be a source of competitive advantage, though our experience is that the value of keeping data infinitely is not as much of an advantage as simply keeping it longer than your competition (but not infinitely).

Ignoring the Cost-Value Data Dilemma, citing the option value of data or claiming competitive advantage through infinite data retention, all potentially have dilutive effects to shareholder value. If the real upside of the decisions (or lack of decisions in the case of ignoring the dilemma) does not create more value than the cost, the decision is suboptimal. In the cases where legislation or regulation requires you to retain data, such as emails or financial transactions, you have little choice but to comply with the letter of the law. But in all other cases, it is possible to assign some real or perceived value to the data and compare it to the costs. Consider the fact that the value is likely to decrease over time and that the costs of data retention, although going down on a per unit basis, will likely increase in aggregate value in hyper-growth companies.

As a real-world analog, your company may be mature enough to associate a certain value and cost to a class of user. Business schools often spend a great deal of time discussing the concept of *unprofitable customers*. An unprofitable customer is a customer that costs you more to keep than you make off of them through their relationship life. Ideally, you do not want to service or keep your unprofitable customers assuming that you have correctly identified them. For instance, a single customer may be unprofitable to you on a standalone basis, but serves to bring in several profitable customers whom you might not have without that single unprofitable relationship. The science and art of determining and pruning unprofitable customers is more difficult in some businesses than others.

The same concept of profitable and unprofitable customers nevertheless applies to your data. In nearly any environment, with enough investigation, you will likely find data that adds shareholder value and data that is dilutive to shareholder value as the cost of retaining that data on its existing storage solution is greater than the value that it creates. Just as we may have customers that are more costly to service than their total value to the company (even when considering the profitable customers that they bring along), so do we have unprofitable and value destroying data.

Making Data Profitable

The business and technology approach for what data to keep and how to keep it is pretty straightforward: architect storage solutions that allow you to keep all data that is profitable for your business, or is likely to be accretive to shareholder value, and remove the rest. Let's look at the most common reasons driving data bloat and then examine ways to match our data storage costs to the value of the data contained within that storage.

Option Value

All options have some value to us. The value may be determined by what we believe the probability is that we will ultimately execute the option to our personal benefit. This may be a probabilistic equation that calculates both the possibility that the option will be executed and the likely benefit of the value of executing the option. Clearly, we cannot claim that the option value is "infinite;" in so doing, we would be saying that the option will produce an infinite value to our shareholders. If that were the case, we should simply disclose our wealth of information and watch our share price rise sharply. What do you think the chance of that is? The answer is that if you were to make such a disclosure, your share price probably wouldn't move noticeably; at least it wouldn't move noticeably as a result of your data disclosure.

The option value of our data then is some noninfinite number. We should start asking ourselves questions like, How often have we used data in the past to make a valuable decision? What was the age of the data used in that decision? What was the value that we ultimately created versus the cost of maintaining that data? Was the net result profitable?

Remember, we aren't talking about flushing all data or advocating the removal of all data from your systems. Your platform probably wouldn't work if it didn't have some meaningful data in it. We are simply indicating that you should evaluate and question your data retention to ensure that all of the data you are keeping is in fact valuable and, as we will discuss later in this chapter, that the solution for storing that data is priced and architected with the data value in mind. If you haven't made use of the data in the past to make better decisions, there is a good chance that you're not going to start using all of it tomorrow. Even when you start using your data, you aren't likely going to use all of it; as such, you should decide which data has real value, which data has value but should be stored in a storage solution of lower cost, and which data can be removed.

Strategic Competitive Differentiation

This is one of our favorite reasons to keep data. It's the easiest to claim and the hardest to disprove. The general thought is that you are better than all of your competitors

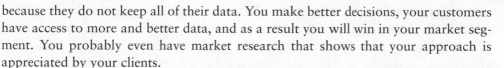

because they do not keep all of their data. You make better decisions, your customers have access to more and better data, and as a result you will win in your market segment. You probably even have market research that shows that your approach is appreciated by your clients.

Let's address the market research first. What do you think the answer will be if you ask your customers if they value having all of their "widgets" available for eternity? Depending upon your industry, they are probably going to respond favorably. There are at least a couple of reasons for this. The first is that they already have a bit of conformational bias working by using your platform over a competitor's and you've just given them a reason to claim why they use your platform. Another reason is that you haven't presented a cost to them, at least not in the question, of having the data infinitely. As such, with no associated cost, they are probably happy with the near infinite storage.

On the other hand, what if we asked questions about what someone would be willing to pay for near infinite storage? Our answers would likely be very different indeed! How about if we were to ask why our customers use our product rather than our competitors and forced them to write an answer in? Our guess is that you may find out that the first thing that comes to mind is not the infinite storage.

The right question here is to determine what the incremental value of "infinite" data storage is over, say, 10 years, or t years. What about the difference between 20 years and 10 years? Our guess is that as the retention period increases, each year adds less value than the previous year. Year 19, for instance, is probably more valuable than year 20, and year 1 is probably more valuable than year 2. As our years increase, the value starts to dwindle to move to zero even as our costs increase relative to the amount of storage. It's starting to appear to us that the company that constrains its storage is very likely going to have a competitive advantage over the company that does not constrain storage. What is that advantage? Greater profitability!

Of course, the preceding comparisons all assume that storage is similarly priced, that all storage solutions are equivalent, and that all types of access require the same service levels for response time, and so on. After we recognize that some data has immense value, some data has lower value, some data "might have value," and some data has no value at all, we can determine a tiered cost storage solution for data with value and remove the data with very low or no value. We can also transform and compact the data to make sure that we retain most of the value at significantly lower costs.

Cost Justify the Solution (Tiered Storage Solutions)

Maybe you have some data that has meaningful business value, but where the cost of storing that data exceeds the value or expected value of the data. This is the time to consider a tiered storage solution. Many young companies settle on a certain type of storage based on the primary needs of their transaction processing systems. The result of this decision is that just about everything else relies upon this (typically) premium storage solution. Not absolutely everything needs the redundancy, high availability, and response of your primary applications. For your lower value, but nevertheless valuable, services and needs, consider moving to tiered storage solutions.

For instance, infrequently accessed data that does not necessarily require immediate response times might be provisioned on the aforementioned massive array of idle disks. Or maybe you just move some of this data to less expensive and slower response network attached storage systems. Potentially, you decide to simply split up your architecture to serve some of these data needs from a y-axis split that addresses the function of "serve archived data." To conserve processing power, maybe the requests to "serve archived data" are made in an asynchronous fashion and emailed after the results are compiled.

You may decide to take all old emails on tape storage for the period of time mandated by current legislation or regulation within your industry. Perhaps you take infrequently accessed customer data and put it on cloud storage systems. Data accessed sometimes (where sometimes is more than infrequently but less than frequently) might go to MAID farms. Data that is frequently accessed but has low corporate value might go onto inexpensive slower speed devices and frequently accessed data of high value might go on your "tier 1" high performance access systems.

Let's return to our example of AllScale and examine how it approaches the problem within its human resource management (HRM) system. The HRM solution allows all correspondence on HR matters to be stored within the company's platform. Some correspondence is searched frequently, and that correspondence tends to be for events happening within the last couple of months. Returns from search results over several months are seldom reviewed and if an email is older than two years, it is almost never viewed. Furthermore, those correspondences are still held within the customer's email systems and are kept by the customer for the period of its user agreements and/or regulatory requirements.

The team decides on a multitier architecture for all storage. Common searches will be precalculated and cached within the platform. The data associated with these searches will be stored in a tiered fashion with the most relevant search results being on high speed local or storage area network storage devices. Less frequently accessed data will be moved progressively to cheaper and slower storage including MAID devices and cloud storage for very infrequently accessed solutions. Very old data simply has records of where the data can be found on the customer managed mail system, and the actual correspondence itself is first archived to tape and permanently purged after no more than five years.

The solution here is to match the cost or cost justify the solution with the value that it creates. Not every system or piece of data offers the same value to the business. We typically pay our employees based on their merit or value to the business, so why shouldn't we approach system design in the same fashion? If there is some, but not much, value in some group of data, simply build the system to support the value. This approach does have some downfalls, such as the requirement that the operations staff will now need to support and maintain multiple storage tiers, but as long as those additional costs are evaluated properly, the tiered storage solution works well for many companies.

Transform the Data

Often, the data we keep for transactional purposes simply isn't in a form that is consumable or meaningful for our other needs. As a result, we end up processing the data in near real time to make it meaningful to corporate decision making or to make it useful to our product and platform for a better customer experience.

As an example of our former case, where we are concerned about making good business decisions, consider the needs of a marketing organization concerned about individual consumer behavior. Our marketing organization might be interested in demographic analysis of purchases over time of any of a number of our products. Keeping the exact records of every purchase might be the most flexible approach to fulfill their needs, but the marketing organization is probably comfortable with being able to match buyer purchases of products by month. All of a sudden, our data requirements have shrunk because many of our customers are repeat purchasers and we can collapse individual transaction records into records indicating the buyer, the items purchased, and the month in which those items were purchased. Now, we might keep online transaction details for four months to facilitate the most recent quarterly reporting needs, and then roll up those transactions into summary transactions by individual for marketing and by internal department for finance. Our data storage requirements might go down by as much as 50%. Furthermore, as we would otherwise perform this summarization during the time of the marketing request, we have reduced the response time of the application generating this data (it is now prepopulated), and as a result increased the efficiency of our marketing organization.

As an example of our latter case, we might want to make product recommendations to our customers while they are interacting with our platform. These product recommendations might give insight as to what other customers bought who have viewed or purchased similar items. It goes without saying that scanning all purchases to develop such a customer affinity to product map would likely be too complex to calculate and present while someone is attempting to shop. For this reason alone, we would want to precalculate the product and customer relationships. However, such calculation also reduces our need to store the details of all transactions over time. As a result in developing our precalculated affinity map, we have not only reduced response times for our customers, we have also reduced some of our long-term data retention needs.

The principles on which data transformation are based are couched within a process data warehousing experts refer to as Extract, Transform, and Load (ETL). It is beyond the scope of this book to even attempt to scratch the surface of data warehousing, but the concepts inherent to ETL can help obviate some of the need for storing larger amounts of data within your transactional systems. Ideally, these ETL processes, besides removing the data from your primary transaction systems, also reduce your overall storage needs as compared to keeping the raw data over similar time periods. Condensing expensive detailed records into summary tables and fact tables focused on answering specific questions helps save space and saves processing time.

Handling Large Amounts of Data

Having spent several pages discussing the need to match storage cost with data value and eliminating data of very low value, let's now turn our attention to a more exciting problem: What do we do when our data is valuable but there is just way too much of it to process efficiently?

If you've ever had an algebra class, and chances are you have, you probably already know the answer to this question. Remember your algebra or calculus teacher or professor reminding you to simplify equations before attempting to solve them? Well, the same advice that would make you successful in solving a math problem will make you successful in solving problems associated with large amounts of data.

If the data is easily segmented into resources or can be easily associated with services, we need only apply the concepts we learned in Chapters 22 through 24. The AKF Scale Cube will solve your needs for these situations. But how about the case when an entire data set needs to be traversed to produce a single answer, such as the count by word within all of the works contained within the Library of Congress, or potentially an inventory count within a very large and complex inventory system? If we want to get through this work quickly, we are going to need to find a way to distribute the work efficiently. This distribution of work might take the form of a multiple pass system where the first pass analyzes (or *maps*) the work and the second pass calculates (or *reduces*) the work. Google introduced a software framework to support distributed processing of such large datasets called MapReduce.[1] The following is a description of that model and an example of how it can be applied to large problems.

At a high level, MapReduce has a Map function and a Reduce function. The Map function takes as its input a key-value pair and produces an intermediate key-value

---

1. Dean, Jeffrey and Sanjay Ghernawat. "Map Reduce: Simplified Data Processing on Large Clusters." http://labs.google.com/papers/mapreduce.html.

pair. This might not immediately seem useful to the layperson, but the intent is that this is a distributed process creating useful intermediate information for another distributed process to compile. The input key might be the name of a document, or remembering that this is a document, the name, or pointer to a piece of a document. The value could be content consisting of all the words within the document itself. In our distributed inventory system, the key might be the inventory location and the value all of the names of inventory within that location with one name for each piece and quantity of inventory. For instance, if we had five screws and two nails, the value would be screw, screw, screw, screw, screw, and nail, nail.

The canonical form of Map looks like this in pseudocode:[2]

```
map(String input_key, String input_value):
// input_key: document name or inventory location name
//input_value: document contents or inventory contents
For each word w (or part p) in input_value:
    EmitIntermediate(w, "1") (or EmitIntermediate(p,"1"));
```

We've identified parenthetically that this pseudocode could work for both the word count example (also given by Google) and the distributed parts inventory example. Only one or the other would exist in reality for your application and you would eliminate the parenthesis. The following input_key and input_values and output keys and values are presented in Figure 27.1. The first example is a set of phrases including the word "red" with which we are fond, and a small set of inventories for different locations.

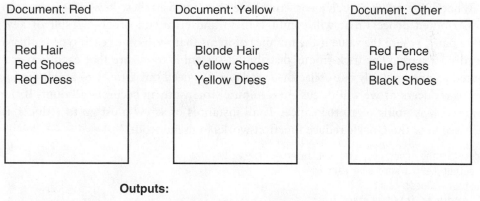

Document: Red	Document: Yellow	Document: Other
Red Hair Red Shoes Red Dress	Blonde Hair Yellow Shoes Yellow Dress	Red Fence Blue Dress Black Shoes

Outputs:

Red 1, Hair 1, Red 1, Shoes 1, Red 1, Dress 1	Blonde 1, Hair 1, Yellow 1, Shoes 1, Yellow 1, Dress 1	Red 1, Fence 1, Blue 1, Dress 1, Black 1, Shoes 1

Figure 27.1 *Input and Output Key-Value Pairs for Three Documents*

---

2. Dean, Jeffrey and Sanjay Ghernawat. "Map Reduce: Simplified Data Processing on Large Clusters." http://labs.google.com/papers/mapreduce-osdi04-slides/index-auto-0004.html.

Outputs:

Nail 1, Screw 1, Pin 1, Nail 1   Screw 1, Nail 1, Pin 1, Pin 1   Pin 1, Screw 1, Nail 1, Screw 1

Figure 27.2 *Input and Output Key-Value Pairs for Inventory in Different Locations*

Note here how Map takes each of the documents and simply emits each word with a count of 1 as we move through the document. For the sake of speed, we had a separate Map process working on each of the documents. Figure 27.2 shows the output of this process.

Again, we have taken each of our initial key-value pairs with the key being the location of the inventory and the value being the individual components listed with one listing for each occurrence of that component per location. The output is the name of the component and a value of 1 per each component listing. Again, we used separate Map processes.

What is the value of such a construct? We can now feed these key-value pairs into a distributed process that will combine them and create an ordered result of key-value pairs, where the value is the number of items that we have of each type (either a word or a part). The trick in our distributed system is to ensure that each key gets routed to one and only one collector or *reducer*. We need this affinity to a reducer (or tier of reducers as we will discuss in a minute) to ensure an accurate account. If the part screw is going to go to reducer 1, all instances of screw must go to reducer 1. Let's see how the Google reduce function works in pseudocode:[3]

```
reduce(String input_key, Iterator intermediate_values):
// output_key: a word or a part name
//output_values: count
For each v in intermediate_values:
    Result  += ParseInt(v);
    Emit(AsString(result));
```

3. Dean, Jeffrey and Sanjay Ghernawat. "Map Reduce: Simplified Data Processing on Large Clusters." See slide 4 at http://labs.google.com/papers/mapreduce-osdi04-slides/.

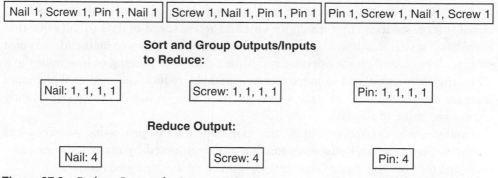

Figure 27.3 *Reduce Output for Inventory System*

For our reduce function to work, we need to add a program to group the words or parts and append the values for each in a list. This is a rather trivial program that will sort and group the functions by key. This too could be distributed assuming that the key-value pairs emitted from the Map function are sent to the same function intended to sort and group and then submit to the reduce function. Passing over the trivial function of sorting and grouping, which is the subject of many computer science undergraduate text books, we can display our reduce function as in Figure 27.3 for our inventory system (we will leave the word count output as an exercise for our readers).

Multiple layers of sorting, grouping, and reducing can be employed to help speed along the process. For instance, if there were 50-map systems, they could send their results to 50 sorters, which could in turn send their results to 25 sorters and groupers, and so on until we had a single sorted and grouped list of parts and value lists to send to our multiple reducer functions. The system is highly scalable in terms of the amount of processors and processing power you can throw at it. We highly recommend that you read the Google Labs MapReduce documentation.

Conclusion

This chapter discussed what to do with large datasets. On one end of the spectrum, we have the paradoxical relationship of cost and value for data. As data ages and data sizes grow, the cost to the organization increases. As this data ages in most companies, its value to the company and platform typically decreases. The reasons for clinging to data past its valuable life to a company include ignorance, perceived option value, and perceived strategic competitive differentiation. Our remedies for perceived option value and perceived competitive differentiation are based in applying real dollar values to these perceived values in order to properly justify the existence (and the cost) of the data.

After we've identified the value and costs of data, we proposed implementing tiered storage solutions that match the cost and access speed of data to the value that it creates for shareholders. On one end of our tiered strategy are high-end, very fast storage devices, and on the opposite end is the deletion or purging of low value data. Data transformation and summarization can help reduce the cost and therefore increase the profitability of data where the reduction in size does not significantly change the value of the data.

Finally, we addressed one approach to parallelize the processing of very large datasets. Google's MapReduce approach is widely adopted by many industries as a standard for how to process large datasets quickly in a distributed fashion.

Key Points

- Data is costly and the cost of data consists of more than just the cost of the storage itself. People, power, capital costs of power infrastructure, processing power, and backup time and costs all impact the cost of data.

- The value of data in most companies tends to decrease over time.

- Companies often keep too much data due to ignorance, perceived option value, and perceived competitive differentiation.

- Perceived option value and perceived competitive differentiation should include values and time limits on data to properly determine if the data is accretive or dilutive to shareholder value.

- Eliminate data that is dilutive to shareholder value, or find alternative storage approaches to make the data accretive. Tiered storage strategies and data transformation are all methods of cost justifying data.

- Applying concepts of distributed computing to large datasets helps us process those datasets quickly. Google's MapReduce is a good example of a software framework to act upon large datasets.

Chapter 28

Clouds and Grids

We cannot enter into alliances until we are acquainted with the designs of our neighbors.

—Sun Tzu

At this point in the book, we need to discuss one of perhaps the most important advances in application scaling that we have seen since hardware started to become commoditized. This most important advancement is the advent of cloud computing. Although most people think of this as a very new technology innovation, the reality is that this has taken well over a decade to become a reality. In this chapter, we are going to cover the history that led up to the launch of cloud computing, provide an overview of both cloud and grid computing, discuss the common characteristics of clouds, and finish the chapter with a comparison of grid and cloud computing.

Cloud computing is important to scalability because it offers the promise of cheap, on-demand storage and compute capacity. As we will discuss in this chapter, this has many advantages, and a few disadvantages, to physical hardware scaling. Grid computing, similar to cloud computing, although utilized differently, offers a method of scaling for computationally intensive applications. To be well versed in scaling applications, you must understand these concepts and how they could be implemented to scale an application or service.

Although the development of the technology and concepts for cloud computing have been in process for many years, the discussion and utilization of it in mainstream technology organizations is still relatively new. Because of this, at times, even definitions of the subject are not always completely agreed upon. We have been fortunate to be around the cloud environment through our clients for quite some time and have seen many players become involved in this field. As with our discussion on technology agnostic designs in Chapter 20, Designing for Any Technology, we believe that it is the architecture and not the technology that is responsible for a product's capability to scale. As such, we consider clouds and grids as architectural components and not as a technology. The particular vendor or type of service is the equivalent of a type of technology chosen to implement the architecture. We will cover some of the technology components so that you have examples and can become familiar with them, but we will focus primarily on the architecture.

History and Definitions

The term *cloud* has been around for decades. No one is exactly sure when it was first used in relation to technology, but it has been around at least as far back as when network diagrams came into vogue. A network diagram is a graphic representation of the physical or logic layout of a network, such as a telecommunications, routing, or neural. The cloud on network diagrams was used to represent unspecified networks. In the early 1990s, *cloud* became a term for ATM networks. Asynchronous Transfer Mode is a packet switching protocol that breaks data into cells and provides OSI layer 2, the data link. ATM was the core protocol used on the public switched phone network. As the World Wide Web began in 1991 as a CERN project built on top of the Internet, the cloud began to be used as a term and symbol for the underlying infrastructure.

OSI Model

The Open Systems Interconnection Reference Model, or OSI Model, is a descriptive abstraction of the layered model of network architecture. It is used to describe the different components of the network and how they are interrelated. There are seven layers, and starting from the lowest layer, they are as follows:

1. *Physical.* This layer contains the physical devices such as cards, cables, hubs, and repeaters.

2. *Data Link.* This layer is responsible for the functional transmission of data between devices and includes protocols such as Ethernet.

3. *Network.* This layer provides the switching and routing functionality and includes protocols such as Internet Protocol (IP).

4. *Transport.* This layer provides the reliability by keeping track of transmission, resending if necessary. It includes the Transmission Control Protocol (TCP).

5. *Session.* This layer controls the communication by establishing, managing, and terminating connections between computers such as with sockets.

6. *Presentation.* This layer provides data presentation and encryption such as with Secure Sockets Layer (SSL).

7. *Application.* This layer interacts between the software application and the network and includes implementation such as Hyper Text Transfer Protocol (HTTP).

Cloud computing can trace its lineage through the application service providers (ASP) of the 1990s, which were the embodiment of the concept of outsourcing computer services. This later became known as Software as a Service (SaaS). The ASP model is an indirect descendant of the service bureaus of the 1960s and 1970s, which were an attempt at fulfilling the vision established by John McCarthy in his 1961 speech at MIT.[1] John McCarthy is the inventor of the programming language Lisp, recipient of the 1971 Turing Award, and credited with coining the term *Artificial Intelligence*.[2]

The idea of the modern cloud concept was extended in October 2001 by IBM in its Autonomic Computing Manifesto.[3] The essence of the paper was that the information technology infrastructure was becoming too complex and that it could collapse under its own weight if the management was not automated. Around this time, the concept of Software as a Service (SaaS) started to grow. SaaS is a software model whereby people pay for software based on usage and demand rather than upfront and recurring license fees. Another confluent event occurred around this time at the beginning of the 21st century, and this was the dot com bubble. As many tech startups were burning through capital and shutting down, those that were ultimately going to survive and thrive were tightening their belts on capital and operational expenditures. Amazon.com was one such company that began modernizing its data centers using early concepts of virtualization over massive amounts of commodity hardware. Having lots of unused capacity most of the time, to deal with peak usage, Amazon decided to sell this as a service.[4]

Out of the offering of spare capacity as a service came the concept and label of Infrastructure as a Service (IaaS). This term started to appear around 2006 and typically refers to offerings of computer infrastructure such as servers, storage, networks, and bandwidth as a service instead of by subscription or contract. This method was a pay-as-you-use model for what previously required either capital expenditure to purchase outright, long-term leases, or month-to-month subscriptions for partial tenancy of physical hardware.

SaaS, PaaS, IaaS, and EaaS

All these concepts of *Blah* as a Service have common characteristics. Among these are paying for what you use instead of buying it up front, scaling the amount you need without prior notice, and multiple tenancy or having many different people use the same service.

---

1. According to Wikipedia, http://en.wikipedia.org/wiki/Application_service_provider.

2. John McCarthy's home page at Stanford University, http://www-formal.stanford.edu/jmc/.

3. The original manifesto can be found at http://www.research.ibm.com/autonomic/manifesto/.

4. *BusinessWeek* article. Nov 13, 2006. http://www.businessweek.com/magazine/content/06_46/b4009001.htm.

- *Software as a Service (SaaS).* This was the original *Blah* as a Service term and started with software such as customer relationship management (CRM) software as some of the earliest offerings. Almost any form of software can be offered in this manner and it can be done either over the Web or via download.

- *Platform as a Service (PaaS).* This model provides all the required components for developing and deploying Web applications and services. These components include workflow management, integrated development environments, testing, deployment, and hosting.

- *Infrastructure as a Service (IaaS).* This is the concept of offering computing infrastructure such as servers, storage, network, and bandwidth for use as necessary by clients. Amazon's EC2 was one of the earliest offerings of this service.

- *Everything as a Service (XaaS or *aaS).* This is the idea of being able to retrieve on demand small components or modules of software that can be pieced together to provide a new Web based application or service. Components could include retail, payments, search, security, and communications.

As these concepts evolve, they will continue to refine their definitions, and subcategories are sure to develop.

From Infrastructure as a Service, we have seen an explosion of *Blah* as a Service offerings. (*Blah* meaning feel free to fill in the blank with almost any word you can imagine.) We even have Everything as a Service (EaaS) now. All of these terms actually do share some common characteristics such as a purchasing model of pay as you go or pay as you use it, on demand scalability of the amount that you use, and the concept that there will be many people or multiple tenants using the service simultaneously.

Grid Computing

Grid computing as a concept has been around for almost two decades. It is used to describe the use of two or more computers processing individual parts of an overall task. The tasks that are most well structured for these types of solutions are ones that are computationally intensive and divisible into smaller tasks. Ian Foster and Carl Kesselman are credited as the fathers of the grid from their book *The Grid: Blueprint for a New Computing Infrastructure* published in 1998 by Morgan Kaufmann Publishers.[5] These two individuals along with others also were instrumental in developing Globus Toolkit. It is an open source product by Globus Alliance and is considered the de facto standard for building grids.

For tasks and jobs to be performed in a grid environment, software must be used to orchestrate the division of labor, monitor the computation of subtasks, and aggre-

---

5. As declared in the April 2004 issue of the *University of Chicago Magazine.* http://magazine.uchicago.edu/0404/features/index.shtml.

gation of completed jobs. This type of processing can be thought of as parallel processing that occurs on a network distributed basis. Before the concept of grid computing, the only way to achieve this scale of parallel processing was on a mainframe computer system. Modern grids are often composed of many thousands of nodes across public or private networks of computers.

Public networks range from volunteers on the Internet allowing the use of their computers' unused CPU clock cycles to pay for usage grids, such as the Sun Grid that was launched in February 2005. Private networks include dedicated farms of small commodity servers used with grid middleware to allow for parallel computing. Other private networks include corporate offices where personal computers are used after hours for parallel computing. One of the most well known public network examples of grid computing is the SETI@home project. This project uses computers connected to the Internet in the Search for Extraterrestrial Intelligence (SETI). Individuals can participate by running a program on their personal computers that downloads and analyzes radio telescope data. It then sends the results back to the central system that aggregates completed jobs. This type of public network grid computing is known as CPU scavenging.

As we mentioned previously, there are several middleware providers for building grid systems. One of the earliest is the Globus Toolkit, but others include the Sun Grid Engine and UNICORE (UNiform Interface to COmputing REsources). Many of these middleware products are used in university, governmental, and industrial applications to create grids.

With all this processing power, how fast can our applications run? Similar in concept to Brooks' Law from the book *The Mythical Man-Month* by Frederick P. Brooks, Jr., applications can only be divided so many times. Although adding more processors to the job probably won't make it actually slow down, as projects do when adding engineers late within a project, it does nothing to accomplish the job faster. There is a law know as Amdahl's Law developed by Gene Amdahl in 1967 that states that the portion of a program that cannot be parallelized will limit the total speed up from parallelization.[6] Stated another way, the nonsequential parts of a program benefit from the parallelization, but the rest of the program does not. There actually was no formula provided in the original paper, but it can be approximated, as shown in Figure 28.1, by the total improvement, a factor of the original run time, equaling the inverse of the sequential parts of the program (s).

$$\text{Improvement} = \frac{1}{s}$$

Figure 28.1 *Amdahl's Law*

---

6. Amdahl, G.M. "Validity of the single-processor approach to achieving large scale computing capabilities." In AFIPS Conference Proceedings vol. 30 (Atlantic City, N.J., Apr. 18-20). AFIPS Press, Reston, Va., 1967, pp. 483–485.

If 75% of the program can be parallelized, leaving 25% that must be executed sequentially, we should see approximately a 4× increase in the total runtime of the application by running it in a parallel computing environment.

As you might expect, there are problems associated with running applications and programs on grid systems. This is especially true on public networks, but can also be problematic on private ones. One of the biggest problems is how to handle the data that is required by the program to execute. Storage management of data, security of the data, and transmission of the data are all areas of concern when dealing with network distributed parallel processing or grid computing. Usually, the amount of data that is sent along with the executable program is small enough that by itself it is neither valuable nor sensitive. Nevertheless, the perceived risk of sending data to computer systems that you do not control can be a tough sell, especially when processing sensitive information such as Personally Identifiable Information (PII).

Public Versus Private Clouds

Some of the largest names in technology are providing or have plans to provide cloud computing services. These companies include Amazon.com Inc., Google Inc., Hewlett-Packard Company, and Microsoft Corporation. These are publicly available clouds, of which anyone from individuals to other corporations can take advantage. However, if you are interested in running your application in a cloud environment but have concerns about a public cloud, there is the possibility of running a private cloud. By private cloud, we mean implementing a cloud on your own hardware in your own secure environment. With more open source cloud solutions becoming available, such as Eucalyptus, this is becoming a realistic solution. There are obviously pros and cons with running your application in a cloud environment. We are going to talk more about these in detail in Chapter 29, Soaring in the Clouds. Some of the benefits and drawbacks are present regardless of whether it is a private or public cloud. Some of the drawbacks are directly related to the fact that it is a public cloud. Similar to the problem with data security in grid computing, even if the public cloud is very secure, there is a perception that the data is not as protected as it would be inside of your network. One of the pros of a cloud is that you can allocate just the right amount of memory, CPU, and disk space to a particular application taking better advantage and improving utilization of the hardware. So, if you want to improve your hardware utilization and not have to deal with security concerns of a public cloud, you may want to consider running your own private cloud.

Characteristics and Architecture of Clouds

At this point in the evolution of the cloud computing concept, there are some basic characteristics that all cloud implementations share. These characteristics have been mentioned briefly before in this chapter, but it is time to understand them in more detail. There are four general characteristics that we find in almost all public cloud implementations, some of which do not apply to private clouds. These characteristics are pay by usage, scale on demand, multiple tenants, and virtualization. Obviously, scaling on demand is an important characteristic when viewing the use of clouds from a scalability perspective, but don't dismiss the other characteristics as unimportant. For cash strapped startup companies paying as you go instead of purchasing hardware or signing multiyear contracts, this could be the difference between surviving long enough to be successful or not.

Pay By Usage

The idea of pay as you go or pay according to your usage is common of Software as a Service (SaaS) and has been adopted by the cloud computing services. Before cloud computing was available, in order to grow your application and have enough capacity to scale, you had limited options. If you were a large enough organization, you probably had servers that you owned or leased that were hosted in a data center or collocation facility. This model requires lots of upfront capital expenditure as well as a pretty healthy monthly expense to continue paying bandwidth, power, space, and cooling costs. An alternative was a hosting service that provided the hardware for you, and you paid them on either a long-term lease or high monthly cost for the use of the hardware. Both models are reasonable and have benefits as well as drawbacks. Many companies still use one or both of these models and will likely do so for many years to come. The cloud offers another alternative. Instead of long-term leases or high upfront capital outlays, the cloud model allows you to have no upfront cost for purchasing hardware and pay by the utilization of either CPU, bandwidth, storage, or possibly all of them.

Scale On Demand

Another characteristic of cloud computing is the ability to scale on demand. As a subscriber or client of a cloud, you have the theoretical ability of scaling as much as you need. This implies that if you need terabytes of storage or gigahertz or more, computing these would be available to you. There are of course practical limits to this that include how much actual capacity the cloud provider has to offer, but with the larger clouds, it is reasonable that you can scale to the equivalent of several hundreds or thousands of servers with no issues on most public clouds. Of course in a private cloud, this becomes your organization's limitations on physical hardware. The time that it takes to do this is almost instant compared to the standard method of provisioning hardware in a data center. Let's look at the typical process first, as if you were hosting your site at a collocation facility and then as if you were running in a cloud environment.

Adding hundreds of servers in a collocation facility or data center can take days, weeks, or months, depending on an organization's processes. For those who have never worked in an organization that hosted with a collocation facility, this is a typical scenario that you might encounter. Most organizations have budgeting and request processes regardless of where or how the site is hosted. After the budget or the purchase order is approved, the process of provisioning a new server in a cloud and one in a collocation facility are almost completely different. For a collocation facility, you need to ensure that you have available the space and power to accommodate the new servers. This can entail going to a new cage in a collocation provider if you do not have any more space or power available in your current cage. If a new cage is required, contracts must be negotiated and signed for the lease of the new space and cross connects are generally required to connect the cage's networks. After the space and power that are necessary are secured, purchase orders for the servers can be placed. Of course, some companies will stockpile servers in anticipation of capacity demand. Others wait until the operations team alerts that capacity is at a point that expanding the server pools is required. If your organization waits, ordering and receiving the hardware can take weeks. After the hardware arrives at the collocation facility, it needs to be placed in the racks and powered up. After this is accomplished, the operations team can get started ghosting, jumpstarting, or kick starting the server depending on the operating system. And when all this is finally accomplished, the latest version of the software can be loaded and the server can be added into the production pool. The total time for this process is at least days in the most efficient operations teams who already have hardware and space available. In most organizations, this process takes weeks or months.

Let's take a look at how this process might go if you were hosting your site in a cloud environment and decided that you needed 10 or 20 more servers for a particular pool. The process would start off similarly with the budget or purchase order request to add to the monthly expense of the cloud services. After this was approved, the operations team would use the control panel of the cloud provider to simply request the number of virtual servers, specifying the size and speed. Within a few minutes, the systems would be available to load the machine image of choice and the latest application code could be installed. The servers could likely be placed into production within a few hours. This ability to scale on demand is a common characteristic of cloud computing.

Multiple Tenants

Although the ability to scale on demand is enticing, all that capacity is not just waiting for you. Public clouds have many users running all sorts of applications on them and the capacity is being shared. This is known as *multitenanting* or having multiple tenants existing on the same cloud. If all works as designed, these users never interact or impact each other. Data is not shared, access is not shared, and accounts are not shared. Each client has its own virtual environment that is walled off from other virtual environments. What you do share with other tenants in a cloud is the physical servers, network, and storage. You might have a virtual dual processor server with 32GB of RAM, but it is likely running on an eight processor with 128GB of RAM that is being shared with several other tenants. Your traffic between servers and from the servers to the storage goes across common networking gear. There are no routers, switches, or firewalls dedicated to individual tenants. The same goes for the storage. Tenants share storage on virtual network-attached storage (NAS) or storage area network (SAN) devices making it appear as if they are the only ones using it. The reality is that there are multiple tenants using that same physical storage device.

Virtualization

All cloud computing offerings implement some form of a hypervisor on the servers that provides the virtualization. This concept of virtualization is the fourth common cloud characteristic and is really the core architectural principle behind clouds. A *hypervisor* is either a hardware platform or software service that allows multiple operating systems to run on a single host server. This is also known as a virtual machine monitor (VMM). There are many vendors that offer hardware and software solutions, such as VMware, Parallels, and Oracle VM. As we covered in the multitenant discussion, this virtualization is what allows multiple users to exist on common hardware without knowing and hopefully without impacting each other. There are other virtualization, separation, or limitation techniques that are used to restrict access of cloud clients to only amounts of bandwidth and storage that they have purchased. The overall purpose of all of these techniques is to control access and provide as much as possible an environment that appears to be completely the client's own. The better this is done the less likely that clients will notice each other's presence.

Common Cloud Characteristics

There are four basic common characteristics of cloud computing services:

1. *Pay as You Go.* Users, subscribers, or clients only pay for the amount of bandwidth, storage, and processing that they consume.

2. *Scale on Demand.* Cloud clients have access to theoretically unlimited capacity for scaling their applications by adding more bandwidth, servers, or storage.

3. *Multiple Tenants.* Clouds service multiple, often many thousands, of clients. Clients share hardware, networks, bandwidth, and storage. Physical devices are not dedicated to clients.

4. *Virtualization.* The way that multitenanting can be accomplished is through virtualization. This is the process by which hardware can have multiple operating systems running on it simultaneously.

Some of these characteristics may or may not be present in private clouds. Let's take a quick look at private cloud implementations. The concept of virtualization is at the core of all clouds regardless of whether it is public or private. The idea of using farms of physical servers in different virtual forms to achieve greater utilization, multitenancy, or any other various reasons is the basic premise behind the architecture of a cloud. The ability to scale as necessary is likely to be a common characteristic regardless of whether it is a private or public cloud. There is a physical restriction on the amount of scale that can occur. This physical restriction is dependent on how large the cloud is and how much extra capacity is built into it.

Having multiple tenants is not required in a private cloud. Tenants in a private cloud can mean different departments or different applications, not necessarily and probably not different companies. Pay as you go is also not required but possible in private clouds. Depending on how cost centers or departments are charged in an organization, each department might have to pay based on usage of the private cloud. If there is a centralized operations team that is responsible for building and running its own profit and loss center, it may very well charge departments or divisions for the services provided. This can include the computational, bandwidth, and storage in a private cloud.

Differences Between Clouds and Grids

Now that we've covered some of the history and basic characteristics of clouds and grids, we are going to conclude this chapter with a comparison of the two concepts. The terms *cloud* and *grid* are often confused and misused. We are going to cover a few of the differences and some of the similarities between the two to ensure that we are all clear on when each should be considered for use in our systems.

Clouds and grids serve different purposes. Clouds offer virtual environments for hosting user applications on one or many virtual servers. This makes clouds particularly compelling for applications that have unpredictable usage demands. When you are not sure if you need 5 or 50 servers over the next three months, a cloud can be an ideal solution. We will cover more pros and cons in Chapter 30, Plugging in the Grid, as well as how to decide if a cloud is really the correct hosting solution for your applications. Clouds, again because of this virtualization architecture, allow users to share the infrastructure. There can be many different users on the same physical hardware consuming and sharing computational, network, and storage resources.

On the other hand, grids are infrastructures for dividing programs into small parts to be executed in parallel across two or more hosts. These environments are ideal for an application that needs computationally intensive environments. Grids are not necessarily great infrastructures to share with multiple tenants. You are likely running on a grid to parallelize and significantly increase the computational bandwidth for your application; sharing the infrastructure simultaneously defeats that purpose. Sharing or multitenancy can occur serially, one after the other, in a grid environment where each application runs in isolation; when completed, the next job runs. This challenge of enabling multitenancy on grids is one of the core jobs of a grid operations team. Grids are also ideal only for applications that can be divisible into elements that can be simultaneously executed. The throughput of a monolithic application cannot be helped by running on a grid. The same monolithic application can likely be replicated onto many individual servers in a cloud, and the throughput can be scaled by the number of servers added. Stated as simply as we can, clouds allow you to expand and contract your architecture; grids decompose work into parallelizable units.

While serving different purposes, there are many crossovers and similarities. The first major one is that some clouds run on top of a grid infrastructure. A good example of this is AppLogic from 3Tera, which is a grid operating system that is offered as software but is also used to power a cloud that is offered as a service. Other similarities between clouds and grids include on demand pricing models and scalable usage. If you need 50 extra servers in a cloud, you can get them allocated quickly and you pay for them for the time that you are using them. The same is the case in a grid environment. If you need 50 more nodes for improving the processing time of the application, you can have this allocated rather quickly and you pay for only the nodes that you use.

At this point, you should understand that clouds and grids are fundamentally different concepts and serve different purposes but have similarities and share common characteristics, and are sometimes intertwined in implementations. One last topic to further analyze these different implementations is the three different types of clouds.

Types of Clouds

There really is no standard categorization for clouds. We like to use three categories to explain the differences between various providers and vendors. These three are service providers, backbones, and virtualization software. Of course, because there is no standardization, many of the vendors cross between these categories.

Starting from the lowest level, the first category is the virtualization software providers. This is software that allows for the hypervisor or the ability to run multiple operating systems on a single server. There are many vendors that offer software in this category. One such software is VMWare. VMWare is used to split physical servers into multiple virtual servers that can be allocated memory, CPU cycles, and disk as if it were a completely separate physical server. Another virtualization software is AppLogic that is offered by 3Tera. AppLogic, as mentioned, is a grid operating system that allows a cloud service to be provided on top of the grid.

The next category of clouds is the backbone providers. These are vendors that provide basic virtualization services, typically on a very large scale. We consider vendors' offerings such as Amazon's EC2, Rackspace's cloud, Google Apps, and Microsoft's cloud to be in this category. These vendors utilize some form, either off-the-shelf, customized, or mostly home grown, virtualization software to provide their clouds.

The last category of clouds is the service provider. Companies that fall in this category offer services on top of backbones. One such vendor is RightScale, who offers an improved management interface for Amazon's EC2 and other services. Another vendor is Mosso, who offers a service on top of Rackspace's cloud. Both of these services have attempted to improve the deployment and management of the backbone offerings.

Many vendors could make an argument that they belong in more than one of these environments. Although a service provider might have a different management interface for a backbone, this doesn't mean that the backbone provider itself does not also have a GUI management interface that is fully functional. Even though this categorization is often blurred in the real world, it does offer a basic framework to help understand the multitude of vendors that have some sort of cloud related offering.

Conclusion

In this chapter, we started by covering the history that led up to the launch of cloud computing and included the background of grid computing. This history dates back several decades, and the concept of the modern-day cloud can be credited to IBM's manifesto. However, the evolution of cloud computing into what it is today has been made possible by many different people and companies including one of the first public cloud services, EC2. We covered many of the "as a Service" offerings including Software as a Service and Infrastructure as a Service.

In the history section, we discussed how the concept of grid computing had been around for almost two decades. Grid computing is used to describe the use of two or more computers processing individual parts of an overall task. Tasks that are most well suited for a grid solution are ones that require intensive computations and those that are divisible. The maximum amount of improvement that can be made by dividing an application up is limited by the amount of sequential processing that is required.

There are four common characteristics of public clouds. These are pay as you go, scale on demand, multiple tenants, and virtualization. We covered each of these in detail and also looked at what characteristics private clouds are likely to have. We concluded that virtualization and scale on demand are two characteristics that private clouds must have. Hosting multiple tenants and pay as you go are possible in private clouds but not necessary.

We concluded the chapter with a comparison of grid and cloud computing. We started by stating that clouds and grids serve different purposes. Clouds offer virtual environments for hosting user applications on one or many virtual servers. Grids, on the other hand, are infrastructures for dividing programs into small parts to be executed in parallel across two or more hosts. Clouds are compelling for applications that have unpredictable usage demands, need to scale quickly, and can scale on independent servers. Grids are more suited for applications that need computationally intensive environments.

The last topic covered under the comparison of grids and clouds was the categorization of cloud providers. We described a three-category hierarchy that started with virtualization software providers, then moved up to backbone providers, and finally ended with service providers. We conceded that although this categorization helps understand all the various offerings, it is excessively restrictive and many vendors cross over between these categories.

As we've pointed out repeatedly in this chapter, clouds and grids are important technologies and concepts to scalability. With a thorough understanding of their characteristics and uses, they can become effective weapons in your arsenal to fight the scalability war.

Key Points

- The term *cloud* has been around for decades and was used primarily in network diagrams.
- The idea of the modern cloud concept was put forth by IBM in its Autonomic Computing Manifesto.
- Developing alongside the idea of cloud computing was the concept of Software as a Service, Infrastructure as a Service, and many more "as a Service" concepts.
- Software as a Service refers to almost any form of software that is offered in a pay as you use model.
- Infrastructure as a Service is the idea of offering infrastructure such as storage, servers, network, and bandwidth in a pay as you use model.
- Platform as a Service provides all the required components for developing and deploying Web applications and services.
- Everything as a Service is the idea of being able to have small components that can be pieced together to provide a new service.
- Grid computing as a concept has been around for almost two decades. It is used to describe the use of two or more computers processing individual parts of an overall task.
- There are three types of cloud vendors: service providers, backbones, and virtualization software providers.

Chapter 29

Soaring in the Clouds

This is called, using the conquered foe to augment one's own strength.

—Sun Tzu

In the previous chapter, we covered the history, characteristics, and comparison of cloud computing and grid computing. We also discussed how important they were to scalability. In this chapter, we are going to cover the benefits and drawbacks of cloud computing. After we've covered this in sufficient detail, we are going to discuss where we think cloud computing makes the most sense in different companies. Lastly, we are going to cover how we recommend you think through the decision of whether to use a cloud computing service for various environments. This will provide you with examples of how you can use cloud computing in your scaling efforts as well as give you a framework for making the decision to use it or not.

There is a lot of excitement about cloud computing services and rightly so. Cloud computing is a significant breakthrough in computing infrastructure and holds the possibility of changing dramatically how many products and services are offered. The reason we believe this and the reason we are going to spend so much time on cloud computing in a book about scalability is that we think clouds are likely to be a key scaling architectural principle in the future. At the same time, we want to be realistic about where cloud computing is in terms of maturity at this point. Making such a significant decision as to forgo a collocation facility in lieu of a cloud computing service should not be done without careful consideration. If you are a Software as a Service (SaaS) company or Web 2.0 business, the future of the entire company likely rests with your system remaining consistently available.

Why is this decision so important? Ultimately, you are striving to maximize shareholder value. If you make a decision to spend capital investing in hardware and data center space, this takes cash away from other projects that you could be investing in. Could that money be spent better by hiring more engineers? On the other hand, if you don't invest in the infrastructure, and you rely on a cloud service that doesn't provide the proper availability or scalability, that can negatively affect shareholder value. This decision is one that can make or break the company and one that you as a leader or member of the technology organization will have the greatest influence over.

Pros and Cons of Cloud Computing

There are benefits and drawbacks to almost everything. Rarely is something just a hundred percent beneficial or problematic. In most cases, the pros and cons can be debated, which makes it more difficult to make decisions for your business. Making it more complex is that the pros and cons do not affect all businesses equally. For example, a software product might have passwords delivered in plain text over the network; if you plan on using the software inside your three-person software shop, this drawback might mean very little to you. If you are planning on using it with 500 engineers spread across three continents, this might be a much more important issue for you. Each company must weigh each of the identified benefits and drawbacks for its own situation. We will get more into how to use the pros and cons to make decisions later in the chapter. To start with, we will cover what we consider the basic and most important of both benefits and drawbacks to cloud computing. Later, we will help put relative weightings to these as we discuss various implementations for different hypothetical businesses.

Pros of Cloud Computing

There are three major benefits to running your infrastructure on a cloud: cost, speed, and flexibility. Each one of these will have varying degrees of importance to your particular situation. You should weight each one in terms of how applicable the benefit is to you. We are going to cover each one in some detail.

Cost The cost model of not outlaying a lot of capital and paying for what you use is a great one. This model works especially well if you are a cash strapped startup. If your business model is one that actually pays for itself as you grow and your expense model is the same, you have effectively eliminated a great deal of risk for your company. There are certainly other models that have limited initial cash outlay, such as managed hosted environments, but where they differ is that you have to purchase or lease equipment on a per server basis and you cannot return it when you are not using it. As a startup, being able to last long enough to become successful is the first step to scaling. At any company, being able to manage cost to stay in line with the volume of business is critical to ensure the ability to scale.

In Figure 29.1, you can see how a normal cost progression occurs. As demand increases, you must stay ahead of that demand and purchase or lease the next server or storage unit or whatever piece of hardware to ensure you are capable of meeting demand. Most organizations are not great at capacity planning. This causes the gap

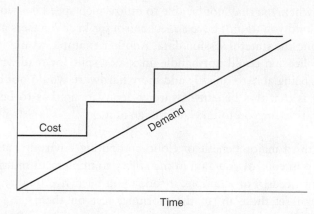

Figure 29.1 *Stepwise Cost Function*

between the cost and demand is either larger than necessary or worse, demand exceeds the capacity and there is a scramble to purchase more equipment all the while your customers are experiencing poor performance. The key when purchasing or leasing in such a manner is to get the cost and demand lines as close as possible without letting them cross. With a cloud cost model, where services are paid for only when used, these lines can be much tighter, almost touching in most cases.

Speed The next benefit that we see from the cloud environment is the speed. Not performance speed as discussed in the cons but rather procurement, provisioning, and deployment speed. Of all the collocation, data centers, managed hosting, or other infrastructure models, there is none faster when it comes to adding another server than in a cloud environment. Because of the virtual nature, this deployment and provisioning is very quick. If you are running a site that expects a spike of traffic over the weekend because of some sporting event, you can throw a couple more virtual hosts into the pool on Friday afternoon and release them back Monday morning. You have them to use over the weekend to add capacity, but you don't pay for them the following week after the spike in traffic is over. The ability to increase an application's usage of virtual hosts very quickly can be used as an effective method of scaling through peak traffic periods.

What clouds do not do yet for deployment and provisioning is augment capacity automatically. Certainly, this is one of the longer term goals of the autonomous infrastructure, but we are not there yet. Even without this happening automatically, it is faster than it has ever been in the past with other models. But this is not to imply that with either it is wise to scale only on the x-axis with additional hardware instances, nor is it always available for applications to scale in this manner. If your application has this capability and you've made a determination that this is a wise strategic architectural decision, this speed adds a lot to your ability to deploy more hosts quickly.

One example of when you may not be able to utilize such speed is if your application maintained state and you do not have a mechanism for keeping users assigned to one host or centralizing the stateful session data. Another example would be on the database. If your application could not handle an x-axis split for read/write or a y-axis split of schemas, being able to quickly add more hardware would not help you scale. The bottom line is that this benefit of speedy deployments has to be able to work with your application for you to take advantage of it.

Flexibility   The third major benefit of cloud computing environments is flexibility. What you give up in control you gain in the ability to implement multiple configurations for different needs. For example, if today you need five quality assurance test instances, you can set these up in the morning, test on them, and remove them tonight. Tomorrow, you can set up a full staging environment to allow your customers to perform user acceptance testing before you roll the code to production. After your customers are satisfied, you can remove the environment and stop paying for it. If you need a load testing environment that requires a bunch of individual hosts to provide multiple connections, the ramping up of a dozen virtual hosts for an hour of load testing is easily done in most cloud environments. This flexibility to add, remove, or change your environments almost at whim is something that we have never had before in previous infrastructures. After a team gets used to this ability to change and reconfigure, they are not going to want to be constrained by physical devices.

Benefits of Cloud Computing

There are three major categories of pros or benefits that we see with cloud computing. These are in no particular order:

- *Cost.* The pay as you use model allows the amount that you spend to stay closer to the actual usage and is particularly helpful for cash strapped companies.

- *Speed.* The speed in procurement, deployment, and provisioning is unmatched with other infrastructure models.

- *Flexibility.* The ability to change an environment from a quality assurance to a staging to a load and performance while not having to pay for three separate environments is advantageous.

The importance of any of these or how much you should weight them when determining whether the cloud is the right environment for you and should be based on your particular company's needs at a particular time.

Cons of Cloud Computing

We think there are five major categories of concern or drawbacks for public cloud computing. These five categories do not all apply to private clouds, but as the greatest utility and greatest public interest is in the use of public clouds, we will stick to using public clouds for our analysis. These categories are security, portability, control, limitations, and performance. These are obviously very broad categories so we will have to delve into each one in more detail to fully understand them.

Security Not a month goes by without us hearing about leaked personal information or a security breach. This causes us to ask the question, "how do cloud providers store and safeguard our information?" The same question can be asked of many of our SaaS vendors. The slight difference is that with a SaaS implementation, the vendor often knows whether it is collecting and storing sensitive information such as personally identifiable information (name, address, social security number, phone number, and so on) and therefore it takes extra precautions and publishes its steps for safeguarding this information. Cloud providers have no idea what is being stored on their systems—that is, whether their customers are storing credit card numbers or blogs—and therefore do not take any extra precautions to restrict or block access to your data by their internal employees. Of course, there are ways around this, such as not storing any sensitive information on the cloud system, but those workarounds add more complexity to your system and potentially expose you to more risks. As stated earlier, this may or may not be a very important aspect for your particular company or application that you are considering hosting on a cloud.

Portability The next category is portability. We long for a day when you can port your application from one cloud to another without code or configuration changes, but this day has not yet arrived, nor do we think it will in the near future because it is not beneficial to the cloud vendors to make this process easy. This is not to say that it is impossible to migrate from one cloud to another or from a cloud to a physical server hosting environment, but those can be nontrivial endeavors depending on the cloud and particular services being utilized. For instance, if you are making use of Amazon's Simple Storage Solution and you want to move to another cloud or to a set of physical servers, you are likely to rework your application to implement storage in a simple database. Although not the most challenging engineering project, it does take time and resources that could be used to work on product features. One of the principles discussed in Chapter 12, Exploring Architectural Principles, was to Use Commodity Hardware; this vendor agnostic approach to hardware is important to scale in a cost-efficient manner. Not being able to port across clouds easily goes against this principle and therefore is a con that should be considered.

Control Any time that you rely solely on a single vendor for any part of your system, you are putting your company's future in the hands of another. We like to control our own destiny as much as possible. Relinquishing a significant amount of control to a third party is a difficult step for us to take. This is probably acceptable when it comes to operating systems and relational database management systems, because hopefully you are using a vendor or product line that has been around for years and you are not likely to build or manage anything better with your engineering team, unless of course you are in the business of operating systems or relational database management systems. When it comes to the hosting environment, many companies move away from managed environments because they get to a point where they have the technical talent on staff to handle the operational tasks required for hosting your own hardware and they get fed up with vendors messing up and causing them pain. Cloud environments are no different. They are staffed by people who are not your employees and who do not have a personal stake in your business. This is not to say that cloud or hosting providers have inferior employees. Quite the opposite, they are usually incredibly talented, but they do not know or understand your business. They have hundreds or thousands of servers to keep up and running. They don't know that this one is any more important than that one; they are all the same. Giving up control of your infrastructure adds an amount of risk into your business.

Continuing with the discussion of control, many cloud vendors are not even to the point of being able to offer guaranteed availability or uptime. When vendors do not stand behind their products with remuneration clauses built-in for failures, it would be wise to always consider their service as best effort, which means you need to have an alternative method of receiving that service. As we mentioned in the portability section, running on or switching between multiple clouds is not a simple task.

Limitations The next cons or drawbacks that we see with cloud computing are limitations due to the nature of virtual environments. The cloud vendors and other cloud service providers are working feverishly to resolve some of these, but nonetheless they still either exist in some or all current cloud environments. Three of the major ones that we are concerned with are IP addresses, load balancing, and certification of third-party software on the clouds. The first limitation on many of the early clouds is lack of public and static IP addresses for your servers. Many clouds have begun to solve this and offer static IP addresses for an additional cost. This still does not solve the problem of not owning your IP space. This may seem a trivial problem to most companies that are not ready to own and manage their own IP space, but for some companies this is very important. As an example, if you send out lots of email and have become a trusted email to major email networks such as AOL, you rely on static IP addresses to accomplish reliable mail delivery. This trusted relationship, until the trusted email open standard (TEOS), or something similar is adopted, is today based on a white list and black list of IP addresses for trusted and untrusted sources, respectively. Remaining on a white list of mail servers is extremely important if you want to continue sending significant amounts of email.

The next major limitation that concerns us with most cloud vendors is the lack of physical load balancers. Most cloud vendors or service providers have implemented software load balancers, but there are some limitations with this when compared to physical devices. The feature sets of software load balancers are always changing and advancing but in general some areas that physical load balancers do better at are distributed denial of service protection, compression, secure socket layer (SSL) termination, connection pooling, caching, and buffering. Like all the concerns that we are raising, these issues might not be important to you. If you happen to be serving billions of advertisements or streaming video, the throughput of your load balancer is going to be very important to you. However, these limitations are often offset in the cloud environment by the capability to add more virtual hardware.

The last issue in the limitations category that we feel strongly about is the lack of certification of other third-party software on cloud computing environments. This third-party vendor software could really be anything that you utilize as a subcomponent or part of your system, but primarily we have concerns over relational database management systems and data warehousing management systems. A lot of these systems will work in virtual environments and more are working toward certifying their systems, but if you have ever been on support calls where the answer to your problem was to upgrade the database version, you can only imagine what the answer will be running on a cloud. What this does is limit your choices of vendors for key components of your system. This may or may not be a major issue for you. As for a database, it probably matters how you are architected. If you are still relying on a very large monolithic database, the limitation of vendors might be problematic. If you already are running on small open source databases split along the x-, y-, or z-axes of the AKF Scale Cube, this limitation probably matters less to you.

Performance The last major category of concerns that we have are regarding performance. From our experiences with our clients on cloud computing infrastructures, the expected performance from an equivalent piece of hard and virtual hardware is not the same. This is obviously very important to the scalability of your application, especially if you have singletons, single instances of batch jobs or parts of your application running on only a single server. Obviously, running a single instance of anything is not an effective way to scale, but it is common for a team to start on a single server and not test the job or program on multiple servers until they are needed. Migrating to a cloud and realizing on the new virtual server the processing of the job is falling behind might put you in panic mode to test and validate that that job can correctly run on multiple hosts.

The virtual hardware underperforms in some aspects by orders of magnitude. The standard performance metrics include memory speed, CPU, disk access, and so on. There is no standard degradation or equivalence among virtual hosts; in fact, it often varies within cloud environments and certainly varies from one vendor to another. Most companies and applications either don't notice this or don't care, but for those making a cost benefit analysis about switching to a cloud computing vendor, you need to test this yourself with your application. Do not take a vendor's word for an equivalent virtual host. Each application has its own sensitivity and bottlenecks with regard to host performance. Some applications are bottlenecked on memory and by slowing down memory even 5% can cause the entire application to scale much more poorly on certain hosts. This matters when you are paying thousands of dollars in computing costs per month. What might have been a twelve month break even now becomes eighteen or twenty-four months in some cases.

Drawbacks of Cloud Computing

There are five major categories of cons or drawbacks that we see with cloud computing. These are in no particular order:

- *Security*. Unlike SaaS companies who know exactly what sensitive or personally identifiable information is being entered into their system, cloud providers don't know and try not to care; but this leaves a potential gap in the security of your data.

- *Portability*. As simple as clouds are to get up and running on, they can be difficult to move to physical servers or other clouds depending on your application's implementation.

- *Control*. Outsourcing your infrastructure is giving a third-party complete control over your application being available or not. Unlike ISPs that can be redundant, redundancy is not easy to accomplish with clouds at this point.

- *Limitations*. Three limitations that we see in some of the cloud vendors' offerings are

  1. *IP addresses*. The early clouds didn't even offer static IP addresses but most do so now. They still do not allow you to own your IP addresses, which may be important to certain applications or services such as email.

  2. *Load balancers*. Most clouds offer software load balancing, which is a great improvement, but there are limitations between software and hardware load balancing.

  3. *Certification*. Other third-party software vendors do not certify their software to run in a cloud environment. This may cause you issues if you are trying to get support for their software.

- *Performance*. Even though clouds are sold on computational equivalencies, the actual performance varies significantly between vendors and physical and virtual hardware. You have to test this yourself to see if it matters to your application.

The importance of any of these or how much you should be concerned with them is determined by your particular company's needs at a particular time.

We have covered what we see as the top drawbacks and benefits of cloud computing as they exist today. As we have mentioned throughout this section, how these affect your decision to implement a cloud computing infrastructure will vary depending on your business and your application. In the next section, we are going to cover some of the different ways in which you may consider utilizing a cloud environment as well as how you might consider the importance of some of the factors discussed here based on your business and systems.

UC Berkeley on Clouds

Researchers at UC Berkeley have outlined their take on cloud computing in a paper "Above the Clouds: A Berkeley View of Cloud Computing."[1] They cover the top 10 obstacles that companies must overcome in order to utilize the cloud:

1. Availability of service
2. Data lock-in
3. Data confidentiality and audit ability
4. Data transfer bottlenecks
5. Performance unpredictability
6. Scalable storage
7. Bugs in large distributed systems
8. Scaling quickly
9. Reputation fate sharing
10. Software licensing

Their article concludes by stating that they believe cloud providers will continue to improve and overcome these obstacles. They continue by stating that ". . . developers would be wise to design their next generation of systems to be deployed into Cloud Computing."

---

1. Armbrust, Michael, et al. "Above the Clouds: A Berkeley View of Cloud Computing." http://www.eecs.berkeley.edu/Pubs/TechRpts/2009/EECS-2009-28.pdf.

Where Clouds Fit in Different Companies

The first item to cover is a few of the various implementations of clouds that we have either seen or recommended to our clients. Of course, you can host your application's production environment on a cloud, but there are many other environments in today's software development organizations. There are also many ways to utilize different environments together, such as combining a managed hosting environment along with a collocation facility. Obviously, hosting your production environment in a cloud offers you the scale on demand ability from a virtual hardware perspective. Of course, this does not ensure that your application's architecture can make use of this virtual hardware scaling, that you must ensure ahead of time. There are other ways that clouds can help your organization scale that we will cover here. If your engineering or quality assurance teams are waiting for environments, the entire product development cycle is slowed down, which means scalability initiatives such as splitting databases, removing synchronous calls, and so on get delayed and affect your application's ability to scale.

Environments

For your production environment, you can host everything in one type of infrastructure, such as a managed hosting, collocation, your own data center, a cloud computing environment, or any other. However, there are creative ways to utilize several of these together to take advantage of their benefits but minimize their drawbacks. Let's look at an example of an ad serving application. The ad serving application consists of a pool of Web servers to accept the ad request, a pool of application servers to choose the right advertisement based on information conveyed in the original request, an administrative tool that allows publishers and advertisers to administer their accounts, and a database for persistent storage of information. The ad servers in our application do not need to access the database for each ad request. They make a request to the database once every 15 minutes to receive the newest advertisements. In this situation, we could of course purchase a bunch of servers to rack in a collocation space for each of the Web server pool, ad server pool, administrative server pool, and database servers. We could also just lease the use of these servers from a managed hosting provider and let them worry about the physical server. Alternatively, we could host all of this in a cloud environment on virtual hosts.

We think there is another alternative, as depicted in Figure 29.2. Perhaps we have the capital to purchase the pools of servers and we have the skill set in our team members to handle setting up and running our own physical environment, so we decide to rent space at a collocation facility and purchase our own servers. But, we also like the speed and flexibility gained from a cloud environment. We decide that since the Web and app servers don't talk to the database very often we are going to

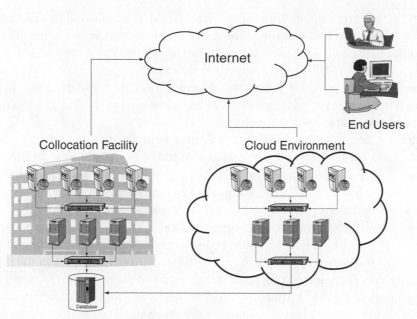

Figure 29.2   *Combined Collocation and Cloud Production Environment*

host one pool of each in a collocation facility and another pool of each on a cloud. The database will stay at the collocation but snapshots will be sent to the cloud to be used as a disaster recovery. The Web and application servers in the cloud can be increased as traffic demands to help us cover unforeseen spikes.

Another use of cloud computing is in all the other environments that are required for a modern software development organizations. These environments include but are not limited to production, staging, quality assurance, load and performance, development, build, and repositories. Many of these should be considered for implementing in a cloud environment because of the possible reduced cost, as well as flexibility and speed of setting up when needed and tearing down when they are no longer needed. Even enterprise class SaaS companies or Fortune 500 corporations who may never consider hosting production instances of their applications on a cloud could benefit from utilizing the cloud for other environments.

Skill Sets

What are some of the other factors when considering whether to utilize a cloud, and if you do utilize the cloud, then for which environments? One consideration is the skill set and number of personnel that you have available to manage your operations infrastructure. If you do not have both networking and system administration skill sets among your operations staff, you need to consider this when determining if you can implement and support a collocation environment. The most likely answer in that case is that you cannot. Without the necessary skill set, moving to a more sophis-ticated environment will actually cause more problems than it will solve. The cloud has similar issues; if someone isn't responsible for deploying and shutting down instances and this is left to each individual developer or engineer, it is very possible that the bill at the end of the month will be much more than you expected. Instances that are left running are wasting money unless someone has made a purposeful deci-sion that the instance is necessary.

Another type of skill set that may influence your decision is capacity planning. Whether your business has very unpredictable traffic or you do not have the neces-sary skill set on staff to accurately predict the traffic, this may heavily influence your decision to use a cloud. Certainly one of the key benefits of the cloud is the ability to handle spiky demand by quickly deploying more virtual hosts.

All in all, we believe that cloud computing likely has a fit in almost any company. This fit might not be for hosting your production environment, but may be rather for hosting your testing environments. If your business' growth is unpredictable, if speed is of utmost urgency, and cutting costs is imperative to survival, the cloud might be a great solution. If you can't afford to allocate headcount for operations management or predict what kind of capacity you may need down the line, cloud computing could be what you need. How you put all this together to make the decision is the subject of the next section in this chapter.

Decision Process

Now that we've looked at the pros and cons of cloud computing and we've discussed some of the various ways in which cloud environments can be integrated into a com-pany's infrastructure, the last step is to provide a process for making the final deci-sion. The overall process that we are recommending is to first determine the goals or purpose of wanting to investigate cloud computing, then create alternative implemen-tations that achieve those goals. Weigh the pros and cons based on your particular situation. Rank each alternative based on the pros and cons. Based on the final tally of pros and cons, select an alternative. Let's walk through an example.

Let's say that our company AlwaysScale.com is evaluating integrating a cloud infrastructure into its production environment. The first step is to determine what goals we hope to achieve by utilizing a cloud environment. For AlwaysScale.com, the goals are lower operation cost of infrastructure, decrease the time to procure and provision hardware, and maintain 99.99% availability for its application. Based on these three goals, the team has decided on three alternatives. The first is to do noth-ing, remain in a collocation facility, and forget about all this cloud computing talk. The second alternative is to use the cloud for only surge capacity but remain in the collocation facility for most of the application services. The third alternative is to move completely onto the cloud and out of the collocation space. This has accomplished steps one and two of the decision process.

Step three is to apply weights to all of the pros and cons that we can come up with for our alternative environments. Here, we will use the five cons and three pros that we outlined earlier. We will use a 1, 3, or 9 scale to rank these in order that we highly differentiate the factors that we care about. The first con is security, which we care somewhat about but we don't store PII or credit card info so we weight it a 3. We continue with portability and determine that we don't really feel the need to be able to move quickly between infrastructures so we weight it a 1. Next, is Control, which we really care about so we rank it a 9. Then, the limitations of such things as IP addresses, load balancers, and certification of third-party software are weighted a 3. We care about the load balancers but don't need our own IP space and use all open source unsupported third-party software. Finally, the last of the cons is performance. Because our application is not very memory or disk intensive, we don't feel that this is too big of a deal for us, so we weight it a 1. For the pros, we really care about cost so we weight it a 9. The same with speed: It is one of the primary goals, so we care a lot about it. Last is flexibility, which we don't expect to make much use of, so we rank it a 1.

The fourth step is to rank each alternative on a scale from 0 to 5 of how well they demonstrate each of the pros and cons. For example, with the "use the cloud for only surge capacity" alternative, the portability drawback should be ranked very low because it is not likely that we need to exercise that option. Likewise, with the "move completely to the cloud" alternative, the limitations are more heavily influential because there is no other environment, so it gets ranked a 5.

The completed decision matrix can be seen in Table 29.1. After the alternatives are all scored against the pros and cons, the numbers can be multiplied and summed. The

Table 29.1 *Decision Matrix*

		Weight (1, 3, or 9)	No Cloud	Cloud for Surge	Completely Cloud
Cons	Security	−3	0	2	5
	Portability	−1	0	1	4
	Control	−9	0	3	5
	Limitations	−3	0	3	4
	Performance	−1	0	3	3
Pros	Cost	9	0	3	5
	Speed	9	0	3	3
	Flexibility	1	0	1	1
Total			0	9	−6

weight of each pro is multiplied by the rank or score of each alternative; these products are summed for each alternative. For example, alternative #2, Cloud for Surge, has been ranked a 2 for security, which is weighted a –3. All cons are weighted with negative scores so the math is simpler. The product of the rank and the weight is –6, which is then summed with all the other products for alternative #2, equaling 9 for a total score: $(2 \times -3) + (1 \times -1) + (3 \times -9) + (3 \times -3) + (3 \times -1) + (3 \times 9) + (3 \times 9) + (1 \times 1) = 9$.

The final step is to compare the total scores for each alternative and apply a level of common sense to it. Here, we have the alternatives with 0, 9, and –6 scores, which would clearly indicate that alternative #2 is the better choice for us. Before automatically assuming that this is our decision, we should verify that based on our common sense and other factors that might not have been included, this is a sound decision. If something appears to be off or you want to add other factors such as operations skill sets, redo the matrix or have several people do the scoring independently to see how a group of different people score the matrix differently.

The decision process is meant to provide you with a formal method of evaluating alternatives. Using these types of matrixes, it becomes easier to see what the data is telling you so that you make a well-informed and data based decision. For times when a full decision matrix is not justified or you want to test an idea, consider using a rule of thumb. One that we often employ is a high-level comparison of risk. In the Web 2.0 and SaaS world, an outage has the potential to cost a lot of money. Considering this, a potential rule of thumb would be: If the cost of just one outage exceeds the benefits gained by whatever change you are considering, you're better off not introducing the change.

Decision Steps

The following are steps to help make a decision about whether to introduce cloud computing into your infrastructure:

1. Determine the goals or purpose of the change.

2. Create alternative designs for how to use cloud computing.

3. Place weights on all the pros and cons that you can come up with for cloud computing.

4. Rank or score the alternatives using the pros and cons.

5. Tally scores for each alternative by multiplying the score by the weight and summing.

This decision matrix process will help you make data driven decisions about which cloud computing alternative implementation is best for you.

The most likely question with regard to introducing cloud computing into your infrastructure is not *whether* to do it but rather *when* and *how* is the right way to do it. Cloud computing is not going away and in fact is likely to be the preferred but not only infrastructure model of the future. We all need to keep an eye on how cloud computing evolves over the coming months and years. This technology has the potential to change the fundamental cost and organization structures of most SaaS companies.

Conclusion

In this chapter, we covered the benefits and drawbacks of cloud computing. We identified five categories of cons to cloud computing including security, portability, control, limitations, and performance. The security category is our concern over how our data is handled after it is in the cloud. The provider has no idea what type of data we store there and we have no idea who has access to that data. This discrepancy between the two causes some concern. The portability addresses the fact that porting between clouds or clouds and physical hardware is not necessarily easy depending on your application. The control issues come from integrating another third-party vendor into your infrastructure that has influence over not just one part of your system's availability but has control over probably the entirety of your site's availability. The limitations that we identified were inability to use your own IP space, having to use software load balancers, and certification of third-party software on the cloud infrastructure. Last of the cons was performance, which we noted as being varied between cloud vendors as well as physical hardware. The degree to which you care about any of these cons should be dictated by your company and the applications that you are considering hosting on the cloud environment.

We also identified three pros: cost, speed, and flexibility. The pay per usage model is extremely attractive to companies and makes great sense. The speed is in reference to the unequaled speed of procurement and provisioning that can be done in a virtual environment. The flexibility is in how you can utilize a set of virtual servers today as a quality assurance environment: shut them down at night and bring them back up the next day as a load and performance testing environment. This is a very attractive feature of the virtual host in cloud computing.

After covering the pros and cons, we discussed the various ways in which cloud computing could exist in different companies' infrastructure. Some of these alternatives included not only as part or all of the production environment but also in other environments such as quality assurance or development. As part of the production environment, the cloud computing could be used for surge capacity or disaster recovery or of course to host all of production. There are many variations in the way that companies can implement and utilize cloud computing in their infrastructure. These examples are designed to show you how you can make use of the pros or benefits of cloud computing to aid your scaling efforts, whether directly for your production environment or more indirectly by aiding your product development cycle. This could take the form of making use of the speed of provisioning virtual hardware or the flexibility in using the environments differently each day.

Lastly we talked about how to make the decision of whether to use cloud computing in your company. We provided a five-step process that included establishing goals, describing alternatives, weighting pros and cons, scoring the alternatives, and tallying the scores and weightings to determine the highest scoring alternative. The bottom line to all of this was that even if a cloud environment is not right for your organization today, you should continue looking at them because they will continue to improve; and it is very likely that it will be a good fit at some time.

Key Points

- Pros of cloud computing include cost, speed, and flexibility.
- Cons of cloud computing include security, control, portability, inherent limitations of the virtual environment, and performance differences.
- There are many ways to utilize cloud environments.
- Clouds can be used in conjunction with other infrastructure models by using them for surge capacity or disaster recovery.
- You can use cloud computing for development, quality assurance, load and performance testing, or just about any other environment including production.
- There is a five-step process for helping to decide where and how to use cloud computing in your environment.
- All technologists should be aware of cloud computing; almost all organizations can take advantage of cloud computing.

Chapter 30

Plugging in the Grid

And if we are able thus to attack an inferior force with a superior one, our opponents will be in dire straits.

—Sun Tzu

In Chapter 28, Clouds and Grids, we covered the basics of grid computing. In this chapter, we will cover in more detail the pros and cons of grid computing as well as where such computing infrastructure could fit in different companies. Whether you are a Web 2.0, Fortune 500, or Enterprise Software company, it is likely that you have a need for grid computing in your scalability toolset. This chapter will provide you with a framework for further understanding a grid computing infrastructure as well as some ideas of where in your organization to deploy it. Grid computing offers the scaling on demand of computing cycles for computationally intense applications or programs. By understanding the benefits and cons of grid computing and providing you with some ideas on how this type of technology might be used, you should be well armed to use this knowledge in your scalability efforts.

As a way of a refresher, we defined grid computing in Chapter 28 as the term used to describe the use of two or more computers processing individual parts of an overall task. Tasks that are best structured for grid computing are ones that are computationally intensive and divisible, meaning able to be broken into smaller tasks. Software is used to orchestrate the separation of tasks, monitor the computation of these tasks, and then aggregate the completed tasks. This is parallel processing on a network distributed basis instead of inside a single machine. Before grid computing, mainframes were the only way to achieve this scale of parallel processing. Today's grids are often composed of thousands of nodes spread across networks such as the Internet.

Why would we consider grid computing as a principle, architecture, or aid to an organization's scalability? The reason is that grid computing allows for the use of significant computational resources by an application in order to process quicker or solve problems faster. Dividing processing is a core component to scaling, think of the x-, y-, and z-axes splits in the AKF Scale Cubes. Depending on how the separation of processing is done or viewed, the splitting of the application for grid computing might take the shape or one or more of the axes.

Pros and Cons of Grids

Grid environments are ideal for applications that need computationally intensive environments and for applications that can be divisible into elements that can be simultaneously executed. With that as a basis, we are going to discuss the benefits and drawbacks of grid computing environments. The pros and cons are going to matter differently to different organizations. If your application can be divided easily, either by luck or design, you might not care that the only way to achieve great benefits is with applications that can be divided. However, if you have a monolithic application, this drawback may be so significant as to completely discount the use of a grid environment. As we discuss each of the pros and cons, this fact should be kept in mind that some of each will matter more or less to your technology organization.

Pros of Grids

The pros of grid computing models include high computational rates, shared infrastructure, utilization of unused capacity, and cost. Each of these is explained in more detail in the following sections. The ability to scale computation cycles up quickly as necessary for processing is obviously directly applicable to scaling an application, service, or program. In terms of scalability, it is important to grow the computational capacity as needed but equally important is to do this efficiently and cost effectively.

High Computational Rates The first benefit that we want to discuss is a basic premise of grid computing—that is, high computational rates. The grid computing infrastructure is designed for applications that need computationally intensive environments. The combination of multiple hosts with software for dividing tasks and data allows for the simultaneous execution of multiple tasks. The amount of parallelization is limited by the hosts available—the amount of division possible within the application and, in extreme cases, the network linking everything together. We covered Amdahl's law in Chapter 28, but it is worth repeating as this defines the upper bound of this benefit from the limitation of the application. The law was developed by Gene Amdahl in 1967 and states that the portion of a program that cannot be parallelized will limit the total speed up from parallelization.[1] This means that nonse-

---

1. Amdahl, G.M. "Validity of the single-processor approach to achieving large scale computing capabilities." In *AFIPS Conference Proceedings*, vol. 30 (Atlantic City, N.J., Apr. 18-20). AFIPS Press, Reston, Va., 1967, pp. 483-485.

quential parts of a program will benefit from the parallelization, but the rest of the program will not.

Shared Infrastructure The second benefit of grid computing is the use of shared infrastructure. Most applications that utilize grid computing do so either daily, weekly, or some periodic amount of time. Outside of the periods in which the computing infrastructure is used for grid computing purposes, it can be utilized by other applications or technology organizations. We will discuss the limitation of sharing the infrastructure simultaneously in the "Cons of Grid Computing" section. This benefit is focused on sharing the infrastructure sequentially. Whether a private or public grid, the host computers in the grid can be utilized almost continuously around the clock. Of course, this requires the properly scheduling of jobs within the overall grid system so that as one application completes its processing the next one can begin. This also requires either applications that are flexible in the times that they run or applications that can be stopped in the middle of a job and delayed until there is free capacity later in the day. If applications must run every day at 1 AM, the job before it must complete prior to this or be designed to stop in the middle of the processing and restart later without losing valuable computations. For anyone familiar with job scheduling on mainframes, this should sound a little familiar, because as we mentioned earlier, the mainframe was the only way to achieve such intensive parallel processing before grid computing.

Utilization of Unused Capacity The third benefit that we see in some grid computing implementations is the utilization of unused capacity. Grid computing implementations vary, and some are wholly dedicated to grid computing all day, whereas others are utilized as other types of computers during the day and connected to the grid at night when no one is using them. For grids that are utilizing surplus capacity, this approach is known as CPU scavenging. One of the most well-known grid scavenging programs has been SETI@home that utilizes unused CPU cycles on volunteers' computers in a search for extraterrestrial intelligence in radio telescope data. There are obviously drawbacks of utilizing spare capacity that include unpredictability of the number of hosts and the speed or capacity of each host. When dealing with large corporate computer networks or standardized systems that are idle during the evening, these drawbacks are minimized.

Cost A fourth benefit that can come from grid computing is in terms of cost. One can realize a benefit of scaling efficiently in a grid as it takes advantage of the distributed nature of applications. This can be thought of in terms of scaling the y-axis, as discussed in Chapter 23, Splitting Applications for Scale, and shown in Figure 23.1. As one service or particular computation has more demand placed on it, instead of scaling the entire application or suite of services along an x-axis (horizontal duplication), you can be much more specific and scale only the service or computation that requires the growth. This allows you to spend much more efficiently only on the capacity that is necessary. The other advantage in terms of cost can come from scavenging spare cycles on desktops or other servers, as described in the previous paragraph referencing the SETI@home program.

Pros of Grid Computing

We have identified three major benefits of grid computing. These are listed in no particular order and are not all inclusive. There are many more benefits, but these are representative of the types of benefits you could expect from including grid computing in your infrastructure.

- *High computation rates.* With the amalgamation of multiple hosts on a network, an application can achieve very high computational rates or computational throughput.

- *Shared infrastructure.* Although grids are not necessarily great infrastructure components to share with other applications simultaneously, they are generally not used around the clock and can be shared by applications sequentially.

- *Unused capacity.* For grids that utilize unused hosts during off hours, the grid offers a great use for this untapped capacity. Personal computers are not the only untapped capacity, often testing environments are not utilized during the late evening hours and can be integrated into a grid computing system.

- *Cost.* Whether the grid is scaling the specific program within your service offerings or taking advantage of scavenged capacity, these are both ways to make computations more cost-effective. This is yet another reason to look at grids as scalability solutions.

These are three of the benefits that you may see from integrating a grid computing system into your infrastructure. The amount of benefit that you see from any of these will depend on your specific application and implementation.

Cons of Grids

We are now going to switch from the benefits of utilizing a grid computing infrastructure and talk about the drawbacks. As with the benefits, the significance or importance that you place on each of the drawbacks is going to be directly related to the applications that you are considering for the grid. If your application was designed to be run in parallel and is not monolithic, this drawback may be of little concern to you. However, if you have arrived at a grid computing architecture because your monolithic application has grown to where it cannot compute 24 hours' worth of data in a 24-hour time span and you must do something or else continue to fall behind, this drawback may be of a grave concern to you. We will discuss three major drawbacks as we see them with grid computing. These include the difficulty in sharing the infrastructure simultaneously, the inability to work well with monolithic applications, and the increased complexity of utilizing these infrastructures.

Not Shared Simultaneously The first con or drawback is that it is difficult if not impossible to share the grid computing infrastructure simultaneously. Certainly, some grids are large enough that they have enough capacity for running many applications simultaneously, but they really are still running in separate grid environments, with the hosts just reallocated for a particular time period. For example, if I have a grid that consists of 100 hosts, I could run 10 applications on 10 separate hosts each. Although you should consider this sharing the infrastructure, as we stated in the benefits section earlier, this is not sharing it simultaneously. Running more than one application on the same host defeats the purpose of massive parallel computing that is gained by the grid infrastructure.

Grids are not great infrastructures to share with multiple tenants. You run on a grid to parallelize and increase the computational bandwidth for your application. Sharing or multitenancy can occur serially, one after the other, in a grid environment where each application runs in isolation and when completed the next job runs. This type of scheduling is common among systems that run large parallel processing infrastructures that are designed to be utilized simultaneously to compute large problem sets.

What this means for you running an application is that you must have flexibility built into your application and system to either start and stop processing as necessary or run at a fixed time each time period, usually daily or weekly. Because applications need the infrastructure to themselves, they are often scheduled to run during certain windows. If the application begins to exceed this window, perhaps because of more data to process, the window must be rescheduled to accommodate this or else all other jobs in the queue will get delayed.

Monolithic Applications The next drawback that we see with grid computing infrastructure is that it does not work well with monolithic applications. In fact, if you cannot divide the application into parts that can be run in parallel, the grid will not help processing at all. The throughput of a monolithic application cannot be helped by running on a grid. A monolithic application can be replicated onto many individual servers, as seen in an x-axis split, and the capacity can be increased by adding servers. As we stated in the discussion of Amdahl's law, nonsequential parts of a program will benefit from the parallelization, but the rest of the program will not. Those parts of a program that must run in order, sequentially, are not able to be parallelized.

Complexity The last major drawback that we see in grid computing is the increased complexity of the grid. Hosting and running an application by itself is often complex enough considering the interactions that are required with users, other systems, databases, disk storage, and so on. Add to this already complex and highly volatile environment the need to run this on top of a grid environment and it becomes even more complex. The grid is not just another set of hosts. Running on a grid requires a specialized operating system that among many other things manages which host has which job, what happens when a host dies in the middle of a job, what data the host needs to perform the task, gathering the processed results back afterward, deleting the data from the host, and aggregating the results together. This adds a lot of complexity and if you have ever debugged an application that has hundreds of instances of the same application on different servers, you can imagine the challenge of debugging one application running across hundreds of servers.

Cons of Grid Computing

We have identified three major drawbacks of grid computing. These are listed in no particular order and are not all inclusive. There are many more cons, but these are representative of what you should expect if you include grid computing in your infrastructure.

- *Not shared simultaneously.* The grid computing infrastructure is not designed to be shared simultaneously without losing some of the benefit of running on a grid in the first place. This means that jobs and applications are usually scheduled ahead of time and not run on demand.

- *Monolithic app.* If your application is not able to be divided into smaller tasks, there is little to no benefit of running on a grid. To take advantage of the grid computing infrastructure, you need to be able to break the application into nonsequential tasks that can run independently.

- *Complexity.* Running on a grid environment adds another layer of complexity to your application stack that is probably already complex. If there is a problem, debugging whether the problem exists because of a bug in your application code or the environment that it is running on becomes much more difficult.

These three cons are ones that you may see from integrating a grid computing system into your infrastructure. The significance of each one will depend on your specific application and implementation.

These are the major pros and cons that we see with integrating a grid computing infrastructure into your architecture. As we discussed earlier, the significance that you give to each of these will be determined by your specific application and technology team. As a further example of this, if you have a strong operations team that has experience working with or running grid infrastructures, the increased complexity that comes along with the grid is not likely to deter you. If you have no operations team and no one on your team had to support an application running on a grid, this drawback may give you pause.

If you are still up in the air about utilizing grid computing infrastructure, the next section is going to give you some ideas on where you may consider using a grid. Although you read through some of the ideas, be sure to keep in mind the benefits and drawbacks covered earlier, because these should influence your decision of whether to proceed with a similar project yourself.

Different Uses for Grid Computing

In this section, we are going to cover some ideas and examples that we have either seen or discussed with clients and employers for using grid computing. By sharing these, we aim to give you a sampling of the possible implementations and don't consider this list inclusive at all. There are a myriad of ways to implement and take advantage of a grid computing infrastructure. After everyone becomes familiar with grids, you and your team are surely able to come up with an extensive list of possible projects that could benefit from this architecture, and then you simply have to weigh the pros and cons of each project to determine if any is worth actually implementing. Grid computing is an important tool to utilize when scaling applications, whether in the form of utilizing a grid to scale more cost effectively a single program in your production environment or using it to speed up a step in the product development cycle, such as compilation. Scalability is not just about the production environment, but the processes and people that support it as well. Keep this in mind as you read these examples and consider how grid computing can aid your scalability efforts.

We have four examples that we are going to describe as potential uses for grid computing. These are running your production environment on a grid, using a grid for compilation, implementing parts of a data warehouse environment on a grid, and back office processing on a grid. We know there are many more implementations that are possible, but these should give you a breadth of examples that you can use to jumpstart your own brainstorming session.

Production Grid

The first example usage is of course to use grid computing in your production environment. This may not be possible for applications that require real-time user interactions such as Software as a Service companies. However, for IT organizations that have very mathematically complex applications in use for controlling manufacturing processes or shipping control, this might be a great fit. Lots of these applications have historically resided on mainframe or midrange systems. Many technology organizations are finding it more difficult to support these larger and older machines from both vendor support as well as engineering support. There are fewer engineers who know how to run and program these machines and fewer who would prefer to learn these skill sets instead of Web programming skills.

The grid computing environment offers solutions to both of the problems of machine and engineering support for older technologies. Migrating to a grid that runs lots of commodity hardware as opposed to one strategic piece of hardware is a way to reduce your dependency on a single vendor for support and maintenance. Not only does this push the balance of power into your court, it is possibly a significant cost savings for your organization. At the same time, you should more easily be able to find already trained engineers or administrators who have experience running grids or at the very least find employees who are excited about learning one of the newer technologies.

Build Grid

The next example is using a grid computing infrastructure for your build or compilation machines. If compiling your application takes a few minutes on your desktop, this might seem like overkill, but there are many applications that, running on a single host or developer machine, would take days to compile the entire code base. This is when a build farm or grid environment comes in very handy. Compiling is ideally suited for grids because there are so many divisions of work that can take place, and they can all be performed nonsequentially. The later stages of the build that include linking start to become more sequential and thus not capable of running on a grid, but the early stages are ideal for a division of labor.

Most companies compile or build an executable version of the checked in code each evening so that anyone who needs to test that version can have it available and be sure that the code will actually build successfully. Going days without knowing that the checked in code can build properly will result in hours (if not days) of work by engineers to fix the build before it can be tested by the quality assurance engineers. Not having the build be successful every day and waiting until the last step to get the build working will cause delays for engineers and will likely cause engineers to not check-in code until the very end, which risks losing their work and is a great way to introduce a lot of bugs in the code. By building from the source code repository every night, these problems are avoided. A great source of untapped compilation capacity at night is the testing environments. These are generally used during the day and can be tapped in the evening to help augment the build machines. This concept of CPU scavenging was discussed before, but this is a simple implementation of it that can save quite a bit of money in additional hardware cost.

For C, C++, Objective C, or Objective C++, builds implementing a distributed compilation process can be as simple as running distcc, which as its site (http://www.distcc.org) claims is a fast and free distributed compiler. It works by simply running the distcc daemon on all the servers in the compilation grid, placing the names of these servers in an environmental variable, and then starting the build process.

Build Steps

There are many different types of compilers and many different processes that source code goes through to become code that can be executed by a machine. At a high level, there are either compiled languages or interpreted languages. Forget about just in time (JIT) compilers and bytecode interpreters; compiled languages are ones that the code written by the engineers is reduced to machine readable code ahead of time using a compiler. Interpreted languages use an interpreter to read the code from the source file and execute it at runtime. Here are the rudimentary steps that are followed by most compilation processes and the corresponding input/output:

- *In* Source code

  1. *Preprocessing.* This is usually used to check for syntactical correctness.

- *Out/In* Source code

  2. *Compiling.* This step converts the source code to assembly code based on the language's definitions of syntax.

- *Out/In* Assembly code

  3. *Assembling.* This step converts the assembly language into machine instructions or object code.

- *Out/In* Object code

  4. *Linking.* This final step combines the object code into a single executable.

- *Out* Executable code

A formal discussion of compiling is beyond the scope of this book, but this four-step process is the high-level overview of how source code gets turned into code that can be executed by a machine.

Data Warehouse Grid

The next example that we are going to cover is using a grid as part of the data warehouse infrastructure. There are many components in a data warehouse from the primary source databases to the end reports that users view. One particular component that can make use of a grid environment is the transformation phase of the extract-transform-load step (ETL) in the data warehouse. This ETL process is how data is pulled or extracted from the primary sources, transformed into a different form—usually a denormalized star schema form—and then loaded into the data warehouse. The transformation can be computationally intensive and therefore a primary candidate for the power of grid computing.

The transformation process may be as simple as denormalizing data or it may be as extensive as rolling up many months' worth of sales data for thousands of transactions.

Processing that is very intense such as monthly or even annual rollups can often be broken into multiple pieces and divided among a host of computers. By doing so, this is very suitable for a grid environment. As we covered in Chapter 27, Too Much Data, massive amounts of data are often the cause of not being able to process jobs such as the ETL in the time period required by either customers or internal users. Certainly, you should consider how to limit the amount of data that you are keeping and processing, but it is possible that the amount of data growth is because of an exponential growth in traffic, which is what you want. A solution is to implement a grid computing infrastructure for the ETL to finish these jobs in a timely manner.

Back Office Grid

The last example that we want to cover is back office processing. An example of such back office processing takes place every month in most companies when they close the financial books. This is often a time of massive amounts of processing, data aggregation, and computations. This is usually done with an enterprise resource planning (ERP) system, financial software package, homegrown system, or some combination of these. Attempting to use off-the-shelf software processing on a grid computing infrastructure when the system was not designed to do so may be challenging but it can be done. Often, very large ERP systems allow for quite a bit of customization and configuration. If you have ever been responsible for this process or waited days for this process to be finished, you will agree that being able to run this on possibly hundreds of host computers and finishing within hours would be a monumental improvement. There are many back office systems that are very computationally intensive—end-of-month processing is just one. Others include invoicing, supply reordering, resource planning, and quality assurance testing. Use these as a springboard to develop your own list of potential places for improvement.

We covered four examples of grids in this section: running your production environment on a grid, using a grid for compilation, implementing parts of a data warehouse environment on a grid, and back office processing on a grid. We know there are many more implementations that are possible, and these are only meant to provide you with some examples that you can use to come up with your own applications for grid computing. After you have done so, you can apply the pros and cons along with a weighting score. We will cover how to do this in the next section of this chapter.

MapReduce

We covered MapReduce in Chapter 27, but we should point out here in the chapter on grid computing that MapReduce is an implementation of distributed computing, which is another name for grid computing. In essence, MapReduce is a special case grid computing framework used for text tokenizing and indexing.

Decision Process

Now we will cover the process for deciding which ideas you brainstormed should be pursued. The overall process that we are recommending is to first brainstorm the potential areas of improvement. Using the pros and cons that we outlined in this chapter, as well as any others that you think of, weigh the pros and cons based on your particular application. Score each idea based on the pros and cons. Based on the final tally of pros and cons, decide which ideas if any should be pursued. We are going to provide an example as a demonstration of the steps.

Let's take our company AllScale.com. We currently have no grid computing implementations but we have read *The Art of Scalability* and think it might be worth investigating if grid computing is right for any of our applications. We decide that there are two projects that are worth considering because they are beginning to take too long to process and are backing up other jobs as well as hindering our employees from getting their work done. The projects are the data warehouse ETL and the monthly financial closing of the books. We decide that we are going to use the three pros and three cons identified in the book, but have decided to add one more con: the initial cost of implementing the grid infrastructure.

Now that we have completed step one, we are ready to apply weights to the pros and cons, which is step two. We will use a 1, 3, or 9 scale to rank these in order that we highly differentiate the factors that we care about. The first con is that the grid is not able to be used simultaneously. We don't think this is a very big deal because we are considering implementing this as a private cloud—only our department will utilize it, and we will likely use scavenged CPU to implement. We weigh this as a –1, negative because it is a con and this makes the math easier when we multiply and add the scores. The next con is the inhospitable environment that grids are for monolithic applications. We also don't care much about this con, because both alternative ideas are capable of being split easily into nonsequential tasks. We care somewhat about the increased complexity because although we do have a stellar operations team, we would like to not have them handle too much extra work. We weight this –3. The last con is the cost of implementing. This is a big deal for us because we have a limited infrastructure budget this year and cannot afford to pay much for the grid. We weight this –9 because it is very important to us.

On the pros, we consider the fact that grids have high computational rates very important to us because this is the primary reason that we are interested in the technology. We are going to weight this +9. The next pro on the list is that a grid is shared infrastructure. We like that we can potentially run multiple applications, in sequence, on the grid computing infrastructure, but it is not that important, so we weight it +1. The last pro to weight is that grids can make us of unused capacity, such as with CPU scavenging. Along with minimizing the cost being a very important goal for us, this ability to use extra or surplus capacity is important also, and we weight it +9. This concludes step 2, the weighting of the pros and cons.

The next step is to score each alternative idea on a scale from 0 to 5 to demonstrate each of the pros and cons. As an example, we ranked the ETL project as shown in Table 30.1, because it would potentially be the only application running on the grid at this time; thus, it has a minor relationship with the con of "not simultaneously shared." The cost is important to both projects and because the monthly financial closing project is larger, we ranked it higher on the "cost of implementation." On the pros, both projects benefit greatly from the higher computational rates, but the month financial closing project requires more processing so it is ranked higher. We plan on utilizing unused capacity such as in our QA environment for the grid, so we ranked it high for both projects. We continued in this manner scoring each project until the entire matrix was filled in.

Step four is to multiply the scores by the weights and then sum the products up for each project. For the ETL example, we multiply the weight −1 by the score 1, add it to the product of the second weight −1 by the score 1 again, and continue in this manner with the final calculation looking like this: $(1 \times -1) + (1 \times -1) + (1 \times -3) + (3 \times -9) + (3 \times 9) + (1 \times 1) + (4 \times 9) = 32$.

As part of the final, we analyze the scores for each alternative and apply a level of common sense to it. In this example, we have the two ideas—ETL and monthly financial closing—scored as 32 and 44, respectively. In this case, both projects look likely to be beneficial and we should consider them both as very good potentials for moving forward. Before automatically assuming that this is our decision, we should verify that based on our common sense and other factors that might not have been included, this is a sound decision. If something appears to be off or you want to add

Table 30.1 *Grid Decision Matrix*

		Weight (1, 3, or 9)	ETL	Monthly Financial Closing
Cons	Not simultaneously shared	−1	1	1
	Not suitable for monolithic apps	−1	1	1
	Increased complexity	−3	1	3
	Cost of implementation	−9	3	3
Pros	High computational rates	9	3	5
	Shared infrastructure	1	1	1
	Unused capacity	9	4	4
Total			32	44

other factors, you should redo the matrix or have several people do the scoring independently.

The decision process is designed to provide you with a formal method of evaluating ideas assessed against pros and cons. Using these types of matrixes, the data can help us make decisions or at a minimum lay out our decision process in a logical manner.

Decision Steps

The following are steps to take to help make a decision about whether you should introduce grid computing into your infrastructure:

1. Develop alternative ideas for how to use grid computing.
2. Place weights on all the pros and cons that you can come up with.
3. Score the alternative ideas using the pros and cons.
4. Tally scores for each idea by multiplying the score by the weight and summing.

This decision matrix process will help you make data driven decisions about which ideas should be pursued to include grid computing as part of your infrastructure.

As with cloud computing, the most likely question is not *whether* to implement a grid computing environment, but rather *where* and *when* you should implement it. Grid computing offers a good alternative to scaling applications that are growing quickly and need intensive computational power. Choosing the right project for the grid for it to be successful is critical and should be done with as much thought and data as possible.

Conclusion

In this chapter, we covered the pros and cons of grid computing, provided some real-world examples of where grid computing might fit, and covered a decision matrix to help you decide what projects make the most sense for utilizing the grid. We discussed three pros: high computational rates, shared infrastructure, and unused capacity. We also covered three cons: the environment is not shared well simultaneously, monolithic applications need not apply, and increased complexity.

We provided four real-world examples of where we see possible fits for grid computing. These examples included the production environment of some applications, the transformation part of the data warehousing ETL process, the building or com-piling process for applications, and the back office processing of computationally intensive tasks. Each of these is a great example where you may have a need for fast and large amounts of computations. Not all similar applications can make use of the grid, but parts of many of them can be implemented on a grid. Perhaps the entire ETL process doesn't make sense to run on a grid, but the transformation process might be the key part that needs the additional computations.

The last section of this chapter was the decision matrix. We provided a framework for companies and organizations to use to think through logically which projects make the most sense for implementing a grid computing infrastructure. We outlined a four-step process that included identifying likely projects, weighting the pros/cons, scoring the projects against the pros/cons, and then summing and tallying the final scores.

Grid computing does offer some very positive benefits when implemented cor-rectly and the drawbacks are minimized. This is another very important technology and concept that can be utilized in the fight to scale your organization, processes, and technology. Grids offer the ability to scale computationally intensive programs and should be considered for production as well as supporting processes. As grid comput-ing and other technologies become available and more mainstream, technologists need to stay current on them, at least in sufficient detail to make good decisions about whether they make sense for your organization and applications.

Key Points

- Grid computing offers high computation rates.
- Grid computing offers shared infrastructure for applications using them sequentially.
- Grid computing offers a good use of unused capacity in the form of CPU scavenging.
- Grid computing is not good for sharing simultaneously with other applications.
- Grid computing is not good for monolithic applications.
- Grid computing does add some amount of complexity.
- Desktop computers and other unused servers are a potential for untapped com-putational resources.

Chapter 31

Monitoring Applications

Gongs and drums, banners and flags, are means whereby the ears and
eyes of the host may be focused on one particular point.

—Sun Tzu

No book on scale would be complete without addressing the unique monitoring
needs of systems that process a large volume of transactions. When you are small or
growing slowly, you have plenty of time to identify and correct deficiencies in the systems that cause customer experience problems. Furthermore, you aren't really interested in systems to help you identify scalability related issues early, as your slow
growth obviates the need for such systems. However, when you are large or growing
quickly or both, you have to be in front of your monitoring needs. You need to identify scale bottlenecks quickly or suffer prolonged and painful outages. Further, small
deltas in response time that might not be meaningful to customer experience today
might end up being brownouts tomorrow when customer demand increases an additional 10%. In this chapter, we will discuss the reason why many companies struggle
in near perpetuity with monitoring their platforms and how to fix that struggle by
employing a framework for maturing monitoring over time. We will discuss what
kind of monitoring is valuable from a qualitative perspective and how that monitoring will aid our metrics and measurements from a quantitative perspective. Finally,
we will address how monitoring fits into some of our processes including the headroom and capacity planning processes from Chapter 11, Determining Headroom for
Applications, and incident and crisis management processes from Chapters 8, Managing Incidents and Problems, and 9, Managing Crisis and Escalations, respectively.

"How Come We Didn't Catch That Earlier?"

If you've been around technical platforms, technology systems, back office IT systems, or product platforms for more than a few days, you've likely heard questions

like, "How come we didn't catch that earlier?" associated with the most recent failure, incident, or crisis. If you're as old as or older than we are, you've probably forgotten just how many times you've heard that question or a similar one. The answer is usually pretty easy and it typically revolves around a service, component, application, or system not being monitored or not being monitored correctly. The answer usually ends with something like, ". . . and this problem will never happen again."

Even if that problem never happens again, and in our experience most often the problem *does* happen again, a similar problem will very likely occur. The same question is asked, potentially a postmortem conducted, and actions are taken to monitor the service correctly "again."

The question of "How come we didn't catch it?" has a use, but it's not nearly as valuable as asking an even better question such as, "What in our process is flawed that allowed us to launch the service without the appropriate monitoring to catch such an issue as this?" You may think that these two questions are similar, but they are not. The first question, "How come we didn't catch that earlier?" deals with this issue, this point in time, and is marginally useful in helping drive the right behaviors to resolve the incident we just had. The second question, on the other hand, addresses the people and process that allowed the event you just had and every other event for which you did not have the appropriate monitoring. Think back, if you will, to Chapter 8 wherein we discussed the relationship of incidents and problems. A problem causes an incident and may be related to multiple incidents. Our first question addresses the incident, and not the problem. Our second question addresses the problem. Both questions should probably be asked, but if you are going to ask and expect an answer (or a result) from only one question, we argue you should fix the problem rather than the incident.

We argue that the most common reason for not catching problems through monitoring is that most systems aren't designed to be monitored. Rather, most systems are designed and implemented and monitoring is an afterthought. Often, the team responsible for determining if the system or application is working properly had no hand in defining the behaviors of the system or in designing it. The most common result is that the monitoring performed on the application is developed by the team least capable of determining if the application is performing properly. This in turn causes critical success or failure indicators to be missed and very often means that the monitoring system is guaranteed to "fail" relative to internal expectations in identifying critical customer impact issues before they become crises.

Note that "designing to be monitored" means so much more than just understanding how to properly monitor a system for success and failure. Designing to be monitored is an approach wherein one builds monitoring into the application or system rather than around it. It goes beyond logging that failures have occurred and toward identifying themes of failure and potentially even performing automated escalation of issues or concerns from an application perspective. A system that is designed to be monitored might evaluate the response times of all of the services with which it interacts and alert someone when response times are out of the normal range for that time of day. This same system might also evaluate the rate of error logging it performs over time and also alert the right people when that rate significantly changes or the composition of the errors changes. Both of these approaches might be accomplished by employing a statistical process control chart that alerts when rates of errors or response times fall outside of N standard deviations from a mean calculated from the last 30 similar days at that time of day. Here, a "similar" day would mean comparing a Monday to a Monday and a Saturday to a Saturday.

When companies have successfully implemented a Designed to Be Monitored architectural principle, they begin asking a third question. This question is asked well before the implementation of any of the systems and it usually takes place in the Architectural Review Board (ARB) or the Joint Applications Design (JAD) meetings (see Chapters 14 and 13, respectively, for a definition of these meetings). The question is most often phrased as, "How do we know this system is functioning properly and how do we know when it is starting to behave poorly?" Correct responses to this third question might include elements of our statistical process control solution mentioned earlier. Any correct answer should include something other than that the application logs errors. Remember, we want the system to tell us when it is behaving not only differently than expected, but when it is behaving differently than normal. These are really two very different things.

Note that the preceding is a significant change in approach compared to having the operations team develop a set of monitors for the application that consists of looking for simple network management protocol (SNMP) traps or *grepping* through logs for strings that engineers indicate are of some importance. It also goes well beyond simply looking at CPU utilization, load, memory utilization, and so on. That's not to say that all of those aren't also important, but they won't buy you nearly as much as ensuring that the application is intelligent about its own health.

The second most common reason for not catching problems through monitoring is that we approach monitoring differently than we approach most of our other engineering endeavors. We very often don't design our monitoring or we approach it in a methodical evolutionary fashion. Most of the time, we just apply effort to it and hope that we get most of our needs covered. Often, we rely on production incidents and crises to mature our monitoring, and this approach in turn creates a patchwork quilt with no rhyme or reason. When asked for what we monitor, we will likely give all of the typical answers covering everything from application logs to system resource utilization, and we might even truthfully indicate that we also monitor for most of the indications of past major incidents. Rarely will we answer that our monitoring is engineered with the same rigors that we design and implement our platform or services. The following is a framework to resolve this second most common problem.

A Framework for Monitoring

How often have you found yourself in a situation where, during a postmortem, you identify that your monitoring system actually flagged the early indications of a potential scalability or availability issue? Maybe space alarms were triggered on a database that went unanswered or potentially CPU utilization thresholds across several services were exceeded. Maybe you had response time monitoring enabled between services and saw a slow increase in the time for calls of a specific service over a number of months. "How," you might ask yourself, "did these go unnoticed?"

Maybe you even voice your concerns to the team. A potential answer might be that the monitoring system simply gives too many false positives (or false negatives) or that there is too much noise in the system. Maybe the head of the operations team even indicates that she has been asking for months that they be given money to replace the monitoring system or given the time and flexibility to reimplement the current system. "If we only take some of the noise out of the system, my team can sleep better and address the real issues that we face," she might say. We've heard the reasons for new and better monitoring systems time and again, and although they are sometimes valid, most often we believe they result in a destruction of shareholder value. The real issue isn't typically that the monitoring system is not meeting the needs of the company; it is that the approach to monitoring is all wrong. The team very likely has a good portion of the needs nailed, but it started at the wrong end of the monitoring needs spectrum.

Although having Design to Be Monitored as an architectural principle is necessary to resolve the recurring "Why didn't we catch that earlier?" problem, it is not sufficient to solve all of our monitoring problems or all of our monitoring needs. We need to plan our monitoring and expect that we are going to evolve it over time. Just as Agile software development methods attempt to solve the problem associated with not knowing all of your requirements before you develop a piece of software, so must we have an agile and evolutionary development mindset for our monitoring platforms and systems. This evolutionary method we propose answers three questions, with each question supporting the delineation incidents and problems that we identified in Chapter 8.

The first question that we ask in our evolutionary model for monitoring is, "Is there a problem?" Specifically, we are interested in determining whether the system is not behaving correctly and most often we are really asking if there is a problem that customers can or will experience. Many companies in our experience completely bypass this very important question and immediately dive into an unguided exploration of the next question we should ask, "Where is the problem located?" or even worse, "What is the problem?"

In monitoring, bypassing "Is there a problem?" or more aptly, "What is the problem that customers are experiencing?" assumes that you know for all cases what systems will cause what problems and in what way. Unfortunately, this isn't often the case. In fact, we've had many clients waste literally man years of effort in trying to identify the source of the problem without ever truly understanding what the problem is. You have likely taken classes in which the notion of framing the problem or developing the right question has been drilled into you. The idea is that you should not start down the road of attempting to solve a problem or perform analysis before you understand what exactly you are trying to solve. Other examples where this holds true are in the etiquette of meetings, where the meeting typically has a title and purpose, and in product marketing, where we first frame the target audience before attempting to develop a product or service for that market's needs. The same holds true with monitoring systems and applications: We must know that there is a problem and how the problem manifests itself if we are to be effective in identifying its source.

Not building systems that first answer, "Is there a problem?" result in two additional issues. The first issue is that our teams often chase false positives and then very often start to react to the constant alerts as noise. This makes our system less useful over time as we stop investigating alerts that may turn out to be rather large problems. We ultimately become conditioned to ignore alerts, regardless of whether they are important.

This conditioning results in a second and more egregious issue: Customers informing us of our problems. Customers don't want to be the one telling you about problems or issues with your systems or products, especially if you are a hosted solution such as an application service provider (ASP) or Software as a Service (SaaS) provider. Customers expect that at best they are telling you something that you already know and that you are deep in the process of fixing whatever issue they are experiencing. Unfortunately, because we do not spend time building systems to tell us that there is a problem, often the irate customer is the first indication that we have a problem. Systems that answer the question, "Is there a problem?" are very often customer focused systems that interact with our platform as if they are our customer. They may also be diagnostic services built into our platform similar to the statistical process control example given earlier.

The next question to answer in evolutionary fashion is, "Where is the problem?" We now have built a system that tells us definitively that we have a problem somewhere in our system, ideally correlated with a single or a handful of business metrics. Now we need to isolate where the problem exists. These types of systems very often are broad category collection agents that give us indications of resource utilization over time. Ideally, they are graphical in nature and maybe we are even applying our neat little statistical process control chart trick. Maybe we even have a nice user interface that gives us a *heat map* indicating areas or sections of our system that are not performing as we would expect. These types of systems are really meant to help us quickly identify where we should be applying our efforts in isolating what exactly the problem is or what the root cause of our incident might be.

Before progressing, we'll pause and outline what might happen within a system that bypassed "Is there a problem?" to address, "Where is the problem?" As we've previously indicated, this is an all too common occurrence. You might have an operations center with lots of displays, dials, and graphs. Maybe you've even implemented the heat map system we alluded to earlier. Without first knowing that there is a customer problem occurring, your team might be going through the daily "whack a mole" process of looking at every subsystem that turns slightly red for some period of time. Maybe it spends several minutes identifying that there was nothing other than an anomalous disk utilization event occurring and potentially the team relaxes the operations defined threshold for turning that subsystem red at any given time. All the while, customer support is receiving calls regarding end users's inability to log into the system. Customer support first assumes this is the daily rate of failed logins, but after 10 minutes of steady calls, customer support contacts the operations center to get some attention applied to the issue.

As it turns out, CPU utilization and user connections to the login service were also "red" in our systems heat map while we were addressing the disk utilization report. Now, we are nearly 15 minutes into a customer related event and we have yet to begin our diagnosis. If we had a monitoring system that reported on customer transactions, we would have addressed the failed logins incident first before addressing other problems that were not directly affecting customer experience. In this case, a monitoring solution that is capable of showing a reduction of certain types of transactions over time would have indicated that there was a potential problem (logins failing) and the operations team likely would have then looked for monitoring alerts from the systems identifying the location of the problem such as the CPU utilization alerts on the login services.

The last question in our evolutionary model of monitoring is to answer, "What is the problem?" Note that we've moved from identifying that there is an incident, consistent with our definition in Chapter 8, to isolating the area causing that incident to identification of the problem itself, which helps us quickly get to the root cause of any issues within our system. As we move from identifying that something is going on to determining the cause for the incident, two things happen. The first is that the amount of data that we need to collect as we evolve from the first to the third question grows. We only need a few pieces of data to identify whether something, somewhere is wrong. But to be able to answer, "What is the problem?" across the entire range of possible problems that we might have, we need to collect a whole lot of data over a substantial period of time. The other thing that is going on is that we are naturally narrowing our focus from the very broad "something is going on" to the very narrow "I've found what is going on." The two are inversely correlated in terms of size, as Figure 31.1 indicates. The more specific the answer to the question, the more data we need to collect to determine the answer.

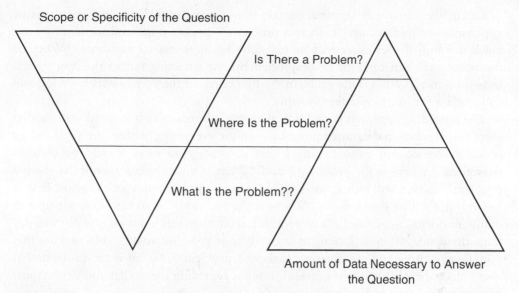

Figure 31.1 *Correlation of Data Size to Problem Specificity*

To be able to answer precisely for all problems what the source is, we must have quite a bit of data. The actual problem itself can likely be answered with one very small slice of this data, but to have that answer we have to collect data for all potential problems. Do you see the problem this will cause? Without building a system that's intelligent enough to determine if there is a problem, we will allocate people at several warnings of potential problems, and in the course of doing so will start to create an organization that ignores those warnings. A better approach is to build a system that alerts on impacting or pending events and then uses that as a trigger to guide us to the root cause.

"What is the problem?" is usually a deeper iteration of "Where is the problem?" Statistical process control can again be used in an even more granular basis to help identify the cause. Maybe, assuming we have the space and resources to do so, we can plot the run times of each of our functions within our application over time. We can use the most recent 24 hours of data, compare it to the last week of data, and compare the last week of data to the last month of data. We don't have to keep the granular by transaction records for each of our calls, but rather aggregate them over time for the purposes of comparison. We can compare the rates of errors for each of our services by error type for the time of day and day of week in question. Here, we are looking at the functions, methods, and objects that comprise a service rather than the operation of the service itself. As indicated earlier, it requires a lot more data, but we can answer precisely what exactly the problem is for nearly any problem we are experiencing.

Often, we can easily segment our three questions into three different types or approaches to monitoring. "Is there a problem?" can often be implemented by finding a handful of user experience or real-time business metrics monitors. "Where is the problem?" can often be accomplished by implementing out of the box system level monitors. "What is the problem?" often relies on the way in which we log and collect data for our proprietary systems.

The preceding approach is methodical in that it forces us first to build systems that identify problems before attempting to monitor everything within our platform or product. We do not mean to imply that absolutely no work should be done in answering "Where is the problem?" and "What is the problem?" until "Is there a problem?" is finished; rather, one should focus on applying most of the effort first in answering the first question. As "Where is the problem?" is so easy to implement in many platforms, applying 20% of your initial effort to this question initially will pay huge dividends, whereas forcing at least 50% of your initial effort to ensuring that you always know and can answer "Is there a problem?" "What is the problem?" is often more difficult and takes careful thought regarding the design and deployment of your proprietary technology.

User Experience and Business Metrics

User experience and business metric monitors are meant to answer the question of "Is there a problem?" Often, you need to implement both of them to get a good view of the overall health of a system, but in many cases, you need only a handful to be able to answer the question of whether a problem exists with a high degree of certainty. For instance, in an ecommerce platform wherein revenue and profits are generated primarily from sales, you may choose to look at revenue, searches, shopping cart abandonment, and product views. You may decide to plot each of these in real time against 7 days ago, 14 days ago, and the average of the last 52 similar weekdays. Any significant deviation from a well-established curve may be used to alert the team that a potential problem is occurring.

Advertising platforms may focus on cost per click by time of day, total clicks, calculated click through rates, and bid to item ratios. These too may be plotted against the values from 7 days ago, 14 days ago, and the average of the last 52 similar week days. Again, the idea here is to identify major business and customer experience metrics that are both early and current indicators of problems.

Third-party providers also offer *last mile* and *customer experience* monitoring solutions that are useful in augmenting business metrics and user experience monitoring. Last mile and user agent monitoring solutions from Keynote and Gomez help us better understand when customers at distant locations can't access our services and when those services are performing below our expectations. User experience solutions such as CA's Wily products and Coradiant's products help us better understand customer interactions, actions, and perceived response times.

Other metrics and thresholds that might affect your business can be considered such as response times and such, but often these are more indicative of "where the problem is" rather than that a problem exists. The best metrics here are directly correlated to the creation of shareholder value. A high shopping cart abandonment rate and significantly lower click through rates are both indicative of likely user experience problems that are negatively impacting your business.

Systems Monitoring

As we've hinted at earlier in this chapter, this is one of the areas that companies tend to cover well. We use the term *systems monitoring* to identify any grouping of hardware and software that share several components. We might have a service consisting of several functions or applications running on a pool of servers and we lump this loose group of hardware and software into a "system." Most monitoring systems and platforms have agents that do this type of monitoring fairly well right out-of-the-box. You simply need to install the agents, configure them for your system, and plug them into your monitoring framework. Where we tend to fail is in augmenting the tools to help us identify where there is a problem. Often, we rely on threshold alerts or highly calibrated eyeballs to identify issues.

The problem with thresholds is that they are too often based on arbitrary values. "We shouldn't go beyond 80% utilization for any given system." A better approach is for us to be alerted when a system is behaving significantly different than the way it has behaved in the past. This variation in approach is the basis for our recommendations to investigate statistical process control, or at the very least, the plotting of values as compared to past values for a similar date and time as a method for identifying issues.

We are relying on systems monitoring to tell us "where the problem is." We have a new problem identified by our end user and business monitoring and, as it is a new problem, we are probably looking for something that is performing differently than it performed before the problem started. Threshold monitoring tells us that something is performing outside of our expectation, but what is even more valuable is for our system to tell us what is performing significantly differently than it has performed in the past.

Application Monitoring

Application monitoring is important to help identify "what is the problem?" Often, to answer the question of "what is the problem?" we need to write some custom monitoring code. To do this well, we probably need to build the code into our product offering itself. Although some out-of-the-box agents will tell us exactly what the problem is, as in the case of a slow I/O subsystem caused by one or more bad disks, it is seldom the case that an out-of-the-box agent can help us diagnose what part of our proprietary application has gone awry. Although the thought of self-healing applications are a bit of a pipe dream and not likely to be cost-effective in terms of development time, the notion that an application can be self-diagnosing for the most common types of failures is both an admirable and achievable aspiration.

For many companies, it is a relatively simple task, if undertaken early in development, to produce a set of reusable tools to help determine the cause of failures. These tools exist as services that are compiled or linked to the application or potentially just services called by the application during runtime. Often, they are at critical chokepoints within the application such as during the emission of an error or the calling of another service or resource. Error logging routines can be augmented to classify error types in a meaningful fashion and keep track of the rate of error counts over time. Methods or functions can keep track of execution times by time of day and log them in a meaningful fashion for other processes to perform calculations. Remote service calls can log the response time of synchronous or asynchronous services on which an application relies.

Monitoring Issues and a General Framework

Most monitoring platforms suffer from two primary problems:

- The systems being monitored were not designed to be monitored.
- The approach to monitoring is bottom up rather than top down and misses the critical question "Is there a problem affecting customers right now?"

Solving these problems is relatively easy:

- Designing your systems to be monitored before implementation.
- Developing monitors to first answer the question "Is there a problem?" These are typically business metric and customer experience monitors.
- Developing monitors to next answer "Where is the problem?" These are typically systems level monitors.
- When completed with the first two questions, developing monitors to answer the question "What is the problem?" Often, these are monitors that you build into your application consistent with your design principles.

It is very important to follow the steps in order, from top down, to develop a world-class monitoring solution.

Measuring Monitoring: What Is and Isn't Valuable?

Remember Chapter 27, Too Much Data? In that chapter, we argued that not all data is valuable to the company and that all data has a cost. Well, guess what? The same is true for monitoring! If you monitor absolutely everything you can think of, there is a very real chance that you will use very little of the data that you collect. All the while, you will be creating the type of noise we described as being the harbinger of death for most monitoring platforms. Moreover, you are wasting employee time and company resources, which in turn cost your shareholders money.

The easiest way to help us understand which monitors provide us value and which do not are to step through our evolutionary monitoring framework in a top-down fashion and describe the value created by each of these tiers and how to limit the cost of implementation.

Our first question was "Is there a problem?" As we previously indicated, there are likely a handful, let's say no less than three and no more than 10 monitors, that will both serve as predictive and current indicators that there will be or currently is a problem. As the number of items that we are tracking is relatively small, data retention should not be that great of a concern. It would be great to be able to plot this data in minute or hourly records as compared to at least the last two weeks of similar days of the week. If today is Tuesday, we probably want the last two Tuesdays' worth of data. We probably should just keep that data for at least the last two weeks but maybe we expand it to a month before we collapse the data. In the grand scheme of things, this data will not take a whole lot of space. Moreover, it will save us a lot of time in predicting and determining if there will be or currently is a problem.

The next question we ask is "Where is the problem?" In Figure 31.1, our pyramid indicates that although the specificity is narrowing, the amount of data is increasing. This should cause us some concern as we will need many more monitors to accomplish this. It is likely that the number of monitors is somewhere between an order of magnitude and two orders of magnitude (10 to 100) greater than our original sets of monitors. In very large, complex, and distributed systems, this might be an even larger number. We still need to compare information to previous similar days, ideally at a granular level. But we are going to need to be much more aggressive in our rollup and archival/deletion strategies. Ideally, we will summarize data potentially first by the hour and then eventually just move the data into a moving average calculation. Maybe we plot and keep graphs but remove the raw data over time. We certainly do not want the raw data sitting around ad infinitum as the probability that most of it will be used is low, the value is low, and the cost is high.

Finally, we come to the question of "What is the problem?" Again, we have at least an order of magnitude increase from our previous monitoring. We are adding raw output logs, error logs, and other data to the mix. This stuff grows quickly, especially in chatty environments. We probably hope to keep about two weeks of the data, where two weeks is determined by assuming that we will catch most issues within two weeks. You may have better information on what to keep and what to remove, but again you simply cannot subject your shareholders to your desire to check up on anything at any time. That desire has a near infinite cost and a very, very low relative return.

Monitoring and Processes

Alas, we come to the point of how all of this monitoring fits into our operations and business processes. Our monitoring infrastructure is the lifeblood of many of our processes. The monitoring we perform to answer the questions of "Is there a problem?" to "What is the problem?" will likely create the data necessary to inform the decisions within many of the processes we described in Part II, Building Processes for Scale, and even some of the measurements and metrics we described within Chapter 5, Management 101.

The monitors that produce data necessary to answer the question of "Is there a problem?" produce critical data for measuring our alignment to the creation of shareholder value. You might remember that we discussed availability as a metric in Chapter 5. The goal is to be able to consistently answer "No" to the question of "Is there a problem?" If you can do that, you have high availability. Measuring availability from a customer perspective and from a business metric perspective, as opposed to a technology perspective, gives you both the tools to answer the "Is there a problem?" question and to measure yourself against your availability goal. The difference between revenue or customer availability and technology availability is important and drives cultural changes that have incredible benefit to the organization. Technologists have long measured availability as a product of the availability of all the devices within their care. That absolutely has a place and is important to such concerns as cost, mean time between failures, headcount needs, redundancy needs, mean time to restore, and so on. But it doesn't really relate to what the shareholders or customers care about most; what these constituents care about most is that the service is available and generating the greatest value possible. As such, measuring the experience of customers and the generation of profits in real time is much more valuable for both answering our first and most important monitoring question and measuring availability. With only a handful of monitors we can satisfy one of our key management measurements, help ensure that we are identifying and reacting to impending and current events, and align our culture to the creation of shareholder and customer value.

The monitors that drive "Where is the problem?" are also very often the sources of data that we will use in our capacity planning and headroom processes from Chapter 11, Determining Headroom for Applications. The raw data here will help us determine where we have constraints in our system and help us focus our attention on budgeting to horizontally scale those platforms or drive the architectural changes necessary to scale more cost effectively. This information also helps feed our incident and crisis management processes of Chapters 8 and 9. It is obviously useful during the course of an incident or crisis and it definitely proves valuable during postmortem activities when we are attempting to find out how we could have isolated the incident earlier or prevented the incident from happening. The data also feeds into and helps inform changes to our performance testing processes.

The data that answers the question of "What is the problem?" is useful in many of the processes described for "Where is the problem?" Additionally, it is useful in helping us test whether we are properly designing our systems to be monitored. The output of our postmortems and operations reviews should be taken by the engineering staff and analyzed against the data and information we produce to help us identify and diagnose problems. The intent is that we feed this information back to our code review and design review processes so that we are creating better and more intelligent monitoring that helps us identify issues before they occur or isolate them faster when they do occur.

That leaves us with the management of incidents and problems as identified within Chapter 8 and the management of crises and escalations as identified in Chapter 9. In the ideal world, incidents and crises are predicted and avoided by a robust and predictive monitoring solution, but at the very least, they should be identified at the point at which they start to cause customer problems and impact shareholder value. In many mature monitoring solutions, the monitoring system itself will be responsible not only for the initial detection of an incident but for the reporting or recording of that incident. In this fashion, the monitoring system is responsible for both the Detect and Report of our DRIER model identified in Chapter 8.

Conclusion

This chapter discussed monitoring. We posited that the primary reasons for most monitoring initiatives and platforms failing repeatedly is that our systems are not designed to be monitored and that our general approach to monitoring is flawed. Too often, we attempt to monitor from the bottom up, starting with individual agents and logs rather than attempting to first create monitors that answer the question of "Is there a problem?"

The best organizations design their monitoring platforms from the top down. These systems first are capable, with a high degree of accuracy, in answering the question of "Is there a problem?" The types of monitors that answer these questions best are tightly aligned with the business and technology drivers that create shareholder value. Most often, these are real-time monitors on transaction volumes, revenue creation, cost of revenue, and customer interactions with the system. Third-party customer experience systems can be employed to augment real-time business metric systems to answer this most important question.

The next step, when we've properly built systems to answer "Is there a problem?" is to answer build systems to answer "Where is the problem?" Often, these systems are out-of-the-box third-party or open source solutions that you install on systems to monitor resource utilization. Some application monitors might also be employed. The data collected by these systems help inform other processes such as our capacity planning process and problem resolution process. Care must be taken to avoid a combinatorial explosion of data, as that data is costly and the value of immense amounts of old data is very low.

Finally, we move to answer the question of "What is the problem?" This very often requires us to rely heavily on our architectural principal Design to Be Monitored. Here, we are monitoring individual components, and often these are proprietary applications for which we are responsible. Again, the concerns of data explosion are present, and we must fight to ensure that we are keeping the right data and not diluting shareholder value.

Focusing first on "Is there a problem?" will pay huge dividends throughout the life of your monitoring system. It is not necessary to focus 100% of your monitoring efforts on answering this question, but it is important to spend a majority (50% or more) of your time on the question until you have it absolutely nailed.

Key Points

- Most monitoring platforms suffer from a failure to properly design systems to be monitored and a bottom-up approach to monitoring that fails to answer the most important questions first.

- Adding Design to Be Monitored as an architectural principle helps fix this problem.

- A change in approach to be top down rather than bottom up solves the second half of the problem.

- Answering the questions of "is there a problem?", "where is the problem?", and "what is the problem?" in that order when designing a monitoring system is an effective top-down strategy.

- "Is there a problem?" monitors are best answered by aligning the monitors to the measurements of shareholder and stakeholder value creation. Real-time business metrics and customer experience metrics should be employed.

- "Where is the problem?" monitors may very well be out-of-the-box third-party or open source solutions that are relatively simple to deploy. Be careful with data retention and attempt to use real-time statistics when employing these measurements.

- "What is the problem?" monitors are most likely homegrown and integrated into your proprietary application.

Chapter 32

Planning Data Centers

Having collected an army and concentrated his forces, he must blend and harmonize the different elements thereof before pitching his camp.

—Sun Tzu

One of the biggest limitations to hyper-growth companies scaling effectively today is the data center. You can absolutely nail everything else in this book including building and incenting the right team and behaviors, developing and implementing the right processes, and architecting the best solutions, and completely fail your customers and shareholders by limiting growth due to ineffective data center planning. Depending upon your needs, approach, and size, it can take anywhere from months to years to bring additional data center or collocation space online. When contrasted with the weeks or months that it might take to make significant architectural changes, management and leadership changes, and process changes, it is easy to see that the data center can very easily and very quickly become your greatest barrier to scale and success.

This chapter will not give you everything you need to know to plan and manage a data center or collocation build out or move; to do so in enough detail to be meaningful to your efforts would require an entire book. Instead, we want to reinforce the need for long-term data center planning as part of your engineering team efforts. We will also highlight some approaches that we hope will be meaningful to reduce your overall costs as you start to implement multiple data centers and mitigate your business risks with disaster recovery and business continuity plans. We will also cover at a high level some of the drivers of data center costs and constraints.

Data Center Costs and Constraints

In the last 15 years, something in data centers changed so slowly that few if any of us caught on until it was just too late. This slow and steady movement should have been obvious to us all as the data was right under our noses if we had only bothered to look at it. But just as a military sniper moves very slowly into a firing position even as the enemy watches but remains unaware of his presence, so did power consumption and constraints sneak up on us and make us scramble to change our data center capacity planning models.

For years, processors have increased in speed as observed by Gordon Moore and as described in Moore's Law. This incredible increase in speed resulted in computers and servers drawing more power over time. The ratio of clock speed to power consumption varies with the technologies employed and the types of chips. Some chips employed technology to reduce clock speed and hence power consumption when idle, and multicore processors allegedly have lower power consumption for higher clock speeds. But given similar chip set architectures, a faster processor will typically mean more power consumption.

Until the mid 1990s, most data centers had enough power capacity that the primary constraint was the number of servers one could shoehorn into the footprint or square footage of the data center. As computers decreased in size in rack units or U's and increased in clock speed, the data center became increasingly efficient. Efficiency here is measured strictly against the computing capacity per square foot of the data center, with more computers crammed into the same square footage and with each computer having more clock cycles per second to perform work. This increase in computing density also increased power consumption on a per square foot basis. Not only did the computers themselves draw more power per square foot, they also required more HVAC to cool the area and as a result even more power was drawn. If you were lucky enough to be in a collocation facility with a contract wherein you were charged by square foot of space, you weren't likely aware of this increase in cost; the cost was eaten by the collocation facility owner causing decreased margins for their services. If you owned your own data center, more than likely, the facilities team identified the steady but slow increase in cost but did not pass that information along to you until you needed to use more space and found out that you were out of power.

Rack Units

A rack unit is a measurement of height in a 19-inch or 23-inch wide rack. Typically labeled as a U and sometimes labeled as an RU, the unit equals 1.75 inches in height. A 2U server is therefore 3.5 inches in height. The term *half rack* is an indication of width rather than height and the term is applied to a 19-inch rack. A half rack server or component, then, is 9.5 inches wide.

This shift where power utilization suddenly constrained our growth caused a number of interesting problems. The first problem manifested itself in an industry once based upon square footage assumptions. Collocation and managed server providers found themselves in contracts for square footage largely predicated on a number of servers. As previously indicated, the increase in power utilization decreased the margins for their services until the provider could renegotiate contracts. The buyers of the collocation facilities in turn looked to move to locations where power density was greater. Successful providers of services changed their contracts to charge for both space and power, or strictly upon power used. The former allowed companies to flex prices based on the price of power, thereby lowering the variability within their operating margins, whereas the former attempted to model power costs over time to ensure that they were always profitable. Often, both would reduce the power and space component to a number of racks and power utilization per rack within a given footprint in a data center.

Companies that owned their own data centers and found themselves constrained by power could not build new data centers quickly enough to allow themselves to grow. As such, they would turn to implement their growth in services within collocation facilities until such time as they could build new data centers, often with more power per square foot than the previous data centers.

Regardless of whether we owned or leased space, the world changed underneath our feet and the new world order was that power, and not space, dictated our capacity planning for data centers. This has led to some other important aspects of data center planning, not all of which has been fully embraced or recognized by every company.

Location, Location, Location

Most of us have heard of the real estate mantra "location, location, location." Nowhere is this mantra more important these days than in the planning of owned or rented space for data centers. Data center location has an impact on nearly everything you do from fixed and variable costs through quality of service and to the risk you impose upon your business.

With the shift in data center constraints from location to power, so came a shift in the fixed and variable costs of our product offerings. Previously, when space was the primary driver and limitation of data center costs and capacity, location was still important, but for very different reasons. When power was not as large a concern as it is today, we would look to build data centers in a place where land and building materials were cheapest. This would result in data centers being built in major metropolitan areas where land was abundant and labor costs were low. Often, companies would factor in an evaluation of geographic risk and as a result, areas such as Dallas, Atlanta, Phoenix, and Denver became very attractive. Each of these areas offered plenty of space for data centers, skills within the local population to build and maintain them, and low geographic risk.

Smaller companies that rented or leased space and services and were less concerned about risk would look to locate data centers close to their employee population. This led to collocation providers building or converting facilities in company dense areas like the Silicon Valley, Boston, Austin, and the New York/New Jersey area. These smaller companies favored ease of access to the servers supporting their new services over risk mitigation and cost. Although the price was higher for the space as compared to the lower cost alternatives, many companies felt the benefit of proximity overcame the increase in relative cost.

When power became the constraining factor for data center planning and utilization, companies started shifting their focus to areas where they could not only purchase and build for an attractive price, but where they could obtain power at a relatively low price, and perhaps as importantly, where they could use that power most efficiently. This last point actually leads to some counterintuitive locations for data centers.

Air conditioning, the AC portion of HVAC, operates most efficiently at lower elevations above sea level. We won't go into the reasons why, as there is plenty of information available on the Internet to confirm the statement. Air conditioning also operates more efficiently in areas of lower humidity, as less work is performed by the air conditioner to remove humidity from the air being conditioned. Low elevation above sea level and low humidity work together to produce a more efficient air conditioning system; the system in turn draws less power to perform a similar amount of work. This is why areas like Phoenix, Arizona, which is a net importer of power and as such sometimes has a higher cost of power, are still a favorite of companies building data centers. Although the per unit cost of power is higher than some other areas, and cooling demands are high in the summer, the efficiency of the HVAC systems through the course of the year and the low winter month demand reduces overall power consumption and makes Phoenix an attractive area to consider.

Some other interesting areas started to become great candidates for data centers due to an abundance of low-cost power. The area served by the Tennessee Valley Authority (TVA), including the state of Tennessee, parts of western North Carolina, northwest Georgia, northern Alabama, northeast Mississippi, southern Kentucky, and southwest Virginia is one such place. Another favorite of companies building data centers is the region called the Columbia River Gorge between Oregon and Washington. Both places have an abundance of low-cost power thanks to their hydroelectric power plants.

Location also impacts our quality of service. We want to be in an area that has easy access to quality bandwidth, an abundance of highly available power, and an educated labor pool. We would like the presence of multiple carriers to reduce our transit or *Internet pipe* costs and increase the likelihood that we can pass traffic over at least one carrier if one of the carriers is having availability or quality problems. We want the power infrastructure not only to be comparatively low cost as described in the preceding paragraphs, but to be highly available with a low occurrence of interruptions due to age of the power infrastructure or environmental concerns. Lastly, we need to have an educated labor pool that can help us build the data center and operate it.

Finally, location affects our risk profile. If we are in a single location with a single data center and that location has high geographic risk, the probability that we suffer an extended outage as a result of that geographic risk increases. A geographic risk can be anything that causes structural damage to our data center, power infrastructure failures, or network transport failures. The most commonly cited geographic risks to data centers and businesses are earthquakes, floods, hurricanes, and tornadoes. But there are other location specific risks to consider as well. Crime rates of an area have the possibility of interrupting services. Extremely cold or hot weather that taxes the location's power infrastructure can cause an interruption to operations.

Even within a general geography, some areas have higher risks than others. Proximity to freeways can cause an increase in the likelihood of a major accident causing damage to our facility or may increase the likelihood that our facility is evacuated due to a chemical spill. Do we have quick and easy access to fuel sources in the area should we need to use our backup generators? Does the area allow for easy access for fuel trucks for our generators? How close are we to a fire department?

Although location isn't everything, it absolutely impacts several areas critical to our cost of operations, quality of service, and risk profile. The right location can reduce our fixed and variable costs associated with power usage and infrastructure, increase our quality of service, and reduce our risk profile.

In considering cost, quality of service, and risk, there is no single panacea. In choosing to go to the Columbia River Gorge or TVA areas, you will be reducing your costs at the expense of needing to train the local talent or potentially bringing in your own talent as many companies have done. In choosing Phoenix or Dallas, you will have access to an experienced labor pool but will be paying more for power than you would be in either the TVA or Columbia River Gorge areas. There is no single right answer for location; you should work to optimize your solution to fit your budget and needs. There are, however, several wrong answers in our minds. We always suggest to our clients that they never choose an area of high geographic risk unless there simply is no other choice. Should they choose an area of high geographic risk, we always ask that they create a plan to get out of that area. It only takes one major outage to make the decision a bad one, and the question is always when, rather than if, that outage will happen.

Location Considerations

When considering a location for your data center or collocation partner, the following are some things to ponder:

- What is the cost of power in the area? Is it high or low relative to other options? How efficiently will my HVAC run in the area?

- Is there an educated labor force in the area from which I can recruit employees? Are they educated and experienced in the building and operation of a data center?

- Are there a number of transit providers in the area and how good has their service been to other consumers of their service?

- What is the geographic risk profile in the area?

Often, you will find yourself making tradeoffs between questions. You may find an area of low power cost, but without an experienced labor pool. The one area we recommend never sacrificing is geographic risk.

Data Centers and Incremental Growth

Data centers and collocation space present an interesting dilemma to incremental growth, and interestingly that dilemma is more profound for companies of moderate growth than it is for companies of rapid or hyper growth. Data centers are, for many of our technology focused clients, what factories are for companies that manufacture product; they are a way to produce the product, they are a limitation on the quantity that can be produced, and they are either accretive or dilutive to shareholder value, depending upon their level of utilization.

Taking and simplifying the automotive industry as an example, new factories are initially dilutive as they represent a new expenditure of cash by the company in question. The new factory probably has the newest available technology, which in turn is intended to decrease the cost per vehicle produced and ultimately increase the gross margin and profit margins of the business. Initially, the amortized value of the factory is applied to each of the cars produced and the net effect is dilutive as initial production quantities are low and each car loses money for the company. As the production quantity is increased and the amortized fixed cost of the factory is divided by an increasing volume of cars, the profit of those cars in aggregate start to offset the cost and finally overcome it. The factory starts to become accretive when the cost of the factory is lower per car produced than the next lowest cost per car factory. Unfortunately, to hit that point, we often have to be using the factory at a fairly high level of utilization.

The same holds true with a data center. The building of a data center usually represents a fairly large expenditure for any company. For smaller companies that are leasing new or additional data center space, that space still probably represents a fairly large commitment for the company in question. In many, if not most, of the cases where new space, rather purchased or lease, is being considered, we will likely put better and faster hardware in the space than we had in most of our other data center space. Although increasing the power utilization and the associated power costs, the hope is that we will reduce our overall spending by doing more with less equipment for our new space. Still, we have to be using some significant portion of this new space before the recurring lease and power costs or amortized property, plant, and equipment costs are offset by the new transactions.

To illustrate this point, let's make up some hypothetical numbers. For this discussion, reference Table 32.1. Let's say that you run the operations of AllScale Networks and that you currently lease 500 square feet of data center and associated power at a total cost of $3,000.00 per month "all in." You are currently constrained by power within your 500 square feet and need to consider additional space quickly before your systems are overwhelmed with user demand. You have options to lease another 500 square feet at $3,000.00 per month, or 1,000 square feet at $5,000.00 per month. The costs to build out the racks and power infrastructure (but not the server or network gear) within the 500 square feet are $10,000.00 and $20,000.00 for the 1,000 square feet. The equipment that you expect to purchase and put into the new space has been tested for your application, and you believe that it will handle about 50% more traffic or requests than your current systems (indexed at 1.5, the original 500 square foot Request Index in Table 32.1), but it will draw about 25% more power to do so (indexed at 1.25% the original Request Index in Table 32.1). As such, given the power density is the same between the cages, you can only rack roughly 80% of the systems you previously had as each system draws 1.25× the power of the previous systems. These are represented as .8 and 1.6 under Space Index in Table 32.1 for the 500 square foot and 1,000 square foot options, respectively. The resulting performance efficiency is (.8 × 1.5 =) 1.2× the throughput for the 500 square foot option and 2.4× for the 1,000 square foot option referenced as the Performance Index. Finally, the performance per dollar spent, as indexed to the original 500 square foot cage, is 1.2 for the 500 square foot and 1.44 for the 1,000 square foot options. This change is due to the addition of 500 square feet more at a reduced price of $2,000 for the 1,000 square foot option. Note that we've ignored the original build out cost in this calculation, but you could amortize that over the expected life of the cage and include it in all of the numbers that follow. We also assume that you are not going to replace the systems in the older 500 square foot cage and we have not included the price of the new servers.

Table 32.1   *Cost Comparisons*

Cage	Cost per Month	Request Index	Power Index	Space Index	Performance Index	Performance Per Dollar
Original 500 sq. ft.	$3,000	1.0	1.0	1.0	1.0	1.0
Additional 500 sq. ft.	$3,000	1.5	1.25	.8	1.2	1.2
Additional 1,000 sq. ft.	$5,000	1.5	1.25	1.6	2.4	1.44

It previously took you two years to fill up your 500 square feet, and the business believes the growth rate has doubled and should stay on its current trajectory. All indicators are that you will fill up another 500 square feet in about a year. What do you do?

We're not going to answer that question, but rather leave it as an exercise for you. The answer, however, is financially based if answered properly. It should consider how quickly the data center becomes accretive or margin positive for the business and shareholders. You should also factor in considerations of lost opportunity for building out data center space twice rather than once. It should be obvious by now that data center costs are "lumpy" in that they are high relative to many of your other technology costs and take some planning to ensure that they do not negatively impact your operations.

How about our previous assertion that the problem is larger for moderate-growth companies than hyper-growth companies? Can you see why we made that statement? The answer is that the same space purchased or leased by a hyper-growth company is going to become accretive faster than that of the moderate-growth company. As such, space considerations are much more important for slower growth companies unless they expect to exit other facilities and close them over time. The concerns of the hyper-growth company are more about staying well ahead of the demand for new space than ensuring that the space hits the accretive point of utilization.

Three Magic Rules of Three

We love simple, easily understood and communicated rules, and one of these is our Rules of Three as applied to data centers. There are three of these rules, hence "Three Magic Rules of Three." The first rule has to do with the costs of data centers, the second has to do with the number of servers, and third has to do with the number of data centers a company should consider implementing.

The First Rule of Three: Three Magic Drivers of Data Center Costs

Our first rule of three concerns the cost of running a data center. The first and most obvious cost within a data center is the cost of the servers and equipment that carries requests and acts upon them. These are the servers and network equipment necessary to run your application or platform. The second cost is the power to run these servers and other pieces of equipment. The third and final cost is the power necessary to run the HVAC for these servers. This isn't a hard and fast rule. Rather, it is intended to focus companies on the large costs of running a data center as too often these costs are hidden within different organizations and not properly evaluated.

These costs tend to increase directly in relationship to the number of servers. Each server obviously has its own cost, as does the power it draws. The HVAC needs also typically increase linearly with the number of servers and the power consumption of those servers. More servers drawing more power create more heat that needs to be moved or reduced. In many companies, especially larger companies, this relationship is lost within organizational budget boundaries.

There are other obvious costs not included within this first rule of three. For instance, we need headcount to run the data center, or we are paying for a contract for someone else to run the data center or it is included within our rental/lease agreement. There are also network transit costs as we are going to want to talk to someone else outside of our data center. There may also be security costs, the costs of maintaining certain pieces of equipment such as FM-200 fire suppression devices, and so on. These costs, however, tend to be well understood and are often either fixed by the amount of area, as in security and FM-200 maintenance, or clearly within a single organization's budget such as network transit costs.

The Second Rule of Three: Three Is the Magic Number for Servers

Many of our clients have included this "magic rule" as an architectural principle. Simply put, it means that the number of servers for any service should never fall below three and when planning data center capacity, you should consider all of the existing services and future or planned services and expect that there will be at least three servers for any service. The thought here is that you build one for the customer, one for capacity and growth, and one to fail. Ideally, the service is built and the data center is planned in such a way that services can expand horizontally per our Scale Out Not Up principle in Chapter 12, Exploring Architectural Principles.

Taken to its extreme for hyper-growth sites, this rule would be applied to data center capacity planning not only for front-end Web services, but for data storage services such as a database. If a service requires a database, and if finances allow, the service should be architected such that at the very least there can be a write database for writes and load balanced reads, an additional read database, and a database that can serve as a logical standby in the case of corruption. In a fault isolative architecture or swim lane architecture by service, there may be several of these database implementations.

It's important to note that no data center decisions should be made without consulting the architects, product managers, and capacity planners responsible for defining, designing, and planning new and existing systems.

The Third Rule of Three: Three Is the Magic Number for Data Centers

"Whoa, hang on there!" you might say. "We are a young company attempting to become profitable and we simply cannot afford three data centers." At first blush, this probably appears to be a ridiculous suggestion and we don't blame you for having such an initial adverse reaction to the suggestion. But what if we told you that you can run out of three data centers for close to the cost that it takes you to run out of two data centers? Few of you would probably argue that you can afford to run out of a single data center forever as most of us recognize that running a single data center for mission critical or revenue critical transactions is just asking for trouble. And if you are a public company, no one wants to make the public disclosure that "Any significant damage to our single data center would significantly hamper our ability to remain a going concern." Let's first discuss the primary architectural shift that allows you to run out of multiple data centers.

In Chapter 12, we suggested designing for multiple live sites as an architectural principle. To do this, you need either stateless systems; or systems that maintain state within the browser (say with a cookie) or pass state back and forth through the same URL/URI. After you establish affinity with a data center and maintain state at that data center, it becomes very difficult to serve the transaction from other live data centers. Another approach is to maintain affinity with a data center through the course of a series of transactions, but allow a new affinity for new or subsequent sessions to be maintained through the life of those sessions. Finally, you can consider segmenting your customers by data center along a z-axis split, and then replicate the data for each data center, split evenly through the remainder of the data centers. In this approach, should you have three data centers, 50% of the data from data center A would move to data centers B and C. This approach is depicted in Figure 32.1. The result is that you have 200% of the data necessary to run the site in aggregate, but each site only contains 66% of the necessary data as each site contains the copy for which it is a master (33% of the data necessary to run the site) and 50% of the copies of each of the other sites (16.5% of the data necessary to run the site for a total of an additional 33%).

Let's discuss the math behind our assertion. We will first assume that you agree with us that you need to have at least two data centers to help ensure that you can survive any disaster. If these data centers were labeled A and B, you might decide to

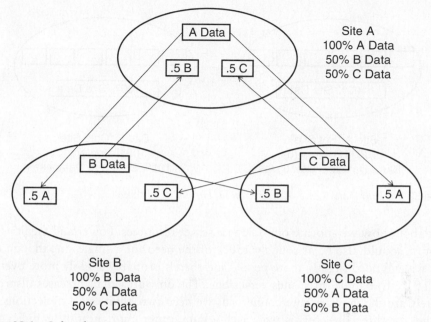

Figure 32.1 *Split of Data Center Replication*

operate 100% of your traffic out of data center A and leave data center B for a warm standby. Back-end databases might be replicated using native database replication or a third-party tool and may be several seconds behind. You would need 100% of your computing and network assets in both data centers to include 100% of your Web and application servers, 100% of your database servers, and 100% of your network equipment. Power needs would be similar and Internet connectivity would be similar. You probably keep slightly more than 100% of the capacity necessary to serve your peak demand in each location in order to handle surges in demand. So, let's say that you keep 110% of your needs in both locations. Any time you buy additional servers for one place, you have to buy for the next. You may also decide to connect the data centers with your own dedicated circuits for the purposes of secure replication of data. Running live out of both sites would help you in the event of a major catastrophe as only 50% of your transactions would initially fail until you transfer that traffic to the alternate site, but it won't help you from a budget or financial perspective. A high-level diagram of the data centers may look as depicted in Figure 32.2.

However, if we have three sites and we run live out of all three sites at once, our cost for systems goes down. This is because for all nondatabase systems, we only really need 150% of our capacity in each location to run 100% of our traffic in the event of a site failure. For databases, we definitely need 200% of the storage as compared to one site, but we only really need 150% of the processing power if we are

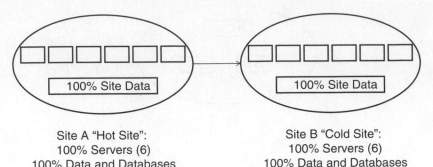

Site A "Hot Site":
100% Servers (6)
100% Data and Databases

Site B "Cold Site":
100% Servers (6)
100% Data and Databases

Figure 32.2 *Two Data Center Configuration, Hot and Cold Site*

smart about how we allocate our database server resources. Power and facilities consumption should also be at roughly 150% of the need for a single site, though obviously we will need slightly more people and there's probably slightly more overhead than 150% to handle three sites versus one. The only area that increases disproportionately are the network interconnects as we need two additional connections (versus one) for three sites versus two. Such a data center configuration is indicated in Figure 32.3 and Table 32.2 shows the relative costs of running three sites versus two. Note that in our Table 32.2, we have figured that each site has 50% of the server

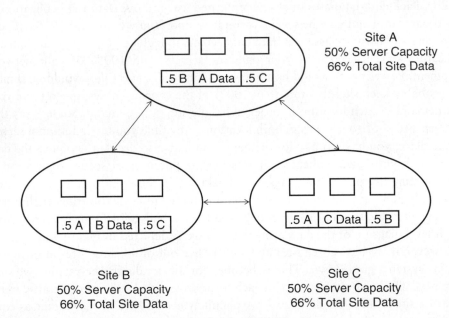

Site A
50% Server Capacity
66% Total Site Data

Site B
50% Server Capacity
66% Total Site Data

Site C
50% Server Capacity
66% Total Site Data

Figure 32.3 *Three Data Center Configuration, Three Hot Sites*

Table 32.2 *Cost Comparisons*

Site Configuration	Network	Servers	Databases	Storage	Network Site Connections	Total Cost
Single Site	100%	100%	100%	100%	0	100%
2 Site "Hot" and "Cold"	200%	200%	200%	200%	1	200%
2 Site Live/Live	200%	200%	200%	200%	1	200%
3 Site Live/Live/ Live	150%	150%	150%	200%	3	~166%

capacity necessary to run everything, and 66% (66.66, but we've made it a round number and rounded down rather than up in the figure) of the storage per Figure 33.3. You would need 300% of the storage if you were to locate 100% of the data in each of the three sites.

Note that we get this leverage in data centers because we expect that the data centers are sufficiently far apart so as not to have two data centers simultaneously eliminated as a result of any geographically isolated event. You might decide to stick one near the West Coast of the United States, one in the center of the U.S., and another near the East Coast. Remember, however, that you still want to reduce your data center power costs and reduce the risks to each of the three data centers so you still want to be in areas of low relative cost of power and low geographic risk.

Maybe now you are a convert to our three-site approach and you immediately jump to the conclusion that more is better! Why not four sites, or five, or 20? Well, more sites are better, and there are all sorts of games you can play to further reduce your capital costs. But at some point, unless you are a very large company, the management overhead of a large number of data centers is cost prohibitive. Each additional data center will give you some reduction in the amount of equipment that you need to have complete redundancy, but will increase the management overhead and network connectivity costs. To arrive at the "right number" for your company, you should take the example of Table 32.2 and add in the costs to run and manage the data centers to determine the right number for your company. While you are performing your cost calculations, remember that there are other benefits to multiple data centers such as ensuring that those data centers are close to end customer concentrations in order to reduce customer response times. Our point is that you should plan for at least three data centers to both give you disaster prevention and reduce your costs relative to a two-site implementation.

Multiple Active Data Center Considerations

We hinted at some of the concerns of running multiple active data centers in our earlier discussion of why three is the magic number for data centers. We will first cover some of the benefits and concerns of running multiple live data centers and then we will discuss three flavors of approaches and the concerns unique to each of those approaches.

The two greatest benefits of running multiple live data centers are the disaster recovery, or as we prefer to call it, disaster prevention, aspects and the reduction in cost when running three data centers versus two. Designing and running multiple data centers also gives you the flexibility of putting data centers closer to your customers and thereby reducing response times to their requests. A multidatacenter approach does not eliminate the benefits you would receive by deploying a content delivery network as described in Chapter 25, Caching for Performance and Scale, but it does benefit those calls that are forced to go directly to the data center due to their dynamic nature. If you are leasing data center space, you also get the benefit of being able to multisource your collocation partners, and as a result, use the market to drive down the negotiated price for your space. Should you ever need or desire to leave one location, you can run live out of two data centers and move to a lower cost or higher quality provider for your third data center. If you are a SaaS (Software as a Service) company, you may find it easier to roll out or push updates to your site by moving traffic between data centers and upgrading sites one at a time during off peak hours. Finally, when you run live out of multiple data centers, you don't find yourself questioning the viability of your warm or cold "disaster recovery site;" your daily operations proves that each of the sites is capable of handling requests from your customers.

Multiple live data centers do add some complexity and will likely increase your headcount needs as compared to running a single data center and maybe even two data centers. The increase in headcount should be moderate, potentially adding one to a few people to manage the contracts and space depending upon the size of your company. Some of your processes will need to change, such as how and when you roll code and how you ensure that multiple sites are roughly consistent with respect to configuration. You will likely also find members of your team travelling more often to visit and inspect sites should you not have full-time employees dedicated to each of your centers. Network costs are also likely to be higher as you add network links between sites for intersite communication.

From an architecture perspective, to gain the full advantage of a multisite configuration, you should consider moving to a near stateless system with no affinity to a data center. You may of course decide that you are going to route customers based on proximity using a geo-locator service, but you want the flexibility of determining when to route what traffic to what data center. In this configuration, where data is present at all three data centers and there is no state or session data held solely within a single data center, a failure of a service or failure of the entire data center allows the end user to nearly seamlessly fail over to the next available data center. This results in the highest possible availability for any configuration possible.

In the case where some state or affinity is required, or the cost of architecting out state and affinity is simply too high, you need to make the choice of whether to fail all transactions or sessions and force them to restart should a data center or service go down or find a way to replicate the state and session to at least one more data center. This increases the cost slightly as now you need to either build or buy a replication engine for the user state information and you will need additional systems or storage to handle it.

Multiple Live Site Considerations

Multiple live site benefits include

- Higher availability as compared to a hot and cold site configuration
- Lower costs compared to a hot and cold site configuration
- Faster customer response times if customers are routed to the closest data center for dynamic calls
- Greater flexibility in rolling out products in a SaaS environment
- Greater confidence in operations versus a hot and cold site configuration

Drawbacks or concerns of a multiple live site configuration include

- Greater operational complexity
- Small increase in headcount needs
- Increase in travel and network costs
- Increase in operational complexity

Architectural considerations in moving to a multiple live site environment include

- Eliminate the need for state and affinity wherever possible
- Route customers to closest data center if possible to reduce dynamic call times
- Investigate replication technologies for databases and state if necessary

Conclusion

This chapter discussed the unique constraints that data centers create for hyper-growth companies, data center location considerations, and the benefit of designing for and operating out of multiple live data centers. As such, when considering options for where to locate data centers, one should consider areas that provide the lowest cost of power with high quality and availability of power. Another major location based criteria is the geographic risk in any given area. Companies should ideally locate data centers in areas with low geographic risk, low cost of power, and high power efficiency for air conditioning systems.

Data center growth and capacity need to be evaluated and planned out months or even years in advance based on whether you lease or purchase data center space and how much space you need. Finding yourself in a position needing to immediately enter into contracts and occupy space puts your business at risk and at the very least reduces your negotiating leverage and causes you to pay more money for space. A failure to plan for data center space and power needs well in advance could hinder your ability to grow.

When planning data centers, remember to apply the *three magic rules of three*. The first rule is that there are three drivers of cost. The first driver is the cost of the server, the second driver is the cost of power, and the third driver is the cost of HVAC. The second rule is to always plan for at least three servers for any service and the final rule is to plan for three or more live data centers.

Multiple active data centers provide a number of advantages for your company. You gain higher availability and lower overall costs relative to the typical hot and cold site disaster recovery configuration. They also allow you greater flexibility in product rollouts and greater negotiation leverage with leased space. Operational confidence in facilities increase as compared to the lack of faith most organizations have in a cold or warm disaster recovery facility. Finally, customer perceived response times go down for dynamic calls when routed to the closest data center.

Drawbacks of the multiple live data center configuration include increased operational complexity, increases in headcount and network costs, and an increase in travel cost. That said, our experience is that the benefits far outweigh the negative aspects of such a configuration.

When considering a multiple live data center configuration, you should attempt to eliminate state and affinity wherever possible. Affinity to a data center closest to the customer is preferred to reduce customer perceived response times, but ideally you want the flexibility of seamlessly moving traffic. You will need to implement some method of replication for databases and should you need to maintain state for any reason, you should also consider using that technology for state replication.

Key Points

- Power is typically the constraining factor within most data centers today.
- Cost of power, quality and availability of power, geographic risk, an experienced labor pool, and cost and quality of network transit are all location based considerations for data centers.
- Data center planning has a long time horizon. It needs to be done months and years in advance.
- The three magic drivers of data center costs are servers, power, and HVAC.
- Three is the magic number for servers: Never plan for a service having less than three servers initially.
- Three is the magic number for data centers: Always attempt to design for at least three live sites.
- Multiple live sites offer higher availability, greater negotiating leverage, higher operational confidence, lower cost, and faster customer response times than traditional hot/cold disaster recovery configurations.
- Multiple live sites tend to increase operational complexity, costs associated with travel and network connectivity, and headcount needs.
- Attempt to eliminate affinity and state in a multiple life site design.

Chapter 33

Putting It All Together

> The art of war teaches us to rely not on the likelihood of the enemy's not coming,
> but on our own readiness to receive him; not on the chance of his not attacking,
> but rather on the fact that we have made our position unassailable.
>
> —Sun Tzu

We started this book with a discussion of how scalability is a combination of *art* and *science*. The art aspect of scaling is seen in the interactions between platforms, organizations, and processes, which impact any structured approach in a company. The science of scalability is embodied within the method by which we measure our efforts and in the application of the scientific method. A particular company's approach to scaling must be crafted around the ecosystem fashioned by the intersection of the technology platform, the uniqueness of the organization, and the maturity and capabilities of the existing processes. Because a one-size-fits-all implementation or answer does not exist, we have focused this book on providing skills and lessons regarding approaches.

It all begins with people. You can't get better or even sustain without the right team, the right leadership, the right management, and the right organizational structure. People are central to establishing and following processes as well as designing and implementing the technology. Having the right people in terms of skill set, motivation, and cultural fit are the essential building blocks. On top of this must be placed the right roles. Even the best people must be placed in the right job that appropriately utilizes their skills. Additionally, these roles must be organized in the right organizational structure and they must receive strong leadership and management in order to perform at an optimal level.

Although people develop and maintain the processes within an organization, the processes control how the individuals and teams behave. Processes are essential because they allow your teams to react quickly to crisis, determine the root cause of failures, determine capacity of systems, analyze scalability needs, implement scalability projects, and many more fundamental needs for a scalable system. There is no single

501

right answer when it comes to processes, and there are many wrong answers. Each and every process must be evaluated first for general fit within the organization in terms of its rigor or repeatability and then specifically for what steps are right for your particular team in terms of complexity. Too much process can stifle innovation and strangle shareholder value, whereas if you are missing the processes that allow you to learn from both your past mistakes and failures, you will very likely at least underachieve and potentially even fail as a company.

Last but not least is the technology that drives the business either as the product itself or the infrastructure allowing the product to be brought to market. There are many methodologies to understand and consider when implementing your scalable solution such as splitting by multiple axes, caching, using asynchronous calls, developing a data management approach, and many others that we've covered in this book. The key is to develop expertise in these approaches so that you appropriately utilize them when necessary. The right people, who understand these approaches, and the right processes, ones that insist on the evaluation of these approaches, are all put together to develop scalable technology.

In the beginning of this book, we introduced the concept of virtuous and vicious cycles (refer to Figure I.1 in the Introduction). The lack of attention to the people and processes can cause poor technical decisions that are what we term a *vicious cycle*. After you start down this path, teams are likely to ignore the people and process more because of the demands on energy and resources to fix the technology problems. The exact opposite is what we called the *virtuous cycle* when the right people and the right process feed each other and produce excellent, scalable technology, thus freeing up resources to continue to improve the overall ecosystem within the organization. After you start down the vicious cycle, it is difficult to stop but with focused intensity you can do it. In Figure 33.1, we have depicted this concept of stopping the downward spiral and starting it back in the other direction.

What to Do Now?

The question that you might have now that you have made your way through all this information about people, processes, and technology is "What to do now?" We have a simple four-step process that we recommend for putting all this information into practice. Note that this process holds true whether you are making technical, process, organizational, or even personal changes (as in changes in you). These steps are

1. Assess your situation.

2. Determine where you need or want to be.

3. Annotate the difference between the two.

4. Make a plan.

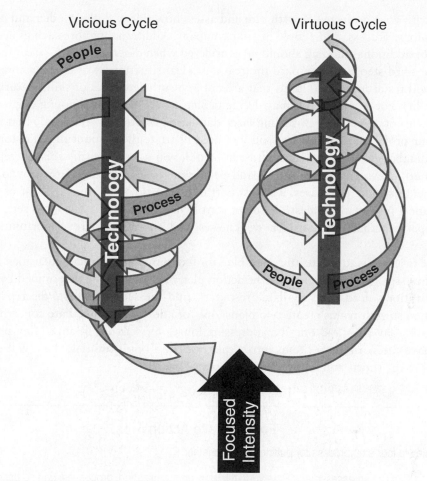

Figure 33.1 *Vicious and Virtual Technology Cycles*

The first step is to assess your current situation. Look at all three aspects of people, process, and technology and make an honest assessment of where you are with each. Answer questions such as what is the caliber of your people, is the structure of your organization optimal, what parts of your technology scale, and are your processes adequately supporting your goals? These assessments are difficult to do from inside the organization. Sometimes, you are just too close to the situation. Our firm AKF Partners is often asked to perform these assessments because we can provide an objective third-party perspective.

After you have the assessment in hand, the second step is to determine where you need to be along those three aspects of people, process, and technology. Do you need to focus on infusing more experience in the engineering team or do you need to dedicate time and energy to developing more robust processes? One approach to this is to start with your projected growth rate and assess how this will place a demand on the technology, process, and people of your company. Additional factors such as acquisitions or additional funding should be considered when determining this ideal state.

The third step is to compare the real and ideal situations within your company. This will result in a list of items that are not at a sufficient level of skill, maturity, or scalability. For example, you may decide in Step 1 that you have a young engineering team with no experience in scaling large databases. In Step 2, you decide that based on your projected growth rate, you will need to triple the amount of data stored in your database in the next 18 months. In Step 3, you would identify this discrepancy and mark down that you need to add people on your engineering team who have experience scaling databases. The last part of Step 3 is to prioritize this list of items from most important to least. We often start by breaking the list into two sets: those discrepancies that we consider weaknesses and those that are opportunities to improve.

The last step is to create an action plan for fixing the discrepancies identified in the previous step. The timeframe for the action plan or plans will be determined by your organization's needs, the available resources, and the severity of the discrepancies. We often suggest teams create two plans: one for addressing immediate concerns in a 30- to 45-day plan and one for addressing longer term issues in a 180-day plan. If you have categorized the items into weaknesses and opportunities, these will correspond to the short- and long-term action plans.

Four Steps to Action

A simple four-step process for putting this all together:

1. *Perform an assessment.* Rate your company on organization, processes, and architecture. Use an outside agent if necessary.

2. *Define where you need to be or your ideal state.* How large is your company going to grow in 12 to 24 months? What does that mean for your organization, processes, and architecture?

3. *List the differences between your actual and ideal situations.* Rank order these differences from most to least severe.

4. *Action plans.* Put together an action plan to resolve the issues identified in the previous steps. This can be in the form of a single prioritized plan, a short-term and long-term plan, or any other planning increments that your company uses.

Case Studies

Throughout this book, we painted a picture of AllScale, a fictional company amalgamating our experiences as advisors and executives, to provide real-world examples. As a last example of how our techniques can be employed to create scalable solutions, we are going to leave AllScale and discuss three companies with which we have personal experience. We chose these three companies to attempt to show how our techniques can be applied to companies in various stages of growth and maturity.

eBay: Incredible Success and a Scalability Implosion

Search for "eBay outage 1999" and you'll get a number of results centered between May and July of 1999. Outages lasting more than five hours were fairly common according to widely published news stories throughout the Internet. Had these outages continued, there is no doubt that eBay would have lost the advantage it enjoyed through at least 2005 as the largest online ecommerce site in gross merchandise sales.

In 1999, Internet commerce was still in its infancy. eBay, Amazon, and Yahoo were blazing new trails in terms of commerce transaction volume on the Internet. Facilitating online auctions also had some attributes unique from other online sites: Time was also a very important element. Regardless of the length of an auction, the most likely time that the auction would be viewed and bid upon was the last several hours of that auction's life. If eBay was down for five hours, it is very likely that certain auctions would close at a final price significantly lower than they would if the site remained available. Unlike most Internet commerce sites, where demand would be scattered over some subset of catalog items even during peak traffic, demand on eBay auctions would be laser focused on an even smaller set of items at any given time. Imagine 1,000 buyers in a 10,000 square foot store all attempting to view and purchase an item in the back corner of the store and for which the store only has a single copy or piece. Further imagine that the number of buyers entering the store doubled sometimes daily and sometimes monthly. The items these buyers were interested in were also doubling, or tripling. Although not unheard of today, this type of growth simply had not been experienced before.

What happened? As we've attempted to point out in this book, it all starts with people. eBay had some of the brightest engineers around in 1999 before and during the outages. But these incredibly bright people didn't have some of the experiences necessary to run platforms at such scale and at such rapid growth. In fact, no one had that type of experience. So, the executive team needed to find folks with different, yet applicable experience to augment the existing team. Meg Whitman brought in Maynard Webb as the President of Technology and Maynard in turn brought in Lynn Reedy and Marty Abbott. The executives established a compelling yet achievable vision to be both highly available and highly scalable. Lynn and Marty hired a number of people to further augment the team over a period of several years including Tom Keeven and Mike Fisher (both now partners in AKF), creating a perpetual cycle of "seed, feed, and weed." Experiences were added to the team and talent was boosted. Great individual contributors and managers were recognized and promoted and some people were asked to leave or left of their own volition if they did not fit into the new culture.

While continuing to focus on ensuring that the teams had the right skills and experiences, the executives simultaneously looked at processes. Most important were the processes that would allow the organizations to learn over time. Crisis management, incident management, postmortem, and change management and control processes were all added within the first week. Morning operations meetings were added to focus on open and recurring incidents and to drive incidents and problems to closure. Project management disciplines were added to keep business and scalability related projects on track.

And of course there was the focus on technology! It is important to understand that although people, process, and technology were all simultaneously focused on, the most important aspects for long-term growth stem from people first and process second. As we've said time and time again, technology does not get better without having the right team with the right experiences, and people do not learn without the right (and appropriately sized) processes to reinforce lessons learned, thereby keeping issues from happening repeatedly.

Databases and applications were split on the x-, y-, and z-axes of scale. What started out as one monolithic database on the largest server available at the time was necessarily split to allow for the system to scale to user demand. Data elements with high read to write ratios were replicated using x-axis techniques. Customer information was split from product information, product information was split into several databases, and certain functions like "feedback" were split into their own systems over the period of a few years.

Quigo: A Young Product with a Scalability Problem

Quigo started out as a company offering a service based on technology. Relying on a proprietary relevance and learning engine, its first product promised to help increase the returns in the nascent search engine marketing industry for direct response advertisers. Leveraging this existing technology, the company branched out into offering a private label contextual advertising platform for premium publishers. AdSonar was born. Early premium branded publishers loved the product and loved the capability to increase their revenue per page over the existing alternatives.

However, within months, the new advertising platform had problems. It simply couldn't handle the demand of the new publishers. How did a new product fail so

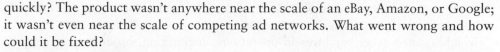

quickly? The product wasn't anywhere near the scale of an eBay, Amazon, or Google; it wasn't even near the scale of competing ad networks. What went wrong and how could it be fixed?

Again, the answer starts with people. The existing team was smart and dedicated, just as with the eBay team. But it missed experience in large-scale operations and designing platforms for hyper growth. This is when two future AKF Partners were brought onboard. The new executives didn't have direct experience with advertising technology, but their experience with commerce and payment platforms was directly applicable. More importantly, they knew how to focus teams on an objective and how to create a culture that would support the needs of a highly scalable site. Consistent with the layout of this book, it all starts with people. The new team created metrics and goals supporting availability, scalability, and cost. It created a compelling vision of the ideal future and gave the team hope that it could be achieved. Where necessary, it added great engineering and managerial talent.

The new executives also set about adding the right processes to support scalability. Scalability summits, operations meetings, incident management processes, and change management processes were all added within a couple of weeks. Joint Application Design and Architecture Review Boards soon followed. Architectural principles focusing the team on the critical elements of scale were introduced and used during Architectural Review Boards.

And of course the team focused on technology. Again, what ultimately became the AKF Scale Cube was employed to split services, resources, and (where necessary) data elements. Fault isolation was employed where possible to increase scalability.

What were the results of all of this work? Within two years, the company had grown more than 100x in transactions and revenue and was successfully sold to AOL.

ShareThis: A Startup Story

ShareThis is a company that is all about sharing. Its products allow people to easily share the things they find online, by consolidating address books and friend lists, so that anything can be shared immediately, without even leaving a Web page. Within six months of launching the ShareThis widget, there were already over 30,000 publishers using it. Witnessing this hyper growth, the cofounder and CEO Tim Schigel met with the AKF Partners to talk about guidance with scalability concerns. Tim is a seasoned veteran of startups having seen them for more than a decade as a venture capitalist and was well aware of the need to address scalability early and from a holistic approach. Michael Fisher from AKF Partners worked with Tim to lay out a short- and long-term plan for scalability. At the top of the list was filling some open positions on his team with great people. One of these key hires was Nanda Kishore as the chief technology officer. Prior to ShareThis, Nanda was a general manager at

Amazon.com and knew firsthand about how to hire, lead, design, and develop scalable organizations, processes, and products.

In addition to other key hires in operations, engineering, product management, and the data warehouse team, there was a dedicated focus on improving processes. Some of the processes that were put in place within the first few weeks were source code control, on-call procedures, bug tracking, and product councils. After people and process were firmly established, they could properly address scalability within the technology.

With a keen focus on managing cost and improving performance, the team worked on reducing the widget payload. It implemented a content delivery network (CDN) solution for caching and moved all serving and data processing into Amazon's EC2 cloud. Because of the ShareThis architecture and need for large amounts of compute processing for data, this combination of a CDN and public cloud worked exceptionally well. Under Nanda's leadership, the team reduced the serving cost by more than 56% while experiencing growth rates in excess of 15% per month. All of this sharing activity resulted in terabytes of data that needs to be processed daily. The team has produced a data warehousing solution that can scale with the ever increasing amount of data while reducing the processing time by 1900% in the past six months.

Less than two years after the launch, the ShareThis widget reached more than 200 million unique users per month and more than 120,000 publisher sites. ShareThis is a scalability success story because of its focus on people, process, and technology.

Again, it's worth repeating a recurring theme throughout this book: You can't scale without focusing on all three elements of people, process, and technology. Too many books and Web sites feature the flavor of the day technical implementation to fix all needs. Vision, mission, culture, team composition, and focus are the most important elements to long-term success. Processes need to support the development of the team and need to reinforce lessons learned as well as rapid learning. Technology, it turns out, is the easiest piece of the puzzle, but unfortunately the one people tend to focus on first. Just as with complex math equations, one simply needs to iteratively simplify the equation until the component parts are easy to solve.

People and organizations are more dynamic and demanding. Although there is no single right solution for them, there is an approach that is guaranteed to work every time. Start with a compelling vision mixed with compassion and hope, and treat your organization as you would your garden. Add in goals and measurements and help the team overcome obstacles.

Process development should focus on those things that help a company learn over time and avoid repeating mistakes. Use process to help manage risks and repeat superior results. Avoid process that becomes cumbersome or significantly slows down product development.

References

We have covered a lot of material in this book. Because of space limitations we have often only been able to cover this material in a summary fashion. Following are a few of the many resources that can be consulted for more information on concepts related to scalability. Not all of these necessarily share our view points on many issues, but that does not make them or our positions any less valid. Healthy discussion and disagreement is the backbone of scientific advancement. Awareness of different views on topics will give you a greater knowledge of the concept and a more appropriate decision framework.

Blogs

AKF Partners Blog: http://www.akfpartners.com/techblog

Silicon Valley Product Group by Marty Cagan: http://www.svpg.com/blog/files/svpg.xml

All Things Distributed by Werner Vogels: http://www.allthingsdistributed.com

High Scalability Blog: http://highscalability.com

Joel On Software by Joel Spolsky: http://www.joelonsoftware.com

Signal vs Noise by 37Signals: http://feeds.feedburner.com/37signals/beMH

Scalability.org: http://scalability.org

Books

Building Scalable Web Sites: Building, Scaling, and Optimizing the Next Generation of Web Applications by Cal Henderson

Guerrilla Capacity Planning: A Tactical Approach to Planning for Highly Scalable Applications and Services by Neil J. Gunther

The Art of Capacity Planning: Scaling Web Resources by John Allspaw

Scalable Internet Architectures by Theo Schlossnagle

The Data Access Handbook: Achieving Optimal Database Application Performance and Scalability by John Goodson and Robert A. Steward

Real-Time Design Patterns: Robust Scalable Architecture for Real-Time Systems (Addison-Wesley Object Technology Series) by Bruce Powel Douglass

Cloud Computing and SOA Convergence in Your Enterprise: A Step-by-Step Guide (Addison-Wesley Information Technology Series) by David S. Linthicum

Inspired: How To Create Products Customers Love by Marty Cagan

Appendices

Appendix A

Calculating Availability

There are many ways of calculating a site's availability. Included in this appendix are five ways that this can be accomplished. In Chapter 6, Making the Business Case, we made the argument that knowing your availability is extremely important in order to make the business case that you need to undertake scalability projects. Downtime equals lost revenue and the more scalability projects you postpone or neglect to accomplish, the worse your outages and brownouts are going to be. If you agree with all of that then why does it matter how you calculate outages or downtime or availability? It matters because the better job you do and the more everyone agrees that your method is the standard way of calculating the measurement, the more credibility your numbers have. You want to be the final authority on this measurement; you need to own it and be the custodian of it. Imagine how the carpet could be pulled out from under your scalability projects if someone disputed your availability numbers in the executive staff meeting.

Another reason that a proper and auditable measurement should be put in place is that for an Internet enabled service, there is no more important metric than being available to your customers when they need your service. Everyone in the organization should have this metric and goal as part of his personal goals. Every member of the technology organization should know the impact on availability that every outage causes. People should question each other about outages and work together to ensure they occur as infrequently as possible. With availability as part of the company's goals, affecting employees' bonus, salary, promotions, and so on, this should be a huge motivator to care about this metric.

Before we talk about the five different methods of calculating availability, we need to make sure we are all on the same page with the basic definition of availability. In our vernacular, *availability* is how often the site is available over a particular duration. It is simply the amount of time the site can be used by customers divided by the total time. For example, if we are measuring availability over one week, we have 10,080 minutes of possibly availability, 7 days × 24 hrs/day × 60 min/day. If our site is available 10,010 minutes during that week, our availability is 10,010 / 10,080 = .9935.

Availability is normally stated as a percentage, so our availability would be 99.35% for the week.

Hardware Uptime

The simplest and most straightforward measurement of availability is calculating it based on device (or hardware) uptime. Using simple monitoring tools that rely on SNMP traps for catching when devices are having issues, organizations can monitor the hardware infrastructure as well as keep track of when the site's hardware was having issues. On whatever time period availability is to be calculated, the team can look back through the monitoring log and identify how many servers had issues and for what duration. A simple method would be to take the total time of the outage and multiply it by a percentage of the site that was impacted. The percentage would be generated by taking the number of servers having issues and dividing by the total number of servers hosting the site. As an example, let's assume an access switch failed and the hosts were not dual homed, so it took out 12 Web servers that were attached to it for 1½ hours until someone was able to get in the cage and swap the network device. The site is hosted on 120 Web servers. Therefore, the total downtime would be 9 minutes calculated as follows:

Outage duration = 1½ hours

Servers impacted = 12

Total servers = 120

90 min × 12/120 = 9 min

With the downtime figured, the availability can be calculated. Continuing our example, let's assume that we want to measure availability over a week and this was our only outage during that week. During a week, we have 10,080 minutes of possibly availability, 7 days × 24 hrs/day × 60 min/hr. Because this is our only downtime of the week, we have 10,080 – 9 = 10,071 of uptime. Availability is simply the ratio of uptime to total time expressed as a percentage, so we have 10,071 / 10,080 = 99.91%.

As we mentioned, this is a very simplistic approach to availability. The reason we say this is that the performance of a Web server is not necessarily the experience of your customers. Just because a server was unavailable does not mean that the site was unavailable for the customers; in fact, if you have architected your site properly, a single failure will likely not cause any customer impacting issues. The best measure of availability will have a direct relation to the maximization of shareholder value; this maximization in turn likely considers the impact to customer experience and the resulting impact to revenue or cost for the company.

This is not meant to imply that you should not measure your servers and other hardware's availability. You should, however, refer back to the goal tree in Chapter 5, Management 101, shown in Figure 5.2. Device or hardware availability would likely be a leaf on this tree beneath the availability of the adserving systems and the registration systems. In other words, the device availability impacts the availability of these services, but the availability of the services themselves is the most important metric. You should use device or hardware availability as a key indicator of your system's health but you need a more sophisticated and customer centric measurement for availability.

Customer Complaints

The next approach to determining availability involves using the customers as a barometer or yardstick for your site's performance. This measurement might be in the form of the number of inbound calls or emails to your customer support center or the number of posts on your forums. Often, companies with very sophisticated customer support services will have real-time tracking metrics on support calls and emails. Call centers measure this every day and have measurements on how many they receive as well as how many they can service. If there is a noticeable spike in such service requests, it is often the fault of an issue with the application.

How could we turn the number of calls into an availability measurement? There are many ways to create a formula for doing this, but they are all inaccurate. One simple formula might be to take the number of calls received on a normal day and the number received during a complete outage; these would serve as your 100% available and 0% available. As the number of calls increases beyond the normal day rate, you start subtracting availability until you reach the amount indicating a total site outage; at that point, you count the time as the site being completely unavailable.

As an example, let's say we normally get 200 calls per hour from customers. When the site is completely down in the middle of the day, the call volume goes to 1,000 per hour. Today, we start seeing the call volume go to 400 per hour at 9:00 AM and remain there until noon when it drops to 150 per hour. We assume that the site had some issues during this time and that is confirmed by the operations staff. We mark the period from 9:00 AM to noon as an outage. The percentage of downtime is 25%, calculated as

Outage duration = 3 hours = 180 min

Normal volume = 200 calls/hr

Max volume = 1,000 calls/hr

Diff (Max − Norm) = 800 calls/hr

Amount of calls above normal = 400 − 200 = 200 calls/hr

Percentage above normal = 200 / 800 = 1 / 4 = 25%

180 min × 25% = 45 min

Although this is certainly closer to a real user experience metric, it is also fraught with problems and inaccuracies. For starters, customers are not likely to call in right away. Most service centers require people to stay on the phone for several minutes or longer waiting before they are able to speak with a real person. Therefore, many customers will not bother calling in because they don't want to be put on hold. Not all customers will call; probably only your most vocal customers will call. While at eBay, for instance, we measured that the customer contact rate would be somewhere in the vicinity of 1% to 5% of the customers actually impacted. This fact skews the metrics toward functionality that is used by your most vocal customers, who are often your most advanced. Another major issue with this measurement is that a lot of Web 2.0 or Software as a Service (SaaS) companies do not have customer support centers. This leaves them with very little direct contact with customers; therefore, the delay in understanding if there is a real problem, the significance of it, and the duration of it are extremely difficult to detect. Another issue with this measurement is that customer calls vary dramatically depending on the time of the day. To compensate for this, you must have a scale for each hour to compare against.

Similar to the hardware measurement discussed earlier, the measurement of customer contacts is a good measurement to keep track of but not a good one to solely rely upon on to gauge your availability. The pulse of the customer or customer temperature, whatever you wish to call this, is a great way to judge how your customer base is responding to a new layout or feature set or payment model. This feedback is invaluable for the product managers to ensure they are focused on the customers' needs and listening to their feedback. For a true availability measurement, we again recommend something more sophisticated.

Portion of Site Down

A third way of measuring availability is monitoring the availability of services on your site. This is obviously more easily accomplished if your site has fault isolation lanes, swim lanes, created to keep services separated. In either case, this is often accomplished by monitoring the ability of a simulated user, usually in the form of a script, to perform certain tasks such as logon, run reports, and so on. This simulated user is then the measure of your availability. As an example, if you want to monitor five services—login, report, pay, post, and logout—you could create five scripts that run every five minutes. If any script fails, it notifies a distribution list. After the service is restored, the test script stops sending failure notices. This way, you have a track through email of the exact downtime and what services were affected.

As an example, let's say we have this monitoring method set up for our five services. We receive problem emails for our login service starting at 9:45 AM and they stop at 11:15 AM. This gives us 1½ hours of downtime on one of our services. A simple method of calculating the availability is to take 1/5 of the downtime, because one of the five services had the problem. This would result in 18 minutes of downtime, calculated as follows

Outage duration = 1½ hours

Services impacted = 1

Total services = 5

90 min × 1/5 = 18 min

This method does have some limitations and downsides, but it can be a fairly accurate way of measuring the impact of downtime upon customers. One of the major limitations with this method is that it only monitors services that you have scripts built for. If you either don't build the scripts or can't accurately simulate real users, your monitoring is less affective. Obviously, you need to monitor the most important services that you provide in your application. It's likely not realistic to monitor every single service, but the major ones should absolutely be monitored. Another limitation is that not all users use all the services equally. For example, a signup flow only gets used by new users, whereas a login flow gets used by all your existing customers. Should each flow get weighted equally? Perhaps you could add a weighting by importance or volume of usage to each flow to help more accurately calculate the impact on your customers for the availability of each flow. Another limitation of this is that if you monitor your application from inside of your network, you are not necessarily experiencing the same customer impact as outside your network. This is especially true if the outage is caused by your Internet service provider (ISP). Even though this does have some limitations, it does offer a pretty good customer centric availability measurement.

Third-Party Monitoring Service

The fourth measurement that we want to present for determining availability is using a third-party monitoring service. This is very similar to the previous measurement except that it overcomes the limitation of monitoring within your own network and potentially has more sophisticated scripting to achieve a more realistic user experience. The principle concepts are very similar in that you set up services that you want to monitor and have it alert a distribution list when there is a problem. There is a wide variety of vendors that offer services including Keynote, Gomez, Montastic, and many others. Some of these services are free and others are fairly costly depending on the sophistication and diversity of monitoring that you require. For example, some of the premium monitoring services have the capability of monitoring from many different peering networks as well as providing user simulation from user's computers, which is about as realistic of a user experience as you can achieve.

The key with using a third-party monitoring service is first determining your requirements for monitoring. Things to consider are how difficult your application or services are to monitor because of their dynamic nature and how many different geographical locations is your site monitored from. Some services are capable of monitoring from almost any Internet peering service globally. Some vendors offer special monitoring for dynamic pages. Others offer dynamic alert that doesn't need thresholds set but instead "learns" what is normal behavior for your application's pages and alerts when they are "out of control," statistically speaking.

Traffic Graph

The last measurement that we want to present was provided as an example in Chapter 6. This is the method of using traffic graphs to determine the impact of an outage on the customer usage of your site based off of network access or traffic graphs. To accomplish this, you must make use of traffic graphs that show the usage reports from your site's network. After you have this setup, each time there is an outage, you can compare a normal day with the outage day and determine how much of your site's traffic and thus users were affected. The way to do this is determine the area between the graphs, and this is representative of the amount of downtime that should be registered.

In Figure A.1, the solid line is a normal day's traffic and the dashed line is the traffic from the day with an outage. The outage began at 9:00 AM and lasted until approximately 3:00 PM when the site was fully recovered. The area between the lines from 9:00 AM to 3:00 PM, marked by light gray, would be considered the outage percentage and could be used in the calculation of downtime. In this case, we would calculate that this area is 40% of the normal traffic and therefore the site had a 40% outage for six hours or 2.4 hours of downtime.

As a continuation of this measurement, we could use it to estimate the cost that the outage caused by not allowing customers to purchase or browse or sign up. To determine the cost that the outage caused, you need to add back in any traffic that came back later in the day because the customers were unable to use the site during the outage. The area marked by dark gray with the dashed line above the solid line from 3:00 PM to 9:00 PM would be traffic that we recovered after the outage. In this

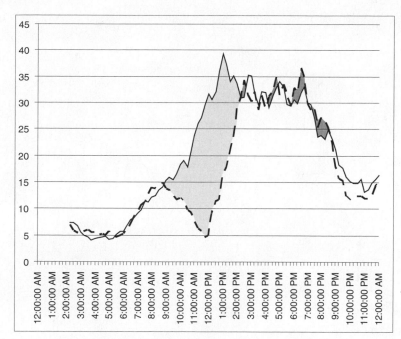

Figure A.1 *Outage Traffic Graph*

case, it is approximately 5% above normal traffic, so we could reduce the 40% by 5% and recalculate the cost of the outage.

Although this approach is much more mathematical and accurate, it still has its limitations and drawbacks. One of these limitations is the reliance on traffic as a representation of user behavior and revenue. This is not necessarily the case. Not all traffic is equal. A new customer signup might be worth $50 in purchases and advertisement revenue over the active span of the customer. A customer interrupted from purchasing a shopping cart is not likely to return and that customer's traffic would be worth a lot more than a customer browsing. The average of all these should equal an average hourly revenue rate, but this can skew the metric during partial outages, such as when new user signup flows are broken but checkouts are still working.

As you can see, measuring availability is not straightforward and can be very complex. The purpose of these examples is not to say which one is right or wrong, but rather to give you several examples that you can choose from or combine together to make the best overall availability metric for your organization. The importance of a reliable and agreed upon availability metric should not be understated as it will be the basis for many recommendations and scalability projects as well as a metric that should be tied directly to people's goals. Spend the time necessary to come up with the most accurate metric possible that will become the authoritative measurement of availability.

Appendix B

Capacity Planning Calculations

In Chapter 11, Determining Headroom for Applications, we covered how to determine the headroom or free capacity that was available for your application. In this appendix, we will walk through a larger example of capacity planning for an entire site, but we will follow the process outlined in Chapter 11. The steps to be followed are

1. Identify components

2. Determine actual and maximum usage rates

3. Determine growth rate

4. Determine seasonality

5. Compute amount of headroom gained through projects

6. State ideal usage percentage

7. Perform calculations

For our example, let's use our made-up company AllScale.com, which provides Software as a Service (SaaS) for human resources professionals. The site is becoming very popular and growing rapidly. The growth is seen in bursts; as new companies sign up for the service, the load increases based on the number of human resource managers at the client company. So far, there are 25 client companies with a total of 1,500 human resource managers that have accounts on AllScale.com. The CTO needs to perform a capacity planning exercise because she is planning for next year's budget and wants accurate cost projects.

Step 1 is to identify the components within the application that we care about sufficiently to include in the analysis. The AllScale.com application is very straightforward with a Web server tier, application server tier, and single database with standbys for failover. AllScale.com was migrated this past year to a new network and the network devices, including the load balancers, routers, and firewalls, were all purchased to scale to 6x current maximum traffic. We will skip the network devices in this capacity planning exercise, but periodically they should be reanalyzed to ensure that they have enough headroom to continue to scale for AllScale.com's growth.

Step 2 is to determine the actual and maximum usage rates for each component. AllScale keeps good records of this and we know the actual peak and average usage for all our components. We also perform load and performance testing before each new code release, and we know the maximum requests per second for each component based on the latest code version.

In Figure B.1, there are the Web server and application server requests that are being tracked and monitored for AllScale.com. You can see that there are around 125 requests per second at peak for the Web servers. There are also around 80 requests per second at peak for the application servers. The reason for the difference is that there are a lot of preprocessed static pages on the Web servers that do not require any business logic computations to be performed. These pages include corporate pages, landing pages, images, and so on. You could make an argument that different types of pages scale differently and should be put on a different set of Web servers or at a minimum be analyzed differently for capacity planning. For simplicity of this example, we will continue to group them together as a total number of requests.

From the graphs, we have put together a summary in Table B.1 of the Web servers, application servers, and the database server. You can see that we have for each component the peak total requests, the number of hosts in the pool, the peak request per host, and the maximum allowed on each host. The maximum allowed was determined through load and performance testing with the latest code base and is the number at which we begin to see diminished response times that are outside of our internal service level agreements.

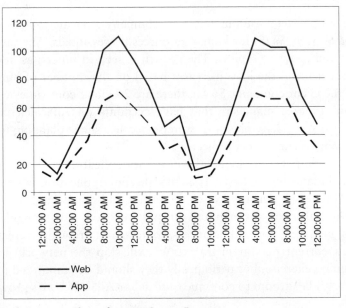

Figure B.1 *Web Server and Application Server Requests*

Table B.1 *Web Server and Application Server Requests Summary*

(a) Web Server

Peak requests per second total	125
Number of servers	5
Peak requests per second per server	25
Maximum requests per second per server	75

(b) Application Server

Peak requests per second total	80
Number of servers	4
Peak requests per second per server	20
Maximum requests per second per server	50

(c) Database

Peak SQL per second total	35
Number of nodes	1
Peak requests per second per server	35
Maximum SQL per second per node	65

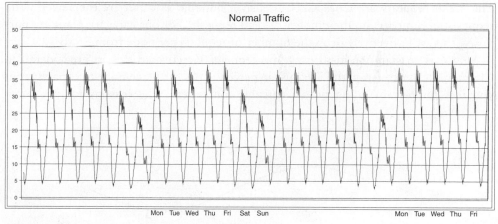

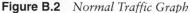

Figure B.2 *Normal Traffic Graph*

Step 3 is to determine the growth rate, and for this we turn to our traffic usage graph that we monitor to show how much traffic the AllScale.com site has each day. We also use the graph to show a percentage growth rate week-over-week. For our traffic, we have a 2% week-over-week growth rate on average throughout the year. This equates to a 280% growth rate annually or approximately 3x growth in traffic each year. This is the combined growth that comes from existing clients using the application more, natural growth, and the growth caused by our sales team signing up new clients, man-made growth. These growth rates are sometimes calculated separately if the sales team can provide accurate estimates for the number of clients that are going to be brought on board each year, or they can be extrapolated from previous year growth rates for new and existing customers.

Step 4 is to determine the seasonality affect on AllScale.com. Because of the nature of the human resource work, a lot of tasks are accomplished during the early part of the year. Items such as annual reviews, salary adjustments, and so on are all done in quarter 1 and therefore that is the largest traffic period for us. AllScale was able to generate the Figure B.3 seasonality graph by gathering traffic data for existing customers but excluding new users. This way, we can eliminate the growth from new users and just see the seasonality effect on existing users. This capacity planning exercise is being conducted in August, which is typically a lower month, and therefore we expect to see a 50% increase in traffic by January based on our seasonality effect.

Step 5 is to compute the headroom that we expect to gain through scalability or headroom projects. The one project that AllScale.com has planned for the fall of this year is to split the database by creating a write master with two read copies, an x-axis split according to the AKF Database Scale Cube. This would increase the number of nodes to three and therefore distribute the existing requests among the three nodes. The write requests are more CPU intensive, but that is offset by the fewer write requests as compared to the number of read requests. For our capacity planning purposes, this will affectively drop the number of requests per node from 35 to 12.

Step 6 is to state the ideal usage percentage. We covered this in great detail in Chapter 11, but to recap, the ideal usage percentage is the percentage of capacity that you feel comfortable using on a particular component. The reasons for not using

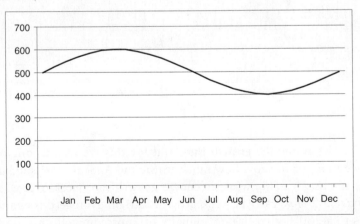

Figure B.3 *Seasonality Traffic Graph*

100% are twofold. The first reason is that there is a percentage of error in our data and calculations. As hard as we try and as much data as we collect, there are sure to be inaccuracies in our capacity plans. Because of this, we need a buffer to accommodate the inaccuracies. The second reason is that as you approach using 100% capacity of any hardware, the behavior becomes erratic and unpredictable. We want to operate in the range of perfectly predictable behavior. For each component, there may be a different Ideal Usage Percentage depending on how accurate you feel you are and how much buffer you need. For our exercise, we are going to use 90% for the database and 75% for the Web and application servers.

Step 7, our final step, is to perform the calculations. You may recall the formula shown in Figure B.4. This formula states that the capacity or headroom of a particular component is equal to the Ideal Usage Percentage multiplied by the maximum capacity of that component minus the current usage minus the sum over the time period of the growth rate, which also includes seasonality, minus projected gains from scalability projects.

As you can see in Table B.2, we have calculated the headroom or capacity for each component. Let's walk through the Web tier in detail. The calculation starts with the

$$\text{Headroom} = (\text{Ideal Usage Percentage} \times \text{Maximum Capacity}) - \text{Current Usage}$$
$$- \sum_{t=1}^{12} (\text{Growth}(t) - \text{Optimization Projects}(t))$$

Figure B.4 *Headroom Equation*

Table B.2 *Capacity Calculation*

(a) Web Server

Peak requests per second total	125
Number of servers	5
Peak requests per second per server	25
Maximum requests per second per server	75
Ideal usage percentage	75%
Scalability projects	0
Growth rate over 12 months	437.5
Headroom = (IUP × max) – usage – sum (growth – projects)	–281.25

(b) App Server

Peak requests per second total	80
Number of servers	4
Peak requests per second per server	20

(continues)

Table B.2 *Capacity Calculation (Continued)*

Maximum requests per second per server	50
Ideal usage percentage	75%
Scalability projects	0
Growth rate over 12 months	280
Headroom = (IUP × max) – usage – sum (growth – projects)	–210
(c) Database	
Peak SQL per second total	35
Number of nodes	3
Peak requests per second per server	11.67
Maximum SQL per second per node	65
Ideal usage percentage	90%
Scalability projects	0
Growth rate over 12 months	122.5
Headroom = (IUP × max) – usage – sum (growth – projects)	18

Ideal Usage Percentage multiplied by the maximum usage; for the Web server tier, this is 75% × 75 requests per second per server × 5 servers, which equals 281.25 requests per second (req/s). This is the total capacity that the AllScale site can handle. The next part of the calculation is to subtract the current usage of 125 req/s, equaling 156.25 req/s. This means that to date we have 156 req/s extra capacity. Now we need to add in the future needs. Sum the growth rate minus any projects planned over the time period to improve scalability. For the Web servers, we have a 3× growth rate annually in traffic and a 50% growth rate from seasonality resulting in a 3.5× total current usage, which equals 437.5 req/s. This final equation is

$$(75\% \times 75 \times 5) - 125 - (3.5 \times 125) = -281.25 \text{ req/s}$$

Because this is a negative number, we know that we do not have enough current capacity based on the number of servers in the pool. We can do several things to correct this. We could add capacity projects over the next year that would increase our capacity on the existing servers to handle the growing traffic. We could also purchase more servers and grow our capacity through a continued x-axis split. The way to calculate how many servers you need is to simply divide the capacity number, 281.25, by the sum of the Ideal Usage Percentage and the maximum usage per server (75% × 75) = 56.25. The result of this 281.25 / 56.25 = 5, means that you need five additional servers to handle the expected traffic growth.

Appendix C

Load and Performance Calculations

In Chapter 17, Performance and Stress Testing, we covered the definition, purpose, variations on themes, and the steps to complete performance testing. We discussed that performance testing covers a broad range of testing evaluations with each sharing the focus on the necessary characteristics of the system rather than the individual materials, hardware, or code. Focusing on ensuring the software meets or exceeds the specified requirements or service level agreements is what performance testing is all about. We emphasized that an important aspect of performance testing included a methodical approach; from the very beginning, we argued for establishing benchmarks and success criteria; and at the very end, we suggested repeating the tests as often as possible for validation purposes. We believe that such a structured and repetitive approach is critical in order to achieve results in which you can be confident and upon which you can base decisions. Here, we want to present an example performance test in order to demonstrate how the tests are defined and analyzed.

Before we begin the example, we want to review the seven steps that we presented for a performance test in Chapter 17. They are the following:

1. *Criteria.* Establish what criteria or benchmarks are expected from the application, component, or system that is being tested.

2. *Environment.* The testing environment should be as close to production as possible to ensure that your results are accurate.

3. *Define tests.* There are many different categories of tests that you should consider for inclusion in the performance test including endurance, load, most used, most visible, and component.

4. *Execute tests.* Perform the actual tests and gather all the data possible.

5. *Analyze data.* Analyzing the data by such methods as comparing to previous releases and stochastic models in order to identify what factors are causing variation.

6. *Report to engineers*. Provide the analysis to the engineers for them to either take action or confirm that it is as expected.

7. *Repeat tests and analysis*. As necessary and possible, validate bug fixes and continue testing.

Our fictitious company AllScale.com, which you may recall provides human resource Software as a Service, has a new release of its code in development. This code base, known internally as release 3.1, is expected out early next month. The engineers have just completed development of the final features and it is now in the quality assurance testing stage. We are joining AllScale just as it is beginning the performance testing phase, which in its company occurs during the later phases of quality assurance after the functional testing has been completed.

The first step that we need to accomplish is determining the benchmarks for the performance test. AllScale.com has performance tested all of its releases for the past year so it has a good set of benchmarks against which comparisons can be made. In the past, it has used the criteria that the new release must be within 5% of the previous release's performance. This ensures that AllScale has sufficient hardware in production to run the application without scaling issues as well as helping it control the cost of hardware for new features. The team confirms with its management that the criteria will remain the same for this release.

The second step is to establish the environment. The AllScale.com team does not have a dedicated performance testing environment and must requisition the use of a shared staging environment from the operations team when it needs to perform testing. The team is required to give one week notice in order to schedule the environment and is given three days in which to perform the tests. Occasionally, if the environment is being heavily used for multiple purposes, the testing is required to be performed off hours, but this time the team has Monday at 9:00 AM through Wednesday at midnight to perform the tests. The staging environment that is used is a scaled down version of production; all of the physical and logical hosts are present, but they are much smaller in size and total numbers than the production environment. For each component or service in production, there is a single server that represents a pool of servers in production. Although such a structure is not ideal and it is preferable to have two servers in a test environment representing a larger pool in production, the configuration is what AllScale.com can afford today and it is better than nothing.

Step three is to define the tests. For the AllScale.com application, the most important performance test to conduct is a load test on the two most critical components: upload of employee information and reporting on employees. If the team completes these two areas of testing and has extra capacity, it will often perform a load test on the welcome screen because it is the most visible component in the application. Further defining the tests that will be performed, there is only one upload mechanism, but there are three employee reports that must be tested. These three reports are all active employees' information: All_Emp, Dep_Emp (department employee information), and Emp_Tng (employee required training). The most computational and database intensive report is the all_emp followed by the emp_tng. Therefore, they are the most likely to have a performance problem and are prioritized in the testing sequence.

The fourth step is to execute or conduct the tests and gather the data. AllScale.com has automated scripts that run the tests and capture the data simultaneously. The scripts run a fixed number of simultaneous executions of a standard data set or set of instructions. This amount has been determined as the maximum amount of simultaneous executions that a particular service will need to be able to handle on a single server. For the upload, the number is 10 simultaneous uploads with data sets ranging from 5,000 to 10,000 employees. For the reports, the number is 20 simultaneous requests per report server. The scripts capture the mean or average response time, the standard deviation of the response times, the number of sql executions, and the number of errors reported by the application.

In Table C.1 are the response time results of the upload tests. The results are from 10 separate runs of the test, each with 10 simultaneous executions of the upload service. In the chart are the corresponding response times.

In Table C.2 are the response times for the All_Emp report tests. The results are from 10 separate runs of the test, each with 20 simultaneous executions of the report. Completed report run times are in the chart area. You can see that the testing scripts provided means and standard deviations for each run as well as for the overall data.

Table C.1 *Upload Test Response Time Results*

	1	2	3	4	5	6	7	8	9	10	Overall
	8.4	2.2	5.7	5.7	9.7	9.2	5.4	7.9	6.1	5.8	
	6.4	7.9	4.4	8.6	10.6	10.4	3.9	8.3	7.3	9.3	
	2.8	10	3	8.5	2	10.8	9.4	2.4	7.1	10.8	
	8.8	5.9	10.2	2.3	10.5	2.6	6	7.1	10.4	8.2	
	9	3.4	7.7	4	4.8	2.7	6.8	7.5	4.5	2.6	
	10.4	3.7	2	7.4	7.5	2.4	9	9.7	5	2.5	
	5.8	9.6	7.9	4.8	8.8	7.9	4.1	2.5	8	8.1	
	6.5	6.2	6.5	9.5	2.4	2.4	10.6	6.6	2.2	5.7	
	6.5	6.2	6.5	9.5	2.4	2.4	10.6	6.6	2.2	5.7	
	5.7	4.1	8.2	7.3	9.7	4.8	3.3	9.1	2.8	7.9	
Mean	7.0	5.9	6.2	6.8	6.8	5.6	6.9	6.8	5.6	6.7	6.4
StDev	2.2	2.6	2.5	2.5	3.6	3.6	2.8	2.5	2.7	2.7	2.7

Table C.2 *All_Emp Report Test Response Time Results*

	1	2	3	4	5	6	7	8	9	10	Overall
	4.2	5.2	3.2	6.9	5.3	3.6	3.2	3.3	2.4	4.7	
	4.4	6.5	1.1	6.7	3.1	4.8	4.6	1.4	2	6.5	
	1.4	3	6.5	2.7	6.2	5.4	1.3	3.7	1.8	2.6	
	3.8	6.9	2.7	2.6	5.8	6.8	1	3.5	1.8	4.9	
	2	6.7	2	4.9	4.1	6	2.3	3.9	6.7	1.3	
	1.3	4.3	2.7	1.4	3.3	3.7	1.7	3.7	6.2	3.9	
	4	6.5	1.4	3.8	5.2	6	5.3	5.5	5.8	5.9	
	6.3	5.7	5.7	6.3	2	7	4.6	1.9	2.9	5.1	
	4.1	6.5	1.2	3.2	4.4	3.6	7	2.5	8.4	4.5	
	1.3	3.9	3.6	4.3	6.5	4.4	3.2	5.1	7.1	7.4	
	9	4.9	2.4	1.8	8.7	7.5	7.8	6.2	7	2.8	
	1.5	3.7	5.5	4	6.8	8.4	2.1	8.3	1.4	8.9	
	4.9	5.2	6.6	6.8	4.6	6.7	1.2	5.4	8	9	
	2.5	5.3	8.3	2.6	8.1	7.7	2	1.9	5.9	2.2	
	7.8	4.8	6	6.4	4.2	8.5	4.5	6.8	7.5	6.5	
	7.8	3.6	8.8	2.9	8.6	3.8	2.6	4.8	5.6	4.1	
	6.7	1.8	2.6	5.5	3.4	8.9	5.2	7.2	6.5	1.5	
	4.3	7.1	3.4	4.1	3.8	2	1.5	5	7.5	2.3	
	4.3	7.1	3.4	4.1	3.8	2	1.5	5	7.5	2.3	
	4.5	1.9	4	2.8	4.3	6.8	4.4	2.9	6.2	3.2	
Mean	4.3	5.0	4.1	4.2	5.1	5.7	3.4	4.4	5.4	4.5	4.6
StDev	2.3	1.7	2.3	1.7	1.9	2.1	2.0	1.9	2.4	2.3	2.1

In Table C.3 are the summary results of the upload and All_Emp report tests for both the current version 3.1 as well as the previous version of the code base 3.0. For the rest of the example, we are going to stick with these two tests in order to cover them in sufficient detail and not have to continue repeating the same thing about all the other tests that could be performed. The summary results include the overall mean and standard deviation, the number of SQL that was executed for each test, and the number of errors that the application reported. The third column for each test is the difference between the old and new versions' performance. This is where the analysis begins.

Step five is to perform the analysis on the data gathered during testing. As we mentioned, Table C.3 has a third column showing the difference between the versions of

Table C.3 *Summary Test Results*

	Upload Test			All_Emp Test		
	v 3.1	v 3.0	Diff	v 3.1	v 3.0	Diff
Simultaneous Executions	10	10		20	20	
Mean Response Time	6.4	6.2	3%	4.6	4.5	3%
Standard Dev Response Time	2.7	2.4	14%	2.1	2.4	–11%
SQL Executions	72	69	4%	240	220	9%
Number of Errors	14	15	–7%	3	2	50%

code for the upload and All_Emp tests. AllScale.com's analysis of the data starts with this comparison. As you can see, both of the tests had a 3% increase in the mean response time. Our stated guidelines were no more than 5% increase per new code version, so this is acceptable. The standard deviation, which measures the variability within the data showing how large or small the spread of individual data points are from the mean, shows that it has increased on the upload test but decreased on the report test. This indicates that there is more variability in the upload than there was previously and is something that we should probably consider looking into further. The number of SQL executions went up on both tests. This information should definitely be pointed out to the engineers to make sure that they indeed added databases queries to both services. If they did not, it should be investigated to determine why the count has increased. The number of application reported errors has gone down on the upload, which is a positive trend indicating that the engineers might have added application logic to handle different data sets. On the report, the number has increased significantly from a percentage standpoint, but the actual number is low, from 2 to 3, so this is likely not a problem but should be pointed out to the engineers and possibly product managers to determine the severity of an error on this report.

To continue the analysis on the variability of the upload data as seen in the increased standard deviation, we can perform some simple statistical tests. One of the first tests that AllScale.com has decided to perform is a paired t-test, which is a hypothesis test for the mean difference between paired observations. The paired t-test calculates the difference for each pair of measurements; for the upload test, this is each test of the datasets. Then the paired t-test determines the mean of these weight changes and determines whether this is statistically significant. We won't go into the details of how to perform this analysis other than to say that you formulate a hypothesis and a null hypothesis. The hypothesis would be that the means of the data sets (v3.1 to v3.0) are the same and the null or alternative hypothesis would be that they are not the same. The result is that these two data sets are statistically different.

Continuing the investigation of the increased variability in v3.1, AllScale.com subjects the data to a control chart. A control chart is a statistical test that measures for special cause variation. There are two types of variation: common cause and special cause. Common cause variation as the name implies is normal variation in a process that exists because of common causes, such as the "noise" inherent in any process. Special cause variation is caused by noncommon causes, such as differences in hardware or software. If a process only has common cause variation, it is considered to be "in control." When special cause variation is present, the process is "out of control."

A control chart is created by plotting the data points on a graph and marking the mean as well as an Upper Control Limit (UCL) and Lower Control Limit (LCL). The UCL is determined by calculating three standard deviations above the mean. The LCL is determined by calculating three standard deviations below the mean. There are many different tests that can be performed to look for special cause variation. The most basic is looking for any point that is above the UCL or below the LCL, meaning that it is more or less than three standard deviations from the mean. In Figure C.1, the version 3.1 upload response time is plotted in a control chart. As you can see, no point is more than three standard deviations away. AllScale could continue on with many other tests to determine how the new version of code should perform compared to the old version, but at this point, it decides to continue to the next step by getting the engineers involved.

Step six is to report to the engineers the results of the tests and analysis. AllScale.com gathers the engineers responsible for the various parts of the code that make up the upload and report services and present their analysis. The engineers

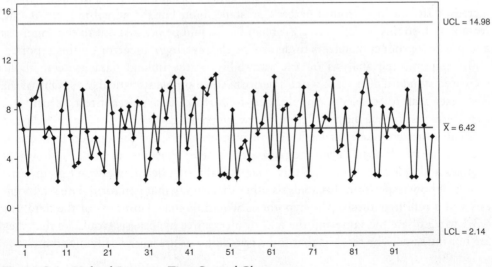

Figure C.1 *Upload Response Time Control Chart*

decide that the increased variation is not concerning but the increase in the number of database queries might be an issue, so they decide to file a bug and investigate.

Step seven is to repeat the tests and analysis as necessary. The AllScale quality assurance and engineering teams continue over the next few weeks to investigate and test the new code repeatedly. They end up running another set of performance tests on version 3.1 of the code before releasing the code to production. Because of their diligence, they feel confident that this version of the code will perform in a manner that is acceptable.

This example has covered the steps of performance testing. We have shown how you might decide which tests to perform, how to gather the data, and how to perform some basic analysis on it. There is a wide spectrum of sophistication that can be demonstrated with performance testing. Much of that depends on the resources both in terms of people and time that your organization can commit to this step in the software development life cycle.

Index

Design Patterns for Succeeding with Enterprise Mashups:
One of Today's Fastest-Growing Areas of Software Development

Mashup Patterns: Designs and Examples for the Modern Enterprise

Michael Ogrinz • ISBN-13: 978-0-321-57947-8

- Contains authoritative insights based on extensive real-world experience, from one of the world's leading innovators in enterprise mashups and integration
- Covers every part of the mashup development lifecycle, from planning core functionality through integration, testing, and much more
- Includes multiple real-world case studies, dozens of patterns, and a full chapter of must-avoid "anti-patterns"

In this book, leading enterprise mashup expert Michael Ogrinz provides more than fifty new patterns that cover virtually every facet of enterprise mashup development, from core functionality through integration, and beyond. These patterns address crucial issues including data extraction and visualization, reputation management, security, accessibility, usability, content migration, load and regression testing, governance, and more. Each pattern is documented with a practical description, specific use cases, and insights into mashup stability.

Learn more at informit.com/title/9780321579478.

The First How-To Guide for Developers who Want to Create
Enterprise-Quality Web 2.0 Mashups

Mashups: Strategies for the Modern Enterprise

J. Jeffrey Hanson • ISBN-13: 978-0-321-59181-4

- Walks enterprise developers step-by-step through designing, coding, and debugging their first mashups
- Surveys all of today's leading technologies and standards for rapidly constructing high-quality mashups
- Includes a full chapter of case studies, as well as an insightful preview of the future of enterprise mashups
- Provides extensive code examples throughout

In this book, J. Jeffrey Hanson guides readers through every step of creating a working enterprise mashup, including design, implementation, and debugging. Each stage is illuminated with detailed sample code. Along the way, Hanson surveys the broad spectrum of technologies and standards that have recently become available to simplify mashup development, helping enterprise developers choose the best options for their projects. Hanson covers topics such as comparing and selecting the right mashup implementation styles; preparing to implement mashups; overcoming technical and business concerns associated with mashups; applying today's best mashup patterns; and much more.

Learn more at informit.com/title/9780321591814.

▲▼Addison-Wesley
informit.com/aw

informIT.com THE TRUSTED TECHNOLOGY LEARNING SOURCE

PEARSON | **InformIT** is a brand of Pearson and the online presence for the world's leading technology publishers. It's your source for reliable and qualified content and knowledge, providing access to the top brands, authors, and contributors from the tech community.

Addison-Wesley Cisco Press EXAM/CRAM IBM Press. QUE PRENTICE HALL SAMS | Safari

LearnIT at InformIT

Looking for a book, eBook, or training video on a new technology? Seeking timely and relevant information and tutorials? Looking for expert opinions, advice, and tips? **InformIT has the solution.**

- Learn about new releases and special promotions by subscribing to a wide variety of newsletters. Visit **informit.com/newsletters**.

- Access FREE podcasts from experts at **informit.com/podcasts**.

- Read the latest author articles and sample chapters at **informit.com/articles**.

- Access thousands of books and videos in the Safari Books Online digital library at **safari.informit.com**.

- Get tips from expert blogs at **informit.com/blogs**.

Visit **informit.com/learn** to discover all the ways you can access the hottest technology content.

Are You Part of the IT Crowd?

Connect with Pearson authors and editors via RSS feeds, Facebook, Twitter, YouTube, and more! Visit **informit.com/socialconnect**.

informIT.com THE TRUSTED TECHNOLOGY LEARNING SOURCE **PEARSON**

Addison-Wesley Cisco Press EXAM/CRAM IBM Press. QUE PRENTICE HALL SAMS | Safari

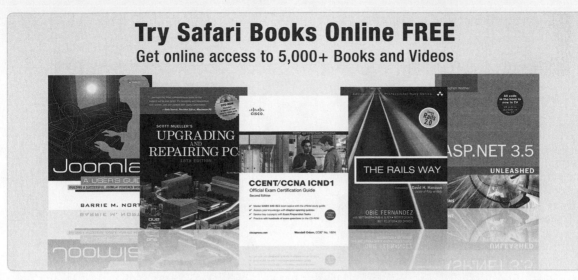

THE ART OF SCALABILITY
Scalable Web Architecture, Processes and Organizations
for the Modern Enterprise

MARTIN L. ABBOTT   MICHAEL T. FISHER

FREE Online Edition

Your purchase of *The Art of Scalability* includes access to a free online edition for 45 days through the Safari Books Online subscription service. Nearly every Addison-Wesley Professional book is available online through Safari Books Online, along with more than 5,000 other technical books and videos from publishers such as Cisco Press, Exam Cram, IBM Press, O'Reilly, Prentice Hall, Que, and Sams.

SAFARI BOOKS ONLINE allows you to search for a specific answer, cut and paste code, download chapters, and stay current with emerging technologies.

Activate your FREE Online Edition at www.informit.com/safarifree

> **STEP 1:** Enter the coupon code: IBXXAZG.

> **STEP 2:** New Safari users, complete the brief registration form.
> Safari subscribers, just log in.

If you have difficulty registering on Safari or accessing the online edition, please e-mail customer-service@safaribooksonline.com

Safari
Books Online